# Diversity and Equity in Canadian Schools

# Diversity and Equity in Canadian Schools

## Fostering Human Flourishing

Edited by
Cathlene Hillier and Wendy D. Bokhorst-Heng

Toronto | Vancouver

**Diversity and Equity in Canadian Schools: Fostering Human Flourishing**
Edited by Cathlene Hillier and Wendy D. Bokhorst-Heng

First published in 2024 by
**Canadian Scholars, an imprint of CSP Books Inc.**
180 Bloor Street West, Suite 1401
Toronto, Ontario
M5S 2V6

www.canadianscholars.ca

Copyright © 2024 Cathlene Hillier, Wendy D. Bokhorst-Heng, the contributing authors, and Canadian Scholars.

All rights reserved. No part of this publication may be reproduced, stored in a retrieval system, or transmitted, in any form or by any means, without the prior written permission of Canadian Scholars, under licence or terms from the appropriate reproduction rights organization, or as expressly permitted by law.

Every reasonable effort has been made to identify copyright holders. Canadian Scholars would be pleased to have any errors or omissions brought to its attention.

**Library and Archives Canada Cataloguing in Publication**

Title: Diversity and equity in Canadian schools : fostering human flourishing / edited by Cathlene Hillier and Wendy D. Bokhorst-Heng.
Names: Hillier, Cathlene, editor. | Bokhorst-Heng, W. D. (Wendy Diana), editor
Description: Includes bibliographical references and index.
Identifiers: Canadiana (print) 20240440145 | Canadiana (ebook) 20240440218 | ISBN 9781773384474 (softcover) | ISBN 9781773384498 (EPUB) | ISBN 9781773384481 (PDF)
Subjects: LCSH: Multicultural education—Canada.
Classification: LCC LC1099.5.C3 D6156 2024 | DDC 370.1170971—dc23

Cover artwork by Chelsea Elaine Hillier, age 16
Cover design by Vivian Lai
Page layout by S4Carlisle Publishing Services

24  25  26  27  28     5  4  3  2  1

Printed and bound in Ontario, Canada

Canadä

# CONTENTS

*Artist Statement by Chelsea Elaine Hillier*     viii
*Acknowledgements*     ix

Introduction: Educating for Diversity and Human Flourishing:
A Conceptual Model, *by Wendy D. Bokhorst-Heng and Cathlene Hillier*     1

**Part I**    Education Policy: A History and Application of Multicultural and Critical Ideologies in Canada     19

     **Chapter 1** · The Evolution of Canadian Multiculturalism: Policy and Legal Considerations, *by David C. Young*     21

     **Chapter 2** · Critical Race Theory in Canadian Educational Praxis, *by Alana Butler, Zuhra Abawi, and Rachel Berman*     40

**Part II**    Ethnicity and Race: Incorporating a Pedagogy of Justice, Liberation, and Care     57

     **Chapter 3** · Cosmopolitan Education and Racial Justice: The Implications of Martha Nussbaum's Philosophy of Education for Forging a Common National Memory in Canada, *by Ben Iheagwara*     59

     **Chapter 4** · Supporting Students to Thrive, Grow, and Flourish: Embracing Their Literate Lives as Liberatory Praxis, *by Ann E. Lopez*     76

     **Chapter 5** · Toward Strengths-Based Culturally Responsive Teaching of Refugee Students with Interrupted Formal Education, *by Hiba Barek, Marja G. Bertrand, and Immaculate K. Namukasa*     93

**Part III**    Socioeconomic Status: Understanding and Responding to Systemic Barriers to Foster Human Flourishing     113

     **Chapter 6** · Socioeconomic Status and Children's Education in Canada: The Importance of Aspirations in Flourishing, *by Cathlene Hillier*     115

     **Chapter 7** · Pedagogical Strategies for Equity and Inclusion: Addressing Low–Socioeconomic Status Students in the Canadian Classroom, *by Sally Abudiab and Ardavan Eizadirad*     133

**Part IV  Gender and Sexual Diversity: Supporting Students' Identity as Important to Human Flourishing**   151
  Chapter 8 • Gender and Sexuality in Education: Critical Considerations, *by Jay Kennedy*   153
  Chapter 9 • Disruptive Stories: Straight Teachers Navigating Queer Allyship in Ontario Schools, *by Leigh Potvin*   170

**Part V  Indigenous Education: Remembering the Past, Acknowledging the Present, Fostering Communities of Flourishing**   185
  Chapter 10 • Tribal Critical Race Theory, *Wâhkôhtowin*, and Decolonizing Canadian Education, *by Joanie Crandall*   187
  Chapter 11 • Fostering Wellness and Redefining Success for All Students through Indigenous Perspectives, *by Lindsay Morcom, Kelly Maracle, Liv Rondeau, and Kate Freeman*   206

**Part VI  Language: Policies and Practices to Support Linguistic Inclusion and Flourishing**   223
  Chapter 12 • Globalization, Decolonization, and the Diversity of Linguistic Identities: A Review of Language Policies and Practices in Canadian K–12 Education, *by Sonya Sachar and Karen A. Krasny*   225
  Chapter 13 • Inclusive Instructional Design within Language Education: Principles and Practices for the Modern Canadian Classroom, *by Renée Bourgoin, Katy Arnett, and Carmelita Duffy*   243

**Part VII  Religion: Understanding, Inclusion, and Flourishing of Religious Diversity**   263
  Chapter 14 • Framing Religious Diversity in the Canadian Classroom, *by Margaretta Patrick and W. Y. Alice Chan*   265
  Chapter 15 • Broadening Understandings of Religion to Support Student Flourishing, *by Margaretta Patrick and Carla L. Peck*   283

**Part VIII   Disability: Nurturing Belonging and Flourishing Among Students with Disabilities   301**

    Chapter 16 • Lived Disability Experience in Canadian Schooling: Essential Knowledge for Fostering Disabled Flourishing, *by Cynthia Bruce*   303

    Chapter 17 • Schools as *Polis*: Fostering Participation and Belonging of Children with Disabilities in Classrooms and Schools, *by Cornelia Schneider*   319

**Part IX   Geography: The Importance of Location in Supporting Students and Teachers   333**

    Chapter 18 • The Landscape of Education Inequalities in Northern and Rural Locations in Canada, *by Cathlene Hillier and David Zarifa*   335

    Chapter 19 • Encountering Rural Narrative/Fiction in Teacher Education: Toward a Conversation, *by Michael Corbett*   356

**Part X   Intersectionality: Teaching the Whole Child in Consideration of Human Flourishing   373**

    Chapter 20 • Implicit Inequities in School Practices: Interdisciplinary Perspectives, *by Monique Somma, Kim Radersma, Jhonel Morvan, and Leigh Potvin*   375

    Chapter 21 • The Things We Carry: Human Flourishing for Students and Educators Through the Equity Backpack Project, *by Vandy Britton, Nerlap Kaur Sidhu, Navtej Nevan Singh Sidhu, and Nathan Ngieng, with Balkaran, Manmeet, Ardra, and Envy*   397

Conclusion: Pedagogy for Flourishing: Preparing and Equipping the Educator, *by Wendy D. Bokhorst-Heng*   413

    *Author Biographies*   433
    *Index*   445

# ARTIST STATEMENT

*Flourishing, 2024*

*Chelsea Elaine Hillier, Age 16*

The cover artist intentionally chose the flora represented. Along with the sweet grass, which is considered a sacred plant among Indigenous groups, the other flowers were chosen for what they traditionally represent: hyacinth (beginnings); red carnation (justice); chamomile (energy in adversity); jasmine (humility and grace); western red lily (love, courage, and passion); marigold (sacred affection); and yellow zinnia (daily remembrance).

# ACKNOWLEDGEMENTS

First, from north to south and east to west, we gratefully acknowledge that we live, work, and flourish on the lands of many diverse First Nations, Métis, and Inuit people. If you would like to learn more about the land that you are situated on, visit www.native-land.ca for more information. Second, as we reflect at the end of this project's journey, before we hand it over to our readers, we are indeed humbled and grateful to have worked with such amazing contributors and reviewers and the people at Canadian Scholars. The authors have shared from their rich experiences and knowledge, willing to reconsider their scholarship in light of human flourishing and make the concept so much richer with exciting possibilities for students. They responded quickly with tight timelines, allowing the project to move on schedule—we are so appreciative. We are also grateful to Isabelle Blais and Haleigh Sears, our research assistants, who helped in managing the project in its early stages, and especially to Haleigh for her intense work as we moved to final submissions, giving that much-needed extra set of eyes on the documents. The various people at Canadian Scholars were so instrumental in moving our initial vision to its fruition, providing encouragement and practical support throughout all the bumps along the way. And thank you to our colleagues and students for all of your involvement in supporting our work over the years and inspiring our thinking. Finally, we are ever so grateful to the most important people in our lives: our families—thank you!

This book has been published with the help of a grant from the Federation for the Humanities and Social Sciences, through the Awards to Scholarly Publications Program, using funds provided by the Social Sciences and Humanities Research Council of Canada.

# INTRODUCTION

# Educating for Diversity and Human Flourishing: A Conceptual Model

*Wendy D. Bokhorst-Heng and Cathlene Hillier*

Since Canada's policy of **multiculturalism** was first enacted in 1971, the country's population has grown in its complexity of demographic diversity and in its understanding of what diversity means. The Council of Ministers of Education Canada's website (n.d.) reports that in 2015 (the most recent year for which these statistics have been reported) approximately 30 percent of Canadian teenagers had an immigrant background. And according to Statistics Canada (2022), the share of second-generation Canadians (children of immigrants) younger than 15 years with at least one foreign-born parent rose from 26.7 percent in 2011 to 31.5 percent in 2021. Indigenous Peoples, who have always been part of Canada's diverse population, have also experienced a population growth—they are the fastest-growing population in Canada, growing by 9.4 percent between 2016 and 2021—and have the youngest population in Canada, with about 28 percent being under the age of 25 in 2021 (Statistics Canada, 2021). The definition of diversity itself has also expanded from a consideration of mostly visible differences like race, ethnicity, and heritage to include other dimensions, some visible and some nonvisible, such as religion, social class, language, sexual orientation, gender identity, and (dis)ability, as well as recognizing intersectionality among these dimensions (Ghosh & Galczynski, 2014).

The implications of this growth can be seen across policies and institutions, including education (e.g., Lam, 2019). As Jule (2019) observes in her discussion of Canadian diversity in education, there are increasing demands on teachers to teach for equity and diversity in addition to teaching the prescribed curriculum. And there are increasing calls for curriculum reform to better prepare students to engage in such diversity within Canadian society, both in their personal and social lives and in their work. Yet many teachers express limited cross-cultural awareness and understanding of culturally responsive teaching and indicate they feel ill-prepared to effectively teach in diverse classrooms (Mahali & Sevigny, 2021). "Too often," Howard (2006) observes, "we expect White teachers to be what they have not learned to be, namely, culturally competent professionals" (p. 6). As you contemplate the realities of your own future or current classroom, you too may feel unprepared and overwhelmed.

Not only are many educators unprepared for the complexities surrounding students' diversity, but they are also often either unaware of their own identities and associated privileges or even ignorant of Canada's history and current realities of racism and discrimination. One of the authors of this chapter recalls one teacher candidate asserting, "There is no racism in Canada." We wondered how to respond to this teacher's ignorance of Canada's history and contemporary realities, realities that shape the everyday lives of many of their future colleagues and students. And we wondered how to respond to the barriers inherent in such a stance that would limit their positionality for deep self-reflection. How can we best engage teacher candidates and teachers in reflection and conversations about concepts like **privilege, discrimination**, and injustice—and do so in ways that open up conversation and increase understanding and compassion? How do we go beyond the guilt and blame that often impede personal and social transformation, particularly for white and male educators? And then how do we engage educators in understanding their role in dismantling the dynamics of privilege?

Such conversations need to go beyond the limiting categorization of constructs within diversity in order to engage all students, regardless of their positions of privilege or nonprivilege, in the conversation. The other author of this chapter recalls one occasion in a course on pre-service teachers' professional development when she devoted several sessions to the topic of white privilege. One of her students, who is Black (we'll call him Carter), passionately recounted his and his family members' and Black friends' everyday experiences with racism and discrimination. However, he was met with strong resistance from another student, who is white and gay (we'll call him William). William wanted to broaden the discussion of discrimination to also engage with constructs of homophobia and heterosexual privilege. Carter interpreted William's demands as an effort to defuse or even deny the realities of his white privilege and at the same time minimize and deny the realities of oppression against Black people. Both were speaking from their own areas of privilege/nonprivilege, locked in what Sen (2006) calls "plural monoculturalism," a compartmentalization that ultimately poses challenges to deeper intercultural dialogue and understanding. (They were fortunately able to, in a side conversation after class, come to a position of mutual understanding and respect.) Multiliteracies theorist Allan Luke (2017) puts it this way: "We cannot talk about race and culture without talking about social class, gender, and sexuality; without talking about geography and place; and without talking about the multiple and complex ways that communities and classes, cultures, genders, and peoples are marginalized, while, indeed, others are privileged without question. We cannot talk about changing the world by expanding or altering pedagogy without also attending to and altering the rules and relationships of the social, institutional, and economic systems where we and our students live and work" (p. 160). He later talks about his early career as a racialized teacher in a small rural school in British Columbia and the "moral challenge" to teach these white rural students "with equity and fairness, to learn from their struggles and life worlds, and to engage them in principled understandings and dialogue about the worlds they would encounter" (p. 165).

And so we realized that, even as teachers must be prepared for the complexities that characterize their students' lives, they must also be guided into deep reflection of how privilege manifests in their own lives and defines their position within Canadian society. They must be prepared for how their identities and positions may influence their role in the classroom and the relationships they have with students and with colleagues. Perhaps you are considering for the first time what it means to be of your particular intersectional identity—your race, gender, religion, social class, and so forth—or perhaps you have had many opportunities for self-reflection but are now thinking about this for the first time in relation to your role as an educator. The purpose of this book is to help prepare you, as a future or current educator, for the complexities that come with diverse student populations and to embrace the opportunities that come with their diversity, providing conceptual foundations with real pedagogical applications, including deep reflection of self.

Taking up Luke's "moral challenge" for all educators, we suggest that Nussbaum's (1997) notion of cultivation in terms of preparing students for **human flourishing** is a way to (re)cast the conversation. She poses the question "What does a life worthy of human dignity require?" (Nussbaum, 2011, p. 32). Put another way, what does a life of flourishing require? This question, we contend, is essential in the context of diversity education. As Carl Grant (2012) argues in his application of Nussbaum's work, "multicultural democratic education puts the cultivation of and attention to students' flourishing and whole lives front and center" (p. 913). He regards "cultivating" as the action—"the work that teachers do for and with their students"—to bring about flourishing.

## HUMAN FLOURISHING IN EDUCATION

The idea of flourishing has a long history, associated with Aristotle's notion of *eudaimonia*, fulfilling one's life potential as a human being within society (see also chapter 3). Whereas Aristotle's ideas are centred more on the individual as he considers a person's quest for the good life, Nussbaum takes a more social approach—for the good of society. This means that not only do we need to think about the whole person when we talk about flourishing, but we also need to think about the whole person *in context* with others. Grant (2012) brings in the ancient Greek notion of "citizens living with and practicing wisdom, beauty, and the common good" (Castoriadis, 1991, p. 123, as cited in Grant, 2012, p. 912). This means that when flourishing is possible for one person, it contributes to the common good. This is particularly poignant when we think about the classroom and cultivating flourishing in the individual and the collective. How we *together* flourish means that students contribute to the flourishing of others, just as they seek their own flourishing. In his 2020 monograph in *The Modern Language Journal*, Levine proposes a "human ecological language pedagogy" within the context of intercultural approaches to language education. His response to Nussbaum's question is that a life worth living requires "the capability to learn from and engage with others in diverse ways throughout our lives" (p. 35); it requires the ability to "create relationships, continuity, and emotional attachments" (p. 35)—and in so doing, to realize one's full human potential. This grounding of human flourishing within human relationship is essential to a view of multicultural education that seeks to engage *all* students. It recognizes the interconnections embedded in human development and personal growth and the intersectionality of diversity that Luke alludes to in his quote given earlier.

It is important to distinguish our understanding of human flourishing from that of Aristotle in another way. As Wolbert and colleagues (2021) point out, Aristotle believed children and youths are not yet capable of experiencing flourishing—life is unpredictable, and many changes can happen along the way, and children and youths have not yet achieved a "full life." He regarded flourishing as an indication that one has lived a "complete" life, which involves thriving long enough to demonstrate they have lived a virtuous life (Wolbert et al., 2021). Furthermore, in Aristotle's view, children and youths are being trained in the "virtues" but have not yet achieved them. However, we argue that, while children and youths may not have achieved a "full life" in the Aristotelian perspective, we know that they can live quite fulfilling lives. It is useful to view flourishing as a "dynamic state," one that is not static but can change and develop in different stages of life (Wolbert et al., 2015, p. 124). Thus, we view the educational focus as one that seeks to prepare children and youths for flourishing lives in the present and into adulthood. At the same time, we are also mindful that a precondition for children and youth to experience flourishing lives is that their basic needs (Maslow, 1970) must first be met.

Nussbaum (1997, 2006) takes her notions of flourishing and human development to the field of higher education, which we argue applies to all levels and types of education. She proposes a three-part model of capabilities that schools should develop in their students: (a) a critical examination of the self; (b) recognition of the importance of and ability to see oneself as a global citizen bound to the flourishing of humanity; and (c) the capacity for compassion and empathy, which requires a narrative imagination or imaginative understanding. These three capabilities, she argues, are essential to prepare students for democracy and engagement in local and global communities of diversity, connected through internationalization, and within those contexts, the "cultivation of humanity." So what exactly are these capabilities?

## Critical Examination of the Self

Even if you have never read Socrates's writings, you have probably heard of his oft-quoted statement that "the unexamined life is not worth living for a human being" (cited in Nussbaum, 1997, p. 21). That is, this life of critical self-examining is an essential characteristic of a worthwhile, meaningful life—of what it means to be human. Nussbaum (1997) provides us with the following context to Socrates's proclamation: "Most of the people Socrates encountered were living passive lives, lives in which, in the most important things, their actions and choices were dictated by conventional beliefs. These beliefs inhabited and shaped them, but they had never made them truly their own, because they had never really looked into them, asking whether there were other ways of doing things, and which ways were truly worthy of guiding them in their personal and political lives. To this extent, they had not made their own selves fully their own" (p. 21). In this description, passivity appears to mean superficiality, lack of curiosity, lack of responsibility for one's beliefs, and as a result, a level of inauthenticity. But as well, we can see how this passivity enables privilege. Privilege thrives when those in such positions do not question or critically self-reflect, when they resist curiosity. This nonquestioning stance of privilege shields them from responsibility and rewards ignorance. What Socrates and Nussbaum argue for is an education that will develop in students the capacity to critically examine their self, their beliefs, and their traditions and to live the life (have a posture of) continual self-examination.

This is not to suggest that, in their call for critical self-examination, Socrates or Nussbaum is advocating for a form of cultural relativism (a critique levelled by many opponents of multiculturalism) that would require abandonment of one's own cultural identity, traditions, and values. As Nussbaum (1997) puts it, there is a misplaced fear that "critical scrutiny of one's own traditions will automatically entail a form of cultural relativism that holds all ways of life to be equally good for human beings and thereby weakens allegiance to one's own" (p. 22). Rather, the goal of critical examination is that students will be able to identify what they believe and know why and that they will be willing to critically assess which views merit their allegiance and which do not. In the end, they may well adhere to the same view that they started with, but they will know why, and this will be principled knowing. Going back to the earlier quote from Socrates, "their own selves" will become "fully their own." This knowledge of self and ownership of their own reasoning and ideas will then enable them to engage in respectful dialogue and deliberation and to then collaborate in a process of respect and dignity for all of humanity (Nussbaum, 2006). They will have the foundation to consider their beliefs, traditions, and selves within the context of others. Rather than populist, emotional reaction that often hardens differences, there will be movement toward dialogue and understanding. Grant (2012) emphasizes the critical evaluation of self (beliefs, values, and traditions) as the first step in creating and cultivating a social justice vision in education. For teachers, this begins with knowing themselves before they ask their students to gaze inward.

## Self-Identification as a Global Citizen

The second tool or capability encompasses "an ability to see oneself as not simply citizens of some local region or group but also, and above all, as human beings bound to all other human beings by ties of recognition and concern" (Nussbaum, 1997, p. 10). This capacity of association, or affiliation, has to do with how we operate as citizens of the world in our local context. It is about recognition and concern for others, understanding who I am in relation to those around me and how my actions are part of a broader social ecology. Nussbaum (2000) puts it well when she says affiliation is about "being able to live with and towards others ... having the social bases for self-respect and non-humiliation; being able to be treated [and treat others] as a dignified being whose worth is equal to that of others" (p. 79). As educators, we play a key role in cultivating in students such "dispositions to act justly" (Wolterstorff, 2004, p. 145). Students do not come to class as a blank slate; rather, they have already been taught or nurtured to act and react in certain ways to the world around them and in response to the social structures that order their lives. For this reason, Wolterstorff (2004) argues, "issues of social justice by their very nature involve issues of social structure" (p. 147) and hence require critical consciousness (Freire, 1970/2000). Critical consciousness asks students to look at the social structures of society and discover the inequality that results among certain groups, both locally and globally. It also asks students to think of their own position within these social structures and their response to their position within these social structures in terms of inequality.

It makes sense, then, that self-identification as a citizen—and more specifically, a global citizen—can be cultivated within the idea of empathy.

There are different conceptualizations of empathy, which we discuss later in this chapter. But here Wolterstorff (2004) brings social justice to the disposition of empathy: "the disposition to struggle against some injustice can often be cultivated by evoking in a person empathy for those suffering under the injustice. And in my experience, one of the most effective ways of doing this is by presenting to the person the human faces and the human voices of suffering: the 'voices of the night'" (Wolterstorff, 2004, pp. 151–152).

Teachers are in an important position to cultivate in all students critical consciousness and a disposition to act justly. Teachers and schools can choose practices and model dispositions that cultivate value and relationships among students and staff to promote flourishing lives and societies. They can help students see themselves as global citizens who respond with empathy to the faces and voices of suffering (using Wolterstorff's words) and to the inequality they see in the world. This position of empathy will then lead to action for social change (Grant, 2012): interactions with social groups, locally and globally, to work toward reform. It means pushing back against injustices and promotes the cultivation of flourishing lives in society. Curren (2014) shares, in his neo-Aristotelian focus on education, justice, and the human good, that "good work is a channelling of one's own capabilities, virtues, and judgment toward something *of value*—in school as in life—and it is sustained in school no less than in life by how much we need to do it to be happy" (p. 94). This capability relates in important ways to the third capability, narrative imagination.

## Narrative Imagination

Nussbaum's (1997) third tool requires students to develop a narrative imagination, which is "the ability to think what it might be like to be in the shoes of a person different from oneself, to be an intelligent reader of that person's story, and to understand the emotions, wishes and desires that someone so placed might have" (p. 11). She draws her thinking from Stoic philosopher Marcus Aurelius, who proposed that as global citizens, gaining knowledge of each other should not be our only response. Rather, we must cultivate a "capacity for sympathetic imagination" so that we can understand differences (e.g., religion, gender, race, class, national origin) in others more fully: "their 'insides,' their desires, thoughts, and ways of looking at the world" (Nussbaum, 1997, p. 85). In so doing, students will also develop a sense of themselves in the world and of human possibility.

Narrative imagination is also a response to the limitations of what novelist Chimamanda Adichie (2009) calls "the single story," often held captive by our assumption that in knowing one story we are now complete knowers. In her TED Talk—which we highly recommend every reader watch—Adichie argues that hearing, or choosing to hear, only a single story about another person robs a person of their dignity and results in a critical misunderstanding, the perpetuation of **stereotypes**. She describes her American roommate, who was surprised at her ability to speak English, as follows: "She had felt sorry for me even before she saw me. Her default position toward me, as an African, was a kind of patronizing, well-meaning pity. My roommate had a single story of Africa: a single story of catastrophe. In this single story, there was no possibility of Africans being similar to her in any way, no possibility of feelings more complex than pity, no possibility of a connection as human equals." Narrative imagination thus requires a more holistic reading and endeavour to see the meaning of a person's narrative as the person intended it.

We used the term *empathy* earlier, but we agree with Levine (2020) and Bloom (2016, as cited in Levine's work) that an important distinction needs to be made here between empathy and the kind of narrative imagination that Nussbaum is talking about. The most common understanding of empathy is the idea of walking in someone else's shoes to feel and experience what you think others are feeling and experiencing. Without going into Bloom's (2016) full argument here, we point out two of his concerns with empathy: (1) empathy comes from a position of privilege, and as such, the power differential makes genuine empathy impossible; (2) empathy is usually incomplete (e.g., the single story) or misaligned with the actual lived experiences of those suffering. To illustrate, he describes a simulation exercise for blindness or other disability that is often used to enable students to experience what others experience. One of the problems with such simulation exercises is that they are obviously undertaken by choice and time-limited; they can be terminated at will. Such simulations clearly cannot really come close to providing a like experience. They also give the false impression that negative aspects of the disability are all there is to being in such a place, leading to the conclusion that "I would hate to be blind"—when in fact, the lived experience of (in this example) one who is visually impaired is much more complex (see chapter 16). Bloom's (2016) alternative to empathy is "rational compassion," which he describes as being "characterized by feelings of warmth, concern and care for the other, as well as a strong motivation to improve the other's well-being" (p. 138). His notion of compassion is similar to Wolterstorff's (2004) conceptualization of empathy, discussed above, and brushes against Nussbaum's notion of narrative imagination. Nussbaum (1997) regards narrative imagination as leading one to compassion: "Compassion involves the recognition that another person, in some ways similar to oneself, has suffered some significant pain or misfortune in a way for which that person is not, or not fully, to blame" and "promotes an accurate awareness of our common vulnerability" (p. 91).

Nussbaum's three capabilities—*critical reflection of self, affiliation as a global citizen*, and *narrative imagination*—are formulated as essential to cultivating humanity and essential to human flourishing. But we also note that they all suggest humanity and flourishing must be seen as embedded in *relationship*. True flourishing of all (speaking in the context of education) can happen only when students critically reflect not only on self, but on their self *in relation* to others around them. What this means is that the flourishing of one can only truly come about with the flourishing of all. In flourishing, there is a necessary understanding of our responsibility for each other.

## GUIDELINES FOR READING

In this book, we will explore the multifaceted nature of diversity in Canadian schools and classrooms and consider what human flourishing might mean in these various experiences. But before we introduce you to our authors and the structure and contents of the book, we invite you to consider the following guidelines to maximize your learning and engagement with the concepts related to flourishing and diversity in Canadian schools. The guidelines have been adapted from Özlem Sensoy and Robin DiAngelo's (2017) guidelines to readers of their book on social justice education.

*Strive for intellectual humility—and with that, curiosity.* In his book *We Can't Teach What We Don't Know*, Howard (2006) reminds us that "we cannot fully and fruitfully engage in meaningful dialogue across the differences of race and culture without doing the work of personal transformation.... We must assume that we will be changed in the process of engagement and dialogue" (p. 6). This transformation begins with humility, with recognizing that there may be gaps or errors in our knowledge, experiences, and beliefs. We must recognize that we all hold various prejudices and stereotypes regarding people who may be different from us—and that these prejudices and stereotypes are premised on versions of a "single story." Their superficiality, incompleteness, and dangers need to be identified in order for transformation to occur. Further, transformation requires genuine curiosity, a desire and disposition to learn about and engage with others and with other ways of knowing and being and to understand their more complete multidimensional story.

*Recognize the difference between opinions and informed knowledge.* Sensoy and DiAngelo (2017) point out that "opinion is the weakest form of intellectual engagement" (p. 9). Undoubtedly, even before reading this book or taking a course related to the topic of diversity and education, we all hold opinions regarding matters of diversity and difference. However, as Sensoy and DiAngelo (2017) argue, opinions don't require understanding or engagement. When we state our opinions, we merely rehearse what we already think without expanding, questioning, or delving deeper into what lies beneath our ideas and beliefs. And so, while sharing opinions is important, it must be for the purpose of critically reflecting on and examining those opinions.

*Let go of personal anecdotal evidence and look at broader societal patterns.* Sensoy and DiAngelo (2017) provide an example of what is meant by this guideline: "Many of us have heard something similar to, 'My cousin tried to get a job, but they hired an unqualified Black guy instead because they had to fill a quota'" (p. 11). Such anecdotes are superficial, mask the deeper systematic ways that social inequality works, and provide little to deepen our understanding. In Rothman's (2014) interview with Peggy McIntosh regarding her work on white privilege, McIntosh referred to a widely debated article by Tal Fortgang (2014) in which he challenged the notion of privilege. He responded angrily to the concept, McIntosh argued, because he "didn't want to see himself systemically" (para. 12). She went on: "In order to understand the way privilege works, you have to be able to see patterns and systems in social life, but you also have to care about individual experiences. I think one's own individual experience is sacred. Testifying to it is very important—but so is seeing that it is set within a framework outside of one's personal experience that is much bigger, and has repetitive statistical patterns in it" (para. 11).

*Notice your own defensive reactions and attempt to use these reactions as entry points for gaining deeper self-knowledge.* The topics and themes covered in this book often touch on emotionally and politically charged issues and can be upsetting, especially if this is the first time you are engaging in a sustained examination of inequality, and even more especially if you are a member of a dominant group. And for individuals who have been victims of oppression, revisiting those experiences and seeing the resistance, and maybe even hostility, of classmates can be painful. It is important to use these reactions as "entry points to deeper self-awareness, rather than as exit points from further engagement" (Sensoy & DiAngelo, 2017, p. 14)—not unlike Carter and William did in their discussion after the painful exchange during class. Going beyond these reactions, then, requires the humility and curiosity discussed earlier.

*Recognize how your own social positionality (such as your race, class, gender, sexuality, ability status) informs your perspectives and reactions to your instructor and the individuals whose work you study in the course.* Drawing again on Howard (2006), we cannot guide our students into flourishing "if we have not unravelled the remnants of dominance that still lingers in our minds, hearts, and habits" (p. 6). It is thus imperative that we continually reflect on our social position and what that means for how we respond to the content of this book.

It is our hope that these guidelines will enable you to engage deeply with the book's content and with our authors and will enable a personal transformation that will equip you to bring your students into a place of flourishing. You will notice that all five guidelines entail critical and deep reflection of self. We recommend the duoethnography exercise described in the conclusion as one way to begin this reflection, positioning you to recognize your own deep-seated assumptions that you bring to the teaching profession and to unpack them on a deeper level in a way that will allow you to develop an understanding of the underlying structural issues that impact your teaching.

## BOOK SUMMARY

The book is organized around eight dimensions of diversity. It presents researchers and educators from across Canada who provide background and practical recommendations for pre- and in-service teachers regarding the incredible and beautiful diversity found in Canadian classrooms. Within their areas of expertise, the authors of this book will guide us through the conceptual, theoretical, and practical components of the dimensions of diversity covered in this volume.

Following this introductory chapter, part I provides the broad context of diversity in Canada, beginning with Young (chapter 1) taking a critical and historical look at Canada's multiculturalism policies in education. Particularly in recent years, critical race theory has become an important framework shaping discussions of racism in education; Butler, Abawi, and Berman (chapter 2) provide an overview of its development and distill for us key components of the theory as they relate to teacher practice. These first two chapters set the stage for the rest of the book.

Part II concerns the dimension of race and touches all three aspects of Nussbaum's capabilities. In chapter 3, Iheagwara asks the people of Canada to look inward at the country's dominant educational philosophies and to look outward to consider a cosmopolitan education facilitating a knowledge of humanity and diminishing prejudice, bias, and racism, building capacity for association as a global citizen. Lopez provides a call for critical examination of self in chapter 4. She challenges education systems to reconsider multicultural education frameworks and reimagine instead liberatory pedagogical praxis to support Black and Indigenous youth to thrive. Liberatory praxis asks teachers to provide opportunities for students to find their voice and gain critical consciousness. And the authors of chapter 5, Barek, Bertrand, and Namukasa, ask teachers to consider practices that combat systemic and structural inequities in schools for students with interrupted formal education (SIFEs), demonstrating the capability of narrative imagination.

Part III is about the dimension of socioeconomic status. In chapter 6, Hillier provides an overview of the status of poverty in Canada, documenting the effect that low-SES circumstances have on children and their education, using Nussbaum's capabilities to frame the discussion. She discusses parents' and children's aspirations as important to human flourishing. Abudiab and Eizadirad continue the conversation in chapter 7, describing both the barriers confronting schools located in low-SES communities and the importance of access and culturally reflective practices in schools for overcoming these barriers and facilitating the conditions of human flourishing for students.

The focus of part IV is on the dimension of gender and sexual diversity. In chapter 8, Kennedy provides the reader with an overview of the terms *gender* and *sexuality* and looks at the history of Western gender norms and stereotypes that informs current understandings. In this examination of history, Kennedy notes that binary and heteronormative conceptions are still dominant in educational discourse and asks educational stakeholders to consider these issues and the implications for students. In chapter 9, Potvin asks straight teachers to learn from the "disruptive stories" shared by teachers, to expand their narrative imagination. These are stories where teachers, who consider themselves allies to

2SLGBTQI+ students, find themselves in a moment of oppression toward the young people they seek to help. Potvin asserts that straight teacher allies need to confront these disruptive stories to truly consider their privilege and move forward to advocate for the human flourishing of 2SLGBTQI+ youth.

Part V is about Indigenous education. In chapter 10, Crandall adds further theoretical depth to the conversation of Indigenizing and decolonizing education with discussion of tribal critical race theory, extending our understanding of critical race theory discussed in chapter 2. Morcom, Maracle, Rondeau, and Freeman (chapter 11) explore how Indigenous perspectives can offer practical strategies to foster wellness in the classroom, introducing us to the concepts of radical decolonial love and two-eyed seeing.

In part VI, the authors discuss the dimension of language. In chapter 12, Sachar and Krasny provide a critical examination of language-in-education policies in K–12 schools. They then discuss the notion of "superdiversity" and plurilingualism as approaches for teachers to respond to language diversity and to address the Calls to Action from the Truth and Reconciliation Commission regarding Indigenous language education. Bourgoin, Arnett, and Duffy's focus in chapter 13 is on Universal Design for Learning and Vygotsky's Zone of Proximal Development to critically examine lesson design to address barriers for minority populations in education and discuss how language learners can best be supported.

In part VII, we turn to a discussion of religion in schools. Patrick and Chan, in chapter 14, look at the history of religion in Canadian schools. They outline the Christianization of schools, the secularization of public spaces, and the changing religious demographics in schools. They then present research conducted in schools by the Centre for Civic Religious Literacy to consider the concept of civic religious literacy in schools. In chapter 15, Patrick and Peck ask teachers to consider themselves, students, and community in the development of student learning about religion and nonreligion, considering the capability of both critical examination of self and the tools of association as global citizens. They offer several recommendations for how teachers can approach talking with students about religion and ways that teachers can engage parents and the community in this process.

The two chapters in part VIII involve the dimension of (dis)ability. In chapter 16, Bruce draws on critical disability studies and disability studies in education to promote the lived experiences of those with disabilities as rich knowledge in informing the fostering of human flourishing. And in chapter 17, Schneider discusses the shift from the medical model to the social or biopsychosocial model of disability that influences teacher education. Educators are asked to consider such tools as the Index for Inclusion to provide an indicator for the level of accessibility in a school and classroom setting. Schneider explores Universal Design for Learning and alternative pedagogies embedded in culturally responsive teaching.

In part IX, the dimension of geography is considered. Hillier and Zarifa, in chapter 18, explore rural and/or northern regions of Canada and the educational achievement and attainment of students in these regions, share initiatives that target these inequalities, and discuss the importance of geographical location in discussions about human flourishing. In chapter 19, Corbett suggests the use of rural narrative and/or fiction in teacher education. He offers a selection of fictional and autobiographical pieces to assist in exercising the narrative imagination in preparing teachers for working in rural communities.

In the last section, part X, we consider the theme of intersectionality, which in many ways is the heart of flourishing. In chapter 20, to challenge the ways that inequities persist in multifaceted ways in the education system, Somma, Radersma, Morvan, and Potvin relate their critical examination of injustices in schooling by presenting four stories to highlight the implications for educators and students. Britton, Sidhu, Sidhu, and Ngieng, along with four students (Balkaran, Manmett, Ardra, and Envy), present the Equity Backpack Project in chapter 21. The Equity Backpack Project is a year-long equity-focused curriculum for middle school students. The project takes students through 10 lessons to help them develop a "narrative imagination" and understand their position in a globally connected society, cultivating Nussbaum's capabilities of critical examination of self, understanding of the self as a global citizen, and social action. Finally, in our conclusion, Bokhorst-Heng shares some practical strategies that can be used in preparing you to both engage with the themes of this book and teach for flourishing in your own practice.

In all these chapters, then, you will be presented with the opportunity to develop your own capabilities of critical examination of self, association as a global citizen, and narrative imagination while at the same time being introduced to practical classroom practices that will enable you to develop those same capabilities in your students. You will be introduced to the main concepts that compose the spectrum of diversity and multicultural education in Canada, with a particular focus on what human flourishing might mean in these contexts. Gibson and Grant (2010) describe a commitment to flourishing in the context of education to be one that "encourages all students—regardless of race, ethnicity, socioeconomic status, language, religion, or gender—to imagine and experience flourishing lives and to discover and cultivate individual talents, interest, aptitudes, and commitments" (cited in Grant, 2012, p. 915). What both Grant and Nussbaum argue is that human flourishing is not just a goal or an act for oneself; rather, human flourishing is for our communities, both local and global. In the context of education, teachers and administrators must work intentionally to work against any barriers that would limit the flourishing of students, particularly those who have been marginalized. It is our hope that this book will inspire ongoing transformative dialogue between educators and students. As Freire (1970/2000) notes, "dialogue further requires an intense faith in human kind, faith in the power to make and remake, to create and recreate, faith in their vocation to be more fully human (which is not the privilege of an elite, but the birthright of all)" (p. 88). As you read this book, we ask you to consider how the idea of flourishing might transform the way you see yourself as a person and as an educator. Also, contemplate how might it transform the way you see your students.

## KEY TERMS

**Discrimination:** Unjust and differential treatment of a person or group based on social categories (e.g., race, gender, social status).

**Human flourishing:** People having positive emotions, experiences, feelings of success, sense of worth, dignity and completeness about their place as an individual and a member of the whole of society; fulfilling one's potential as a human being.

**Multiculturalism:** A principle of diversity based on the inclusion of multiple cultures, races, and ethnicities within a space (e.g., political boundary, classroom).

**Privilege:** Built-in and unearned advantage given to a certain person or group.

**Stereotype:** General belief about a specific group of people that is based on various social categories (e.g., race, religion, sexual orientation).

## DISCUSSION QUESTIONS AND ACTIVITIES

1. Have you encountered a time when you had difficulty reflecting on your own privilege or discussing privilege with someone else? Discuss this encounter with a colleague.
2. View or read the transcript of Chimamanda Ngozi Adichie's TED Talk, *The Danger of a Single Story* (www.ted.com/talks/chimamanda_ngozi_adichie_the_danger_of_a_single_story [includes transcript]). As you watch, complete a double-entry journal: a T-chart on which, in the left column, you write key quotes, concepts, or moments in the video, and in the right column, you write your own personal reflections, responses, or questions to what you have written in the left column. Discuss your responses with a peer or in a group

of four. When everyone in your group has shared, discuss the following with each other: What is one thing you can do in your future or current classroom to combat the "dangers of the single story"? (You can read more about the double-entry journal strategy at www.adlit.org/in-the-classroom/strategies/double-entry-journals.)
3. Of Nussbaum's three capabilities presented in this chapter, which one do you think aligns the most with what you have done in the classroom or what you have seen other teachers do in the classroom? Why? Which have you noticed the least? Why do you think that is?

## REFERENCES

Adichie, C. N. (2009). *The danger of a single story.* www.ted.com/talks/chimamanda_ngozi_adichie_the_danger_of_a_single_story/transcript?language=en

Bloom, P. (2016). *Against empathy: The case for rational compassion.* HarperCollins.

Council of Ministers of Education Canada. (n.d.). *Education in Canada: An overview.* www.cmec.ca/299/education-in-canada-an-overview/index.html

Curren, R. (2014). A neo-Aristotelian account of education, justice, and the human good. In K. Meyer (Ed.), *Education, justice and the human good* (pp. 80–99). Routledge.

Fortgang, T. (April 2, 2014). *Checking my privilege: Character as a basis of privilege.* The Princeton Tory. www.theprincetontory.com/checking-my-privilege-character-as-the-basis-of-privilege/

Freire, P. (2000). *Pedagogy of the oppressed.* Continuum International. (Original work published in 1970).

Ghosh, R., & Galczynski (2014). *Redefining multicultural education: Inclusion and the right to be different.* Canadian Scholars.

Grant, C. A. (2012). Cultivating flourishing lives: A robust social justice vision of education. *American Educational Research Journal, 49*(5), 910–934. doi.org/10.3102/0002831212447977

Howard, G. R. (2006). *We can't teach what we don't know: White teachers, multiracial schools* (2nd ed.). Teachers College Press.

Jule, A. (Ed.). (2019). *The compassionate educator: Understanding social issues and the ethics of care in Canadian schools.* Canadian Scholars.

Lam, M. (2019). Effects of Canada's increasing linguistic and cultural diversity on educational policy, programming and pedagogy. *Journal of Contemporary Issues in Education, 14*(2), 16–32. doi.org/10.20355/jcie29370

Levine, G. (2020). Why a human ecological language pedagogy? *The Modern Language Journal, 104* (Supplement). doi.org/10.1111/modl.12608

Luke, A. (2017). No grand narrative in sight: On double consciousness and critical literacy. *Literacy Research: Theory, Method and Practice, 66*, 157–182. doi.org/10.1177/2381336917718805

Mahali, S. C., & Sevigny, P. R. (2021). Multicultural classrooms: Culturally responsive teaching self-efficacy among a sample of Canadian preservice teachers. *Education and Urban Society*, 1–23. doi.org/10.1177/00131245211062526

Maslow, A. H. (1970). *Motivation and personality* (2nd ed.). Harper & Row.

Nussbaum, M. C. (1997). *Cultivating humanity: A classical defense of reform in liberal education.* Harvard University Press.

Nussbaum, M. C. (2000). *Women and development: The capabilities approach.* Cambridge.

Nussbaum, M. C. (2006). Education and democratic citizenship: Capabilities and quality education. *Journal of Human Development, 7*(3), 385–395.

Nussbaum, M. C. (2011). *Creating capabilities: The human development approach.* Harvard University Press.

Rothman, J. (2014). The origins of white privilege. *New Yorker.* www.newyorker.com/books/page-turner/the-origins-of-privilege

Sen, A. (2006). *Identity and violence.* Allan Lane.

Sensoy, Ö., & DiAngelo, R. (2017). *Is everyone really equal? An introduction to key concepts in social justice education* (2nd ed.). Teachers College Press.

Statistics Canada. (2021). *Indigenous peoples.* www12.statcan.gc.ca/census-recensement/2021/rt-td/indigenous-autochtones-eng.cfm

Statistics Canada. (October 26, 2022). *Immigrants make up the largest share of the population in over 150 years and continue to shape who we are as Canadians.* The Daily. www150.statcan.gc.ca/n1/daily-quotidien/221026/dq221026a-eng.htm

Wolbert, L., de Ruyter, D., & Schinkel, A. (2015). Formal criteria for the concept of human flourishing: The first step in defending flourishing as an ideal aim of education. *Ethics and Education, 10*(1), 118–129. doi.org/10.1080/17449642.2014.998032

Wolbert, L., de Ruyter, D., & Schinkel, A., (2021). The flourishing child. *Journal of Philosophy of Education, 55,* 698–709. doi.org/10.1111/1467-9752.12561

Wolterstorff, N. (2004). Teaching for justice: On shaping how students are disposed to act. In C. W. Joldersma & G. Goris Stronks (Eds.), *Education for shalom: Essays on Christian higher education* (pp. 135–154). William B. Eerdmans.

# PART I

## EDUCATION POLICY: A HISTORY AND APPLICATION OF MULTICULTURAL AND CRITICAL IDEOLOGIES IN CANADA

## Introduction

- Teachers must be aware of intersectional identities
- flourishing - fulfilling ones life potential
  ↳ basic human needs must first be met in order to experience this
- 3 things school should teach students
  ↳ examination of self - exposed to ways of being being then self
  ↳ recognition as citizen - how actions affect others
  ↳ compassion & empathy - not stereotyping based on one story/scenario.

- you cant teach what you dont know
- transformation requires genuine curisioty

# CHAPTER 1
# The Evolution of Canadian Multiculturalism: Policy and Legal Considerations

*David C. Young*

Among the many conceptions or misconceptions—depending on one's perspective—of Canadians is that we are polite and have an over-reliance on the use of the word *eh*. While one might lament these generalizations as being overly simplistic, they are, for better or worse, part of the larger social fabric that defines what it is to be a resident of this country. In a similar way, Canada is regarded as a diverse country. As Gibbon put it in 1938, Canada was a "**mosaic**," standing in stark contrast to the American idea of a "**melting pot**." Today we have the idea and the promise of Canada as a **multicultural** country where people from different backgrounds and cultures have the potential to live together and flourish (Jansen, 2005). Here the reference to flourishing is based on the Aristotelian (Aristotle et al., 2009) notion that by living and doing well, we realize our full human capacities.

Building on earlier research (Mangan & Young, 2010; Young, 2008; Young & Gottschall, 2019), this chapter will examine the evolution of Canadian multiculturalism. As Brosseau and Dewing (2018) argue, multiculturalism can be interpreted descriptively (as a fact sociologically), prescriptively (as ideology), or politically (policy). This chapter embraces the last interpretation, with a focus on policy and litigation, with reference to education. Attention will also be devoted to addressing how, where applicable, multicultural education can contribute to a sense of human flourishing.

# THE EVOLUTION OF CANADIAN MULTICULTURALISM: POLICY CONSIDERATIONS

Writing in 1986, Milner warns of the inherent dangers in trying to write a historical educational narrative in a single chapter. Certainly, there might be a temptation to undertake such an initiative, but all efforts to produce a definitive and all-encompassing account have been resisted. Rather, the approach adopted here has been to highlight the key moments and themes in this evolution, thus offering a snapshot of what has preceded the contemporary scene. And of course, one should not lose sight of the fact that multiculturalism is complex and not a static concept. As Leung (2015) notes, multiculturalism "is not only a moving target, but also a multidimensional entity" (p. 107).

Through a survey of the literature (see Brosseau & Dewing, 2018; Fleras & Elliott, 1992), one can see that there appears to be general agreement that multicultural policy in this country has evolved through three distinct phases: (1) the incipient stage (pre-1971); (2) the formative period (1971–1981); and (3) institutionalization (1982–present). It is important to remember that multicultural policy in each of these phases was/is a reflection of initiatives pursued by various levels of government and other para-public organizations. While it is hoped that the effect of these initiatives is policy coherence, and this is often the case, there are times when contradictions in policy also play a role (Ryan, 2010). Ultimately, development of policy in the sphere of multiculturalism is a "process in a constant state of negotiation, compromise, and accomplishment" (Fleras & Elliott, 1992, p. 71).

## Incipient Stage

In looking specifically at the incipient stage, it is first important to recognize that for centuries, many cultures have existed in this country, with the original inhabitants being Indigenous Peoples in various nations (Ghosh & Galczynski, 2014). The arrival of European settlers—primarily from France and England—from the 1500s onward led to the emergence of French and English dominance, with the French and English languages both being enshrined in the 1867 British North America Act (Fleras & Elliott, 1992). At the same time, "the cultures of other groups—in particular, those of native peoples and immigrants from other nations—were, if not dismissed, at least considered to be of little consequence" (Jansen, 2005, p. 25). With nation-building being a central goal post-1867, "preference was given to assimilation and Anglo-conformity as building blocks of Canadian society" (Fleras & Elliott, 1992, p. 71).

In the years following **Confederation**, change was a constituent feature of Canadian society. As new provinces joined the union, Canada experienced growth in both a geographic and a demographic sense. By the 1960s, traditional Canadian immigration patterns, which had largely been dominated by those originating from France and Britain, gave way to those from other European countries. In all actuality, Canada was already becoming a multicultural society—albeit still largely European—although this was not officially enshrined in policy (Jansen, 2005). Some posit that this shift in immigration was the "parent" of policies related to multiculturalism (MacKay & Richard, 1998, p. 268). However, other factors, including greater activism by the state (federal and provincial/territorial governments) in the social policy sphere, also played a role. The 1960 enactment of the Canadian Bill of Rights and the 1970 ratification by the federal government of the International Convention on the Elimination of All Forms of Racial Discrimination helped establish the groundwork for a domestic multicultural policy (Lee & Johnstone, 2021).

Among all these competing factors, perhaps none warranted greater import than the rise of French-Canadian **nationalism** in Quebec in the 1960s. As a result, in 1963 the federal government established the Royal Commission on Bilingualism and Biculturalism, which found that francophones were experiencing inequality when compared with English-speaking Canadians. In its preliminary report, released in 1965, the commission recommended that Canada should have two official languages: French and English. "With the passing of the Official Languages Act [in 1969], the first of Canada's two major intergroup building blocks—bilingualism—was dropped into place" (Bibby, 1990, p. 49).

The demands of minority ethnocultural groups for increased rights also played a significant role in the abandonment of the earlier assimilationist policies and the development of multiculturalism in Canada (Ghosh & Abdi, 2004, p. 103). Building on this, a second intergroup issue addressed by the commission in 1969 dealt with the integration of non-Indigenous, non-French, and non-English ethnic groups (Brosseau & Dewing, 2018). Essentially, ethnocultural groups would now have a full and equal opportunity to participate in Canada's institutional structure (Fleras & Elliott, 1992). "The report of the Royal Commission on Bilingualism and Biculturalism spoke to the growing multicultural nature of Canadian society and provided a basis for an official policy that recognized the multicultural reality and promoted cultural retention and ethnic diversity as part of the policy shift from assimilation to integration in dealing with the 'other' Canadians: immigrants and refugees" (Galabuzi, 2011, p. 69).

## Formative Period

In terms of the evaluation of multiculturalism in Canada, the 1969 recommendation by the commission helped to usher out the incipient period and paved the way for the emergence of the formative period. In 1971, "the second ... of two critical Canadian building blocks—multiculturalism—was set in place beside bilingualism" (Bibby, 1990, p. 49). In a statement made in the House of Commons on October 8, 1971, Prime Minister Pierre Elliott Trudeau announced that multiculturalism would become official government policy. While it was recognized that Canada had a linguistic duality, the country "had no official culture, and no ethnic group took precedence over another" (Jansen, 2005, p. 25). In sum, "bilingualism within a multicultural framework was an attempt by the Canadian state to establish a flexible basis for unity and a comprehensive nationhood" (Ghosh & Galczynski, 2014, p. 32).

As Galabuzi (2011) notes, the federal government committed to supporting the policy of multiculturalism through various initiatives, including the following:

- removing any cultural barriers that prevented full participation in Canadian society
- funding ethnocultural groups to support cultural maintenance
- encouraging cultural interchanges
- providing language training for immigrants in either French or English

Certainly, these policy initiatives would require significant federal funding, and to that end, between 1971 and 1987, the government earmarked nearly $200 million to promote linguistic and cultural maintenance. In addition, a Multicultural Directorate was established in 1972, and its mandate was to assist in the implementation of multicultural policies and programs. A year later, a Ministry of Multiculturalism was created to provide oversight of the programs being implemented within government departments (Brosseau & Dewing, 2018; Fleras & Elliott, 1992).

## Institutionalization Phase

By the early 1980s, the institutionalization phase in the evolution of Canadian multiculturalism had arrived. Immigration of visible minorities largely from non-European countries had increased, and with this came a need to rethink the country's multicultural policy. While the concern with language and culture remained, a new emphasis on employment, housing, education, and nondiscrimination began to occupy centre stage (Brosseau & Dewing, 2018; Fleras & Elliott, 1992).

The adoption of the Charter of Rights and Freedoms in 1982 was a watershed moment in the history of this country. Section 27 is particularly relevant in that it stated that the Charter was to "be interpreted in a manner consistent with the preservation and enhancement of the multicultural heritage of Canadians." Further, in Section 15(1), the Charter expressly prohibited discrimination based on race or ethnic origin.

By the mid-1980s, it was glaringly apparent that existing multiculturalism frameworks were outdated. In 1987, the Parliamentary Standing Committee on Multiculturalism referred specifically to the 1971 policy as "floundering" (Fleras & Elliott, 1992, p. 75). As a result, in 1988 the Canadian Multiculturalism Act, introduced by Brian Mulroney's government, was enacted, thus providing explicit statutory expression for the policy of official multiculturalism. This act "sought to assist with cultural and language preservation, to reduce discrimination, to enhance intercultural awareness and understanding, and to promote culturally sensitive institutional change at federal levels" (Fleras & Elliott, 1992, p. 75). Fleras and Elliott (1992) argue that "multiculturalism serves as a positive instrument of change that is no longer concerned only with the ethnic sidestream. It is aimed at the removal of those barriers that preclude the involvement, equity, access, and representation of all citizens in Canada's institutions. The 1988 act recognizes the need to increase minority participation in society by mainstreaming Canada's major institutions, that is, by bringing diversity into the institutions as a natural, normal, and positive component of decision-making, resource allocation, and the setting of priorities" (p. 78).

In the more than 30 years that have elapsed since the introduction of the Canadian Multiculturalism Act, governments at all levels have been engaged in developing and implementing policies around multiculturalism, with some provinces enacting official legislation that supports and promotes multiculturalism. Although efforts to achieve multiculturalism will never be complete, the country continues to respond and adapt to emerging realities. As an example, in 1997, after a comprehensive review of existing policies undertaken by the Department of Canadian Heritage, the federal government announced its intent to focus on three objectives: (1) social justice; (2) civic participation; and (3) identity. Further, the federal government has undertaken the recognition of past wrongs, an example being the 2016 apology for the *Komagata Maru* incident of 1914, in which the South Asian passengers of a Japanese ship were denied entry to Canada due to the immigration policy in effect that that time (Brosseau & Dewing, 2018). As a consequence of this denial of entry, most on board the ship were ultimately forced to return to India, where some met with death and others imprisonment.

From a policy perspective, critics of official multiculturalism (see, as an example, Bissoondath, 2002) still lament the difficulties associated with it. As Dickinson (1997) writes, "one cannot expect the nation's social history to be repudiated.... The trick is to ensure that, as history continues to be written and our social roots extend, the values, contributions, and interests of all members of our contemporary society are properly reflected and protected. That is the promise but also the challenge of multiculturalism" (p. 8). And despite our best efforts and intentions, under certain circumstances, legal wranglings involving multiculturalism have arisen during the institutionalization phase, with the courts often drawn upon to provide some semblance of clarity.

The struggle between competing old and new constitutional values has surfaced in various Charter cases, many concerned with education (Young & Gottschall, 2019). Among the most noteworthy are *Zylberberg et al. v. Sudbury Board of Education* (1988), *Corporation of the Canadian Civil Liberties Association v. Ontario (Minister of Education) and Elgin County Board of Education* (1990), and *Adler v. Ontario (Minister of Education)* (1992–1996). These cases, which are collectively referred to as "the trilogy," involved challenges to religious and funding regulations and policies. According to Dickinson and Dolmage (1996), the addition of *Bal v. Ontario* (1994) and *Islamic Schools Federation of Ontario v. Ottawa Board of Education* (1997) to the equation results in this "trio" becoming a "quintet." It is worth noting that in terms of this discussion, religion has largely become a proxy for culture, and as such, much of the focus of this chapter will be on cases that deal with religion.

One of the seminal Charter cases dealing with religion and education was *Zylberberg et al. v. Sudbury Board of Education* (1988). This case dealt with a regulation under the Ontario Education Act mandating that opening and closing school exercises must involve the reading of scriptures or other appropriate readings or the recitation of the Lord's Prayer or a similar prayer. Ultimately, the Ontario Court of Appeal struck down the regulation, finding that one religion cannot be given priority and that opening and closing exercises in schools must be consistent with the multicultural nature of the province (Brown & Zuker, 1994, p. 110; Young, 2017).

The case of *Corporation of the Canadian Civil Liberties Association v. Ontario (Minister of Education) and Elgin County Board of Education* (1990) revolved around an Ontario regulation that mandated two periods of religious instruction per week. In addition, it was alleged that the Elgin County Board of Education's religious instruction curriculum displayed a Christian point of view, which was tantamount to a form of religious indoctrination. In the end, the Ontario Court of Appeal reversed a Divisional Court decision, noting that the regulation and curriculum effectively permitted religious indoctrination (Green, 1991; Young, 2008). The conclusion to be drawn from *Zylberberg* and *Elgin County* is that "public schools were [and are] to be secular" (Dickinson & Dolmage, 1996, p. 370).

*Adler v. Ontario (Minister of Education)* (1992–1996) involved the right of minority groups to have their children educated in schools consistent with their faith and to be able to do so without having to endure undue economic hardship. Two groups of parents (Jewish and Christian Reformed) opted, for religious reasons, to send their children to private schools. The parents argued that not providing funding for a private school option was a violation of their Charter rights. The Supreme Court of Canada rejected the argument but did note governments were not prohibited from extending funding to private schools (Young & Gottschall, 2019). Considering the *Adler* decision, some commentators lament the fact that denying individuals rights enjoyed by others is prima facie discriminatory and casts a dark shadow over the Canadian mosaic (Farmy, 2004; Ogilvie, 1997).

*Bal v. Ontario* (1994) arose from the earlier decision in *Elgin County*, which prohibited school boards from operating alternative religion-specific schools. The applicants in *Bal* believed that because of this, their freedom of religion and conscience and freedom of expression were impacted detrimentally. The Ontario Court of Appeal found that the government was not obliged to fund these alternative schools and that denying the applicants the right to promote their religious beliefs within the public school system did not constitute a Charter violation (Dickinson & Dolmage, 1996; Foster & Smith, 2001).

The final case in the quintet is the 1997 *Islamic Schools Federation of Ontario v. Ottawa Board of Education* (see Dickinson, 1997), which involved a 1994 decision by the Ottawa Board of Education to postpone the start of the school year by two days to accommodate Rosh Hashanah. The Islamic Schools Federation of Ontario requested that the board's schools (or at least some of them) be closed on the Muslim holy days of March 3 and May 11, 1995, and that these days be designated as professional activity days. When the board rejected this request, an application for judicial review was then brought by the Islamic Schools Federation, with the Ontario Divisional Court finding that there was no breach of Charter rights because students were permitted to be absent from school on holy days (Young, 2008).

The quintet of cases that arose during the institutionalization phase is an important signpost in the evolution of multicultural policy. The principle reinforced by the courts that schools are to be secular and indoctrination in education will not be permitted is important in establishing schools as a safe place where human flourishing can reside. And although not every judicial decision will appease all parties, the courts have done their level best to respect the rights of all as enshrined in such documents as the Charter. This is not to suggest that all is resolved, since, as Dickinson (2006, p. 171) points out, "Canada's policy of official multiculturalism is still undergoing what could be described as growing pains and at worst as entrenched resistance."

## MULTICULTURAL EDUCATION: AN EVOLVING CONCEPT

Before we turn our attention specifically to the nature of education, it is important to recognize that education does not exist in a vacuum and is to a degree a reflection of larger societal trends. Further, as James and Wood (2005) point out, education in this country has developed in a rather uneven way as each province/territory has developed a system that is a response to its own unique circumstances. In sum, "multicultural education is neither a uniform nor homogeneous process" (Fleras & Elliott, 1992, p. 189).

However, in a general sense, it might not come as a complete surprise that schooling during the incipient stage (as discussed previously) was largely monocultural. That is, assimilation and Anglo-conformity (at least in English Canada) tended to be constituent features of the educational enterprise, with the overarching goal being to strip immigrant children of both their language and their culture. Relatedly, during this period First Nations peoples were also expected to assimilate, with many forced to attend residential schools (Fleras & Elliott, 1992). These schools, which were largely administered by the federal government and various religious denominations, provided an industrial education with little emphasis placed on academic subjects. Rather, the goal was to denigrate "First Nations cultures and society in an attempt to remake them in the colonizers' image" (Ghosh & Galczynski, 2014, p. 45). Oftentimes, residential schools were "overcrowded, riddled with disease, and the source of numerous other problems" (Ghosh & Abdi, 2013, p. 128). Further, "many students experienced brutal abuse, both physical and sexual, at the hands of nuns and priests in these schools" (King, 2023, p. 106). The intergenerational trauma associated with these residential schools continues to this day (Akkari & Radhouane, 2022), and as mass graves have recently been discovered/uncovered by archaeologists at the former sites of some of these schools, we are reminded of their horrible legacy (James, 2023). Murray Sinclair, the chair of the Indian Residential School Truth and Reconciliation Commission from 2009 until 2015, has likened the residential schools to a form of "genocidal" practice (cited in King, 2023, p. 107).

Certainly, the above approach was antithetical to human flourishing. Far from allowing the realization of one's full potential, the forced assimilation that accompanied residential schools instead stifled and, in many ways, tried to extinguish what made people unique.

However, as policy developments arose during the formative period and institutionalization phase, educational policies also adapted and responded to emerging realities. Certainly, demographic, political, and social pressures have been accompanied by a recognition and acceptance of diversity as a core feature of the education system and an attendant effort by schools to develop and enact policies reflective of the pluralistic character of Canada. This effort is manifested in many areas, such as curricula, textbooks, and teacher pedagogy (Fleras & Elliott, 1992).

Trying to encapsulate what multicultural education looks like in schools is no easy task, but Fleras and Elliott (1992) offer a useful typology to understanding its evolution since the 1970s. In a somewhat cautionary note, they remind us that although they propose four distinct perspectives (compensation, enrichment, enhancement, and empowerment), there is much overlap between and among them. As such, the temptation to think of these in a purely chronological or restrictive ideological sense must be resisted. To borrow a nautical metaphor, the perspectives are not to be thought of as watertight compartments.

The compensatory perspective is seen as the earliest prototype of later multicultural education policies and is regarded as multicultural in the loosest sense of the term. Generally, the emphasis was on minority children, with the philosophy being that these students were disadvantaged because of their background, so remediation was necessary to assist them in adapting and integrating into the mainstream. In essence, minority students were singled out as a "social problem" that inhibited educational success, so the school system was tasked with applying "corrective measures" (Fleras & Elliott, 1992). In present day, the compensatory perspective seems relatively anachronistic, so its use in schools is highly questionable. Further, it seems safe to say that, like that found during the incipient stage, the compensatory perspective did little if anything to promote human flourishing.

The enrichment perspective is much more expansive than the compensatory perspective in that it focuses on all students, not just those from minority ethnic backgrounds. Consistent with the philosophy of enrichment, students are exposed to a variety of different cultures as part of their educational experience. This perspective, likened to a celebration of diversity, is premised on the belief that increased exposure to diversity will necessarily lead to positive attitudes toward others, improve minority self-image, reduce bigotry and discrimination, and foster social harmony (Fleras & Elliott, 1992). The development of a positive attitude is encouraging and equates with Nussbaum's (1997) idea that we must recognize that we are all bound together by ties of concern. This would seem, at least superficially, to support human flourishing. However, there remains the possibility that celebrating diversity leads to trivialization, which is highly problematic.

Critics have also warned that the enrichment perspective does little to tackle the root causes of racism and fails to provide students with the tools they need to deal with the realities of a pluralistic society. Thus, some advocate for an enhancement perspective, in which everyone has a cross-cultural understanding that provides the ability and capacity to interact with other cultural groups. This perspective also advocates analyzing the school itself to bring to the surface the racism inherent within the organization, including the hidden curriculum. Attention can then be focused on "reducing racism and discriminatory barriers that students may experience because of their physical or cultural differences" (Fleras & Elliott, 1992, p. 193). Again, borrowing from the work of Nussbaum (1997), we are reminded that in cultivating human flourishing, thinking critically about one's own culture and traditions is critical, and this appears to correspond with the enhancement perspective. As Ghosh (2023) reminds us when discussing the role educators can play, "teachers [will] need to examine their own assumptions, ways of knowing, biases, and prejudices, which may be difficult to do" (p. 27). Gorski's (2016) work around equity literacy is particularly salient in this regard, as the tenets of this framework argue for being aware of the many ways access and opportunity can be negatively impacted by factors such as race, class, gender identity, (dis)ability, and language.

The final perspective, empowerment, argues for a restructuring of the entire educational system so that minority needs, concerns, and aspirations are a primary focus. According to the tenets of empowerment, schools must provide minority students with the skills and resources required to control their own destiny. And as James and Wood (2005) posit, students who lack the necessary social and cultural capital are less likely to experience success in school unless the organization is responsive to their needs. For some, the empowerment perspective can be equated with having control over one's education, with commentators noting this has an interesting parallel to the quest for First Nations to have control over their education (Fleras & Elliott, 1992). In this regard, human flourishing might well rest upon the ability to empathize or walk a mile in the shoes of another, which Nussbaum (1997) refers to as "narrative imagination." But perhaps even more importantly, "changes that individuals are expected to make, will not be productive, unless the institution's policies, programs, and practices are not simultaneously examined, challenged, and altered as individuals do the same with their values, attitudes, and behaviours" (James, 2023, p. 513).

While the preceding discussion has focused on English Canada, it is important to also address the situation in French Canada. Quebec has always maintained a distrust of and opposition to Canadian multiculturalism, instead preferring to embrace the notion of interculturalism. According to this approach, schools are to prepare students in the French language to develop a new common identity. Interestingly, it has been observed that although multiculturalism and interculturalism differ in practical terms, they are quite similar in a philosophical sense (Ghosh & Galczynski, 2014; James & Wood, 2005).

In thinking about multicultural education, it seems that elements of compensation, enrichment, enhancement, and empowerment stand as features of contemporary pedagogy. "In reality, educational institutions are known to juxtapose several of these perspectives" (Fleras & Elliott, 1992, p. 197). And this pluralistic approach, much like the very nature of multiculturalism, can lend itself nicely to helping a diverse student population experience human flourishing.

## ONGOING ISSUES: A PEEK BEYOND THE QUINTET

### Funding

In certain provinces in Canada, denominational (religious) rights have been frozen in time. This has resulted in a constitutional convention that public funding is normally extended only to public school boards and Roman Catholic separate school boards. As a result, in Ontario, Saskatchewan, and Alberta, Roman Catholic separate school boards are treated as public in the sense that they receive funding from the provincial government but are generally established to provide an education to students of the Roman Catholic faith. As Axelrod (2005) notes, it does seem paradoxical to provide full public funding for only Roman Catholic (denominational) school boards in a country that endorses the tenets of multiculturalism. According to the principle of religious parity, it logically follows that if Roman Catholic school boards are funded, then this funding should also be extended to other private religious or faith-based schools.

In addition to *Adler*, which was discussed previously, the 1999 case of *Waldman v. Canada* dealt with the issue of extending funding to a parent who opted to send his children to a private Jewish day school. The United Nations Human Rights Committee, in hearing the case, found that the government of Ontario's denial of funding was discriminatory given that the province already provided full funding for Roman Catholic schools. Even though *Waldman* resulted in a victory for those who support private schools, the case has had little practical impact because the United Nations Human Rights Committee lacks an enforcement mechanism (Young, 2017).

Across the country, variation in terms of funding is the norm. While some jurisdictions, such as Nova Scotia and Ontario, provide little or no funding for private school options, British Columbia, Alberta, Saskatchewan, Manitoba, and Quebec provide various levels of funding (Winton & Staples, 2022). In the end, what we are left with is a situation where funding for private school options remains at the discretion of the province/territory, and the courts have been quite clear that the Charter cannot be used as a tool to require jurisdictions to extend public funding to institutions beyond those afforded protections via Section 93 of the Constitution (Ginn et al., 2020). Consequently, it might be argued that human flourishing is dealt a blow when the discussion turns to private school options.

Despite this, the issue of funding private schools continues to resurface. A 2017 Angus Reid survey found that 31 percent of Canadians believe faith-based schools should be entitled to receive government funding equivalent to that extended to the public education system. An additional 30 percent of those surveyed were in favour of these schools receiving some amount of government funding. The survey data also revealed that support for extending full funding was strongest in Alberta, Saskatchewan, and Ontario and weakest in Quebec (Angus Reid Institute, 2022a).

As far back as the 2007 provincial election campaign in Ontario, then Conservative leader John Tory promised, if elected, to extend funding to faith-based schools provided they agreed to follow the provincial curriculum, employed licensed teachers, and participated in standardized student testing. More recently, Andrew Scheer, while campaigning for the leadership of the federal Conservative Party, suggested that parents who send their children to private and religious schools should be entitled to a $4,000 personal income tax deduction. Even though Tory and Scheer were unsuccessful in their bids to lead Ontario and Canada, respectively, the issue of funding remains an ongoing constituent feature of the educational puzzle.

## Religious Freedom

In addition to this funding debate, in thinking about multiculturalism in the context of education, another important point to keep in mind is that the reasonable accommodation of one's beliefs and the right to express said beliefs are continuing policy considerations. As Clarke (2005) notes, the "expression of one's reasonable and legitimate beliefs needs to be accommodated in our public schools to promote toleration and respect for diversity" (p. 373). This remains consistent with the religious freedom safeguards in the Charter of Rights and Freedoms. Still, it is important to remember that the duty to accommodate is not absolute or unfettered; rather, one must accommodate to the point of "undue hardship," which includes such factors as financial and safety concerns (Bowlby & Reesor, 2017, pp. 281–282).

The Supreme Court of Canada, in the 1985 case of *R. v. Big M Drug Mart*, defined religious freedom as "the right to entertain such religious beliefs openly and without fear of hindrance or reprisal, and the right to manifest belief by worship and practice or by teaching and dissemination" (as cited in Buckingham, 2014, p. 24). The quintet of cases has shaped this debate, but it might be going too far to suggest that religious freedom is tantamount to human flourishing, so work remains.

In the 2006 case of *Multani v. Commission scolaire Marguerite–Bourgeoys*, the Supreme Court of Canada struck down the decision by a school board to prohibit the wearing of a kirpan while at school. In its finding, the court rested its decision on a violation of freedom of religion as guaranteed by section 2(a) of the Charter (Clarke, 2005; Smith, 2006; Young, 2008). Perhaps Chandler (2006) describes it best when he argues that *Multani* "should not be viewed as anything other than a triumph for freedom of religion and tolerance of minority beliefs in Canadian society" (p. 33).

It is worth noting that the decision in *Multani* runs parallel with a decision reached in 1992 by the Ontario Divisional Court in *Ontario Human Rights Commission and Harbhajan Singh Pandori v. Peel Board of Education*. This case stemmed from a prohibition by the Peel Board of Education regarding the wearing of kirpans while at school. In its findings, the Ontario Divisional Court indicated a ban of this nature was contrary to the Ontario Human Rights Code because it denied one's freedom of religion (Tymochenko, 2017; Young, 2008). Taken together, *Multani* and *Pandori* are important because the courts in both cases reaffirmed the multicultural nature of Canada, which in turn facilitates human flourishing.

Any discussion around religious accommodation would be incomplete without also considering recent developments in Quebec. In the 2012 case of *S. L. v. Commission scolaire des Chenes,* the Supreme Court of Canada denied a request from a group of Quebec parents to exempt their children from an ethics and religious culture program. The court found that exposing children to a variety of religious facts does not infringe religious freedom and, further, that exempting children would amount to a rejection of the multicultural reality of Canadian society (Peters, 2017). As the court stated, "the suggestion that exposing children to a variety of religious facts in itself infringes their religious freedom or that of their parents amounts to a rejection of the multicultural reality of Canadian society" (cited in MacKay et al., 2013, p. 54). Following on the heels of this decision, in 2013 the Parti Québécois government introduced the Quebec Charter of Values. Under the Charter, all overt religious symbols and emblems would be banned. Not surprisingly, there was much opposition to the legislation, and it was eventually dropped when the Quebec Liberal Party assumed power in 2014 (Peters, 2017).

However, this effort to secularize Quebec was rekindled in 2017 when the government passed Bill 62 (the religious neutrality law), which prevented individuals from covering their faces when working in the public sector or receiving public services. While this bill was struck down by the courts, the government of Quebec invoked the notwithstanding clause (Section 33) of the Charter of Rights and Freedoms to override this ruling. Subsequently, Bill 21 (An Act Respecting the Laicity of the State) was introduced in 2019. This legislation instituted a ban on all religious symbols for public sector workers, including teachers, and those who receive public services. Specifically, Bill 21 articulates that Quebec is to be a lay state. As Hunter and Clarke (2022) note, the laicity of the state rests on four principles: separation of state and religions; religious neutrality of the state; equality of all citizens; and freedom of conscience and freedom of religion.

As a final analysis, "the Laicity Act argues for a strict deconfessionalization, no accommodation for religious purposes when offering public educational or legal services, and a strict demarcation between church and state" (Hunter & Clarke, 2022, p. 194). While this legislation has detractors and detrimentally impacts human flourishing, an Angus Reid poll conducted in 2019 revealed that 64 percent of Quebec citizens support the act overall (Angus Reid Institute, 2022b). It is worth noting that the government of Quebec recently signalled its intention to reinvoke the notwithstanding clause to further safeguard Bill 21 from judicial oversight.

## CONCLUSION

In a statement issued on October 8, 2021, Prime Minister Justin Trudeau recognized the 50 years that had elapsed since his father proclaimed the policy of official multiculturalism in 1971. As he noted, "while the policy continues to give vitality to Canadian society, reflect its multicultural reality, and inspire people and countries around the world, we still have work to do to make Canada inclusive, fair, and equitable for all" (Prime Minister of Canada Justin Trudeau, 2022). And if we truly value human flourishing, everyone must take up the fight to ensure Canadian multiculturalism is characterized by inclusivity, fairness, and equity. In this regard, Gorski (2016) argues that equity literacy can be an important element in tackling inequity. More particularly, we must be able to embrace and operationalize the following principles: (1) recognize inequity; (2) respond to inequity; (3) redress inequity; and (4) sustain equity. Through enacting these principles, "we become a threat to the existence of inequity" (Gorski, 2016, p. 20).

As Fielding (2008) notes, "our *modus vivendi*, or how we live together in disagreement, will be the central challenge for Canada's ever-changing, multicultural society" (p. 50). But disagreement does not have to always be seen as a negative. In fact, it might provide the fertile conditions needed for real and impactful change that will lay the foundation for a society where all citizens can realize their full capabilities, thus resulting in human flourishing moving to the fore.

## KEY TERMS

**Confederation:** The 1867 act of union that united New Brunswick, Nova Scotia, Upper Canada (Ontario), and Lower Canada (Quebec).

**Melting pot:** A multicultural theory positing that immigrant groups will melt together by giving up their individual cultures, thus assimilating into the dominant culture. The melting pot theory is often associated with the United States.

**Mosaic:** A multicultural theory in which immigrants retain their own culture while immersing themselves in a new society. The mosaic theory is often associated with Canada.

**Multiculturalism:** A sociological concept referring to several ethnic or cultural groups within a single society.

**Nationalism:** An ideology based on the principle that allegiance or loyalty to one's nation is paramount.

## DISCUSSION QUESTIONS AND ACTIVITIES

1. In thinking about the multicultural character of Canada, do you believe it is fair that full public funding for education is normally extended only to Roman Catholic or public school boards? Why or why not?
2. How would you, as a teacher, enact multiculturalism within your practice? Remember to think about the perspectives of compensation, enrichment, enhancement, and empowerment to frame your response.
3. What are the greatest challenges currently facing Canadian multiculturalism?
4. The KAIROS Blanket Exercise can be used as a means to explore the relationship between Indigenous and non-Indigenous people in Canada. By stepping on blankets that represent the land, participants will assume the role of First Nations, Inuit, and Métis people. The activity will conclude with a talking circle. It is important to note that although this activity can be done in person or virtually, it should be conducted by a trained facilitator. More information about the Blanket Exercise can be found at www.kairosblanketexercise.org/v-kbe/.

## REFERENCES

*Adler v. Ontario*, 1996 3 SCR 609.

Akkari, A., & Radhouane, M. (2022). *Intercultural approaches to education: From theory to practice*. Springer.

Angus Reid Institute. (2022a). *Funding religious schools: The majority of Canadians say at least some public dollars should be provided*. https://angusreid.org/funding-religious-schools-majority-canadians-say-least-public-dollars-provided/

Angus Reid Institute. (2022b). *Quebecers support religious symbols ban, but are divided on how—or even whether—to enforce it*. https://angusreid.org/quebec-bill-21-religious-symbols/

Aristotle, Ross, W. D., & Brown, L. (2009). *The Nicomachean ethics*. Oxford.

Axelrod, P. (2005). Public money for private schools? Revisiting an old debate. *Education Canada, 45*(1), 17–19. https://eric.ed.gov/?id=EJ736049

*Bal v. Ontario*, 1994, 21 OR (3d) 681.

Bibby, R. W. (1990). *Mosaic madness: The poverty and potential of life in Canada*. Stoddart.

Bissoondath, N. (2002). *Selling illusions: The cult of multiculturalism in Canada*. Penguin Canada.

Bowlby, B., & Reesor, L. (2017). Special education law in Canada. In D. C. Young (Ed.), *Education law in Canada: A guide for teachers and administrators* (pp. 259–285). Irwin Law.

Brosseau, L., & Dewing. M. (2018). *Canadian multiculturalism: Background paper*. Library of Parliament.

Brown, A. F., & Zuker, M. A. (1994). *Education law*. Carswell.

Buckingham, J. (2014). *Fighting over God: A legal and political history of religious freedom in Canada*. McGill-Queen's University Press.

Chandler, B. (2006). Freedom of religion: The Supreme Court and the kirpan. *Education Canada, 46*(3), 33.

Clarke, P. (2005). Religion, public education and the Charter: Where do we go now? *McGill Journal of Education, 40*(3), 351–381. https://mje.mcgill.ca/article/view/578

*Corporation of the Canadian Civil Liberties Association et al. v. Ontario (Minister of Education) and Board of Education of Elgin County*, 1990 37 OAC 93 (CA). https://ca.vlex.com/vid/cdn-civil-liberties-assoc-680850329

Dickinson, G. M. (1997). School holidays: Days of worship or common pause days? *Education Law, 3*(4), 2–8.

Dickinson, G. M. (2006). Balanced on a knife's edge: School safety meets religious freedom at the Supreme Court of Canada. *Education Law Journal, 7*(3), 171–180. https://heinonline.org/HOL/LandingPage?handle=hein.journals/edulj2006&div=45&id=&page=

Dickinson, G. M., & Dolmage, W. R. (1996). Education, religion, and the courts in Ontario. *Canadian Journal of Education, 21*(4), 363–383. doi.org/10.2307/1494891

Farmy, M. (2004). The private school funding debate: A second look through Charter first principles. *Education & Law Journal, 13*(3), 397–431. https://www.proquest.com/scholarly-journals/private-school-funding-debate-second-look-through/docview/212957155/se-2

Fielding, A. (2008). When rights collide: Liberalism, pluralism and freedom of religion in Canada. *Appeal, 13*, 28–50. https://heinonline.org/HOL/LandingPage?handle=hein.journals/appeal13&div=9&id=&page=

Fleras, A., & Elliott, J. L. (1992). *Multiculturalism in Canada: The challenge of diversity*. Nelson Canada.

Foster, W. F., & Smith W. J. (2001). Religion and education in Canada: Part II—an alternative framework for the debate. *Education & Law Journal, 11*(1), 37–67. www.proquest.com/scholarly-journals/religion-education-canada-part-ii-alternative/docview/212956718/se-2

Galabuzi, G. (2011). Hegemonies, continuities, and discontinuities of multiculturalism and the Anglo-Franco conformity order. In M. Chazan, L. Helps, A. Stanley, & S. Thakkar (Eds.), *Home and native land: Unsettling multiculturalism in Canada* (pp. 58–82). Between the Lines.

Ghosh, R. (2023). Critical multicultural education as a platform for social justice education in Canada. In A. Abdi (Ed.), *Social justice education in Canada: Select perspectives* (pp. 17–29). Canadian Scholars.

Ghosh, R., & Abdi, A. A. (2004). *Education and the politics of difference: Canadian perspectives*. Canadian Scholars.

Ghosh, R., & Abdi, A. A. (2013). *Education and the politics of difference: Select Canadian Perspectives* (2nd ed.). Canadian Scholars.

Ghosh, R., & Galczynski, M. (2014). *Redefining multicultural education: Inclusion and the right to be different*. Canadian Scholars.

Gibbon, J. (1938). *Canadian mosaic: The making of a northern nation*. McClelland & Stewart.

Ginn, D., Garcia Oliva, J., & Lewis, E. R. (2020). Religion in Canadian public schools: Constitutionalized anomalies. *Education & Law Journal, 28*(3), 267–295. www.proquest.com/openview/bd3fa2b9d287b842606d545a5920af70/1?pq-origsite=gscholar&cbl=44752

Gorski, P. C. (2016, May). Re-examining beliefs about students in poverty. *School Administrator*, 17–20. www.aasa.org/resources/resource/re-examining-beliefs-about-students-in-poverty

Green, M. A. (1991). Ontario Court of Appeal strikes down regulation mandating religious instruction. *Education & Law Journal, 3*, 97–100.

*Human Rights Commission (Ont.) et al. v. Board of Education of Peel*, 1991 47 OAC 234 (DC).

Hunter, D., & Clarke, P. (2022). Quebec's laicity act, teachers, and dress codes in Canadian case law: Introspection before legal action. *Education & Law Journal, 31*(2), 169–199. https://www.proquest.com/openview/f018de1d7af7d92e7bab21e268b7f02d/1?pq-origsite=gscholar&cbl=44752

*Islamic Schools Federation of Ontario v. Ottawa Board of Education*, 1994, Ontario Court (General Division), Court File No. 84372/94.

James, C. E. (2023). What did the multicultural policies of the last century promise that need to be re-imagined in today's DEDI post-secondary world? *Canadian Journal of Education, 46*(3), 502–516. doi.org/10.53967/cje-rce.6233

James, C. E., & Wood, M. (2005). Multicultural education in Canada: Opportunities, limitations and contradictions. In C. E. James (Ed.), *Possibilities & limitations: Multicultural policies and programs in Canada* (pp. 93–107). Fernwood.

Jansen, C. J. (2005). Canadian multiculturalism. In C. E. James (Ed.), *Possibilities & limitations: Multicultural policies and programs in Canada* (pp. 21–33). Fernwood.

King, A. L. (2023). Social justice through Indigenization and anti-oppressive teaching. In A. Abdi (Ed.), *Social justice education in Canada: Select perspectives* (pp. 103–116). Canadian Scholars.

Lee, E., & Johnstone, M. (2021). Lest we forget: Politics of multiculturalism in Canada revisited during COVID-19. *Critical Sociology, 47*(4–5), 671–685. doi.org/10.1177/08969205211000116

Leung, H. H. (2015). Canadian multiculturalism in the 21st century. In S. Guo & L. Wong (Eds.), *Revisiting multiculturalism in Canada: Theories, policies and debates* (pp. 107–119). Sense.

MacKay, A. W., & Richard, M. C. (1998). Multiculturalism: Who needs it? *Education & Law Journal, 8*(3), 265–293. www.researchgate.net/profile/A-Mackay/publication/317725828_Multiculturalism_Who_Needs_It/links/594abb13a6fdcc89090cc216/Multiculturalism-Who-Needs-It.pdf

MacKay, A. W., Sutherland, L., & Pochini, K. D. (2013). *Teachers and the law: Diverse roles and new challenges* (3rd ed.). Emond Montgomery.

Mangan, J. M., & Young, D. C. (2010). Multiculturalism in Canada: Context, policy, and law. In J. M. Mangan (Ed.), *Social foundations of education coursebook, 2010–2011* (pp. 195–202). Althouse Press.

Milner, H. (1986). *The long road to reform: Restructuring public education in Quebec.* McGill-Queen's University Press.

*Multani v. Commission scolaire Marguerite-Bourgeoys*, 2006 1 SCR 256.

Nussbaum, M. C. (1997). *Cultivating humanity: A classical defense of reform in liberal education.* Harvard University Press.

Ogilvie, M. H. (1997). Adler v. Ontario: Preconceptions, myths (or prejudices) about religion in the Supreme Court of Canada. *National Journal of Constitutional Law, 9*(1), 79–95.

Peters, F. (2017). The legal and administrative framework of education in Canada. In D. C. Young (Ed.), *Education law in Canada: A guide for teachers and administrators* (pp. 19–58). Irwin Law.

Prime Minister of Canada Justin Trudeau. (2022). *Statement by the prime minister on the 50th anniversary of Canada's multiculturalism policy.* https://pm.gc.ca/en/news/statements/2021/10/08/statement-prime-minister-50th-anniversary-canadas-multiculturalism

Ryan, P. (2010). *Multicultiphobia.* University of Toronto Press.

Smith, W. J. (2006). Private beliefs and public safety: The Supreme Court strikes down a total ban on the kirpan in schools as unreasonable. *Education & Law Journal, 16*(1), 83–112. www.thecharterrules.ca/resources/smith_private_beliefs_and_public_safety.pdf

Tymochenko, N. (2017). Student rights. In D. C. Young (Ed.), *Education law in Canada: A guide for teachers and administrators* (pp. 113–150). Irwin Law.

*Waldman v. Canada*, 67th Sess., UN Human Rights Committee, CCPR/C/67/D/694/1996 (5 November 1999).

Winton, S., & Staples, S. (2022). Shifting meanings: The struggle over public funding or private schools in Alberta, Canada. *Education Policy Analysis Archives, 30*(15), 1–17. doi.org/10.14507/epaa.30.7002

Young, D. C. (2008). Education law and multiculturalism: Beyond the quintet. In J. M. Mangan (Ed.), *Social foundations of education coursebook, 2008–2009* (pp. 197–203). Althouse Press.

Young, D. C. (2017). Educator rights and duties. In D. C. Young (Ed.), *Education law in Canada: A guide for teachers and administrators* (pp. 83–111). Irwin Law.

Young, D. C., & Gottschall, K. (2019). Viewing with compassion: Religious responsiveness in Canadian schools. In A. Jule (Ed.), *The compassionate educator: Understanding social issues in Canadian schools* (pp. 212–227). Canadian Scholars.

*Zylberberg et al. v. Board of Education of Sudbury et al.*, 1988 29 OAC 23 (CA).

# CHAPTER 2
# Critical Race Theory in Canadian Educational Praxis

*Alana Butler, Zuhra Abawi, and Rachel Berman*

Residential schooling in Canada began in the 1870s, and its enduring legacy of abuse and cultural genocide has resulted in intergenerational trauma for Indigenous persons (Battiste & Youngblood Henderson, 2009). There were also efforts to segregate non-Indigenous non-charter groups from the white Canadian population. Walker (1997) notes the history of segregated schools in Nova Scotia, which were legalized by the Education Act of 1836. The act allowed local commissioners to establish separate schools for "Blacks or people of colour." In Ontario, the Common School Act of 1850 permitted separate schools for Black people if at least 12 heads of families (i.e., white husbands and fathers) made such a request (Walker, 1997). Aylward (1999) writes that segregation provisions remained in the legislation until the mid-1960s and that de facto forms of segregation still exist.

After the elimination of segregation in schools, segregation took the form of streaming within schools. In the 1980s, studies found that Black children were streamed into basic courses 50 percent more often than white children were (Walker, 1997). The topic of streaming in schools is one that readily lends itself to an analysis grounded in critical race theory (CRT). In this chapter, we will define CRT, outline its history, and provide an overview of CRT in Canada. We will then discuss how it can be a helpful theoretical lens to understand educational praxis contexts, focusing on Canada in particular. Finally, we will explore how educators can utilize CRT as part of their anti-oppressive, anti-racist pedagogy. These pedagogical approaches will contribute to students' psychological well-being and sense of belonging, which are important factors in human flourishing (Dahl et al., 2020). We (the authors of this chapter) have delivered many workshops for teachers and educators. Teachers and other practitioners always ask for strategies that they can readily adapt for the classroom, but we caution that it is imperative that the teachers develop their theoretical knowledge by developing an understanding of the theories before attempting to *apply* them.

## WHAT IS CRITICAL RACE THEORY?

Critical race theory is a theoretical approach to the study of race that grew out of critical legal studies in the United States (Delgado & Stefancic, 2017). Social scientists acknowledge that race is a social construct through which societies allocate privilege and status (Dei, 2011; Delgado & Stefancic, 2017; Goldberg, 2009; Omi & Winant, 2014). CRT thus rejects the idea that any institutions, laws, or policies can be race-neutral. In the United States, there has been a recent backlash against the theory, with several states banning the teaching of CRT in K–12 schools and some higher educational institutions prohibiting the topic as well (Arnett, 2022; Kelly, 2023; Miller et al., 2023). Cammaerts (2022) observes that the anti-woke culture war by politically conservative parties as well as right-wing media demonstrates how social justice struggles like anti-racism, anti-sexism, and pro-2SLGBTQI+ rights, and, more recently, diversity, equity, and inclusion (DEI) efforts, are being positioned as extreme deviant political positions. Cammaerts (2022) also notes that freedom of speech laws are being weaponized to protect racist speech and silence the marginalized. CRT as a theoretical tool has been incorporated into research in many fields and disciplines, including law; social sciences; humanities; child, ethnic, and women's studies; and education (Berman, 2020; Crenshaw, 2011; Delgado & Stefancic, 2017; Gillborn & Ladson-Billings, 2010; Goldberg, 2009; Solórzano & Yosso, 2002).

## HISTORY OF CRITICAL RACE THEORY

Critical race theory emerged in the late 20th century within the field of critical legal studies (Bell, 1973; Crenshaw, 1989; West et al., 1995). The original objective of CRT was to analyze how race and racism become embedded in laws, policies, and institutional practices. In his seminal work titled *Race, Racism and American Law*, Bell (1973) studied the impact of racial discrimination in the area of civil rights, criminal justice, and property rights. One of his key arguments is that the American legal system has perpetuated systemic racism. He further introduced the concept of *interest convergence*, a concept that has become central to CRT and is applicable to immigration laws, labour laws, and civil rights protections. Interest convergence refers to the idea that racial justice can happen only if it aligns with the interests of the dominant white society. For example, racist immigration laws existed until labour shortages necessitated the admission of non-Europeans to the United States (Bell, 1973). In the 1980s and 1990s, scholars such as Kimberlé Crenshaw (1989, 2011) further contributed to CRT when they provided a Black feminist critique within feminist legal studies that included a robust analysis of CRT in law and politics. Goldberg (2009) is a renowned critical race theorist from South Africa who brought a global perspective to CRT, drawing on South Africa's racial apartheid policies to explore how CRT could be applied to them. From about 2010 to the present, CRT has been integrated as a theoretical tool to understand racial disparities in education, health sciences, social work, business, computer science, literature, media, and many other areas (Lin, 2023).

Although CRT is a well-established theory with several decades of scholarly research, it has been criticized by certain scholars who argue that too much social significance is given to race relative to social class (Walton, 2020). Based on the work of Karl Marx, Marxism is a theory that focuses on the class conflict between the working class and the upper-class owners of production (Cole, 2020). Neo-Marxists insist that social class inequalities account for social inequality and have broader implications than race. Others have argued that CRT focuses too much on white supremacy and ignores other permutations of racism, such as racism between minority groups (Cole, 2020). Political leaders in the United States have also used opposition to CRT to justify eliminating or reducing ethnic studies programs, including African American history (Arnett, 2022; Kelly, 2023).

## KEY TENETS OF CRITICAL RACE THEORY

Rather than seeing racism as anomalous or atypical, CRT posits that racism is an endemic aspect of societal institutions. The main tenets, as outlined by Delgado and Stefancic (2017), are summarized in this section, with examples of how they may manifest within the educational system.

### Racial Realism, Interest Convergence, and Material Determinism

Racial realism means that race is a primary way that societies allocate privilege and status. This greatly impacts life outcomes in employment, health, and well-being. Students are embedded in social systems, so both inside and outside the classroom, race serves as a visible marker that may shape their lived experiences. As noted earlier, interest convergence means that racial gains occur only if they also benefit the majority white society. For example, labour laws protecting racial minorities from employment discrimination occurred when there was a decline in European migration and their labour was needed. Material determinism means that your ascribed status in terms of race, class, and gender affects your social mobility by shaping opportunities that are available to you throughout your life. For example, teacher expectations are influenced by a student's race, class, and gender, and this may have long-term impacts on the student's educational achievement (Carter et al., 2018; Gershenson et al., 2021).

## Revisionist History

History is re-examined and interrogated through the lens of the marginalized, not the dominant, culture, whose victories and gains—which have come at the expense of others—have been recorded. An example of this is the current attempt, which privileges Eurocentric perspectives of history, to restrict the teaching of subjects related to race and slavery in the Americas (Pendharkar, 2022). A revisionist history approach would support the teaching of these subjects to focus on the perspectives of the marginalized voices.

## Critique of Liberalism

CRT theorists argue that liberal ideologies of equality and fairness obscure racial injustices. Colour-blind ideologies permeate liberal policies and discourses. The existence of rights is procedural rather than substantive and disproportionately disadvantages those who are disenfranchised from exercising those rights. In education, this indicates a need to make a distinction between equality and equity.

## Structural Determinism

There are structural elements in society, for example poverty, that may lead to adverse outcomes regardless of a person's individual disposition. Oppressive social structures contribute to racial inequality. Educators need to acknowledge how structural systems interact with race to produce inequities for students.

## Counter-Storytelling and Intersectionality

Other contributions from CRT include the importance of counter-storytelling as evidence of the lived experiences of marginalized groups. Solórzano and Yosso (2002) contend that the voices of the marginalized are ignored or obscured by the dominant culture. Counter-storytelling is a way for nondominant populations to challenge racial stereotyping, deficit framing, and ahistoricity. Crenshaw (1989) is also credited with introducing the theory of **intersectionality**.

Intersectionality refers to the idea that our interlocking social identities of gender, race, social class, sexuality, and religion, among others, cannot be easily separated (Crenshaw, 1989).

Now that we have considered some of the key tenets of CRT, in the next section we will look more closely at how CRT has been understood within the context of education. Since policies and practices in the United States often influence educational debates and policy in Canada (e.g., Maharaj et al., 2022), we begin with a brief discussion of some of the key moments of CRT's history and educational debate in the United States.

## THE HISTORY OF CRITICAL RACE THEORY IN U.S. EDUCATION

Ladson-Billings (2005) observes that CRT shifted from a focus solely on law to a focus on education around 1994. For close to three decades, scholars have been integrating theoretical approaches to CRT in the field of education (Busey et al., 2023), particularly applying it to explain differences in educational outcomes by race (Gillborn & Ladson-Billings, 2010; Parker et al., 1999). CRT posits that racism is ingrained within all aspects of our society. Since racism is so pervasive, mainstream classroom practices also reinforce race, class, and gender oppressions (DeCuir-Gunby, 2020). CRT sheds light on the injustices evident in the expanding disparity in academic performance among marginalized **racialized** youth and the perpetuation of racial stereotypes (Ladson-Billings, 2005).

However, while CRT has been a powerful theoretical tool in making systemic racism in education transparent, it has also become both politicized and weaponized through relentless campaigns to silence race-related pedagogical content across the educational landscape. Under Donald Trump's presidency in 2020, Executive Order 13950 was passed to effectively outlaw the teaching of CRT, and many governors followed suit, passing similar state-level laws. Although the legislation was revoked under Biden's leadership in 2021, widespread bans remain intact at local and state levels, the most notorious example being Florida, where not only have books on race been banned and teachers reprimanded for engaging in discussions pertaining to race (Alexander, 2023), but the social studies curriculum now teaches students that slavery was beneficial to African Americans (Breen, 2023). Thus, the curriculum has enacted structural violence by silencing America's long and brutal legacy of the transatlantic slave trade. Using textbooks that minimize the scale and impact of slavery or ignoring the topic altogether perpetuates anti-Black racism by ignoring these histories.

# CRITICAL RACE THEORY IN CANADA: CONVERGENCES WITH AND DIVERGENCES FROM THE UNITED STATES

Similarly to CRT's beginnings in the United States, CRT in Canada originated in critical legal studies (Aylward, 1999). The first known Canadian book to be published on the topic was *Canadian Critical Race Theory: Racism and the Law* (Aylward, 1999). The author notes that Canadian Black scholars and other scholars of colour were attracted to the critical legal studies movement because of its recognition that objective laws could be oppressive. The adoption of CRT in Canada has been challenged by national mythologies about Canada as a welcoming nation that values cultural differences, particularly exemplified by the Multiculturalism Act of 1988, and the mythology of Canada being an egalitarian nation.

Prime Minister Pierre Elliott Trudeau first introduced Canada's official multiculturalism policy in 1971 (Guo & Wong, 2015). This represented a significant policy shift from assimilation to integration. The national discourse of multiculturalism valorizes the ideals of the "founding" nations of Britain and France. Canadian sociologist John Porter (1992) claims that Canadian society is a vertical mosaic, with each ethnic group occupying a hierarchical level and the top representing those who are closest to the British and French "founding" ethnic groups. This, of course, obscures the impact of colonialism on the pre-existing Indigenous populations, who are excluded from the mythology of the "founding" ethnic groups (Bannerji, 2000; Denga, 2020).

Another challenge to the mythology of Canada as an egalitarian nation is the existence of slavery. With the Underground Railroad and the so-called rescuing of Black Loyalists from the American Revolution being central to the Canadian narrative, many Canadians tend to be unaware of or ignore the realities of slavery in Canada's history. However, Black and Indigenous Peoples were enslaved under policies in New France from around 1607. Olivier Le Jeune was the first enslaved African brought directly from Africa recorded in the historical documents (Aylward, 1999). In 1709, slavery received full approval from France, and under British rule, it further expanded until it was officially abolished in 1834 (Aylward, 1999).

Critical legal scholars have also challenged the mythology of the egalitarian Canadian nation through their study of jurisprudence (Aylward, 1999; Backhouse, 1999; Walker, 1997). Walker (1997) reveals that Canada had its own version of American Jim Crow laws mandating segregation in public spaces such as theatres, churches, housing, orphanages, funeral homes, cemeteries, and others. Canada's Viola Desmond, now commemorated on the $10 bill, became famous for protesting a racially segregated theatre in Nova Scotia in 1946 (MacLeod, 2018).

A significant barrier for legal equity was the fact that Black people were excluded from law schools in Canada. According to Aylward (1999), while a Black Nova Scotian graduated from Dalhousie Law School in 1898, it would be 54 years before another Black man, named George Davis, did so. A 1989 Royal Commission report recommended that visible minority students be encouraged to pursue law. At the time, Nova Scotia had seven lawyers who were not able to practise law because of racial discrimination (Aylward, 1999). The lack of Black representation in law is one of the ways critical race theorists contend that racism is allowed to perpetuate in the legal system.

Like the United States, Canada—a settler-colonial nation with a history of slavery, genocide, and segregation—has experienced strong opposition to the teaching of CRT in public education. In Ontario, Canada's largest and most diverse province, the Waterloo Region District School Board and Durham Catholic District School Board, among others, encountered fierce backlash from parents and trustees alike who expressed their discomfort with terms including *white supremacy* and *colonialism* being used in the classroom. Such discomforts are driven by white racial fears and anxieties about coming to terms with Canada's racism, underpinned by **settler-colonialism** (James & Shah, 2022). For CRT pedagogies and epistemic approaches to be centred in classrooms, structural whiteness informing the teaching profession must be unpacked.

Following the horrific murder of George Floyd, a Black man, by Derek Chauvin, a white police officer in Minneapolis, Minnesota, many white people were forced to come to terms with their whiteness, as organizations responded reactively with a rapid increase in equity, diversity, and inclusion training initiatives. The impact was felt in Canada as well. School boards, especially in Ontario, were charged with changing educator practice following scathing ministry reviews—the most notable being the 2020 review of the Peel District School Board, which uncovered epidemic levels of anti-Black racism (Raza, 2022). As noted earlier, extant literature outlines strong correlations between race and disciplinary practices, streaming processes, and chronically low teacher expectations, which especially disenfranchise Black students (James & Turner, 2017; Ledesma & Calderon, 2015; Matias et al., 2014). White women have been instrumental in such settler-colonial "civilizing roles," constituting the majority of residential school workers, nuns, missionaries, and teachers (Abawi, 2021;

Eizadirad et al., 2023). As such, deviations from and nonconformity to whiteness are weaponized and not only shape the content taught in classrooms but also actively reinforce social, behavioural, developmental, and parental norms that students, families, and the community are told to adhere to. Further, the normative structures of whiteness in education dictate which bodies are suitable to teach (read: white, feminine, and heteronormative). Since society upholds whiteness as the norm when thinking about teacher identities, Black, Indigenous, and other racialized communities have faced steep barriers and have had to navigate extensive gatekeeping mechanisms just to access the teaching profession. Those who enter the profession are often pushed out for resisting whiteness and embedding CRT, ostracized for leading anti-racism work, and continually passed over for promotions in favour of white educators (Abawi & Eizadirad, 2020).

## CANADIAN SCHOLARS' USE OF CRT AS A FRAMEWORK IN EDUCATION

Although critical race theory originated in the United States, Canadian scholars have found it a helpful framework to understand racism in schools, particularly the explicitly racist legal policies related to the schooling of Black and Indigenous students. This section will explore how scholars have used CRT in their educational research, along with implications for teaching praxis.

Most Canadian provinces have some form of streaming for secondary school courses that offer both applied/basic tracks and academic tracks. The academic tracks are designed to prepare students for post-secondary education, and research has found that Black and Indigenous students are disproportionately streamed into lower academic tracks (James & Turner, 2017; Parekh et al., 2016). Dei (2008) has, in his body of scholarly work, documented how Black students are "pushed out" by systemic anti-Black racism within the Ontario elementary and secondary school systems. This process is connected to the school-to-prison pipeline, where school disengagement leads to the juvenile and potentially the adult criminal justice system.

The largest and most diverse school board in Ontario is the Toronto District School Board (TDSB). It is one of the few boards to systemically collect race-based data, although several other boards have begun developing surveys to collect race-based data (Parekh et al., 2016). James and Turner (2017) conducted a review of the TDSB and found that only 53 percent of Black students (compared to 81 percent of white students and 80 percent of other racialized students) were in the academic program stream. Through a lens of CRT, educators should question what the overt and covert ways are in which Black students may be deemed less academically capable and encouraged to enrol in lower academic tracks. What are the structural barriers in place that disproportionately affect Black students? Disparities also exist in school discipline. Black students are twice as likely as their white and other racialized peers to be suspended at least once during high school (James & Turner, 2017).

Using a critical race theoretical lens, it is evident that systemic racism has played a role in how Black students are disciplined for similar behaviours as those demonstrated by white students, how they are perceived as less academically competent and thus streamed into lower tracks, and how these factors can culminate in higher dropout rates. These school policies are ostensibly race-neutral, but in practice they result in racial disparities (James & Turner, 2017; Parekh et al., 2016). Dei (2008) asserts that scholarly literature is replete with terms like *at risk*, *dropout*, and *disadvantaged* to describe Black youth and to explain why Black youth struggle or demonstrate lower academic achievement in schools. He argues that the essence of education should involve nurturing a sense of identity within one's culture and community while also incorporating ancestral cultural knowledge.

The TDSB released a document in 2020 aimed at supporting Black student achievement and dismantling anti-Black racism in its schools, and in March of 2023, the Ontario Human Rights Commission (OHRC) announced an initiative to respond to the pervasive and rising anti-Black racism in Ontario's publicly funded education system (TDSB, 2020).

Many scholars have also argued that CRT provides a useful lens through which to examine curriculum in both secondary and post-secondary institutions. For example, Douglas et al. (2022) contend that CRT should be included in medical education to address health disparities, given that racism is one of the social determinants of health (Barr, 2019).

## CRT INFORMED PEDAGOGY

There is no quick-fix strategy to integrate CRT in one's pedagogy without a commitment to ongoing learning. Embedding CRT in the classroom is essential to honouring the diversity of intersecting identities of students and educators, repositioning and rethinking epistemologies through the centring of voices that are often silenced, and disrupting the hegemony of whiteness. According to the original conceptualization by Lynn (1999) and expanded by later scholars, such as Parker and Gillborn (2020), CRT-informed pedagogies entail four fundamental components: the understanding of the myriad ways that racism undergirds all facets of education; the recognition of power relations that are built on racial hierarchies and reinforced by whiteness; the importance of self-reflective practice for educators; and the centring of emancipatory and transformative teaching practices guided by **counter-narratives** that recentre marginalized voices and allow for the flourishing of all students (Ledesma & Calderon, 2015). Elsewhere, Lynn and Parker (2006) conceptualize CRT pedagogy as follows: critical race studies in education could be defined as a critique of racism as a system of oppression and exploitation that explores the historic and contemporary constructions and manifestations of race in our society, with particular attention to how these issues are manifested in schools (p. 282).

Infusing CRT into classrooms requires teachers to engage in self-reflective praxis to unpack their own intersecting identities and develop racial self-awareness. We argue that, rather than a simple classroom tool, CRT is a conceptual lens. Through self-reflective practice, teachers are encouraged to critically reflect on their own positionalities, ways of knowing, and lived experiences as well as to "excavate" any biases or pre-conceived notions they may consciously or subconsciously harbour (Lopez, 2013). Such teacher self-reflection is integral to the elevation of Black, Indigenous, and other racialized student voices through counter-narratives and storytelling as pedagogy (Delgado & Stefancic, 2017; Ladson-Billings & Tate, 1995; Lopez, 2013; Solórzano & Yosso, 2002). Simply stated, counter-narratives affirm the identities of students whose identities are erased, marginalized, or denigrated in their everyday lives and through their educational experiences. A teacher could engage students in a critical examination of a textbook to help them explore which identities are represented and which are not. How could the teacher supplement or replace the textbook content to better reflect the identities of those students?

Because the majority of teachers in Ontario are white and student demographics are increasingly racialized, it is vital for educators to name whiteness and acknowledge whiteness as a racial identity that intersects with other positionalities rather than a marker of normalcy (Abawi, 2021). Teacher attitudes and dispositions greatly impact if and how CRT is taught and interwoven into curricular programming. Such critical awareness is needed not only to prevent the minimization of racism and **microaggressions**, but also to circumvent harmful practices such as **white saviourism** (Ledesma & Calderon, 2015). As Miller and colleagues (2020) posit, counter-narratives provide great opportunities for students and teachers of colour to voice their oppressed experiences, which can lead to further critical analysis of the educational system and the society at large by both people of colour and the white majority (p. 284).

Counter-narratives and storytelling as a pedagogical tool must be rooted in the lived experiences of people of colour to dismantle white normative worldviews and stereotypes about minoritized populations (Miller et al., 2020). Counter-narratives or counter-realities (Delgado, 1995) recentre the perspectives, histories, and memories of Black, Indigenous, and other racialized students. For example, rather than being taught lessons on historical events, geographies, social studies, and so on informed by power relations that privilege whiteness, students are allocated space to draw on their own cultural experiences, teachings, and perspectives of such events. A teacher could also engage the students in a discussion about how the perspectives of the marginalized might differ from the perspective of a member of the white-dominant society for any given topic. The utilization of counter-narratives through storytelling thus challenges the notion that realities and memory are fixed and thereby legitimizes the perspectives of people of colour (Solórzano & Yosso, 2002). By challenging racialized stereotypes and dominant narratives of people of colour, counter-narratives provide space for transformative change, which means that both students and teachers are able to develop new understandings that change their approaches. Using a CRT lens, teachers can approach assessment, curricula, and student, family, and community engagement in a manner that is cognizant of the ways that race may influence outcomes. This challenges the colour-blind orientation of many teacher practices.

Educators will be able to shift their practices from blaming students and families through deficit constructions to recognizing their strengths and supporting them. This will help the students to flourish within an educational system that presents many barriers.

## CONCLUSION

The widespread resistance to and political retaliation against CRT in educational systems are rooted in the overarching unwillingness of settler-colonial societies to name, acknowledge, and dismantle white supremacy. This speaks to a widespread pattern of anti-wokeness, whereby the feelings and validations of white people are centred at the expense of the traumas of Black, Indigenous, and other racialized folks. The interrogation of white supremacist underpinnings of the educational system, and social structures in general, disrupts the status quo through which such inequities are normalized and rationalized. Hindering CRT in pedagogical approaches only impedes opportunities for students to flourish by widening and reproducing racial inequities in educational systems and society at large. Despite the onslaught of educational policy initiatives implemented in Ontario, many of these policies can be characterized as stagnant and performative. Not only are these policies subject to the political climate the province finds itself engulfed in, but they also deflect responsibilities on to the education system, where white supremacy and dominance remain intact. In addition to the negative outcomes noted previously, students and staff of colour report lower levels of well-being than their white counterparts, speaking to the ongoing coloniality of educational spaces that are hostile to minoritized students (Shah et al., 2022). While the province has come under pressure to diversify its educator workforce, such diversification alone is not sufficient; educators of colour also need to critically engage in self-reflective practice to support student well-being and success.

Whiteness in settler-colonial contexts is often internalized by educators of various social locations. As noted, Canada is often praised for embracing diversity; however, stark educational inequities in this country will continue to be exacerbated if **colour-blindness**, meritocracy, and racism are not challenged. As such, teaching and embedding CRT in educational contexts as resistance is more crucial than ever against the backdrop of rising populism, racialized violence, and concerted efforts to erase the histories and lived experiences of people of colour. Counter-narratives as CRT pedagogy are more vital than ever, considering current systematic efforts to erase the memory, histories, and perspectives of Black, Indigenous, and racialized people. CRT is about both social justice and epistemological justice, which are essential to foster human flourishing.

## KEY TERMS

**Colour-blindness:** A term that refers to not seeing or ignoring people's skin colour. It perpetuates racial inequities and power structures by ignoring race and the lived realities of racialized people in an attempt to treat everyone equally. This ideology claims to not notice race and in the process often reinforces racist practices.

**Counter-narratives:** Narratives and perspectives that are grounded in the lived experiences, histories, and memories of those who have historically been and continue to be marginalized from dominant forms of knowledge production.

**Intersectionality:** A term coined by Kimberlé Crenshaw that asserts that people are made up of various positionalities (e.g., race, gender, age, social-economic status) that intersect and that these intersecting identities create unique experiences and facets of discrimination.

**Microaggression:** Subtle verbal or nonverbal acts that serve to diminish individuals based on their race, gender, ability, class, or other social identity.

**Racialization:** The assigning of various markers to a collective group of people based on their actual or perceived racial identity. Such processes often result in inequitable treatment based on perceived racial attributes.

**Settler-colonialism:** A system founded upon the erasure and uprooting of Indigenous Peoples, lands, and resources. Settler-colonialism differs from other forms of colonialism in that there is no formal decolonization process in which land and autonomy is restored, and settlers remain permanent occupiers of the land.

**White saviourism:** The paternalistic view that racial minorities can succeed only if white people save them by imparting their own cultural values. The implication is that racial minorities are always in need of assistance by white individuals.

## DISCUSSION QUESTIONS AND ACTIVITIES

1. In what ways do the histories of settler-colonial racism in the United States and Canada converge and/or diverge? How might these intersections challenge the narrative of multiculturalism in Canada?
2. How might the politicization of CRT in education contribute to ongoing processes of white supremacy and settler-colonial erasure?
3. Why is it important for teachers to engage in critical self-reflective practice to embed CRT pedagogical practices in their classrooms? How can we hold teachers accountable?
4. Textbook curriculum analysis: In small groups, explore a section of a school textbook. Discuss the images: who is included or excluded? Next, explore the written content with the same thing in mind (who is included or excluded?). How does this perpetuate white supremacy/dominance?
5. Educational policy analysis: Examine the Ministry of Education policies for the province or territory in which you teach. After analyzing these policies, discuss how racial bias within these policies may shape the outcomes for diverse members of the student population.

## REFERENCES

Abawi, Z. (2021). Privileging power: Early childhood educators, teachers, and racial socialization in full-day kindergarten. *Journal of Childhood Studies, 46*(1), 1–12. doi.org/10.18357/jcs00202119594

Abawi, Z., & Eizadirad, A. (2020). Bias-free or biased hiring? Racialized teachers' perspectives on educational hiring practices in Ontario. *Canadian Journal of Educational Administration and Policy, 193*. https://journalhosting.ucalgary.ca/index.php/cjeap/article/view/68280

Alexander, T. N. (2023). *Efforts to ban critical race theory have been put forth in all but one state—and many threaten schools with a loss of funding.* The Conversation.

https://theconversation.com/efforts-to-ban-critical-race-theory-have-been-put-forth-in-all-but-one-state-and-many-threaten-schools-with-a-loss-of-funds-200816

Arnett, A. A. (2022). The CRT debate. *Diverse: Issues in Higher Education, 38*(21), 28–30. link.gale.com/apps/doc/A698309472/EAIM?u=anon~6321eae1&sid=bookmark-EAIM&xid=309712c8

Aylward, C. A. (1999). *Canadian critical race theory: Racism and the law.* Fernwood.

Backhouse, C. (1999). *Colour-coded: A legal history of racism in Canada, 1900–1950.* University of Toronto Press.

Bannerji, H. (2000). *The dark side of the nation: Essays on multiculturalism, nationalism, and gender.* Canadian Scholars.

Battiste, M., & Youngblood Henderson, J. (2009). Naturalizing Indigenous knowledge in Eurocentric education. *Canadian Journal of Native Education, 32*(1), 5–17. doi.org/10.14288/cjne.v32i1.196482

Barr, D. A. (2019). *Health disparities in the United States: Social class, race, ethnicity, and the social determinants of health* (3rd ed.). Johns Hopkins University Press.

Bell, D. (1973). Race, racism and American law. *Stanford Law Review, 26*(3), 713–714. doi.org/10.2307/1227685

Berman, R. (2020). Critical race theory. In D. T. Cook (Ed.), *The Sage encyclopedia of children and childhood studies* (pp. 572–575). Sage.

Breen, K. (2023). *Read Florida's Black history teaching standards document to get details on controversial new curriculum.* CBS. www.cbsnews.com/news/florida-Black-history-curriculum-document-pdf-new-teaching-standards-slavery-education/

Busey, C. L., Duncan, K. E., & Dowie-Chin, T. (2023). Critical what? A theoretical systematic review of 15 years of critical race theory research in social studies education, 2004–2019. *Review of Educational Research, 93*(3), 412–453. doi.org/10.3102/00346543221105551

Cammaerts, B. (2022). The abnormalisation of social justice: The "anti-woke culture war" discourse in the UK. *Discourse & Society, 33*(6), 730–743. doi.org/10.1177/09579265221095407

Carter, R., Mustafaa, F. N., & Leath, S. (2018). Teachers' expectations of girls' classroom performance and behavior: Effects of girls' race and pubertal timing. *The Journal of Early Adolescence, 38*(7), 885–907. doi.org/10.1177/0272431617699947

Cole, M. (2020). A Marxist critique of Sean Walton's defence of the critical race theory concept of "white supremacy" as explaining all forms of racism, and some comments on critical race theory, Black radical and socialist futures. *Power and Education, 12*(1), 95–109. doi.org/10.1177/1757743819871318

Crenshaw, K. (1989). Demarginalizing the intersection of race and sex: A Black feminist critique of antidiscrimination doctrine feminist theory and antiracist politics. *University of Chicago Legal Forum, 1*(8), 139–167. https://chicagounbound.uchicago.edu/cgi/viewcontent.cgi?article=1052&context=uclf

Crenshaw, K. (2011). Twenty years of critical race theory: Looking back to move forward. *Connecticut Law Review, 43*(5), 1253–1352. https://digitalcommons.lib.uconn.edu/law_review/117/

Dahl, C. J., Wilson-Mendenhall, C. D., & Davidson, R. J. (2020). The plasticity of well-being: A training-based framework for the cultivation of human flourishing. *Proceedings of the National Academy of Sciences, 117*(51), 32197–32206. doi.org/10.1073/pnas.2014859117

DeCuir-Gunby, J. T. (2020). Using critical race mixed methodology to explore the experiences of African Americans in education. *Educational Psychologist, 55*(4), 244–255. doi.org/10.1080/00461520.2020.1793762

Dei, G. S. (2008). Schooling as community: Race, schooling, and the education of African youth. *Journal of Black Studies, 38*(3), 346–366. doi.org/10.1177/0021934707306570

Dei, G. S. (2011, Spring). Defense of official multiculturalism and recognition of the necessity of critical anti-racism. *Canadian Issues*, 15–19. https://www.proquest.com/docview/1008913710?sourcetype=Scholarly%20Journals

Delgado, R. (1995). *The Rodrigo chronicles: Conversations about America and race*. NYU Press.

Delgado, R., & Stefancic, J. (2017). *Critical race theory: An introduction* (2nd ed.). New York University Press.

Denga, B. (2020). Racism and anti-racism in Canada. *Cultural and Pedagogical Inquiry, 11*(3), 148–149. doi.org/10.18733/cpi29516

Douglas, D., Ndumbe-Eyoh, S., Osei-Tutu, K., Hamilton-Hinch, B. A., Watson-Creed, G., Nnorom, O., & Dryden, O. H. (2022). Black health education collaborative: The important role of critical race theory in disrupting anti-Black racism in medical practice and education. *Canadian Medical Association Journal, 194*(41), E1422–E1424. doi.org/10.1503/cmaj.221503

Eizadirad, A., Abawi, Z., & Campbell, A. B. (2023). Disrupting the weaponization of difference with intentionality: What it means to be an activist and anti-racist educator. In A. Eizadirad, Z. Abawi, & A. B. Campbell (Eds.), *Enacting anti-racism and activist pedagogies in teacher education: Canadian perspectives* (pp. 1–19). Canadian Scholars.

Gershenson, S., Hansen, M. J., & Lindsay, C. A. (2021). *Teacher diversity and student success: Why racial representation matters in the classroom*. Harvard Education Press.

Gillborn, D., & Ladson-Billings, G. (2010). Education and critical race theory. In M. Apple, S. Ball, & L. Gandin (Eds.), *The Routledge international handbook of sociology of education* (pp. 37–47). Routledge.

Goldberg, D. T. (2009). *The threat of race: Reflections on racial neoliberalism*. Wiley-Blackwell.

Guo, S., & Wong, L. (Eds.). (2015). *Revisiting multiculturalism in Canada: Theories, policies and debates*. Sense. doi.org/10.1007/978-94-6300-208-0

James, C. E., & Shah, V. (2022). *Why critical race theory should inform schools*. The Conversation. https://theconversation.com/why-critical-race-theory-should-inform-schools-185169

James, C. E., & Turner, T. (2017). *Towards race equity in education: The schooling of Black students in the Greater Toronto Area*. York University. https://edu.yorku.ca/files/2017/04/Towards-Race-Equity-in-Education-April-2017.pdf

Kelly, L. B. (2023). What do so-called critical race theory bans say? *Educational Researcher, 52*(4), 248–250. doi.org/10.3102/0013189X231159382

Ladson-Billings, G. (2005). The evolving role of critical race theory in educational scholarship. *Race, Ethnicity and Education, 8*(1), 115–119. doi.org/10.1080/1361332052000341024

Ladson-Billings, G., & Tate, W. F. (1995). Toward a critical race theory of education. *Teachers College Record, 97*, 47–68. doi.org/10.1177/016146819509700104

Ledesma, M. C., & Calderon, D. (2015). Critical race theory in education: A review of past literature and a look to the future. *Qualitative Inquiry, 21*(3), 206–222. doi.org/10.1177/1077800414557825

Lin, J. C. P. (2023). Exposing the chameleon-like nature of racism: A multidisciplinary look at critical race theory in higher education. *Higher Education, 85*, 1085–1100. doi.org/10.1007/s10734-022-00879-9

Lopez, A. E. (2013). Embedding and sustaining equitable practices in teachers' everyday work: A framework for critical action. *Teaching and Learning, 7*(3), 1–15. doi.org/10.26522/TL.V7I3.421

Lynn, M. (1999). Toward a critical race pedagogy, a research note. *Urban Education, 33*, 606–626. doi.org/10.1177/0042085999335004

Lynn, M., & Parker, L. (2006). Critical race studies in education: Examining a decade of research on US schools. *The Urban Review, 38*, 257–290. doi.org/10.1007/s11256-006-0035-5

MacLeod, E. (2018). *Meet Viola Desmond*. Scholastic Canada.

Maharaj, S., Tuters, S., & Shah, V. (2022). *Even school boards are now experiencing severe political polarization*. The Conversation. https://theconversation.com/even-school-boards-are-now-experiencing-severe-political-polarization-191102

Matias, C. E., Viesca, K., Garrison-Wade, D. F., Tandon, M., & Galindo, R. (2014). "What is critical whiteness doing in OUR nice field like critical race theory?" Applying CRT and CWS to understand the white imaginations of white teacher candidates. *Equity and Excellence in Education, 47*(3), 289–304. doi.org/10.1080/10665684.2014.933692

Miller, R., Liu, K., & Bale, A. F. (2020). Critical counternarratives as transformative methodology for educational equity. *Review of Research in Education, 44*, 269–300. doi.org/10.3102/0091732X20908501

Miller, V., Fernandez, F., & Hutchens, N. H. (2023). The race to ban race: Legal and critical arguments against state legislation to ban critical race theory in higher education. *Missouri Law Review, 88*(1). https://papers.ssrn.com/sol3/papers.cfm?abstract_id=4227952

Omi, M., & Winant, H. (2014). *Racial formations in the United States: From the 1960s to the 1980s*. Routledge.

Parekh, G., Flessa, J. J., & Smaller, H. (2016). The Toronto District School Board: A global city school system's structures, processes, and student outcomes. *London Review of Education, 14*(3), 65–84. doi.org/10.18546/LRE.14.3.06

Parker, L., Deyhle, D., & Villenas, S. A. (1999). *Race is—race isn't: Critical race theory and qualitative studies in education*. Westview Press.

Parker, L., & Gillborn, D. (Eds.). (2020). *Critical race theory in education*. Routledge.

Pendharkar, E. (2022, May 19). A school openly discusses race in a state that bans it. *Education Week, 41*(36). www.edweek.org/leadership/a-school-openly-discusses-race-in-a-state-that-bans-it/2022/05

Porter, J. (1992). *The vertical mosaic: An analysis of social class and power in Canada*. University of Toronto Press. doi.org/10.3138/9781442683044

Raza, A. (2022, April 13). *Being Black in school: Peel students open up about the racism they face in the classroom*. CBC. www.cbc.ca/news/canada/toronto/peel-students-racism-panel-1.6408851

Shah, V., Aoudeh, N., Cuglievan-Mindreau, G., & Flessa, J. (2022). Subverting whiteness and amplifying anti-racisms: Mid-level district leadership for racial justice. *Journal of School Leadership, 32*(5), 456–487. doi.org/10.1177/10526846221095752

Solórzano, D. G., & Yosso, T. J. (2002). Critical race methodology: Counter-storytelling as an analytical framework for education research. *Qualitative Inquiry, 8*(1), 23–44. doi.org/10.1177/107780040200800103

Toronto District School Board. (2020). *Supporting Black student achievement and dismantling anti-Black racism at the TDSB*. www.tdsb.on.ca/Portals/ward8/docs/Shelley%20Laskin/2020%2007%20Supporting%20Black%20Student%20Achievement%20and%20Dismantling%20Anti-Black%20Racism.pdf

Walker, J. W. S. G. (1997). *"Race," rights and the law in the Supreme Court of Canada: Historical case studies*. Osgoode Society for Canadian Legal History and Wilfrid Laurier University Press.

Walton, S. (2020). Why the critical race theory concept of "white supremacy" should not be dismissed by neo-Marxists: Lessons from contemporary Black radicalism. *Power and Education, 12*(1), 78–94. doi.org/10.1177/1757743819871316

West, C., Crenshaw, K., Gotanda, N., Peller G., & Thomas K. (1995). *Critical race theory: The key writings that formed the movement*. New Press.

# PART II

## ETHNICITY AND RACE: INCORPORATING A PEDAGOGY OF JUSTICE, LIBERATION, AND CARE

# CHAPTER 3
# Cosmopolitan Education and Racial Justice: The Implications of Martha Nussbaum's Philosophy of Education for Forging a Common National Memory in Canada

*Ben Iheagwara*

One of the main objectives of education is to champion human flourishing. As a multicultural society with a **colonial legacy**, providing an education and a learning environment that foster human flourishing for all learners and educators, especially those from racialized communities, remains challenging for Canada. Despite the implementation of multicultural education across school boards in Canada, many in racialized communities feel that the education system fails to incorporate their viewpoints and experiences on equal footing with the Euro-Canadian community (LeMarquand, 2021). The prevailing view among racialized communities about Canada's educational philosophy is that it remains Eurocentric and systemically racist.

This chapter discusses how multicultural education, as currently constituted, overwhelmingly reflects the perspective of the Euro-Canadian community in Canada. In so doing, it perpetuates the racial injustices faced by racialized communities, consolidates the advantages of the Euro-Canadian community, and creates a discordant conception of the national public memory and the sense of equal citizenship concomitant with it.

I will provide a sketch of the Eurocentric flavour of the dominant narrative of Canada and its alienating impact on racialized communities. I will also examine multicultural education to demonstrate that, in spite of the commendable progress attained through multiculturalism, it still fails to combat systemic racism and decolonize the curriculum. To address this shortcoming, this chapter will show that the conception of cosmopolitan education rooted in Martha Nussbaum's capabilities approach provides a path for constituting an education system that combats systemic racism, decolonizes the curriculum, and establishes the conditions for hermeneutical and epistemic justice, the conditions without which racial justice will continue to remain elusive. It provides a model of education that enables the flourishing of all learners and facilitates the fashioning of a common national memory. The key question this chapter hopes to answer is this: How does cosmopolitan education enable racial justice and complement multicultural education?

## THE HEGEMONIC HOLD OF THE EURO-CANADIAN NARRATIVE OF CANADA

George Erasmus, the former co-chair of the Royal Commission on Aboriginal Peoples, said, "Where common memory is lacking, where people do not share in the same past, there can be no real community. Where community is to be formed, common memory must be created" (cited in Charles, 2015, p. 1). Erasmus's clamour for the forging of a common memory is a subtle critique of the fragmented official narrative of Canada invented and propagated by shapers of the Euro-Canadian conception of Canada.

Principally manufactured by Anglo-Canadian historians and policy-makers, the Euro-Canadian (principally French and British) narrative of Canada frequently begins Canadian history with the arrival of Europeans. This grand narrative sidesteps the pre-European history of Indigenous Peoples in Canada, choosing instead to tell early stories of Canada as a combat between the French and British Empires. The grand narrative paints what is now called Canada as a massive mysterious land, a terra nullius destined to be a place of refuge, a haven of opportunity for ordinary people fleeing persecution from their homelands or seeking freedom elsewhere. The narrative depicts European pioneers and settlers as visionary, enterprising, and courageous risk-takers forging a new nation with a scattering of savages. As Stanley (2000) observes, the grand narrative has become "the stuff of popular and official histories, Heritage Minutes, beer commercials, public school teaching. It also is the device for organizing university courses, textbooks, and tenure-track positions" (p. 83).

The reach of the Anglo-Canadian narrative of Canada is ubiquitous. It is a well-established feature of the dominant educational pool of interpretive tropes and pedagogical lexicon for making sense of the idea of Canada. The plotting and scripting of the narrative was not an innocent undertaking. Today, it remains a project in Eurocentric-oriented education at the service of nation-building. The architects of this grand project knew that, as Said (1993) observes, "nations are narrations. The power to narrate, or to block other narratives from forming and emerging, is very important to culture and imperialism" (p. xiii). Indeed, the narrative is a part of the colonial and neocolonial educational project to shape the public memory and fashion the popular imagination in terms that portray Euro-Canadians as a civilized people.

The power of memory manipulation is at the core of the Euro-Canadian hegemonic dominance of knowledge production. It has produced far-reaching untoward consequences for the education of both Euro-Canadians and Canadians of non-European stock. Memory manipulation has negatively impacted the prevailing educational philosophy of Canada in that it is rooted in the silencing of non-European voices. Consequently, it has left a legacy of Euro-Canadian **hegemony**, the most damaging of which is the persistence of **white supremacy** (see also chapter 2). Born from this Eurocentric narrative is an incoherent public memory, one that is incapable of forging a socially cohesive society. Compared to that of Euro-Canadians (especially the French and the British), the memory of nonwhite Canadians, members of racialized communities (principally Indigenous, Black, and Chinese), remains unflattering. Consequently, it is incapable of engendering a strong sense of belonging and inculcating a sense of equal citizenship for racialized Canadians.

Indigenous Peoples' memory of Canada has been largely one of plunder, pillage, theft of lands, broken Treaties, creation of reserves, a draconian pass system, the Sixties Scoop, forced assimilation, cultural genocide, mass incarceration, economic marginalization, and intergenerational trauma (Facing History and Ourselves, 2015). Battiste (2013) observes that the "education system has not yet ensured that non-Indigenous children develop an accurate understanding of the Indigenous peoples in Canada and their knowledge systems" (p. 32). The same could also be said of the history of Black enslavement in Canada as well as the Chinese exclusion.

As a matter of interest, the legacy of this Eurocentric narrative furtively undergirds the policies of multiculturalism and multicultural education. Consequently, the noble goals of multiculturalism and multicultural education continue to remain elusive. To fulfill its promise, multicultural education must be repackaged and redesigned to reflect the voices and viewpoints of racialized communities. Before we delve into this, we should have a clear understanding of what multicultural education is.

## WHAT IS MULTICULTURAL EDUCATION?

Multicultural education is a reform movement in education designed to transform the school to reflect the diversity of Canada. It aims to promote educational equity, decolonize, and overhaul the Eurocentric orientation of education by integrating the stories, beliefs, experiences, and contributions of minorities into the curriculum to expose learners to the viewpoints of racialized communities (Banks, 2019). Ghosh and Galczynski (2014) observe that multicultural education aims to foster the full development of children irrespective of ethnicity, gender, race, sexual orientation, class, and physical ability.

Multicultural education in Canada emerged from the formal institutionalization of the policy of multiculturalism within a bilingual framework by the federal government in 1971. The Multiculturalism Act of 1988 reinforced the federal government's commitment to building a society in which people of all ethnicities, religions, and races could preserve their identities while integrating into Canadian society. Against this changing social landscape, provincial ministries of education and school boards across the country began to redesign their curriculum to accommodate the perspectives of racialized communities. The evolution and implementation of multicultural education remain varied and gradual across the country. In Alberta, Manitoba, and Saskatchewan, schools try to provide instruction in French, Cree, Ukrainian, and Hebrew, among other languages (Ghosh & Galczynski, 2014, pp. 32–35). In Quebec, multicultural education was forged against the background of the rise of Quebec nationalism in the face of Anglo-Canadian dominance. Multicultural education in Quebec operates within the framework of a protectionist policy for the French language, especially since the passage of Bill 101 in 1977.

Undoubtedly, multicultural education is on the trajectory of multiculturalizing the curriculum and diversifying the background of educators and educational administrators. Multicultural education helps racialized communities engender a sense of pride in their identity and, through this, foster a sense of positive self-evaluation and hopefully mitigate the damaging effects of Eurocentric education. For learners and educators of Euro-Canadian provenance, multicultural education offers opportunities for enlightenment on the experiences and perspectives of racialized communities. A key feature of multicultural education is the practice of dedicating so-called heritage months to celebrating and educating learners on racialized community members' history, culture, achievements, and contributions to Canadian society. Prominent among these heritage months is Black History Month. The key question to ask is whether multicultural education has attained its objective of promoting equity, reducing prejudice, and fostering the dignity of racialized communities in meaningful and profound ways, as opposed to focusing on the shallow and cosmetic activities characteristic of it.

On the strength of multiple facts, it is plausible to hold that the goals of multicultural education remain unsuccessful. Multiple examples from some school boards in Canada provide compelling evidence that, after many decades, multicultural education has failed in crushing systemic racism in the education system. Racism, discriminatory streaming of students into divergent academic programs, the laissez-faire approach to including Black and Indigenous history in the curriculum, and so on demonstrate the inefficacy of multicultural education.

The first report of the Human Rights Office of the Toronto District School Board to assess the school board's progress in meeting its mission of creating a discrimination-free learning environment came up with a troubling finding: "The data clearly indicates that the Board continues to have a serious racism problem. *Race or race related grounds* is the most frequent ground of complaint received by the Human Rights Office making up 54 percent of all complaints alleging a human rights violation" (Toronto District School Board, 2020). Similarly, a study undertaken to ascertain why Black students in the Greater Toronto Area disproportionately experience poor educational outcomes compared to their Euro-Canadian peers found that the practice of streaming—classifying and channelling students into different post-secondary tracks on the basis of academic ability—is to blame (James & Turner, 2017; see also chapter 2). The streaming program places students in either the academic program (which prepares students for enrolment in universities) or the applied program (which prepares students for enrolment in community colleges). The study found that 53 percent of Black students were streamed to the academic program, as opposed to 81 percent of their Euro-Canadian peers. In the applied program, Black students accounted for 39 percent of the placement, compared to 16 percent of their Euro-Canadian peers (James & Turner, 2017). In a statement to the Canadian Broadcasting Corporation (CBC), Ontario Minister of Education Stephen Lecce confirmed that the discriminatory practice exists in Ontario school boards. In Lecce's words, "it is clear there is systemic discrimination built within the education system, whether it be streaming of racialized students, suspensions overwhelmingly targeting Black and Indigenous kids, or the lack of merit-based diversity within our education workforce" (Powers, 2020).

In many school boards across Canada, Black and Indigenous history is routinely taught as an optional curriculum intervention. A CBC news report on the Black history curriculum in the Prairie provinces found that Black history remains optional. In Manitoba, for instance, the curriculum offers teachers the option to teach Black history under the all-inclusive theme of human rights (Omayra, 2022). To regard Black history as an optional topic to be taught under the broad category of human rights invites both students and teachers to place Black history and Black people in the category of marginality. The policy of keeping Black history optional demonstrates the irrefutable centrality of *white privilege*. If a school board grants schools the licence to opt out of teaching Black and Indigenous history while requiring them to teach the official narrative of Canada, isn't that demonstrably a case of white privilege? Do Black and Indigenous learners in the education system have the privilege of opting out from learning about the Euro-Canadian narrative of Canadian history?

Instead of having that privilege, Indigenous learners in the education system are exposed to whitewashed portrayals of what happened in the residential school system. For instance, in the fall of 2020, a teacher asked their grade 6 students, in a middle school in the Abbotsford School District in British Columbia, to submit *at least five positive facts or stories about residential schools* (Britten, 2020). Assignments such as this not only deny the incontrovertible fact of the *cultural genocide* visited on Indigenous Peoples through the ignoble residential school system, they also retraumatize descendants of victims of the residential school system and damage the possibility for realizing reconciliation and healing.

These examples, drawn from Ontario, British Columbia, and the Prairie provinces, incontrovertibly demonstrate that multicultural education remains rooted in a Eurocentric and systemically racist educational philosophy. The **Eurocentrism** of multicultural education mirrors the Eurocentrism of multiculturalism. A lot of what goes on in the name of multicultural education refrains from critically engaging with difficult subjects, urgent matters bearing on, for example, settler-colonialism, expropriation of Indigenous lands, enslavement, and cultural imperialism. Multicultural education principally adopts a descriptive approach to culture. Over-dependence on culture as an omnibus category stifles its ability to isolate, sequester, and adopt a targeted approach to interrogating the systemic racism inherent in the education system (Thornhill, 1999).

In other words, multicultural education as currently implemented is not adequately critical. It lacks abrasiveness and seeks to turn away from uncomfortable subjects to avoid bringing discomfort to learners from the Euro-Canadian community.

To be sure, multicultural education has produced notable positive outcomes. Through multicultural education, members of Euro-Canadian communities have learned some elements of the cultural and religious beliefs and practices of racialized communities. The multicultural encounters that multicultural education sets up foster cross-cultural learning. The celebration of diversity represents the outstanding achievement of multicultural education. Nevertheless, multicultural education as an effective tool for achieving racial justice remains elusive.

So why does multicultural education resist **decolonization**? The key reason is that multicultural education is permeated by systemic racism. Quite frequently, the charge of the persistence of systemic racism stirs up controversy and resistance. Skeptics like Lau (2023) argue that the charge paints a negative image of society, suggesting that a considerable number of the members of the Euro-Canadian community are demonstrably racist. To counter this charge, Lau employs the so-called *few bad apples argument*—the notion that racism exists only through the occasional acts of self-proclaimed white supremacists or the personal prejudices of people working within institutions. For Lau, systemic racism died or at least declined significantly with the abrogation of overtly racist laws and policies.

What skeptics like Lau fail to realize is that systemic racism is versatile, resilient, and evasive. It can be reinvented and repackaged to appear nonthreatening. Systemic racism hides in the safety of white-controlled boardrooms and classrooms. It resides in the unreachable sphere of unconscious prejudice and is disguised in the welcoming smiles and reassuring attitudes of members of the Euro-Canadian community in the education system in their interactions with colleagues from racialized communities.

To be sure, the persistence of systemic racism doesn't mean that the education system is staffed by racist teachers and administrators. Like an invisible force, it eludes the poorly examined curriculum, policies, and assumptions of well-meaning teachers and administrators in the execution of their duties. Considering this, multicultural education, as currently implemented, not only falls short of its goal; it has also failed in constituting a common national memory. Accordingly, multicultural education needs to be complemented by an approach that invites broad scrutiny of Eurocentrism, facilitates a healthy patriotism, and supports the development of the capabilities and well-being of racialized communities. Canada is both multicultural and cosmopolitan. Our education system shouldn't just be multicultural; it should also be cosmopolitan. I will show that Martha Nussbaum's conception of cosmopolitan education complements multicultural education (Hébert, 2013).

## MARTHA NUSSBAUM'S CONCEPTION OF COSMOPOLITAN EDUCATION

Cosmopolitan education as conceived by Martha Nussbaum adopts a critically robust approach to education inspired by Socratic self-scrutiny, Stoic cosmopolitanism, and Nussbaum's distinctive articulation of the capabilities approach. Her perspective on cosmopolitan education aims to create conditions that facilitate *eudaimonia*—the idea of human flourishing and human well-being. Human flourishing evokes the idea of an objectively desirable and worthwhile life, one that elevates the socioeconomic quality of life for humans regardless of their race, gender, sexual orientation, nation, religion, sex, and ethnicity. She develops this idea from the Stoic view that human flourishing should not be left to luck. The Stoics hold that one's place of birth or status is morally irrelevant. Nussbaum (1997) concurs, noting that "the accident of where one is born is just that, an accident; any human being might have been born in any nation" (p. 58). Much of the problem arising from racism and ethnocentrism derives from the erroneous ascription of undue significance to personal characteristics that are due to accidents of birth. Malignant patriotism, racism, ethnocentrism, sexism, and heterosexism frequently originate from oppressive systems of social hierarchy that valorize and naturalize what is socially constructed.

Nussbaum's conception of cosmopolitan education draws from a liberal egalitarian philosophy. The egalitarian worldview champions anti-racist and anti-oppressive pedagogy. Nussbaum's view of cosmopolitan education rests on two approaches: *diagnostic* and *empowerment*, respectively. The diagnostic approach aims to ferret out the sources of parochialism, Eurocentrism, sexism, Islamophobia, racism, and so on that foster oppression and vitiate the education system. The diagnostic approach uses the method of sympathetic imagination to accomplish this goal. The empowerment approach is twofold: battling the demeaning image of racialized learners as consumers of knowledge and passive bystanders in history and promoting the image of racialized learners as agents, producers, and creators of knowledge by creating the conditions for achieving their capabilities. It is worthwhile to stress that the two approaches belong together since the nucleus of the diagnostic approach—the method of the sympathetic imagination—is implicit. The seeds of cosmopolitan education lie buried in the capabilities approach. I will demonstrate this connection while discussing the empowerment approach to cosmopolitan education, for that is where the connection is visible. For the purposes of chronology, I will first discuss Nussbaum's diagnostic approach to cosmopolitan education since her perspective on cosmopolitan education was developed independently of the capabilities approach.

## Nussbaum's Diagnostic Approach to Cosmopolitan Education

Nussbaum's (1994) project in cosmopolitan education began as a forceful critique of divisive patriotism and parochial education systems. Divisive patriotism arises when citizens lack a cohesive conception of their national narrative. Nussbaum's cosmopolitan education engages discordant patriotism by way of diagnosis, a sort of root cause analysis undertaken to see, feel, hear, and understand from different viewpoints. The approach proceeds outward from curiosity about the self and ultimately to curiosity about the world. For Nussbaum, cosmopolitan education helps engender and deepen self-knowledge and knowledge of humanity in all its guises—the strange and the familiar, the near and the far, the racialized and the nonracialized. Cosmopolitan education helps learners cultivate the ability "to understand something of the history and character of the diverse groups that inhabit" the world (Nussbaum, 2010, p. 80). The means by which self-knowledge and knowledge of humanity are undertaken is sympathetic imagination.

Sympathetic imagination is one of the pillars on which cosmopolitan education stands. For Nussbaum, cultivating sympathetic imagination entails learning to imaginatively enter another's sufferings and feelings by learning and understanding their story to experience a kind of kinship with them. It entails vicariously participating in the emotions and predicament of another. In Nussbaum's words, it is "a curious questioning, and receptive demeanor that says in effect, 'Here is another human being. I wonder what he (or she) is seeing and feeling right now'" (Nussbaum, 2012, p. 139). Animated by an egalitarian and nonoppressive impulse, the method of sympathetic imagination aims to decentre the self and dismantle the centrality, the hegemony, of the dominant viewpoint, with a view to establishing equitable standing for suppressed, oppressed, and misrepresented perspectives.

One example Nussbaum uses to elucidate the idea of sympathetic imagination is the condition of African Americans, one with which members of racialized communities in Canada can identify. Borrowing from the opening passage of Ralph Ellison's novel *Invisible Man*, Nussbaum stresses the importance of cultivating our *inner eyes*. In the novel, Ellison describes his experience as a Black man in America as that of an embodied being who is equipped with flesh, blood, fibre, and bones but who ironically remains invisible to the "diseased" eyes of white gazers. Ellison (1947) laments that his corporeality escapes the notice of white eyes: "I am invisible, understand, simply because people refuse to see me.… When they approach me they see only my surroundings, themselves, or figments of their imagination—indeed, everything and anything except me. That invisibility to which I refer occurs because of a peculiar disposition of the eyes of those with whom I come in contact. A matter of construction of the *inner eyes*, those eyes with which they look through their physical eyes upon reality" (p. 3). This passage provides a lucid metaphorical portrait for appreciating why systemic racism in education remains elusive despite the efforts of multicultural education. It is a diagnostic metaphor that portrays a curious condition of partial selective blindness that sees everything but Black bodies. The metaphor speaks to the state of *nobodiness* of Black bodies and, by extension, racialized bodies. The diagnosis highlights the *peculiar disposition of the inner eyes*, an optical pathology that is moral and epistemic in nature. The pathology is moral because it fails to see the common humanity, the equal moral status of racialized bodies. It is epistemic because it denies the existence of what is demonstrably perceptible. It evokes the idea of testimonial dishonesty, one that disavows the indubitable existence of racialized bodies.

Cosmopolitan education invites learners and educators to dig deep into the unconscious to unearth the roots of racial prejudices. Digging into the unconscious is undertaken to vicariously identify with another regardless of race, gender, or ethnicity. It is an exercise for sensitizing oneself to being morally attuned to the humanity of strangers, saying, as Nussbaum urges, *Here is another human being. I wonder what they are seeing and feeling right now.* Sympathetic imagination is a device for unearthing the unconscious, enlightening the self about others, and broadening the bounds of the moral circle of concern. The device of the sympathetic imagination isn't a one-time activity; it is an ongoing process for cultivating one's humanity and recognizing, *seeing* the equal dignity of others, and advocating for their capabilities.

Cosmopolitan education goes beyond diagnosis; it includes empowerment for racialized and nonracialized people. I now turn to the empowerment approach to demonstrate how an education system rooted in the capabilities approach offers racialized learners the opportunity for a decolonized and egalitarian learning environment.

## Nussbaum's Empowerment Approach to Cosmopolitan Education

Nussbaum's empowerment approach to cosmopolitan education imagines learners of all races, ethnicities, religions, and genders as endowed with internal capabilities in need of a system that supports their development and flourishing. Her capabilities approach represents her substantive liberal egalitarian theory of human well-being.

The capabilities approach is a theory of justice articulated for making comparative quality-of-life assessments across the programs of different societies by asking, *What is each person able to do and be?* Rooted in liberal egalitarianism, the capabilities approach aims to foster people's power for defining themselves by combating deep-seated social injustices and inequalities, such as racial injustice, that result from discrimination and marginalization (Nussbaum, 2011, pp. 18–19). For Nussbaum, capabilities are best understood in terms of substantive freedoms. Capabilities include the abilities with which a person is endowed as well as the "opportunities created by a combination of personal abilities and the political, social, and economic environment" (Nussbaum, 2011, p. 20). To appreciate this definition, it is helpful to note that Nussbaum's conception of capabilities is best understood as comprising basic, internal, and combined capabilities. Basic capabilities are innate capacities, while internal capabilities are developed potentials. Internal capabilities are cultivated from pre-existing basic capabilities through education and training. Combined capabilities consist of the interplay between internal capabilities and the external conditions that make the exercise of a capability feasible. Combined capabilities are the social conditions in which internal capabilities are nurtured. So, in the context of the capabilities approach, a person genuinely flourishes when their internal capabilities are cultivated in an enabling environment.

It is plausible to maintain that a Eurocentric education system, understood as the interaction between internal capabilities and the social environment, does not provide an enabling environment for the flourishing of racialized learners since it remains systemically racist. I have provided multiple examples to show that the system of multicultural education, as currently run, does not create an enabling environment for learners from racialized communities to flourish. In short, a Eurocentric education system is not conducive for combined capabilities. Through the empowerment approach, cosmopolitan education challenges the belittling image of members of racialized communities as consumers of knowledge and passive bystanders in history. How is this so?

I noted earlier that the seeds of cosmopolitan education lie buried in the capabilities approach. The seeds can be unpacked from a list of 10 central capabilities that Nussbaum insists a politically just society must provide for its citizens as a threshold level for guaranteeing their flourishing. Particularly relevant to the link between cosmopolitan education and the sympathetic imagination are the fifth, sixth, and seventh capabilities:

> *Senses, imagination, thought.* Being able to use the senses; being able to imagine, to think, and to reason—and to do these things in ... a way informed and cultivated by an adequate education ...; being able to use imagination and thought in connection with experiencing, and producing expressive works and events of one's own choice ...
> *Practical reason.* Being able to form a conception of the good and to engage in critical reflection about the planning of one's own life.
> *Affiliation.* Being able to live for and in relation to others; being able to imagine the situation of another and to have compassion for that situation; having the capability for both justice and friendship.... Being able to be treated as a dignified being whose worth is equal to that of others. (Nussbaum, 2011, p. 33)

Notice that these capabilities indicate the importance of the imagination as a tool for understanding another's predicament. Moreover, compared to the belittling portrait of racialized people in the Eurocentric education system, the capabilities approach uses the language of agency and ability to envision people. Persons are, so to speak, pictured as having the capacity for pursuing their aims in life. Portrayed as such, the capabilities approach could be employed as a tool of empowerment for racialized learners, positioning them to see themselves and their forebears as producers, creators, and givers of knowledge in the knowledge production system.

Underpinned by an egalitarian foundation, a capabilities approach–based cosmopolitan education focuses its critique against the racial injustice of Eurocentric education by advancing a conception of an education system in which all learners and teachers of all groups, racialized and nonracialized, are genuinely represented as equals in the curriculum, in the administration of education, and in the entire education system. What this means, in essence, is that cosmopolitan education provides an enabling environment for learners by decolonizing the curriculum. Decolonizing the current Eurocentric education system involves unlearning the old ways of thinking about racialized learners and the viewpoints they can offer to the education system. It entails rethinking, reconceiving, reimagining, and reconstituting education in ways that integrate non-European knowledge systems. Marie Battiste's (2013) book *Decolonizing Education: Nourishing the Learning Spirit* is a good case in point. Battiste's thesis is that decolonizing education entails establishing a new knowledge system, a knowledge system that consists of a reflective articulation of the epistemology of the constituent communities of Canada.

Battiste's point here is that a truly decolonized education system is one in which the knowledge repertoire of racialized communities is accorded equal standing in the knowledge production system. Racialized communities are represented as having the capability to produce, contribute to, and enrich the common knowledge and hermeneutical pool (Fricker, 2015). In this connection, a capabilities approach–driven cosmopolitan education could be said to be a cross-pollination of knowledge systems animated by a liberal egalitarian ethos.

Cosmopolitan education supervenes on a capacious moral foundation, aiming as it does to widen the reach of one's moral concern and broaden the scope of one's epistemic and hermeneutical pool. Racial injustice in education endures in education systems that are plagued with exclusionary negligence and resistance to the voices whose viewpoints might ultimately bring fresh ideas for understanding the pains of one's compatriots and healing the wounds of a fragmented society. Cosmopolitan education serves as a kind of public good, one that furnishes the public with more epistemic and hermeneutical resources for solving urgent problems that have a bearing on racial injustice. Indeed, cosmopolitan education is invaluable for establishing an egalitarian education system, fostering the flourishing of learners, and forging a common national memory.

The idea of flourishing stretches beyond Nussbaum's view of cosmopolitan education. Flourishing looms large in her ethical thought, and she uses it to advance her theories of domestic and international justice. In fact, her conception of cosmopolitan education derives from the ancient Greek tradition of flourishing (*eudaimonia*)—having good fortune. The Stoics held that human beings deserve to be treated with equal respect because all are endowed with reason and the capacity for moral choice. For Aristotle, flourishing meant living well and doing well. Flourishing evokes the idea of an objectively desirable and worthwhile life for human beings. Nussbaum (2006) appropriates this motif from Aristotle and the Stoics to articulate an ethic of human well-being by which she means a life "worthy of the dignity of the human being" (p. 70).

The concept of flourishing is a triad that encompasses three ideas: abolition, equality, and development. Abolition and equality pertain to the social structures that inhibit or enable flourishing. Development pertains to the personal; it is agent-relative. The first idea is *abolitionist* in that it aims to abolish ascriptive privileges arising from any form of group membership, such as race, that establishes and perpetuates the historical advantages of certain racial groups in society. The second idea is *egalitarian* in that it aims to foster the sense of the equality of human beings in society. In so doing, it makes equal citizenship a reality for racial and cultural minorities who have been excluded from the goods that enable human well-being, development, and flourishing. The third idea is *developmentalist* in that it consists of the exercise and enjoyment of one's cognitive, social, emotional, and physical capabilities in order to live a dignified life.

Social context and egalitarian social institutions create the conditions for human flourishing. Human flourishing is not only dependent on personal qualities and preferences. The background conditions in which people live make this possible. To flourish, human beings need access to social goods, social capital, the networks that govern access to political power, cultural capital, jobs, business connections, egalitarian education systems, and so on. Put in other words, flourishing is steeped in the ethic of human rights.

## CONCLUSION

Multicultural education remains the dominant education approach in Canada. Despite its commendable results, it fails to deliver a learning experience that makes learners of racialized communities feel seen, understood, and respected by the system. Multicultural education lacks the ability to disrupt the Eurocentrism of the education system. If we want better outcomes for racialized learners in the education system, then we must complement multicultural education with cosmopolitan education. I have shown in this chapter that the conception of cosmopolitan education articulated by Nussbaum provides a promising model for decolonizing the Eurocentric vestiges of multicultural education.

A capabilities approach–based cosmopolitan education sees education as a vehicle for social change, one that promotes dialogue on implementing curriculum decolonization in a transparent manner, diversifying the composition of school boards, and hiring and empowering teachers from racialized communities. As a change-making education system, cosmopolitan education does not preserve the asymmetry of power and achievement gap between learners from the Euro-Canadian community and those from racialized communities. Cosmopolitan education encourages ongoing critical dialogue among racialized communities, school boards, and education policy-makers.

## KEY TERMS

**Colonial legacy:** The long-lasting structural, political, economic, and cultural disadvantages impacting Indigenous Peoples and descendants of enslaved people in countries colonized by European settlers. In Canada, some of the lasting impacts of colonial rule include the residential school system, economic inequality, and intergenerational trauma.

**Decolonization:** A twofold anti-colonial process that involves uprooting, unlearning, and dismantling Eurocentric ideas that persist in the education system and replacing them with ideas drawn from the heritage of Indigenous and racialized people to affirm their equal dignity and humanity.

**Eurocentrism:** A mindset that views the civilization of European or Western societies as superior to that of non-Western societies. This mindset also tends to portray European and Western societies as the model of human progress and reason by virtue of their economic, political, and technological achievements.

**Hegemony:** The enduring domination of one social group by another social group via the spread of the beliefs, values, worldviews, stereotypes, history, and norms of the dominant group through schools, the media, religious institutions, and so on.

**White supremacy:** A multidimensional social system that concentrates economic, political, and cultural power around white people while consciously and unconsciously reproducing ideas of white superiority across the society. This system persists despite the official abolition of explicitly racist laws and policies.

## DISCUSSION QUESTIONS AND ACTIVITIES

1. In what ways can teachers help students from racialized communities see themselves as agents, producers, and creators in the making of Canadian history?
2. Provide two reasons why Canadians from racialized communities might view the education system as Eurocentric.
3. In groups of two or three, create a Venn diagram with "Multicultural Education" in one circle and "Cosmopolitan Education" in the other, and note the distinct features of each. In the centre, where the circles overlap, indicate the commonalities of multicultural and cosmopolitan education in Canada.

## REFERENCES

Banks, J. A. (2019). *An introduction to multicultural education*. Pearson.

Bannerji, H. (2000). *The dark side of the nation: Essays on multiculturalism, nationalism and gender*. Canadian Scholars.

Battiste, M. (2013). *Decolonizing education: Nourishing the learning spirit*. Purich.

Britten, L. (2020, November 25). *Homework assignment to list "positive" stories about residential schools under investigation*. CBC News. www.cbc.ca/news/canada/british-columbia/residential-school-homework-assignment-1.5816491

Charles, M. (2015, April 28). *Mark Charles: Our common memory from our traumatized past*. Indianz. www.indianz.com/News/2015/04/28/mark-charles-our-common-memory.asp

Ellison, R. (1947). *Invisible man.* Vintage Books.

Facing History and Ourselves. (2015). *Stolen lives: The Indigenous peoples of Canada and the Indian residential schools.* www.facinghistory.org/en-ca/resource-library/stolen-lives-indigenous-peoples-canada-indian-residential-schools-0

Fricker, M. (2015). Epistemic contribution as a central human capability. In G. Hull, *The equal society: Essays on equality in theory and practice* (pp. 73–90). Lexington Books.

Garcea, J. (2008). Postulations on the fragmentary effects of multiculturalism in Canada. *Canadian Ethnic Studies, 40*(1), 141–160. doi.org/10.1353/ces.0.0059

Ghosh, R., & Galczynski, M. (2014). *Redefining multicultural education: Inclusion and the right to be different.* Canadian Scholars.

Hébert, Y. (2013). Cosmopolitanism and Canadian multicultural policy: Intersection, relevance, and critique. *Encounters/Encuentros/Rencontres on Education, 14,* 3–19. doi.org/10.24908/eoe-ese-rse.v14i0.4088

James, C. E., & Turner, T. (2017). *Towards race equity in education: The schooling of Black students in the Greater Toronto Area.* https://edu.yorku.ca/files/2017/04/Towards-Race-Equity-in-Education-April-2017.pdf

Lau, M. (2023). Is Canada systemically racist? In M. Milke (Ed.), *The 1867 project: Why Canada should be cherished—not cancelled* (pp. 61–74). Friesens.

LeMarquand, A. (2021). The colonization of Canada's curriculum and its effects on our societal knowledge. *Journal of School & Society, 7*(1), 118–122. www.johndeweysociety.org/the-journal-of-school-and-society/files/2021/03/11.pdf

Nussbaum, M. C. (1994, October 1). Patriotism and cosmopolitanism. *Boston Review.* https://bostonreview.net/articles/martha-nussbaum-patriotism-and-cosmopolitanism/

Nussbaum, M. C. (1997). *Cultivating humanity: A classical defense of reform in liberal education.* Harvard University Press.

Nussbaum, M. C. (2006). *Frontiers of justice: Disability, nationality, species membership.* Belknap Press.

Nussbaum, M. C. (2010). *Not for profit: Why democracy needs the humanities.* Princeton University Press.

Nussbaum, M. C. (2011). *Creating capabilities: The human development approach.* Belknap Press.

Nussbaum, M. C. (2012). *The new religious intolerance: Overcoming the politics of fear in an anxious age.* Belknap Press.

Omayra, I. (2022, January 24). *Bringing Black history into Prairie classrooms.* CBC News. www.cbc.ca/newsinteractives/features/bringing-black-history-into-prairie-classrooms

Powers, L. (2020, July 6). *Ontario to end "discriminatory" practice of academic streaming in grade 9.* CBC News. www.cbc.ca/news/canada/toronto/ontario-streaming-high-school-racism-lecce-1.5638700

Royal Commission on Bilingualism and Biculturalism. (1969). *The report of the Royal Commission on Bilingualism and Biculturalism*. Queen's Printer.

Said, E. W. (1993). *Culture and imperialism*. Vintage Books.

Stanley, T. (2000). Why I killed Canadian history: Towards an anti-racist history in Canada. *Histoire Sociale / Social History*, *33*(65), 79–103. www.researchgate.net/publication/292241304_Why_I_killed_Canadian_history_Towards_an_anti-racist_history_in_Canada

Thornhill, E. M.A. (1999). Multicultural and intercultural education: The Canadian experience. *Revue Québécoise de droit international*, *12*, 79–89. www.persee.fr/doc/rqdi_0828-9999_1999_num_12_1_1915

Toronto District School Board. (2020). *Human rights update: Annual report 2018–2020*. https://pubtdsb.escribemeetings.com/filestream.ashx?DocumentId=8102 www.tdsb.on.ca/Portals/0/docs/HRO%20Report_March%202021.pdf

# CHAPTER 4
# Supporting Students to Thrive, Grow, and Flourish: Embracing Their Literate Lives as Liberatory Praxis

*Ann E. Lopez*

In this chapter, addressing forms of oppression and connecting with students' lived experiences—in other words, creating teaching and learning spaces that value their histories, cultures, and ancestral knowledges, and decentre Eurocentricity—are positioned as central to students flourishing in schools. Schools are tasked with educating a diverse population of students from different backgrounds and experiences; however, some are not fulfilling this task. Schools have long been plagued with systemic inequities that prevent some students from achieving their full potential. We know from research that students thrive when they see themselves in the curriculum and feel connected to the teaching and learning process, and when teaching and learning occur in contexts free from **oppression**. In an era of standardization, accountability measures, and competency tests—and, more recently, challenges to diversity, inclusion, equity, and anti-racist initiatives—engaging in teaching and learning that affirms diverse learners has been a challenging task. After the murder of George Floyd in 2020, critical approaches, policies, and practices that named the harmful impact of white supremacy and the legacy of colonization on education and schooling were prominent in the discourse, not only in the United States, but also in other Western countries (see also chapter 2). Since that time, right-wing advocates in the United States, the anti-woke and anti-CRT movements, have sought to roll back gains made toward greater equity in education and schooling, which has had implications for what are seen and valued as valid pedagogical practices. Within the Canadian context, we have seen a rise in challenges to equity, anti-racist, and inclusive education. This is not surprising, as trends in the United States tend to find their way to Canada. Education and schooling continue to be the site of anti-Blackness and anti-Black racism. Black students and families are often constructed as the problem and pathologized; they bear the brunt of harsh school discipline, and families are not perceived as resourceful and knowledgeable (Lopez & Jean-Marie, 2021). If Black students are to flourish and achieve their full potential in education systems and schools, it is important that educators examine how Black learners are impacted by systemic anti-Black racism and anti-Blackness, and how these practices are perpetuated (Ohito, 2016). This holds true in Canada, where some school boards are acknowledging anti-Black racism and its impact on students, and education workers and students are developing anti-Black racism policies to address the issue.

Furthermore, inequities persist for certain learners (Black, Indigenous, and refugee students and students from low-resourced communities), and there are significant disparities between groups in Canada (Potvin, 2017). An important pedagogical challenge faced by educators in Canada today is how to repair inherited colonial policies and practices that continue to harm some students (Donald, 2021). Canada officially embraced multiculturalism through the Canadian Multiculturalism Act (1985), and a national discourse exists of Canadians valuing and embracing diversity (see chapter 1 in this volume for a historical overview). Notwithstanding this official policy of acknowledging the diversity within Canadian society, many argue that Canada remains a racist society where Black and Indigenous Peoples and people from global majority communities experience racism in their daily lives (Satzewich & Liodakis, 2021). Malhi and Boon (2007) argue that racism is embedded in Canada's history through slavery, the destruction of Africville, the Chinese head tax, settler-colonialism, residential schools, the *Komagata Maru* incident, World War II Japanese internment camps, and other atrocities and that racism continues to exist at both individual and structural levels in current Canadian society. In Canada, there is a pervasiveness of myths of Canada as an open and inclusive society despite evidence to the contrary (Bailey, 2016). It is imperative that Canada adopts a more forward-thinking approach to combating the effects of racism rather than the lack of acknowledgement of race and racism (Williams et al., 2022). James and Turner (2017) found ongoing acts of discrimination and oppression impacting Black students within the education system in Ontario. They argue that the white racial frame informs interactions in society, policies, and practices within public institutions. This frame also interprets and informs how racial disparities influence, for example, high dropout rates, poor educational outcomes, and attitudes of teachers and administrators toward Black students. Because of embedded inequities in education and schooling, Black children are more likely to be enrolled in under-resourced schools, receive harsher discipline, and be streamed into nonacademic programming regardless of academic potential and capability; they are also less likely to attend university despite wishing to do so (Cameron & Jefferies, 2021). These realities impact how students experience education and schooling. The colonial and white supremacist nature of schooling in Canada must be named, with an intentional shift away from fixing students and toward fixing the educational structures that unfairly impact Indigenous and Black students (Kerr, 2023).

Despite the challenges that educators face within current contexts, research has shown that students benefit when teaching and learning are connected and relevant to their lived experiences, decentre Eurocentric knowledge, and disrupt the taken-for-granted traditional modes of learning. Paulo Freire (1970), in *Pedagogy of the Oppressed*, argues for pedagogy that challenges the status quo and develops **critical consciousness** in students. These approaches are not inspired by standardized-test preparation or through instruction in basic skills; instead, they arise from enriching learning spaces that push students to their intellectual limits and connect them to meaningful, authentic ways to express their ideas (Scorza et al., 2013). These pedagogical approaches allow students to thrive and flourish in teaching and learning spaces. Nussbaum (1997) argues for spaces to support students to flourish and suggests that students should (a) be supported in critical examination of self; (b) see themselves as part of a global citizenry; and (c) develop "narrative imagination"—building capacity for others. Students develop critical consciousness when they are able to critically examine their own actions and have connections and empathy for others. Students' literate lives are an integral part of their lived experiences that impact their teaching and learning experiences. This means that when students' literate lives outside the classroom are valued and included in what takes place in the classroom, they feel a sense of belonging and engagement increases.

In this chapter, I theorize how embracing students' literate lives outside and inside the classroom can be a form of **liberatory praxis** that challenges oppressive practices and allows students—particularly those marginalized by the education system—to flourish by supporting their educational achievements. Such an approach, I argue, is essential for all students to flourish and journey in their full potential as human beings. Willen (2022) suggests that the notion of flourishing must be understood within critical and cultural contexts, as "what flourishing looks or feels like, what makes flourishing possible, or what might stand in people's way and thwart their ability to flourish" is important (p. 3). Questions concerning inequities in power and resources, matters of justice, and structural conditions must be part of understanding what it means to flourish and people's ability to reach their full potential.

## POSITIONALITY

Increasingly, critical scholars, academics, and practitioners are seeking to disrupt the status quo, positing their voices and experiences as valuable spaces and ways of learning in ways that depart from the expected norms. In this chapter, I "step outside of boundaries … to exemplify both the process and the impact of fully engaging liberatory praxis" (Richardson, 2023, p. 3). In this regard, I draw not only on research, but also on my own ontology and journey of learning and unlearning as a critical educator in educational spaces and community. I am a Black woman, a descendant of the enslaved, born and raised in Jamaica. I completed my undergraduate degree in Jamaica before immigrating to Canada. My life was filled with the love of my parents and extended family. My grandfather, who died when I was still very young, doted on me and my sister and would always share his hard dough bread and coffee with me. He grew coffee and cocoa, hence my love of coffee to this day. My grandmother was my first teacher. She was a product of the descendants of the enslaved and the Scottish that colonized Jamaica. She not only taught me to read, but also taught me about social justice and the importance of embracing an ethic of care for others. She shared with me many stories of her experience growing up. We talked about ways that colonialism had impacted our small district, from the availability of water to land ownership and more. She shared many stories of her mother, grandmother, father, and older brothers and sisters. She told of her father's connections to colonizers from Scotland who owned property and of his mother, who was a Black woman, and how he was not given any land because he married a Black woman, my great-grandmother. My grandmother also shared stories of her grandmother and her experiences as a Black woman growing up in a colonized Jamaica. My grandmother made sure that I could speak the "Queen's English" in addition to Jamaican patois. She was fully aware of the power of literacy in all forms. My grandmother and her mother were readers, and she instilled that love of reading in me and all her grandchildren. Those within the society who did not have a good command of the colonizer's language were often seen as "not well educated" or "uneducated" and experienced language and other forms of bias. My relationship with my grandmother and listening to her stories had a profound impact on how I came to understand the world and notions of literacy.

When I started secondary school, the education I received was grounded in Eurocentric knowledge, and the General Certificate of Education that we took in fifth and sixth forms was sent to Britain to be graded. I also realized that the books we were reading and our formal education were all from the colonizers' perspectives. The traditions and knowledge of my West African ancestors were not represented in the formal education curriculum. The education system was never designed to fully educate the descendants of the enslaved about their own histories and the knowledge of their ancestors. It was not until I arrived at the University of the West Indies, in Kingston, and was exposed to books written by Walter Rodney, Frantz Fanon, and other post-colonial authors that I began to make the connections between my grandmother's stories of her concern for those who were "less fortunate," as she would say, and inequities grounded in colonization. Later, as a classroom teacher in Ontario, Canada, and teacher educator at the Ontario Institute for Studies in Education, University of Toronto, the importance of including the lived experiences of students in the teaching and learning process—and its impact on student outcomes—was amplified. I began to understand how the various forms of literacies that my grandmother engaged in—stories, songs, proverbs, and customs outside of the scripted curriculum—informed my educational journey and who I am as an educator. As a descendant of the enslaved, liberatory praxis means for me decentring Eurocentric knowledge and centring the epistemologies grounded in African Indigenous Knowledge.

## STUDENTS' LITERATE LIVES MATTER

The ways in which educators take up, understand, and deconstruct notions of literacy impact how we understand what it means to be literate. In other words, by *literate lives*, we mean the experiences, knowledge, and emerging forms of literacies that are being included and excluded as we come to understand what it means to be literate. According to Perry (2012), literacy is "what people do with reading, writing, and texts in real world contexts and why they do it" (p. 54). I further argue that students' literate lives matter in how they provide a pathway for students' flourishing and full development as human beings. There are three aspects of literate lives that I argue are essential for students to flourish: acknowledging multiple literacies, disrupting canons, and challenging all forms of oppression.

## Acknowledging Multiple Literacies

By understanding the idea that creating spaces does not always refer to *physical spaces*, we can understand the literate lives of students to include multiple forms of literacy, such as texts, oral communication, and their daily experiences. Their literate lives involve orature or oral literature—stories and songs, often used in many cultures to pass on traditions and customs. They include other spaces, such as online chat groups and social media, to enhance the meanings of literacy and literacy learning (Howard et al., 2017). Furthermore, stories are relevant to their literate lives (McKinney & Giorgis, 2009). Indeed, all forms of literacy practices serve as the tools for shaping the literacy identities individuals construct, enact, and explore in various situations (Moje & Luke, 2009).

Bomer and Fowler-Amato (2014) argue that classroom environments should be spaces where students can read and write together and share multiple perspectives that cause them to think critically about their experiences and about how these experiences shape their literacy identities. Similarly, Ladson-Billings (2016) argues that while we rail about students' failure to read traditional texts and write in standard forms, we cannot be ignorant of current forms of communication. We cannot "decry the demise of English because the youth are inventive with language ... one of the advantages of this new media and creative language use is that youth have been able to connect the broader social and civic concerns of their lives in ways that school literacy has failed to do" (p. 65). In some instances, students are coming to see schools as increasingly irrelevant to their lives and look to other spaces for learning and belonging. When teachers know more about the literate lives of their students outside of the classroom, they are more able to set up positive connections between home and school; however, gaps remain in teachers' knowledge about what literacies students are engaged in outside of school and the people, tools, and practices that support their learning (Baroutsis & Woods, 2018). Knowing about the literate lives of students and valuing and centring the knowledge that they bring helps to shatter deficit notions that some educators have about students and their communities (Alford & Woods, 2017).

## Disrupting the Canon

On my own educational journey, I was not particularly focused on literacy and the literate lives of students. However, efforts to understand and implement culturally relevant pedagogy (CRP) practices in classrooms that involve students in all aspects of teaching and learning and literacy is central to this. As a teacher educator, I embarked on research focused on CRP and critical literacy in diverse English classrooms (Lopez, 2011, 2014) with teachers in a large suburban school in Southern Ontario. This research project highlighted the importance of literacy in challenging inequities in education and schooling, and its centrality in equity pedagogies that challenge all forms of oppression. In that study, I observed two teachers of English in diverse classrooms who were intentional in implementing CRP approaches. They used diverse texts written by Black and Brown authors and performance poetry from various contexts. The students also wrote their own poetry. The teachers deliberately moved away from the canons of literary expressions grounded in Eurocentric knowledge and included different forms that represented the students' lived experiences and their interests. They described their agency in encouraging students to engage in critical thinking and reflections, connecting to stories in the texts, challenging ideas, and constructing their own literary texts. Students in both classes wrestled with issues such as forms of racism and stereotypes and how these impacted their lives. In the media literacy class (Lopez, 2011), the teacher used critical media texts (Morrell & Duncan-Andrade, 2006) to engage students in dialogic exchanges about similarly difficult issues. Findings of the study revealed that students became more interested in the courses, disciplinary issues were reduced, and overall performance improved (Lopez, 2011, 2014).

## Challenging All Forms of Oppression

We are seeing a new space for literacy emerging directly from youth culture such as hip-hop. Hip-hop is an innovative and exciting youth art form that allows literacy to be the site of real self-expression and creativity (Ladson-Billings, 2016). Teachers seeking a critical approach to engage youth in alternative forms of literacies have been embracing hip-hop, performance poetry, and digital literacies. Ladson-Billings argues that the "expression of youth culture is a part of the 'cultural competence' and 'sociopolitical consciousness' components of CRP" (p. 147). She explores ways that the hip-hop reinvents and revolutionizes culturally relevant pedagogy by incorporating youth culture as essential ingredients in "students' academic, social, cultural, and civic success" (p. 147). In doing so she draws attention to what it means to think intentionally about students marginalized by the education system, and in particular Black students, and what it means to develop "Black Literate Lives" (p. 146). Students' access and relationship to information are extraordinary, and still most classrooms make little or no use of these resources, as educators fail to recognize how different the experiences of today's students are (Ladson-Billings, 2013). In an era when anti-Black racism and other forms of oppression and exclusion continue to impact the lives of students and their success, literacies that acknowledge their lived experiences and artistic expressions become forms of agency and empowerment.

Acknowledging multiple literacies, disrupting canons, and challenging all forms of oppression provide a pathway for liberatory praxis in education and schooling, and ultimately for students' flourishing. We require multiple literacies to communicate and participate in the times in which we find ourselves as the youth continue to invent new forms of literacies as part of their literate lives and identity formation. In exploring the literate lives of students, we must intentionally also learn from them. We must listen to and engage with students, make connections, and create space for them to bring together their literate lives outside of school with their lives inside schools. Comber and Woods (2018) suggest that in listening to and working with students' ideas and literate experiences outside of the classroom, we can inform classroom experiences in positive ways and develop a sense of belonging within students' educational spaces. Creating space for students to draw on their interests and lived experiences enhances the goals of equitable education, which intentionally focuses on policies and practices in education systems that prevent some students from thriving and achieving to their full potential. Equity education is not a list of strategies but a perspective, a way of thinking, guided by a set of commitments. This perspective is captured in the notion of *liberatory praxis*.

## LIBERATORY PRAXIS

**Praxis,** according to Freire (2000), comprises the amalgamation of one's "critical consciousness"—meaning an awareness of unjust disparities due to an unequal distribution and use of power and resources—with political action (p. 34). Engaging in liberatory educational praxis means operating outside of the formal curriculum and the limiting boundaries of the status quo and questioning whether practices are equitable for all students. It means finding spaces to challenge and better understand the social systems of oppression and supporting students in understanding and challenging those systems. This involves engaging students in critical consciousness and creativity to nurture critical reflection and action (Freire, 2000). It also involves the inclusion of student voices as central and valid in the process of discovery and learning (Richardson, 2023). Liberatory praxis is an approach to teaching and learning that provides students with agency and acknowledges their realities and experiences and the ways that oppressive policies and practices hinder their progress (Pipe & Stephens, 2021). It means disrupting the canons and engaging in praxis that frees not only our actions, but our souls and spirits. Teachers should not be seen as either only nurturers or strict purveyors of information; they also need to strike a balance between the two because our students need love in the process of learning (Freire, 2000).

Liberatory praxis disrupts the notion of neutrality in education and takes the approach that teaching is inherently a political act. This involves teachers "intentionally striving to have critical awareness of, and sensitivity to, broad power dynamics, understanding their own and their students' positional power, or lack thereof … taking pedagogical steps to empower marginalized students while bolstering all students along a path of critical thinking, growth, and self-definition" (Wilson et al., 2019, p. 347). Giroux (França, 2019) suggests that "those arguing that education should be neutral are really arguing for a version of education in which nobody is accountable" (p. 1). Neutrality therefore becomes a political choice and is one that supports, if not strengthens, the status quo (Filippakou, 2022). "This defense of neutrality" makes invisible its own codes and values and in doing so prevents readers from understanding "the role that education plays ideologically, in producing particular forms of knowledge, power, social values, modes of agency, and narratives about the world" (França, 2019, p. 3). Giroux (2020) writes the following:

> The notion of a neutral, objective education is an oxymoron. Education and pedagogy do not exist outside of relations of power, values, and politics. Ethics on the pedagogical front demands an openness to the other, a willingness to engage a "politics of possibility" through a continual critical engagement with texts, images, events, and other registers of meaning as they are transformed into pedagogical practices both within and outside of the classroom. Pedagogy is never innocent, and if it is to be understood and problematized as a form of academic labor, cultural workers have the opportunity not only to critically question and register their own subjective involvement in how and what they teach in and out of schools, but also to resist all calls to depoliticize pedagogy through appeals to either scientific objectivity or ideological dogmatism. (p. 210)

Giroux (2020) argues further that "education is not just about empowering people, the practice of freedom, it's also in some ways about killing the imagination" (p. 2). Liberatory praxis enables students to draw on their imaginations, releasing them from the boundaries of the formal and scripted curriculum. Enacting liberatory pedagogical praxis involves teachers wilfully exercising their influence and agency to engender freedom and equity with academic learning (Wilson et al., 2019).

By creating a nexus between students' literate lives outside of classrooms and what happens inside classrooms, teachers help students to connect what they learn in school to civic agency and empowerment outside of school. In this regard, teachers use various forms of literacies to foster students' critical thinking, political awareness, and ability to critique issues that affect them and their communities (Mirra & Morrell, 2011). Liberatory praxis is also about teachers developing authentic relationships with students (Richardson, 2023). In fact, critical equity, anti-racist, decolonizing education work does not exist outside of relationships. This is collaborative work where teachers and students reimagine and co-create, where they grow, learn, and unlearn together and become empowered in the process of teaching and learning (Lopez, 2018). Liberatory pedagogical praxis requires teachers to "transgress" divisive relational boundaries related to their identities and ideologies and to resist teaching approaches that are "mired in structures of domination" (hooks, 1994, p. 18).

## ACTIONS TO SUPPORT AND SUSTAIN LIBERATORY PRAXIS

As teachers focus on students' literate lives within current contexts where equity initiatives are under attack (e.g., the banning of books on Black history in some schools), the classroom must remain a space of hope. This in and of itself is liberatory praxis. Praxis connects theory to practice and action. Without action, knowledge remains at the intellectual level and real change cannot take place or be sustained. The following are posited as strategies that teachers can embrace on their journey of liberatory pedagogical praxis.

### Engage in Critical Reflexivity

Teaching and learning that are liberatory start with the self, by recognizing how aspects of our identity intersect with those of our students and examining what needs to be learned and unlearned (see conclusion in this volume). All journeys focused on dismantling systems of oppression begin with the self, examining our positionality in many areas: epistemologically, socially, politically, and otherwise. Reflexivity creates space for our emotions and critical examination of the environments in which teaching and learning occur and is a way of "nourishing our spirit" (Rodney et al., 2023). Through critical reflexivity, educators examine what they bring into their roles, including their personal histories (Lopez, 2015). Critical reflexivity is "a process of recognizing one's own position in the world in order both to better understand the limitations of one's own knowing and to better appreciate the social realities of others" (Ng et al., 2019, p. 1124). It involves continual internal dialogue and critical self-evaluation of one's positionality as well as active acknowledgement and explicit recognition that this position may affect others (Berger, 2015). Critical reflexivity is important for teachers as their socialization and social locations, which are sometimes at dissonance with those of the students they teach, impact students' learning. Teachers must critically examine their beliefs, assumptions, and worldviews to learn about areas that might be vulnerabilities and unexamined biases and ideologies that might be held.

## Develop Authentic and Respectful Relationships with Communities

Much of what students bring into classrooms as representation of their literate lives comes from their communities. Liberatory praxis is the valuing of this knowledge as part of teaching and learning. In the research that I conducted with teachers, implementing CRP connections with community was an important aspect of their work. One teacher utilized a book that was written about a South Asian girl coming into adolescence instead of using Shakespeare as the literature study. Members of the South Asian community were invited into the classroom to share their ideas about the issues raised in the book and answer questions from students, including addressing stereotypes about the community (Lopez, 2014). Offering students opportunities to leverage their funds of knowledge and their family, community, and cultural histories in classroom activities and assignments boosts the relevance of students' learning (Wilson et al., 2019). Teachers must intentionally support students whose educational, economic, and social circumstances are challenging. This means unlearning some practices and learning new ones, including engaging with popular culture. Affirming language must be used when talking about students and communities. Historically, we know that certain communities have been positioned within deficit discourses. For example, when speaking about Black children, the focus should be on Black excellence and not the stereotypical tropes used to describe Black children.

## Develop Sociopolitical and Cultural Vision

Teachers must be aware of how political discourses and dominant narratives inform what is read, written, and offered as knowledge in classrooms. Living literate lives means seeing one's history in written form in texts but also through other media, such as movies, dance, art, and so on—all these inform and enrich our literate lives. It is important for teachers to raise students' awareness of historical and contemporary social issues, engage with the complexities, and engage in dialogic conversations to build deeper understanding. How history is represented at home might be in dissonance with the experiences of others, especially those who have been colonized and oppressed by other groups. Acknowledging this tension and supporting students to make space for this enhances their literate lives and creates cross-cultural understanding. Presenting contemporary struggles not as events of modern times but as part of ongoing struggles for freedom and justice can contextualize issues in a such a way that develops students' understanding of contemporary issues (Wilson et al., 2019).

## Embrace Digital Literacies as a Critical Tool of Change

Within contemporary contexts, liberatory praxis must be broadened to include digital literacies. As we have seen from movements and uprisings around the world fighting for justice, equity, and liberation, social media is playing a large role. We are in a moment when social media, citizen journalism, and instant communication platforms are the main organizing tool of students' literacy lives. As well, with the emergence of artificial intelligence, educators will need to rethink how they embrace this technology and what questions around equity need to be asked. Teachers must learn how to leverage these digital platforms and technologies to enhance teaching and learning within the classroom. One of the advantages of these new media is that youth have been able to connect to broader social and civic concerns of their lives in ways that school literacy has failed to do (Ladson-Billings, 2016). In research conducted with teachers implementing CRP in a grade 12 media literacy classroom, the students used social media and various platforms to listen to performance poetry from other contexts to inform their own understanding and engaged with challenging issues such as bullying, gang violence, and other issues affecting the youth. Their own performance poetry that they wrote as a summative assessment for the course reflected their own lives and struggles (see Lopez, 2011). Within current contexts, we have witnessed developments after the murder of George Floyd in 2020, youths responding to social issues in Canada and around the world, and a new sense of activism among young people. Ladson-Billings (2016) argues that "the vehicle for that activism has been the social media platforms that recruit this new literacy our youth embrace. More than [taking] selfies ... or pictures of restaurant meals, youth are organizing, strategizing, and cooperating via social media" (p. 146). This emerging literacy supports liberatory praxis that seeks advanced justice, challenges oppression in its many forms, and supports students in flourishing in their teaching and learning contexts.

## CONCLUSION

Changing their pedagogical stance to embrace the lived realities of students, with a goal of challenging injustices, can be challenging for teachers. Teachers are encouraged to develop a loving and caring community where they can share both the pain and the joys of the work. This kind of space is crucial in offering support and sharing resources and can become a space of healing. The work can be emotionally charged and time-consuming, but it is essential to enriching students' well-being, learning, and engagement (Howard & Milner, 2014). Implementing liberatory pedagogical praxis is collective work to which everyone fighting for justice and equity should contribute. It is important that we, as educators, affirm students' humanity and cultivate their sense of belonging, freedom, and transformative possibilities in schools and in a contentious world (Richardson, 2023). As Gloria Ladson-Billings (2016) argues, literacy is crucial for liberation, especially among those who have been marginalized in society. This is collective and collaborative work. We must become more expansive and creative in creating space for all forms of expression; only then will equity be achieved. Teaching that embeds liberatory pedagogical praxis is a vital form of resistance that seeks to mitigate the harmful effects of standardization, competition, and meritocracy, and high-stakes testing that places children, particularly those marginalized by the system, in challenging and oppressive situations. Liberatory praxis and spaces offer hope.

## KEY TERMS

**Critical consciousness:** A term made popular by Paulo Freire when he wrote about *conscientization*. Critical consciousness focuses on developing an understanding of the world that raises one's social and political awareness of contradictions that exist in society and using this understanding to act against all forms of oppression, particularly in education and schooling. Critical educators draw on critical consciousness to frame pedagogy and praxis.

**Liberatory praxis:** Educators operating outside of the scripted curricula, connecting theory to praxis in ways that centre voices and experiences that are on the margins. It is education that has as its aim justice and freedom from oppression in teaching and learning spaces.

**Oppression:** The unjust treatment of people through institutional power, prejudice, and white supremacy logics that lead to marginalization and exclusion. People can be oppressed through various aspects of their identities, which can be overlapping. In other words, people can experience oppression in multiple ways. Oppression can be experienced individually through institutions and society.

**Praxis:** Connecting theory to action. In other words, how the actions that emanate from understanding and theorization frame one's thinking. Praxis includes reflection and action, not only to become aware but to be transformative.

## DISCUSSION QUESTIONS AND ACTIVITIES

1. What challenges might educators experience in classrooms where social dissonance exists between educators' positionality and students' positionality? How might this be overcome?
2. Engaging in critical praxis that names and addresses forms of oppression and exclusion that students experience in teaching and learning can be challenging for some educators. What are some of the ways that teachers might sustain this journey and avoid engaging in performative actions?
3. Actions to support liberatory praxis are outlined in this chapter. How might schools develop communities of practice to engage in this kind of teaching? In what ways might communities be involved?
4. Disrupting the formal and scripted curricula in an era of standardization and pushback against equity education can be daunting. What resources would be needed to implement culturally relevant and equitable curricula in schools? How might formal school leaders, such as administrators, support this?
5. Drawing on the examples in this chapter, in collaborative groups, develop a curriculum, lesson plan, or unit grounded in liberatory praxis. How might you include students' literate lives in all subject areas?

## REFERENCES

Alford, J., & Woods, A. (2017). Constituting "at risk" literacy and language learners in teacher talk: Exploring the discursive element of time. *Australian Journal of Language and Literacy, 40*, 7–15. doi.org/10.1007/BF03651980

Bailey, K. A. (2016). Racism within the Canadian university: Indigenous students' experience. *Ethnic and Race Studies, 39*(7), 1261–1279. doi.org/10.1080/01419870.2015.1081961

Baroutsis, A., & Woods, A. (2018). Children resisting deficit: What can children tell us about literate lives? *Global Studies of Childhood, 8*(4), 325–338. doi.org/10.1177/2043610618814842

Berger, R. (2015). Now I see it, now I don't: Researcher's position and reflexivity in qualitative research. *Qualitative Research, 15*(2), 219–234. doi.org/10.1177/1468794112468475

Bomer, R., & Fowler-Amato, M. (2014). Expanding adolescent writing: Building upon youths' practices, purposes, relationships, and thoughtfulness. In K. A. Hinchman & H. K. Sheridan-Thomas (Eds.), *Best practices in adolescent literacy instruction* (2nd ed., pp. 154–168). Guilford Press.

Cameron, E. S., & Jefferies, K. (2021). Anti-Black racism in Canadian education: A call to action to support the nest generation. *Healthy Populations Journal, 1*(1) 11–15. doi.org/10.15273/hpj.v1i1.10587

Canadian Multiculturalism Act. R.S.C. 1985, c. 24 (4th Supp.). https://laws-lois.justice.gc.ca/eng/acts/c-18.7/page-1.html

Comber, B., & Woods, A. (2018). Pedagogies of belonging in literacy classrooms and beyond: What's holding us back? In C. Halse (Ed.), *Interrogating belonging for young people in schools* (pp. 263–283). Palgrave.

Donald, D. (2021). We need a new story: Walking and the wâhkôhtowin imagination. *Journal of the Canadian Association for Curriculum Studies, 18*(2), 53–63. doi.org/10.25071/1916-4467.40492

Filippakou, O. (2022). Higher education and the myth of neutrality: Rethinking the cultural politics of research in the age of instrumental rationality. *Review of Education, Pedagogy, and Cultural Studies, 45*(1), 77–89. doi.org/10.1080/10714413.2022.2091396

França, J. (2019). Henry Giroux: "Those arguing that education should be neutral are really arguing for a version of education in which nobody is accountable." CCCB Lab. https://lab.cccb.org/en/henry-giroux-those-arguing-that-education-should-be-neutral-are-really-arguing-for-a-version-of-education-in-which-nobody-is-accountable/

Freire, P. (1970). *Pedagogy of the oppressed*. Seabury Press.

Freire, P. (2000). *Pedagogy of the oppressed* (30th ed.). Bloomsbury Academic.

Giroux, H. A. (2020). *On critical pedagogy* (2nd ed.). Bloomsbury.

hooks, b. (1994). *Teaching to transgress: Education as the practice of freedom*. Routledge

Howard, C. M., Adams-Budde, M., Myers, J., & Jolliff, G. (2017). Shaping our literate lives: Examining the role of literacy experiences in shaping positive literacy identities of doctoral students. *International Journal for the Scholarship of Teaching and Learning, 2*(11), Article 8. doi.org/10.20429/ijsotl.2017.110208

Howard, T. C., & Milner, H. R., IV. (2014). Teacher preparation for urban schools. In H. R. Milner IV & K. Lomotey (Eds.), *Handbook of urban education* (pp. 199–216). Routledge.

James, C. E., & Turner, T. (2017). *Towards race equity in education: The schooling of Black students in the Greater Toronto Area*. York University.

Kerr, J. (2023). Transformational opportunities through new(er) stories: Research addressing educational inequalities. *Canadian Journal of Education, 46*(1), i–iv. www.erudit.org/en/journals/cje/1900-v1-n1-cje07967/1099118ar.pdf

Ladson-Billings, G. (2013). "Stakes is high": Educating new century students. *Journal of Negro Education, 82*(2), 105–110. doi.org/10.7709/jnegroeducation.82.2.0105

Ladson-Billings, G. (2016). #Literate lives matter: Black reading, writing, speaking, and listening in the 21st century. *Literacy Research: Theory, Method, and Practice, 65*(1), 141–151. doi.org/10.1177/2381336916661526

Lopez, A. E. (2011). Culturally relevant pedagogy and critical literacy in diverse English classrooms: Case study of a secondary English teacher's activism and agency. *English Teaching Practice and Critique, 10*(4), 75–93. https://eric.ed.gov/?id=EJ962607

Lopez, A. E. (2014). Re-conceptualizing teacher leadership through curriculum inquiry in pursuit of social justice: Case study from the Canadian context. In C. Shields & I. Bogotch (Eds.), *International handbook of educational leadership and social (in)justice* (pp. 465–484). Springer.

Lopez, A. E. (2015). Navigating cultural borders in diverse contexts: Building capacity through culturally responsive leadership and critical praxis. *Multicultural Education Review, 7*(3), 171–184. doi.org/10.1080/2005615X.2015.1072080

Lopez, A. E. (2018). Disruptive pedagogy: Critical approach to diversity in teacher education. In A. E. Lopez and E. Olan (Eds.), *Transformative pedagogies for teacher education: Moving towards critical praxis in an era of change* (pp. 157–174). Information Age.

Lopez, A. E., & Jean-Marie, G. (2021). Challenging anti-Black racism in everyday teaching, learning and leading: From theory to practice. *Journal of School Leadership, 31*(1–2), 50–65. doi.org/10.1177/1052684621993115

Malhi, R. L., & Boon, S. D. (2007). Discourses of "democratic racism" in the talk of South Asian Canadian women. *Canadian Ethnic Studies, 39*(3), 125–149. doi.org/10.1353/ces.0.0026

McKinney, M., & Giorgis, C. (2009). Narrating and performing identity: Literacy specialists' writing identities. *Journal of Literacy Research, 41*(1), 104–149. doi.org/10.1080/10862960802637604

Mirra, N., & Morrell, E. (2011). Teachers as civic agents: Toward a critical democratic theory of urban teacher development. *Journal of Teacher Education, 62*(4), 408–420. doi.org/10.1177/0022487111409417

Moje, E. B., & Luke, A. (2009). Literacy and identity: Examining the metaphors in history and contemporary research. *Reading Research Quarterly, 44*(4), 415–437. doi.org/10.1598/RRQ.44.4.7

Morrell, E., & Duncan-Andrade, J. (2006). Popular culture and critical media pedagogy in secondary literacy classrooms. *The International Journal of Learning Annual Review, 12*(9), 273–280. doi.org/10.18848/1447-9494/CGP/v12i09/48068

Ng, S. L., Wright, S. R., & Kuper, A. (2019). The divergence and convergence of critical reflection and critical reflexivity: Implications for health professions education. *Academic Medicine, 94*(8), 1122–1128. doi.org/10.1097/ACM.0000000000002724

Nussbaum, M. C. (1997). *Cultivating humanity: A classical defense of reform in liberal education*. Harvard University Press.

Ohito, E. O. (2016). Making the emperor's new clothes visible in anti-racist teacher education: Enacting a pedagogy of discomfort with white preservice teachers. *Equity & Excellence in Education, 49*(4), 454–467. doi.org/10.1080/10665684.2016.1226104

Perry, K. H. (2012). What is literacy? A critical overview of sociocultural perspectives. *Journal of Language and Literacy Education, 8*(1), 50–71. https://eric.ed.gov/?id=EJ1008156

Pipe, L. M., & Stephens, J. T. (2021). Toward a liberated learning spirit: A model for developing critical consciousness. *Journal of Scholarship, Teaching, and Learning, 21*(2), 121–139. doi.org/10.14434/josotl.v21i2.29148

Potvin, M. (2017). *How equitable is Canada's education system?* EdCan Network. www.edcan.ca/articles/equitable-canadas-education-system/

Richardson, C. O. (2023). Being about it: Engaging liberatory educational praxis. *Education Sciences, 13*(6), 1–17. doi.org/10.3390/educsci13060625

Rodney, R., Hinds. M., Bonilla-Damptey, J., Khan, A., & Forde, A. (2023). Anti-oppression as praxis in the research field: Implementing emancipatory approaches for researchers and community partners. *Qualitative Research*. doi.org/10.1177/14687941231196382

Satzewich, V., & Liodakis N. (2021). *Race and ethnicity in Canada: A critical introduction*. Oxford University Press.

Scorza, D. A., Mirra, N., & Morrell, E. (2013). It should just be education: Critical pedagogy normalized as academic excellence. *The International Journal of Critical Pedagogy, 4*(2), 15–34. https://libjournal.uncg.edu/ijcp/article/view/337/365

Willen, S. S. (2022). Flourishing and health in critical perspective: An invitation to interdisciplinary dialogue. *SSM-Mental Health, 2*. doi.org/10.1016/j.ssmmh.2021.100045

Williams, M. T., Khanna Roy, A., MacIntyre, M. P., & Faber, S. (2022). The traumatizing impact of racism in Canadians of colour. *Current Trauma Reports, 8*, 17–34. doi.org/10.1007/s40719-022-00225-5

Wilson, C. M., & Hanna, M. O., & Li, M. (2019). Imagining and enacting liberatory pedagogical praxis in a politically divisive era. *Equity & Excellence in Education, 52*(2–3), 346–363. doi.org/10.1080/10665684.2019.1656563

# CHAPTER 5
# Toward Strengths-Based Culturally Responsive Teaching of Refugee Students with Interrupted Formal Education

*Hiba Barek, Marja G. Bertrand, and Immaculate K. Namukasa*

During the last decade, we have witnessed a global increase in war, political conflicts, corruption, and post-COVID economic degradation. These crises have often resulted in an augmented refugee movement toward many countries, including Canada. Refugees flee their war-torn countries hoping for a better life for themselves, but more so for their children. Canada has been regularly welcoming refugees for many years; however, the literature shows that there have been challenges in responding to the needs of refugee students in Canadian classrooms (e.g., Barek, 2020; Gagné et al., 2017). Since 2015, the influx of refugees with interrupted formal education into Canada, particularly following the war in Syria, has revealed the need to understand the ways in which teachers respond to the cultural, linguistic, and ethnic diversity of refugee students with interrupted formal education (SIFEs) and create appropriate learning opportunities for them. In this chapter, we specifically examine the practices and perspectives of English literacy development (ELD) teachers. We address the question *What practices and pedagogies are enacted in ELD classrooms that build teacher capacity to address systemic and structural inequities in schools for refugee SIFEs?*

An intersection of various factors characterizes the experiences of Syrian refugee SIFEs and their teachers in Canadian classrooms (e.g., sudden enrolment of high numbers of Syrian refugee SIFEs in Canadian classrooms, interruption of students' formal education, language barriers, Middle Eastern culture, [predominant] Islamic religious belief, visible minority status of refugees, war trauma, loss of family members, teachers' lack of preparedness for teaching refugee SIFEs, teachers feeling overwhelmed). Studying the practices and pedagogies that build teacher capacity for teaching refugee SIFEs in ELD classrooms promises to extend the knowledge about refugee education more broadly in Canadian classrooms.

We begin this chapter by providing an overview of the recent trends regarding the experiences of refugee students and their teachers in Canadian schools. We then present the main tenets of critical theory and culturally responsive teaching. After, we describe how teachers build caring and culturally responsive relationships with their students and create culturally responsive learning opportunities for them. We discuss findings from a research project that we conducted on teachers' experiences with Syrian refugee SIFEs in Southwestern Ontario. To conclude, we provide theoretical and practical implications for curriculum development and teacher education that we hope will contribute to refugee youths' holistic well-being and their flourishing.

## REFUGEE STUDENTS' AND TEACHERS' EXPERIENCES IN CANADIAN CLASSROOMS

Since 2015, Canada has welcomed Syrian refugees, including children, some of whom have suffered from years of interrupted formal education. As a result, Canadian educators have been found to be overwhelmed by the increasing number of refugee SIFEs in their classrooms (Barek, 2020; Dufresne, 2015), which raises questions about support for teachers' preparedness to assist these students and lead them to achieve academic success. According to He et al. (2008), teachers' struggles might be related to their own context-based knowledge about their students' backgrounds juxtaposed with the latter's linguistic, cultural, and ethnic diversities. Thus, teachers find it difficult to relate to their students' experiences and consequently struggle to create supportive classroom practices and learning opportunities for them (Gay, 2000, 2010; Ladson-Billings, 1994). Barek (2020) has come to a similar conclusion. Based on her review of the literature, she observes that teachers' limited context-based knowledge about Syrian refugee SIFEs' migration journeys (including pre- and post-migration) has made it challenging for teachers to understand their experiences and create adequate learning opportunities with/for them. Gay (2018) asserts that educators cannot teach their students if they lack knowledge about the students' life history and needs. Furthermore, Brewer and McCabe (2014) propose that teachers' attitudes toward refugee students, their lack of preparedness for and awareness about ways to support such students in the classroom, and poor inclusion practices may have led to refugee students' isolation and marginalization in Canadian classrooms. Refugee students' experiences in Canada, they conclude, have been affected by the "ongoing legacies of colonialism, capitalism, and racism" (Brewer & McCabe, 2014, p. 2). Yet, while trying to create meaningful and culturally responsive learning opportunities for their students, ELD teachers in Canadian high schools struggle (Barek, 2020; Clark, 2017; Gagné et al., 2017; Ghosh et al., 2019). According to the Government of Canada (2017), Canadian stakeholders and teachers of Syrian refugee students were not provided with sufficient information about the needs of government-sponsored refugees, nor were the teachers prepared to deal with refugee students' mental health issues. Teachers' struggles are thus further complicated by their lack of awareness of, and expertise in, professional training opportunities related to teaching SIFEs as well as their misconceptions about refugee SIFEs in general (Barek, 2020; Gay, 2002; Vavrus, 2008). Consequently, Canadian teachers need to be more prepared to identify the needs of their refugee students (Barek, 2020; Clark, 2017; Ghosh et al., 2019; Kaur & Szorenyi, 2022; Rossiter & Rossiter, 2009; Yau, 1996; Yu, 2012). Based on the literature and in response to Clark's (2017) fundamental question—"Are we ready?"—we created a diagram (figure 5.1) to illustrate some of the reasons why teachers are not well prepared to support Syrian refugee SIFEs in Canadian classrooms. Teachers benefit from additional professional development training in order to interact appropriately with refugee SIFEs and adapt their curricula to accommodate their specific needs (Barek, 2020; Rossiter & Rossiter, 2009; Yau, 1996; Yu, 2012).

As these accounts make clear, teachers need to know general information about the Syrian refugee SIFEs enrolled in their classrooms to be adequately equipped to develop students' capabilities to flourish and fulfill present and future aspirations: to live with dignity and contribute meaningfully to society (Nussbaum, 1997) in Canada. It is, then, crucial for teachers to help refugee students embrace their identities, beliefs, and principles while they find connections, relationships, and a place in their new home.

Despite the challenges outlined in figure 5.1, the literature also reveals the successful experiences of teachers of refugee students that are worth highlighting

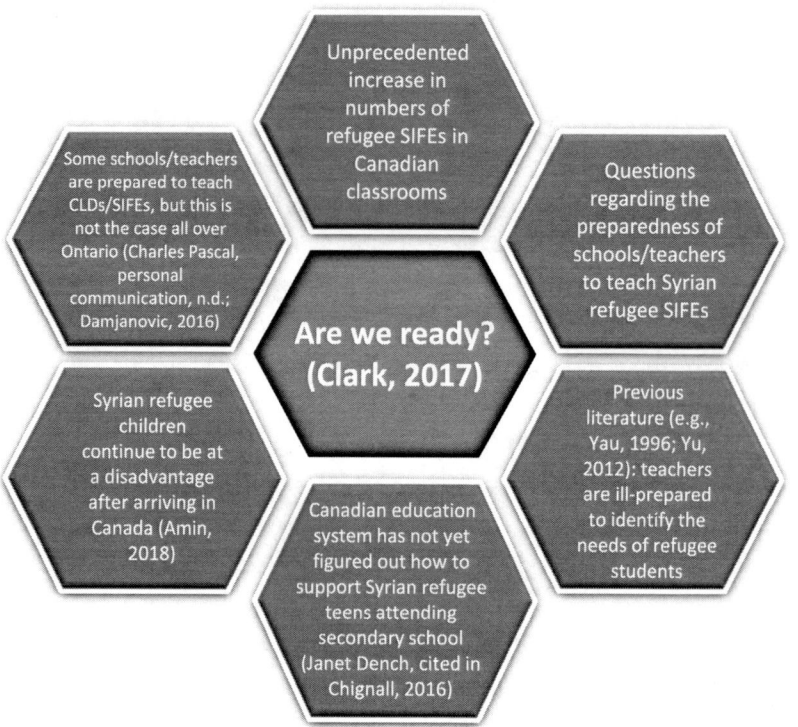

**Figure 5.1:** The Transition of Refugee Students, K–12, into Canadian Classrooms
*Source:* Compiled by the authors.

and building upon (e.g., Barek, 2020; Gagné et al., 2017). There is, thus, an urge to explore such positive experiences and pedagogical practices of teachers—and specifically in this discussion, ELD teachers. Highlighting them may benefit other teachers, researchers, curriculum developers, and policy-makers in implementing strategies to improve support for refugee SIFEs in Canadian schools that match refugee students' needs and experiences and inspire them to academic success (Barek, 2020; Clark, 2017; Kovinthan, 2016).

The purpose of this chapter, then, is to document such experiences. Our discussion is based on a qualitative case study project conducted in ELD classrooms in two urban secondary schools with high numbers of refugee SIFEs in a mid-size Canadian city in Southwestern Ontario. Our discussions with the teachers included seven participants: five ELD teachers, one English as a second language (ESL) teacher, and one school settlement worker. These participants were teaching Syrian refugee SIFEs in ELD classes during the study or had previously taught ELD classes. Before we discuss participants' perspectives and experiences, we will discuss the theoretical frameworks that guided the study: critical theory and culturally responsive teaching.

## CRITICAL THEORY AND CULTURALLY RESPONSIVE TEACHING FRAMEWORK

We used the framework of critical theory and **culturally responsive teaching**, and we drew on what we learned from the analysis of the data collected to contribute to the discussion on multicultural education and to support the success and flourishing of youth in Canada (see table 5.1).

Furthermore, we utilized Gay's (2010, 2018) five tenets of culturally responsive teaching to better understand teachers' experiences when teaching refugee SIFEs (see table 5.2).

Culturally responsive teaching addresses the sustained academic struggles and challenges of marginalized populations. Further, it integrates students' wealth of knowledge and previous experiences into the curriculum and classroom practices.

Table 5.1: A Summary of the Main Components of Critical Theory and Culturally Responsive Teaching

| CRITICAL THEORY (CT) | CULTURALLY RESPONSIVE TEACHING (CRTE) |
|---|---|
| Eisner (1992) defines critical theory as "an approach to the study of schools and society that has as its main function the revelation of the tacit values that underlie the enterprise" (p. 314). CT (Cummins, 2000; Eisner, 1992) provides a framework that—through pointing to inequality in selecting, evaluating, and disseminating knowledge—helps to conceptualize the ways in which, and the conditions under which, knowledge is created in ELD classrooms. | CRTe (Gay, 2000) is a student-centred pedagogy that frames an approach to empower students intellectually, academically, socially, psychologically, emotionally, and politically (Ladson-Billings, 1994). It honours the cultural backgrounds of excluded and marginalized students (Vavrus, 2008), and it uses their cultural knowledge and prior educational experiences as a *conduit* to support the teaching and learning process (Gay, 2000). CRTe provides the framework to examine how ELD teachers respond (or not) to their students' socio-emotional and academic needs. |
| *Curriculum*: focuses on power and privileges in hidden curriculum | *Curriculum*: focuses on knowledge and content |
| *Culture*: integrates coercive relations of power, majority language | *Culture*: integrates culture and communication |
| *Structure*: includes exclusionary structures of schooling | *Structure*: includes both instructions and caring practices |

**Table 5.2: Gay's (2010, 2018) Five Components of Culturally Responsive Teaching and Instruction**

| COMPONENT | BRIEF DESCRIPTION |
|---|---|
| Cultural diversity knowledge base | Seeking information about students' backgrounds, cultures, and prior experiences |
| Ethnic and culturally diverse curriculum content | Making curriculum content accessible to students by connecting it to their lives outside of school |
| Culturally responsive caring | Caring for, instead of about, students |
| Culture and communication in the classroom | Understanding, accepting, and respecting students' cultural communication styles |
| Ethnic diversity in the delivery of instruction or cultural congruity in teaching and learning | Conveying knowledge through students' learning styles |

# SYSTEMIC AND STRUCTURAL INEQUITIES EMBEDDED IN SOCIOCULTURAL AND EDUCATIONAL STRUCTURES

The analysis of the teacher interviews showed several systemic and structural inequities embedded in sociocultural and educational structures. These include issues related to (a) teachers' education; (b) the lack of representation of refugee SIFEs' voices in the **programmatic curriculum** and under-representation of refugee SIFEs' experiences in pedagogical practices and school activities; and (c) the cultural divide between schools and society for SIFEs. These inequities lead to unpleasant experiences and negative feelings for refugee SIFEs in the classrooms, including feelings of exclusion, disappointment in the education system, and lack of a sense of belonging. As a result, refugee SIFEs dropped out of school and faced academic and eventually professional uncertainty, which in turn caused harm to their well-being and negatively affected their families and communities.

## Teachers' Preparedness from Education Programs

The teachers we talked to agreed that neither their academic training nor their prior classroom experiences had adequately prepared them to teach refugee SIFEs. They felt that teaching Syrian refugee SIFEs, for instance, had proved to be quite fulfilling, although the teachers were not initially adequately prepared and lacked the resources to teach ELD students. One of the teachers, Mark, explained, "Initially, I didn't have the slightest clue of what ELD meant or that there were sheltered courses for our English Language Learners." Similarly, Suzan posited the following:

> We can all agree that while we were at Teachers College taking our ESL [course] we had no idea that there is this special section of ESL which is called ELD ... I was ignorant when I came into this secondary school, I knew that there were refugee students here, but I didn't know how interrupted their education was. I had no knowledge about what I am getting myself into ... Teachers College did not prepare me [to teach ELD].

Cummins (2000) critiques teacher education programs in Canada that do not prepare educators to cater to minorities. The lack of preparation for Canadian teachers to teach nonwhite minority students represents, according to Cummins (2000), "a sociological phenomenon that can be analyzed only in terms of the persistence of coercive relations of power hiding behind meaningless multicultural rhetoric" (p. 7).

## Lack of Relevance and Representation in the Programmatic Curriculum

Culturally responsive pedagogy and curricula are key resources for putting culturally responsive teaching practices into effect (see also chapter 4). The teachers in our study asserted that the ELD curricula do not consider the Syrian refugee SIFEs' needs, identities, culture, backgrounds, or prior experiences. Suzan, for example, said, "Unfortunately, it [the programmatic curriculum] doesn't reflect the students' backgrounds." Many of the teacher participants noted that the ELD curricula and the Ontario education system are not supportive of refugee SIFEs and do not promote their academic success. In this regard, Cynthia said, "The system doesn't work and is not meant for them [refugee SIFEs] to psychologically succeed." Similarly, Mark mentioned that he realized early on "that many of those students [Syrian refugee SIFEs] were not graduating and in turn, they needed some type of skills as they entered the workforce." Further, Rina, a settlement worker in the school board, asserted, "The first wave of Syrian GARs [government-assisted refugees] arrived at [the school] in 2016. The majority have been placed in ELD classes ... the majority of the youth who enrolled during the first wave dropped out or were advised to go to adult ESL if they were over 18."

The way Syrian refugee SIFEs were assigned to the teachers' classes also showed a lack of caring and responsiveness to these students' prior experiences and knowledge. Lynn and Suzan recognized and acknowledged that their students had different academic backgrounds and abilities and that they should not be placed randomly into ELD classrooms without some sort of diagnostic assessment (oral and/or written). Lynn said, "You have kids that if their education wasn't interrupted because of war, they would've been in academic[-level courses] going into college or university and then we have workplace[-level students who plan to go straight into the workforce after high school].… But they aren't being streamed that way and they are all in one class."

Besides the lack of proper course-level assignment with respect to refugee SIFEs, there was also a disconnect between the ELD curriculum, where students are taught elementary school content, and the evaluation, where they are assessed at the secondary level. Lynn and Suzan felt that this disconnect hindered the academic success of the Syrian refugee SIFEs. Suzan explains:

> I think of our students, we are teaching them at an elementary level. I find it so unfair to say like you are at 45 [percent] because you are unable to do all this, but look at all the things you are doing and you are doing that well to build up here. So, the board will not take away the numbers but for the ELD students, 45, for example, is so disappointing and it just sets them back a lot more than pushes them forward.

In addition, Jennifer explained that the "expectations need to be broken down and modelled, not expected from the start as they are in mainstream classes." Jennifer, Lynn, and Suzan stated that the time frame planned by the school board for Syrian refugee SIFEs to succeed in their ELD courses and start their ESL courses was not sufficient. They thought that the students needed more time to learn English and adjust to the Canadian education system.

To address the gap between the curriculum and students' evaluated reading levels, Lynn and Suzan embraced the guided reading program as a way to provide the students with "certain criteria to move up" (Suzan) and potentially succeed academically, as it gave students time to progress and set their own goals (Barek, 2020).

### Cultural Divide between School and Society

Three teachers in particular (Lynn, Suzan, and Jasmine) described a divide at school and in society between minority and majority population groups. Further, all participants emphasized that one of their tasks as teachers of refugee SIFEs was to support and aid these students' integration into the greater school community and Canadian society. Lynn, Suzan, and Jasmine especially went into detail in describing a divide at school and in society between minority and majority population groups and the strategies they used to address this divide. I am "the person to go to if [they are] having issues with other teachers ... and helping them [to] navigate this world" was how Suzan described her role. Besides teaching the refugee students the curricular content, Lynn intentionally modelled for them and provided positive examples of Canadians who are empathetic, inclusive, and accepting of people who are different from themselves. She said, "We hope that they see that's what Canadians could be like, this is what we are." Suzan and Lynn underlined how crucial it is for refugee SIFEs to understand how to navigate the Canadian education system and culture and to be able to work with people of diverse backgrounds and perspectives. As such, Suzan explained to them that there are two kinds of Canadians: those who accept and respect minorities and those who appear to be biased or prejudiced against people who are ethnically or racially different. Suzan shared how she prepared her students to face these challenges:

> Because not all Canadians are going to have the same mentality as us and that's OK ... but ... there is also a lot of Canadians to find that help people and who want to help you and they care, and when you find it, enjoy it, and embrace it.... It really doesn't matter where you're going in the world, it doesn't matter where you go, you are going to run into issues where people don't necessarily like you, and it doesn't matter. You know what your background is, you will just find people who don't like you and you need to find out how to handle it.

Lynn and Suzan taught their refugee SIFEs how to cope when faced with racism, social inequities, and prejudices and how to channel their uncomfortable feelings, such as anger, when they are treated unfairly. They told their students, "We are here for you guys ... you will have bad experiences with racism, ... but this is anywhere.... We want them to know that there are people like us who care, but ... the world around them may not be that safe or as accepting and [we want to] give them a zone ... where they can calm [themselves], relax and just breathe."

Specifically, Jasmine noted that one of Syrian refugee SIFEs' challenges was "being accepted into Canadian society." Although each teacher described themselves as caring, compassionate, and empathetic, they recognized that this may not be the case with all ELD and mainstream teachers. In their schools, there appeared to be a divide between some mainstream teachers and ESL/ELD teachers in their approach to teaching refugee SIFEs. Lynn said, "If you ask other teachers in the [school] board, they wouldn't know what ELD is, we didn't know what ELD was until we started. It really is a minority [of] teachers that know this.... You have some mainstream teachers versus the ESL/ELD teachers. There is still, within the school, a divide."

The teachers expressed their concerns about the different ways in which the systemic and structural inequities embedded in the sociocultural and educational structures discussed above would hinder the academic success and well-being of Syrian refugee SIFEs. To counter this hindrance, all educators need to be better prepared through training to address harmful prejudices such as racism. They need to "become critically conscious of their cultural socialization, and how it affects their attitudes and behaviors toward the cultures of other ethnic groups" (Gay, 2002, p. 619). When teachers ignore the sociocultural realities of systemic racism and how its harm affects many SIFEs' lives, they are in effect asking students to defend their cultural practices, religious beliefs, and identities against the dominant cultural norms to which they are expected to assimilate to.

## EFFECTIVE CLASSROOM PRACTICES CREATED BY ELD TEACHERS

The teachers we spoke with increased their capacity to challenge systemic inequities in schools by enacting anti-racist pedagogical practices and culturally responsive teaching techniques. For example, they respectively engaged in self-reflection, cultivated their students' critical thinking and consciousness, participated in political discussions with their students, and represented them in the curriculum. As a result, they encouraged equity and social justice in the classroom. Gay's (2010, 2018) five components of culturally responsive teaching (see table 5.2) provided a way for us to reflect on effective instructional practices in ELD classrooms.

### Building on Refugee SIFEs' Prior Knowledge and Experiences

Teachers told us they drew on students' prior knowledge and experiences to create a supportive learning environment through culturally responsive learning opportunities that validated, affirmed, and celebrated refugee SIFEs' identities, languages, and backgrounds. Teachers shared that they wanted to learn more about their students' backgrounds. Jennifer stated, "The first few weeks ... should be full of conversations and observations so that my planning can be based on the learners.... The more I know about their journeys and challenges, the better I'm able to tailor my teaching and approach to their needs."

Teachers from both schools relied primarily on their daily interactions with the students to learn more about them and to tailor their instructions and lesson plans accordingly by building on the students' strengths and accommodating their individual needs. Susan reflected, "It is crazy how well even though they can't speak English we know more about these students than we know about [the mainstream] students."

The teachers' pedagogical approach, which built on their students' prior knowledge, motivated them to collect information about their students and helped them have a better understanding of their students' backgrounds, history, and culture; this was despite the fact that initially the information was scarce and the government was unable to provide sufficient details. The teachers' pedagogical approach helped them perceive the hidden potential and resilience that their refugee SIFEs had. Consequently, they identified these potentials, focused on developing them, and predicted that their students' resilience would guide them toward realizing their full potential and achieving academic success.

## Providing Ethnic and Culturally Diverse Curriculum Content and Differentiated Instructions

Teachers from both schools confirmed that the ELD programmatic curriculum did not reflect any of the refugee SIFEs' cultures, languages, identities, backgrounds, prior experiences, or religions. To meet the varying needs of refugee SIFEs, teachers provided ethnic and culturally responsive curriculum content and used differentiated instructions and diverse adaptations, recognizing that students may have varying levels of proficiency in English and different educational backgrounds. Lynn explained, "We don't want them to lose their language, we don't want them to lose their culture … we want them to embrace it."

For instance, most of the teachers said that they tried to link the stories they worked on in the classroom to the lives of their students. Two teachers (Lynn and Suzan) said that they asked their ELD students questions such as "Do you have a personal story, what does this remind you of? … Does this relate to you in any way?" Both affirmed that providing students with the opportunity to share their stories and make a connection to their culture, language, identity, and background was key to understanding them.

Cynthia shared that she incorporated students' "heritage, pictures, and first language when applicable." Further, Cynthia, Jennifer, and Lynn organized classroom activities in which they connected the lessons to refugee SIFEs' cultural characteristics. For instance, Cynthia shared the following:

> When designing a culturally responsive lesson, I invite[d] students to ... [bring] in different foods and cultural outfits and music.... Looking up pictures and maps from their cities back home and involving them in discussions ... we focused on positive images from days they were proud of and were so happy to talk about and excited to show me which cities they are from.

The teachers contended that such material helped students engage authentically in texts and sparked genuine discussions in their classes. Further, Jennifer mentioned that she often planned her course content with a focus on culturally significant topics for her students. "For instance, we may read and discuss articles related to [religious topics such as] Mecca, Eid, etc. I look for documentaries and other media which reflect some of what my students experience in Canada, for instance, *14 & Muslim*, a CBC documentary about adapting to Canadian schools and deciding between public and religious education."

According to the Ontario Ministry of Education (OME, 2020), "in an inclusive education system, students must see themselves reflected in the curriculum, their physical surroundings, and the broader environment, so that they can feel engaged in and empowered by their learning experiences" (p. 19). Similarly, *Supporting English Language Learners with Limited Prior Schooling: A Practical Guide for Ontario Educators, Grades 3 to 12* (OME, 2008) emphasizes that ELD students "need to see the connections between who they are, what they value, and what they are learning in school in order to make sense of the learning and integrate it into their whole being" (p. 35). Teachers in the ELD program agreed with these statements and created learning opportunities for their ELD students accordingly. However, they doubted that these principles were respected and considered in the ELD programmatic curriculum. They found that there was a lack of representation of refugee SIFEs in the curriculum and an under-representation of their experiences in pedagogical practices and that certain provisions needed to be included in the curriculum in order to incorporate refugee SIFEs' voices, cultures, languages, identities, and backgrounds.

## Fostering Culture, Communication, and Critical Consciousness in the Classroom

Culture and communication are interrelated. Gay (2018) asserts that "communication cannot exist without culture, culture cannot be known without communication, and teaching and learning are more effective for ethnically diverse students when classroom communication is culturally responsive" (p. 89). According to the teachers, integrating culturally responsive material into the curriculum resulted in heightened engagement for the SIFEs in classroom practices and sparked genuine discussions in the classroom. Cynthia mentioned that she had realized the message was hard to get through using English only. Thus, she conveyed that she "uses all kinds of ways including pictures, sign language, acting and translations to get the kids to understand the content."

Jennifer said that she was learning to listen more and self-reflect: "Listening, letting students express their ideas and tell their stories. Apologize and change my approach if I have misrepresented or offended any learner ... I try to be as considerate and responsive in my teaching and planning as possible." Lynn and Suzan mentioned that they were "learning to be culturally aware." The teachers agreed that it does not make sense to ask students about topics that do not relate to their prior experiences (e.g., "Tell [me/us] about ... [an] experience in the snow" when they have never seen snow before).

Teachers confirmed that they respected and took into consideration students' backgrounds, religions, and cultures when navigating discussions in the classroom. For instance, Suzan and Lynn said they paid special attention to the words they used and the texts they selected. These teachers asserted that they knew their students originated from conservative families with traditional and religious beliefs; thus, they tried to use words and expressions that students were familiar with and that did not create cultural misunderstanding.

In addition, teachers managed to foster their SIFEs' critical thinking through discussions of social justice issues. The teachers' practices were meant to cultivate capabilities needed by the students to better integrate into their schools and communities, channel their potential to reach their goals, negotiate their cultural identities, question social inequities, and lead flourishing lives.

## Implementing Ethnically Diverse Instructions

Teacher participants said they attempted to understand their students' ways of knowing and created culturally responsive learning opportunities for them by acknowledging, celebrating, and intentionally planning for the specific and unique contexts of refugee SIFEs. Jennifer explained, "I constantly reimagine lessons so that they are more culturally relevant and applicable to my ELD learners." Some teachers said they used translations in the classroom, and others mentioned that they differentiated their instructions (e.g., using "differentiated and tiered-type pedagogy when teaching Syrian SIFEs" [Mark]) and modified the curriculum to engage their students. The instructions and programs (e.g., guided reading program and ELD co-op program) that teachers implemented appeared to greatly enhance students' learning, achievements, and outcomes. These findings corroborate research by Gay (2018) on the benefit of such instructions for the education of culturally and linguistically diverse students and align with Ladson-Billings's (1994) acknowledgement that modified, differentiated, or translingual instructions empower minority students intellectually, academically, socially, psychologically, and emotionally.

## Fostering Positive Teacher-Student Relationships through Culturally Responsive Caring

The nature of the teacher-student relationship has a significant impact on refugee SIFEs' academic achievement and well-being. Gay (2018) suggests that teachers who underestimate or do not prioritize the importance of relationship-building struggle to connect with their students and often have trouble addressing the unique socioemotional and academic needs of minority students or students at risk. From the teachers' self-reported data, it appears the teachers succeeded in building positive and supportive relationships with their students. Consequently, they created a sense of belonging and trust among their students, which in turn enhanced students' well-being and fostered their engagement and academic achievement.

Teachers also demonstrated unequivocal advocacy (e.g., "I am an ally when needed" [Jennifer]), endless efforts, and authentic commitment to ensure that learning in their ELD classrooms was responsive to students' socioemotional and academic needs within and beyond the classroom walls. For instance, Mark showed **culturally responsive caring** when he noticed that to thrive in Canadian society, most of his students needed hands-on and practical experience in addition to their paper-and-pencil academic learning. According to Mark, his students had already entered the workforce while still in school. However, they were lacking the necessary basic knowledge to successfully navigate the workplace. Mark posited, "Early on, I realized that many of these students were not graduating and in turn needed some type of skills as they entered the workforce. As such I helped create an ELD/ESL co-op program." He went on: "Perhaps more hands-on or co-op type programs can be offered to help provide these students with skills that will help them in the real world. We need to build on their strengths.... Why not try to build on their strengths so they can be strong, contributing members of society."

Most teachers said they engaged in self-monitoring and self-reflection when they were teaching ELD students. For instance, Jennifer asserted the following:

> Each year I am learning more about how I can best serve these students. I try to remember all that I don't know about each student—the trauma and disruptions many of my students face, the day-to-day frustrations and challenges, the homesickness.... From experience, I've learned not to take any education background for granted (e.g., using a dictionary, pencil, locker) since some students have not had access to the most basic of educational resources or experiences.

Lynn and Suzan practised culturally responsive caring beyond their ELD classrooms to advocate for refugee SIFEs in the mainstream, non-ELD classroom, by fighting negative stereotypes. This required shifting mindsets and constant reflection on common biases and preconceived assumptions (Nussbaum, 1997; Sasakamoose, 2021) linked to the education of refugee SIFEs. Suzan hoped that other teachers "can see ... that students aren't troublemakers, they are either bored or they don't understand what is happening and they only need a caring adult to help them and understand that they are worth it ... you have students who are at the university level and, in the same class, students who are working at a kindergarten level. [Teachers] are trying to work out their classroom to the best of their abilities." These perspectives of the ELD teacher participants support research from Gay (2000). According to Gay (2000), culturally responsive pedagogy "teaches to and through the strengths" (p. 29) of culturally and linguistically diverse students, and culturally responsive caring places "teachers in an ethical, emotional, and academic partnership with ethnically diverse students" (p. 52).

The teachers modelled care for their students. They showed openness to questioning preconceived assumptions and knowledge. They deployed personal efforts to acquire knowledge about their students' culture, needs, interests, and desires. They showed sustained interest in students' welfare and maintained caring nonhierarchical teacher-student relationships. There were no indicators of imbalanced teacher-student power relationships. The teachers said that they constantly had high expectations for their refugee SIFEs and that there were still consequences for students' inappropriate behaviours and academic carelessness. Those expectations and consequences were normalized by the teachers, not from a power standpoint, but rather from a culturally caring standpoint, to bring out the best in their refugee SIFEs. Teachers' practices showed authentic caring (Gay, 2010; Noddings, 2003) for refugee SIFEs. Beyond aesthetic caring, teachers' authentic caring for minority students (Barek, 2020; Gay, 2018) and radical compassion (Barek et al., 2021) proved to enhance the students' overall well-being and academic achievement.

## CONCLUSION

In countries where systemic inequities continue to disrupt the education of historically marginalized students, especially those countries that receive immigrants and refugees, educators have the ethical responsibility to act as agents of social change. In these countries, educators also need to reflect on, examine, and confront unjust sociopolitical and sociocultural realities in order to disrupt the cycle of oppression and inequality (Nieto, 2004, p. xxii) and create more advantageous conditions for historically marginalized groups such as refugee SIFEs to flourish within education institutions.

Overall, the culturally responsive and inclusive practices and pedagogies enacted by the teacher participants in this study validated the identities, languages, prior knowledge, and backgrounds of refugee SIFEs; they potentially allowed the students to live with dignity while making connections and building relationships with others as well as contributing meaningfully to Canadian society. These practices also helped to build teachers' capacity to challenge and combat systemic and structural inequities in the educational system and to support the successful integration of refugee SIFEs into the Ontario classrooms and schools in which the study was carried out.

Our dialogues with the teachers helped us unveil the systemic and structural inequities perpetuating an unjust social order in Ontario schools and specifically in the two secondary schools that participated in our study. We also were able to document ELD teachers' experiences of cultural responsiveness, agency, and advocacy and to underscore the importance of positive, caring teacher-student relationships as a key factor in promoting the holistic well-being and academic success of refugee SIFEs.

This chapter thus offers a strengths-based perspective where teachers build on refugee SIFEs' prior experiences, ways of knowing, culture, and first language to facilitate students' flourishing. The perspective offered has theoretical and practical implications for curriculum development and teacher education. Teacher education programs and in-service professional development offerings need to train teachers (present and future) in teaching diverse students using a culturally responsive teaching model in all classrooms where refugee SIFEs are present. Policy-makers, curriculum developers/designers, and stakeholders are invited to consider and represent in curriculum and materials the voices and experiences of the teachers of refugee SIFEs when planning future policy implementations and programs in classrooms. If they fail to meet these conditions, the academic and professional future of refugee SIFEs in Canada will be at risk.

## KEY TERMS

**Culturally responsive caring:** Caring for students' well-being that goes beyond caring for their academic achievement. This is a process of actively building positive teacher-student relationships grounded in reciprocal respect and mutual compassion.

**Culturally responsive teaching:** A pedagogy that uses culturally and linguistically diverse students' backgrounds, experiences, characteristics, and ways of knowing as tools to better respond to these students' needs and aspirations.

**Programmatic curriculum:** Curriculum materials and documents that help translate the ideas of the institutional curriculum into classroom curriculum planning.

## DISCUSSION QUESTIONS AND ACTIVITIES

1. How can the findings from this chapter be extended to other minorities, immigrants, and refugee K–12 students in Ontario classrooms?
2. How can we modify our practices based on what we learned about the Canadian educational system—specifically as it relates to ELD classrooms—from the experiences of ELD teachers?
3. How can educators, researchers, curriculum developers, and policy-makers use the ELD teachers' experiences when planning policies and programs that are more inclusive, representative, and equitable in the classroom?
4. How can we, as educators and researchers, bridge the gap between theory and practice with respect to the Canadian education system for minorities, immigrants, and refugee students?
5. Group activity: Using Gay's five components of CRTe (table 5.2), create a concept map to brainstorm ideas of what these five concepts would look like in the classroom or within a lesson plan. Note: Possible online platforms to use for this are GitMind (gitmind.com), MindMeister (www.mindmeister.com), and Canva (www.canva.com). Alternatively, use physical sticky notes or chart paper. This can also be done in small groups or as a class, collaboratively brainstorming ideas and creating a concept map.

## REFERENCES

Amin, N. (2018). *Successes and challenges of Syrian refugee children in Canada: Language and literacy* [Master's thesis, Wilfrid Laurier University]. https://scholars.wlu.ca/etd/2066

Barek, H. (2020). *Exploring the experiences of high school Syrian refugee students with interrupted formal education and their teachers in ELD classrooms* [Doctoral dissertation, Western University]. https://ir.lib.uwo.ca/etd/7532/

Barek, H., Namukasa, I., & Ravitch, S. (2021). *Pedagogies of care in precarity*. MethodSpace. www.methodspace.com/blog/pedagogies-of-care-in-precarity

Brewer, C. A., & McCabe, M. (2014). *Immigrant and refugee students in Canada*. Brush Education.

Chignall, S. C. (2016). Children of refugees thrive in Canada: StatsCan study. *IPolitics*. https://ipolitics.ca/2016/04/25/children-of-refugees-thrive-incanada-statscan-study/

Clark, K. (2017). *Are we ready? Examining teachers' experiences supporting the transition of newly-arrived Syrian refugee students to the Canadian elementary classroom* [Master's research paper, University of Toronto]. https://tspace.library.utoronto.ca/handle/1807/76952

Cummins, J. (2000). *Language, power, and pedagogy: Bilingual children in the crossfire* (Vol. 23). Multilingual Matters.

Damjanovic, J. (2016). *Syrian refugees in public school: OISE experts say one size does not fit all*. University of Toronto News. www.utoronto.ca/news/syrian-refugees-public-school-oise-experts-sayone-size-does-not-fit-all

Dufresne, S. (2015, December 1). *Canadian researcher worries teachers unprepared for Syrian students*. CBC News. www.cbc.ca/news/canada/manitoba/teachers-unprepared-syrian-refugees-1.3345253

Eisner, E. W. (1992). Curriculum ideologies. In P. W. Jackson (Ed.), *Handbook of research on curriculum* (pp. 302–326). Macmillan.

Gagné, A., Schmidt, C., & Markus, P. (2017). Teaching about refugees: Developing culturally responsive educators in contexts of politicised transnationalism. *Intercultural Education*, 28(5), 429–446. doi.org/10.1080/14675986.2017.1336409

Gay, G. (2000). *Culturally responsive teaching: Theory, research, and practice*. Teachers College Press.

Gay, G. (2002). Culturally responsive teaching in special education for ethnically diverse students: Setting the stage. *International Journal of Qualitative Studies in Education*, 15(6), 613–629. doi.org/10.1080/0951839022000014349

Gay, G. (2010). *Culturally responsive teaching: Theory, research, and practice* (2nd ed.). Teachers College Press.

Gay, G. (2018). *Culturally responsive teaching: Theory, research, and practice* (3rd ed.). Teachers College Press.

Ghosh, R., Sherab, D., Dilimulati, M., & Hashemi, N. (2019). Creating a refugee space in the Canadian school context: The approach of an inclusive society. In A. W. Wiseman, L. Damaschke-Deitrick, E. L. Galegher, & M. F. Park (Eds.), *Comparative perspectives on refugee youth education* (pp. 102–130). Routledge. doi.org/10.4324/9780429433719-5

Government of Canada. (2017, April 20). *Syrian refugee resettlement initiative—looking to the future* [Service description]. www.canada.ca/en/immigration-refugees-citizenship/services/refugees/welcome-syrian-refugees/looking-future.html

He, M. F., Phillion, J., Chan, E., & Xu, S. (2008). Immigrant students' experience of curriculum. In F. M. Connelly (Ed.), *The Sage handbook of curriculum and instruction* (2nd ed., pp. 219–239). SAGE. http://ebookcentral.proquest.com/lib/west/detail.action?docID=996458

Kaur, S., & Szorenyi, J. (2022). The role of educators in supporting the development of refugee students' sense of belonging. *Journal of Belonging, Identity, Language and Diversity, 6*(2), 41–62. Bild-lida.ca/journal/wp-content/uploads/2022/06/J-BILD_6-2_Kaur_Szorenyi.pdf

Kovinthan, T. (2016). Learning and teaching with loss: Meeting the needs of refugee children through narrative inquiry. *Diaspora, Indigenous, and Minority Education, 10*(3), 141–155. doi.org/10.1080/15595692.2015.1137282

Ladson-Billings, G. (1994). *The dreamkeepers: Successful teachers of African American children.* Jossey-Bass.

Nieto, S. (2004). *Affirming diversity: The sociopolitical context of multicultural education* (4th ed.). Pearson/Allyn & Bacon.

Noddings, N. (2003). *Caring: A feminine approach to ethics and moral education.* University of California Press.

Nussbaum, M. C. (1997). *Cultivating humanity: A classical defense of reform in liberal education.* Harvard University Press.

Ontario Ministry of Education. (2008). *Supporting English language learners with limited prior schooling: A practical guide for Ontario educators grades 3 to 12.* www.edu.gov.on.ca/eng/document/manyroots/ell_lps.pdf

Ontario Ministry of Education. (2020). *The Ontario curriculum grades 1–8: Mathematics.* www.dcp.edu.gov.on.ca/en/curriculum/elementary-mathematics

Rossiter, M. J., & Rossiter, K. R. (2009). Diamonds in the rough: Bridging gaps in supports for at-risk immigrant and refugee youth. *Journal of International Migration and Integration / Revue de l'integration et de la migration internationale, 10*(4), 409–429. doi.org/10.1007/s12134-009-0110-3

Sasakamoose, J. (2021, July 13). *Finding a better way: Strengths-based trauma-informed practice* [Webinar]. Western University. www.vawlearningnetwork.ca/webinars/recorded-webinars/2021/webinar-2021-4.html

Vavrus, M. (2008). Culturally responsive teaching. In L. T. Good (Ed.), *21st century education: A reference handbook* (pp. 519–528). Sage. doi.org/10.4135/9781412964012

Yau, M. (1996). *Refugee students in Toronto schools: An exploratory study: No. 211.* Toronto Board of Education, Research Services. doi.org/10.25071/1920-7336.21886

Yu, H. (2012). *The language learning of refugee students in Canadian public elementary and secondary schools* [Doctoral dissertation, Western University]. Ir.lib.uwo.ca/cgi/viewcontent.cgi?article=2002&context=etd

# PART III

## SOCIOECONOMIC STATUS: UNDERSTANDING AND RESPONDING TO SYSTEMIC BARRIERS TO FOSTER HUMAN FLOURISHING

# CHAPTER 6
# Socioeconomic Status and Children's Education in Canada: The Importance of Aspirations in Flourishing

*Cathlene Hillier*

One of the most significant predictors of children's flourishing in all aspects of life is **socioeconomic status** (SES). Not only does family SES have a significant impact on students' education and future outcomes, but it can also determine present and future physical health, mental health, and social and emotional learning. Thus, poverty and low-SES circumstances can hinder full human flourishing. These effects are exacerbated when SES intersects with other areas where students may be marginalized in education and society (e.g., physical or cognitive disabilities, race). In education, SES is a strong predictor of children's educational achievement, future education, and career outcomes. On average, students from high-SES homes tend to do better academically and achieve higher levels of post-secondary education and occupation (Aurini & Hillier, 2018). They also tend to have higher future **aspirations** than their low-SES counterparts, and these aspirations are positively related to academic achievement and attainment (Davies & Aurini, 2013; Hillier, 2021).

Martha Nussbaum's (2001) concept of human flourishing emphasizes the importance of cultivating human capabilities. She notes that humans have innate capacities that enable them to live fulfilling lives, but these capacities can be fully realized only in a society that values them (Nussbaum, 2001). Human flourishing is not just about material well-being. Rather, it is about individuals living meaningful and fulfilling lives in which they can pursue their own goals and develop their own unique talents and abilities. However, among the core aspects of flourishing that Nussbaum (2011) outlines, those goals would be difficult for families living in poverty or low-SES circumstances to achieve. In this chapter, I will first outline the status of poverty and low-income families in Canada and discuss Nussbaum's 10 capabilities in relation to SES. After this, I will discuss the effect that low-SES circumstances have on education as well as the importance of parents' and children's aspirations to human flourishing.

## POVERTY AND LOW-INCOME FAMILIES IN CANADA

Canada's official poverty line is based on the Market Basket Measure, which indicates that a family lives in **poverty** when they "cannot afford the cost of a specific basket of goods and services in their community" (Statistics Canada, 2023a). This "basket" includes the necessities related to a basic standard of living (e.g., food, clothing, shelter, transportation). The Market Basket Measure is priced for 53 geographical areas as cost of living varies by community size and location (Statistics Canada, 2022c). In 2021, 7.4 percent of Canadians were living in poverty, and this percentage had increased from 6.4 percent in 2020 (Statistics Canada, 2023a). Further, this number will continue to increase due to current inflation.

It is important to note that poverty statistics do not include those who are **low income**, such as those who live in "hidden poverty"—above the official poverty line but still unable to afford food, utility bills, childcare, and other basic needs (Canada without Poverty, n.d.)—and undocumented people, such as those who are unhoused. Table 6.1 presents the rates of poverty and low income for families in Canada. Since children living in lone-parent families are more likely to live in low-income situations than those in couple families, these percentages are also included in the table. The first column represents overall poverty rates, including people with and without children. The next two columns show the low-income rates for couple families and lone-parent families (one parent and one or more children). The provinces and territories are listed from highest poverty rate to lowest. Notably, the poverty rates in 2020 are lower than in previous years because of COVID-relief money from Canadian governments (Statistics Canada, 2022b).

Table 6.1 clearly demonstrates the importance of considering geography when considering SES (see chapter 18). Due to its remote northern location, Nunavut has high living costs, which result in extremely high poverty and low-income rates—in addition to the realities of scarce job opportunities and limited access to education and training (Nunavut Roundtable on Poverty Reduction, 2023).

Table 6.1: Poverty and Low-Income Rates in Canada, 2020

| | OVERALL PERCENTAGE OF POVERTY[1] | PERCENTAGE OF COUPLE FAMILIES IN LOW INCOME[2] | PERCENTAGE OF LONE-PARENT FAMILIES IN LOW INCOME[2] |
|---|---|---|---|
| **Canadian Provinces** | | | |
| British Columbia | 9.8 | 11.1 | 33.5 |
| Nova Scotia | 9.8 | 10.5 | 27.3 |
| Prince Edward Island | 8.7 | 12.5 | 35.0 |
| Manitoba | 8.6 | 8.4 | 24.7 |
| Saskatchewan | 8.4 | 12.1 | 31.0 |
| Ontario | 8.3 | 15.2 | 45.0 |
| Newfoundland and Labrador | 8.2 | 15.2 | 46.0 |
| New Brunswick | 8.1 | 11.3 | 33.9 |
| Alberta | 8.1 | 10.8 | 35.6 |
| Quebec | 6.4 | 11.2 | 30.0 |
| **Canadian Territories** | | | |
| Nunavut | 29.1 | 28.6 | 53.0 |
| Northwest Territories | 10.2 | 12.7 | 35.9 |
| Yukon | 8.8 | 6.7 | 20.5 |

*Sources:* (1) Provinces: Statistics Canada (2022b). Northwest Territories and Yukon: Statistics Canada (2022a). Nunavut: Nunavut Roundtable on Poverty Reduction (2023). (2) Statistics Canada (2023b).

The other two territories experience these same issues. Quebec has the lowest poverty level due to more affordable living costs (Statistics Canada, 2022b).

Additionally, intersectionality is important to consider in the discussion of poverty and low-SES families. Groups historically marginalized tend to have higher levels of poverty and low income than other individuals. The following points reflect the poverty statistics of various marginalized groups in Canada. While these are statistics for the entire population and not specifically focused on families with children, they reflect the economic circumstances that families who are included in these groups may have.

- In 2018, 19.5 percent of Indigenous people residing off reserve lived in poverty (Government of Canada, 2022).
- Among racialized people, 10.8 percent of South Asian Canadians, 15.3 percent of Chinese Canadians, and 12.4 percent of Black Canadians lived in poverty in 2020 (Statistics Canada, 2022b).

- Newcomers and refugees had a poverty rate of 9.1 percent in 2020 and were more likely to live in poverty than Canada-born citizens (Statistics Canada, 2022b).
- In 2018, 16.6 percent of people with disabilities lived in poverty (Government of Canada, 2022).
- Lone-parent families headed by a woman with a child or children aged zero to five have the highest poverty rate (31.3 percent) among family types (Statistics Canada, 2022b).
- Transgender men (12.9 percent) and transgender women (12 percent) have higher poverty rates than cisgender men and women. Also, 20.6 percent of nonbinary people lived in poverty in 2020 (Statistics Canada, 2022b).

Notably, while basic needs are crucial, attaining a full and dignified life is equally important. According to the United Nations (n.d.), "Poverty entails more than the lack of income and productive resources to ensure sustainable livelihoods. Its manifestations include hunger and malnutrition, limited access to education and other basic services, social discrimination and exclusion, and lack of participation in decision-making."

Additionally, the stress and anxiety of living in poor or low-income circumstances can sometimes affect parenting skills and lead to long-term trauma (e.g., neglect, abuse) in the family (Bishop, 2019). Nussbaum's (2011) notions of flourishing are thus essential in considering how SES affects students' opportunities to do the following:

- live with dignity and respect
- participate in social and political processes
- develop one's personality and talents
- obtain equal access to education
- have good health and basic nutritional needs met
- form intimate relationships and have a family
- participate in and appreciate cultural activities and art
- engage in work that is meaningful and not exploitive
- be able to enjoy leisurely pursuits
- access basic needs, such as food, shelter, and clothing

This list highlights the fact that education is a fundamental part of human flourishing (Nussbaum, 2011). Schools play a key role in connecting with families, not only in relation to their children's education but also by providing them with the information they need to access other support. This includes helping families access facilities and resources within the community for children and youth, such as community centres, libraries, playgrounds, family support centres, summer programs, after-school homework programs, food banks, and clinics (see chapter 7).

## CHALLENGES IN EDUCATION

Children from low-SES families often face challenges in education that affect their academic performance and future opportunities. They may have limited access to educational resources such as books, computers, tutoring services, and quiet spaces to work (Ciuffetelli Parker & Conversano, 2021). They are more likely to suffer from mental health problems, chronic illnesses, and malnutrition, which can limit their ability to learn and achieve in school (Bishop, 2019). Over time, poverty and low-SES circumstances can impact life outcomes such as mental health, academics, social functioning and relationships, and physical health (Ferguson et al., 2007). In the following sections, I outline the research on academic achievement and parent engagement in relation to children living in poverty or low-income environments.

**Academic Achievement**

Students from low-SES families are more likely to have lower academic achievement compared to their peers from higher-SES families (Ferguson et al., 2007). Before they enter kindergarten, children from poor or low-SES homes are already on an educational trajectory of lagging behind their high-SES peers in vocabulary and other areas of school readiness such as behaviour regulation and ability to follow instructions (Bradbury et al., 2015). They are more likely to have lower reading and math skills in comparison to their high-SES counterparts (Hillier et al., 2022), lower high school graduation rates (Brownell et al., 2010), and lower rates of post-secondary enrolment (Zarifa et al., 2018), which can lead to a cycle of economic disadvantage within families (Phipps & Lethbridge, 2006). Dropping out of high school and not attending post-secondary school leads to unemployment, precarious employment, lower paying jobs, and/or low satisfaction with one's occupation. At the high school level in the Toronto District School Board, low-SES students are overrepresented among those receiving special education services and in other programs generally considered to be non-university track (Parekh et al., 2011).

One explanation of these findings is that higher-SES families can afford more quality preschool care, which prepares children for school, and families living in poverty or low-SES have less access to the resources to create enriching home learning environments. Also, some parents lack the support and the types of parenting skills that are beneficial to setting preschoolers on a track for school readiness (e.g., setting consistent routines) (Ferguson et al., 2007). While children from poor or low-SES homes often enter school at a disadvantage, they may catch up to their peers during the school year. However, summer learning research demonstrates that students from socioeconomically underresourced backgrounds often fall further behind during the summer months when they are away from the structure and educational stimulation that school provides (Davies & Aurini, 2013; Davies et al., 2023; Hillier, 2021).

Further, these gaps may remain throughout the children's schooling. Caro et al. (2009) found, using Canada's National Longitudinal Study of Children and Youth data, that educational achievement gaps between low-SES and high-SES children remain relatively stable from ages 7 to 11 but then increasingly widen from age 11 up to age 15. Haeck and Lefebvre (2021) report that while they lessen in some years, SES achievement gaps have been stable over time from 2000 to 2018 (seven cycles of Programme for International Student Assessment [PISA] test scores in reading, math, and science). While Canada is one of the top-performing countries in the PISA, the within-country differences by province (poorer provinces compared to richer ones) and within-family differences by SES are still a concern.

### Parent Engagement in Children's Education

Parent engagement refers to the overall involvement of parents in their children's schooling, including communicating with the school, volunteering, attending school functions, and supporting learning at home (e.g., reading, helping with homework, setting expectations for educational achievement) (Epstein, 1995). It is viewed as a means for parents to align with schooling processes and continue learning opportunities at home (Hillier, 2018). School boards, schools, and parent engagement policies encourage parents to be involved in schooling and emphasize the importance of the home learning environment as an incubator for achievement (e.g., Ontario Ministry of Education, 2010). The Canadian Teachers' Federation emphasizes the importance parents have in preparing children for school and encourages parents to read with their children daily, enrol children in sports, and encourage physical activity (cited in Rogova et al., 2016).

However, parent engagement itself can be a source of unequal opportunities (Aurini & Hillier, 2018; Hillier, 2021). Poor and low-SES families struggle to provide educational resources in the home and establish a home learning environment (Lyche, 2010). For a variety of reasons (e.g., work schedules, unemployment, their own negative school experiences, low literacy levels, mental health issues), parents and caregivers might not feel that they can be full participants in "parental engagement" activities—as they are defined by schools—such as attending school events, meeting with the teacher, and helping with homework. Focusing on immediate concerns such as providing care, food, and shelter is often the priority for low-SES families. Sociological research examining parents' and students' interactions with teachers and schools have found differences in the way that low-SES families engage with schooling in comparison to their high-SES counterparts (e.g., Calarco, 2018). This body of research reveals inequalities in these interactions, particularly by demonstrating how students and parents enact their personal resources of economic, social, and cultural capital to ensure academic success—resources that high-SES families have greater access to (Aurini & Hillier, 2018).

In an educational setting, social capital refers to the connections parents have with teachers, principals, and other parents (see Coleman, 1988). It can help parents learn how schools work, what the academic expectations are, where to get resources, and how to effectively navigate institutional processes (Lareau, 2011). For example, parents who are present at various school functions demonstrate their support of the school, which may strengthen relationships with teachers and lead to deeper conversations about their children's progress. Ongoing parent-teacher contact can alert parents early regarding their child's struggles in school and inform them of strategies they can use at home to facilitate academic support. Often due to more flexible work schedules and other advantages, higher-SES parents are more likely to participate in social-capital-building activities (Ream & Palardy, 2008), resulting in networks that allow them to gain knowledge about programs and school supports that would benefit their children.

Cultural capital, as conceptualized by Bourdieu (1998), incorporates other types of nonfinancial investments that parents make in their children's education. Bourdieu's concept of the cultural customs of the dominant class (e.g., classical music and literature) has evolved into parents' overall understanding of social norms and habitus, or "way of being" (Hillier, 2018). Applying this definition to a school setting, higher-SES families are more likely to have the type of cultural capital that facilitates school success. This includes a greater understanding of how the education system works (e.g., test-taking strategies, getting a child into a gifted program) and a view of teachers as equals to maximize advantages for their children (e.g., Lareau, 2011). In addition, cultural capital may encompass differences in the "learning environments" that are cultivated within homes (e.g., home reading habits). It can also include the extent to which students request help from the teacher when they struggle with schoolwork and the way that parents "coach" their children in how to talk to teachers (Calarco, 2018).

Social and cultural capital can be enacted when children are considering post-secondary education and future occupations. High-SES parents may have more know-how in what their children need to do to successfully attain higher education and what courses to take in relation to specific occupations. Low-SES parents may not have attended post-secondary education themselves and therefore may not have knowledge of institutional processes to draw on. Considering how families start to convey ideas of future education to children is important, given the documented inequality in post-secondary attendance by social class and the disparity in career outcomes and income earned between those with a high school diploma and those with post-secondary education credentials (Johnson & Hitlin, 2017). Despite this fact, parents and children from all socioeconomic levels have aspirations, and schools can be a crucial part of fostering these goals for human flourishing.

## PARENTS' AND CHILDREN'S ASPIRATIONS

One dimension of parent engagement that consistently predicts children's academic achievement and attainment is parental and student aspirations (the highest level of education or occupation they hope to achieve) (Hillier, 2021). In this section, I present quotes from interviews that I conducted with parents and children as a part of a larger study on summer learning programs in Ontario (Davies et al., 2023). I explore parents' and children's future aspirations and how these aspirations inform parents' approaches to engagement in schooling. The goal is to express family aspirations in terms of future flourishing and conclude with what schools can do in response.

Drawing on 27 interviews with children (ages 5–8, including three sets of siblings) and 24 interviews with their parents from two urban elementary schools in lower-SES neighbourhoods, I explore the conversations about future education that occur at home (Hillier, 2018). Parents with post-secondary aspirations for their children are more likely to have conversations with them about future education. These parents also display a more interconnected approach with their children's education at school and at home. They link schooling to future socioeconomic mobility, job security, and career and life satisfaction. Because more proactive lower-SES families with post-secondary aspirations are anxious about their children's future, they rely on resources, information, and social connections provided by schools and the community.

Eight parents stated that there were no barriers to goals for their children's future education, while finances and academics were mentioned by three and five parents, respectively. The most cited barrier, by nine parents, was developmental or personal characteristics. This included waning self-confidence in high school, peer pressure, and changing attitudes about schooling or future endeavours, suggesting that parents acknowledged that, at some point, children's agency may override parental expectations.

## Parental Guidance on the Role and Importance of Education

Parental guidance on the role and importance of education may manifest itself in the expectations parents have for children's present education, such as in the direction a parent gives to a child for how to manage schoolwork, reminding children about homework, or providing a quiet place to do homework (Hillier, 2018). This includes how the child's day is organized beyond school, such as free time to play, read, do homework, or spend time with family. Also, rules concerning screen time, homework completion, or reading can convey to children the importance that parents place on education.

Most parents hope that their children will exceed their own life outcomes. Of the 24 families represented in my study, 11 parents expressed that they view education as a way for their children to accomplish this goal. This sentiment was shared by parents with both high school graduation and post-secondary education aspirations, but for those who did not graduate from high school, this belief that education is a way for children to have a better life was felt more acutely. For them, graduating from high school was the first hurdle to overcome; seeing their children surpass their accomplishments was an important goal. After stating high school as the main goal, some of these parents mentioned trade apprenticeships, college, and/or university, but these were often considered icing on the cake. Parents with high school graduation aspirations talked about their own educational experiences with their children as a cautionary tale. For example, Matthew, a single parent who dropped out of high school in grade 11 and lives on government assistance, talked about his own struggles with school and how he got "mixed in with the wrong group." Matthew articulated that he would like his daughter, Chloe (grade 2), to complete high school and secure a government job. Matthew described his daughter as smart and said she loved school. He did not have any rules regarding homework or reading since he felt that Chloe would tell him if she needed help. In my interview with Chloe, she said that her favourite activity to do with her father was watching him play video games. At home, she mostly read books on her own when assigned for homework and asked her father for help when she encountered a difficult word.

In contrast, low-SES parents who aspire for their children to attend post-secondary education have discussions with their children about the importance of education. When children share their preferred future occupation, these parents talk with their children about the type of training required for that vocation and the importance of staying in school and doing well. Other conversations with children include the value of post-secondary education in finding an enjoyable career and not struggling like their parents. As Elizabeth stated, "I have a job. I like my job. I go to my job. It does what I need it to do, but it's not a career ... I don't love it. I could have been something else. I didn't pick it and that's what I want for them, to pick something just that they love." In another example, Audrey's (grade 3) mother, Cynthia, talked about saving up for her daughter's future education with the help of her father. Cynthia shared that she liked school up until high school, and due to extreme shyness and feeling overwhelmed, she took longer to complete high school and college. While Cynthia did not talk about her own schooling experiences with Audrey, she mentioned discussing Audrey's aspirations to become a veterinarian and the education she would need to accomplish that goal. Audrey shared that a typical school evening for her involved homework and reading—both of which her mother ensured were completed.

Parental guidance can also involve some pressure from parents stemming from their own concerns that their children will end up like them. This was especially prevalent among parents who saw their work in more instrumental terms: it pays the bills but is not necessarily the occupation they would choose if they had more education or the opportunity to advance. Cheryl, Lily's (grade 1) mother, reflected on schooling, her job, and how she would like things to be different for her three daughters:

> Oh no, no, no [laughs], I was not a good student at all. So, I think a lot of it is I get anxious because I want her to do better than I did because I know the downfall of not getting the education, not going through the schooling. You know? Because I don't mean to put myself down, but I'm a school bus driver at 38. I want her to be able to get the job that she wants.... That was very

important to me. From the beginning, I actually sat down when she was a year old and started her education plan. Uh, with all my kids, they all have a savings, education savings. And, we also put away about, when we can, about five dollars a week for them for when they get older and when they start going to college. That way they can buy books. They can have the extra money if they need it.

The desire to help their children improve their lives heightens the pressure parents feel to emphasize the importance of education. Cheryl described working with Lily on reading and homework as "a fight." However, she viewed it as a non-negotiable part of their daily routine. Cheryl described herself as a reader, said she read in front of her children often, and stressed the importance of reading outside of school hours: "During the summer, if I don't read to them, they don't read at all." These stories illustrate parents' overall involvement in their children's present schooling in relation to the aspirations they have for their children.

## Parents' Interactive Engagement in Schooling

Parents' interactive engagement in schooling is evident in the home learning environment and parents' actions (e.g., learning activities, reading) related to their children's education. Of the 17 families in my study who indicated post-secondary aspirations for their children, 11 engaged in *both* school and home learning. The parents in these families shared that their children also had reading setbacks and/or learning disabilities, but most of them described an interconnected learning approach between what happens at school and what happens at home. For example, Elizabeth has a high school diploma and works in hospitality at the local university. To Elizabeth, parent engagement means being there, helping with homework, doing activities, and having conversations. She felt the school's role was to "provide a safe environment for my child to learn to the best of their ability." The parent's role is to "start them out with the moral fibre and the standard, expectations, that kind of thing and reinforce what the teachers teach … if I didn't do my work properly, then the school can't do their job properly." As a child, Elizabeth was diagnosed with dysphonetic dyslexia, and her parents struggled to teach her. She shared that she did not learn how to read completely on her own until she was almost 12. She "lost the drive" to continue with her schooling because of the frustration she and her parents felt with schoolwork. Consequently, she pushed through with her children's schooling because she did not want them to feel exasperation or to give up on school. Elizabeth felt her primary role was ensuring her children were successful and had the best opportunities. This was why she emphasized education and regular reading at home:

> Yeah, yeah, I don't want to look back and think I could have done so much more if I was given a little bit more motivation, and instead of pouring that energy into myself and making my life super great, you know, and missing time with my kids, I'd rather just invest in them and give them that. Yeah, they're my investment. I want to see them smile. I don't know. Isn't that what every parent wants?

The parents in my study with post-secondary aspirations and high engagement aligned more closely with Lareau's (2011) description of "concerted cultivators" who engage in every aspect of their child's schooling and seek extracurricular opportunities outside of school to develop their child's skills and talents. Lareau attributes this parenting approach to high-SES families. However, I found the low-SES parents in my study who had post-secondary aspirations were quite involved and saw what they did as an investment in their children's future success.

As Devine (1998) notes, it is not fair to say that low-SES families have a "poverty of aspirations" (p. 31), but they do make decisions within the context of their current social landscape and previous schooling experiences. While the primary focus of aspirational research has been on adolescents, the parents and children in my study started talking about future careers and post-secondary education at early ages. Leaving direction about future aspirations solely to parents and children will only continue to exacerbate social class gaps due to the inequalities in capital. Thus, reaching both children and parents at earlier ages with the resources to support their aspirations will help to build social and cultural capital in low-SES families.

## CONCLUSION

The first part of this chapter considered the overall picture of poverty and low-SES prevalence in Canada and the adversities that low-SES families face in relation to everyday existence, educational outcomes, and flourishing. The second part of this chapter considered the perspectives of families and the aspirations they have for their children—parents who are living with hope for their children's future flourishing. Indeed, aspirations are an important part of flourishing for present and future education in children's lives. As aspirations are associated with higher educational outcomes, schools in low-SES communities can encourage high aspirations and success among students. In her investigation of a successful school in a low-SES community, Bishop (2019) reports that the main goal of the school was to help students "progress and lead prosperous lives" and that "students had the right to be cared for and strongly supported by schools, families, and society: students deserved good learning and life chances" (p. 263). There are several ways that schools can support families in coming alongside them and promoting academic achievement and high aspirations as a part of flourishing.

First, equalizing opportunities is crucial in addressing systemic barriers in schools. Early interventions—prenatal and postnatal support, high quality preschools, and addressing early learning difficulties are key (Haeck & Lefebvre, 2021). In addition, Ciuffetelli Parker and Conversano (2021) recommend "enhancing professional practice; building a school culture of care[; and] developing partnerships and relationships" with external programs that can support schools (p. 1). Reducing class sizes for the emerging literacy years can also be beneficial for schools in low-SES communities in addition to providing ongoing professional development for teachers (Haughey et al., 2001). Professional development opportunities could include educating schools about a trauma-informed teaching, the realities of living in poverty, and working with parents "where they're at" on ways that they are able to support their child (Ciuffetelli Parker & Conversano, 2021; Hillier, 2018). Also, quality school-based after-school and summer tutoring/learning camps staffed by certified teachers and teacher-education candidates can help address learning gaps (Davies et al., 2023). Research on programs that support students, such as extracurricular activities and peer programs, emphasize the potential they have in raising social and cultural capital (e.g., Kisida et al., 2014).

Second, focusing on culturally relevant pedagogy—which advocates educating with high expectations for all students—is crucial to fostering future aspirations and human flourishing (Mitton & Murray-Orr, 2021). Students should be talked to early about their educational and career aspirations. All children dream and aspire—even when they may seem not to or when they are "checked out" of school. Finding out what their passions are and offering open-ended assignments in which they can explore some of those interests can empower students in the learning process. Having students present their learning portfolio in parent-teacher meetings is another way to centre the learner and cultivate agency. Teachers should also talk to parents about their aspirations for their children: What are their dreams and goals for their children? How do they see education as a part of that?

Third, just as early interventions are mentioned above, later interventions in high school are important (Ferguson et al., 2007). Strengthening learning support and providing affordable extracurricular opportunities for students can help them feel engaged and explore other interests. Destreaming is also recommended to equalize opportunities for students. As Ferguson and colleagues (2007) note, "a key to making schools more effective at raising the performance of low SES students is to keep schools heterogeneous with regard to the SES of their students (i.e., all types of streaming result in markedly poor outcomes for disadvantaged children and youth)" (p. 704). Further, career days could have professionals from the community talk about their work. These outreach efforts can build on children's aspirations and provide them with opportunities to learn about various careers and understand more about the related degrees or diplomas they might need to pursue in university or college. Bozick and colleagues (2010) find that when secondary school students maintain long-term post-secondary education aspirations, they are more likely to attend post-secondary schooling. Therefore, schools and teachers could foster this longevity in low-SES students' and parents' high aspirations by providing information and support (e.g., addressing their learning needs, offering learning opportunities outside of school time).

Education can be a powerful force in helping students from low-SES backgrounds flourish as humans. By providing access to knowledge, skills, and support systems, education can break down barriers, foster personal growth, and empower students to have high aspirations and reach their personal goals.

## KEY TERMS

**Aspirations:** The hopes and goals that parents/children have for future education (the highest level of education they hope to achieve) and/or occupation (future employment or career).

**Low income:** In Canada, a family is considered low income if their after-tax income falls below 50 percent of the total population median after-tax income (Statistics Canada, 2023b). The median is the middle income of the census population. See the Statistics Canada chart referenced in the Discussion Questions and Activities for recent low-income numbers.

**Poverty:** In Canada, the Market Basket Measure determines that a family lives in poverty if they "cannot afford the cost of a specific basket of goods and services in their community" (Statistics Canada, 2023a).

**Socioeconomic status:** A measure of a person's social class. Socioeconomic status considers an individual's income, highest level of education, and occupation, when all this information is available. In most of the educational research, students' socioeconomic status is measured by their parent's or caregiver's income and level of education. This is a more comprehensive measure than simply examining family income because parental education levels can inform a family's approach to education.

## DISCUSSION QUESTIONS AND ACTIVITIES

1. Referring to Statistics Canada's chart on low income for different sizes of families (www150.statcan.gc.ca/t1/tbl1/en/tv.action?pid=1110023201) and using a local grocery website, as a class, determine a rough estimate of what a week's worth of groceries that meets Canada's Food Guide recommendations (https://food-guide.canada.ca/en/) would cost for a four-person family. Take that number and figure out how much money would go toward food in a year and subtract that from the income for a four-person family on the Statistics Canada chart. Since this exercise is for a low-income family, think about the implications for a family living in poverty.
2. As a current or future teacher, what are some ways you could discuss aspirations with students? Extending this, how could you have these discussions with parents?
3. As a class, make a list of supports in your area that are available for families (e.g., food banks, low-cost preschools, parent support centres, libraries, free extracurricular programming). Think of a school in a low-SES area in your city and map out the distance between these family supports and the community. (Note: Because many low-SES families may not have vehicles, this activity illustrates the importance of having these supports in the communities that need them most.)

## REFERENCES

Aurini, J., & Hillier, C. (2018). Re-opening the black box of educational disadvantage: Why we need new answers to old questions. In J. Mehta & S. Davies (Eds.), *Education in a new society: Renewing the sociology of education* (pp. 309–333). University of Chicago Press.

Bishop, P. (2019). Compassion in high poverty schools: Socially just educational leadership in action. In A. Jules (Ed.), *The compassionate educator: Understanding social issues and the ethics of care in Canadian schools* (pp. 251–270). Canadian Scholars.

Bourdieu, P. (1998). The forms of capital. In A. H. Halsey, H. Lauder, P. Brown, & A. Stuart Wells (Eds.), *Education: Culture, economy and society* (pp. 46–58). Oxford University Press.

Bozick, R., Alexander, K., Entwisle, D., Dauber, S., & Kerr, K. (2010). Framing the future: Revisiting the place of educational expectations in status attainment. *Social Forces, 88*(5), 2027–2052. doi.org/10.1353/sof.2010.0033

Bradbury, B., Corak, M., Waldfogel, J., & Washbrook, E. (2015). *Too many children left behind: The U.S. achievement gap in comparative perspective.* Russell Sage Foundation.

Brownell, M. D., Roos, N. P., MacWilliam, L., Leclair, L., Ekuma, O., & Fransoo, R. (2010). Academic and social outcomes for high-risk youths in Manitoba. *Canadian Journal of Education, 33*(4), 804–836. https://journals.sfu.ca/cje/index.php/cje-rce/article/view/2188

Calarco, J. M. (2018). *Negotiating opportunities: How the middle class secures advantages in school.* Oxford University Press.

Canada Without Poverty. (n.d.). *Facts about poverty*. https://cwp-csp.ca/poverty/just-the-facts/

Caro, D. H., McDonald, J. T., & Willms, J. D. (2009). Socio-economic status and academic achievement trajectories from childhood to adolescence. *Canadian Journal of Education, 32*(3), 558–590. https://psycnet.apa.org/record/2010-16661-007

Ciuffetelli Parker, D., & Conversano, P. (2021). Narratives of systemic barriers and accessibility: Poverty, equity, diversity, inclusion, and the call for a post-pandemic new normal. *Frontiers in Education, 6*, 1–19. doi.org/10.3389/feduc.2021.704663

Coleman, J. S. (1988). Social capital in the creation of human capital. *American Journal of Sociology, 94*, s95–s120. www.jstor.org/stable/2780243

Davies, S., & Aurini, J. (2013). Summer learning inequality in Ontario. *Canadian Public Policy, 30*(2), 287–307. doi.org/10.3138/CPP.39.2.287

Davies, S., Aurini, J., & Hillier, C. (2023). Reproducing or reducing inequality? The case of summer learning programs. *Canadian Journal of Education, 45*(4), 1055–1083. doi.org/10.53967/cje-rce.5311

Devine, F. (1998). Class analysis and the stability of class relations. *Sociology, 32*(1), 23–42. www.jstor.org/stable/42855896

Epstein, J. L. (1995). School/family/community partnerships. *Phi Delta Kappan, 76*(9), 701–712. www.scirp.org/reference/referencespapers?referenceid=1081438

Ferguson, H. B., Bovaird, S., & Mueller, M. P. (2007). The impact of poverty on educational outcomes for children. *Paediatrics & Child Health, 12*(8), 701–706. doi.org/10.1093/pch/12.8.701

Government of Canada. (2022). *Building understanding: The first report of the National Advisory Council on Poverty*. www.canada.ca/en/employment-social-development/programs/poverty-reduction/national-advisory-council/reports/2020-annual.html#h2.03

Haeck, C., & Lefebvre, P. (2021). Trends in cognitive skill inequalities by socio-economic status across Canada. *Canadian Public Policy, 47*(1), 88–116. doi.org/10.3138/cpp.2019-039

Haughey, M., Snart, F., & da Costa, J. (2001). Literacy achievement in small grade 1 classes in high-poverty environments. *Canadian Journal of Education, 26*(3), 301–320. doi.org/10.2307/1602210

Hillier, C. (2018). *A seasonal research design examining macro-level factors and micro-understandings of parent engagement and children's literacy achievement* [Doctoral dissertation, University of Waterloo]. https://uwspace.uwaterloo.ca/handle/10012/13980

Hillier, C. (2021). A seasonal comparison of the effectiveness of parent engagement on student literacy achievement. *Canadian Journal of Education, 44*(2), 496–529. doi.org/10.53967/cje-rce.v44i2.4551

Hillier, C., Zarifa, D., & Hango, D. (2022). Mind the gaps: Examining youth's reading, math and science skills across northern and rural Canada. *Rural Sociology, 87*(1), 264–302. doi.org/10.1111/ruso.12401

Johnson, M. K., & Hitlin, S. (2017). Family (dis)advantage and life course expectations. *Social Forces, 95*(3), 997–1022. doi.org/10.1093/sf/sow094

Kisida, B., Greene, J. P., & Bowen, D. H. (2014). Creating cultural consumers: The dynamics of cultural capital acquisition. *Sociology of Education, 87*(4), 281–295. https://eric.ed.gov/?id=EJ1040480

Lareau, A. (2011). *Unequal childhoods: Class, race, and family life* (2nd ed.). University of California Press.

Lyche, C. S. (2010, November 9). *Taking on the completion challenge: A literature review on policies to prevent dropout and early school leaving.* Organization for Economic Co-operation and Development. doi.org/10.1787/19939019

Mitton, J., & Murray-Orr, A. (2021). Identifying the impact of culturally relevant pedagogy: Evidence of academic risk-taking in culturally and economically diverse Nova Scotia classrooms. *Canadian Journal of Education, 44*(4), 1084–1115. doi.org/10.53967/cje-rce.v44i4.4811

Nunavut Roundtable on Poverty Reduction. (2023). *Poverty in Nunavut: Understanding and combating it.* Makiliqta. www.makiliqta.ca/#:~:text=In%20Canada%2C%20poverty%20is%20measured,Nunavut%2C%20it%20was%2029.1%25

Nussbaum, M. C. (2001). *The fragility of goodness: Luck and ethics in Greek tragedy and philosophy.* Cambridge University Press.

Nussbaum, M. C. (2011). *Creating capabilities: The human development approach.* Belknap Press.

Ontario Ministry of Education. (2010). *Parents in partnership: A parent engagement policy for Ontario schools.* www.edu.gov.on.ca/eng/parents/involvement/PE_Policy2010.pdf

Parekh, G., Killoran, I., & Crawford, C. (2011). The Toronto connection: Poverty, perceived ability, and access to education equity. *Canadian Journal of Education, 34*(3), 249–279. https://journals.sfu.ca/cje/index.php/cje-rce/article/view/941

Phipps, S. A., & Lethbridge, L. (2006). *Income and the outcomes of children.* Statistics Canada. www150.statcan.gc.ca/n1/en/catalogue/11F0019M2006281

Ream, R. K., & Palardy, G. J. (2008). Reexamining social class differences in the availability and the educational utility of parental social capital. *American Educational Research Journal, 45*(2), 238–273. doi.org/10.3102/0002831207308643

Rogova, A., Pullman, A., Iglesias, C. B., & Bryce, R. (2016, January 19). *Inequality explained: The hidden gaps in Canada's education system.* Open Canada. https://opencanada.org/inequality-explained-hidden-gaps-canadas-education-system/

Statistics Canada. (2022a). *Canadian income survey: Territorial estimates, 2020.* www150.statcan.gc.ca/n1/daily-quotidien/221103/dq221103d-eng.pdf

Statistics Canada. (2022b). *Disaggregated trends in poverty from the 2021 census of population.* www12.statcan.gc.ca/census-recensement/2021/as-sa/98-200-X/2021009/98-200-X2021009-eng.cfm

Statistics Canada. (2022c). *Market basket measure (MBM)*. www12.statcan.gc.ca/census-recensement/2021/ref/dict/az/Definition-eng.cfm?ID=pop165

Statistics Canada. (2023a). *Dimensions of poverty hub*. www.statcan.gc.ca/en/topics-start/poverty

Statistics Canada. (2023b). *Table 11-10-0018-01: After-tax low income status of tax filers and dependents based on census family low income measure (CFLIM-AT), by family type and family type composition*. doi.org/10.25318/1110001801-eng

United Nations. (n.d.). *Ending poverty*. www.un.org/en/global-issues/ending-poverty#:~:text=Poverty%20entails%20more%20than%20the,of%20participation%20in%20decision%2Dmaking

Zarifa, D., Kim, J., Seward, B., & Walters, D. (2018). What's taking you so long? Examining the effects of social class on completing a bachelor's degree in four years. *Sociology of Education, 91*(4), 290–322. doi.org/10.1177/0038040718802258

# CHAPTER 7
# Pedagogical Strategies for Equity and Inclusion: Addressing Low–Socioeconomic Status Students in the Canadian Classroom

*Sally Abudiab and Ardavan Eizadirad*

This chapter will explore pedagogical strategies that teachers can implement to teach for equity with a focus on supporting students from low–socioeconomic status (SES) backgrounds. Additionally, it highlights relevant Canadian resources available to teachers to help them support students living in poverty. Throughout the chapter, we explore the question *How does one teach for equality and equity?* How can teachers ensure that their students from low-SES backgrounds will not be marginalized in the curriculum? How can teachers work with community agencies in lower-SES and racialized communities to mitigate opportunity gaps perpetuated by systemic inequities? Thematic analysis outlining key barriers within the literature is combined with a case study from the Jane and Finch community in Toronto, Canada. As a collective, they outline how equitable resource allocation and culturally reflective teaching can mitigate the opportunity gap for students experiencing poverty, allowing them to overcome systemic barriers and flourish. Overall, the chapter outlines various resources, pedagogical strategies, and Canadian organizations to help educators provide equitable and culturally reflective opportunities to support students, parents, and schools situated in lower-SES communities.

In Canada, promoting **equity** and inclusion in education is of paramount importance. By employing pedagogical strategies that prioritize their students' needs and inclusion, educators can create an equitable learning environment that supports the academic success and flourishing of all students relative to who they are and their circumstances. The Colour of Poverty—Colour of Change (2019) fact sheets outline that "Canada has most often used the Low-Income Cut-Off (LICO) to measure financial hardship. The LICO shows how many households are spending a higher than average percentage of their income on the necessities of food, shelter and clothing. The After-Tax Low-Income Measure (LIM-AT) shows how many households have an income that is less than half the national median income for a similar-sized household" (p. 1). The face of poverty in Canada is diverse and multifaceted (Colour of Poverty—Colour of Change, 2019; Tranjan, 2018). While poverty affects individuals and families across various demographic groups, certain segments of the population are more vulnerable than others, particularly people of colour and Indigenous communities. The experiences of rural poverty are also different than those of urban poverty. Additionally, recent immigrants, particularly those who have arrived within the past five years, face higher poverty rates than Canadian-born individuals (see chapter 6). Single-parent households, predominantly headed by women, experience a greater risk of poverty (United Way, 2019; chapter 6). Therefore, it is essential to consider these specific groups when addressing poverty-related policies, pedagogies, and interventions to ensure equitable outcomes for all Canadians.

Students in communities associated with low SES and increased levels of poverty experience more learning barriers, such as limited access to resources and infrastructure and widening achievement and **opportunity gaps** (Eizadirad, 2020; Gorski, 2012). At a neighbourhood level, those living in poverty are more likely to experience trauma related to violence, crime, homelessness, and/or transitional housing (McMurtry & Curling, 2008). Furthermore, the COVID-19 pandemic intensified the impact of systemic inequities, widening the disparity in educational opportunities between schools in lower- and higher-SES communities (Eizadirad & Sider, 2020; Gallagher-Mackay et al., 2021).

## LITERATURE REVIEW EXAMINING THE PANDEMIC'S IMPACT ON HIGH-POVERTY NEIGHBOURHOODS

In our selective literature review, we identified key studies between 2020 and 2023 that addressed COVID-19, SES, race, and its impact on marginalized communities. Within the articles retrieved, three main themes emerged: (1) limited access to resources and infrastructure; (2) socioeconomic inequities and achievement/opportunity gaps; and (3) community and family influences (Ciuffetelli Parker & Conversano, 2021; Eizadirad & Sider, 2020; Silva-Laya et al., 2020; see also chapter 6).

## Limited Access to Resources and Infrastructure

Schools situated in low-SES communities often struggle with limited financial resources, outdated infrastructure, and inadequate learning materials (Borup et al., 2020; Hoglund et al., 2015; Muijs et al., 2004). Insufficient funding restricts the ability of these schools to provide quality educational opportunities and leads to overcrowded classrooms, outdated texts, and a lack of access to modern technologies. These can serve as barriers to students flourishing and achieving their full potential. According to a Canadian study by the Organisation for Economic Co-operation and Development (OECD, 2018), schools in disadvantaged communities are more likely to have inadequate physical facilities and fewer learning resources, thereby hindering student engagement and achievement. Students from low-income, rural, and First Nations households experience more challenges, with competing needs for devices and connectivity (Gallagher-Mackay et al., 2021; Royal Society of Canada, 2021; Toronto Foundation, 2021; see also chapter 18). In addition to affecting student achievement outcomes, the **digital divide** affects students' mental health through increased feelings of boredom, frustration, and isolation. This was evident during the COVID-19 pandemic when many students had to learn in isolation due to restrictions for gatherings and the shift to online learning.

## Socioeconomic Inequities and Achievement/Opportunity Gaps

Students from low-SES communities face a range of systemic barriers that affect their academic success and well-being. Factors such as limited access to healthcare, unstable housing, food insecurity, and higher levels of stress can hinder their ability to concentrate, participate, and learn effectively (Eizadirad et al., 2023; McCoy & Hanno, 2023). These external barriers impact access to opportunities and career trajectories in terms of students flourishing based on their passions and interests. A study by Reardon and Portilla (2016) revealed that SES disparities contribute significantly to achievement and opportunity gaps. Moreover, the stigma associated with poverty can also negatively impact students' self-esteem, motivation, and participation in school activities, further widening the achievement gap (Reyna, 2008).

### Community and Family Influences

Communities grappling with poverty often lack the resources and support systems necessary to foster a positive and inclusive learning environment. Limited community engagement, higher crime rates, and limited access to extracurricular activities can further isolate students and hinder their growth and educational outcomes (McMurtry & Curling, 2008; Nubani et al., 2023; O'Brien et al., 2021). Additionally, the lack of parental involvement and support, often due to economic constraints or low educational attainment, can impede students' academic progress or extent of supports available at home (Đurišić & Bunijevac, 2017; Fenton et al., 2017; Hillier et al., 2019; Sheridan et al., 2011). This points to the need for strong family-school partnerships to create continuity of care between school and home environments so students can thrive by constantly feeling supported.

## PEDAGOGICAL STRATEGIES FOR TEACHING FOR EQUITY

Pedagogical strategies for teaching for equity are of paramount importance in creating an inclusive and just educational environment, particularly for schools situated in communities with higher levels of poverty (Gorski, 2012; Milner, 2017). These strategies recognize the diverse needs, backgrounds, and abilities of students—and the unique extent to which systemic barriers impact the community where the school is situated—to ensure equitable access to opportunities. The remainder of this section details a range of resources, teaching strategies, and Canadian institutions (also see the Discussion Questions and Activities section of this chapter for additional resources) that teachers can use to offer equitable and culturally relevant and responsive opportunities to support students, parents, and schools in lower-SES communities. By employing such resources and pedagogical strategies, educators can actively counteract systemic inequalities and promote fairness in the classroom. They go beyond a one-size-fits-all approach, instead valuing individual differences and tailoring instruction to meet the specific needs of each student to support them in flourishing. Pedagogical strategies for teaching for equity not only cultivate a culture associated with educational excellence but also foster a more just society by preparing students to be compassionate, empathetic, and socially aware global citizens.

### Culturally Responsive Teaching

Culturally responsive teaching can be used to discuss relevant community issues and how the intersection of SES, poverty, race, and ethnicity impacts the school and the unique experiences of each student. Culturally responsive teaching is characterized by three key principles. First, it recognizes and values the diverse cultural backgrounds, experiences, and perspectives of students and creates spaces to discuss lived experiences as valuable knowledge. Second, it promotes a positive and inclusive classroom environment that fosters respect, equity, and social justice to explore different perspectives. Third, it incorporates culturally relevant content and instructional strategies that reflect students' identities, interests, and lived experiences (see Ladson-Billings, 1995). Overall, teachers can employ culturally responsive teaching practices to bridge the cultural gap between students and the curriculum.

Oftentimes, the contents of the official curriculum, which tends to be Eurocentric, do not reflect all students' lived experiences, especially students from equity-deserving groups, including those experiencing poverty on a daily basis. Therefore, as educators, it is important to critically analyze the curriculum and pay particular attention to who is (re)presented, not represented, and misrepresented and how you can bring in supplementary external sources and guest speakers to prioritize and centre voices impacted by specific social issues, such as poverty (Tsang & Eizadirad, 2023). Implementing lessons or curriculum projects that examine complexities of identity and family histories is a great way to legitimize lived experiences as important knowledge. This approach incorporates students' diverse backgrounds, experiences, and perspectives into the classroom, making the learning process more relatable and meaningful for all students, particularly those who have become disengaged by a predominantly Eurocentric Canadian curriculum (Milner, 2017; see also chapter 3). This also includes seeing students as experts on their own lives who can make a difference in their community. Educators are encouraged to provide options for learners to apply what they are learning to real-life contexts in the hopes they can use these skills to change their lives and better their communities. Creating brave spaces where students can share their lived experiences and how they can take action on issues that impact them is empowering, especially discussions on how to address the underlying structural issues that perpetuate inequities in their communities. This is essential to becoming a global citizen. Inviting parents to be guest speakers in the classroom and have input in securing diverse books for the classroom can also create a more inclusive classroom environment. A great resource that outlines a range of educational resources for equity, diversity, inclusion, and Indigenization, grouped by grade and recommended age, is the following website, curated by the Equity, Diversity, Inclusion and Indigenization Coalition in the Faculty of Education at Wilfrid Laurier University: www.wlu.ca/academics/faculties/faculty-of-education/assets/resources/edi-resources-for-educators.html.

### Differentiated Instruction

While poverty affects individuals and families across various demographic groups, certain segments of the population are more vulnerable. Therefore, teachers must be intentional in how they support students to meet their unique needs. Differentiated instruction allows teachers to tailor their teaching methods, curriculum content, and assessments to the individual needs of students and their preferred learning styles relative to each student's living circumstances and the resources and supports they have access to at home. For example, using closed captioning in videos shown in class helps those with hearing impairments or other exceptionalities, but it can also be helpful for English language learners and students who have attention deficits. This approach in providing support for all students through empathy and an ethics of care aligns with Universal Design for Learning principles (see CAST, 2018). A useful website that provides practical suggestions for accommodations and modifications, including how to differentiate instruction based on student exceptionalities, is the following: www.teachspeced.ca/node/1.

Educators can further identify, through student and class profiles, how each student best learns and can be supported to flourish through relationship-building with students and their families. This relevant information should be incorporated into decisions about what content is used in the classroom and in what ways. This includes being mindful of topics that can be triggering (e.g., discussions on poverty and healthy eating habits that may be unaffordable for some families) and ensuring that students are connected with support if triggered. Another strategy to differentiate instruction can be the infusion of storytelling as a form of pedagogy in which students are encouraged to explore their connections to the land they are on and their family histories. This creates opportunities for dialogue and discussions from different perspectives related to understanding what it means to decolonize and Indigenize education relative to each student's positionality and intergenerational history. Overall, by recognizing and accommodating diverse learning styles, abilities, and interests, educators can create a classroom that values and supports the unique strengths and lived experiences of all students.

### Prioritizing Social-Emotional Learning

Prioritizing social-emotional learning (SEL) in the classroom helps foster a supportive and inclusive environment (Durlak et al., 2011). This is significant for students who experience poverty and are from single-parent households as they likely experience more trauma as part of their daily realities. No person wants to be the spokesperson for the historical or current trauma of their social group. As an educator, provide opportunities for discussion, but do not pressure or force anyone to speak. This can be done through circle sharing or restorative practices with options to pass. Silence itself is a form of response and at times is a coping mechanism for survival. There is no such thing as a safe space; therefore, educators should strive to create brave spaces where students are willing to come out of their comfort zone, talk about their emotions, and be vulnerable (see Eizadirad & Campbell, 2021, for more details about brave spaces and their key characteristics; see also chapter 10). Within brave spaces, (un)learning and growth can take place when social issues (e.g., challenges of living in poverty and lack of access to opportunities) are explored from different perspectives. When educators normalize talking about emotions in the classroom, students can become better at recognizing their triggers and learning that it is okay to ask for help, which counters what dominant discourse in society teaches them (e.g., being emotional is a form of weakness). To encourage students to be vulnerable and to build trust with students, educators should model and speak about their emotions and past and current lived experiences. Educators can find suggestions on how to implement various fun socioemotional learning games as part of character development via the following website: https://proudtobeprimary.com/social-emotional-learning-games/.

## Collaborative Learning

By encouraging collaborative learning, educators provide opportunities for students to explore different perspectives rooted in varied lived experiences. Collaborative approaches in the classroom are more student-centred. Projects or assignments involving different roles can be implemented using a strengths-based approach where people can take leadership roles based on what they are good at. This creates opportunities for students to help out one another and turn areas for improvement into strengths in a supportive environment where it is okay to make mistakes. Cooperative group projects, peer tutoring and mentorship, and inclusive classroom discussions foster a sense of community, respect, and shared responsibility among students. They also create opportunities for students to tell their own narrative rooted in their lived experiences versus others speaking on their behalf. A great website to check out, which provides many collaborative project-based lessons, is Lessons from the Earth and Beyond: www.lessonsfromearthandbeyond.ca/.

## Connecting Students and Families with Additional Resources to Support Their Needs

The COVID-19 pandemic highlighted how a lack of resources, particularly access to digital technologies, private nonshared spaces, and a high-speed Internet connection can disadvantage students from lower-SES backgrounds (Eizadirad & Sider, 2020). Therefore, it is important that educators identify students who may face financial barriers and provide them with extra resources, such as additional learning materials or access to technology. Educators can collaborate with school administrators, community organizations, or local initiatives to secure additional supports for students in need and their families (Jennings & Rentner, 2020). Educators can support families with system navigation, connecting parents to resources that they may not know about or have the cultural or social capital to find on their own. Building strong partnerships with families and communities ensures a holistic approach to student support. Educators need to consistently communicate with parents via different media that are accessible and convenient (e.g., texts, phone calls, emails, and/or feedback via a planner) to understand their needs, involve them in decision-making processes, and connect them with relevant community resources to address their concerns and unmet needs. This can lead to greater parental involvement and student engagement, particularly for families from lower-SES backgrounds (Hillier et al., 2019). BGC Canada (formerly the Boys and Girls Clubs of Canada) and Pathways to Education are useful Canadian organizations to connect families with to support their children's needs outside of school hours (see the Discussion Questions and Activities section of this chapter for more details).

In the following section, we shift to examine a case study from the Jane and Finch community in Toronto, Canada, to learn how, through equitable resource allocation and culturally reflective teaching, a specialized math program was adapted during the COVID-19 pandemic to remain accessible and support students in flourishing to their full potential. We share this case study to emphasize how the strategies discussed in this section intersect with one another—rather than being separate and compartmentalized actions—in the realm of application.

# CASE STUDY: YOUTH ASSOCIATION FOR ACADEMICS, ATHLETICS, AND CHARACTER EDUCATION AND THE COMMUNITY SCHOOL INITIATIVE

In this section, through a case study in the Jane and Finch community in Toronto, Canada, we examine how low-SES students were supported to flourish, with various stakeholders working together to advocate for equitable outcomes. This involved identifying with intentionality the local needs of a community and then strategically implementing pedagogical strategies to support the students and their families. The focus of the research project, funded by the Social Sciences and Humanities Research Council of Canada, was to explore how community-based programming could be adapted and mobilized during the pandemic to mitigate opportunity and achievement gaps for Black people, Indigenous Peoples, and people of colour (BIPOC) and families from lower-SES backgrounds.

The Youth Association for Academics, Athletics, and Character Education (YAAACE) is a Black-led, Black-focused, and Black-serving nonprofit community organization in the Jane and Finch neighbourhood that has been operating since 2007. It serves approximately 1,000 students and families annually through a range of programs in academics, athletics, expanded opportunities, and violence prevention and intervention. Jane and Finch is considered one of Canada's most under-resourced neighbourhoods. To put this into context, the Learning Opportunities Index produced by the Toronto District School Board ranks each school based on measures of external challenges affecting student success, with the school with the greatest level of external challenges being ranked number one and described as highest on the index. Of more than four hundred elementary schools assessed, three of the top five schools are located in the Jane and Finch community, indicating that there are extensive systemic barriers at the community level that impact educational achievement, such as high poverty rates, low parental education levels, and a large number of single-parent households (Toronto District School Board, 2023).

The Community School Initiative (CSI) is a partnership between YAAACE (yaaace.com) and the for-profit enterprise Spirit of Math (spiritofmath.com). It delivered a structured math curriculum to students in grades 2 to 8, aged 8 to 14 years old, from September 2020 to May 2021 at a subsidized cost and supported by a team of caring adults, including teachers, coaches, parents, and volunteers. Spirit of Math has been operating for 35 years and typically offers a structured math curriculum to high-performing and gifted students in kindergarten to grade 11 as a private service. The organization serves more than 11,000 students across 40 campuses in 20 cities in North America and Pakistan. The foundation of the Spirit of Math curriculum is based on four elements: drills, problem-solving, core curriculum, and cooperative learning. The length of the CSI program was nine months (36 weeks), and families had access to the program for a fraction of what the Spirit of Math program generally costs as a private support service ($3,000) because the cost was subsidized at $100 per participant. CSI started off with in-person programming, switched to remote delivery due to COVID-19 public health restrictions, and then made the switch to a hybrid model. Students participated in a two-hour Saturday learning session that was followed by a one-hour remote drop-in session on a weeknight to receive further assistance. Students were initially grouped by age. After diagnostic assessments, some students were identified as lacking in certain age-appropriate math skills, and as a result, some older pupils were placed into lower-level classes. To deliver the program, Spirit of Math instructors trained and assisted YAAACE teachers. Students were evaluated on a weekly basis through homework, math exercises, examinations, and a final exam.

Surveys were conducted with 35 Black parents and 35 students to examine YAAACE's transition to remote learning. Insights from their experiences helped identify how programming offered by YAAACE and similar community organizations could be tailored to reflect students' and parents' needs in a manner that was accessible and feasible in relation to circumstances caused by COVID-19 as well as adaptation for programming post-COVID. Surveys and a focus group were also conducted with the eight teachers who delivered the program curriculum to understand what they felt was needed to engage students and increase the quality of YAAACE's programs, particularly with remote teaching.

### Findings from the Case Study

All data were examined by the research team, who looked for key words and re-emerging big ideas expressed by the research participants involving the students, parents, and teachers. Similar codes were grouped together to identify main themes. This included themes related to holistic and **culturally reflective teaching and learning**, structured programming, communication and parental engagement, digital divide and inequality, and effective pedagogies.

Each student was provided with an individualized binder to keep track of their progress. This allowed teachers to spend less time preparing lessons and more time supporting students. Teachers also expressed that the consistency in the program's structure helped identify struggling students who needed additional support. Parents echoed similar sentiments about the structure and consistency of the curriculum being a positive aspect of the program. One parent stated, "Accountability, responsibility, ownership, pride, confidence all developed from program consistency." Teachers further emphasized that the technologies and resources made available to the students as part of the program, such as "iPads, AppleTV, laptops, and applications such as Brightspace, Microsoft Teams, and ActiveInspire," were very helpful. These were resources that many of the students did not have access to or would have been unable to afford if it were not for the subsidized program. Recognizing that similar programs exist but at a much higher price, one parent expressed gratitude, stating that "programs outside of YAAACE do not fit the budget."

Another integral characteristic of the program was the fact that it was offered through people who had established trust and rapport with the community and who understand the local needs of the neighbourhood, including the magnitude of systemic inequities influencing learning conditions. For example, one teacher shared the following:

> I don't know if it was so much the points system that was getting these kids on board or if it was the coaches. The coaches were a phenomenal resource because when they came online to support homework help, they would see who wasn't there. They would disappear for a bit, and then all of a sudden kids would just start popping up into the homework help and the coach would come back to hold them accountable.

Another teacher similarly said, "When we first started, we didn't have the coaches and it was like night and day in terms of the difference in terms of behaviour when the coaches got involved and were present."

One major challenge with program implementation was that teachers had difficulties supporting students who did not have adequate access to technologies and the Internet at home. Once this was recognized, YAAACE provided devices on loan to help mitigate the digital divide and enhance student engagement for distance learning. YAAACE also created how-to videos to support students and parents in navigating the learning platform. One parent observed that "remote learning is not an ideal model for a child with ADHD [attention deficit hyperactivity disorder]," and another parent also noticed that it was "harder to focus and learn compared to in-person learning." Teachers stated that teaching remotely made gauging student engagement, supporting students one on one, and collecting student work more difficult. Body language was not observable when cameras and mics were turned off during the online learning sessions. Teachers also noticed more inconsistent attendance from the students in a remote context, which made it challenging to progress through the Spirit of Math curriculum expectations.

Overall, teachers working in lower-SES schools can play a critical role in mitigating the opportunity gap by partnering with community agencies to support families beyond the individual in the classroom (see chapter 6). After-school hours, weekends, and summertime are crucial times for programs to connect with families. Schools can partner with local community organizations or actively promote their programs and services to families to meet their unique needs and create continuity of care. Low-SES communities not only need these programs, but they need them to be accessible and culturally reflective.

Findings from both the literature review and the case study highlight the importance of connecting students and their families with holistic and socio-culturally relevant community organizations to help students develop their well-being, health, achievement, and capacity for continued success (Eizadirad, 2019; Kearney & Graczyk, 2014; Samuels, 2018). Findings emphasize the significance of structured education programs offered by nonprofits in mitigating the impact of learning loss from the pandemic, particularly for racialized and under-resourced students and communities (Gallagher-Mackay et al., 2021; James, 2020; Toronto Foundation, 2021). This is where there is potential for synergetic collaborative partnerships between the public/nonprofit and the private sector to work together to mitigate systemic barriers impeding student achievement and flourishing of the community. This will differ for each community, and by extension each postal code, as every neighbourhood has its own unique challenges driven by systemic inequities such as the intersection of poverty and racism.

## CONCLUSION

To continue to understand how teachers can work with community agencies in lower-SES schools to mitigate the opportunity gap perpetuated by systemic inequities, first, it is important to put greater investments into facilitating access to programs that are affordable, accessible, and led by diverse educators and practitioners who reflect the community demographics. This is essential for ensuring the flourishing of not only students, but also their families and the larger community where the school is situated. Second, it is important to invest in holistic and culturally reflective teaching and learning that reward diverse identities and lived experiences and to prioritize relationships and have people with trusted connections in the community involved with program delivery (e.g., BIPOC teachers and coaches working together with students and families). Third, teachers and leaders in the education system must provide multiple avenues to help parents navigate educational platforms to support their children remotely and at home, with consideration for digital literacy (e.g., information letters, how-to videos, and administrative support).

In conclusion, addressing the opportunity gap in racialized and under-resourced communities with high levels of poverty requires a multifaceted approach that involves collaboration between educators and community agencies to ensure that students, families, and the entire community flourish. Teachers can work with community agencies to identify students who would benefit from local programs and connect them with the appropriate resources to create continuity of care between school hours, evenings, and weekends. Part of this is also recognizing and identifying what systemic barriers impact students and impede their flourishing so actions taken can be intentional. Finally, educators need to be proactive in creating a classroom environment and culture of excellence that promote equity and inclusion. This involves incorporating diverse perspectives and experiences into the curriculum; creating opportunities for students to engage in meaningful dialogue around issues of race, equity, and social justice; and fostering a sense of belonging and community in the classroom. By implementing pedagogical strategies that prioritize inclusivity and implementing resources designed to support students living in poverty, educators can create an environment where all students can thrive and flourish regardless of their socioeconomic status.

## KEY TERMS

**Culturally reflective teaching and learning:** A strengths-based approach to teaching that views Black people, Indigenous Peoples, and people of colour (BIPOC) as innately diverse, works with their strengths, and considers their unique lived experiences for optimal teaching and learning conditions.

**Digital divide/gap:** The gap between people who can easily access and use information and communication technologies (e.g., computers, tablets, the Internet) in their daily lives and people who cannot.

**Equity:** Practices, processes, and policies that promote and ensure fair access to opportunities and outcomes for diverse identities within an institution.

**Opportunity gap:** The way that systemic inequities create barriers to minoritized identities and communities accessing opportunities to achieve to their full potential.

## DISCUSSION QUESTIONS AND ACTIVITIES

1. What challenges do you think schools in low-income areas face? What would be some alternative approaches and innovative solutions to support students attending schools in communities with high levels of poverty?
2. How can schools work better with community agencies and nonprofit organizations to more holistically support students and their families outside of school hours, particularly during evenings and on weekends, to create continuity of care?

3. How can schools deliver programming and services so that they are accessible and culturally reflective of the demographics of the communities they serve? What resources would be needed for implementation, and how can such resources be secured through equitable allocation by school boards?
4. As a class or school faculty, find local organizations and/or resources that you can share with families in your school community as part of community asset mapping. Add these to the list in question 5. Make this a living document so that resources can be continually added and updated. Discuss how you can share these resources with families and what relevant media you can share them through.
5. The following are various resources and organizations for supporting students living in poverty. In small groups, consider how these resources could be introduced and used in the classroom.

    *Pathways to Education* (www.pathwaystoeducation.ca/): A national organization dedicated to supporting students living in low-income communities by providing a comprehensive set of academic, financial, social, and advocacy supports.

    *BCG Canada* (www.bgccan.com/): A nationwide network of clubs that offer affordable after-school programs, mentorship, and support services to children and youth, including those from low-income backgrounds. Children and youth can experience new experiential opportunities, overcome barriers, build positive relationships, and develop confidence and skills for life.

    *Canada's History* (www.canadashistory.ca/education/classroom-resources#/?page=1&format=8b1b6045-2cae-47c2-b646-03ff251302b9): Access a range of free lesson plans and activities related to history. A search can be done by themes, grade level, and type of resource (e.g., webinar, podcast, lesson plan, video, book, or article).

    *Google Earth: Canada's Residential Schools* (https://earth.google.com/web/data=CiQSIhlgYTBINWFkNDVhMjBiMTFIN2IzZmQzZjBhY2YwNDZiOWE): A collaboration between *Canadian Geographic* and the National Centre for Truth and Reconciliation. Students can read about the history of residential schools while being taken to corresponding locations on Google Earth.

    *Wilfrid Laurier University's Educational Resources for Equity, Diversity, Inclusion, and Indigenization* (www.wlu.ca/academics/faculties/faculty-of-education/assets/resources/edi-resources-for-educators.html): This collection draws on a range of English and French digital sources and includes a variety of resources suitable for educator self-growth and teaching in K–12 classrooms grouped by the following categories: anti-discrimination, celebrating identity, diversifying knowledge, Indigenization, and library resources. It is a living collection that is monitored and updated annually.

    *Lessons from the Earth and Beyond* (www.lessonsfromearthandbeyond.ca/): This comprehensive resource aims to bring about important conversations and critical inquiries into the importance of Indigenous Knowledge systems in alignment with the Ontario curriculum for different subjects. This resource presents project-based critical explorations of how multiple knowledge systems come into dialogue with one another.

*TVO Learn Mathify* (https://mathify.tvolearn.com): This website provides free online math help for Ontario students in grades 4–12. Students can access the math tutoring website from any digital device to get homework help, prepare for math tests, get clarity on math concepts, or visually sketch math problems.

*Exploring by the Seat of Your Pants* (www.exploringbytheseat.com/): This organization seeks to inspire the next generation of scientists and explorers by bringing those on the front lines of science, exploration, adventure, and conservation live into classrooms with virtual guest speakers and field trips. What they offer is always free for classrooms everywhere.

## REFERENCES

Borup, J., Jensen, M., Archambault, L., Short, C., & Graham, C. (2020). Supporting students during COVID-19: Developing and leveraging academic communities of engagement in a time of crisis. *Journal of Technology and Teacher Education, 28*(2), 161–169. https://eric.ed.gov/?id=EJ1257158

CAST. (2018). *Universal design for learning guidelines version 2.2*. http://udlguidelines.cast.org

Ciuffetelli Parker, D., & Conversano, P. (2021). Narratives of systemic barriers and accessibility: Poverty, equity, diversity, inclusion, and the call for a post-pandemic new normal. *Frontiers in Education, 6*, 704663. doi.org/10.3389/feduc.2021.704663

Colour of Poverty—Colour of Change. (2019). *Fact sheet #2: An introduction to racialized poverty*. https://colourofpovertyca.files.wordpress.com/2019/03/cop-coc-fact-sheet-2-an-introduction-to-racialized-poverty-3.pdf

Đurišić, M., & Bunijevac, M. (2017). Parental involvement as an important factor for successful education. *Center for Educational Policy Studies Journal, 7*(3), 137–153. https://eric.ed.gov/?id=EJ1156936

Durlak, J. A., Weissberg, R. P., Dymnicki, A. B., Taylor, R. D., & Schellinger, K. B. (2011). The impact of enhancing students' social and emotional learning: A meta-analysis of school-based universal interventions. *Child Development, 82*(1), 405–432. doi.org/10.1111/j.1467-8624.2010.01564.x

Eizadirad, A. (2019). *Decolonizing educational assessment: Ontario elementary students and EQAO*. Palgrave Macmillan.

Eizadirad, A. (2020). Closing the achievement gap via reducing the opportunity gap; YAAACE's social inclusion framework within the Jane and Finch community. In P. Trifonas (Ed.), *Handbook of theory and research in cultural studies and education* (pp. 275–297). Springer.

Eizadirad, A., & Campbell, A. (2021). Visibilizing our pain and wounds as resistance and activist pedagogy to heal and hope: Reflections of 2 racialized professors. *Diaspora, Indigenous, and Minority Education, 15*(4), 241–251. doi.org/10.1080/15595692.2021.1937600

Eizadirad, A., Hagerman, B., Dawe, L., Hall, S., Long, T., Skop, M., Hodson, E., Mehta, B., Daly, M., & Beer, J. (2023). The summer of the pivot: Prioritizing equity in remote instruction through a multidisciplinary community of practice initiative at a Canadian university. *Journal of Leadership, Equity, and Research, 9*(1), 100–114. http://journals.sfu.ca/cvj/index.php/cvj/index

Eizadirad, A., & Sider. S. (July 2020). *Schools after coronavirus: Seize "teachable moments" about racism and inequities.* The Conversation. https://theconversation.com/schools-after-coronavirus-seize-teachable-moments-about-racism-and-inequities-142238

Fenton, P., Ocasio-Stoutenburg, L., & Harry, B. (2017). The power of parent engagement: Sociocultural considerations in the quest for equity. *Theory into Practice, 56*(3), 214–225. doi.org/10.1080/00405841.2017.1355686

Gallagher-Mackay, K., Srivastava, P., Underwood, K., Dhuey, E., McCready, L., Born, K., & Sander, B. (2021). COVID-19 and education disruption in Ontario: Emerging evidence on impacts. *Science Briefs of the Ontario COVID-19 Science Advisory Table, 2*(34), 1–36. doi.org/10.47326/ocsat.2021.02.34.1.0

Gorski, P. C. (2012). Perceiving the problem of poverty and schooling: Deconstructing the class stereotypes that mis-shape education practice and policy. *Equity & Excellence in Education, 45*(2), 302–319. doi.org/10.1080/10665684.2012.666934

Hillier, C., Milne, E., & Aurini, J. (2019). "It's not just helping your kid with homework anymore": The challenges of aligning education policy with parents and teachers. *Canadian Public Policy, 45*(4), 497–510. doi.org/10.3138/cpp.2019-004

Hoglund, W. L., Klingle, K. E., & Hosan, N. E. (2015). Classroom risks and resources: Teacher burnout, classroom quality and children's adjustment in high needs elementary schools. *Journal of School Psychology, 53*(5), 337–357. doi.org/10.1016/j.jsp.2015.06.002

James, C. E. (2020). *Racial inequity, COVID-19 and the education of Black and other marginalized students.* Royal Society of Canada Working Group on the Impact of COVID-19 in Racialized Communities. https://rsc-src.ca/en/themes/impact-covid-19-in-racialized-communities

Jennings, J., & Rentner, D. S. (2020). Supporting students and families through chronic absenteeism. *Phi Delta Kappan, 102*(6), 45–50. doi.org/10.1177/003172170608800206

Kearney, C. A., & Graczyk, P. (2014). A response to intervention model to promote school attendance and decrease school absenteeism. *Child & Youth Care Forum, 43*, 1–25. doi.org/10.1007/s10566-013-9222-1

Ladson-Billings, G. (1995). Toward a theory of culturally relevant pedagogy. *American Educational Research Journal, 32*(3), 465–491. doi.org/10.2307/1163320

McCoy, D. C., & Hanno, E. C. (2023). Systemic barriers and opportunities for implementing school-based social–emotional learning interventions in low-income and conflict-affected settings. *Frontiers in Psychology, 14*, 1–6. doi.org/10.3389/fpsyg.2023.1011039

McMurtry, R., & Curling, A. (2008). *The review of the roots of youth violence.* https://youthrex.com/wp-content/uploads/2019/05/The-Roots-of-Youth-Violence-vol.-1-Findings-Analysis-and-Conclusions-2008.pdf

Milner, H. R. (2017). *Rac(e)ing to class: Confronting poverty and race in schools and classrooms.* Harvard Education Press.

Muijs, D., Harris, A., Chapman, C., Stoll, L., & Russ, J. (2004). Improving schools in socioeconomically disadvantaged areas—a review of research evidence. *School Effectiveness and School Improvement, 15*(2), 149–175. doi.org/10.1076/sesi.15.2.149.30433

Nubani, L., Fierke-Gmazel, H., Madill, H., & De Biasi, A. (2023). Community engagement in crime reduction strategies: A tale of three cities. *Journal of Participatory Research Methods, 4*(1). doi.org/10.35844/001c.57526

O'Brien, D. T., Hill, N. E., & Contreras, M. (2021). Community violence and academic achievement: High-crime neighborhoods, hotspot streets, and the geographic scale of "community." *PLoS ONE, 16*(11). doi.org/10.1371/journal.pone.0258577

Organisation for Economic Co-operation and Development. (2018). *Equations and inequalities: Making mathematics accessible to all.* www.oecd.org/publications/equations-and-inequalities-9789264258495-en.htm

Pathways to Education. (n.d.). *The impacts of socioeconomic status and educational attainment on youth success.* www.pathwaystoeducation.ca/the-impacts-of-socioeconomic-status-and-educational-attainment-on-youth-success/

Reardon, S. F., & Portilla, X. A. (2016). Recent trends in socioeconomic and racial school readiness gaps at kindergarten entry. *AERA Open, 6*(3). doi.org/10.1177/2332858416657343

Reyna, C. (2008). Ian is intelligent but Leshaun is lazy: Antecedents and consequences of attributional stereotypes in the classroom. *European Journal of Psychology of Education, 23*(4), 439–458. doi.org/10.1007/BF03172752

Royal Society of Canada. (2021). *Children and schools during COVID-19 and beyond: Engagement and connection through opportunity.* https://rsc-src.ca/sites/default/files/C%26S%20PB_EN_0.pdf

Samuels, A. J. (2018). Exploring culturally responsive pedagogy: Teachers' perspectives on fostering equitable and inclusive classrooms. *SRATE Journal, 27*(1), 22–30. https://eric.ed.gov/?id=EJ1166706

Sheridan, S. M., Knoche, L. L., Kupzyk, K. A., Edwards, C. P., & Marvin, C. A. (2011). A randomized trial examining the effects of parent engagement on early language and literacy: The getting ready intervention. *Journal of School Psychology, 49*(3), 361–383. doi.org/10.1016/j.jsp.2011.03.001

Silva-Laya, M., D'Angelo, N., García, E., Zúñiga, L., & Fernández, T. (2020). Urban poverty and education. A systematic literature review. *Educational Research Review*, 29, 100280. doi.org/10.1016/j.edurev.2019.05.002

Toronto District School Board. (2023). *The 2023 Learning Opportunities Index: Questions and answers*. www.tdsb.on.ca/Portals/research/docs/reports/LOI2023.pdf

Toronto Foundation. (2021). *Toronto's vital signs: 2021 report*. https://torontofoundation.ca/vitalsigns2021/

Tranjan, R. (2018). *Poverty measures: Opportunity or distraction?* Canadian Centre for Policy Alternatives. https://policyalternatives.ca/sites/default/files/uploads/publications/Ontario%20Office/2018/08/Poverty%20Measures.pdf

Tsang, J., & Eizadirad, A. (2023). Disrupting the colonizing gaze and mobilizing for systemic decolonization: 2020 world events and the curriculum of critical consciousness. In P. P. Trifonas & S. Jagger (Eds.), *Handbook of curriculum theory and research* (pp. 1–16). Springer International Handbooks of Education. doi.org/10.1007/978-3-030-82976-6_38-1

United Way. (2019). *Rebalancing the opportunity equation*. www.unitedwaygt.org/wp-content/uploads/2021/10/2019_OE_fullreport_FINAL-1.pdf

# PART IV

## GENDER AND SEXUAL DIVERSITY: SUPPORTING STUDENTS' IDENTITY AS IMPORTANT TO HUMAN FLOURISHING

# CHAPTER 8
# Gender and Sexuality in Education: Critical Considerations

*Jay Kennedy*

Whether the average teacher is aware of it or not, education is a pivotal venue for the transmission of knowledge about gender and sexuality. Teachers exert significant influence on school culture and students' experience, often with little explicit training about gender or sexuality (Action Canada, 2019). Curriculum also plays a role, determining the content to which students are formally exposed and dictating a baseline of acceptable knowledge. Curriculum and teachers' understanding of gender are both informed by the wider culture and the popular understanding of histories of gender and sexuality. Therefore, in this chapter, I discuss the topics of gender and sex by looking back briefly at the history of Western gender norms and stereotypes that inform our current popular understandings. Despite some apparent changes to gender norms, the predominant popular conceptions of gender and sexuality largely remain binary and heteronormative, presenting limits to human flourishing. The harms experienced by all students due to prescriptive gender and sexuality norms are discussed, with special attention given to the experiences of **2SLGBTQI+** students and educators late in the chapter. The chapter ends with a discussion of pertinent gender and sexuality issues that require consideration by all teachers, teacher candidates, faculties of education, and school boards to promote student flourishing.

A brief note: I, the author, am a white, cisgender, heterosexual, middle-class, able-bodied man. I have intentionally chosen the citations in this chapter both to elevate voices or viewpoints from marginalized communities that have informed my perspective and to focus, to the extent possible within the available literature, on the Canadian context. My hope is that the citations will help to represent the authors who have added to the knowledge on these topics and spur greater discussion of their work.

## SEX AND GENDER

In contemporary Western society, sex is considered by many people to be a binary concept, with humans being assigned as male or female by biology. Biological sex is often viewed as the signal that indicates appropriate behaviours and expectations for individuals gendered as men and women (Fine, 2010). However, these expectations, when assumed to be natural or inherent, confuse biological sex with the expectations imposed on sex categories by the social context (Fine, 2010). Collections of context-specific social expectations, often associated with the sexes, form the concept of gender. In Western society, the genders historically were **essentialized** and assumed to be complementary opposites (Connell, 2005). These ideas were supported by religious dogma and political mechanisms to maintain a gender hierarchy (Benayon, 2012; Kimmel, 1995), typically favouring men and masculine gender enactment, while devaluing women, the feminine, and any divergent gender expressions (Foucault, 1990). I regularly teach a Bachelor of Education course on social justice topics that examines these ideas, and I often find that some students are incredulous that current concepts of gender and sexuality are influenced by religious and political forces, exactly because of how natural and obvious these norms appear. However, it bears remembering that in Canadian residential schools, from 1883 to 1996, white Eurocentric binary gender norms were enforced for Indigenous students, whose cultures often considered gender differently (Driskill, 2010). In this case, these students, who were not initially socialized into Western gender norms, were forced to learn them. This specific gender training, which remains more common than we might think, along with deliberately chosen portrayals of gender in mass media and the classification, until recently, of divergent gender expression as a form of mental illness (Drescher, 2010) likely accounts for the "naturalness" of the binary conception of gender in at least the last century or so. Over time, and because of various social incentives, these ideas became everyday or common-sense knowledge.

Sexuality in the West has likewise been linked to the binary conception of sex and gender and filtered through a lens of religion (particularly Christianity in Canada) and liberal political philosophy (Connell, 2005). Although the average citizen might consider current Canadian society and government to be secularized, it bears considering that when I was younger (I'm now 45 years old), I was read the Christian Bible in public school and all stores in Ontario were legally required to close on Sunday for the Christian Sabbath (see chapter 1 for further discussion on religion in Canadian society). I add this point to highlight that not that long ago (the 1980s and early 1990s) Judeo-Christian religious ideals were a significant part of public life and likely have lingering, if not altogether obvious, influences on our norms and practices today (leaving aside, of course, the fact that multiple provinces in Canada still fully or partially fund public Catholic schools; Rymarz, 2017; chapters 1 and 14). As a result of such influences, sexuality expressed beyond the boundaries of a fairly strict and parochial heterosexuality was, until quite recently, considered aberrant and pathologized (Drescher, 2010). This notion of sexuality ignores a broad variety of sexual expressions and concepts of gender beyond the binary that have existed for millennia, as documented in multiple societies (Golden & Toohey, 2019; Pyle, 2020).

With these factors in mind, I argue that so-called traditional notions of gender and sexuality are far from universal, with significantly different definitions of each demonstrated in a variety of cultures. In fact, researchers note that expectations have changed for the Western binary gender roles throughout history, and multiple changes have occurred in Western gender norms in the past 300 years (Greig, 2012; Kimmel, 1995). These shifts in gender expectations and performances have often accompanied dramatic changes in the economy and/or social structure (Greig, 2012; Kimmel, 1995). Examples include the rise of the more androgenous short-haired flapper style for women and the increasing focus on men's appearance introduced by the growing consumer culture of the early 20th century (Nicholas, 2012). A more recent example is the fashion of thick beards (Oldstone-Moore, 2017) and men's protein-gobbling gym bodies, which became increasingly popular following (and perhaps in response to) the 2008 financial crisis (Hakim, 2018).

Although there were major shifts to gender theory and gender roles in the 20th century, the values assigned to each gender in Western culture have remained relatively stable (Connell, 2005; Fine, 2010). Similarly, although explicit homophobia has lessened in North American society, it has simply morphed to operate more subtly (Diefendorf & Bridges, 2020). Qualities popularly associated with men, and therefore deemed masculine, are competitiveness, aggression, toughness, emotional stoicism, physicality, logic, rationality, and individualism (Connell, 2005; Kimmel, 1995). Stereotypically feminine characteristics, including softness, caring, deference, emotionality, subjectivity, irrationality, and nature, are often considered to be inferior and opposite to masculine ones (Connell, 2005). Owing to the historical and cultural factors described above, stereotypically masculine traits have tended to be valued in society, while feminine traits have typically been denigrated (Connell, 2005).

## DISPUTING SEX AND GENDER CLAIMS

Despite the recent increasing visibility of trans and nonbinary individuals (J. W. Skelton, 2022) in Western society, many still perceive sex and gender in binary terms. For this reason, the early part of this chapter considers that binary. Another reason is an attempt to use "strategic essentialism" (Beasley, 2019, p. 37). Although some authors suggest that continued mention of the binary only further supports it, strategic essentialism deliberately discusses the binary to call attention to the inequality that results from the associated gender norms.

Sex can variously be defined in numerous terms, such as by physical anatomy, chromosomes, and hormone levels, which, for any given person, may not all point in the same direction (Fine, 2010). As noted above, a popular notion is that a person's sex determines how they think and act. However, researchers who examined the body of biological research found that "sex differences on almost every psychological trait measured, are either non-existent or fairly small" (Connell, 2005, p. 21). Not only does the evidence not support widespread sex differences in psychology or behaviour, but there are also multiple studies that have documented women acting in stereotypically masculine ways (e.g., risk-taking via gambling, sexual promiscuity, aggression) in non-Western cultures.

These studies were published but have received little attention (Fine, 2010). Even more concerning, a recent review found that many research findings were denied publication because their results contradicted established wisdom (Eliot, 2010). In contrast, many studies with more suspect research methods that supported sex differences were published (Fine, 2010). As much as we would like to believe that academic publishing is based entirely on merit, this is simply not true; power relationships and people's biases do play a part. This publication bias may partly explain the tenacity of stereotypical gender norms in Western society. These findings simultaneously support the effects of gendered assumptions on the interpretation of research findings and the notion that a wider spectrum of gender expressions than commonly considered is possible.

The findings mentioned above serve to highlight the socially constructed nature of gender, meaning that as individuals we learn how to act in what are popularly considered sex-congruent ways based on social cues, both subtle and explicit (Fine, 2010; Rippon, 2019). Rather than being a simplistic essential nature rooted in biology, the process of gender instruction is socially complex. Individuals act, influence their environments, and receive feedback from that context, learning through trial and error which performances generate approval and status. On the other hand, the way we act is also subject to surveillance and **policing** by others (Foucault, 1990) in overt and subtle ways, resulting in seemingly inevitable gender expressions within a given context.

## GENDER IN EDUCATION

Formal schooling is a common venue for the policing of gender and sexual norms (Fine, 2010; Paterson, 2014). The curriculum can promote both stereotypical gender norms and heteronormativity by demonstration or promotion of certain normative ideas about gender and sexuality. For example, literacy readings or health curriculum examples can often portray certain family types (e.g., a mother and father) and gender identities and exclude others. Moreover, multiple assumed strict, natural rules are presented in some aspects of the science curriculum, particularly in biology (James, 2019). In addition, certain subjects have been construed as specifically gendered. From the Enlightenment onward, maths and sciences have been considered masculine subjects and have therefore become high-status. In fact, women were discouraged from studying these subjects in both policy and in practice in the 19th and 20th centuries (Acker & Oatley, 1993).

Girls have recently been encouraged into nontraditional school subjects and are consequently less limited in their choices, particularly in math (Van der Vleuten et al., 2016). Statistics show that girls have increased their participation and achievement in STEM (science, technology, engineering, and mathematics) subjects, though a gender gap remains (Wall, 2019). Although that trend is encouraging, within the broad subject of science gendered divisions exist. Girls tend toward participation in the life sciences (e.g., biology), and boys prefer physical sciences (e.g., physics, chemistry) and computer science (Wall, 2019). Although some variations exist between primary, secondary, and post-secondary levels, the gendered trend in science specialization is reasonably consistent (Kollmayer et al., 2018). Gender expectations play a role in student choices, and can result in social exclusion in both school programs (Wall, 2019) and the labour market (Chan et al., 2021) if an individual chooses outside of their gendered subject. This social punishment for not adhering to gendered subjects has been raised as a significant issue contributing to the gender gap among STEM subjects.

Another subject that is often gendered, English literacy, is included in required curricular subjects in most Canadian school boards and is prominently featured on many provincial standardized tests. There has long been a narrative that English literacy is a feminine subject at which girls "naturally" excel, which disadvantages boys (Greig, 2012). This narrative persists despite ample evidence that there is little or no gender difference in literacy skills (Fine, 2010). Categorizing literacy as feminine is somewhat paradoxical as books chosen by teachers tend to present strong or dynamic male characters and relatively passive and unexciting girl characters (when girl characters are included at all), reinforcing dominant gender stereotypes (Paterson, 2014). The use of these stories in read-alouds and literacy lessons has been found to increase children's gender-stereotyped behaviours (Ashton, 1983).

French language learning is similarly feminized in Canada (Frank et al., 2003). Associations with femininity mean that some boys, even those quite skilled in French, avoid the subject to limit negative backlash from peers (Kissau, 2006). In addition, boys and men may actually gain gender credibility among peers by doing poorly in subjects they consider feminized. Fine (2017) calls the ability to gain social capital from demonstrated inability in a non-gender-congruent activity "failure as an asset" (p. 295). In this way, boys' academic choices can also be limited by gender expectations, though these effects are also influenced by social class and other factors.

A final subject to consider is physical education (PE). Learning activities in PE often support stereotypically masculine concepts of strength, speed, and competition (Anderson & White, 2018) for boys, while simultaneously devaluing girls' sporting performances (Kirk, 2002). These norms around PE can lead boys to think that they must demonstrate ability in sport to be considered adequately masculine (Atkinson & Kehler, 2010; Metcalfe, 2018) and can cause some girls and other genders to disengage from sport and physical activity entirely (Metcalfe, 2018). In addition, PE teachers often promote stereotypical notions of gender (Preece & Bullingham, 2022), and teachers, as well as students, police dominant notions of gendered activities, physical ability, and gendered "athletic" bodily forms (Atkinson & Kehler, 2010; Metcalfe, 2018). PE success criteria often promote gender norms, meaning the curriculum itself supports these stereotypes (Preece & Bullingham, 2022). The same is true of outdoor education through expectations about gendered skills (Warren et al., 2019) and teachers' assumptions about students' capacities (Weaver-Hightower, 2010).

Interestingly, despite these gender pressures that influence students' academic choices, a persistent narrative in popular media has arisen decrying the "boy-crisis" (Greig, 2012, p. 316) in schools. According to this idea, boys are underachieving because they cannot relate to feminine teaching methods employed by women teachers, particularly at the primary school level. This situation, according to the narrative, undervalues boys' "natural" interests and styles of learning. According to the "boy-crisis," boys' recent lagging academic performance and their comparatively poor rates of post-secondary school attendance (Greig, 2012; Wall, 2019) are evidence of this phenomenon. However, these narratives have been used regularly in media since at least 1870 and tend to reliably resurface during periods of social, political, and economic instability (Greig, 2012). Essentially, boys will stop trying in school as a way to save face (Greig, 2012) and will instead tend to place their focus more on sports prowess and general physical activity, viewing academic success as feminizing (Schiffrin-Sands, 2021). In doing this, some boys are explicitly using masculine gender norms as a tool to gain social status in the short term, placing long-term limits on their educational outcomes. Although it is true that some men are choosing not to attend post-secondary education, the intersections of class, race, and other social factors play significant roles in this decline.

The common ideas about gendered learning styles, such as those promoted by the "boy-crisis" narrative, clearly serve to define gender in binary and opposite terms (C. Skelton, 2010). Similarly, certain curricular aspects, or teachers' interpretation thereof, support gendered or heteronormative notions. Unfortunately, teachers in general can lack understanding of gendered social barriers for students (C. Skelton, 2010) or of the heteronormativity fostered by the curriculum. What's more, even teachers who are aware of the need to counter these stereotypes will often still accept and subtly support them because they are commonly viewed as "natural" or common sense (Riley, 2014).

## TEACHERS' MAINTENANCE OF GENDER ROLES

It seems clear from the previous section that binary gender stereotypes can be harmful to students by limiting academic choice and biasing teachers' perceptions. It is likely that many teachers reading this would state that they do not prejudge students based on gender or sexuality and that they work to engage every student as an individual. This may be true; however, well-worn everyday practices, such as addressing groups of young students as "boys and girls," not only reinforce the binary conception of gender (J. W. Skelton, 2022) but also signal the fundamental difference between these groups and further reinforce gender difference (J. W. Skelton, 2022).

These actions may seem trivial, but the perception of gender differences by teachers has very material consequences. In the regular classroom, studies have demonstrated that teachers' gender biases affect their perceptions of students (Burusic et al., 2012), including gendered differences in need of support and attention (Sadker & Zittleman, 2009) and students' academic potential (Bianco et al., 2011). These perceptions can lead to teachers producing biased recommendations for placement in courses for the following academic year. These biases can occur at all levels of schooling (Riley, 2014). For example, a Canadian study of pre-kindergarten learners found that, due to teachers' gender socialization, they judged students' social ability and academic potential based on stereotypical gender norms (e.g., men teachers viewed physical aggression as indicative of these characteristics; women teachers held the opposite view) (Bosacki et al., 2015). Further, Riley (2014) states that, due to stereotypical gender norms, boys are perceived to be more likely to exhibit problematic behaviour. The author posits that such a perception of boys might lead to decreased academic expectations and negative impacts on boys' self-concept, particularly for those from marginalized communities, as other biases might intersect with and compound teachers' negative attitudes.

Students' behaviours and academic outcomes are affected not only by teachers; peers play a significant role in the maintenance of binary gender norms in schools. Whereas teachers' gender biases tend to be demonstrated in formal learning activities and classroom arrangement, students' maintenance of gender norms often occurs informally, by creating social discomfort or exclusion for students who do not adequately adhere to gender expectations (Blenkinsop et al., 2018; Schiffrin-Sands, 2021). Gendered pressures can also result in bullying and rejection, which result in absenteeism for students who are 2SLGBTQI+ (Crothers et al., 2017) or who do not strictly adhere to stereotypical gender norms (J. W. Skelton, 2022).

Students' influence is not limited to peers; it also affects teachers' gender expectations and enactment. Martino (2008) reports that two male teachers managed their masculine presentation to be accepted by their students. What's more, one of the teachers hid his 2SLGBTQI+ status, wanting to avoid sanction or questioning by students and their parents. Student and parent expectations raise interesting questions for teachers about their displays of their gender and sexuality in the classroom. For example, one student in my university's Bachelor of Education program recently complained that 2SLGBTQI+ pre-service teachers were told in a seminar by a visiting speaker to avoid discussions or displays of their personal life, such as family photos, in their classrooms to avoid negative student or parent reactions.

The promotion, either formal or informal, of normative gender and heteronormative sexuality can be limiting to all school stakeholders in multiple ways, as demonstrated above. It also reinforces the notion that there are competing interests between genders (Ringrose, 2007), which only supports othering and zero-sum thinking. These ideas limit flourishing by limiting freedom of self-expression and development of oneself as a whole person. There is evidence that some students are becoming more critical of the limitations of the gender binary and support non-normative displays of gender and sexuality. In addition, a growing number of students are reporting gender identities or expressions beyond the binary (Diamond, 2020). The questioning of dominant gender norms and the increasing visibility of 2SLGBTQI+ students can act as motivation for educators to do and learn more. However, this impetus may be problematic as it is reactive rather than proactive. Given the current and ongoing reports of homophobic language, (verbal, physical, and sexual) harassment faced by 2SLGBTQI+ students in Canadian schools (Peter et al., 2021), and the resulting mental health challenges (Lucassen et al., 2017), teachers need to work to create environments in which students feel free to express themselves and continue the often messy process of personal development. Fostering these cultures can be challenging, particularly since 2SLGBTQI+ youth often report feeling unsupported by their teachers. However, *unsupported* is a vague term in practical settings. What does it mean? For starters, some research findings indicate that teachers perceive less bullying and verbal harassment than is reported by 2SLGBTQI+ youth (Crothers et al., 2017) and are ineffective at addressing such issues (Peter et al., 2021). Another issue is that teachers have reported avoiding discussion of non-normative gender and sexuality because they do not want to stir controversy, offend students, or inadvertently support stereotypical ideas of gender and sexuality (Malins, 2016). In addition, teachers may also assume that no 2SLGBTQ+-identifying students are present in their classes and therefore decide not to implement more inclusionary language and practices. Moreover, teachers may have specific notions of what sexual minority or transgender students look like (i.e., what outward displays count as gender nonconforming) both in their personal conceptions and in board policies. Such notions limit even well-intentioned teachers' understanding of students who are gender nonconforming (or who would like to express themselves in nonconforming ways but are not yet comfortable doing so) and their ability to provide support (Airton, 2023). If that is the situation, and teachers genuinely do not hear or see the issue, make assumptions, or are reluctant to address such issues for fear of being wrong, how can they adequately support students?

## SUPPORTS FOR TEACHERS AND STUDENTS

Awareness is important. Pride days and Pink Shirt Day bring attention to 2SLGBTQI+ issues and gender norms. However, this awareness can be just that: simple recognition that these issues exist, without context or nuanced understanding of the issues (Airton, 2023). The result often promotes simple tolerance, as opposed to more genuine acceptance or inclusion. The objective should be to foster genuine flourishing, enabling each student to fulfill their life's potential, and to foster a more supportive society focused on the collective good. To enable such flourishing, though, proactive strategies are required to support 2SLGBTQI+ students in schools.

The establishment of gay-straight alliances (GSAs) is one method of making schools safer for 2SLGBTQI+ students (Marx & Kettrey, 2016) and spurring deeper discussion of 2SLGBTQI+ issues. Through GSAs, teachers can learn about the experiences of 2SLGBTQI+ students and their student allies. These interactions can act as a method to bridge the teacher–student perception gap about 2SLGBTQI+ bullying and harassment. GSAs are also a dedicated space, authorized by administration, where 2SLGBTQI+ issues can be discussed. This means that teachers can engage in dialogue with students with less worry about student or parent objections. However, GSAs are not a simple fix. Since they are often supported by teachers already passionate about advocating for 2SLGBTQI+ issues, teachers without much knowledge of such issues receive little exposure to new perspectives or additional information. Also, teachers participating in GSAs, and those who simply identify themselves as allies in less formal ways, need to be reflective about their assumptions, the possibility of committing missteps, and taking the spotlight away from 2SLGBTQI+ students (Potvin, 2021; see also chapter 9) to avoid saviour thinking. Lastly, teacher allies can feel alone among their colleagues and unsupported by administration (Malins, 2016). For this reason, more training for teachers about issues of gender and sexuality is recommended by research (Potvin, 2021; J. W. Skelton, 2022) and 2SLGBTQI+ advocacy groups (GLSEN, n.d.).

Another issue faced by Canadian teachers who want to teach about gender norms and sexuality in the classroom is worry over parental backlash due to religious, cultural, or political beliefs (Malins, 2016). Malins (2016) advocates for structural support from administration and ministries of education. Support from these sources would help to increase teachers' knowledge around gender and sexuality issues, providing a degree of confidence in addressing those topics in the classroom. In addition to training, curriculum is often mentioned as a method of support. One example is the recent change to the Ontario health and physical education curriculum, which has helped to raise awareness and provided supportive cues and examples for some teachers as they learn how to engage with nonbinary or transgender students (Martino et al., 2022).

Typically, across Canada, gender and sexuality topics are contained in health curricula, in what are commonly called sex-ed strands or units. Action Canada produced a report in 2019 assessing the curricula of all provinces against UNESCO (2018) guidelines (stated in UNESCO's *International Technical Guidelines of Sexuality Education* document). Action Canada promotes updating curriculum Canada-wide to both better inform students and limit heteronormative language and examples, and provide resources and support to teachers. In recent years, new curricula and policy have been introduced in some provinces, including Ontario, British Columbia, and New Brunswick, that contain content about gender expression and sexuality. However, some provinces and territories still have sex-ed curricula that have little or no consideration of these topics (Action Canada, 2019). Moreover, considerable backlash occurred following the implementation of these curricula, with conservative political parties accusing them of "indoctrination" (Nash & Browne, 2021, p. 75) of youth, disputing the influence of "gender ideologies" (Nash & Browne, 2021, p. 76), and arguing for a maintenance of childhood innocence and for the upholding of parental rights.

The notion of parental rights has also been invoked in Saskatchewan and New Brunswick, both of which, in 2023, instituted policies overturning previous laws that permitted students to use nonlegal names and pronouns in school. The new policies require teachers to use the names and pronouns for students that are stated on the students' birth certificates unless given written parental permission. These moves have been criticized as harmful to 2SLGBTQI+ students' self-expression, resulting in the outing of students who may not be ready to discuss such issues with their parents, while simultaneously placing teachers in a precarious position between wanting to support students and adhering to current government policy.

Despite parental backlash to curriculum and rollbacks of some protections in policy, the majority of parents in Canada are supportive of sex-ed for their children (Action Canada, 2019). One issue of concern, particularly with the 2019 Ontario health and physical education curriculum, is the opt-out option provided to parents who do not feel comfortable with some topics. This option means that not all students will receive the full curriculum. To help avoid having students miss content due to opt-outs and to avoid siloing gender and sexuality topics into only one curriculum, the integration of sex-ed topics, particularly 2SLGBTQI+ issues, into all curricular subjects is recommended (Kalarikkal, 2020).

## CONCLUSION

I have outlined the harms of policing gender expression and sexuality in some detail. However, rather than focusing on the negative academic and health outcomes, collaborative work toward student flourishing through supportive and affirming approaches is likely more productive (J. W. Skelton, 2022). It is no surprise that teachers are influential in students' lives in many ways. Teachers at all grade levels can choose to either support or critically engage with limiting and prejudicial norms. Both actions will affect students' perceptions of gender and sexuality. As teachers, our job is to create environments in which our students can flourish. However, to accomplish this goal we must be critical of the norms that surround us. Also, we need to believe students when they describe their needs (J. W. Skelton, 2022). Further, as many effective teaching approaches advocate, we need to allow students freedom to explore their self-expression, which may change over time. This freedom applies both in curricular subjects and in their daily gender expression. Finally, lifelong learning is a professional expectation for teachers. Work to ensure that you avoid assumptions or narrow understandings of gender and/or sexuality; learn not only from workshops, curriculum documents, and formal professional development sessions, but also daily from your students.

## KEY TERMS

**Essentialized:** Considered to be integral or naturally occurring in someone or something (i.e., part of one's essential nature).

**Policing:** Using a variety of punishments, whether obvious or subtle, physical or social, to enforce rules or codes of behaviour.

**2SLGBTQI+:** An acronym for Two-Spirit, lesbian, gay, bisexual, transgender, queer, and intersex. The "+" symbol indicates additional nonheterosexual or noncisgender identities. I use this acronym because of its current recommended use by the Government of Canada, through engagement and consultation with 2SLGBTQI+ communities.

## DISCUSSION QUESTIONS AND ACTIVITIES

1. What are some dominant gender norms to which you adhere (consider appearance, activities, mannerisms)? In what ways might you have been limited by norms surrounding gender expression or sexuality?

2. As a teacher, what can you do to support students' flourishing in terms of gender and sexuality? Avoid platitudes in your response (e.g., "I will accept every student for who they are"). Instead, list tangible actions you can take or resources you can consult.

3. What aspects of gender and sexuality do you feel uninformed about (or feel uncomfortable talking about)? Why do you feel uninformed (i.e., why might it be that you were not provided with this information)? Also, research and list sources you could use to find out more about this topic.
4. Ask students to split into groups based on their teachable subjects. Once in groups, ask students to look through their curriculum and find two or more possible examples of heteronormativity in their curriculum expectations or examples. Ask the class to discuss these examples, why they may persist, and how they might be resisted or questioned.

## REFERENCES

Acker, S., & Oatley, K. (1993). Gender issues in education for science and technology: Current situation and prospects for change. *Canadian Journal of Education, 18*(3), 255–272. doi.org/10.2307/1495386

Action Canada. (2019). *State of sex-ed report*. www.actioncanadashr.org/resources/reports-analysis/2020-04-03-state-sex-ed-report

Airton, L. (2023). You don't know me: Welcoming gender diversity in schools via an ethic of hospitality. *Curriculum Inquiry, 53*(2), 148–168. doi.org/10.1080/03626784.2023.2200810

Anderson, E., & White, A. (2018). *Sport, theory and social problems: A critical introduction*. Routledge.

Ashton, E. (1983). Measures of play behaviour. The influence of sex-role stereotyped children's books. *Sex Roles, 9*, 43–47. doi.org/10.1007/BF00303108

Atkinson, M., & Kehler, M. (2010). Boys, gyms, locker rooms and heterotopia. In M. Kehler & M. Atkinson (Eds.), *Boys' bodies: Speaking the unspoken* (pp. 73–90). Peter Lang.

Beasley, C. (2019). Feminism and men/masculinities scholarship: Connections, disjunctions, and possibilities. In L. Gottzén, U. Mellström, & T. Shefer (Eds.), *Routledge international handbook of masculinity studies* (pp. 30–40). Routledge.

Benayon, M. (2012). "Raise them Jewish, raise them proud!": Gay Jewish fathers in contemporary Israeli and Canadian Jewish society. In C. Greig & W. Martino (Eds.), *Canadian men and masculinities: Historical and contemporary perspectives* (pp. 878–977). Canadian Scholars.

Bianco, M., Harris, B., Garrison-Wade, D., & Leech, N. (2011). Gifted girls: Gender bias in gifted referrals. *Roeper Review, 33*(3), 170–180. doi.org/10.1080/02783193.2011.580500

Blenkinsop, S., Piersol, L., & Sitka-Sage, M. D. D. (2018). Boys being boys: Eco-double consciousness, splash violence, and environmental education. *Journal of Environmental Education, 49*(4), 350–356. https://eric.ed.gov/?id=EJ1182917

Bosacki, S., Woods, H., & Coplan, R. (2015). Canadian female and male early childhood educators' perceptions of child aggression and rough-and-tumble play. *Early Child Development and Care, 185*(7), 1134–1147. doi.org/10.1080/03004430.2014.980408

Burusic, J., Babarovic, T., & Seric, M. (2012). Differences in elementary school achievement between girls and boys: Does the teacher gender play a role? *European Journal of Psychology of Education, 27,* 523–538. doi.org/10.1007/s10212-011-0093-2

Chan, P. C., Handler, T., & Frenette, M. (2021). *Gender differences in STEM enrolment and graduation: What are the roles of academic performance and preparation?* Statistics Canada. www150.statcan.gc.ca/n1/pub/36-28-0001/2021011/article/00004-eng.htm

Connell, R. (2005). *Masculinities* (2nd ed.). University of California Press.

Crothers, L. M., Kolbert, J. B., Berbary, C., Chatlos, S., Lattanzio, L., Tiberi, A., Wells, D. S., Bundick, M. J., Lipinski, J., & & Meidl, C. (2017). Teachers', LGBTQ students', and student allies' perceptions of bullying of sexually-diverse youth. *Journal of Aggression, Maltreatment & Trauma, 26*(9), 972–988. doi.org/10.1080/10926771.2017.1344344

Diamond, L. M. (2020). Gender fluidity and nonbinary gender identities among children and adolescents. *Child Development Perspectives, 14*(2), 110–115. doi.org/10.1111/cdep.12366

Diefendorf, S., & Bridges, T. (2020). On the enduring relationship between masculinity and homophobia. *Sexualities, 23*(7), 1264–1284. doi.org/10.1177/1363460719876843

Drescher, J. (2010). Queer diagnoses: Parallels and contrasts in the history of homosexuality, gender variance, and the *Diagnostic and Statistical Manual. Archives of Sexual Behavior, 39,* 427–460. doi.org/10.1007/s10508-009-9531-5

Driskill, Q. L. (2010). Doubleweaving Two-Spirit critiques: Building alliances between Native and queer studies. *GLQ: A Journal of Lesbian and Gay Studies, 16*(1–2), 69–92. doi.org/10.1215/10642684-2009-013

Eliot, L. (2010). *Pink brain, blue brain: How small differences grow into troublesome gaps—and what we can do about it.* Oneworld.

Fine, C. (2010). *Delusions of gender: How our minds, society, and neurosexism create difference.* Norton.

Fine, C. (2017). *Testosterone rex: Myths of sex, science, and society.* Norton.

Foucault, M. (1990). *The history of sexuality: An introduction* (Vol. 1). Vintage.

Frank, B., Kehler, M., Lovell, T., & Davison, K. (2003). A tangle of trouble: Boys, masculinity and schooling—future directions. *Educational Review, 55*(2), 119–133. http://doi.org/10.1080/0013191032000072173

GLSEN. (n.d.). *Developing LGBTQ-inclusive classroom resources.* www.glsen.org/sites/default/files/2019-11/GLSEN_LGBTQ_Inclusive_Curriculum_Resource_2019_0.pdf

Golden, M., & Toohey, P. (2019). *Sex and difference in ancient Greece and Rome.* Edinburgh University Press.

Greig, C. (2012). Boys' underachievement in school in historical perspective: Exploring masculinity and schooling in the postwar era, 1945–1960. In C. Greig & W. Martino (Eds.), *Canadian men and masculinities: Historical and contemporary perspectives* (pp. 400–451). Canadian Scholars.

Hakim, J. (2018). "The spornosexual": The affective contradictions of male body-work in neoliberal digital culture. *Journal of Gender Studies, 27*(2), 231–241. doi.org/10.1080/09589236.2016.1217771

James, K. (2019). Mapping sexual orientation and gender identity (SOGI) inclusion through curriculum and practice in a Canadian teacher education program. *Canadian Journal of Education, 42*(4), 957–991. https://journals.sfu.ca/cje/index.php/cje-rce/article/view/3899L

Kalarikkal, G. (2020). *LGBTQ issues in Canadian schools*. Pride and Joy Foundation. www.prideandjoyfoundation.com/blog/lgbtq-issues-in-canadian-schools

Kimmel, M. (1995). *Manhood in America: A cultural history*. Free Press.

Kirk, D. (2002). Physical education: A gendered history. In D. Penney (Ed.), *Gender and physical education: Contemporary issues and future directions* (pp. 24–40). Routledge.

Kissau, S. (2006). Gender differences in motivation to learn French. *Canadian Modern Language Review, 62*(3), 401–422. doi.org/10.1353/cml.2006.0020

Kollmayer, M., Schober, B., & Spiel, C. (2018). Gender stereotypes in education: Development, consequences, and interventions. *European Journal of Developmental Psychology, 15*(4), 361–377. doi.org/10.1080/17405629.2016.1193483

Lucassen, M. F., Stasiak, K., Samra, R., Frampton, C. M., Merry, S. N. (2017). Sexual minority youth and depressive symptoms or depressive disorder: A systematic review and meta-analysis of population-based studies. *Australian & New Zealand Journal of Psychiatry, 51*(8), 774–787. doi.org/10.1177/0004867417713664

Malins, P. (2016). How inclusive is "inclusive education" in the Ontario elementary classroom? Teachers talk about addressing diverse gender and sexual identities. *Teaching and Teacher Education, 54*, 128–138. doi.org/10.1016/j.tate.2015.11.004

Martino, W. (2008). Male teachers as role models: Addressing issues of masculinity, pedagogy and the re-masculinization of schooling. *Curriculum Inquiry, 38*(2), 189–223. doi.org/10.1111/j.1467-873X.2007.00405.x

Martino, W., Omercajic, K., & Kassen, J. (2022). "We have no 'visibly' trans students in our school": Educators' perspectives on transgender-affirmative policies in schools. *Teachers College Record, 124*(8), 66–97. doi.org/10.1177/01614681221121522

Marx, R., & Kettrey, H. (2016). Gay-straight alliances are associated with lower levels of school-based victimization of 2SLGBTQI+ youth: A systematic review and meta-analysis. *Journal of Youth and Adolescence, 45*(7), 1269–1282. doi.org/10.1007/s10964-016-0501-7

Metcalfe, S. (2018). Adolescent constructions of gendered identities: The role of sport and (physical) education. *Sport, Education and Society, 23*(7), 681–693. doi.org/10.1080/13573322.2018.1493574

Nash, C. J., & Browne, K. (2021). Resisting the mainstreaming of LGBT equalities in Canadian and British schools: Sex education and trans school friends. *Environment and Planning C: Politics and Space, 39*(1), 74–93. doi.org/10.1177/2399654419887970

Nicholas, J. (2012). Representing the modern man: Beauty, culture, and masculinity in early twentieth century Canada. In C. Greig & W. Martino (Eds.), *Canadian men and masculinities: Historical and contemporary perspectives* (pp. 139–195). Canadian Scholars.

Oldstone-Moore, C. (2017). *Of beards and men: The revealing history of facial hair.* University of Chicago Press.

Paterson, K. (2014). "It's harder to catch a boy because they're tougher": Using fairytales in the classroom to explore children's understandings of gender. *Alberta Journal of Educational Research, 60*(3), 474–490. https://www.researchgate.net/publication/292849217_It's_harder_to_catch_a_boy_because_they're_tougher_Using_fairytales_in_the_classroom_to_explore_children's_understandings_of_gender

Peter, T., Campbell, C. P., & Taylor, C. (2021). *Still in every class in every school: Final report on the second climate survey on homophobia, biphobia, and transphobia in Canadian schools.* Egale Canada Human Rights Trust.

Potvin, L. (2021). It's not all rainbows and unicorns: Straight teacher allies reflect on privilege. *Journal of LGBT Youth, 18*(3), 273–286. doi.org/10.1080/19361653.2020.1719952

Preece, S., & Bullingham, R. (2022). Gender stereotypes: The impact upon perceived roles and practice of in-service teachers in physical education. *Sport, Education And Society, 27*(3), 259–271. doi.org/10.1080/13573322.2020.1848813

Pyle, K. (2020). Reclaiming traditional gender roles: A Two-Spirit critique. In S. Nickel & A. Fehr (Eds.), *In good relation: History, gender, and kinship in Indigenous feminisms* (pp. 109–121). University of Manitoba Press.

Riley, T. (2014). Boys are like puppies, girls aim to please: How teachers' gender stereotypes may influence student placement decisions and classroom teaching. *Alberta Journal of Educational Research, 60*(1), 1–21. doi.org/10.11575/ajer.v60i1.55729

Ringrose, J. (2007). Successful girls? Complicating post-feminist, neo-liberal discourses of educational achievement and gender equality. *Gender and Education, 19,* 471–89. doi.org/10.1080/09540250701442666

Rippon, G. (2019). *Gender and our brains: How new neuroscience explodes the myths of the male and female minds.* Random House Canada.

Rymarz, R. (2017). Considering governance of Catholic schools in Canada: Some insights for Australia. *eJournal of Catholic Education in Autraliasia, 3*(1), 1–20. https://researchonline.nd.edu.au/ecea/vol3/iss1/3

Sadker, D., & Zittleman, K. (2009). *Still failing at fairness: How gender bias cheats girls and boys in school and what we can do about it.* Scribner.

Schiffrin-Sands, L. (2021). He said he said: Boysplaining in a primary classroom. *Gender and Education, 33*(6), 661–675. doi.org/10.1080/09540253.2020.1831442

Skelton, C. (2010). Gender and achievement: Are girls the "success stories" of restructured education systems? *Educational Review, 62*(2), 131–142. doi.org/10.1080/00131910903469536

Skelton, J. W. (2022). Schools often fail to expect trans and nonbinary elementary children: What gender independent, nonbinary, and trans children desire. *Teachers College Record, 124*(8), 244–274. doi.org/10.1177/0161468122112624

UNESCO. (2018). *International technical guidelines of sexuality education.* www.unfpa.org/sites/default/files/pub-pdf/ITGSE.pdf

Van der Vleuten, M., Jaspers, E., Maas, I., & van der Lippe, T. (2016). Boys' and girls' educational choices in secondary education: The role of gender ideology. *Educational Studies, 42*(2), 181–200. doi.org/10.1080/03055698.2016.1160821

Wall, K. (2019). *Persistence and representation of women in STEM programs.* Statistics Canada. www150.statcan.gc.ca/n1/pub/75-006-x/2019001/article/00006-eng.htm

Warren, K., Mitten, D., D'Amore, C., & Lotz, E. (2019). The gendered hidden curriculum of adventure education. *Journal of Experiential Education, 42*(2), 140–154. doi.org/10.1177/1053825918813398

Weaver-Hightower, M. B. (2010). Oatmeal facials and sock wrestling: The perils and promises of extra-curricular strategies for "fixing" boys' education. *Discourse: Studies in the Cultural Politics of Education, 31*(5), 683–697. doi.org/10.1080/01596306.2010.516953

# CHAPTER 9
# Disruptive Stories: Straight Teachers Navigating Queer Allyship in Ontario Schools

*Leigh Potvin*

Schools are microcosms, institutions that reflect and reproduce the norms and values of society at large (Wotherspoon, 2004). Foucault (1978) argues that all spaces, both public and private, are guided and informed by relations of power (the way that power exists and is exercised in relation to others). Building on Foucault, Delpit (1988) argues that relations of power govern institutions such as schools and that teacher allies have access to power by virtue of the authority assigned to them by the institution. This becomes increasingly complex when factors like gender, sexuality, class, and race are taken into consideration (McCall, 2005). In other words, straight white teachers benefit from systemic advantage. Teacher allies, Delpit (1998) suggests, can "agitate for change—pushing gatekeepers to open their doors to a variety of styles and codes" (p. 292). I suggest here that the work of opening these doors for Two-Spirit/lesbian/gay/bisexual/transgender/queer/questioning/intersex/asexual (2SLGBTQIA+) students is integral to their development so they may flourish and reach their full potential as human beings. Indeed, schools are frequent sites of homophobia and transphobia—both systemic and incidental. These injustices reinforce hegemonic patriarchal narratives about gender and sexuality and hamper students' growth and flourishing.

In this chapter, straight teachers discuss their actions as allies for 2SLGBTQIA+ students, including their disruptive stories of allyship. This is especially important given the fact that homophobia, **heterosexism**, and **heteronormativity** continue to dominate in everyday school life, all three of which regulate how straightness is performed, protected, and valorized (Kosciw et al., 2012; Taylor

& Peter, 2011; Taylor et al., 2015; Yep, 2002). Through this discussion of the factors that influence and affect straight teacher allies and their advocacy, and their so-called disruptive stories of allyship, I aim to shed light on the complexity of ally experiences. I showcase these narratives to demonstrate ways in which allies are not consistently effective supporters for the marginalized youth with whom they work. For, if allies are positioned as heroes, 2SLGBTQIA+ students remain targets, victims, and martyrs (Rofes, 2004).

## SITUATING MYSELF

I am a queer white cisgender university professor and parent. The research that informs this manuscript was conducted for my doctoral dissertation; during this time, I publicly identified as a straight ally, having not yet fully realized (in all senses of the word) my queer bisexual identity. Before entering academia full-time, I was a secondary school teacher in Ontario (Canada). As a teacher, I led gay-straight alliances (GSAs) and worked with 2SLGBTQIA+ youth on advocacy initiatives, entering this work alongside 2SLGBTQIA+ youth with institutional authority and a lot of social privilege. I have written in detail elsewhere about a formative experience in which I used Twitter (now known as X) to tell a joke that was homophobic (Potvin, 2019, 2020). I was called out by my peers. I apologized. This experience from transgression to call-out to apology formed the basis of my doctoral dissertation work. It helped me pose questions (to myself and others) about what I perceived at the time as the static nature of an ally identity.

In Margaret's (2010) study of settler-Indigenous allyship, she claims that being an ally is "a practice and a process—not an identity. It is an on-going practice that is learned and developed through experience" (p. 12). Being an ally is meaningless as a concept if it is not put into practice (Margaret, 2010). Key qualities of allies include courage and endurance, or what Margaret understands as "messing up, learning, picking up and keeping on" (p. 12). Huelskamp (2014) also describes a process of stumbling through allyship. In this chapter, I explore the way educators move through the messiness of ally experiences. Before so doing, some context of the oppressive forces in schools and the importance of those willing to resist them, including allies, is warranted.

## WHY ARE TEACHER ALLIES IMPORTANT?

Anti-oppressive education is rooted in the notion that all forms of oppression in educational contexts are linked (Kumashiro, 2000, 2002, 2004). Teachers can resist oppression to create safer learning environments for all students.

Kumashiro's (2000) anti-oppressive pedagogy provides a mechanism for confronting heteronormativity, specifically in schools and classrooms. It suggests a platform for educators who seek to end discrimination in all its many forms and intersections—including, but not limited to, sexism/heterosexism, racism, classism, and ableism—within their classrooms and schools. Being able to name oppression is a first critical step in the process, and it requires seeing inequity and/or relations of power playing out in a systematically disadvantageous way for individuals or groups in a school or classroom. Addressing oppressions in an intersectional way means educators should confront all forms of oppression (sexism, racism, classism, homophobia, and heterosexism) simultaneously and together. Changing oppressive dynamics rooted in these power inequities requires what Kumashiro (2004) calls *disruptive knowledge* not as an end, but rather as "a means toward the always-shifting end/goal of learning more" (p. 34). I frame the pedagogically rich stories of the teacher allies included in this manuscript as *disruptive stories*. They are often the kinds of stories that allies would rather not tell for fear that they will invite criticism or because they feel shame about them. These stories disrupt the narrative of allyship as a simple series of actions and/or as a static identity category. Bringing disruptive stories to the fore, I highlight their enriching potential to shift the course of allyship.

Yep (2002) outlines the violent impact of homophobia, heterosexism, and heteronormativity on everyday life for 2SLGBTQIA+ students. Like other scholars critical of the dominance of heterosexuality (see Martino, 1999; Meyer, 2007; Rodriguez & Pinar, 2007), Yep (2002) explains that heteronormativity is powerful because of its "invisibility disguised as 'natural,' 'normal,' 'universal'—its 'it-goes-without-saying' character" (p. 168). Heterosexuality maintains its hegemony in schools as long as it remains uncontested and unquestioned (Ingraham & Saunders, 2016). Finley (2011) argues that heteronormativity and heteropatriarchy (heterosexual and male dominance) are key features of a colonized society. Put differently, the normalization of straightness and male dominance are joint forces under colonization. Heteronormativity and heteropatriarchy are key areas of focus to challenge colonialism. Finley (2011) and Barker (2017) demonstrate how queer politics and anti-colonial (decolonizing) movements are rooted in resistance to intersectional oppressions, which also exist within schools. Often, the leaders of social change in schools are students and teaching staff and not the formalized leadership of administrators (Kitchen & Bellini, 2013; LaPointe, 2014). Griffin and Ouellett (2002) contend that institutional leaders and policies should guide these social changes. Many 2SLGBTQIA+ youth and adults work toward greater equity in schools as part of GSAs or on administrative or policy-developing committees (Griffin & Ouellett, 2002; Kitchen & Bellini, 2013; Ngo, 2003). There are also many straight-identified staff and student allies who participate in GSAs (Kitchen & Bellini, 2013; Kosciw et al., 2012; LaPointe, 2014; Taylor & Peter, 2011; Taylor et al., 2015; see also chapter 8).

Short (2013) challenges people outside schools to assume responsibility and shift heteronormative culture, emphasizing that teachers and principals alone should not be responsible for creating this change. What follows is a presentation of straight teacher ally experiences (and ideas) about allyship in schools. The teachers shed light on their experiences in schools and within some of their stories demonstrate the queer work being done in their schools and what some of them think needs to be done to continue pushing the boundaries of normalized heterosexuality in schools.

As homophobia, heterosexism, and heteronormativity remain pervasive forces in school and society, it is important for queer teachers and their allies to resist these norms. Noteworthy, however, is the reality that with violence (systemic and individual) toward 2SLGBTQIA+ communities in Canada (and the United States), the role of conscientious allies is increasingly important as queer educators (and students) may not be safe to come out in their professional lives or otherwise. Teacher allies occupy an important space of leveraging their privilege to start conversations, advocate for policy changes, and create curricula that support the flourishing of queer students and teachers in schools (LaPointe, 2014). It is also important for these same teacher allies to remain rigorous in their reflexive practice to ensure that allyship does not become complacent and static (Potvin, 2020). I present disruptive stories here to deepen a collective understanding of the messiness of allyship and the ways that disruptive stories—like my own shared above—can enrich one's commitment to allyship rather than being a highlight reel of good deeds.

## TEACHERS' STORIES

The participants in this study are teachers from rural and urban regions across Ontario, Canada's most populous province. Participants range in age from 25 to 60 years. Their teaching, and consequently teacher ally, experiences are varied; some have two years' teaching experience and others have more than 25 years' experience.

### Making Sense of Allyship: Disruptive Stories

I argue elsewhere (Potvin, 2016) that allies have much to learn from their more challenging experiences, their disruptive stories. Too often, allies want to tell the story of the great work they did to positively affect lives; these are what could be called their "good stories." I think, however, that people tend to learn from their stumbling and fumbling throughout allyship (Huelskamp, 2014; Margaret, 2010). In sharing the stories of these mishandled events, allies maintain a sense of humility in their practices. Thus, during the interviews, I intentionally elicited stories that reflect this stumbling and fumbling or the messy work of living in a way that is allied with 2SLGBTQIA+ students (and colleagues). Allies (and people with privilege) are often eager to share stories that portray them as benevolent and successful in their social justice activities. At the same time, they are reticent to share stories that might expose ignorance about their unacknowledged privilege.

Homophobic parents, overly cautious administrators, and their own stumbles as allies are sources of great concern for participants. One participant shared how her students' sexism and homophobia perturbed her:

> [These situations] made me start to really dislike the kids in question because I felt they were also disrespecting me as a woman and that they were laughing at me behind my back. I connected with the gay teachers, who were generous enough to be open and vulnerable about their identities, only to be mocked by a group of students I had taught and known from the time they were in kindergarten. It hurt me that none of my lessons over the years about kindness and equity had sunk in.

For another participant, recognizing one's capacity to work effectively as an ally was evident in an observation that "I have had to come to terms with the limits of my own understanding of the issues affecting trans students." Working in a school where a large part of the student body came from conservative religious families, another participant shared the following:

> Working alongside a queer colleague, I did a lot of anti-homophobia work. However, we received a fair bit of pushback from parents and the admin. Constantly, I was told by the VP that it wasn't "in their culture" to accept (let alone celebrate) the 2SLGBTQIA+ experience. Many students didn't show up (or were pulled out by parents) on our workshop day. It was difficult and frustrating because my work as an ally intersected with all kinds of other issues of race, religion, culture, etc. It was tough to navigate my own privilege in that environment, while still pushing for a more inclusive school for the 2SLGBTQIA+ population.

An element of this response that is troubling is the way the participant presents the tension between conservative religious forces (perceived or otherwise) and anti-homophobia education. There are ways to navigate these tensions in a collaborative way with community groups, such as working with mentors and/or leaders within the community. However, the language the participant uses here does seem less collaborative and more divisive.

In terms of overall impact of their allyship and the capacity to assist students in making lifelong changes to their behaviour, one participant pondered, "I'm troubled that I'm only changing local [classroom] behaviours and not changing minds." And the concerns go beyond students for this study's participants, as is revealed in the following reflection: "sometimes I'm afraid to challenge 'macho' behaviour in the schools that I work in … I'm not proud of it and I'm especially unlikely to speak up around older colleagues." Many of these statements are resonant with my own experiences of both personal failure to challenge colleagues' language or assumptions and unexpressed distaste for students' homophobic or sexist stances (Potvin, 2011). The discourse of professionalism is relevant to participants (Meyer, 2007) and lack of teacher training regarding challenging heterosexism in schools (Ngo, 2003). This highlights the pervasive pressure within schools to conform to heteronormativity and heterosexism, which reinforces the need for straight allies to play an integral part in resisting them. Without that resistance from the privileged vantage point that allies offer, how can caring educators expect their 2SLGBTQIA+ students to feel safe and comfortable to grow and flourish fulsomely into and through their queer identities?

One participant candidly shared their thoughts about a personal behaviour that they found very difficult to reconcile with their stance as an ally, and one that many people would find troubling and shocking: "Something that troubles me is the choice of words or jokes I'll make that don't align with my values and beliefs. I think a lot of it comes from years of calling everything *gay* in the place of *lame, stupid, boring* as a teen and pre-teen. Even recently, I've found myself using the term *faggot*, which is to reference a person who is behaving like a terrible human being."

This response is shocking to uncover because I assumed that if a person identified as an ally enough to participate in a study about allyship in schools, then the participant group would not include people who actively use homophobic language. As such, I present this quotation not as exemplary ally behaviour but, rather, as an indication of a need for continued reflexivity for the participant and, hopefully, behavioural changes. This participant's story highlights the complexity of experiences for allies, reinforces calls from marginalized groups for allies to consider their privilege before self-identifying as allies, and significantly probes the limitations of simply self-identifying as an ally. This example also problematizes the notion that calling oneself or identifying as an ally is enough. For many, simply calling oneself an ally or calling one's classroom a safe space is insufficient and short-sighted. The work of true allyship is to walk the walk of one's commitment to social justice, equity, and queer liberation within schools.

## The Messiness of Allyship: Disrupting Self-Perception

*Samuel:* Some of Samuel's most rewarding moments as an ally occur at provincial and national conferences for allies, where he represents his school and school board. A conference he recently attended (before the interview), however, involved a negative experience over which he felt considerable shame and remorse:

> I had a student who I took to a conference last month and I was speaking. I was one of the guest speakers at [the conference] and my topic [which focused on how to be an effective ally and what it means to be an ally] was meant for teachers and there were some students who were in the group and I made the colossal mistake of not giving a trigger warning [because I was going to talk about some sensitive material, like suicide]. And I mentioned about the suicide of a student from our school, [maybe five or six years ago] and it was the loss of that student that really lit the fire under me to work toward reconciliation with our native students and also bridging the gaps between our queer students and the rest of the school. She was both Anishinaabekwe [from *Anishinaabe*, which, in English, translates to *Ojibwe and female*] and lesbian. And she took her own life because of not being accepted by members of the community and her family. I made the colossal mistake of not making that trigger warning known and without reading the crowd and one of my students was at the back of the room and she was her cousin.

The fallout of this incident involved psychological trauma for the student, including suicidal thoughts. Samuel and the other practitioners at the conference helped the student access counselling support. While this action did not erase the severity of the initial mistake, it helped the student cope with the fallout of Samuel's misstep. In our interview, the student disclosed to Samuel that she was identifying him to her counsellor as part of her support network. In other words, a closer student-teacher relationship emerged from this very frightening situation.

*Julia:* Throughout our interview, Julia demonstrated humility and a commitment to growth as an ally. The bad story she recounted took place at a dinner party:

> I don't even have the right vocabulary sometimes, like I don't even have the words to say what I want to say, but part of my learning was becoming okay with my ignorance around it and being, admitting uncertainty. I have a friend who is transgender, which I didn't realize. I had known her as a woman my whole life, [we've] been close forever. I didn't realize that now she was identifying as a man so *he* in *his* circle of friends is known as he and I didn't realize that. I was making a toast at his birthday, and I said, "You know she's the most wonderful woman" and the room was just like silent, and I was like, "Oh shit! I didn't know." But making these mistakes and being okay with these mistakes and learning to … learning that your ignorance is okay as long as you are trying to be reflective and understand.

I relate to Julia's self-reflexive thinking here; however, it is important to note that the ignorance of a privileged straight ally can have serious consequences for marginalized people. Hopefully, thoughtful reflection leads to more thoughtful actions with less negative impact.

*Lucy:* At the outset of her interview, Lucy recounted a story from the teacher education program she entered after graduate school. In this program, she focused many of her studies on feminist politics and her privileged identity as a white woman. One day, a course instructor brought in a guest speaker to discuss the significance of the hijab for Muslim women. Most of the students in her class (including Lucy) were white; there was only one female Muslim student. Lucy described the course as "sensitivity training for different issues—all the issues that we might encounter in schools."

> [The instructor] brought in an outside group of young Muslim women to [speak to our class]. The first problem [was that] it wasn't laid out what they were there to do. We [the pre-service teachers in the class] thought [the guest speakers were there to] tell us about how to interact with Muslim students and parents. So, [the guest speakers] came in feeling like we hadn't done our research and we shouldn't even ask about veils [because it is] none of our fucking business and [the implication was that we were] a bunch of white teachers [living in a big city, why] don't you know how to deal with this?

In a later class, while the (mostly white) teacher candidates were debriefing the experience, short-sighted opinions (including Lucy's) about hijab-wearing women emerged. Lucy elaborated:

> I used to feel sorry for women in veils [a word sometimes used to describe the hijab and niqab] and not that I would ever say anything, but I kind of agree in the sense that "yeah, I don't understand why a woman ... why a culture would support suppressing women in this way" and so I stood up and I don't remember what I said but I do know there was a Muslim girl who stood up and said, "I'm so sick of you white people, shut up, I can't handle this" and I said, "Well why don't you explain it to us?" and she said, "Don't single me out! I'm not a token Muslim here to explain my culture or my religion to you!" and ran out crying. And so, then I immediately was like, "No, no! wait! I'm sorry!" ... I just wanted to know how not to do what I did in that moment.

Lucy's story of her experience in her pre-service teacher training program shaped her thinking as a straight white person. While this example is not about 2SLGBTQIA+ issues, it demonstrates how even supportive, well-informed allies can forget their privilege. Lucy went on to say that this experience shaped the way she teaches critical issues in her classroom so that marginalized students feel safe and not centred out like the student was in her teacher education course.

*Trueman:* Trueman struggles with his commitment to his allyship, a point that is demonstrated in his use of homophobic language:

> For some reason my go-to to describe the behaviour [of a person acting like a jerk is to call him] a faggot. And [I] said it with angry conviction. [That's] the only time that word ever comes out [of my mouth], when someone is behaving like a total asshole. That's [the] word I think suits their behaviour.

As a self-identified ally, Trueman should consider a greater commitment to anti-homophobia, especially in his school and community. Effective and responsible allies need to put their intentions into action. In the interview, which occurred over Skype using video, I expressed my shock at his use of homophobic language. I did not verbalize much in response, but my facial expressions said it all. I encouraged Trueman to think about what motivates him to use inappropriate language and to consider his **straight privilege**. I suggested that he consider his role as an ally beyond having some gay friends and going to queer nightclubs. This was difficult to do as an interviewer because, due to the voluntary nature of the interview, I did not want to critique Trueman too harshly. I relied on our conversation about straight privilege to begin to unpack his ideas. At the end of our interview, he expressed gratitude at having the opportunity to discuss these experiences and to be able to examine them a little. He also acknowledged that he had never considered his straight privilege before. I tried to use the opportunity to educate Trueman rather than condemn him.

*Kelly:* At the start of her teaching career, Kelly lived with a roommate and friend. During this time, they watched a popular movie with a scene where two friends jokingly refer to each other using homophobic slurs, something Kelly and her friend would re-enact with each other at home. She decided to re-enact these scenes in the staff room at work and to other staff members. Now that Kelly is a committed ally, she says it "makes me cringe to think about it" and "makes me want to puke when I think about it." Kelly hopes that "nobody remembers [me re-enacting these scenes] now that I publicly identify as an ally. I hope people don't remember me that way." She works in school administration, providing leadership and training for staff on 2SLGBTQIA+ rights. Kelly uses this example to demonstrate that "without doing work on privilege, it's impossible" to be an ally.

The disruptive stories participants shared with me in the interviews reflect their learning as allies, which is ongoing. The most difficult part of these stories for the majority of the participants is where they acted in a discriminatory way and/or perpetuated stereotypes. I relay participants' disruptive stories here to highlight the complexity of ally experiences. In some cases, their stories involve perpetuating homophobia, racism, and/or transphobia. These narratives demonstrate the prominence of heteronormativity and straight, white, cisgender privilege even among well-intentioned allies. A pressure can exist for allies to be perfect and to never make mistakes, as these mistakes can significantly affect the very people someone is seeking to ally themselves with. All participants were uncomfortable and embarrassed about telling their stories. For example, Lucy said she felt uncomfortable telling hers but related to my own story, and so she felt more comfortable sharing her own bad story. In fact, it was one of the first things she discussed in her interview. She wanted to "get it out there and over with." Julia referred to herself as "dumb" and to the embarrassment she felt when recounting her story. I argue, however, that the discomfort in retelling is a necessary part of the process of acknowledging straight privilege. This recognition is a concrete step toward challenging heteronormativity and heterosexism in schools. I believe, in general, that the participants' discomfort was alleviated by the fact that I had told them my own disruptive story in video format. It created an openness and willingness to share challenging moments and to avoid presenting ourselves as perfect educators and allies. Lucy and Kelly especially used these stories (and experiences), much like me, as fodder for better allyship. These cringeworthy and frustrating moments demonstrate some components of allyship that may not be at the core of every conversation about the good work that allies do. Nevertheless, they are powerful experiences that shape the way that allies themselves frame their work and, in some cases, begin to understand straight privilege and heteronormativity.

## CONCLUSION

These shared stories help create a fuller picture of what it means to be a teacher ally in K–12 schools in Ontario. Using Margaret's (2010) idea of allyship involving messing up, learning, picking up, and keeping on as well as Huelskamp's (2014) idea of stumbling through allyship, this chapter helps extrapolate on the experiences of straight teachers in K–12 schools. It's also setting the table for, or inviting, teachers and teacher candidates to consider how they can support queer people and queerness in the schools where they work and the communities where they live. Participants who seem to bring the most critical or queered pedagogy focus on the role that their own straight privilege plays in their ally role. Disruptive stories of allyship present a more nuanced perspective of what it means to be an ally and of what learning as an ally looks like: multifaceted and fraught with tensions (Pinar, 1998; Seidman, 1994). I urge allies to deepen their commitment to queer school spaces and disrupt the status quo, business-as-usual heterosexism, homophobia, and heteronormativity that fester in schools. To see the lived oppression of 2SLGBTQIA+ youth in schools and do nothing is a salient example of straight privilege at work. In other words, it is from a position of luxury that one can choose, or not, to be involved in working to make schools safer, more equitable places. Wells (2007) articulates the impact of the teachers, his "silent tormentors," those who failed speak out and act out against oppression. The toxic silence around gender- and sexuality-based harassment in schools must be broken, and I think that straight allies can be well situated to do so. Few things grow—or flourish—from a base of toxicity. In other words, what might be the positive impact for 2SLGBTQIA+ students who were supported, nurtured, and cared for in ways that nourished their identities and interests? We must provide them with a foundation from which to flourish and realize their full potential as human beings.

## KEY TERMS

**Heteronormativity:** Normalized straightness or heterosexuality, often working in tandem with anti-gay (homophobic) sentiments and heterosexism.

**Heterosexism:** Presumed straightness or heterosexuality, particularly expressed in ways that mobilize discrimination toward 2SLGBTQIA+ people.

**Straight privilege:** Unearned systemic opportunities and advantage on the basis of heterosexuality/straightness that are often unseen and unacknowledged.

## DISCUSSION QUESTIONS AND ACTIVITIES

1. Do you have a "disruptive story" like some of those shared in this chapter? If so, share it with a colleague or the class. Were you the speaker or the listener? What did you learn from this incident?
2. How can you queer your classroom and/or curriculum? What approaches can you take to ensure that queer students feel safe and supported?
3. How have you encountered homophobia, heterosexism, and/or heteronormativity in the past? Are there particular tools or strategies that have worked? How can these strategies be mobilized in a school or learning context?
4. Several teacher stories were shared in this chapter. In small groups, consider one teacher's story as a case study. Read the story. Consider the main problem or lesson to be learned in the story. What are some next steps you would recommend in the classroom or school? How do these stories help others to understand allyship as a complex experience rather than a static identity?

## REFERENCES

Barker, J. (2017). Introduction: Critically sovereign. In J. Barker (Ed.), *Critically sovereign: Indigenous gender, sexuality, and feminist studies* (pp. 1–44). Duke University Press.

Delpit, L. (1988). The silenced dialogue: Power and pedagogy in educating other people's children. *Harvard Educational Review, 58*(3), 280–299. doi.org/10.17763/haer.58.3.c43481778r528qw4

Finley, C. (2011). Decolonizing the queer Native body (and recovering the Native bull-dyke): Bringing "sexy back" and out of Native studies' closet. In Q. L. Driskill, C. Finley, B. Gilley, & S. L. Morgensen (Eds.), *Queer Indigenous studies: Critical interventions in theory, politics, and literature* (pp. 32–42). University of Arizona Press.

Foucault, M. (1978). *The history of sexuality* (Vol. 1). Random House.

Griffin, P., & Ouellett, M. L. (2002). Going beyond gay-straight alliances to make schools safe for lesbian, gay, bisexual, and transgender students. *ANGLES: The Policy Journal of the Institute for Gay and Lesbian Strategic Studies, 6*, 1–8. https://api.semanticscholar.org/CorpusID:151302578

Huelskamp, B. (2014). On creating and framing cissexual advocacy with trans* community in higher education. *The Vermont Connection, 35*(1), 55–61. http://scholarworks.uvm.edu/tvc/vol35/iss1/7

Ingraham, C., & Saunders, C. (2016). Heterosexual imaginary. *The Wiley Blackwell Encyclopedia of Gender and Sexuality Studies*, 1–4. doi.org/10.1002/9781118663219.wbegss762

Kitchen, J., & Bellini, C. (2013). Making schools safe and inclusive: Gay-straight alliances and school climate in Ontario. *Canadian Journal of Educational Administration and Policy, 146*(1), 1–37. www.umanitoba.ca/publications/cjeap/pdf_files/kitchen_bellini.pdf

Kosciw, J. G., Greytak, E. A., Bartkiewicz, M. J., Boesen, M. J., & Palmer, N. A. (2012). *The 2011 National School Climate Survey: The experiences of lesbian, gay, bisexual and transgender youth in our nation's schools*. GLSEN. www.glsen.org/sites/default/files/2020-04/2011%20GLSEN%20National%20School%20Climate%20Survey.pdf

Kumashiro, K. K. (2000). Toward a theory of anti-oppressive education. *Review of Educational Research, 70*(1), 25–53. doi.org/10.3102/00346543070001025

Kumashiro, K. K. (2002). *Troubling education: "Queer" activism and anti-oppressive pedagogy*. Routledge.

Kumashiro, K. K. (2004). *Against common sense: Teaching and learning toward social justice*. Routledge.

LaPointe, A. A. (2014). Gay–straight alliance (GSA) members' engagement with sex education in Canadian high schools. *Sex Education, 14*(6), 1–11. doi.org/10.1080/14681811.2014.914024

Margaret, J. (2010). *Working as allies: Winston Churchill fellowship report*. www.lynngehl.com/uploads/5/0/0/4/5004954/jenmargaret.pdf

Martino, W. (1999). "It's okay to be gay": Interrupting straight thinking in the English classroom. In W. J. Letts IV & J. T. Sears (Eds.), *Queering elementary education: Advancing the dialogue about sexualities and schooling* (pp. 137–150). Rowman & Littlefield.

McCall, L. (2005). The complexity of intersectionality. *Journal of Women in Culture and Society, 30*(3), 1771–1800. www.jstor.org/stable/10.1086/426800

Meyer, E. (2007). "But I'm not gay": What straight teachers need to know about queer theory. In N. M. Rodriguez & W. Pinar (Eds.), *Queering straight teachers: Discourse and identity in education* (pp. 15–29). Peter Lang.

Ngo, B. (2003). Citing discourses: Making sense of homophobia and heteronormativity at Dynamic High School. *Equity & Excellence in Education, 36*(2), 115–124. doi.org/10.1080/10665680303513

Pinar, W. F. (1998). Introduction. In W. F. Pinar (Ed.), *Queer theory in education* (pp. 1–39). Lawrence Erlbaum Associates.

Potvin, L. (2011). *Masculinity goes to class: Gender performances and anti-oppressive perspectives in a secondary classroom* [Master's thesis, Lakehead University]. http://lurepository.lakeheadu.ca:8080/handle/2453/454

Potvin, L. (2016). Radical heterosexuality: Straight teacher activism in schools: Does ally-led activism work? *Confero: Essays on Education, Philosophy and Politics*, *4*(1), 9–36. doi.org/10.3384/confero.2001-4562.160614

Potvin, L. (2019). Straight teacher allies: Lessons from compassionate educators. In A. Jule (Ed.), *The compassionate educator: Understanding social issues and the ethics of care in Canadian schools* (pp. 73–90). Canadian Scholars.

Potvin, L. (2020). It's not all rainbows and unicorns: Straight teacher allies reflect on privilege. *Journal of LGBT Youth*, *18*(3), 273–286. doi.org/10.1080/19361653.2020.1719952

Rodriguez, N. M., & Pinar, W. (2007). *Queering straight teachers: Discourse and identity in education*. Peter Lang.

Rofes, E. (2004). Martyr-target-victim: Interrogating narratives of persecution and suffering among queer youth. In M. L. Rasmussen, E. Rofes, & S. Talburt (Eds.), *Youth and sexualities: Pleasure, subversion, and insubordination in and out of schools* (pp. 41–62). doi.org/10.1057/9781403981912_3

Seidman, S. (1994). Queer-ing sociology, sociologizing queer theory: An introduction. *Sociological Theory*, *12*(2), 166–177. doi.org/10.2307/201862

Short, D. (2013). *"Don't be so gay!" Queers, bullying, and making schools safe*. UBC Press.

Taylor, C., & Peter, T. (2011). *Every class in every school: Final report on the first national climate survey on homophobia, biphobia, and transphobia in Canadian schools*. Egale Canada. http://egale.ca/wp-content/uploads/2011/05/EgaleFinalReport-web.pdf

Taylor, C., Peter, T., Campbell, C., Meyer, E., Ristock, J., & Short, D. (2015). *The Every Teacher Project on 2SLGBTQIA+-inclusive education in Canada's K–12 schools: Final report*. Teachers' Society. http://news-centre.uwinnipeg.ca/wp-content/uploads/2016/01/EveryTeacher_FinalReport_v12.pdf

Wells, K. (2007). Diverse threads in social fabrics: Autobiography and arts-informed educational initiatives for social justice. In I. Killoran & K. P. Jimenez (Eds.), *"Unleashing the unpopular": Talking about sexual orientation and gender diversity in education* (pp. 117–128). Association for Childhood Education International.

Wotherspoon, T. (2004). *The sociology of education in Canada: Critical perspectives*. Oxford University Press.

Yep, G. A. (2002). From homophobia and heterosexism to heteronormativity: Toward the development of a model of queer interventions in the university classroom. *Journal of Lesbian Studies*, *6*(3–4), 163–176. doi.org/ 10.1300/J155v06n03_14

# PART V

## INDIGENOUS EDUCATION: REMEMBERING THE PAST, ACKNOWLEDGING THE PRESENT, FOSTERING COMMUNITIES OF FLOURISHING

# CHAPTER 10
# Tribal Critical Race Theory, *Wâhkôhtowin*, and Decolonizing Canadian Education

*Joanie Crandall*

Tribal critical race theory (**TribalCrit**), which extends critical race theory (CRT), serves as a frame by which learners and educators can come to understand and co-participate in redefining approaches to Indigenizing and decolonizing education. TribalCrit supports the enactment of Indigenizing, decolonizing, inclusive, multicultural, anti-racist, anti-oppressive education. In conjunction with TribalCrit, it is useful to explore Elder Albert Marshall's (2018) work—building on *Etuaptmumk* or two-eyed seeing—which makes the case for **apoqnmatultl'k jiksktuali'lk**, or learning together by learning to listen to each other, and as such, I suggest, helps to render TribalCrit more accessible for educators from a wide range of linguistic and cultural backgrounds.

TribalCrit and *apoqnmatultl'k jiksktuali'lk* are mutually supportive entry points for decolonizing and Indigenizing education. Considered in relation to Marshall's (2018) listening approach, Donald's (2021) framework of **wâhkôhtowin** offers a place from which both Indigenous and non-Indigenous can walk together and explore their unique cultural capital (Bourdieu, 2011), which contributes to richer educational contexts. In this chapter, I use the term *Indigenous* as inclusive of First Nations, Métis, and Inuit people in the land now known as Canada. Employing TribalCrit, building meaningful relationships through walking together and listening to each other's stories of experience, and drawing on Indigenous resources have the potential to create positive educational shifts. Exemplars used in the Arctic of Canada include the *Dene Kede Education: A Dene*

*Perspective* (Northwest Territories Department of Education, Culture and Employment, 1993; hereafter referred to as *Dene Kede*), *Inuuqatigiit: The Curriculum from the Inuit Perspective* (Northwest Territories Department of Education, Culture and Employment, 1996; hereafter referred to as *Inuuqatigiit*), and *Inuit Qaujimajatuqangit: Education Framework for Nunavut Curriculum* (Nunavut Department of Education, 2007; hereafter referred to as *Inuit Qaujimajatuqangit*), as well as *Ilitaunnikuliriniq: Foundation for Dynamic Assessment as Learning in Nunavut Schools* (Nunavut Department of Education, 2008a) and *Inuglugijaittuq: Foundation for Inclusive Education in Nunavut Schools* (Nunavut Department of Education, 2008b; hereafter referred to as *Ilitaunnikuliriniq* and *Inuglugijaittuq* respectively). Together, TribalCrit, *apoqnmatultl'k jiksktuali'lk*, and *wâhkôhtowin* can be employed to expand current pedagogical practices and support learners in critically engaging in their own culture, becoming more inclusive global citizens, creating connections across cultural boundaries, and flourishing (Nussbaum, 2002, 2006).

As this chapter unfolds, I provide an overview of TribalCrit, share my positionality, and outline the navigation of critical self-reflexivity. I discuss engaging with TribalCrit in teaching and learning contexts. I explore considerations for pre- and in-service educators in K–12 classrooms, building capabilities for the flourishing of all students, and building educator capacity. I then examine structures, policies, curriculum, and pedagogies that can promote flourishing.

## AN OVERVIEW OF TRIBAL CRITICAL RACE THEORY

Extending critical race theory (Ladson-Billings, 1998; Matias et al., 2014), TribalCrit (Brayboy, 2005) draws on counter-storytelling (Brayboy & Chin, 2019) and responds to the gap in CRT as a theory by which learners and educators can co-participate in redefining approaches to decolonizing and Indigenizing education. TribalCrit seeks to address the legal, political, and social liminality of American Indians—the common term used to refer to Indigenous Peoples in the United States—and "is rooted in the multiple, nuanced, and historically- and geographically-located epistemologies and ontologies found in Indigenous communities" (Brayboy, 2005, p. 427). TribalCrit offers the opportunity for a deeper engagement with topics and issues particularly related to Indigenous communities. Although Brayboy's writings are grounded in the American context, they apply to Canada and other countries that colonized local Indigenous Peoples. There is still a great amount of work to be done to explore the multiplicity of Indigenous epistemologies and ontologies within the borders of what is now known as Canada.

Brayboy (2005) identifies nine tenets that are essential to understand to fully engage TribalCrit in the classroom context:

- Racism and colonization and the ensuing negative effects on Indigenous Peoples are endemic in American society (p. 430).
- American hegemonic and imperialistic policies demonstrate the wide divergences between the concepts of Indigenous stewardship and white settler ownership in relation to land (p. 431).
- Indigenous Peoples living in the United States occupy a space of liminality that impacts their legal, political, and racialized identities (p. 432).
- Indigenous Peoples desire to have tribal autonomy, with decision-making power over land, resources, and tribal boundaries as well as the ability to engage nation to nation; self-determination (i.e., rejecting the role of the American government in the oversight of Indigenous Peoples); self-identification (i.e., the legitimacy for Indigenous groups to self-define); and tribal sovereignty (i.e., freedom from governmental control) (pp. 433–434).
- An Indigenous lens impacts conceptualizations of culture, knowledge, and power such that they are dialogic, both situated and dynamic (pp. 434–436).
- Governmental and educational policies are grounded in assimilationist goals, and it is important to support the interweaving of Indigenous Knowledge with non-Indigenous education (pp. 436–437).
- Indigenous tribal philosophies, beliefs, traditions, and visions for the future must underpin an understanding of Indigenous Peoples' lived realities and their resilience and inform self-education and self-determination (pp. 437–439).
- Oral narratives are valuable, representing cumulative knowledge, and are interconnected with theory—and the hearer of narratives bears responsibility for engaging thoughtfully and empathically with the narrative (pp. 439–440).
- Theory and practice are interrelated and demand that one expose and deconstruct inequalities and participate in enacting social change through activism, which will ultimately support tribal sovereignty (pp. 440–441).

Similarly, in Canada, the effects of colonization continue to be felt in urban and reserve Indigenous communities. Indigenous Peoples continue to experience marginalization in healthcare, education, and social justice and continue to fight for the rights of self-determination, self-identification, and tribal sovereignty. Indigenous communities continue to assert the need for engaging with language, culture, and traditional knowledge and continue to fight assimilationist educational goals. The last residential school in Canada closed only in 1996. Learning about Indigenous cultures underpins understanding Indigenous Peoples' lived realities and their resilience. The richness of Indigenous oral narratives requires close, careful attention as a responsible listener. It also must be recognized that theory and practice are interrelated. Here in Canada, as elsewhere, it is necessary to take responsibility for exposing and deconstructing inequalities and to participate in enacting social change.

While correlations for each of these tenets can easily be made between the American and Canadian contexts, the particular contexts of Indigenous Peoples across the country now known as Canada must each be considered individually while recognizing the similar challenges each community faces in accordance with the tenets above. It is worth deeper consideration of how individual lessons (do Amaral & Windchief, 2019), subject curriculum (Krueger, 2021), and places of learning can be reshaped through TribalCrit and the ideas of *apoqnmatultl'k jiksktuali'lk* and *wâhkôhtowin*, whether one is an Indigenous or non-Indigenous educator of kindergarten or post-secondary learners. Furthermore, advocating to expand decolonizing efforts at the district level is beneficial in ensuring that schools are more inclusive to Indigenous learners through district-supported, culturally relevant, and contextually responsive professional development (Campbell-Daniels, 2021), thus providing locally specific knowledge, building on existing skills, and increasing confidence in engaging in or extending equity, diversity, inclusion, and decolonization (EDID) initiatives.

## POSITIONALITY

I am a non-Indigenous person. Before I became a grades 7–12 teacher in an Indigenous community, my knowledge of Indigenous people was limited to what I had learned in school. However, through a focus on listening in my travels throughout Canada as an educator and administrator, I have learned to speak a little Nêhiyawêwin, Inuktitut, Inuvialuktun, Gwich'in, Dene, Tłı̨chǫ, Wolastoqey, Mi'kmaq, Anishininiimowin, Anishinaabemowin, Saulteaux, Kanien'kéha, Dakelh, and Michif, and to each of my teachers I am grateful. I recognize the privilege of that which I have gained from the experiences I have had working in Indigenous communities and the simultaneously privileged and partial nature of what I have learned as a non-Indigenous person. I have learned much through the process of extended listening in the communities in which I have lived and worked and the personal relationships and in-person and online classes into which I have been welcomed. I have had the opportunity to incorporate Indigenous resources, curricula, and frameworks into educational contexts from kindergarten to graduate-level classes. My experiences have reinforced the belief that wherever possible, local culturally relevant resources, curricula, and frameworks should be employed, and I agree with Lamb and Godlewska (2021) that this approach is necessarily going to involve increasing resources for building capacity in Indigenous communities and supporting pre-service and in-service educators. In my journeys to learn about Indigenous Knowledge, language, and culture, I continue to learn about where to find provincial/territorial resources to build my knowledge, and I continue to build reciprocal relationships with community members and language teachers. Engaging with texts and topics through supportive mentoring relationships and friendships and developing awareness of Indigenous languages, epistemologies, and methodologies, I have learned, helps strengthen one's awareness of the need to further social justice in a wide range of learning contexts and to become more conscious of one's own cultural framework. This chapter represents my effort to share part of my learning-journey-in-progress and acknowledge my responsibility to participate in positive educational change to decolonize education.

## NAVIGATING CRITICAL SELF-REFLEXIVITY

Practising critical self-reflexivity is necessary as a non-Indigenous educator engaging in learning about Indigenous cultures, languages, and knowledges. The notion of self-reflexivity needs to be explored in some detail here as self-reflexivity is arguably particularly important when engaging with TribalCrit. Within the context of intercultural communication and social justice (Akkari & Radhouane, 2022), self-reflexivity offers a means of developing intercultural sensitivity (Wallin & Scribe, 2022). Métissage, for example, is one approach that supports intercultural learning as it seeks to navigate the complexities of relationality through awareness of historical, cultural, and social contexts (Donald, 2012). I echo here the ongoing calls that have been made for attention to cultural specificity (Womack, 1999; Younging, 2018) and for respecting the complexities of cultural boundaries (Vowel, 2016) in building mutually respectful relationships. Further, I have come to believe that teaching learners how to engage in self-reflexivity is increasingly valuable as a means of enacting EDID. Pursuing approaches informed by EDID can enact strong connections between curriculum, culture, language, and place.

Self-reflexivity also means acknowledging one's learned relationship to different ways of knowing and being, such as familiarity with Eurocentric approaches to learning and the historical exclusion of Indigenous languages, cultures, epistemologies, ontologies, and pedagogies from most mainstream schools in Canada. Change is possible, however, by learning together in positive and productive ways. TribalCrit and *apoqnmatultl'k jiksktuali'lk*, then, contextualize in critical terms Freire's (1985) teacher-learner/learner-teacher framework. Despite the limitations of Freire's work in relation to colonial ideologies, critical pedagogy continues to be relevant as a means of Indigenous resistance (Kee & Carr-Chellman, 2019). Engaging with TribalCrit amplifies Indigenous resistance and helps to provide the lens through which to reshape pedagogy.

These exhortations are not intended to be prescriptive but rather seek to invite people—particularly non-Indigenous educators such as myself—to consider the significance of their geographical location and local Indigenous language(s) and culture(s) and how they might be respectfully incorporated, alongside other EDID supporting practices, into one's own professional praxis. What is included in learning opportunities must not be merely superficial. As a non-Indigenous person, positioning oneself as a learner alongside students, amplifying Indigenous voices rather than disenfranchising or subjugating them through neocolonial practices, can open doors to deeper dialogue. Creating a community of like-minded educators who can collaboratively move beyond the idea of a safe space to supporting each other in creating a brave space (Ali, 2017) in which they can collectively engage with TribalCrit, *apoqnmatultl'k jiksktuali'lk*, and *wâhkôhtowin* can be a compelling experience. The Office of the Treaty Commissioner (n.d.) has stated that "We Are All Treaty People," and as non-Indigenous people, that entails responsibility for learning about how to improve one's own context. Together, in the brave space created as a learning community of educators, learning about the Treaties established in the land now known as Canada, specifically the Treaties of the area in which one lives, for example, can be a powerful experience. Education is a foundational Treaty right, and delivering education that supports EDID requires contextualization. Non-Indigenous educators like me who wish to explore their own linguistic and cultural identity and engage in TribalCrit and EDID from a relational, learning perspective can also do so through such means as reflexive inquiry (Cunliffe, 2016), narrative inquiry (Clandinin & Connelly, 2004), or autoethnography (Bochner & Ellis, 2016). TribalCrit presents a way to take a positive step forward (Masta, 2022) through deepening relationships and advocating for schools, boards, and governments to make positive changes related to decolonizing education.

## ENGAGING WITH TRIBAL CRITICAL RACE THEORY IN TEACHING AND LEARNING CONTEXTS

It is important to shape educational initiatives to meet all learners' needs, and TribalCrit offers a helpful lens through which to engage in such initiatives even when one is not Indigenous. TribalCrit provides a lens by which one can reflect upon one's own cultural lens and biases and connect with Indigenous Peoples and cultures in respectful terms, and, from this vantage point, become a more critically conscious citizen (Nussbaum, 2002, 2006). Recognition of the need for centring Indigenous Knowledge in places of education (Kovach, 2009) and the centrality of intergenerational, relational, and land-based pedagogies in Indigenous Knowledge systems (Carpena-Méndez et al., 2022) supports enacting positive change through Indigenization, a significant element of EDID initiatives that seek to create flourishing for all learners. Language, furthermore, is a significant cultural resource (Chiblow & Meighan, 2021), and it is important to look for opportunities to learn and incorporate Indigenous language as a form of language activism, which can support different forms of Indigenous knowing (Matsaw et al., 2020). As Williamson and Vizina (2017) have pointed out, because most current education systems do not accommodate local Indigenous cultures, there is a corresponding negative effect on Indigenous identity. While they write of an Arctic context, from the lens of my own experience supporting Indigenous learners, this assertion is valid beyond the Arctic. Employing TribalCrit can help to centre Indigenous cultures and identities.

It is important to recognize the political nature of and responsibility intrinsic to the use of Indigenous ontologies by non-Indigenous people because of the risk of recentring or reinforcing non-Indigenous ontologies, epistemologies, methodologies, and axiologies (Cameron et al., 2014, p. 24). As a non-Indigenous educator, I recognize this risk but wish to make a case here for learning from and drawing upon Indigenous ontologies in a respectful way, acknowledging one's own limitations while also celebrating being able to learn about and share what one learns, opening the door to further dialogue. It is my intention to encourage other non-Indigenous educators to engage similarly while schools continue their work to build capacity with higher numbers of Indigenous educators so that, in the interim, Indigenous approaches and texts are not minimized or excluded.

## CONSIDERATIONS FOR PRE- AND IN-SERVICE EDUCATORS IN K–12 CLASSROOMS

When engaging TribalCrit in the classroom, the practical considerations must be context-specific. Consider the value of engaging in ongoing personal and professional development opportunities to learn about Indigenous critical pedagogies, curricula, frameworks, texts, and supporting resources that are specific to the local community/communities and languages (Battiste & Henderson, 2009) as part of ongoing efforts to decolonize classrooms (Wallace-Casey, 2022). Studies have shown that white educators continue to have limited cross-cultural awareness or experience (Richter et al., 2023; Sit et al., 2017; Sleeter, 2001) and increased attention to critical race consciousness in teacher education programs continues to be required (Baidoo-Anu et al., 2023; Lee & Lee, 2020). Personally, I did not think critically about the curriculum I learned in school because it reflected my cultural experience. While I was exposed to anti-racist/anti-oppressive frameworks as a pre-service teacher, it was only when I went to teach in a remote northern reserve community that I realized the breadth of the gap between the experience and knowledge of the learners I was there to support and my own curricular experience. Kitchen and Hodson (2013) have argued for the need for and impact of culturally responsive models of teaching while acknowledging the challenges of the colonial legacy, both in Canada and other colonized countries, in enacting this goal fully and how educators must become agentic in support of culturally responsive education for Indigenous learners. In Kitchen and Hodson's study, five themes of significance emerged: relational knowing, promoting self-identity and cultural identity, teaching through language and culture, curriculum and pedagogical expertise, and epistemic conversations with Indigenous staff. These themes all lend themselves to more extensive research in relation to TribalCrit but are beyond the scope of this chapter. While Kitchen and Hodson's work demonstrates that some movement has followed Sleeter's (2001) call for further research and more professional development on multicultural teacher education, much is left to be done to connect pre-service education to community-based learning and school reform. Educators and educational leaders must necessarily continue to engage in acts of **solidarity** to advocate for expanded opportunities for learners to flourish. In Nêhiyawêwin (Cree Plains or Y dialect), for example, *flourish* is *awiyak ka miyowepiniket* in Standard Roman Orthography or ᐊᐃᔭᐠ ᑲ ᒥᔪᐁᐱᓂᑫᐟ in syllabics (Nehiyaw Masinahikan, n.d.). The direct translation of the verb phrase means "someone who works or physically moves well," and a holistic approach informed by TribalCrit and a sense of solidarity will help learners to learn, work, and move well and thus gain further opportunities to flourish. Drawing upon TribalCrit, *apoqnmatultl'k jiksktuali'lk*, and *wâhkôhtowin*, then, educators have opportunities to connect with organizations to extend their awareness of local Indigenous language(s), culture(s), and history and to amplify them in school contexts. As schools and districts are increasingly demonstrating, building and extending relationships with local Indigenous communities and Elders can facilitate incorporating Indigenous Knowledge in a good way. This supports educators in reshaping community in positive ways (Hextrum et al., 2022), a significant consideration in the wake of repeated COVID-19-related school closures.

## BUILDING CAPABILITIES FOR THE FLOURISHING OF ALL STUDENTS

Employing multifaceted approaches can be effective in building learners' capabilities to flourish. Good teaching that seeks to engage in acts of reconciliation in Canada incorporates recognition of Indigenous languages and cultures, particularly when they are not the majority language or culture (Keskitalo et al., 2012). TribalCrit, *apoqnmatultl'k jiksktuali'lk*, and *wâhkôhtowin* can inform lesson planning, learning activities, and assessments so that learning can occur and be demonstrated in different ways. Educators are often advised to question the curriculum and take the initiative to address the gaps. This is neither to critique nor vilify curriculum writers but to explore through supported dialogue how individual understandings of the world can be different based on positionality. There are rich opportunities to question whose knowledge is given a voice and why and to learn to read against the grain through this process. It follows that the questions raised can be used to inform one's teaching practice and develop a context in which more students can flourish (Deng, 2022). Schools and districts are responding to calls for increased support in decolonizing and Indigenizing activities and assessments, and it follows that individual educators are responsible for participating in this process of reconciliation as well.

## BUILDING EDUCATOR CAPACITY

TribalCrit supports educators and learners in engaging critically in multicultural, anti-racist education (Stavrou & Murphy, 2021) and in the exploration of contemporary Indigenous issues (Krueger, 2021) as a means of flourishing. As Kee and Carr-Chellman (2019) have asserted, "cultures are not discrete categories, but are, instead, porous, rhizomatic, and marked by experiential and epistemological border crossings" (p. 101). TribalCrit offers opportunities to build critical awareness through such border crossings and what Garcia-Olp et al. (2019) have referred to as Heart Work, a deep consciousness of relationship, which can underpin strong pedagogy. I advocate for deeper learning about Indigenous cultures and languages in school contexts as a way for schools and individual educators to contribute to the Truth and Reconciliation Commission's (TRC's) Calls to Action (2015).

Seeking out professional association opportunities and advancing dialogue on decolonization can be another way that educators can get involved (Aho & Quaye, 2018), as can advocating within such associations for decolonizing and Indigenizing committee work. Using the lens of TribalCrit, *apoqnmatultl'k jiksktuali'lk*, and *wâhkôhtowin*, personal learning opportunities offer other ways for educators to learn how to be collaborators and allies (Anthony-Stevens, 2017). Post-secondary Indigenous language offerings are increasing at many universities, and some schools support language classes for non-Indigenous educators. Alternatively, there are many high-quality, free, noncredit virtual classes available as well as groups on social media that one can join; these are fun and interactive ways to learn about Indigenous languages and cultures.

## ADDRESSING STRUCTURES THAT LIMIT FLOURISHING

Educators at all levels are being urged to think in new and creative ways to decolonize structures and promote flourishing. TribalCrit can be a strong lens for this work. Watson (2007) has made a compelling case for thinking about buildings as inclusive spaces of potential for physical and virtual transformation, spaces that embrace imaginative technology and architecture that enables—rather than inhibits—new forms of and approaches to learning. Schools must work to cultivate a sense of welcoming for Indigenous learners (Gallop et al., 2023), since a long history of structural oppression has hindered Indigenous students' learning and sense of belonging (Kokka, 2018). As many school boards and districts are demonstrating in their efforts to reimagine education and educational spaces, it is important to include Indigenous Elders, Indigenous educators, and Indigenous community members in the dialogue and decision-making processes of building renovations or the design of new spaces in a good way.

## ADDRESSING POLICIES THAT LIMIT FLOURISHING

School policies became more fluid during the height of the COVID-19 pandemic as districts tried to meet the needs of learners and support educators who often had not been trained in the technologies suddenly needed to deliver lessons. As Kendi (2019) has affirmed, "every policy in every institution in every community in every nation is producing or sustaining either racial inequity or equity, racial justice or injustice" (p. 21). The gaps created by inequitable educational policies became more evident during the height of the pandemic, and there are opportunities for educators, administrators, parents, and community members to urge educational policy-makers at various levels to enact and promote ongoing EDID-informed changes. As Barrero Jaramillo (2023) has asserted, it is educators' responsibility to push back against deficit discourses wherever they appear and to recognize how policies negatively impact Indigenous learners as well as other racialized learners. Engaging in acts of solidarity that advance reconciliation and recognize the significance of local context (Wotherspoon & Milne, 2022) can promote the flourishing of all learners. Furthermore, advocating for and supporting the inclusion of Indigenous representatives on policy committees are crucial. Becoming involved in committees and initiatives as an ally means that one can influence policies and further EDID, *apoqnmatultl'k jiksktuali'lk*, and *wâhkôhtowin*. TribalCrit offers a lens through which to do this work.

## ADDRESSING CURRICULA THAT LIMIT FLOURISHING

Resources such as *Dene Kede, Inuuqatigiit, Ilitaunnikuliriniq, Inuglugijaittuq*, and *Inuit Qaujimajatuqangit*, currently used in Arctic classrooms, can be employed to expand current pedagogical practices and support learners in flourishing. Lamb and Godlewska (2021) have pointed out that decolonizing education must not be reduced to an additive approach (p. 105) and that a decolonizing approach can transform relations between Indigenous and non-Indigenous people (p. 117). It is incumbent upon non-Indigenous educators such as I to seek ways to self-educate (Leddy & O'Neil, 2022) rather than to place the burden on Indigenous communities. Although Prest and Goble (2021) have noted the linguistic challenges that accompany Indigenization, Indigenous Peoples should not be burdened with the core responsibilities for re-education. Rather, Indigenous Peoples' ideas should lead change, and the majority of the work should be done by non-Indigenous people acting in solidarity.

There are ways to advocate for including local Indigenous Knowledge as curriculum alongside provincial/territorial curriculum. New or additional locally relevant Indigenous learning resources that can be used similarly to *Dene Kede*, *Inuuqatigiit*, *Inuit Qaujimajatuqangit*, *Ilitaunnikuliriniq*, and *Inuglugijaittuq* will strengthen educational opportunities for flourishing for all learners. In the meantime, consider how curricular gaps that limit flourishing can be addressed through incorporating the lenses of TribalCrit, *apoqnmatultl'k jiksktuali'lk*, and *wâhkôhtowin*. Everyone is responsible for challenging dominant narratives and amplifying Indigenous voices to support social justice for all learners (McCarty et al., 2018).

## ADDRESSING PEDAGOGIES THAT LIMIT FLOURISHING

TribalCrit counters limitations to learners' flourishing because when Indigenous voices are amplified, the pedagogies that oppress Indigenous Knowledge and language become more evident, and those oppressive practices can then be replaced with EDID-informed pedagogies. The deeper knowledge gained through employing TribalCrit then invites educators to continue to improve practices to help more students flourish. Decolonizing pedagogies incorporate Indigenous Knowledge, resources, and curriculum (Chrona, 2022). Privileging Indigenous Knowledge and calling for critical Indigenous pedagogy, resources, and curriculum can be firmly grounded in TribalCrit. Decolonization demands the examination of inequities, the enactment of more visible and audible spaces for Indigenous Knowledge, and more nuanced educational experiences for learners. As Thomas King offered in his Massey lecture, "The Truth about Stories" (CBC Radio, 2003), "it's yours. Do with it what you will…. But don't say in the years to come that you would have lived your life differently if only you had heard this story. You've heard it now" (51:27–51:44). There are ways in which pedagogy, teaching philosophy, and instructional leadership might be lived differently and expanded through reciprocity to address the gaps that limit flourishing (Osmond-Johnson & Turner, 2021). Then, by taking learning outside and paying attention to the shifts that can occur, drawing upon TribalCrit, *apoqnmatultl'k jiksktuali'lk*, and *wâhkôhtowin*, new stories can almost certainly be expected to follow.

## CONCLUSION

Learning about TribalCrit is a step that can potentially help in expanding one's consciousness of and participation in EDID initiatives. TribalCrit invites a shift in interpreting the world. This shift can lead to a parallel shift in pedagogical practices and the ability to support learners more holistically as they critically engage in familiar and unfamiliar cultures, build connections across cultural boundaries, flourish, and expand their understanding of their responsibilities as global citizens (Nussbaum, 2002, 2006). Furthermore, as Nussbaum (2006) has asserted, this can happen from the earliest years of learning. Employing TribalCrit, engaging in critical self-reflection, and acknowledging how positionality shapes values, expectations, and approaches can help to identify gaps in curriculum and current teaching practices to help move forward in a good way. Student capabilities can be expanded in tandem with one's own capabilities as an educator through *apoqnmatultl'k jiksktuali'lk* and *wâhkôhtowin*. There are many ways to learn about local Indigenous languages, cultures, and approaches that can make teaching and schools more inclusive and equitable and that will contribute to decolonizing learning. Every educator is responsible for committing to ongoing learning and amplifying calls for responses to the TRC's Calls to Action (2015). Every educator can seek out opportunities to include Indigenous Knowledge, language, texts, resources, frameworks, and curricula in respectful ways. The more voices that advocate in solidarity for the creation of locally specific Indigenous resources, the sooner positive change will occur. Continuing to engage in dialogue about pedagogy with other educators is necessary—in classrooms, in hallways, in staff rooms, in learning communities, at conferences, in person, and online—so that collaborations can develop to address challenges together. Everyone is responsible for calling out policies and structures that negatively impact learners and demanding that changes occur to promote EDID in places of education. Systemic change can occur through collaborative effort to help students to flourish and thus, together, *mino-bimaadizi giinawa*: live well, you all (The Ojibwe People's Dictionary, n.d.a, n.d.b).

## ACKNOWLEDGEMENTS

This chapter was written on the traditional lands of the Wabanaki Confederacy, the Wolastoqiyik-Maliseet First Nation, and the Mi'kmaq and was revised on the unceded ancestral lands of the Lheidli T'enneh. Thank you to my language and culture teachers, who have helped me to appreciate the places in which I live.

Dedicated to Seana and Deanna. *Nikatakonin kiyawâw kâkike pihci nimiteh.* I will carry you in my heart forever.

With my humble appreciation to Nell Beaudry McLachlan, MLIS, and Sarah van Sickle, Yorkville University librarians, for their help in bringing this research to fruition.

## KEY TERMS

***apoqnmatultl'k jiksktuali'lk:*** Elder Albert Marshall's (2018) Mi'kmaw articulation of the possibilities within learning together through Indigenous and non-Indigenous people learning to listen to one other.

**Solidarity:** Enacting unity and relationship; in this chapter, I refer specifically to the possibilities of working alongside Indigenous Peoples as a non-Indigenous educator through collaboration.

**TribalCrit:** A term coined by Lumbee academic Bryan McKinley Jones Brayboy, it is an interdisciplinary critical praxis grounded in critical race theory, anthropology, political and legal theory, political science, Indigenous literatures, education, and Indigenous studies (Brayboy, 2005).

***Wâhkôhtowin:*** Dwayne Donald (2021) uses this Cree word to explore the concept of how good relations can be developed between Indigenous and non-Indigenous people through moving forward together. This term also speaks to more extensive interconnectedness that is part of Indigenous ontology and epistemology.

## DISCUSSION QUESTIONS AND ACTIVITIES

1. How do you self-locate? How will you engage in self-reflexivity and in the creation of brave spaces in your context?
2. What Indigenous community/communities is/are nearest to you? How might you forge authentic and lasting connection with local Indigenous community/communities?
3. What print or digital Indigenous resources and curriculum documents are available to you? How might you create a community of educator-learners to continue learning about how to decolonize and Indigenize pedagogy and curriculum? Where might you look to find opportunities to learn local Indigenous Teachings and language(s)? How might you seek mentorship in using Indigenous Teachings and Indigenous print resources in a good way? What would be an appropriate way to demonstrate thanks to your mentor(s)?
4. Look at the local school board's website and explore the resources that are made available there. In a small group, brainstorm and develop a mind map (or another graphic organizer) and sketch out some ideas for a lesson plan that connects locally relevant Indigenous resources and the provincial/territorial curriculum. If time permits, develop this outline into a full lesson plan.

# REFERENCES

Aho, R. E., & Quaye, S. J. (2018). Applied critical leadership: Centering racial justice and decolonization in professional associations. *Journal of Critical Scholarship on Higher Education and Student Affairs, 3*(3), 8–19. https://ecommons.luc.edu/jcshesa/vol3/iss3/2/

Akkari, A., & Radhouane, M. (2022). *Intercultural approaches to education: From theory to practice.* Springer Nature.

Ali, D. (2017). Safe spaces and brave spaces. *NASPA Research and Policy Institute, 2,* 1–13. https://eric.ed.gov/?id=ED594535

Anthony-Stevens, V. (2017). Cultivating alliances: Reflections on the role of non-Indigenous collaborators in Indigenous educational sovereignty. *Journal of American Indian Education, 56*(1), 81–104. doi.org/10.1353/jaie.2017.a798931

Baidoo-Anu, D., Gyamerah, K., Mahama, I., & Ofori-Sasu, E. (2023). Towards classroom inclusivity: Exploring K–12 teachers' sensitivity to cultural diversity. *Culture and Education, 35*(4), 938–975. doi.org/10.1080/11356405.2023.2200590

Barrero Jaramillo, D. M. (2023). Achievement as white settler property: How the discourse of achievement gaps reproduces settler colonial constructions of race. *Education Policy Analysis Archives, 31*(13), 1–21. doi.org/10.14507/epaa.31.7131

Battiste, M., & Henderson, J. Y. (2009). Naturalizing Indigenous knowledge in Eurocentric education. *Canadian Journal of Native Education, 32*(1), 5–18. doi.org/10.14288/cjne.v32i1.196482

Bochner, A., & Ellis, C. (2016). *Evocative autoethnography: Writing lives and telling stories.* Routledge.

Bourdieu, P. (2011). The forms of capital. In M. Granovetter & R. Swedberg (Eds.), *The sociology of economic life* (pp. 78–92). Routledge.

Brayboy, B. M. J. (2005). Toward a tribal critical race theory in education. *The Urban Review, 37*(5), 425–446. doi.org/10.1007/s11256-005-0018-y

Brayboy, B. M. J., & Chin, J. (2019). A match made in heaven: Tribal critical race theory and critical Indigenous research methodologies. In J. T. DeCuir-Gunby, T. K. Chapman, & P. A. Schutz (Eds.), *Understanding critical race research methods and methodologies: Lessons from the field* (pp. 51–63). Routledge.

Cameron, E., De Leeuw, S., & Desbiens, C. (2014). Indigeneity and ontology. *Cultural Geographies, 21*(1), 19–26. doi.org/10.1177/14744740135002

Campbell-Daniels, S. (2021). *Culturally responsive/relevant professional development: Impacts on pre-service and in-service educator perceptions and practice* [Doctoral dissertation, University of Idaho].

Carpena-Méndez, F., Virtanen, P. K., & Williamson, K. J. (2022). Indigenous pedagogies in a global world and sustainable futures. *Anthropology & Education Quarterly, 53*(4), 308–320. doi.org/10.1111/aeq.12447

CBC Radio. (2003, November 7). *The 2003 CBC Massey Lectures, "The truth about stories: A Native narrative."* Part 5 [Audio podcast episode]. www.cbc.ca/radio/ideas/the-2003-cbc-massey-lectures-the-truth-about-stories-a-native-narrative-1.2946870

Chiblow, S., & Meighan, P. J. (2021). Language is land, land is language: The importance of Indigenous languages. *Human Geography, 15*(2), 206–210. doi.org/10.1177/19427786211022899

Chrona, J. (2022). *Wayi wah! Indigenous pedagogies: An act for reconciliation and anti-racist education*. Portage & Main Press.

Clandinin, D. J., & Connelly, F. M. (2004). *Narrative inquiry: Experience and story in qualitative research*. John Wiley & Sons.

Cunliffe, A. (2016). "On becoming a critically reflective practitioner" redux: What does it mean to be reflective? *Journal of Management Education, 40*(6), 740–746. doi.org/10.1177/1052562916668919

Deng, Z. (2022). Powerful knowledge, educational potential and knowledge-rich curriculum: Pushing the boundaries. *Journal of Curriculum Studies, 5*(54), 599–617. doi.org/10.1080/00220272.2022.2089538

do Amaral, B., & Windchief, S. (2019). The pathway to achieving classroom equity: Computational and critical thinking through storytelling and 3D models. *Educational Research, 30*(1), 62–66. https://eric.ed.gov/?id=EJ1248538

Donald, D. (2012). Indigenous métissage: A decolonizing research sensibility. *International Journal of Qualitative Studies in Education, 25*(5), 533–555. doi.org/10.1080/09518398.2011.554449

Donald, D. (2021). We need a new story: Walking and the wâhkôhtowin imagination. *Journal of the Canadian Association of Curriculum Studies, 18*(2), 53–63. doi.org/10.25071/1916-4467.40492

Freire, P. (1985). Reading the world and reading the word: An interview with Paulo Freire. *Language Arts, 62*(1), 15–21. https://www.jstor.org/stable/41405241

Gallop, C. J., Turner, D., Arshinoff, J., Bullee, M., & Arcand, R. (2023). Sticks and stones may break our bones and names can also hurt us: Alumni of the Plains Indians Cultural Survival School reflect on their experiences. *Critical Education, 14*(2), 22–45. doi.org/10.14288/ce.v14i2.186682

Garcia-Olp, M., Nelson, C., & Saiz, L. (2019). Conceptualizing a mathematics curriculum: Indigenous knowledge has always been mathematics education. *Educational Studies, 55*(6), 689–706. doi.org/10.1080/00131946.2019.1680374

Hextrum, K., Suresh, M. S., & Wagnon, J. D. (2022). Honoring TribalCrit in higher education: Survival and sovereignty in the wake of anti-CRT bills. *Philosophy and Theory in Higher Education, 4*(3), 29–48. doi.org/10.3726/ptihe.032022.0003

Kee, J. C., & Carr-Chellman, D. J. (2019). Paulo Freire, critical literacy, and Indigenous resistance. *Educational Studies, 55*(1), 89–103. doi.org/10.1080/00131946.2018.1562926

Kendi, I. X. (2019). *How to be an antiracist*. One World.

Keskitalo, P., Uusiautti, S., & Määttä, K. (2012). How to make the small Indigenous cultures bloom? Special traits of Sámi pedagogy in Finland. *Current Issues in Comparative Education, 15*(1), 52–63. doi.org/10.52214/cice.v15i1.11464

Kitchen, J., & Hodson, J. (2013). Living alongside: Teacher educator experiences working in a community-based Aboriginal teacher education program. *Canadian Journal of Education / Revue canadienne de l'éducation, 36*(2), 144–174. https://journals.sfu.ca/cje/index.php/cje-rce/article/view/1249

Kokka, K. (2018). Radical STEM teacher activism: Collaborative organizing to sustain social justice pedagogy in STEM fields. *Educational Foundations, 31*(1–2), 86–113. https://files.eric.ed.gov/fulltext/EJ1193676.pdf

Kovach, M. (2009). *Indigenous methodologies: Characteristics, conversations, and contexts*. University of Toronto Press.

Krueger, J. (2021). TribalCrit, curriculum mining, and the teaching of contemporary Indigenous issues. *Multicultural Perspectives, 23*(2), 78–86. doi.org/10.1080/15210960.2021.1914048

Ladson-Billings, G. (1998). Just what is critical race theory and what's it doing in a nice field like education? *International Journal of Qualitative Studies in Education, 11*(1), 7–24. doi.org/10.1080/095183998236863

Lamb, C., & Godlewska, A. (2021). On the peripheries of education: (Not)learning about Indigenous peoples in the 1995–2010 British Columbia curriculum. *Journal of Curriculum Studies, 53*(1), 103–123. doi.org/10.1080/00220272.2020.1774806

Leddy, S., & O'Neil, S. (2022). Learning to see: Generating decolonial literacy through contemporary identity-based Indigenous art. *International Journal of Education & the Arts, 23*(9/10), 1–19. doi.org/10.26209/ijea23n9

Lee, A. Y., & Lee, A. J. (2020). Experience with diversity is not enough: A pedagogical framework for teacher candidates that centers critical race consciousness. *Journal of Curriculum Studies Research, 2*(2), 40–59. doi.org/10.46303/jcsr.2020.9

Marshall, A. (2018). Network voices / Voix du réseau. *Education Canada, 58*(2), 6–7.

Masta, S. (2022). Theory-to-practice: Researching Indigenous education in the United States. *International Journal of Multicultural Education, 24*(1), 1–17. doi.org/10.18251/ijme.v24i1.1937

Matias, C. E., Viesca, K. M., Garrison-Wade, D. F., Tandon, M., & Galindo, R. (2014). "What is critical whiteness doing in OUR nice field like critical race theory?" Applying CRT and CWS to understand the white imaginations of white teacher candidates. *Equity & Excellence in Education, 47*(3), 289–304. doi.org/10.1080/10665684.2014.933692

Matsaw, S., Hedden-Nicely, D., & Cosens, B. (2020). Cultural linguistics and Treaty language: A modernized approach to interpreting Treaty language to capture the tribe's understanding. *Environmental Law, 50*(2), 415–446. https://digitalcommons.law.uidaho.edu/faculty_scholarship/411/

McCarty, T. L., Nicholas, S. E., Chew, K. A., Diaz, N. G., Leonard, W. Y., & White, L. (2018). Hear our languages, hear our voices: Storywork as theory and praxis in Indigenous-language reclamation. *Daedalus, 147*(2), 160–172. doi.org/10.1162/DAED_a_00499

Nehiyaw Masinahikan. (n.d.). *awîyak ka miyowepiniket*. Nehiyaw Masinahikan: Online Cree Dictionary. www.creedictionary.com/

Northwest Territories Department of Education, Culture and Employment. (1993). *Dene kede: Education: A Dene perspective*. www.ece.gov.nt.ca/en/services/curriculum/dene-kede-and-inuuqatigiit

Northwest Territories Department of Education, Culture and Employment. (1996). *Inuuqatigiit: The curriculum from the Inuit perspective*. www.ece.gov.nt.ca/sites/ece/files/resources/inuuqatigiit_k-12_curriculum.pdf

Nunavut Department of Education. (2007). *Inuit Qaujimajatuqangit: Education framework for Nunavut curriculum*. Nunavut Department of Education: Curriculum and School Services Division. https://www.gov.nu.ca/sites/default/files/publications/2024-01/Inuit%20Qaujimajatuqangit%20ENG.pdf

Nunavut Department of Education. (2008a). *Ilitaunnikuliriniq: Foundation for dynamic assessment as learning in Nunavut schools*. Nunavut Department of Education: Curriculum and School Services Division. https://www.gov.nu.ca/sites/default/files/publications/2024-01/Dynamic%20Assessment%20ENG.pdf

Nunavut Department of Education. (2008b). *Inuglugijaittuq: Foundation for inclusive education in Nunavut schools*. Nunavut Department of Education: Curriculum and School Services Division. https://www.gov.nu.ca/sites/default/files/publications/2022-03/inuglugijaittuq_eng.pdf

Nussbaum, M. C. (2002). Education for citizenship in an era of global connection. *Studies in Philosophy and Education, 21*, 289–303. doi.org/10.1023/A:1019837105053

Nussbaum, M. C. (2006). Education and democratic citizenship: Capabilities and quality education. *Journal of Human Development, 7*(3), 385–395. doi.org/10.1080/14649880600815974

Office of the Treaty Commissioner. (n.d.). www.otc.ca

The Ojibwe People's Dictionary. (n.d.a). *Giinawaa*. In *The Ojibwe People's Dictionary*. http://ojibwe.lib.umn.edu

The Ojibwe People's Dictionary. (n.d.b). *Mino-bimaadizi*. In *The Ojibwe People's Dictionary*. http://ojibwe.lib.umn.edu

Osmond-Johnson, P., & Turner, P. (2021). Weetutoskemitowin: Conceptualizing positive leadership for flourishing schools through an Indigenous lens. In K. D. Walker, B. Kutsyuruba, & S. Cherkowski (Eds.), *Positive leadership for flourishing schools* (pp. 355–370). Information Age.

Prest, A., & Goble, J. S. (2021). Language, music, and revitalizing Indigeneity: Effecting cultural restoration and ecological balance via music education. *Philosophy of Music Education Review, 29*(1), 24–46. doi.org/10.2979/philmusieducrevi.29.1.03

Richter, N. F., Schlaegel, C., Taras, V., Alon, I., & Bird, A. (2023). Reviewing half a century of measuring cross-cultural competence: Aligning theoretical constructs and empirical measures. *International Business Review, 32*(4), 102122. doi.org/10.1016/j.ibusrev.2023.102122

Sit, A., Mak, A. S., & Neill, J. T. (2017). Does cross-cultural training in tertiary education enhance cross-cultural adjustment? A systematic review. *International Journal of Intercultural Relations, 57*, 1–18. doi.org/10.1016/j.ijintrel.2017.01.001

Sleeter, C. E. (2001). Preparing teachers for culturally diverse schools: Research and the overwhelming presence of whiteness. *Journal of Teacher Education, 52*(2), 94–106. doi.org/10.1177/0022487101052002002

Stavrou, S., & Murphy, M. S. (2021). Methodological landscapes: Mapping narrative inquiry, critical race theory, and anti-racist education. *Journal of Critical Race Inquiry, 8*(1), 1–21. https://jcri.ca/index.php/CRI/article/view/14359

Truth and Reconciliation Commission of Canada. (2015). *Truth and Reconciliation Commission of Canada: Calls to action.* http://trc.ca/assets/pdf/Calls_to_Action_English2.pdf

Vowel, C. (2016). *Indigenous writes: A guide to First Nations, Métis & Inuit issues in Canada.* Highwater Press.

Wallace-Casey, C. (2022). Teaching and learning the legacy of residential schools for remembering and reconciliation in Canada. *History Education Research Journal, 19* (1), 4. doi.org/10.14324/HERJ.19.1.04

Wallin, D. C., & Scribe, C. (2022). Wahkohtowin: Decolonizing teacher preparation for rural, urban and first nations schools. *Australian and International Journal of Rural Education, 32*(2), 59–74. doi.org/10.47381/aijre.v32i2.318

Watson, L. (2007). Building the future of learning. *European Journal of Education, 42*(2), 255–263. doi.org/10.1111/j.1465-3435.2007.00299.x

Williamson, K. J., & Vizina, Y. (2017). Indigenous peoples and education in the Arctic region. In United Nations, *State of the world's Indigenous peoples* (pp. 39–73). doi.org/10.18356/66ce8e42-en

Womack, C. (1999). *Red on red: Native American literary separatism.* University of Minnesota Press.

Wotherspoon, T., & Milne, E. (2022). Cosmopolitanism and decolonization: Contradictory perspectives on school reform to advance reconciliation with Indigenous peoples. *International Journal for Talent Development and Creativity, 10*(1), 45–58. doi.org/10.7202/1099940ar

Younging, G. (2018). *Elements of Indigenous style: A guide for writing by and about Indigenous peoples.* Brush Education.

# CHAPTER 11
# Fostering Wellness and Redefining Success for All Students through Indigenous Perspectives

*Lindsay Morcom, Kelly Maracle, Liv Rondeau, and Kate Freeman*

In this chapter we examine flourishing from Haudenosaunee and Anishinaabe perspectives through a binding framework of **radical decolonial love,** and we explore how we can apply these perspectives in a Western educational context through **two-eyed seeing** (Bartlett et al., 2015; Iwama et al., 2009; Marshall et al., 2015). We discuss how schools can work with Indigenous communities and supports to help ensure student wellness, create family and community connections, and contribute to students', teachers', and families' potential to thrive, while at the same time respecting and understanding Indigenous ways of knowing, being, and doing. We also consider what this means for the fundamental values that schools, teachers, and boards espouse and for standards of professionalism and classroom structure. While there are overlaps between Western and Indigenous perspectives on wellness, we believe that an Indigenous approach can contribute significantly to a richer understanding of wellness within school and community environments in ways that better serve both Indigenous and non-Indigenous students.

## RADICAL DECOLONIAL LOVE AS A BINDING FRAMEWORK

As researchers of Anishinaabe, Haudenosaunee, and settler ancestry, we come to this work with diverse perspectives. It is vital to state that Anishinaabe and Haudenosaunee beliefs and values, though similar in some ways, are distinct.

We begin with the concept of radical decolonial love as a bridge that brings these perspectives together.

As a concept, radical decolonial love is based in Black, Latinx, and Indigenous decolonial scholarship. Originally coined by Sandoval (2000), decolonial love involves engaging people to build connection across differences. It pushes back against colonially imposed hierarchies and divisions such that we come to work together for mutual emancipation. This approach requires action and purposeful connection with others (Moreno, 2019; Recollet, 2015; Ureña, 2017) and requires deep commitment to morality and equality in the face of a society that drives us toward competitiveness and self-interest (West, 1993). Dismantling the colonial concept of love as weakness comes through understanding that living and teaching with relationships at the forefront is an act of vulnerability, full humanity, and strength. This is particularly true for Indigenous, Black, and other marginalized communities, including those marginalized through socio-economics and disability, who have been dehumanized through colonial structures (Morcom & Butler, 2023). Biana (2021) describes the following tenets of decolonial love: love is an act of care; we teach each other how to love and mirror the love we receive; loving is an act of resistance against oppressive colonial structures; and love is not limited to people but extends to the universe and the healing of the world. We embrace this as not just decolonial love but *radical* decolonial love because it is based in fierce compassion and unending acceptance of our students and ourselves. Radical decolonial love calls us, and our students, to see the best in one another and to be accountable in our own responsibilities and actions to honour connections to each other and the world in which we live. This way of being in the classroom is decolonial because it stands in contrast to colonial education structures based on dehumanization, domination, hate of ourselves and others, division, the imposition of hierarchies and binaries, and the teaching of inauthentic or untrue knowledge to hold up colonial power structures (Ureña, 2017; West, 1993).

hooks (1994, 2003) states that embracing love in a radical way in the classroom is risky, an act of epistemic disobedience. Teachers seeking to foster radical decolonial love in their classrooms must stand up against dominant attitudes that are present in teacher training, schools, and wider society. This means questioning Western perceptions of both school success and well-being. With respect to school success, increasing emphasis has been placed societally on standardized test scores, "catching up" to grade-level expectations, and "back to basics" education focused on core skills of literacy and numeracy (Walters, 2022). This approach is bolstered by media reports and government policies. For example, in Ontario, the recently passed Bill 98: Better Schools and Student Outcomes Act (2023), states, "The Government is committed to re-focusing Ontario's education system on student achievement, prioritizing hands-on learning and skills development in reading, writing, and math.... The Government believes that these reforms would ensure students graduate with a competitive advantage while learning modern curricula in modern schools, preparing them for the jobs of the future" (Preamble). Bill 98, which mentions mental health only in passing, demonstrates an emphasis on neoliberal measures of educational success, such as earning potential and competitiveness. This reinforces a fixation on grades and teachers' approval and buttresses the predatory nature of colonial culture by telling students that they must defeat one another to prove their superiority. That attitude, rooted in colonial dehumanization, prevents the development of meaningful community in which real learning can thrive (hooks, 2003).

In Western culture, well-being has been conceptualized mainly as a product of our personal choices and behaviours—an individual-level approach and responsibility (Cabanas & Illouz, 2019; Joshanloo et al., 2021). For example, Holder and Lannon (2020) describe a state of well-being as an active process of making choices toward a healthy life. Access to healthy foods, sleep, and necessities such as clothing and shelter are the bare minimum that young people, and their families, need to have to begin to access learning, let alone achieve academic success. In thinking this way, well-being is seen as personal and private, an internal feeling that we have personal control of and accountability for (Joshanloo et al., 2021). Happiness, as Joshanloo et al. (2021) state, is seen as a mindset that can be engineered through willpower. The focus on the individual and their choices, or their perceived desire to achieve wellness, implies that people, and in this case young people, Indigenous or not, have a choice in whether to be well. This is an incredibly unfair and unrealistic expectation to place on individuals, let alone young people. Many students and families do not have continued and stable access to the choices that lead to wellness. Supports and services often have long wait times, lines, and end dates to accommodate other families and students. Educators, schools, school boards, and other institutions are influenced by colonial structures, policies, and systemic and institutionalized racism. The Western worldview and ingrained systemic issues thereby influence policies, procedures, strategies, and reports related to mental health and wellness. In understanding what has been ingrained through Western society as a means for dealing with mental health and wellness, we can understand how this cultural mindset has impacted policies, systems, and supports at all levels of education.

In contrast, an approach to education rooted in radical decolonial love, arising from a sense of mutuality, requires us to build alliances based on equality between ourselves and our students, making the development of relationships and the well-being of students and colleagues the primary priority, before any curricular considerations or skills development (Biana, 2021). This does not preclude academic achievement but rather supports it because students who are well and accepted are better able to learn and because students who feel safe in the classroom and who have compassion and care for each other will take risks, listen, challenge inequalities, and support one another's growth (Maluleka, 2023). For all students, but particularly those who are marginalized through race, disability, or other factors, it is crucial to focus not only on their challenges but also on their gifts and life potential. That does not negate their difficulties but rather places them in a position of equality with other learners who also have struggles and gifts.

In a Western educational context, professional standards laid out for teachers require a degree of distancing between teachers and their students to maintain the domination of teacher over students and to create a compartmentalization between teachers' professional and personal selves (hooks, 2003). Teachers are cautioned that a breach of distancing will compromise classroom management and will cause teachers to lose their objectivity in their evaluation of their students. Certainly, student and teacher safety must be paramount in embracing an ethic of radical decolonial love in the classroom. It does not mean that students and teachers should not put boundaries in place to protect their own wellness. However, hooks (2003) writes, "Contrary to the notion that love in the classroom makes teachers less objective, when we teach with love we are better able to respond to the unique concerns of individual students while simultaneously integrating those of the classroom community" (p. 133). The result is a classroom where teachers can step away from curriculum to embrace meaningful learning opportunities and where they can demonstrate that conflict and critical discussion can take place in a caring atmosphere (hooks, 2003). Such an approach is most effective when whole schools embrace it, thus magnifying positive affect.

In keeping with Indigenous understandings, radical decolonial love requires us to go beyond the students and the classroom to understand our responsibilities to wider humanity and the natural world. As students come to understand themselves and everyone around them as worthy of love, they naturally come to see the need to fight against colonial inequalities that pervade global society (Makuleka, 2023; Ureña, 2017). For Black, Indigenous, and other marginalized students, this is particularly important because colonial structures have taught these students to dehumanize and hate themselves and their communities (see also chapters 2, 3, and 4). Embracing radical decolonial love liberates these students from colonial violence and empowers them to fight for recognition of their worth and the validity of their emotions and experiences (Makhubu & Mbongwa, 2019; Moreno, 2019; Ureña, 2017; West, 1993). It also inspires students to understand colonial oppression beyond their own solipsistic experience and thereby to fight for an end to systemic domination (hooks, 1994). This is the only way that real decolonization can occur, as through decolonial love "the search for truth and knowledge, the accomplishment of liberty and equality, and the satisfaction of demands for the recognition of identity respond ... to the humanizing task of building a world in which genuine ethical relations become the norm and not the exception" (Maldonado-Torres, 2008, p. 244). From the perspective of both Indigenous epistemologies and radical decolonial love, that liberation extends beyond the human to the land and more-than-human, requiring us to fight for the well-being of the world to which our wellness is inextricably connected (Biana, 2021; Moreno, 2019). As Kimmerer (2015) states, from an Indigenous perspective, "all of our flourishing is mutual" (p. 166).

## INDIGENOUS PERSPECTIVES ON FOSTERING STUDENTS' WELLNESS AND FLOURISHING

As researchers of Anishinaabe, Haudenosaunee, and settler ancestry, we look to teachings from these Nations through the principle of radical decolonial love to guide our path forward.

From an Anishinaabe perspective, as we understand it, connection is at the heart of what it means to flourish—to live a good life, or *mino-bimaadiziwin* (Bouchard & Martin, 2009; Rheault, 1999; Stark, 2021). Everything in creation is related, and honouring interconnectedness through good relations is central to Anishinaabe lifeways and spirituality (Stark, 2021). The importance of connection and relationship is clear in Anishinaabe spiritual teachings, namely the Medicine Wheel and the **Seven Grandfather Teachings** (Benton-Banai, 1988; Bouchard & Martin, 2009; Chartrand, 2012; Corbiere, 2000; Morcom, 2017; Ray & Cormier, 2012). First, the Medicine Wheel offers us a greater understanding that, as humans, we are more than our minds and our bodies; we must recognize and teach to the intellectual, physical, spiritual, and emotional elements of ourselves and one another. A holistic understanding of the world extends beyond the self to the family and community as well as the other-than-human, the earth, and the sacred, with the understanding that the relationships between everything

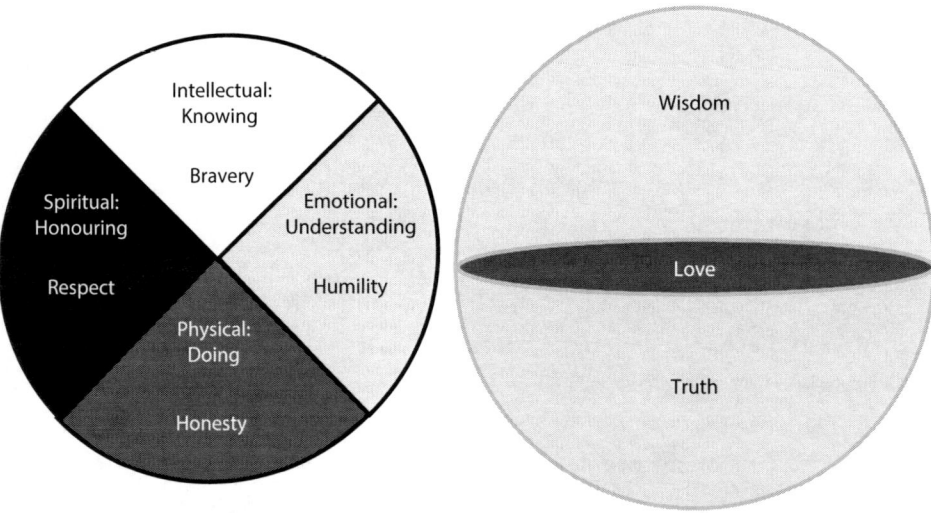

**Figure 11.1: The Medicine Wheel and Seven Grandfather Teachings**
*Source:* Morcom and Freeman (2018). Used with permission.

around us are more important than each element separately (Chartrand, 2012; Ermine, 1995; Morcom, 2017; Ray & Cormier, 2012). The Seven Grandfather Teachings of honesty, humility, respect, bravery, wisdom, truth, and love provide guidance about how to live *mino-bimaadiziwin* in connection and reciprocity. These have even deeper meaning when considered in the Anishinaabemowin language. For example, *manaaji'idiwin* (respect) more accurately means "to go easy on one another and all of Creation" (Seven Generations Education Institute [SGEI], 2021). The Seven Grandfather Teachings map onto the four directions three-dimensionally, with the addition of above, below, and within to create a sacred cosmology that further reminds Anishinaabek of their connection to the world both within and beyond themselves (Bouchard & Martin, 2009; Morcom & Freeman, 2018). Both Anishinaabe teachings and scholars of radical decolonial love point out that our interconnectedness calls us to ethical relationship with each other and the wider world (Biana, 2021; Kimmerer, 2015; Maldonado-Torres, 2008; Moreno, 2019). In this context, learning about each other and the world around us is an act of radical decolonial love (hooks, 2003). See figure 11.1.

From a Haudenosaunee perspective, Johnson (1996) outlines key elements of Haudenosaunee ontology that are fundamental to the culture, which include keeping **a good mind, relational responsibility, and a sense of reverence and gratitude**. These elements are integral to how we experience and participate in the world around us. *Ka'nikonhri:yo*, or a good mind, is a state of being that

Haudenosaunee people strive to emulate. Waterman (2023) states it is to remind ourselves and encourage others to always approach people, situations, and the world as if intentions are good and with the knowledge of how things can be done in a positive way. When we look at others, we attempt to see the best in them. Johnson (1996) describes relational responsibility as our mutual responsibility and commitment to take care of each other and all of creation. We have a duty to all living things around us, an understanding that we need to take care of each other as equals and relatives. As all living things in creation help to provide for us, we also need to take care of creation. This leads us to the third value: gratitude. At the start of the day, at an event, ceremony, or gathering, Haudenosaunee people recite the *Ohenton Karihwatehkwen*, or the Words That Come before All Else. In these moments of intentional gratitude, thanks and acknowledgement are given to all parts of creation for their role and necessary contribution to the interwoven aspects that we all depend on, not just for survival, but for a good life.

We find that these principles provide valuable guidance to serve school communities and support student wellness for Indigenous—and all—students. As Waterman (2023) notes, the basis of goodness means that one tries to maintain good relationships to do good work and that when using a good mind, we are not to make decisions based on anger or revenge. Waterman (2023) goes on to discuss the importance of a good mind, the necessity of building students' confidence instead of admonishing struggling students, and the importance of relationships with students, colleagues, and community. This philosophy encourages educators to focus on student strengths and approach students as if they all can and will do well, while striving to find and utilize each student's individual gifts. Longboat (2018) highlights the connection between "head, heart, and hands" as a foundational premise of Indigenous Knowledge and essential to the work of building meaningful community and change. He says, "Both Haudenosaunee and Anishinaabe teachings emphasize caring about the emotional, physical and spiritual health of the person, alongside their intellectual growth, and honouring holistic interconnections between family, community, place, and the more-than-human."

Indigenous understandings, like radical decolonial love, hold that reciprocal, respectful, and meaningful connection in the classroom based in caring and personal responsibility is a prerequisite for an effective learning environment (Battiste, 2013; Chartrand, 2012; Morcom, 2017; Ray & Cormier, 2012). Such insights also show that emotion and spirituality are not superfluous to learning or barriers to learning but essential pathways to learning. Western education is limited by a refusal to move beyond the observable and recognize knowledge that comes from emotional or spiritual sources. A commitment to the myth of objectivity, rather than an understanding that all interpretation of knowledge is based in the learner's connections, experiences, and relationships, is inauthentic to human experience and dishonest, even dangerous, in its misrepresentation of how we know and how we exist in relationship to the world that we are a part of (Hampton, 1995; Stonechild, 2016).

As an example of the practical application of Indigenous concepts of well-being, the First Nations Health Authority provides several resources on wellness, including a document titled *First Nations Perspective on Health and Wellness* (2012). It offers an in-depth understanding of how health and wellness are supported from an Indigenous worldview. The visual depiction of this approach is framed within a circle, with each layer of the circle serving a purpose in understanding mental health and well-being through Indigenous ways of knowing, being, and doing (see figure 11.2).

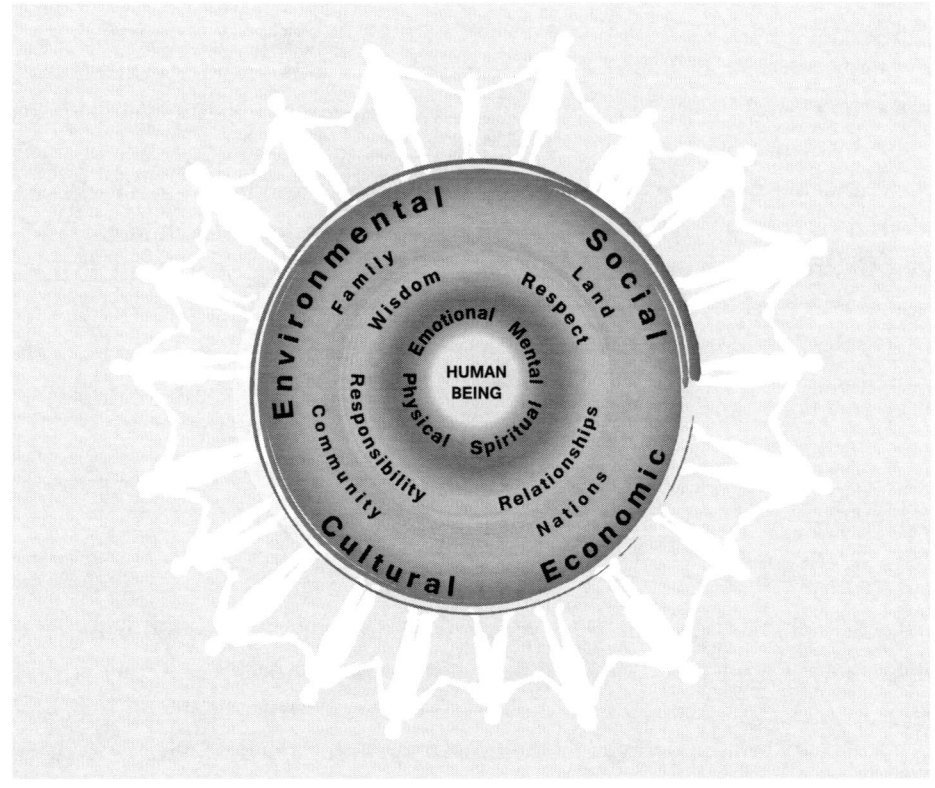

**Figure 11.2: Visual Depiction of** *First Nations Perspective on Mental Health and Wellness*
*Source:* First Nations Health Authority (2012). Used with permission.

The centre circle represents our individual wellness and the understanding that to begin to heal, we must take responsibility for our own health and wellness. The second circle focuses on the importance of mental, emotional, spiritual, and physical health, which teaches us about the value of living a healthy and well-balanced life in all four areas. If we can do this, then we can achieve holistic well-being. The third circle demonstrates the overarching values that support and uphold wellness: respect, wisdom, responsibility, and relationships. Each of these values is connected to us, our families, our communities, the land, our languages, traditions, cultures, medicines, and more. These values teach the importance of thinking not only of ourselves but also of how we live in reciprocity with others and how, in turn, our relationships sustain us in healthy, nurturing, and positive ways. The fourth circle depicts the people who surround us and the places we come from. Encompassed in this circle are the land, community, family, and nations, which are all critical components to health and well-being. Again, this circle demonstrates that mental health and well-being are not an individual responsibility but start with an individual who is surrounded by many relations who care for, sustain, and value them. The fifth circle outlines the various determinants of mental health and well-being: social, environmental, cultural, and economic. In this, it can be understood that each of these four elements, again, has an impact on an individual's wellness. Finally, the last circle depicts the people who make up a person's support system: children, families, Elders, and people in communities. This framework demonstrates that, as opposed to a Western perspective of wellness, an Indigenous perspective asserts that maintaining positive mental health and well-being does not have to be solely an individual's responsibility but rather is a collective responsibility that all have to support, care for, sustain, and work on to uplift one another.

## APPLYING A BROADER UNDERSTANDING OF WELLNESS

Most school boards in Ontario have programming dedicated to well-being that focuses mostly on mental and physical health. A significant concept that has been given more attention over the past few years is that of belonging, or the concept that everyone should feel they are an integral, valued, and respected part of the school community to participate in school activities and increase learning. Belonging, which reflects connectedness, is also central to a mindset based in radical decolonial love and Indigenous perspectives on wellness. Schools focus on mental health and wellness through a variety of practical initiatives, such as breakfast and lunch programs, education and awareness-building programs around mental health, and the incorporation of services such as school counsellors. The School Mental Health Ontario site highlights school and classroom strategies for providing a welcoming atmosphere, inclusion, student engagement, and understanding. These include mental health literacy and knowing students, as well as promotion through teaching and learning and partnerships with community supports and services. So we have seen some progress in expanding notions of what flourishing entails.

An understanding of well-being and access to services and supports to help achieve and maintain well-being are necessary for students to participate in the day-to-day activities leading to success in school. If we define academic success from a Western perspective, we focus on measurable metrics such as grades, attendance, and credit accumulation. However, well-being is much harder to measure but looking at the whole student is integral to doing so, rather than measuring academic success alone. Instead of focusing on individuals and their perceived choice of whether to be well, school communities might benefit from the notion that if they strengthen the community, wellness will be more attainable for individuals. Whitlow et al. (2019) outline *Onkwehon:we* (or original) ways of knowing that focus on holism and community support. They go on to note that cultural knowledge is paramount to creating better mental health outcomes for young people: "A well-balanced focus that goes beyond simple intellectual pursuit and requires action, emotion, and spiritual expression brings us into wholistic alignment with decolonization according to the tenets of Onkwehonwe'neha (the teachings and practice of original ways of being)" (p. 559).

The metrics of success discussed earlier, such as standardized test scores, measure the intellectual pursuit and ignore, or are unable to measure, the other realms that foster wellness in people and lead to healthier communities overall. Healthier communities are better able to support individuals who need more focus on well-being.

Community and belonging are expansive concepts; human beings, like all things in nature, rely on an intricate web of relationships to all living things in our environment. Engaging more fully and developing a deep connection with our environment is also a requirement if we are to flourish. Children are spending more time than ever inside and are increasingly occupied with electronic devices (Sturdy, n.d.). As well, students in economically deprived urban areas may experience an increased lack of access to the natural world, which may have serious mental health impacts (de Figueiredo et al., 2021), so it is important to find ways to take the classroom outside. From a practical standpoint (and at bare minimum), connection with nature and exposure to sunlight have both physical and psychological benefits. As de Figueiredo et al. (2021) note, exposure to nature benefits children in terms of lower stress levels, better physical health development, improved self-control and fewer inappropriate behaviours in class, better communicative and social development, and improved cognitive development, including greater curiosity and creativity. For some urban young people, school may be one of few places offering access to nature (e.g., through local land-based education and field trips). We benefit from understanding that there exists in our world something larger than ourselves. As Odawa educator Dr. Cecil King said, "there's a greater world beyond where [people] are and if they're totally in tune with the environment, then there's hope" (cited in Coleman, 2022). A commitment to radical decolonial love ensures that we act in the best interests of our students' holistic wellness, including fostering a connection to the natural world and helping our students understand their responsibilities to each other and to nature. By drawing on Indigenous perspectives of wellness as connectedness and adopting a mentality of radical decolonial love, schools could continue to be a place where positive changes in support of a broader understanding can be made.

This requires an understanding of both the (primarily Western) education system and its goals and Indigenous perspectives based on relationships and interconnectedness. The concept of two-eyed seeing, or *Etuaptmumk*, recognizes the beneficial outcomes of merging two or more perspectives, specifically Western or Eurocentric and Indigenous seeing (Bartlett et al., 2015; Iwama et al., 2009; Marshall et al., 2015). Marshall et al. (2015) explain that the gift of multiple perspectives is treasured by many Indigenous Peoples. They describe two-eyed seeing as learning to see from one eye the strengths of Indigenous Knowledges and ways of knowing and learning to see from the other eye the strengths of Western knowledges and ways of knowing. Most importantly, Marshall et al. (2015) emphasize that we must learn to see with both eyes together, for the benefit of all peoples. Iwama et al. (2009) stress that two-eyed seeing respectfully and meaningfully asks that people bring together different ways of knowing in order to motivate others, Indigenous and non-Indigenous. Two-eyed seeing aims to achieve the goal of leaving the world a better place and not compromising the opportunities for youth. Iwama et al. (2009) encourage this model of thinking to solve problems in our communities, especially the damage done to health through the loss of traditional language and connectedness. A two-eyed seeing approach to mental health and well-being allows the opportunity to bring in culturally sustainable and land-based initiatives that will support students in their journey toward wellness. Adopting a two-eyed seeing approach to developing documents or strategies to support mental health and well-being at a school-based level supports moving away from an individualistic mental health and wellness approach and toward one that acknowledges and infuses Indigenous ways of knowing, being, and doing.

## RECOMMENDATIONS AND CONCLUSION

According to the *Opening Minds Interim Report*, published by the Mental Health Commission of Canada (MHCC) (2013), schools are an ideal place to provide universal mental health promotion in teaching coping skills and providing early intervention for students who may not otherwise receive treatment. The MHCC (2013) reports that youth are at a high risk of being stigmatized, and the fear of stigma often delays the reception of a diagnosis or treatment. For this reason, working with schools to identify, evaluate, and then replicate successful anti-stigma programs is critical (MHCC, 2013). Schools can make a difference and have a positive impact on a student's mental health and well-being when supports and interventions are provided. By balancing the pervasive Western cultural understanding of well-being with Indigenous perspectives through a model of two-eyed seeing, we can develop holistic, individually relevant, and culturally reflective ways to foster not only academic development but also wellness in each student's emotional, physical, spiritual, and intellectual dimensions.

Indigenous perspectives can inform school communities on how to support learners' whole selves in classrooms and schools, but incorporating Indigenous Knowledges must be done appropriately and with respect. Educators must have a good understanding of local community and a willingness to acknowledge Indigenous ways of knowing, being, and doing. Knowing where knowledge comes from and how to incorporate it in a good way must be at the forefront of the work being done in schools and classrooms.

Working with Indigenous community members is important to promote collective and wraparound support that nourishes the social, emotional, mental, physical, and spiritual wellness of a person. We offer several recommendations for how schools can mobilize this framework and consider adopting an Indigenous worldview on mental health and well-being.

- Identify the need for mental health and well-being supports through student, staff, family, and community voice.
- Gather data in culturally sustainable ways (e.g., talking circles, offering a meal).

- Acknowledge each individual's cultural protocols (e.g., tobacco, cloth) and offer that to them as a request to support Indigenous students and staff.
- Ensure that teachers have knowledge of and access to Indigenous Education Leads and Indigenous-vetted activities and resources available through their local boards of education.
- Work with Indigenous community members to provide cultural safety training to staff so that they can better understand how to work with Indigenous students, families, and communities.
- Invite Indigenous community members to speak about Indigenous approaches to mental health and well-being. This may include providing knowledge on ways of knowing, being, and doing, including the Seven Grandfather Teachings and the Great Law of Peace as teachings for how we maintain positive relationships with ourselves and others.
- Understand how the land supports our well-being and work with Indigenous community members to bring more land-based learning opportunities to the classroom.
- Engage families and community members in mental health and well-being initiatives.
- Create safe spaces in schools where students can participate in cultural wellness opportunities such as smudging.

Through engaging in the practices noted above, we can promote a shift away from individualistic responsibility for mental health and well-being and instead adopt a mindset that provides collective and community-based support for all members of our communities and acknowledges that the land, community, family, nation, culture, and environment impact our mental health and wellness.

Indigenous perspectives and practices have much to offer to support a broader comprehension of flourishing. Challenging deep-seated values and assumptions is required to move beyond mainstream notions of success measured by competitive advantage to an understanding that honours all our relations and acknowledges that well-being is fully possible only when all of our flourishing is mutual.

## KEY TERMS

**A good mind, relational responsibility, and a sense of reverence and gratitude:** Key elements of Haudenosaunee ontology that integrally inform Haudenosaunee ways of understanding the world and living in harmony with it. This requires a commitment to seeing and acting in a positive way; dedication to living in reciprocity with other humans, other-than-human relatives, and the earth; and intentional gratitude for all parts of creation.

**Radical decolonial love:** A purposeful approach to relationships that recognizes love as a way to build connections and dismantle oppressive colonial systems. It is radical in that it requires fierce commitment to belonging, equality, and reciprocity in the face of Western epistemologies that demand the opposite.

**Seven Grandfather Teachings:** Sacred Anishinaabe teachings of *dabasendiziwin* (humility); *gwayakwaadiziwin* (honesty); *manaaji'idiwin* (respect); *zoongide'ewin* (courage); *nibwaakaawin* (wisdom); *debwewin* (truth); and *zaagi'idiwin* (love) (SGEI, 2021). These teachings are important to many Anishinaabe people and communities who use them as guiding principles to live *mino-bimaadiziwin* (a good life).

**Two-eyed seeing:** *Etuapmtumk* in Mi'kmaq, a way of learning from the best of two or more perspectives and bringing these perspectives together harmoniously for the benefit of people and the natural world.

## DISCUSSION QUESTIONS AND ACTIVITIES

1. Focusing on Indigenous Knowledges from the land on which you live, how can you shift/decolonize your perspective of wellness?
2. How does this understanding compare with Western perspectives, and how can two-eyed seeing bring these perspectives together? What opportunities, challenges, and risks do you see in taking this approach?
3. How can the concept of radical decolonial love inform your perspective on relationships among students, teachers, and broader human and more-than-human relatives? How can this concept be translated into praxis or policy in your experience?

## REFERENCES

Bartlett, C., Marshall, M., Marshall, M., & Iwama, M. (2015). Integrative science and two-eyed seeing: Enriching the discussion framework for healthy communities. In L. K. Hallstrom, N. Guehlstorf, & M. Parkes (Eds.), *Ecosystems, society and health: Pathways through diversity, convergence, and integration* (pp. 280–326). McGill-Queen's University Press.

Battiste, M. (2013). *Decolonizing education: Nourishing the learner spirit*. UBC Press.

Benton-Banai, E. (1988). *The Mishomis book: The voice of the Ojibway*. Red School House.

Biana, H. T. (2021). Love as an act of resistance: bell hooks on love. In S. Hongladarom & J. J. Joaquin (Eds.), *Love and friendship across cultures: Perspectives from east and west*. (pp. 127–140). Springer. doi.org/10.1007/978-981-33-4834-9

Bill 98: Better Schools and Student Outcomes Act. (2023). Royal assent received June 8, 2023, 43rd legislature, Ontario. www.ola.org/en/legislative-business/bills/parliament-43/session-1/bill-98

Bouchard, D., & Martin, J. (2009). *Seven sacred teachings: Niizhwaaswi gagiikwewin*. More than Words.

Cabanas, E., & Illouz, E. (2019). *Manufacturing happy citizens: How the science and industry of happiness control our lives*. Wiley.

Chartrand, R. (2012). Anishinaabe pedagogy. *Canadian Journal of Native Education, 35*(1), 144–162. doi.org/10.14288/cjne.v35i1.196534

Coleman, C. (2022, February 21). *New memoir details how Cecil King went from humble beginnings to celebrated Indigenous educator in Saskatchewan*. CBC News. www.cbc.ca/news/canada/saskatchewan/new-memoir-cecil-king-1.6359454

Corbiere, A. I. (2000). Reconciling epistemological orientations: Toward a wholistic Nishnaabe (Ojibwe/Odawa/Potowatomi) education. *Canadian Journal of Native Education, 24*(2), 113–119. https://eric.ed.gov/?id=ED467707

Crenshaw, K. (1991). Demarginalizing the intersection of race and sex: A Black feminist critique of antidiscrimination doctrine feminist theory and antiracist politics. *University of Chicago Legal Forum, 1*(8), 139–167. https://chicagounbound.uchicago.edu/cgi/viewcontent.cgi?article=1052&context=uclf

Davis, L., Hare, J., Hiller, C., Morcom, L. A., & Taylor, L. (2023). Pedagogies of inheriting: Kitchen table conversations. *Contingencies, 1*(2). doi.org/10.33682/8kwh-ug1q

de Figueiredo, C. S., Sandre, P. C., Portugal, L. C. L., Mázala-de-Oliveira, T., da Silva Chagas, L., Raony, Í., Ferreira, E. S., Giestal-de-Araujo, E., dos Santos, A. A., & Bomfim, P. O. S. (2021). COVID-19 pandemic impact on children and adolescents' mental health: Biological, environmental, and social factors. *Progress in Neuro-Psychopharmacology and Biological Psychiatry, 106*, 110171. doi.org/10.1016/j.pnpbp.2020.110171

Ermine, W. (1995). Aboriginal epistemology. In M. Battiste & J. Barman (Eds.), *First Nations education in Canada: The circle unfolds* (pp. 101–112). UBC Press.

First Nations Health Authority. (2012). *First Nations perspective on health and wellness*. www.fnha.ca/wellness/wellness-for-first-nations/first-nations-perspective-on-health-and-wellness

Hampton, E. (1995). Memory comes before knowledge: Research may improve if researchers remember their motives. *Canadian Journal of Native Education, 21*. doi.org/10.14288/cjne.v21i.195782

Holder, S., & Lannon, A. (Eds.). (2020). *Student wellness and academic libraries: Case studies and activities for promoting health and success*. Association of College & Research Libraries.

hooks, b. (1994). *Outlaw culture: Resisting representations*. Routledge.

hooks, b. (2003). *Teaching community: A pedagogy of hope*. Routledge.

Iwama, M., Marshall, M., Marshall, A., & Bartlett, C. (2009). Two-eyed seeing and the language of healing in community-based research. *Canadian Journal of Native Education, 32*(2), 3–23. doi.org/10.14288/cjne.v32i2.196493

Johnson, P. (1996). *Native voices on Native science: Mohawk perspectives on the concept, practice, and meaning of a knowledge production system rooted in traditional Native thought* [Master's thesis, Wilfrid Laurier University].

Joshanloo, M., Van de Vliert, E., & Jose, P. E. (2021). Four fundamental distinctions in conceptions of well-being across cultures. In M. L. Kern & M. L. Wehmeyer (Eds.), *The Palgrave handbook of positive education* (pp. 675–703). Springer Nature. doi.org/10.1007/978-3-030-64537-3_26

Kimmerer, R. W. (2015). *Braiding sweetgrass: Indigenous wisdom, scientific knowledge, and the teachings of plants.* Milkweed Editions.

Longboat, D. (2018, June 29). *Interview with Dan Longboat.* The National Centre for Collaboration in Indigenous Education. www.nccie.ca/story/interview-with-dan-longboat/

Makhubu, N., & Mbongwa, K. (2019). Radical love as decolonial philosophy: In conversation with Khanyisile Mbongwa. *Journal of Decolonising Disciplines, 1*(1), 10–26. https://upjournals.up.ac.za/index.php/jdd/article/view/53/9

Maldonado-Torres, N. (2008). *Against war: Views from the underside of modernity.* Duke University Press. doi.org/10.1215/9780822388999

Maluleka, P. (2023). Teaching and learning sensitive and controversial topics in history through and with decolonial love. *Yesterday & Today, 29*, 30–51. doi.org/10.17159/2223-0386/2023/n29a3

Marshall, M., Marshall, M., & Bartlett, C. (2015). Two-eyed seeing in medicine. In M. Greenwood, S. de Leeuw, N. M. Lindsay, & C. Reading (Eds.), *Determinants of Indigenous peoples' health in Canada: Beyond the social* (pp. 16–24). Canadian Scholars.

Mental Health Commission of Canada. (2013, November 18). *Opening minds: Interim report.* https://mentalhealthcommission.ca/wp-content/uploads/2021/05/opening_minds_interim_report_0.pdf

Morcom, L. A. (2017). Indigenous holistic education in philosophy and practice, with wampum as a case study. *Foro de Educación, 15*(23), 121–138. doi.org/10.14516/fde.572

Morcom, L. A., & Butler, A. (2023, February). *Anti-racism and decolonization: Why it matters* [Conference presentation]. Harmony Movement 2023 Educators' Anti-Racism Conference, York University, Toronto, ON.

Morcom, L. A., & Freeman, K. (2018). Niinwi-Kiinwa-Kiinwi: Building non-Indigenous allies in education. *Canadian Journal of Education, 41*(3), 584–609. https://eric.ed.gov/?id=EJ1192156

Moreno, S. (2019). Love as resistance: Exploring conceptualizations of decolonial love in settler states. *Girlhood Studies: An Interdisciplinary Journal, 12*(3), 116–133. doi.org/10.3167/ghs.2019.120310

Ray, L., & Cormier, P. N. (2012). Killing the Weendigo with maple syrup: Anishnaabe pedagogy and post-secondary research. *Canadian Journal of Native Education, 35*(1), 163–176. doi.org/10.14288/cjne.v35i1.196535

Recollet, K. (2015). Glyphing decolonial love through urban flash mobbing and *Walking with Our Sisters*. *Curriculum Inquiry, 45*(1), 129–145. doi.org/10.1080/03626784.2014.995060

Rheault, D. R. R. I. (1999). *Anishinaabe mino-bimaadiziwin (the way of a good life)* [Master's thesis, Trent University].

Salzman, P. C. (2017, February 13). *Yes, Canada does have a culture: Philip Carl Salzman for Inside Policy*. McDonald Laurier Institute. https://macdonaldlaurier.ca/yes-canada-does-have-a-culture-philip-carl-salzman-for-inside-policy/

Sandoval, C. (2000). *Methodology of the oppressed*. University of Minnesota Press.

School Mental Health Ontario. (2023, April 20). *Mentally healthy schools and learning environments*. https://smho-smso.ca/educators-and-student-support-staff/mentally-healthy-classrooms/

Seven Generations Education Institute. (2021, February 3). *Seven grandfather teachings*. www.7generations.org/seven-grandfather-teachings/

Stark, K. J. (2021). Anishinaabe inaakonigewin: Principles for the intergenerational preservation of mino-bimaadiziwin. *Montana Law Review, 82*(2), 293–341. https://scholarworks.umt.edu/mlr/vol82/iss2/2/

Stonechild, B. (2016). *The knowledge seeker: Embracing Indigenous spirituality*. University of Regina Press.

Sturdy, J. (n.d.). *Screen time vs. green time*. Nature Canada. https://naturecanada.ca/enjoy-nature/for-children/screen-time-vs-green-time/

Ureña, C. (2017). Loving from below: Of (de)colonial love and other demons. *Hypatia, 32*(1), 86–102. doi.org/10.1111/hypa.12302

Walters, A. S. (2022). School absenteeism in the post-pandemic world. *The Brown University Child and Adolescent Behaviour Letter, 39*(1), 8. doi.org/10.1002/cbl.30684

Waterman, S. J. (2023). "They won't do it the way I can": Haudenosaunee relationality and goodness in Native American postsecondary student support. *Journal of Diversity in Higher Education, 16*(4), 437–446. https://psycnet.apa.org/doi/10.1037/dhe0000352

West, C. (1993). *Race matters*. Vintage Books.

Whitlow, K. B., Anderson, V. O. K., Brozowski, K., Tschirhart, S., Charles, D., & Ransom, K. (2019). Yehyatonhserayenteri: A Haudenosaunee model for Onkwehon:we (Indigenous) education. *Canadian Journal of Education, 42*(2), 553–575. https://journals.sfu.ca/cje/index.php/cje-rce/article/view/3725

# PART VI

## LANGUAGE: POLICIES AND PRACTICES TO SUPPORT LINGUISTIC INCLUSION AND FLOURISHING

# CHAPTER 12
# Globalization, Decolonization, and the Diversity of Linguistic Identities: A Review of Language Policies and Practices in Canadian K–12 Education

*Sonya Sachar and Karen A. Krasny*

Globalization prompts a reassessment of new ideas, views, and aspects of language and culture. In line with Blommaert and Rampton's (2011) assertion that globalization has "altered the face of social, cultural, and linguistic diversity in societies all over the world" (p. 1), this chapter explores the impact of globalization on language and culture. Specifically, it examines how national language policies influence educational policies and practices in Canadian K–12 classrooms and schools. The focus is on navigating the transformed landscape, characterized by dynamic "superdiversity" (Vertovec, 2007, 2019), and emphasizing an orientation toward the promise of *plurilingualism* (Krasny & Sachar, 2017). We maintain that the implementation of national language policies in Canada is a direct result of the 1960s' Royal Commission on Bilingualism and Biculturalism, which enshrined official French and English language rights and the Trudeau government's 1971 policy of multiculturalism within a bilingual framework. These frameworks served to bolster a view of Canada as a cultural mosaic—one of ethnic inclusiveness of diverse yet distinct linguistic and ethnic communities. However, they fell short of respecting the plurality of linguistic, national, and cultural perspectives within the individual. **Superdiversity** attempts to account for a large increase in the categories of migrants in countries such as Canada "not only in terms of nationality, ethnicity, language, and religion, but also in terms of motives, patterns and itineraries of migration, [and] processes of insertion into the labor and housing markets of the host societies" (Vertovec, 2007, p. 1025). The range of migratory influences contributes to increasing numbers of students in Canada whose language repertoire and practices draw from a myriad of cultural and linguistic experiences. In response, publicly funded schools in Canada have attempted to embrace diversity through the integration of culturally reflective and responsive practices that honour students' lived experiences and identities, albeit with varying degrees of success (Krasny & Sachar, 2017). For educators in K–12 schools, the variables associated with increasingly complex patterns of migration affect "where, how, and with whom people teach and learn" (Gogolin, 2011, p. 241).

In this chapter, we explore policies and practices enacted in the Canadian context that reflect a changing landscape and demographics. Specifically, we provide a review of national language policies in Canada, and in doing so we consider how a respect for superdiversity and plurilingualism might enhance schools' capacity to deliver on the educational recommendations of the Truth and Reconciliation Commission's Calls to Action (2015) in service of decolonizing education through land-based curriculum. Finally, in our critical review of current language policy and practice in K–12 schools, we consider how recurring pivots between in-person and remote learning lend yet another dynamic dimension to an increasingly complex educational landscape and examine the burgeoning influence of artificial intelligence (AI) on language learning in Canada.

## SUPERDIVERSITY

Vertovec (2007) originally coined the term *superdiversity* in response to changing patterns observed in British migration data, calling attention to "differential legal statuses and their concomitant conditions, divergent labour market experiences, discrete configurations of gender and age, patterns of spatial distribution, and mixed local area responses by service providers and residents. The dynamic interaction of these variables is what is meant by 'superdiversity'" (p. 1025).

Similar to what has happened in Britain, globalization has rendered Canadian K–12 classrooms superdiverse. In fact, it is estimated that in 2031, nearly half the population in Canada will be first- or second-generation immigrants, a third will have a first language other than English or French, and a third will be racialized minorities (Statistics Canada, 2022). However, while we recognize that superdiversity aims to account for the complex formation and intersection of cultural and linguistic identities among migrant populations, it also falls short in some significant ways. Vertovec (2019) himself has recognized the need to expand interests and uses for the concept of superdiversity to arrive at better ways to describe and analyze new and varied social patterns, forms, and identities. But his definitional extension still derives from migration-driven diversification. As it is currently defined, then, superdiversity cannot immediately be extended to Indigenous Peoples and others without considerable qualification that recognizes the liminal existence forced upon Indigenous Peoples and those cast on the borders of nationhood. As such, we still see a definite need to better acknowledge the dominant role of imperialism and colonization on cultural and linguistic subjugation, which have determined, for example, how Indigenous populations and those inhabiting cultural borderlands (e.g., francophone-minority milieux) also reflect superdiversity associated with the liminality of a bilingual existence. We view this conceptual shortcoming of superdiversity as an opportunity for educators to build upon and further think about the growing number of definitions and exceptions to productively advance our understanding of the complexity of emerging cultural and linguistic identities beyond migration-driven data.

## THE PROMISE OF PLURILINGUALISM

The Council of Europe (2007) defines plurilingualism as considering "languages not as objects but from the point of view of those who speak them. It refers to the repertoire of varieties of language which many individuals use, and is therefore the opposite of monolingualism; it includes the language variety referred to as 'mother tongue' or 'first language' and any number of other languages or varieties. Thus, in some multilingual areas some individuals may be monolingual and some may be plurilingual" (p. 8). We define **plurilingualism** within the Canadian educational context as the capacity to leverage the dynamism and interconnectedness of language competencies and knowledge in order to engage in social, cultural, and economic activity. It needs to be clearly stated, however, that the ability to recognize and leverage one's linguistic competence across a range of experiences—and plurilingualism's potential contribution to individuals' self-efficacy and how they deploy such knowledge—is highly subject to economic and political power. In many countries, this ability alone does not guarantee language rights or basic human freedoms. For these reasons and others explored in this chapter both within and outside of the Canadian context, we focus on the potentiality or *promise of plurilingualism*. We maintain that the promise of plurilingualism is dependent on the extent to which individuals can freely engage as social actors to access their knowledge of languages in interactive ways as a form of cultural, intellectual, and social capital. In this regard, fostering plurilingualism in Canadian classrooms and communities is consistent with motivational concepts in Aristotle's notion of human flourishing or eudaimonic living that emphasize the pursuit of intrinsic goals and values and satisfying the need for competence, relatedness, and autonomy (Ryan et al., 2008). The capacity to flourish in culturally and linguistically superdiverse classrooms depends, therefore, on the right of students to cultivate their linguistic identities as they freely negotiate competing discourses and varying points of view.

Historically, **multilingualism** throughout the world was a function of power differentials closely tied to colonization and processes of nation-building whereby monolingual white elites determined language norms (Flores & Rosa, 2015; Garcia & Otheguy, 2020; Makoni & Pennycook, 2007; Rosa & Flores, 2017). Monolingual elites wanting to learn another language did so as part of their educational formation in schools and focused on target languages that were held separate from what is still often referred to as the first language or "mother" tongue. In this regard, we draw an important distinction between the idea of multilingualism composed of first (L1) and second language (L2), performed separately, where at least one of these is a dominant European language (e.g., English, French, Spanish) (Garcia & Otheguy, 2020), and the kind of unified practices of languaging we associate with the promise of plurilingualism. It needs to be said, therefore, that while mastery of another language is an admirable goal, it is not necessarily the fulfillment of the promise of plurilingualism. That said, it would be foolhardy not to acknowledge that, for many immigrants and for migrants seeking refuge, language competency in one of Canada's two official languages is a fundamental requirement on the road to citizenship and commonly seen as necessary to full economic integration and fulfillment of their aspirations for their children. These requirements make for a strong motivation for language learning.

In her work on Ukrainian language and identity just prior to the 2014 Euromaidan revolution, Krasny (2009) explored Bourdieu's notion of "embodied capital" to describe how the intersections of language and cultural traditions contribute to a complex sense of self and ways of acting in the world. In this way, one's communicative ability in many languages, in accordance with an individual's needs, is an important form of embodied capital. Bourdieu sees embodied capital as being inherited and acquired, though not in the genetic sense, but rather through a process of socialization whereby time, culture, and traditions are bestowed intergenerationally within and across families. Access to such capital is thus linked to social stratification and reproduction of power.

We ask readers to contemplate how an orientation toward understanding language and language traditions as a form of embodied capital might serve as a decolonizing principle. In particular, this perspective can help educators begin to redress the cultural and linguistic genocide of First Nations, Inuit, and Métis peoples in seeking to deliver on the educational recommendations outlined in the *Truth and Reconciliation Commission of Canada: Calls to Action* (2015) section on education and language and culture. Later in this chapter, we provide an example of Indigenous language learning at a public high school in Western Canada to explore how language and discourse practices can reflect Indigenous approaches and ways of knowing and a land-based learning curriculum while responding to the very real needs of urban Indigenous students. But first we present an overview of language policies in Canada.

## LANGUAGE POLICIES IN CANADA: FROM OFFICIAL LANGUAGE RIGHTS TO PLURILINGUALISM

This section provides an overview of how various Canadian national policies related to cultural and linguistic diversity have evolved. First, we will describe the policies and why they are important to review and evaluate as educators. We then move into an overview of Canadian national policies from the 1960s to present to bring to light the importance of how these policies inform language learning in Canadian classrooms and how we must rethink national policies and projects to reflect the complex and diverse social, cultural, and linguistic histories of various communities more fully.

To provide a single definition of policy is challenging because in varying contexts this term carries with it different connotations. Ozga (2000) argues "that there is no fixed, single definition of policy" (p. 2). Instead, Ozga interprets "policy as a *process* rather than a product, involving negotiation, contestation or struggle between different groups of people who may lie outside the formal machinery of official policy making" (p. 2). Within education, Krasny and Sachar (2017) argue, policies serve to institutionalize spaces and practices that educators use within their classrooms. Analyzing these policies offers an assessment of the educational system and a basis on which to provide recommendations and improvements at various levels of jurisdiction (e.g., school, board, provincial ministry, and federal government). Additionally, Krasny and

Sachar (2017) contend that analyses that are aimed at understanding language policies and outcomes are important for education because they reveal how these policies are used as "mechanisms of power and manipulation" (p. 37). Shohamy (2006) argues, "Language policy (LP) is the primary mechanism for organizing, managing and manipulating language behavior as it consists of decisions made about languages and their uses in society" (p. 45). In this regard, we ask educators to critically think about and examine how past and present Canadian national language policies influence curriculum and classroom practices. And more importantly, how do we as educators recognize the importance of language revitalization and maintenance for individuals and communities?

## Royal Commission on Bilingualism and Biculturalism (1963–1970)

In Canada, the 1960s signified a growing recognition of diversity on the part of the federal government. It was during this period that a change in federal immigration policies brought increased numbers of non-European immigrants, contributing to greater linguistic and cultural diversity across Canada (Anderson & Jaafar, 2006; Haque & Patrick, 2015). For example, in 1963, under the authority of Lester Pearson, the Royal Commission on Bilingualism and Biculturalism (commonly known as the B and B Commission) was established. This has been noted as the "most influential commission in Canadian history" (Laing, 2013) as it resulted in a policy not only to reflect changing demographics but also to maintain the status of French and English within Canada as official languages: the 1969 Official Languages Act and the 1971 multiculturalism policy (multiculturalism within a bilingual framework). The B and B Commission aimed to foster a greater sense of belonging among Canadians while addressing the following three areas of interest: "radical changes to immigration policy, the federal government's ongoing attempts to abolish the Indian Act, and the rise of Quebec linguistic nationalism and independence movements" (Krasny & Sachar, 2017, p. 38). The commission also recommended steps to strengthen Canadian confederation of the two languages while taking into consideration "the contribution made by the other ethnic groups to the cultural enrichment of Canada" (Royal Commission on Bilingualism and Biculturalism, 1967, p. xxi). Although these recommendations were made, the B and B Commission failed to recognize the marginalization of Indigenous groups and the languages and rich histories that were already existent in the Canadian landscape. As Haque and Patrick (2015) argue, language ideologies underpinning the B and B Commission's policies positioned English and French "as superior and indigenous languages as 'primitive' and as barriers to 'civilisation' and modernity" (p. 28). Additionally, by defining separate and unequal groups, such as "founding races" (pp. 4–5) and "other ethnic groups" (pp. 50–60), the B and B Commission's policies silenced Indigenous Peoples and helped perpetuate the very policies of assimilation that dominated residential schooling in support of settler nation-building (Barman, 1986; Castellano, 2008; Chrisjohn & Young, 1994; Milloy, 1999; Sassen, 2014). In short, the B and B Commission contributed to the maintenance of a racial hierarchy and the reinscription of English and French dominance.

## Official Languages Act (1969)

In 1969 the Official Languages Act declared Canada a bilingual country with French and English as its official languages. This act affirmed that bilingualism was to be reflected in federal and provincial levels of government in Canada and their administrative bodies. For education, this policy was seen as a means of legitimizing one's ability to fully participate in Canadian society (Krasny & Sachar, 2017). Accordingly, parents had the right to educate their children in either French or English, but all children were to learn these languages, and French became a mandatory part of the curriculum (Anderson & Jaafar, 2006). The act validated terms such as *mother tongue* and *official languages* that ultimately shaped the educational fabrication with regards to languages in schools. Furthermore, the act set time limits for implementation of bilingualism in provincial and federal government offices, including nominations and promotions by the Public Service Commission of relevant personnel who "effectively worked to incentivize French instruction in English schools across Canada for years to come" (Krasny & Sachar, 2017, p. 38). The Official Languages Act continued to cause divisiveness between various linguistic groups and communities throughout Canada. It was seen to discourage other groups from using their linguistic practices and created a linguistic and cultural hierarchy in which terms such as *biculturalism* and *bilingualism* legitimized the view that Canada had only two national groups (French Canadians and English Canadians) (Krasny & Sachar, 2017; Martel, 2019). Through community representatives, individuals voiced some of these challenges. For example, large numbers of families who had immigrated to Canada, including the Ukrainian community, expressed the view that bilingualism was exclusionary and questioned why, in places such as Western Canada, where the percentage of francophones was around only 2 percent, bilingualism was being imposed (Martel, 2019). More importantly, the act failed to recognize Indigenous languages and ultimately continued to reinforce a "no status" agenda (Haque & Patrick, 2015; Martel, 2019). In 1971, Canada embarked upon the national project known as multiculturalism within a bilingual framework in an attempt to curb ongoing and rising tensions.

## Multiculturalism within a Bilingual Framework (1971) and Canada's Policy on Multiculturalism

In 1971, under Pierre Elliott Trudeau's leadership, the Liberal government established a national policy of multiculturalism within a bilingual framework. The framework asserted that "there are two official languages, there is no official culture, nor does any ethnic group take precedence over any other. No citizen or group of citizens is other than Canadian" (Canada. House of Commons Debates, 1971, p. 8545). While this initiative sought to alleviate tensions about divisiveness among other language groups in Canada and give recognition to the two official languages, it continued to integrate citizens into an already existing "radicalized hierarchy of belonging and citizenship rights" (Haque, 2012, p. 6). More importantly, the policy failed to recognize Indigenous groups in Canada and their languages. In fact, the preservation and promotion of Indigenous languages remained unrealized within Canadian policies until later in the 20th century. While constitutions and policies in later years (e.g., Canadian Charter of Rights and Freedoms and the Multiculturalism Act) were established to reflect the changing demographics of the languages spoken in Canada to be more inclusive and to alleviate inequality, they continued to exclude languages other than French and English by categorizing them as *nonofficial*. Due to this, the definition of nonofficial languages included Indigenous and immigrant languages. As a direct consequence of this, the term **heritage language**, which first appeared in the Canadian Heritage Languages Institute Act of 1991, refers to "language, other than one of the official languages of Canada, that contributes to the linguistic heritage of Canada" (Government of Canada, 1991). These languages are most often associated with newcomers, settlers, and immigrants to Canada, and "heritage refers to knowledge of an ancestral language" (Eaton & Turin, 2022, p. 788). The term *heritage language* does include Indigenous languages and recognizes languages that have been brought to Canada through immigration; however, Canadian Indigenous communities do not see their languages as heritage languages and prefer to use terms such as *Indigenous languages* (Cummins, 2005).

## Heritage Language Programs in Canadian Schools

After the enactment of the Multiculturalism Act, Canadian schools implemented educational programming that supported heritage languages and/or international language education. Many schools presently provide heritage language and international language learning, starting as early as kindergarten. The range of offerings and conditions governing their provision are province-specific, and models include regularly scheduled language classes similar to core French or more substantive half-day immersion programs. For example, since 1979, Manitoba's Public Schools Act has provided for instruction in languages other than English or French for up to 50 percent of the school day. Such programs meet criteria for bilingual heritage language programming whereby language arts, social studies, art, and physical education may be taught in the target heritage language from kindergarten through grade 6 (Manitoba Education, n.d.). Languages of study presently offered in Manitoba include Arabic, Cree, Filipino, German, Hebrew, Japanese, Mandarin, Ojibwe, Portuguese, Punjab, Spanish, and Ukrainian, with bilingual heritage programs offered in Cree, Filipino, German, Hebrew, Ojibwe, Spanish, and Ukrainian. Since 1977, Ontario has provided a variety of offerings in support of its Heritage Languages Program and its International Languages—Elementary Program, including Cantonese, German, Hebrew, Italian, Korean, Mandarin, Portuguese, Punjabi, Spanish, Tamil, Ukrainian, Urdu, and dozens of other languages spoken in immigrant communities (Nagy, 2021). The general goal of all heritage language programs is the preservation of the language, culture, and identity, and significant numbers of students participate in these programs (Baker, 2011). Although there is government support for such programs in the provinces that have chosen to mandate them, there are other provincial governments that oppose public funding for such programs (e.g., Prince Edward Island, Newfoundland and Labrador). Additionally, there are variations across provinces and school boards regarding policies, course offerings, and the number of students enrolled in these programs. Although these programs emphasize the importance of preserving one's identity through language maintenance, they continue to pose an issue as they do not adequately describe an individual's linguistic experiences and histories. For example, learning a heritage or international language through these programs does not provide enough information about one's existing linguistic repertoire, known languages, and languages that are spoken (Sachar, 2017). Additionally, there is not always a clear understanding of parental and community aspirations for children's enrolment into such programs. Sachar's (2017) doctoral ethnographic study of a private Russian language school in an Ontario suburb reveals that language maintenance did not hold singular or primary importance among parents of students residing in a Russian-speaking community and that, in fact, for some students, Russian was not their first language. Sachar noted that the creation of the small Russian language school was in direct response to parental aspirations and their commitment to providing their children with a STEM curriculum that more closely corresponded to shared educational aims for mathematics and sciences experienced in post-Soviet countries. Heritage language and international language programs continue to pose a larger systemic question of whose languages count as heritage and, more broadly, whose heritage counts.

This review of Canadian national and educational language policies offers a critical overview for teachers, as stakeholders in education, to further think about their own positionality and pedagogy in relation to changing student demographics while continuing to reflect on larger forces that will continue to govern and legitimize what can be taught in the classroom. Furthermore, we ask teachers to consider how students can enact their knowledge of multiple languages in linguistically diverse classrooms in ways that more fully recognize students' identities. More importantly, how have such policies continued to create assimilative practices that have led to the erasure of Indigenous languages, and what is our responsibility as educators to deliver on the educational recommendations of *Truth and Reconciliation Commission of Canada: Calls to Action*?

## INDIGENOUS LANGUAGES AND THE TRUTH AND RECONCILIATION CALLS TO ACTION

As of March 2023, Statistics Canada reported that there are 70 distinct Indigenous languages that are currently spoken by First Nations people, Métis, and Inuit across Canada. The United Nations Educational, Scientific and Cultural Organization's (UNESCO's) *Atlas of the World's Languages in Danger* (Moseley, 2010) identifies all Indigenous languages spoken in Canada as being considered at risk; they have been classified as either "vulnerable," "definitely endangered," "severely endangered," or "critically endangered" (definitions of language endangerment can be found in Moseley, 2010, pp. 11–12). While Canadian language policies have influenced Canadian education, they continue to enforce national unity and control, producing forms of exclusion and maintaining a white-settler nation (Haque, 2014). Over the past six decades, there has been little progress because official language policies remain enshrined in settler-colonial sovereignty as Indigenous communities continue to make efforts to reclaim, revitalize, and maintain their languages. In 2015, the Truth and Reconciliation Commission of Canada (TRC) issued 94 Calls to Action. In redressing the ongoing legacy of the residential school system, reconciliation emphasizes the importance of recognizing and implementing rights related to Indigenous languages. Specifically, Calls to Action 13 and 14 demand the acknowledgement of Aboriginal (the term used in the Calls to Action) language rights and the rebuilding of Canada's relationship with Indigenous Peoples, predicated on the following five principles:

- Aboriginal languages are a fundamental and valued element of Canadian culture and society, and there is an urgency to preserve them.
- Aboriginal language rights are reinforced by the Treaties.
- The federal government is responsible for providing sufficient funds for Aboriginal-language revitalization and preservation.
- The preservation, revitalization, and strengthening of Aboriginal languages and cultures are best managed by Aboriginal people and communities.
- Funding for Aboriginal language initiatives must reflect the diversity of Aboriginal languages. (Truth and Reconciliation Commission of Canada, 2015, p. 2)

In response to these Calls to Action, on July 21, 2019, the Indigenous Languages Act was passed by Parliament and received Royal Assent. The act was established to "preserve, promote and revitalize Indigenous languages in Canada" and "to support the efforts of Indigenous peoples to reclaim, revitalize, maintain and strengthen their languages" (Government of Canada, 2019). With the implementation of the act, the Government of Canada has stated that this Call to Action is completed; however, the act further sets out several purposes and mechanisms (see the Government of Canada's website: https://laws-lois.justice.gc.ca/eng/acts/i-7.85/page-1.html). Additionally, UNESCO (2021) declared 2022 to 2032 the International Decade of Indigenous Languages to draw attention to the critical loss of Indigenous languages and the urgent need to preserve and promote them nationally and internationally. This mandate is important for the Canadian context as Statistics Canada (2023) recently reported that "approximately 237,420 Indigenous people in Canada reported they could speak an Indigenous language well enough to conduct a conversation in 2021, down by 10,750, or 4.3 percent, from 2016." As outlined in the TRC Calls to Action, education has and is a fundamental approach to fostering reconciliation and the maintenance and revitalization of Indigenous languages (see also chapter 10).

A number of long-standing Indigenous language programs and dedicated public schools predate the TRC and its Calls to Action. Note that Calls to Action 62 to 65 specifically focus on education for reconciliation. Children of the Earth High School in Winnipeg was established by the Winnipeg School Division in

1991. For more than 30 years, the school has provided Indigenous language programming (Cree and Ojibwe) for students in grades 9 to 12. The programs and initiatives have evolved over time and continue to be responsive to the students and the community the school serves from its inner-city location. Consistent with the idea in plurilingualism that meaningful language learning and communicative interactions can thrive among nonfluent and fluent speakers, heritage language programming at Children of the Earth aims to build upon various levels of reading and writing skills throughout a student's time at the school. Language outcomes for students are embedded in cultural content and real-world contexts. Children of the Earth's website features a monthly calendar of ceremonies and gatherings (e.g., medicine gathering, pipe ceremonies, Sweat Lodge ceremonies) that engage Elders in instructional life and community events (Winnipeg School Division, 2021). The school also supports several career-building initiatives, including the Omazinibii'gig Artist Collective, in which student artists partner with Indigenous artists working professionally to create and market their work in an "exciting journey of artistic expression, entrepreneurship and self-discovery" (Winnipeg School Division, 2022). The examples provided demonstrate important and necessary steps the Winnipeg School Division has taken in response to the TRC's Calls to Action 62 and 63. While there is no federal department of education and no national integrated system of education in Canada, there is ongoing work that each provincial and territorial government can take on in collaboration with Indigenous community members in the process of decolonizing and Indigenizing education across Canada.

## FROM PLURILINGUALISM TO TRANSLANGUAGING IN CANADIAN CLASSROOMS

We conclude this chapter by noting that any attempt to disrupt hegemonic linguistic structures in Canadian classrooms will always be subject to uneven power structures. By providing a historical review of Canadian language and multicultural policy and how it has shaped educational practice in Canadian schools, we propose that educators further think about their future pedagogies and practices that advance a critical understanding of plurilingualism—specifically in reference to the wide range and numbers of Indigenous, minority, and heritage language groups living in Canadian provinces and territories. While these groups are inherently diverse within their social, cultural, and linguistic histories, we ask educators to consider **translanguaging theory** as a reconceptualization to language learning. In contrast to monolingual approaches to language that continue to be implemented in Canadian classrooms, operating from a translanguaging lens provides educators with a way to understand students' language practices and encourages learners to draw on their existing linguistic resources and experiences to negotiate communicative contexts and make meaning (Canagarajah, 2011). Garcia and Wei (2014) further argue that "translanguaging does not refer to two separate languages nor to a synthesis of different language practices or to a hybrid mixture. Rather, translanguaging refers to *new* language practices that make visible the complexity of language exchanges among people with different histories, and releases histories and understandings that had been buried within fixed language identities constrained by nation-states" (p. 21). In this way, students can meet their communicative needs while exercising their linguistic and cultural identities. For example, Krasny's (2002) early theoretical research on Bakhtinian dialogism and its applications to classrooms enhances our understanding of an intersubjective existence and how to ethically engage in more open communication. Dialogism counters monolingualism as language and permits "a multiplicity of social voices and a wide variety of their links and interrelationships" (Bakhtin & Holquist, 1981, p. 263). In many regards, translanguaging is circumscribed by context insofar as students may speak one language at home (and even here may be selective about which language to speak to which family member), another when socializing in the community, and yet another school. This is not a new phenomenon. Within classrooms, students will invariably encounter limits imposed on the freedom to engage fully in a chosen language. While the aim is not to transform bilingual subjectivities into mastery of an official language (Garcia & Otheguy, 2020), there are some practical ways to engage plurilingualism. For example, students can collaborate on creating bilingual books for their peers or for read-aloud or performance to younger students. Dramatic presentations and storytelling with multilingual dialogue (not translations) can be an effective way to foster creative expression as students explore their developing understanding of multiple languages.

We expect that language expansion and the degree to which students build communicative competences—as their knowledge of language contributes, interrelates, and interacts—will vary according to a range of geographical, political, cultural, and social factors and depend upon our educational commitment to students' right to exercise linguistic agency within a range of intercultural interactions. Given that we are writing at a time when artificial intelligence (AI) is dominating both academic and public discourse on media and communication, we cannot ignore the implications for languaging in Canadian classrooms.

We have both encountered unprecedented situations where students have engaged with AI to produce assignment submissions using translation applications. The critical distinction thus far in several cases has been whether the application was transparently and strategically used to scaffold a student's linguistic understanding and ability to personally express ideas or whether it was applied in ways meant to deceive. Across Canada, schools and post-secondary institutions are engaged in making policy about the use of AI. Educators will have to carefully consider the ethical parameters of using AI applications while considering the possibilities such applications have for building students' (and instructors') knowledge of and competence in languages to communicate effectively and promoting translanguaging exchanges. There are undoubtedly contingencies we have yet to encounter, but we have both found that more sophisticated translation apps have been instrumental in helping us regain confidence in languages that we have let lapse. They serve to scaffold our prior knowledge toward more independence in crafting our message. It would be foolish not to acknowledge, however, the looming temptation for anyone to simply give the critical work to AI to create, and this is something that will continue to invariably occupy our attention. As assistive technological extensions, ChatGPT and translation apps are a bit like the introduction of calculators to math classrooms in the 1970s, whereby their legitimate instructional use demands that students still possess knowledge about operations or statistical formulae to critically select and apply to problem-solve across a range of contexts.

## KEY TERMS

**Heritage language:** A language learned and spoken within a home and/or community, where the speaker has an ancestral relationship to that language.

**Multilingualism:** The ability of societies, institutions, groups, and individuals to engage with more than one language in their day-to-day life.

**Plurilingualism:** An individual's ability to speak several languages in various social situations. The term also captures the nature of the individual language user's/learner's connectedness to their linguistic and cultural repertoires. In this way, users/learners are seen as social actors that draw upon their linguistic and cultural repertoires as resources for intercultural interactions.

**Superdiversity:** As globalization has altered social, cultural, and linguistic diversity, superdiversity attempts to account for the large increase in the categories of migrants in countries such as Canada and the United States. This is not exclusively in terms of nationality, ethnicity, language, and religion, but also in terms of motives, patterns, and itineraries of migration. The migratory patterns contribute to increasing numbers of students in North America whose language repertoire and practices draw from a myriad of cultural and linguistic experiences.

**Translanguaging theory:** First coined in 1994 by Cen Williams in Welsh (*trawsieithu*) to refer to pedagogical practices in which students in bilingual Welsh/English classrooms used these languages for different activities and intentions—for example, reading in one language and writing in another (Williams, 1994). Translanguaging theory is a reconceptualization of language learning. In contrast to monolingual approaches to language that continue to be implemented in Canadian classrooms, operating from a translanguaging lens provides educators with a way to understand students' language practices and encourages learners to draw on their existing linguistic resources, experiences, and histories to negotiate communicative contexts and make meaning.

## DISCUSSION QUESTIONS AND ACTIVITIES

1. In this chapter, how do Sachar and Krasny distinguish between multilingualism and plurilingualism? Why do they focus on the promise of plurilingualism, and what does it mean in connection to human flourishing for our communities, both local and global?
2. In response to the TRC's Calls to Action in education, as a group of four, construct three to five ways that you, as future or current educators, can work with your students to Indigenize the curriculum and approach to learning.
3. After reviewing the article "What Is Translanguaging?" (https://ealjournal.org/2016/07/26/what-is-translanguaging/) and the various examples of incorporating translanguaging practices in the classroom, consider what two or three pedagogical strategies are that you could use within your own classroom to promote translanguaging in the Canadian context.

## REFERENCES

Anderson, S. E., & Jaafar B. S. (2006). *Policy trends in Ontario education 1990–2006*. Ontario Institute for Studies in Education, University of Toronto.

Baker, C. (2011). *Foundations of bilingual education and bilingualism* (5th ed.). Multilingual Matters.

Bakhtin, M. M., & Holquist, M. (1981). *The dialogic imagination: Four essays by M. M. Bakhtin*. University of Texas Press.

Barman, J. (1986). Separate and unequal: Indian and white girls in All Hallows School, 1884–1920. In J. Barman, Y. Hebert, & D. McCaskill (Eds.), *Indian education in Canada: The legacy*, vol. 1 (pp. 110–131). University of British Columbia Press.

Blommaert, J., & Rampton, B. (2011). Language and superdiversity. *Diversities, 13*(2), 1–22. doi.org/10.58002/v6r9-1476

Canada. House of Commons Debates. (1971, October 8). *28th Parliament, 3rd Session*, vol. 8 (pp. 8545–8585). Queen's Printer. https://parl.canadiana.ca/view/oop.debates_HOC2803_08

Canagarajah, S. (2011). Translanguaging in the classroom: Emerging issues for research and pedagogy. *Applied Linguistics Review, 2*(1), 1–28. doi.org/10.1515/9783110239331.1

Castellano, M. B. (2008). *From truth to reconciliation: Transforming the legacy of residential schools*. Aboriginal Healing Foundation.

Chrisjohn, R. D., & Young, S. L. (1994). *The circle game: Shadows and substance in the Indian residential school experience in Canada*. Theytus.

Council of Europe. (2007). *From linguistic diversity to plurilingual education: Guide for the development of language education policies in Europe*. Language Policy Division. https://rm.coe.int/CoERMPublicCommonSearchServices/DisplayDCTMContent?documentId=09000016802fc1c4

Cummins, J. (2005). A proposal for action: Strategies for recognizing heritage language competence as a learning resource within the mainstream classroom. *The Modern Language Journal, 89*(4), 585–592. www.jstor.org/stable/3588628

Eaton, J., & Turin, M. (2022). Heritage languages and language as heritage: The language of heritage in Canada and beyond. *International Journal of Heritage Studies, 28*(7), 787–802. doi.org/10.1080/13527258.2022.2077805

Flores, N., & Rosa, J. (2015). Undoing appropriateness: Raciolinguistic ideologies and language diversity in education. *Harvard Educational Review, 85*(2), 149–171. doi.org/10.17763/0017-8055.85.2.149

Garcia, O., & Otheguy, R. (2020). Plurilingualism and translanguaging: Commonalities and divergences. *International Journal of Bilingual Education and Bilingualism, 23*(1), 17–35. doi.org/10.1080/13670050.2019.1598932

García, O., & Wei, L. (2014). *Translanguaging: Language, bilingualism and education*. Palgrave Macmillan.

Gogolin, I. (2011). The challenge of super diversity for education in Europe. *Education Inquiry, 2*(2), 239–249. doi.org/10.3402/edui.v2i2.21976

Government of Canada. (1991). *Canadian heritage languages institute act* (S.C. 1991, c. 7). Justice Laws Website. https://laws-lois.justice.gc.ca/eng/acts/C-17.6/

Government of Canada. (2019). *Indigenous languages act* (S.C. 2019, c. 23). Justice Laws Website. https://laws-lois.justice.gc.ca/eng/acts/i-7.85/FullText.html

Haque, E. (2012). *Multiculturalism within a bilingual framework: Language, race, and belonging in Canada*. University of Toronto Press.

Haque, E. (2014). Multiculturalism within a bilingual framework: A retrospective. *Canadian Ethnic Studies, 46*(2), 119–125. doi.org/10.1353/ces.2014.0034

Haque, E., & Patrick, D. (2015). Indigenous languages and the racial hierarchisation of language policy in Canada. *Journal of Multilingual and Multicultural Development, 36*(1), 27–41. doi.org/10.1353/ces.2014.0034

Krasny, K. A. (2002). *Dialogic spaces: Bakhtin's social theory of utterance in reader response* [Master's thesis, University of Manitoba].

Krasny, K. (2009). Intentional threads: Connecting the ordinary in autobiographical and fictional narratives. In P. Burke (Ed.), *Women and pedagogy: Education through autobiographical narrative*. Educators' International Press.

Krasny, K., & Sachar, S. (2017). Legitimizing linguistic diversity: The promise of plurilingualism in Canadian schools. *Language and Literacy, 19*(1), 34–47. doi.org/10.20360/G2G02K

Laing, G. (2013). Royal Commission on Bilingualism and Biculturalism. *The Canadian Encyclopedia*. www.thecanadianencyclopedia.ca/en/article/royal-commission-on-bilingualism-and-biculturalism

Makoni, S., & Pennycook, A. (2007). Disinventing and reconstituting languages. In S. Makoni & A. Pennycook (Eds.), *Disinventing and reconstituting languages* (pp. 1–41). Multilingual Matters, Clevedon.

Manitoba Education. (n.d.). *Education and early childhood learning: International and heritage languages*. Manitoba Education. www.edu.gov.mb.ca/k12/cur/languages/index.html

Martel, M. (2019). The 1969 Official Languages Act: A turning point, but for whom. *The Canadian Historical Review, 100*(2), 208–222. doi.org/10.3138/chr.2018-0082-1

Milloy, J. S. (1999). *A national crime: The Canadian government and the residential school system, 1879 to 1986*. University of Manitoba Press.

Moseley, C. (Ed.). (2010). *Atlas of the world's languages in danger*. UNESCO. https://unesdoc.unesco.org/ark:/48223/pf0000187026

Nagy, N. (2021). Heritage languages in Canada. In M. Polinsky & S. Montrul (Eds.), *The Cambridge handbook of heritage languages and linguistics* (pp. 178–204). Cambridge University Press. doi.org/10.1017/9781108766340.010

Ozga, J. (2000). *Policy research in educational settings: Contested terrain*. Open University Press.

Rosa, J., & Flores, N. (2017). Unsettling race and language: Toward a raciolinguistic perspective. *Language in Society, 46*(5), 621–647. doi.org/10.1017/S0047404517000562

Royal Commission on Bilingualism and Biculturalism. (1967). *Book I: The official languages*. Queen's Printer. https://publications.gc.ca/collections/collection_2014/bcp-pco/Z1-1963-1-5-4-1-eng.pdf

Ryan, R., Huta, V., & Deci, E. (2008). Living well: A self-determination theory perspective on eudaimonia. *Journal of Happiness Studies, 9*, 139–170. doi.org/10.1007/s10902-006-9023-4

Sachar, S. (2017). *Legitimizing languages in the classroom: A case study of an Ontario private school for Russian-speaking students* [Doctoral dissertation, York University].

Sassen, S. (2014). *Expulsions: Brutality and complexity in the global economy*. Belknap Press.

Shohamy, E. G. (2006). *Language policy: Hidden agendas and new approaches*. Routledge.

Statistics Canada. (2022). *Increasing diversity of languages, other than English or French, spoken at home*. www150.statcan.gc.ca/n1/pub/11-627-m/11-627-m2022051-eng.htm

Statistics Canada. (2023). *Indigenous languages across Canada*. www12.statcan.gc.ca/census-recensement/2021/as-sa/98-200-X/2021012/98-200-X2021012-eng.cfm

Truth and Reconciliation Commission of Canada. (2015). *Truth and Reconciliation Commission of Canada: Calls to action*. https://publications.gc.ca/collections/collection_2015/trc/IR4-8-2015-eng.pdf

United Nations Educational, Scientific and Cultural Organization. (2021). *International decade of Indigenous languages*. www.unesco.org/en/decades/indigenous-languages

Vertovec, S. (2007). Super-diversity and its implications. *Ethnic and Racial Studies, 30*, 1024–1054. doi.org/10.1080/01419870701599465

Vertovec, S. (2019). Talking around super-diversity. *Ethnic and Racial Studies, 42*(1), 125–139. doi.org/10.1080/01419870.2017.1406128

Williams, C. (1994). *Arfarniad o Ddulliau Dysgu ac Addysgu yng Nghyd-destun Addysg Uwchradd Ddwyieithog* [An evaluation of teaching and learning methods in the context of bilingual secondary education] [Doctoral dissertation, University of Wales].

Winnipeg School Division. (2021, February 4). *Aboriginal language program (Cree and Ojibwe)*. www.winnipegsd.ca/childrenoftheearth/page/657/heritage-languages

Winnipeg School Division. (2022, July 14). *Omazinibii'gig Artist Collective*. www.winnipegsd.ca/childrenoftheearth/page/729/omazinibii-igeg-indigenous-artist-collective

# CHAPTER 13
# Inclusive Instructional Design within Language Education: Principles and Practices for the Modern Canadian Classroom

*Renée Bourgoin, Katy Arnett, and Carmelita Duffy*

In the world of language education, Canada enjoys a celebrated status for its contributions, especially its French immersion (FI) program. Since its inception in the 1960s, FI has become an integral part of the Canadian educational landscape, boasting steadily increasing enrolment numbers and reaching 450,000 students in 2021 (Canadian Parents for French, 2021). Canada's strong reputation in language education has also been burnished for other reasons, including (1) the near-universal expectation that all kindergarten to grade 12 students study a second language (L2); and (2) the country's deliberate attention to growing its population through immigration, a strategy that sees more and more newcomer students learning either or both of Canada's official languages (French and English).

In this chapter, we first review current realities with respect to language education and inclusion. We recognize that language learners are not only those enrolled in language programs or taking language classes. With increased immigration, language learners also make up part of our mainstream classes, and even so-called native English speakers can be language learners. We find language learners in all our classes, including sciences, math, and social studies. We then make the case for language learning for all before shifting our attention to theoretical and practical frameworks that support inclusive pedagogies for language learners. Specifically, we examine instructional design for language learners through the theoretical underpinnings of Universal Design for Learning (Rose & Meyer, 2002) and the application of sociocultural theory as linked to the work of Vygotsky (1962). These principles help us reconceptualize how we view students' access to the language of instruction. We also critically examine typical principles of lesson design in hopes of deconstructing the **barriers** that perpetuate the marginalization of some language learners, barriers that limit students' ability to flourish. We demystify the implementation of supports to better include all learners in the experience of developing proficiency. Finally, based on our earlier work (Arnett & Bourgoin, 2017; Bourgoin & Arnett, 2020; Hennessey, 2016), we take a closer look at inclusive classroom-based instructional practices that support language learners in different contexts, including those in language programs and in mainstream classes. We demonstrate, through practical examples, strategies designed to level the playing field and help students access the language of instruction so they may flourish. We hope that building teacher capacity around inclusive language education will reduce barriers that limit students' capacities to achieve their own level of success.

## LANGUAGE EDUCATION

### Language Education in Mainstream Programs

Over the years, Canada has continued to see steady growth in immigration. According to 2021 data, 23 percent of the population were foreign-born immigrants, most originating from India, the Philippines, and China, but also from Middle Eastern, European, African, Caribbean, Central American, and Southern American countries (Statistics Canada, 2011, 2021). With such demographic shifts away from traditionally English-speaking countries, the percentage of allophones (i.e., Canadians reporting a mother tongue other than French or English) continues to increase. More and more children are entering French or English Canadian schools speaking a minority language at home and learning one or both official languages at school. Language education in Canada is no longer limited to those teaching in L2 programs (e.g., FI, intensive English, core French, Cree immersion). Increasingly, teachers outside of language programs are teaching language learners. Snow and colleagues' claim in 1989 that "every teacher is a language teacher" is more accurate than it has ever been. However, the reality is that most Canadian classroom teachers have not been prepared to work with linguistically diverse student populations. Further, even within language programs, many teachers report never having had any sort of deep professional learning around inclusive practices that support students' language development (Canadian Association of Immersion Professionals, 2018; Lapkin et al., 2006). Supporting the professional learning needs of *all* classroom teachers (pre- and in-service), irrespective of the program and courses they teach, is increasingly imperative.

**Language Education in Language Programs**

Although Canadian education systems boast of being inclusive, they have a history of actively limiting students' access to language education. Beginning in the 1970s, questionable research, burgeoning understandings of learning disabilities, and societal attitudes about the potential of individuals with disabilities contributed to numerous policies and de facto practices that restricted some students' access to and/or continued enrolment in immersion or other L2 programs or led to some students being exempted from requirements to study other languages (Arnett, 2013; Mady, 2007). Although research supports the inclusion of a wide range of learners in language programs (see Arnett, 2003, 2008; Genesee, 2007 for a fuller review), many still believe that language learning may not be suitable for specific groups of learners, including allophone students, students with low academic ability, or students who have specific learning needs or disabilities. As a result, some students have been limited in their ability to join, be supported in, and/or flourish in immersion or other L2 programs, on the basis that they first "need" to develop proficiency in the dominant language (Mady, 2007), often to the point that this limitation is common practice (Arnett, 2013). The residual impact of such exclusionary policies and practices contributes to persistent misunderstandings of L2 learning (Dicks & Kristmanson, 2008) and affects how language programs are delivered and how language learners are supported (or not) within these programs.

## POSITIONING AND CONTEXT

We support language learning for all—the notion that language learning should not be an endeavour open to a selected few deemed appropriate for language learning. We advocate for language learners and supporting their unique language needs in classrooms. We view every teacher as a language teacher (Snow et al., 1989) and recognize that each one has a role to play in inclusive language education. Language teachers can play a vital role in "guiding and facilitating the process of L2 acquisition," which is critical "in assisting learners to achieve advanced levels of target language proficiency" (Loewen, 2012, p. 1). We concur with Loewen (2012) on the important role of teachers in language learning but also believe that they are central to fostering inclusive language education. We draw on our research, our own experiences teaching in French as a second language contexts, and our work as teacher educators and regular facilitators of professional learning experiences for in-service language educators to offer insights on designing inclusive lessons for language learners. Our proximity to language teachers and classrooms has allowed us to toggle between learning about issues through our own research, applying those insights to our work with pre-service and in-service educators, and gaining new understandings via that work with educators. We acknowledge that *inclusion* encompasses social inclusion, academic inclusion, cultural and religious inclusion, physical inclusion, and so on, but in this chapter we focus on the inequalities that exist in classroom with respect to language needs (although this is not mutually exclusive of other types of inclusion) in order to design lessons that are more inclusive for all language learners.

## UNDERPINNINGS OF LESSON DESIGN FOR LANGUAGE LEARNERS

### Principles of Language Acquisition

We know that, within L2 language learning contexts, the role of oral language in the development of literacy skills is vital (e.g., Le Bouthillier et al. 2022; Shanahan, 2016; Tedick & Wesely, 2015). The importance of oral language in content classes is also well documented (e.g., Ballinger & Lyster, 2011; Cormier & Turnbull, 2009; Genesee, 1994). Oral language encompasses social and academic interactions, oral production and comprehension, and the ability to critically interpret messages and participate in exchanges (Soucy, 2016). There are several theoretical and instructional principles that underpin L2 acquisition, including the need for lots of exposure to the target language (input) and opportunities for sustained, meaningful output. Classroom input needs to be rich and comprehensible, that is, just above students' current ability levels. "Extended output" opportunities that are authentic and meaningful (e.g., meaning-making, risk-taking, negotiating) are essential to facilitate language learning (Krashen, 1982; Swain, 1993).

### Universal Design for Learning

In 2004, the Center for Applied Special Technology (now known as CAST) published the first Universal Design for Learning (UDL) guidelines, introducing three broad principles to guide educators' thinking and work around accessibility and inclusivity of learning experiences (Rose & Meyer, 2002). UDL can be defined as instructional practices, strategies, and materials that are "usable" by as many students as possible (Burgstahler, 2007). By acknowledging student differences, UDL principles advocate for students to have access to multiple means of engagement, of representation, and of expression to access, build, and internalize learning. This broader attention to the structure and components of a learning experience is designed to create accessible experiences for the full complement of individuals within an experience rather than simply for the students assumed to have a specific disability or unique learning need. Though these principles are applicable to every student in the classroom, they often lack specificity with respect to the lesson-building process. In our work with both pre-service and in-service teachers, this lack of explicit direction on how to translate UDL principles to lesson planning is regularly lamented. To that end, we turn to the theoretical underpinnings and concepts of instructional design to offer a pathway to such conceptualization.

## Sociocultural Theory

Sociocultural theory (SCT), traced to the early work of Lev Vygotsky (1962), is a theoretical model that is applied in both language education and inclusive education. Kraker (2000) cites three tenets of SCT that are relevant to both: (1) cultural, historical, societal, familial, and institutional contexts surrounding a child define their learning; (2) interactions carried out within those contexts alter a child's development; and (3) a child's development is formed and transformed through the use of language and other tools that mediate meaning. In L2 research, SCT tends to focus on interactions between the teacher and students and the supports (or scaffolds) used in those interactions to build student competency in the target language (e.g., Antón & DiCamilla, 1998; DiCamilla & Antón, 1997). A scaffold is said to be present when, in the moment of trying to mediate thinking/knowledge in the target language—via output—the student encounters a gap in their capacity to express an idea, and they receive a prompt, cue, or resource that helps them address that gap directly. Scaffolds are highly situational and are unique to that interaction and the needs/goals of the learner's output in that exchange.

When SCT is applied to conversations around inclusive practice, the focus on the interactions remains central. Differences in abilities and skills are acknowledged and accepted neutrally. Differences are viewed as part of a broader continuum of normal rather than something that is lacking, different, or otherwise negative. SCT acknowledges that these differences are alleviated or compounded because of the interactions or actions that occur within a particular context and considers how different elements within the setting interact with each other to create access or lower barriers to the setting. For example, this conceptualization would be interested in how teacher belief systems around learner differences and disability might influence the general accessibility of a learning experience, as highlighted in the following studies. Lambert and Tan's (2020) meta-analysis of research on the educational experience of students with disabilities in mathematics education found that an overwhelming majority adopted a medical/deficit view of disability (an attitudinal barrier), viewing students as likely "not capable" of learning. Jordan et al. (1997) explored links between low success rates of students with disabilities and the following: teachers' views of disability, teachers' perception of their ability to respond to learner needs, and the quality of interactions they had with students.

Interactions within the classroom are ostensibly occurring to support student progress toward and/or achievement of a particular learning goal. Interactions between the teacher and students, or among students, are designed to facilitate linguistic and conceptual understandings within the classroom. Though many of these interactions are spontaneous, their success in supporting the learning goal(s) of the lesson often is dependent upon teachers' skill with instructional design. In the next section, we highlight a particular approach to instructional design that is known to facilitate attention to and implementation of broader practices that enhance accessibility in classrooms, making it more likely that teachers apply principles of UDL to their instruction of L2 learners.

## INSTRUCTIONAL DESIGN THAT FACILITATES INTERACTIONS

Developed by Wiggins and McTighe (2005), the three-step model of Understanding by Design (UBD) is notable for how it links student needs, learning outcomes, assessments, and instruction. It is colloquially termed *backwards design* because it requires teachers, in step one of the instructional planning process, to define where students are expected to end up with their knowledge or skills at the end of the instructional sequence. After identifying the outcomes, teachers consider the "essential questions" students will explore or answer, the "enduring understandings" they will gain, and the prior knowledge and skills they need to bring to the exploration. Teachers must consider students' current proficiency to ensure that goals are relevant, realistic, and the same for all (equal outcomes). Tomlinson and McTighe (2006) explored how backwards design can be combined with pedagogical approaches of "differentiation" to create equitable paths for attaining learning goals. Step two focuses on identifying the "proof" teachers need to gather that demonstrates that students have met the learning goals. Teachers need to think about the task students will perform, the success criteria, and any other evidence needed to gauge mastery of the content/skill. Although the proof needs to align with learning outcomes, at this phase we can introduce ideas about differentiation by articulating options for the proof that students can offer as mastery (Tomlinson & McTighe, 2006). In step three, instructional events or activities are planned to help students explore and apply concepts and skills related to the learning objectives. The goal is to offer students rich and varied ways to engage with the concepts and skills by applying differentiation principles that create equitable paths to attaining the learning goals. At this stage of the planning process, teachers are invited to think through the three key elements of UDL—multiple means of representation, expression, and engagement—as ways to reduce or eliminate barriers and maximize learning.

## Designing Inclusive Second-Language Learning Experiences

We conducted a multi-year action research project to examine how teachers who work with language learners can further support their students' language needs. This work led to the development of **Universal Language Actions** (Arnett & Bourgoin, 2017; Bourgoin & Arnett, 2020; Hennessey, 2016). Underpinned by principles of Universal Design for Learning and Vygotsky's notion of scaffolding, this list of universal actions was found to bridge the gap between theory and practice by integrating principles of L2 development, instructional design, and inclusive teaching practice. Universal Language Actions (ULAs) are defined as "gestures, procedures, and operations that help create the most favorable and accessible environment in which to learn a language" (Arnett & Bourgoin, 2017, p. 83). ULAs, which help facilitate language comprehension and production, have been designed for use across different grade levels and subjects to support content and language learning.

Teacher-participants felt that ULAs were easy to implement in classroom practice and could easily be adapted to different instructional contexts (i.e., grade levels and subject areas) and for different types of language learners (i.e., varying proficiency levels, EAL students, and immersion students). When using ULAs in lesson design and delivery, teachers found renewed ways of offering and advocating for inclusionary practices within L2 contexts. Through this study, teacher-participants gained practical experience with instructional techniques emblematic of inclusive language practice and, largely, aligned with supporting interactions in the classroom. Equipped with specific ways of supporting language learning, teachers felt a sense of empowerment in moving inclusive language education forward and finding an increased voice in pushing against existing power structures that can perpetuate the marginalization of certain learner groups within language education.

## Translating Research into Practice—Inclusive Lesson Planning for Language Learners

In this section, we present important insights gained from this study and our work in inclusive language education. We highlight key principles and strategies of inclusive lesson design that promote access to language learning and better include language learners in the experience of developing proficiency in the target language.

### Key Principle 1: Reflecting on Our Beliefs

The first step in beginning the critical work of planning inclusive lessons and instruction for language learners is to reflect on our beliefs and acknowledge the often-oppressive influences of traditions that can marginalize language learners (or groups of language learners) and limit their ability to flourish. It is important to acknowledge our belief systems and where we position ourselves with respect to the following principles:

- All classrooms are language classrooms regardless of the subject being taught.
- All teachers are language teachers.
- Not all students will learn the target language in the same way.
- Not all students will learn the target language at the same rate.
- All teachers can and should be inclusive teachers.
- Explicit attention to and use of teaching practices that support access and equity are needed.
- Teaching for inclusion requires teachers to be intentional and reflective.
- Teachers need to be proactive (not reactive) toward students' language needs.
- Inclusion is something that continuously needs tending to.

### Key Principle 2: Recognizing That Every Lesson Is a Language Lesson

When it comes to working with language learners, every lesson is a language lesson regardless of the subject being taught (e.g., reading, science, mathematics). In terms of input, lessons are filled with oral explanations, presentations, and oral comprehension tasks. Students are exposed to large amounts of oral input that is often complex and/or unfamiliar. Students also need to work through large amounts of written language. Texts are used to present information, strengthen understanding, or convey new knowledge and skills. Output demands are also embedded in any given lesson. Students need to produce a lot of language, whether it be oral or written. They are expected to share their ideas, opinions, feelings, and questions; retell events; describe and compare; and explain concepts, solutions, problems, and phenomena. As teachers, we need to seize these opportunities and view them as critical components of lesson design. In doing so, we can begin to question how inclusive our lessons are from a language perspective. We can address this by (1) reorienting the lesson (regardless of subject) toward a better (and dare we say, greater) balance between content and language objectives and (2) planning for and providing greater support for the language demands of the lesson.

*Key Principle 3: Acknowledging Learner Differences and Barriers to Access*
Inclusive lesson design requires teachers to consider the unique needs of language learners and consider whether they truly have access to the learning. To offer ways of facilitating supports to students so they can meet their greatest potentials, we need to ask ourselves the following questions:

- Can all of our students access the language being presented? That is, are we facilitating their understanding of the material presented orally or in writing?
- Are all of our students afforded the same opportunities, through scaffolds, to engage with others in ways that support language acquisition?
- Are our classroom-based language activities truly inclusive and differentiated for different language abilities?
- Are more and less skilled language learners being exposed to language that meets their current language needs?

These questions allow for an introspective look into how we can design and deliver lessons with the necessary classroom-based supports needed to level the playing field and allow for less or more skilled language learners to engage in classroom activities, discussions, and learning opportunities in meaningful ways.

*Key Principle 4: Being Proactive in Supporting Students' Needs*
In line with UDL principles, when planning lessons for language learners, teachers need to be proactive in anticipating and supporting unique language needs. ULAs are a critical tool in this regard. Although ULAs can be deployed by the teacher as needs arise in the classroom (a reactive approach), they should be central in the design of lessons—that is, when lessons are being conceptualized and

planned. Teachers who plan for embedded supports are proactive in their approach to inclusive education. ULAs can and should be integrated throughout the learning cycle—when the teacher is providing instruction, during learning opportunities (when students develop skills, knowledge, and understanding), and when students demonstrate their learning—to allow students greater access to the target language and the curriculum. Embedding ULAs in lesson design requires that teachers know their language learners—their strengths and their needs. It also requires that teachers recognize the components of the lessons that may pose language challenges and where additional supports may be needed to understand the material (comprehension), to work through concepts, and/or to show understanding.

*Key Principle 5: Being Intentional and Purposeful*
Inclusionary classroom practices require teachers to be deliberate in their choice and use of ULAs if students are to access the language of instruction and flourish in our classrooms. There are many ULAs to choose from—it is important that they are carefully selected during the lesson planning process and implemented with purpose and intent (see Box 13.1: Sample List of ULAs).

The intentional use of ULAs enables teachers to be proactive and accountable to the needs of language learners. It is quite possible that certain ULAs will need to be implemented for an extended period for learners to reap their full benefits, while other ULAs may be limited to specific lessons. The intentionality of ULA use, as part of inclusive instructional design, recognizes that inclusion is something that needs continuous attention. As Valle and Connor (2010) state, "'inclusion' is not something we put in place structurally, then sit back and hope for the best" (p. ix). Students change, situations change, needs change, and school systems and supports change. As such, adapting our inclusive strategies ensures that they continue to be purposeful.

## EXAMPLES OF INCLUSIVE LESSON PLANNING PROCESS AND DESIGN

As a concluding element to this chapter, we offer two excerpts from a recent instructional planning exercise with teacher candidates to demonstrate how teachers—either in-service or pre-service—can begin to transform their planning practices to be more explicitly inclusive of a range of learner needs. As the starting point for inclusive lesson design, we asked teacher candidates to design typical lesson plans. As they learned about inclusive lesson design and specific ULAs, they were asked to go back to their original lessons to re-examine and

> **Box 13.1: Sample List of Universal Language Actions**
>
> 1. Use gestures and visuals (images, pictures, drawing, and objects).
> 2. Assess students' prior knowledge and fill in "language/learning gaps."
> 3. Adjust the complexity of language used or presented.
> 4. Provide wait time when presenting information, asking questions, and before tasks.
> 5. Provide expectations, examples, and exemplars of oral and written tasks.
> 6. Use graphic organizers to support oral and written output.
> 7. Co-create accessible linguistic resources.
> 8. Repeat directions and explanations; rephrase students' comments and answers.
> 9. Choose grouping arrangements that favour peer communication.
> 10. Identify and make accessible the required language/vocabulary.
> 11. Offer planning strategies before assigning tasks.
> 12. Review useful learning strategies and/or steps to complete tasks.
> 13. Use predictable pedagogical and language production routines.
> 14. Recycle and reuse pedagogical material for additional exposure.
> 15. Provide specific listening intentions and reading intentions.
> 16. Do frequent comprehension checks; chunk activities into smaller steps.
> 17. Use different modalities or formats to present information.
> 18. Explain the relevance of what is being taught; provide connections to real-world applications.
> 19. Summarize and take stock of key points of lessons or activities.
> 20. Explain vocabulary using examples, synonyms, antonyms, and teacher definitions.

*Source:* Adapted from Arnett and Bourgoin (2017).

analyze their work. We asked them to reflect on the initial supports offered to deeply consider language learner needs and what should be offered to students to make the lessons more inclusive. By doing so, teacher candidates engaged in critical reflection on their lesson design in support of language learning.

## Example 1

The following excerpt is from a closure activity planned by teacher candidate Carmelita Duffy (third author) for an elementary language arts lesson. In the

> **Box 13.2: Initial Planning for Closure Activity**
>
> Carmelita Duffy
> Subject: English language arts
> Grade level: 2
> Teaching/learning objective(s):
>
> - the concept of word families, specifically -ot, -at, -ain, -ake
> - how to create a variety of words by changing the constant/prefix of a word
>
> Lesson Closure/Wrap-Up
> Teacher will
>
> - individually have students select a word from each of the word families covered (from our graph charts created earlier) to create a sentence using all four of the words they selected

lesson, students were learning specific sound families. Students were read stories that featured specific sounds, and the closure activity was designed to offer a summarizing moment for the students. Box 13.2 presents Carmelita's initial plans for the closure activity, in which students were asked to create a sentence using one of the words they identified during the text exploration.

After all teacher candidates submitted their initial lesson plans, they explored a range of ULAs that support students' language production in the target language in their Bachelor of Education course. They were then invited to revise their individual lesson plans to incorporate some ULAs and to reflect on their choice of ULAs and the likely impact of this change on students' learning. Box 13.3 presents Carmelita's revision of the closure activity to include attention to specific ULAs, followed by her reflection (Box 13.4).

In this concrete example, an inclusive instructional strategy (ULA) became embedded within the instructional design and delivery to make the target (written) language more accessible to language learners. Further, this example shows how the teacher candidate confronted the assumptions that sometimes underlie initial decisions of lesson components and relates that to potential barriers in the classroom.

## Box 13.3: Revised Planning for Closure Activity

Lesson Closure/Wrap-Up
Teacher will

- have students select a word from each of the word families covered (from our graph charts created earlier) to create sentences using two to three of the words they selected
- prior to getting students to do this wrap-up activity, model an example sentence *and* review with students various strategies to use when writing sentences

Embedded ULAs:

- co-create "accessible" linguistic resources
- offer planning strategies before a task

## Box 13.4: Teacher Candidate's Reflection on Use of ULAs within Closure Activity

Offering planning strategies before a task: *Prior to the lesson closure, we will formulate a list of strategies to help students write strong sentences. During a class discussion, the teacher will work with students to generate ideas for strategies we can use to create strong sentences and we will formulate our list collectively as a class. Since these strategies will be visually displayed, we can even keep this list hung up in the classroom for future reference. It is important to ensure that all students understand and know that these strategies are applicable to different learning opportunities, and that they are not just for students who struggle with writing.*

*As we have learned throughout the course, as teachers it is important that we never make assumptions of the students' capabilities. Therefore, we do not want to assume students know all the strategies for writing strong sentences or how to apply these strategies in their writing. Reminding students of these strategies and how to use them in their writing will help all students be able to accomplish the writing tasks. This is an important action that can benefit all learners in the classroom.*

**Example 2**

Similarly, in the next excerpt, a previously designed lesson was re-examined in light of the aforementioned five key principles of inclusive lesson design. Through reflection, Carmelita Duffy, who was a teacher candidate at the time, recognized the extent of the language demands embedded within this content lesson and reframed language as a critical component of the lesson. By reflecting on how language was being presented and used, she was able to intentionally embed specific ULAs to support learner needs. These ULAs provided students access to the language and the content by scaffolding comprehension and language output. Box 13.5 contains her revised plan, and Box 13.6 contains her reflection.

### Box 13.5: Revised Plan for Activity (with Embedded ULAs)

Carmelita Duffy
Subject: Social studies
Grade level: 6
Teaching/learning objective(s):

- identify key elements of social and cultural elements of societies
- compare and contrast elements of different societies

Step 1—Teacher will

- teach cultural/social elements of a country/region and their importance (e.g., food, transportation, shelter)
- present a slide show that defines *sustainability* and *sustainable lifestyle*; encourage students, for each slide, to ask questions and share their thoughts about the concepts presented; summarize students' contributions by recording key discussion points on each slide
- do a final comprehension check before moving on
- explain the activity—comparing/contrasting elements of different societies using different sources of information
- model the activity using a Venn diagram; present and model what kind of language should be used to investigate the similarities and differences between this area and other ancient societies (from previous lessons)
  - *I noticed that …; This is the result of …; I think that …; This is similar to/different than …; Ancient societies had …*

- invite students to do the activity using the Venn diagram to compare/contrast ideas and document their learning

Embedded ULAs:

- summarize key points of the lesson or activity
- give students time to absorb information
- use graphic organizers to support language production
- make the required language accessible

**Box 13.6:** Teacher Candidate's Reflections on Embedding ULAs

Summarize key points of the lesson or activity (in this case, summarizing discussion): *We will pause after each slide so students can share their thoughts and questions. Having students' comments documented where they were discussed during the presentation can be useful for future reference when completing other assignments and lessons regarding this subject. This is also an effective strategy to connect oral language and written language, as the teacher will be writing as students share their ideas. This can be an important tool in helping students visualize a conversation, since there are many students who find it challenging to follow a conversation without any sort of visual supports. Documenting the discussion points directly on the presentation slides will provide students the visual support they need.*

Use graphic organizers to support language production: *Prior to getting students in small groups, the teacher will model each section of the Venn diagram as well as the sentence frames they can use. This is to ensure every student can see how the graphic organizer (and required language) could be used and feel successful with this task. The use of graphic organizers [is] incredibly important and [they are] useful tools to academically support all types of students in the classroom. They provide a specific, clear, and organized way of seeing the expectations. Since graphic organizers are consistent amongst students, they provide all students equal opportunities for success, yet still allow open opportunities to explain their learning in the most effective way for them. The use of various graphic organizers can enhance the learning of all students and be a supportive tool to help students organize and share their thoughts on the information that has been taught to them.*

We have found that such an approach to instructional design with teacher candidates has been most effective in counteracting the assumption that *just good teaching* is enough to create an inclusive environment. Explicit attention to teaching strategies that support access and equity (e.g., proactively embedding ULAs in lesson design) is needed to help teachers understand that inclusive practice requires more deliberate attention. In doing so, we avoid defaulting to a few instructional methods that inherently exclude some students from the experience right from the outset.

## CONCLUSION

Reimagining our roles in increasing our inclusive language teacher mindset requires us to critically reflect on our own teaching practices, traditions we uphold, and beliefs we have about teaching and learning. Through this examination of inclusive lesson design in support of language learners, we aimed to foster a sense of empowerment for teachers in moving inclusive language education forward. This commitment to professional self-reflection and to supports for all language learners is central to students flourishing in the target language. We concur with Bokhorst-Heng and Hillier (in the introduction to this volume) that teachers "must work intentionally to work against any barriers that would limit the flourishing of students." In this chapter, we addressed barriers in language education and offered ways forward by drawing on our ongoing work related to inclusion and inclusive practice within French second-language programs for students with disabilities, broad learning differences, and profiles that may have been previously cited as being unsuitable or otherwise not representative of the idea of the so-called good language learner.

It is our contention that these universal second-language classroom supports, along with appropriate **differentiated instruction**, exemplary L2 instructional practices, and strong monitoring and data collection techniques, have the potential to impact the way language programs are promoted, delivered, and supported. Many teachers we have worked with or had as teacher-participants in our studies reported never having any sort of deep professional learning around inclusive practices that support language development. Teacher education programs, school districts, and professional associations need to join forces to address this need in the field more systematically. If teacher education programs do not rise to this challenge, then school districts and professional associations will need to regularly offer such professional learning to their teachers.

## KEY TERMS

**Barriers:** Practical, attitudinal, technological, linguistic, and/or structural elements that limit a student's access to or participation within the learning event or environment.

**Differentiated instruction:** Distinct and varied pathways (e.g., tasks) toward a common learning goal that allow for equitable learning experiences.

**Universal Language Actions:** "gestures, procedures, and operations that help create the most favorable and accessible environment in which to learn a language" (Arnett & Bourgoin, 2017, p. 83).

## DISCUSSION QUESTIONS AND ACTIVITIES

1. Review a lesson plan or activity that you have designed and/or used in your classroom. Working with the list of Universal Language Actions offered in Box 13.1, revise the plan or activity to incorporate at least one ULA and reflect on or explain the rationale for incorporating that teaching action.
2. What barriers have you encountered in your classroom that may be limiting some language learners' access to the learning experience? How might you minimize or reduce those barriers?
3. Using the broad learning goal *I can express my preferences about sports and activities*, generate a list of (1) the success criteria for this activity and (2) the possible types of evidence a teacher could collect to verify that a student is making progress toward or meeting this learning goal.
4. As you process the content of this chapter, which of the elements (e.g., sociocultural theory, backwards design, Universal Design for Learning, Universal Language Actions) stands out to you as the anchor for creating inclusive learning experiences for language learners?

## REFERENCES

Antón, M., & DiCamilla, F. (1998). Socio-cognitive functions of L1 collaborative interaction in the L2 classroom. *Canadian Modern Language Review, 54*, 314–342. doi.org/10.3138/cmlr.54.3.314

Arnett, K. (2003). Teacher adaptations in core French: A case study of one grade 9 class. *The Canadian Modern Language Review, 60*(2), 173–198. doi.org/10.3138/cmlr.60.2.173

Arnett, K. (2008). Exploring the use of student perspectives to inform topics in teacher education: Issues in creating an inclusive core French classroom. *Canadian Journal of Applied Linguistics, 11*(1), 63–81. https://journals.lib.unb.ca/index.php/CJAL/article/view/19910

Arnett, K. (2013). The genesis and perpetuation of exemptions and transfers from French second language programs for students with diverse learning needs: A preliminary examination and their link to inclusion. In K. Arnett & C. Mady (Eds), *Minority populations in Canadian second language education* (pp. 103–117). Multilingual Matters.

Arnett, K., and Bourgoin, R. (2017). *Access to success: Making inclusion work for language learners*. Pearson Education Canada.

Ballinger, S., & Lyster, R. (2011). Student and teacher oral language use in a two-way Spanish/English immersion school. *Language Teaching Research, 15*(3), 289–306. doi.org/10.1177/1362168811401151

Bourgoin, R., & Arnett, K. (2020). Practices for supporting inclusive language teaching: Lessons from New Brunswick, Canada. *The Language Educator*. www.thelanguageeducator.org/actfl/library/item/february_march_2020/3800228/

Burgstahler, C. (2007). *Universal design of education: An approach to ensure educational programs support all students*. University of Washington.

Canadian Association of Immersion Professionals. (2018). Rapport final consultation pancanadienne. *Journal de l'immersion, 40*(2). https://www.acpi.ca/wp-content/uploads/2020/05/Vol40_n1_Printemps_2018_final_fr_web-1.pdf

Canadian Parents for French. (2021). *French as a second language enrolment statistics 2016–2017 to 2020–2021*. cpf.ca/wp-content/uploads/CPF_Nat_EnrolementStats_20162021_v4_FINAL.pdf

CAST. (2018). *Universal design for learning guidelines version 2.2*. http://udlguidelines.cast.org

Cormier, M., & Turnbull, M. (2009). Une approche littératiée: Apprendre les sciences et la langue en immersion. *Canadian Modern Language Review / Revue canadienne des langues vivantes, 65*(5), 817–840. doi.org/10.3138/cmlr.65.5.817b

DiCamilla, F., & Antón, M. (1997). Repetition in the collaborative discourse of L2 learners: A Vygotskian perspective. *Canadian Modern Language Review, 53*, 609–633. doi.org/10.3138/cmlr.53.4.609

Dicks, J., & Kristmanson, P. (2008). French immersion: When and why? In *The state of French-second-language education in Canada 2008* (p. 16). Canadian Parents for French.

Genesee, F. (1994). *Integrating language and content: Lessons from immersion*. Center for Research on Education, Diversity and Excellence. http://escholarship.org/uc/item/61c8k7kh

Genesee, F. (2007). French immersion and at-risk students: A review of research evidence. *Canadian Modern Language Review / Revue canadienne des langues vivantes, 63*(5), 655–687. doi.org/10.1353/cml.2008.0004

Hennessey, K. (2016). *L'exploration des actions pedagogiques universelles en immersion francaise* [Unpublished master's thesis, University of New Brunswick, Fredericton, Canada].

Jordan, A., Lindsay, L., & Stanovich, P. (1997). Classroom teachers' instructional interactions with students who are exceptional, at risk, and typically achieving. *Remedial and Special Education, 18*(2), 82–93. doi.org/10.1177/074193259701800202

Kraker, M. J. (2000). Classroom discourse: Teaching, learning, and learning disabilities. *Teaching and Teacher Education*, *16*, 295–313. doi.org/10.1016/S0742051X(99)00063-3

Krashen, S. (1982). *Principles and practice in second language acquisition*. Pergamon Press.

Lambert R., & Tan P. (2020). Does disability matter in mathematics educational research? A critical comparison of research on students with and without disabilities. *Mathematics Education Research Journal*, *32*, 5–35. doi.org/10.1007/s13394-019-00299-6

Lapkin, S. McFarlane, A., & Vandergrift. L. (2006). *Teaching French in Canada: FSL teachers' perspectives*. Canadian Teachers Federation.

Le Bouthillier, J., Bourgoin, R., & Dicks, J. (2022). L'acquisition de la langue orale par l'entremise de tâches de centres d'apprentissage de littératie dans des classes d'immersion française. *Canadian Modern Language Review*, *78*(2), 91–105. doi.org/10.3138/cmlr-2020-0116

Loewen, S. 2012. The role of feedback. In S. M. Gass & A. Mackey (Eds.), *The Routledge handbook of second language acquisition* (pp. 24–40). Routledge.

Mady, C. (2007). The suitability of core French for recently arrived adolescent newcomers to Canada. *Canadian Journal of Applied Linguistics*, *10*(2), 177–196. https://journals.lib.unb.ca/index.php/CJAL/article/view/19741

Rose, D. H., & Meyer, A. (2002). *Teaching every student in the digital age: Universal design for learning*. Association for Supervision and Curriculum Development.

Shanahan, T. (2016). Relationships between reading and writing development. In C. MacArthur, S. Graham, & J. Fitzgerald (Eds.), *Handbook of writing research* (2nd ed., pp. 194–207). Guilford Press.

Snow, M., Met, M., & Genesee, F. (1989). A conceptual framework for the integration of language and content in second/foreign language instruction. *TESOL Quarterly*, *23*(2), 201–217. doi.org/10.2307/3587333

Soucy, E. (2016). Quelle place pour l'oral dans les centres de littératie? *Language and Literacy*, *18*(2), 1–16. doi.org/10.20360/G2SC72

Statistics Canada. (2011). *Immigration and ethnocultural diversity in Canada*. www12.statcan.gc.ca/nhs-enm/2011/as-sa/99-010-x/99-010-x2011001-eng.cfm

Statistics Canada. (2021). *Focus on geography series, 2021 census of population*. www12.statcan.gc.ca/census-recensement/2021/as-sa/fogs-spg/page.cfm?lang=E&topic=9&dguid=2021A000011124

Swain, M. (1993). The output hypothesis: Just speaking and writing aren't enough. *Canadian Modern Language Review*, *50*(1), 158–164. doi.org/10.3138/cmlr.50.1.158

Tedick, D., & Wesely, P. (2015). A review of research on content-based foreign/second language education in US K–12 contexts. *Language, Culture and Curriculum*, *28*(1), 25–40. doi.org/10.1080/07908318.2014.1000923

Tomlinson, C., & McTighe, J. (2006). *Integrating differentiated instruction and understanding by design.* Association for Supervision and Curriculum Development.

Valle, J., & Connor, D. (2010). *Rethinking disability: A disability studies approach to inclusive practices.* McGraw Hill.

Vygotsky, L. S. (1962). *Thought and language.* MIT Press.

Wiggins, G., & McTighe, J. (2005). *Understanding by design* (2nd ed.). Association for Supervision and Curriculum Development.

# PART VII

## RELIGION: UNDERSTANDING, INCLUSION, AND FLOURISHING OF RELIGIOUS DIVERSITY

# CHAPTER 14
# Framing Religious Diversity in the Canadian Classroom
*Margaretta Patrick and W. Y. Alice Chan*

When her children entered the Canadian school system, Momina Khan (2021) "began to realize my state of being as a racialized mother burdened by unfamiliarity, foreignness, and newness" (p. 260). A self-described poet, scholar, and Canadian citizen who emigrated from Pakistan in 2000, Khan speaks of the pain that students and parents confront when educators discount or ignore experiential and worldview differences rather than viewing them as opportunities for learning. Rejecting cultural and institutional systemic silencing, Khan undertakes the daunting task of truth telling, of speaking about the pain. In doing so, Khan and her children are "replacing victim-narratives with counter-narratives [that] arise from a place of wakefulness and gracefulness" (p. 261) in their efforts to transform educational and other public spaces.

Research echoes Khan's experiences. Afshan Amjad (2018), who studies newcomer experiences with Canadian education systems, asked newcomer Muslim students in urban Alberta to share stories about their elementary school experiences. Generally, the students encountered teachers who desired to help them adjust to Canadian schools, although some teachers did not understand cultural differences. For example, one student, Amina, explained how she was a quiet student and avoided direct eye contact with the teacher "because this was considered a quality of a good child in Muslim culture" (p. 321). According to Amina, her teacher concluded Amina was asocial and dumb, suspecting her of cheating on an essay when Amina's writing skills exceeded expectations. Other students remembered when teachers' comments about wearing hijab, sharia law, or terrorism unintentionally reinforced anti-Muslim stereotypes or racist attitudes among peers. Although the students were hurt by their teachers' lack of knowledge, they expressed appreciation for teachers who helped students distinguish between Muslims and terrorists.

Amjad's research provides several takeaways:

- *Teachers need to examine their own biases, understanding, or lack thereof.* Chapter 15 provides more details about this process.
- *Students can become disconnected from their teacher and peers.* At least one student shared this sentiment when partial or inaccurate information about Islam was presented or when teachers did not take the alternative experiences and interpretations offered by the Muslim students seriously.
- *Teacher knowledge about religion must extend beyond the media.* Students found that teachers over-relied on the media as a source of religious knowledge.

We know that teachers want all their students to flourish (Niyozov & Pluim, 2009). Teachers committed to student flourishing recognize and develop capacities within each individual student, including abilities grounded in diverse cultures and perspectives, and enable individual students to work collectively and engage in relationships with others (Grant, 2012). Lack of knowledge about students' religious identity, then, can cause harm. To help teachers understand the religious aspect of identity, this chapter presents **religious literacy** as a framework for thinking about the evolving religious diversity in Canadian education. The first section outlines the current conversations about the role and place of **religion** in Canadian school systems and a conception of teaching about religion in the form of cross-cultural religious literacy. The second section studies the notion of religious literacy more deeply and presents a made-in-Canada model.

## EDUCATION AND RELIGION IN CANADA

Religion always exists within a context as it is lived and practised by people who live in social, cultural, political, and economic circumstances. Thus, questions pertaining to the relationship between education and religion are specific to individual countries, regions, and communities. In Canada, this relationship is shaped by the historical role of Christianity, the narratives of religion and secularism, and social changes, including those informed by immigration policies that, starting in the 1970s, expanded immigration beyond Europe.

## History of Religion and Education in Canada

From Confederation in 1867 until the 1980s, public schools in most English-speaking provinces and territories were nonsectarian Protestant Christian with provisions for minority, mostly Catholic, separate schools. If provinces funded separate systems at the time they entered Confederation, such schools were constitutionally protected. Exceptions included Manitoba's dual Catholic and Protestant systems until 1890, Newfoundland's denominational system until 1997, Quebec's dual Catholic and Protestant systems until 2000, and provinces that did not fund separate schools when they entered Confederation (British Columbia, New Brunswick, Nova Scotia, and Prince Edward Island, although the Maritime provinces quickly reached compromises about Catholic schools) (Robson, 2012, chapter 3).

Beginning in the late 1980s, non-Christian parents in Ontario challenged mandated Christian instruction and daily opening exercises that included students reciting the Lord's Prayer (Hoverd et al., n.d.; see also chapter 1). Courts in Ontario ruled in favour of the parents, and changes were made to the school curriculum and schedules. This process can be described as secularization, although educational institutions retain a Christian structure in that holidays follow a Christian calendar and constitutional protections for funding religious schools remain limited to Christian schools (Seljak, 2005). Other provinces followed Ontario in de-Christianizing the most obvious elements of their school systems, such as morning prayers.

In response, some parents from various religious traditions challenged what they perceived to be the dominance of secular humanism in Ontario public schools. Those belonging to non-Christian religious communities sometimes found secular schools to be "inhospitable" (Seljak, 2005). Ultimately unsuccessful, the legal challenge nevertheless raised pertinent questions about the degree to which "religiously neutral" education is possible.

Religion remains contentious throughout Canada. Here we reference just a few examples:

- *Multani v. Commission Scolaire Marguerite Bourgeoys (2006)*: School authorities in a Quebec school prohibited a Sikh student from wearing a kirpan (ceremonial dagger) to school. The case was concluded by the Supreme Court of Canada, which ruled that Sikh students can wear the kirpan to school provided they meet specific conditions.
- *Expanding public funding for faith-based schools in Ontario*: In the 2007 provincial election, the Ontario Conservative Party, under John Tory,

promised to extend public funding for faith-based schools beyond the Roman Catholic school system. The platform was unpopular and contributed to Tory's loss. Seljak et al. (2008) argue that Islamophobia was "the elephant in the room" as opponents used negative stereotypes of Islam and racialized Muslim immigrant communities in Europe to stoke fear of publicly funded Islamic schools (p. 15).

- *Ontario protest against prayer rooms*: During the 2017 controversy regarding Muslim prayer rooms in the Peel District School Board, a media source reported that many of the South Asian opponents of such rooms based their objections on Hindu-Muslim conflicts in India (Bascaramurty & Alphonso, 2017).
- *Quebec's Bill 21*: In 2019, Quebec prohibited teachers, lawyers, judges, and police officers from wearing religious symbols while working, negatively impacting Muslims and Sikhs the most.
- *Servatius v. Alberni School District No. 70 (2022)*: A mother in British Columbia sued the local school board, claiming her children's religious freedoms were violated when they observed two Indigenous ceremonies, a smudge and a hoop dance with a prayer. The BC courts ruled against the parent on the grounds that (a) the children did not participate in the ceremony presentations, (b) the justices agreed with the Indigenous interpretation of the ceremonies as cultural rather than spiritual, and (c) the ceremonies are consistent with the curricular goals of integrating Indigenous worldviews.

Some of these legal and policy changes have had a chilling effect on education about religion and have contributed to rising religious illiteracy among Canadians (Seljak, 2005). Today we need more, not less, religious literacy given the increase in rates of hate-based violence.

Most hate-based violent crimes are committed based on race and ethnicity; religion is the second most common basis (see figure 14.1). It is important to view these categories as related because identities intersect and overlap. For example, it is difficult for police to categorize violence against Black Muslim women, as in such instances the reasons of race/ethnicity, religion, and sex all pertain. Jews are consistently the group targeted for the highest number of hate crimes based on religion, followed by Muslims. Figure 14.1 shows alarming increases in hate crimes in 2021. Police-reported hate crimes involving religion increased by 67 percent, or 354 incidents, over the previous year. Hate crimes involving Jews rose by 47 percent to 487 reported incidents altogether, Muslims by 71 percent

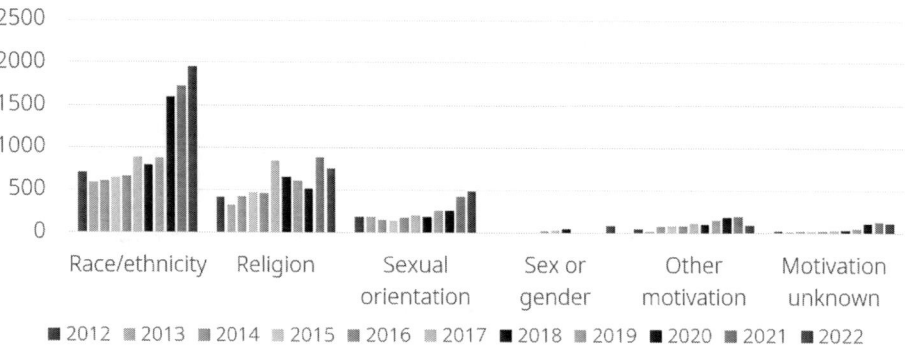

Figure 14.1: Number of Police-Reported Hate Crimes in Canada, by Type of Motivation, from 2012 to 2022
Source: Compilation by the Centre for Civic Religious Literacy. Used with permission. Created with data from Statistics Canada (2024).

to 144 incidents, and Catholics by 260 percent to 155 incidents—a unique occurrence and a result of an increase in crimes targeting Catholic institutions after the discovery of unmarked graves on the sites of several former residential schools (Statistics Canada, 2022d).

## Religion and Secularism

In the context of such tensions, the question must be asked: *How do we live together well across our differences?* This common yet challenging question requires individuals to consider their own development, well-being, and flourishing in relation to those of others while in view of the common good for society at large—a complex but important endeavour as we all live in relation with others in one form or another. The research by Khan (2021) and Amjad (2018) and the legal cases referenced above indicate ongoing tensions surrounding religious diversity. A first step is to unpack the terms *religion* and *secularism*.

What is religion? On the one hand, many public and scholarly actors recognize that religions are not "coherent blocks" but rather "lived, transactional, and steeped in fluid, located meanings and beliefs" (Baker & Dinham, 2017, p. 10). This recognition is embedded with specific understandings. Firstly, religious traditions are internally heterogeneous; that is, not all Sikhs, Buddhists, or adherents from any religious or nonreligious tradition observe and believe in the same manner. Secondly, dichotomies between religion and science, religion and the secular, and public and private are blurring. Religious practice is changing as many adherents are less committed to institutional forms and beliefs, preferring informal and fluid practices, rituals, and identities that open new spaces for religion and the sacred, such as in nature or online (Baker & Dinham, 2017; Wilkins-Laflamme, 2023).

On the other hand, preoccupations about religious violence and controversies continue, often exacerbated by legal disputes. When policy-makers and public institutions like schools use outdated interpretations of religion, the resulting structures are often inadequate to meet current realities (Baker & Dinham, 2017). Religion is dynamic, informed by place and time, elastic in definition, and increasingly seen at the local level in the lives of adherents rather than the statements of belief issued by institutional leaders.

The term *secularism* is equally fluid and dynamic. Historically posited as the opposite of religion, the realm of nonreligion, science, and rationality, it is increasingly "seen as a presence. It is *something* … rather than merely the absence of religion" (Calhoun et al., 2011, p. 5). Dinham (2020) describes the supposed nonreligiousness of public or shared space as full "of other normativities, beliefs and worldviews, revolving around liberal and neo-liberal commitments" (p. 143).

Contemporary global contexts speak to the dynamic natures of both religion and secularism. As Western countries become increasingly secular, religious impulses are reshaping societies and communities. Consider the following:

- The growth of Pentecostalism around the world. Pentecostals account for 600 million of the 2 billion Christians worldwide and the religion sees a growth of approximately 35,000 converts every day in countries as diverse as Brazil and Nigeria (*Current Affairs*, 2022).
- The 50 Muslim-majority countries, found in the Middle East, North Africa, Central Asia, Southeast Asia, and elsewhere (Nations Online, n.d.)
- The complex religious dynamics in India, where Hindus are in the majority and Muslims make up a much smaller minority in comparison, though they are still the third-largest Muslim population in the world, behind Indonesia and Pakistan (Nations Online, n.d.)
- The increase of Protestantism in China, where Christianity has expanded from 1 million to an estimated 100 million in four decades (Chalufour, 2023)

These dynamics are important to Canadian teachers as India, the Philippines, China, and Nigeria are the top countries of origin for newcomers, including new students (Statistics Canada, 2022c).

Despite these realities, belief in the public irrelevance of religion continues to dominate Western assumptions. Too often, religion is perceived as a problem to be solved rather than an aspect of lived realities to be engaged.

## Education and Religious Literacy

In the maelstrom of religion and secular realities is education, a key institution through which society instills knowledge, values, and attitudes. Although educational systems address diversity in a variety of ways (i.e., structural diversity that offers worldview choice [Hiemstra & Brink, 2006]), for the purposes of this chapter we will focus on providing a framework for thinking through education about religion in ways that promote active engagement with diversity through relationships. Relationships contribute to flourishing, as through them individuals learn about their neighbours; engage in collective action, including social justice for those who are religiously marginalized; and build such democratic competencies as listening, meaning-making, and cooperation (Grant, 2012).

Research has found that relationships are essential to religious literacy. The concept of literacy as it pertains to cultural or financial literacy has come to signify an ability of "reading the world" and "navigat[ing] a complex range of social practices" (Biesta et al., 2019, pp. 11, 19). Engaging literacies critically "involves an ability to question offered domains and take responsibility for defining them" (p. 12). Religious studies scholars define religious literacy in different ways, and we follow the Centre for Civic Religious Literacy (n.d.) in defining it as content knowledge and a skill set of understanding akin to media literacy and digital literacy. Understanding identities, people, topics, and institutions is critical to recognizing discrimination in Canada that is based on religion and racialization of religion, which occurs when observable characteristics (e.g., race and dress) are associated with a particular religion or religions and lead to notions of inferiority or superiority about that group (Joshi, 2016). Implicit in religious literacy is a rejection of assumptions such as the following: secularization is inevitable in modern societies, most people in the West are secular, secularism is belief-neutral, and the religious landscape can be described in the simple binaries of religious/secular or public/private (Dinham & Francis, 2016).

Relationships, by their definition, are active; people engage in them. They involve more than discrete bits of information. Shaw's (2022) advocacy for worldview literacy, which builds on religious literacy, involves "a process of dialogical encounter with difference, an educational praxis that brings the pupil to a greater understanding of the diversity and dynamism of worldviews and of themselves as actors therein" (Introduction). Although we retain the term *religious literacy*, which encompasses diverse worldviews, including the spiritual and nonreligious, we take from Shaw the emphasis on transformative dialogue as an important element of religious literacy. The transformative nature of religious literacy guides one to be mindful of an individual's experience in flourishing; language and lenses may shift when describing an individual's worldview as they journey through different parts of their development. This recognition offers students the space to explore, express, and understand their growth in a genuine manner that reflects who they are at any given time.

But how can this happen in a classroom when so many content and social demands already exist? We believe that the work of several scholars at the Institute for Global Engagement (IGE) offers glimpses at the answer through their visions for cross-cultural religious literacy and **covenantal pluralism**. Important to note is that these approaches do not add more to the already full curriculum and classrooms. Instead, they suggest a reframing of the teaching that is already occurring.

### Cross-Cultural Religious Literacy

Cross-cultural religious literacy is grounded in the idea of pluralism rather than diversity, the latter described as "the presence of difference" (Seiple & Hoover, 2021, p. 6). Promoters of pluralism, such as Diana L. Eck (n.d.) of the Harvard Pluralism Project, go further, insisting that pluralism involves (1) energetically engaging with diversity, (2) moving beyond tolerance to actively seek understanding across difference, (3) rejecting relativism in favour of encounters with commitments, and (4) pursuing dialogue. The IGE presents pluralism in stark contrast to tolerance:

- Tolerance intimates that the person doing the tolerating has privilege over the person being tolerated, suggesting condescension. "No one wants merely to be 'tolerated,' as if their presence is only grudgingly and tenuously accepted within the socio-political order" (Stewart et al., 2022, p. 25).
- Tolerance "can reveal an alarming degree of religious illiteracy" (Stewart et al., 2022, p. 26) that oversimplifies religion or religious differences—for example, either saying that all religions are the same and welcome or that they are all false and "poisonous."
- Tolerance is "too easily coupled with indifference" rather than engagement with differences (Stewart et al., 2022, p. 26).

Building on Eck's work, Seiple and Hoover (2021) posit pluralism as going beyond tolerance to active engagement with diversity, meaning that pluralism needs careful attention and cannot be assumed. Religious literacy, they submit, provides a model for pluralism and, as such, requires several skills, one of which is understanding "of the other's motivations and interests, and some self-awareness of one's own" (p. 7). Other skills include judgment and flexibility as contexts and individuals change and vary, and building relationships, which are central to the entire enterprise. Relationships, in turn, require the three fundamental skills of evaluation (to assess what is occurring), negotiation, and communication.

The fact that cross-cultural interactions are firmly rooted in relationships and depend on an understanding of self and others is a familiar concept for teachers. Parker Palmer (1997) points out that we teach who we are. If we are to avoid indoctrination and ensure that students encounter multiple perspectives, teachers must know their own beliefs, assumptions, and motivations. Palmer's dictum is also a crucial aspect of student flourishing because teachers capable of self-reflection and interpretation of their own life experiences are better able to support student introspection, healthy attitudes of self, and questioning (Grant, 2012). Seiple and Hoover (2021) are quick to point out that religious literacy is not an end in itself; rather, the goal is pluralism, active engagement to support "social flourishing and pluralistic peace" (p. 10). In this way, cross-cultural religious literacy has civic goals and serves a larger purpose of covenantal pluralism.

## Covenantal Pluralism

"Covenantal pluralism embodies the humility, patience, empathy, and responsibility to engage, respect, and protect the other—albeit without necessarily lending moral equivalency to the beliefs and behaviors of others" (Seiple & Hoover, 2021, p. 11). Cross-cultural literacy is one aspect of covenantal pluralism. Elsewhere, Stewart et al. (2020) describe it as "characterized by a constitutional order of equal rights and responsibilities and by a culture of reciprocal commitment to engaging, respecting, and protecting the other—albeit *without* necessarily conceding equal veracity or moral equivalence to the beliefs and behaviors of others. The envisioned end-state is neither a thin-soup ecumenism nor vague syncretism, but rather a positive, practical, non-relativistic pluralism" (para. 6).

Here *covenantal* is used in a secular rather than religious sense, moving beyond the rules-bound contract to embrace relationships. It can respect communities that make exclusive truth claims (such as "Jesus Christ is the only way to the truth" and "nothing is true unless proven by science"), while at the same time insisting on the respect and fairness embedded in a pluralist covenant. It preserves differences to recognize that not all religions or worldviews are the same (Prothero, 2010) and encourages the virtues of humility, courage, and empathy (Stewart et al., 2020). "This is a pluralism that requires a humble posture of openness to people who make exclusive truth claims, who are deeply embedded in communities with particularistic identities and guarded boundaries, whose beliefs and practices are not as 'negotiable' as consumer-market choices" (Stewart et al., 2022, p. 31).

## A CANADIAN MODEL OF RELIGIOUS LITERACY

Cross-cultural religious literacy and covenantal pluralism may appear abstract to some teachers or common sense to others who promote an inclusive classroom where students engage with one another. However, a deeper exploration of each concept reveals its complexity. How can one teach students to be religiously literate so that they are discerning but flexible? What does it mean to evaluate, negotiate, and communicate in relation to religious diversity? How can one implement covenantal pluralism by concretely fostering the humility, patience, empathy, and responsibility needed to engage, respect, and protect the other? Approaching these bigger questions begins with a deeper understanding of religious literacy.

The team at the Centre for Civic Religious Literacy (CCRL) has created a made-in-Canada model so that the approach to religious literacy in Canada is context-specific (Dinham & Francis, 2016; Jackson, 1997). Though the CCRL does not refer to its approach as "cross-cultural religious literacy," its lens and premise to promote understanding, engagement, and dialogue across, between, and within cultural groups have the same intention. Like the work at IGE, the work at the CCRL echoes Eck's (n.d.) conceptualization of pluralism, which goes beyond diversity and holds a civic purpose and commitment.

In Canada, religious literacy is an academic framework to perceive and analyze the complexity within identity and society. The context-specific content includes discrimination, such as anti-Indigenous racism, which is informed by our colonial history by region, group, Treaty, international politics, religious traditions, and economic development, among other aspects of history. The CCRL's Canadian conception includes five principles.

### Internal Diversity Exists within All Religious, Spiritual, and Nonreligious Worldviews

Each worldview community is diverse in race, ethnicity, gender, sexual orientation, class, immigration status, and so on. In this way, intersectionality—the concept that each identity factor is embedded with different aspects of power and that one's set of overlapping identities informs the power dynamics they experience (Crenshaw, 1991; Hill-Collins & Bilge, 2016)—is embedded in religious literacy. For example, this principle recognizes the diversity among Indigenous Peoples: some are anti-religion due to Canada's colonial history, while others are Christians, which can lead to discrimination within Indigenous communities based on religious differences. As such, religious literacy offers the lens and skills to perceive the basis of this conflict and the language to engage with this tension in some Indigenous communities.

## Worldviews Are Externally Diverse

Worldviews are distinct despite actual and perceived similarities. For example, Diwali is celebrated by many South Asians, including Hindus, Sikhs, and Muslims, among others, but each group is distinct.

## Worldviews Are Not Static—They Inform All Spheres of Society and Are Informed by Them

Worldviews inform all spheres of society (religious, political, social, and economic), historically and currently, and are informed by them. This principle promotes the analytical ability to recognize the profoundly discriminatory influence of worldviews, such as how Christian leadership (religious, political, social, and economic) informed the cultural genocide of Indigenous Peoples in Canada as well as the impetus for generosity in times of need, including that displayed by Christian groups and churches that sponsored Syrian refugees to Canada regardless of their religious backgrounds. This principle helps individuals acknowledge emotions and frustrations behind negative experiences and details regarding religious groups without ignoring the contributions that members of the group may have made.

## Religious Literacy in Canada Must Include Nonreligious Worldviews and Indigenous Spiritualities

A Canadian discussion must include nonreligious worldviews and Indigenous spiritualities, as 34.6 percent of Canadians are not religiously affiliated and the Indigenous population grew 9.4 percent between 2016 and 2021, at almost double the rate of non-Indigenous people in the same period (Statistics Canada, 2022a, 2022b).

## Worldviews Hold a Significant Personal Meaning for Each Individual and Need to Be Discussed from Their Distinct Lens

Worldviews hold a significant personal meaning for each person, which requires us to discuss them from an individual's and their worldview's distinct lens and not from the worldview of others; this includes the language individuals may use to express a deep sense of belonging and connection with something greater than themselves (Michaelson, 2021).

The fact that worldviews hold personal meaning is perhaps most important for teachers focused on relationship building as this reality speaks to the inability to separate religious, ethnic, and cultural identity for some (e.g., consider the embeddedness of Judaism in ethnically Jewish communities). It also speaks to the affective and holistic reality of one's being, recognizing the interconnectedness between one's social-emotional, mental, physical, and spiritual well-being.

In 2019, the CCRL hosted a one-hour Queering Religion workshop for Ontario secondary students at the Peel District School Board's You Are Not Alone conference, created to support gay-straight alliance clubs across its schools. The aim of the workshop was to offer space, time, and support to 2SLGBTQI+ students and allies to discuss the lived reality of being 2SLGBTQI+ and religious, and the CCRL met students who simply needed the space and were evaluating, negotiating, and communicating ideas pertaining to various aspects of the topic. Students spoke about the challenges of living at the crux of that internal diversity within their religious community. Some shared that they were from mixed religious homes, which made it even more difficult. The CCRL's role was to frame the conversation by introducing the religious literacy framework, helping students understand that internal diversity includes those who are religious and 2SLGBTQI+, and providing students with the language and lens to know how to discuss their lived reality or those of their friends. CCRL facilitators created a space for covenantal pluralism that went deeper than other parts of the conference, which was made evident as many teachers who spoke with us afterward were extremely interested in the workshop progress and expressed that they had no idea how to engage on that intersection of identity with their students.

Also in 2019, the CCRL hosted an in-class workshop for Montreal secondary students at a local public (not religiously affiliated) high school, co-hosted with the Canadian Race Relations Foundation. The workshop was framed as an all-day ethics fair embedded into the students' regular ethics and religious culture class that day. The CCRL talked about prejudice, stereotypes, and many types of discrimination. Though the term *religious literacy* was never used, the workshop was an opportunity to engage with past and present aspects of Canadian history and identify where prejudice, stereotypes, and discrimination harmed people (e.g., the *Komagata Maru* incident and anti-Semitism within well-known institutions such as McGill University). Present-day examples revolved around local Montreal statistics, including the report *Xenophobic and Notably Islamophobic Acts of Hate* by the Quebec Commission for Human Rights and Rights of Youth (2019), about Islamophobia in Quebec. During the workshop, students participated in grade-appropriate degrees of evaluation and negotiation, and the ethics fair encouraged students to promote covenantal pluralism in their lives to counter local prejudices, stereotypes, and discrimination by discussing the misunderstandings and internal diversities in religious, ethnic, racialized, and socioeconomic groups.

Despite the existence of religious, spiritual, and nonreligious individuals in society, many K–12 and post-secondary programs continue to exclude religious literacy—to the detriment of the student and society because this limits covenantal pluralism and relationship building. In a review of three top Canadian teacher training programs, we (Patrick & Chan, 2022) found that two programs do not make any online reference to religion or spirituality, despite their commitments to reconciliation or to teaching students holistically. The third program references religion and spirituality minimally. This reflects a lack of understanding or a lack of desire to recognize that religion, spirituality, and nonreligion are intertwined in our colonial past and present history and our identities. As humanity looks toward contemporary needs, such as climate action, disengaging from religious literacy omits a recognition of many communities working toward climate action based on their religious, spiritual, and nonreligious commitments. In turn, omitting this aspect of identity and society in class discussions inhibits students from recognizing or working in partnership with climate action partners of particular worldviews.

## CONCLUSION

This chapter offers Canadian teachers a framework to think about religion within the reality of increasing religious diversity in classrooms. We are familiar with the fears many teachers have about teaching about religion but consider religious literacy essential if all students in classrooms are to flourish. If religion matters to the identity of many students, then teachers need to recognize and resist stereotypes, ensure that correct information about religion is shared in the classroom, and view religious diversity as a means to learning about our neighbours and the world rather than viewing it as a problem to be solved. It is about moving beyond tolerance, which can be positive if viewed as creating space for everyone but is too often reduced to platitudes and indifference. Instead, we offer cross-cultural religious literacy that takes both difference and social cohesion seriously and works toward actively learning and engaging in the democratic practices of evaluating, negotiating, and communicating via the skills of humility, patience, empathy, and responsibility to engage, respect, and protect the other. The ever-expanding work of the CCRL indicates that there is a desire among various sectors in society, including educators and students, to learn more about religion so citizens can participate in respectful, knowledgeable, and empathetic relationships in society. Such interest is not surprising, as all human beings wish to be understood, to create meaning in their contexts, and to engage in meaningful relationships. Religious literacy is an avenue to promote such flourishing.

## KEY TERMS

**Covenantal pluralism:** "A robust, relational, and non-relativistic paradigm for living together peacefully and productively, in the context of our deepest differences" (Stewart et al., 2022, p. 21). This concept "embodies the humility, patience, empathy, and responsibility to engage, respect, and protect the other—albeit without necessarily lending moral equivalency to the beliefs and behaviors of others" (Seiple & Hoover, 2021, p. 11).

**Religion:** A complex term that encompasses many details and does not have an agreed-upon definition among scholars. However, from our discussion, we can summarize that religions are not static blocks but rather "lived, transactional, and steeped in fluid, located meanings and beliefs" (Baker & Dinham, 2017, p. 10) because religious traditions are internally heterogeneous. The dichotomies between religion and that which is not religion are blurring, and religious practice is changing. Religion, then, is dynamic, informed by place and time, elastic in definition, and increasingly seen at the local level in the lives of adherents rather than the statements of belief issued by institutional leaders.

**Religious literacy:** This includes content knowledge and a skill set of understanding akin to media literacy and financial literacy. Understanding identities, people, topics, and institutions is critical to recognizing discrimination based on religion and racialization of religion, which occurs when observable characteristics (e.g., race and dress) are associated with a particular religion or religions and lead to notions of inferiority or superiority about that group (Joshi, 2016).

## DISCUSSION QUESTIONS AND ACTIVITIES

1. Activity: Create a living graph and indicate whether specific policies and events contribute to covenantal pluralism or divisiveness. For example, a history of Canadian immigration policies can be found at the Canadian Museum of Immigration at the Pier 21 website (https://pier21.ca). The same activity could be done with policies for multiculturalism, trade policies, foreign affairs, and more.
2. Discussion question for in-service teachers: How can religious literacy be incorporated into various school subjects in ways that fit naturally within the curriculum? The point is for religious literacy to be embedded within the context and content of the curriculum rather than being an add-on.
3. Discussion question for pre-service teachers: Can you benefit from learning about diverse religious and nonreligious worldviews? What might such education look like? Reference case studies designed by Harvard University's Pluralism Project, found here: https://pluralism.org/case-studies.

## REFERENCES

Amjad, A. (2018). Muslim students' experiences and perspectives on current teaching practices in Canadian schools. *Power and Education*, *10*(3), 315–332. doi.org/10.1177/1757743818790276

Baker, C., & Dinham, A. (2017). New interdisciplinary spaces of religions and beliefs in contemporary thought and practice: An analysis. *Religions*, *8*, Article 16. doi.org/10.3390/rel8020016

Bascaramurty, D., & Alphonso, C. (2017). A community divided. *Globe and Mail*. www.theglobeandmail.com/news/toronto/a-community-divided-the-fight-over-canadian-values-threatens-to-boil-over-inpeel/article34852452

Biesta, G., Adridge, D., Hannam, P., & Whittle, S. (2019). *Religious literacy: A way forward for religious education?* Brunel University London & Hampshire Inspection and Advisory Service. doi.org/10.13140/RG.2.2.24170.47047

Calhoun, C., Juergensmeyer, M., & VanAntwerpen, J. (2011). Introduction. In C. Calhoun, M. Juergensmeyer, & J. VanAntwerpen (Eds.), *Rethinking secularism* (pp. 3–30). Oxford University Press.

Centre for Civic Religious Literacy. (n.d.). *What is civic religious literacy in Canada?* https://ccrl-clrc.ca/work/civic-religious-literacy/

Chalufour, M. (2023). *What's behind boom of Christianity in China?* The Brink. www.bu.edu/articles/2023/why-is-christianity-growing-in-china/

Chan, W. Y. A., Mistry, H., Reid, E., Zaver, A., & Jafralie, S. (2019). Recognition of context and experience: A civic-based Canadian conception of religious literacy. *Journal of Beliefs & Values*, *41*(3), 255–271. doi.org/10.1080/13617672.2019.1587902

Crenshaw, K. (1991). Mapping the margins: Intersectionality, identity politics, and violence against women of color. *Stanford Law Review*, *43*(6), 1241–1299. doi.org/10.2307/1229039

*Current Affairs*. (2022). The rise of Pentecostal Christianity. www.currentaffairs.org/2022/04/how-pentecostal-christianity-is-taking-over-the-world

Dinham, A. (2020). Reimagining religion and belief in the public sphere. *Modern Believing*, *61*(2), 141–151. doi.org/10.3828/mb.2020.9

Dinham, A., & Francis, M. (2016). Religious literacy: Contesting an idea and practice. In A. Dinham & M. Francis (Eds.), *Religious literacy in policy and practice* (pp. 3–25). Policy Press.

Eck, D. L. (n.d.). *What is pluralism?* The Pluralism Project. https://pluralism.org/about

Grant, C. A. (2012). Cultivating flourishing lives: A robust social justice vision of education. *American Educational Research Journal*, *49*(5), 910–934. http://www.jstor.org/stable/23319631

Hiemstra, J. L., & Brink, R.A. (2006). The advent of a public pluriformity model: Faith-based school choice in Alberta. *Canadian Journal of Education*, *29*(4), 1157–1190. https://eric.ed.gov/?id=EJ766908

Hill-Collins, P., & Bilge. S. (2016). *Intersectionality*. Polity Press.

Hoverd, W., LeBrun, E., & Van Arragon, L. (n.d.). *Religion and education in the provinces of Quebec and Ontario*. http://religionanddiversity.ca/media/uploads/religion_and_education_in_the_provinces_of_quebec_and_ontario_report.pdf

Jackson, R. (1997). *Religious education: An interpretive approach*. Hodder & Stoughton.

Joshi, K. Y. (2016). Racialization of religion and global migration. In J. Saunders, E. Fiddian-Qasmiyeh, & S. Snyder (Eds.), *Intersections of religion and migration: Issues at the global Crossroads* (pp. 123–149). Palgrave Macmillan. doi.org/10.1057/978-1-137-58629-2_5

Khan, M. (2021). Pedagogy of pain: Pulling passion, potential, and possibility from the pain of silence and truth telling. *Diaspora, Indigenous, and Minority Education*, *15*(4), 252–262. doi.org/10.1080/15595692.2021.1944087

Michaelson, V. (2021). Developing a definition of spiritual health for Canadian young people: A qualitative study. *International Journal of Children's Spirituality*, *26*(1–2), 67–85. doi.org/10.1080/1364436X.2020.1856048

*Multani v. Commission Scolaire Marguerite Bourgeoys* (2006) 1 S.C.R. 256, 2006 SCC 6. https://scc-csc.lexum.com/scc-csc/scc-csc/en/item/15/index.do

Nations Online. (n.d.). *Islamic world*. www.nationsonline.org/oneworld/muslim-countries.htm

Niyozov, S., & Pluim, G. (2009). Teachers' perspectives on the education of Muslim students: A missing voice in Muslim education. *Curriculum Inquiry*, *39*(5), 637–677. doi.org/10.1111/j.1467-873X.2009.00463.x

Palmer, P. (1997). *The courage to teach: Exploring the inner landscape of a teacher's life.* Jossey-Bass.

Patrick, M., & Chan, W. Y. A. (2022). Can I keep my religious identity and be a professional? Evaluating the presence of religious literacy in education, nursing, and social work professional programs across Canada. *Education Sciences, 12*(8), 543. doi.org/10.3390/educsci12080543

Prothero, S. R. (2010). *God is not one: The eight rival religions that run the world.* HarperOne.

Quebec Commission for Human Rights and Rights of Youth. (2019). *Les actes haineux à caractère xénophobe, notamment islamophobe: résultats d'une recherche menée à travers le Québec* [Xenophobic and notably Islamophobic acts of hate]. www.cdpdj.qc.ca/fr/publications/les-actes-haineux-a-caractar

Robson, K. L. (2012). *Sociology of education in Canada.* https://ecampusontario.pressbooks.pub/robsonsoced/

Seiple, C., & Hoover, D. R. (2021). A case for cross-cultural religious literacy. *The Review of Faith & International Affairs, 19*(1), 1–13. doi.org/10.1080/15570274.2021.1874165

Seljak, D. (2005). Education, multiculturalism, and religion. In P. Bramadat & D. Seljak (Eds.), *Religion and ethnicity in Canada* (pp. 178–200). Pearson Lonqman.

Seljak, D., Schmidt, A., Stewart, A., & Bramadat, P. (2008). Secularization and the separation of church and state in Canada. *Canadian Diversity, 6*(1), 6–24.

*Servatius v. Alberni School District No. 70* (2022) BCCA 421. www.bccourts.ca/jdb-txt/ca/22/04/2022BCCA0421.htm

Shaw, M. (2022). Worldview literacy as intercultural citizenship education: A framework for critical, reflexive engagement in plural democracy. *Education, Citizenship and Social Justice, 18*(2), 197–213. doi.org/10.1177/17461979211062125

Statistics Canada. (2022a). *The Canadian census: A rich portrait of the country's religious and ethnocultural diversity.* www150.statcan.gc.ca/n1/daily-quotidien/221026/dq221026b-eng.htm

Statistics Canada. (2022b). *Indigenous population continues to grow and is much younger than the non-Indigenous population, although the pace of growth has slowed.* www150.statcan.gc.ca/n1/daily-quotidien/220921/dq220921a-eng.htm

Statistics Canada. (2022c). *Nearly one in five recent immigrants were born in India, the highest proportion from a single place of birth since 1971.* www150.statcan.gc.ca/n1/daily-quotidien/221026/g-a005-eng.htm

Statistics Canada. (2022d). *Police-reported crime statistics in Canada, 2021.* www150.statcan.gc.ca/n1/pub/85-002-x/2022001/article/00013-eng.htm

Statistics Canada. (2024). *Police-reported hate crime, by type of motivation, selected regions and Canada (selected police services).* https://doi.org/10.25318/3510006601-eng

Stewart, W. C., Seiple, C., & Hoover, D. R. (2020). To advance international human rights, first promote covenantal pluralism. *London School of Economics and Political Science, Religion and Global Society* [Blog]. https://blogs.lse.ac.uk/religionglobalsociety/2020/12/to-advance-international-human-rights-first-promote-covenantal-pluralism/

Stewart, W. C., Seiple, C., & Hoover, D. R. (2022). Covenantal pluralism: Toward a world of peaceable neighborhoods. In C. Seiple & D. R. Hoover (Eds.), *The Routledge handbook of religious literacy, pluralism, and global engagement* (pp. 21–37). Routledge. doi.org/10.4324/9781003036555-4

Wilkins-Laflamme, S. (2023). *Religion, spirituality and secularity among millennials: The generation shaping American and Canadian trends*. Routledge.

# CHAPTER 15
# Broadening Understandings of Religion to Support Student Flourishing

*Margaretta Patrick and Carla L. Peck*

Whether we are personally aware of it or not, religion is a key part of Canadian society and is often central to debates in the public sphere, including in schools. For example, on the day Amrit Kaur graduated as a teacher in the spring of 2019, she realized she would have to move out of the province of Quebec if she wished to teach (Somos, 2019). Quebec's National Assembly had just passed Bill 21, the Act Respecting the Laicity of the State, which prohibits some public service workers, including teachers, from wearing religious symbols while working. As a Sikh, Kaur wears a turban and thus faced the choice of either moving out of Quebec or not teaching. A subsequent survey in 2022 clarified that Muslims, Sikhs, and Jews are disproportionately and negatively impacted by the bill, with two-thirds of the Muslim women surveyed reporting that they feel "significantly less safe" than they did prior to the bill's passing (Rubertucci, 2022). One researcher described the increase in hate incidents in Quebec as the result of "sort of state sanctioned Islamophobia" enabled by the bill (Rubertucci, 2022).

In March 2021, the Ministry of Education in Alberta released a new draft kindergarten to grade 6 social studies curriculum as part of a suite of curriculum revisions undertaken by the Jason Kenney government. While all subjects were widely criticized, the draft social studies curriculum received the most scrutiny, with local, national, and international experts denouncing it due to fundamental flaws related to its content and design (Peck, 2022). One key area of criticism was how the draft social studies curriculum treated religion, which one of us described as "inadequate and harmful" (Patrick, 2023). As a result of this overwhelming criticism, the draft social studies curriculum was eventually pulled for further revision. A new draft, released on March 14, 2024, eliminated the study of specific religions and instead included the terms *religions* and *beliefs* in lists of elements of cultures and civilizations.

Whether the question is about who is allowed to teach in schools or what is being taught, it is clear that Canadians would benefit from a deeper understanding of religion. Many governments recognize the benefits of students learning about religion. For example, the Government of Manitoba (2019) describes the intent of the grade 12 elective course, World of Religions: A Canadian Perspective, as "the development of understanding and appreciation for the diversity of religious belief systems and practices, and their roles in society and people's lives. The current course also aims to challenge misinformation and biases, both explicit and implicit, that learners may have developed or to which they may have been exposed" (p. 1).

We recognize that teaching about religion can feel like dangerous ground, particularly within public school systems, which are intended to be nonreligious. We want to clarify that when we write *teaching about religion*, we do not mean teaching students to enter into a particular faith tradition. Rather, our focus is on teaching students *about* "world" religions in an effort to build understanding of religious diversity in their community, province, country, and the world. When we speak of religious diversity or religious literacy, we include nonreligious worldviews, communities, and individuals. Those who are nonreligious can hold to their beliefs, practices, rituals, and/or identities as strongly as some who are religious, and both religious and nonreligious identities can inform how teachers and students view the world, their role in it, **controversial public issues**, current events, and so on. In this chapter we hope to equip and empower educators by providing a self-reflection tool, information about religion helpful to teachers, and pedagogical suggestions so they feel comfortable and confident teaching about religion in their classrooms.

The first section of the chapter provides context by examining how religious diversity impacts teachers and school leaders, students, and caregivers. The second and third sections aim to support teachers as they create inclusive classrooms in which all students can flourish. In preparation for planning how to teach about religion, the second section provides a process for teacher self-reflection on their beliefs and assumptions about religion and nonreligion, followed by some remarks on the reflection questions by scholars of religion. The third section offers some pedagogical approaches and strategies to use when teaching about religion. We present suggested strategies that are similar to strategies used when teaching other topics in an effort to normalize discussions about religion in the classroom.

## THE IMPACTS OF RELIGIOUS DIVERSITY ON VARIOUS CLASSROOM PARTICIPANTS

### Teachers and School Leaders

In 2020, on the eve of the 19th anniversary of 9/11, @hqdada (Haroun, 2020) posted a tweet asking, "With 9/11 tmrw, what was the shittiest thing a teacher said or let other students say in front of you?" There was a flood of responses from those who appeared to live in the United States. Now adults, people remembered both the words and the silences of their teachers. They wrote about being called "Osama bin Laden" and being referred to as terrorists. In one instance, a principal called six- and eight-year-old brothers into the office and "interrogated" them after a mom reported that their grandmother, who had dropped them off at school, seemed "suspicious" because she was wearing a headscarf. On the other hand, some students encountered teacher allies, like the student whose teacher told stories of the discrimination experienced by his partner of Middle Eastern ethnicity. Our point here is not to call out bad teacher behaviour. Rather, we wish to emphasize the importance of teacher responses to religion because religion and religious identities matter to many students (see also chapter 3).

Delegitimizing, marginalizing, and silencing students' religious identity negatively impacts student **flourishing**. When religion is a deeply held aspect of identity, as it was for many of the first- and second-generation newcomer elementary students Parker (2016) studied, "some students may need to feel explicitly invited to contribute their personal knowledge to discussion, especially when they may be unsure of whether personal religious perspectives are respected in publicly funded, mainstream classrooms" (p. 81). Research suggests that students as young as 10 recognize when their religious identities are not welcomed in a classroom (Keller et al., 2017). Parker views student engagement with **religious diversity** in secular contexts as peacebuilding education in which purposeful dialogic pedagogy teaches students to engage with conflicting perspectives. Such education, argues Parker, "can encourage young people to develop and deepen their awareness of religious plurality and critical multiculturalism" (2016, p. 136). Peacebuilding education promotes student flourishing as it develops students' critical examination of how people and religious traditions are portrayed in textbooks and supports their learning about multiple perspectives, conflict, and power structures.

Clearly, teachers and school leaders play a foundational role in how students experience religious diversity and citizenship in the classroom and school writ large and whether these are safe spaces to discuss controversial and meaningful issues that are pertinent to students' identities. If teachers and school leaders are to plan such curricular and pedagogical encounters, they must go through their own processes of self-reflection and critical understanding of their worldviews, particularly as they relate to religion. Such a process is developed in the following sections.

## Students

An increasing number of students are nonreligious. According to the 2021 Canadian census (Statistics Canada, 2022), the number of children under the age of 10 who were born in Canada and are growing up in homes with no religious affiliation is contributing (and will continue to contribute) to the number of Canadians who self-identify as religiously "none." At the same time, newcomers are more likely than those born in Canada to identify as religious, have higher rates of religious participation, and view their religious and spiritual beliefs as influential in their lives (Cornelissen, 2021).

Religious newcomer students and their families have mixed experiences in Canadian school systems. Similarly to Khan (2021), introduced in the previous chapter, Alameddine (2021) calls for teachers to "critically examine how classrooms are perpetuating injustices by discrediting Muslim students' personal experiences considering the discourse surrounding Muslims" (p. 26). Khan and Alameddine call on teachers to pay attention to the stories and histories of Muslim students, with Alameddine further asking teachers to self-reflexively examine biases, prejudicial beliefs, and the power derived from current perspectives.

Listening to newcomer stories can interrogate assumptions. Haque's (2019) research with young adult, mostly Sunni, Muslims in Canada about their experiences with sexual health education in the varied spaces of school-based sex-ed; informal sex-ed from friends, parents, and online; and Islamic sex-ed is an example of research upending assumptions. Survey participants ranged in age from 18 to over 30, with 106 participants born in Canada and 145 born elsewhere (p. 17). Despite opt-out options, 76.8 percent of the survey respondents in public schools attended the sex-ed classes (p. 34). Several respondents desired more age-appropriate education and greater focus on healthy relationships, including interpersonal skills (p. 47). They reported sex-ed programs based solely on either safe sex or abstinence as insufficient (p. 48) and advocated for sex-ed in all contexts to be more culturally and religiously sensitive, a sensitivity that they insisted should include 2SLGBTQI+ content (pp. 131–132). The significance of Haque's research is that strong religious identities are not something to fear and that stereotypes should be avoided. Some of these young people exhibited well-developed capacities for critical thinking and had "adopted ideas of equality and diversity enshrined in Canadian conceptions of multiculturalism, and ... they are willing to act towards others according to these ideas" (pp. 133–134).

## Parents/Caregivers

The debate over Alberta's draft social studies curriculum mentioned above brought parents and child caregivers into curriculum conversations like no other debate has done in recent memory. For the first time, Alberta's social studies curriculum included the study of religious traditions, primarily in grades 2 and 6. Albertans were concerned about the lack of representation for the 40 percent of the population who identify as nonreligious (Statistics Canada, 2022), how religious "facts" for some traditions were misrepresented, and how religion was defined primarily as beliefs (Patrick, 2023).

Parental responses were polarized and at times based on stereotypes, as evidenced in the responses to an op-ed published in the spring of 2021 in both the *Calgary Herald* and the *Edmonton Journal* (Nicolai-deKoning & Patrick, 2021). On one end of the spectrum were those who opposed any education about religion in public education, arguing that such education belonged in *religious schools*. One commenter responding to the *Edmonton Journal* wrote, "If you do not teach children about religion; [sic] how are they supposed to know what to run away from?" The latter part of the statement about knowing "what to run away from" precludes that there is anything positive to be learned from religion. On the other end of the spectrum, those who supported some education about religion did so for different reasons. One person responding to the *Calgary Herald* wrote, "Absolutely schools need to instill Christian values onto [sic] our children. They should learn a basic sense of being a decent person and family values. Its [sic] much better than what they are learning right now, especially in their health class about sexuality." Another took a more historical perspective, also writing in response to the *Calgary Herald*, "It [religion] has historical, cultural, political and philosophical implications that are important to acknowledge."

Throughout the public conversation, however, there were few references to the increasing religious diversity of the province and the need to address negative religious and nonreligious stereotypes. Rarely was it mentioned that students flourish when they see people like themselves—including their religious and nonreligious selves—in the curriculum, making the topic of this chapter even more pertinent.

# CULTIVATING STUDENT FLOURISHING: TEACHER SELF-REFLECTION

Ultimately it is teachers who create classroom spaces in which students flourish as they plan activities and create safe and inclusive classroom spaces. However, we believe that before this can occur, teachers must first engage in a process of self-reflection to determine their own views of religion, including identifying misconceptions and gaps in knowledge.

## Teacher Self-Reflection

Teachers hold beliefs about many aspects of education, from the purpose of education to how students learn to which issues are controversial and which ones are settled (Peck & Herriot, 2015). Often these beliefs operate beneath the surface where they nevertheless influence content and pedagogical decisions. To help bring beliefs and assumptions about religion to the fore in preparation for planning how to teach about religion, it is helpful for teachers to think through their responses to these questions before reading the thoughts of religious studies scholars that follow:

- *How do you define religion?* Is religion primarily a thing in and of itself, or is it socially constructed? Is it institutional or lived at the level of individual life? Is it primarily about beliefs? Is it a meaning-making system?
- *How do you perceive the role of religion in society?* Is religion inevitably a source of conflict, or can it contribute to peacebuilding? Is it repressive, especially against women and Indigenous Peoples?
- *Is religion a private affair?* Should religion be privatized? Can all religious adherents privatize their beliefs and practices?
- *To what degree does your context shape your understanding of religion?* What population cohort are you in? Did you grow up in a religious or secular household? How did these formative experiences shape your views about religion?
- *Do all students benefit from dialogue about religion?* Should nonreligious students learn about religion and vice versa? What are the benefits and concerns for all students learning about religion and nonreligion?

The literature on these topics is extensive, so teachers reading the following responses to the questions articulated above should bear in mind that, due to space constraints, these responses represent an introduction rather than a fulsome exploration of the issue at hand. Readers are therefore encouraged to continue their learning by referring to the references provided at the end of this chapter.

## How Should Religion Be Defined?

Despite many attempts to define religion, there is no absolute definition accepted by all scholars and/or practitioners. Lincoln (2003) identifies four elements of religion, with each element present to varying degrees in any given religion: a discourse, a set of practices, a community, and an institution. This is a *substantive* definition, an attempt to define what religion *is*. Others focus on *functionalist* definitions, identifying what religion *does*. For example, Moon (2008) defines religion as "[orientating] the individual in the world, shaping her perception of the social and natural orders and providing a moral framework for her actions" (p. 234). Creating an authoritative definition of religion is difficult for the following reasons:

*Religions, indeed, all worldviews, are dynamic*, changing over time and full of internal differences (such as Shi'a and Sunni Islam or Catholic and Protestant Christianity). Some of the changes are shaped by migrant experiences. For example, Banerjee and Coward (2005) describe how Hindus in Canada shifted from practising Hinduism in their homes to erecting temples to facilitate marriage celebrations and death rites. Over time, worship became congregational, with Sunday meeting times.

*So-called world religions are dissimilar.* Buddhism has no divine being, while Hinduism has a pantheon of gods and goddesses "through which the Divine has revealed itself in the Hindu tradition" (Banerjee & Coward, 2005, p. 32). Discussions about whether such "Eastern" religions as Confucianism, Daoism, and Buddhism should be considered religions are ongoing (Cohen et al., 2016). One reason for the dissimilarities is colonization. When European countries encountered philosophies and worldviews that functioned like Christianity, they were identified as religious even though some local languages had no word similar to *religion*. Colonialism privileges the assumption that all act and function like Christianity, and often this means privileging belief (Asad, 1993). Privileging belief marginalizes worldviews and communities that focus on traditions and rituals and more communally based religions, such as Judaism, Islam, or Catholicism, although one must be aware of essentializing both religious traditions and cultures as more or less communal (Cohen et al., 2016).

## What Is the Role of Religion in Society?

According to Sears and Herriot (2016), "there is a pervasive belief that religion is almost always a negative force in public life; in the words of the late Christopher

Hitchens ..., it 'poisons everything'" (p. 299). There is no doubt that much violence has been committed in the name of religion: consider Christian Church involvement in Indian residential schools in Canada, radical Islamists and the events of 9/11, the role of militant Buddhists in Sri Lanka, and the oppression of women, just to name a few. Additionally, religious groups and individuals can both experience discrimination and discriminate against others, frequently in relation to the same people and/or groups (p. 287).

However, religion is no more violent than nonreligious worldviews. One need only think of the atrocities committed by the Nazis or communism, especially during the Cultural Revolution and under Stalin in the Soviet Union. Like nonreligious traditions, religion contains the potential for good as well as bad. Religions contribute to the common good through their engagement in education, health, and social services and increasingly in environmental sustainability. For example, a Pew Research Centre (2016) report titled *Religion and Education around the World* evaluated the levels of education among adults in religious and unaffiliated groups and found that education levels among women in all religions had increased faster than education levels among men, although region matters, as socioeconomic factors greatly impact education. Even though attitudes toward the education of women are changing, recent developments in Afghanistan are a reminder that setbacks for women and girls are an ongoing concern (UNESCO, 2023).

### *Is Religion a Private Affair?*

Many people today think of religion within a secular/religious binary in which religion references the superstitious, emotional, and irrational, whereas the secular is the sphere of science and the rational. If religion is perceived as irrational, it can be dangerous, and if it is seen as superstitious, it has no role in the public sphere. Therefore, many in developed countries believe religion must be relegated to private life. However, political science and religious studies scholar Elizabeth Shakman Hurd (2011) argues that this binary has its own politics: "The practices, institutions, and ways of being designated as secular sustain and shape the contours of public life and the modern organisation of social-scientific knowledge. These traditions do not merely reflect social reality; they help to construct it" (p. 169). To reiterate a point elaborated in the previous chapter, secularism is not the absence of religion but a worldview with its own set of values that influences the nature of religion and knowledge.

When teachers reject a simplistic binary and instead recognize the political, social, economic, and historical roles of religion and the secular, they can better understand and teach about the following:

- the religious and secular underpinnings of citizenship and social justice (Sears & Herriot, 2016)
- both secular and religious Canadians' contributions to the development of immigration policy that recognizes refugees as a distinct category and to the implementation of Canada's refugee sponsorship program, as well as their suggestions for reform (Melnyk & Parker, 2021)
- the religious and secular motivations that animate the environmental/creation care movements

All people have value systems, whether religious, nonreligious, or spiritual. Yet typically only religious people are asked to bracket their worldview when engaging in the public sphere. If public spaces are seen as plural rather than secular spaces, then more people can engage in public conversations, each from their own identity, and no one is forced to privatize what may be central to their identity.

*Does Context Shape One's Understanding of Religion?*

The population cohort to which one belongs influences how one views and experiences religion, with older generations reporting higher rates of religious affiliation and participation (Cornelissen, 2021). Scholar Sarah Wilkins-Laflamme (2023) studies the beliefs of Millennials. Although the birth year range of the cohort varies among scholars, Wilkins-Laflamme uses data for those born between 1986 and 2005, who grew up in the most ethnically and religiously plural society to date. Wilkins-Laflamme describes them as more "inclined toward nonbelief and a nonreligious, nonspiritual worldview" (p. 27), due at least in part to the emergence of the "cradle nonreligious" (p. 146): those who were born into nonreligious homes and subsequently are indifferent toward religion and lack knowledge about it.

Religious disaffiliation does not mean that Millennials are nonreligious, but it does mean that religion and spirituality look different among Millennials than among previous generations. For example, some observe the presence of what is called a moralistic therapeutic deism among older Millennials, which continues to allow for a creating God who desires that people be good but is not involved in individual lives. It is a worldview that emphasizes happiness and feeling good and claims that upon death those who are good go to Heaven or another good place (Wilkins-Laflamme, 2023, p. 25).

Given that many teachers are Millennials, it is helpful to understand how their generational cohort understands religion. For those raised in nonreligious homes, a lack of knowledge of and familiarity with religion may lead some to assume that religion is not important. Yet that is not the case for all students.

### Do All Students Benefit from Studying about Religion?

The website Teaching for Diversity (Peck, n.d.) is intended for use by K–12 teachers and addresses myths and misconceptions about diversity. The site engages with such misconceptions as "My students are all White. I don't really need to teach about diversity here" and "It is enough for me to teach to the diversity that exists in my classroom or school." In response, website creator Carla Peck reminds educators that they are required to "teach students about the full range of diverse peoples in Canada ... even if these groups are not represented in their current classrooms." Peck encourages educators to create learning experiences in which students confront their misconceptions through, for example, literature about and written by people from diverse ethnic groups.

The same rationales apply to education about religion. Educators may not know the religious and nonreligious worldviews and lived experiences present in a classroom, school, or community. Students may form misconceptions about religious and nonreligious worldviews, particularly when there is no instruction to counter these misconceptions. As the Government of Manitoba (2019) states in the introduction to its grade 12 course on religion discussed above, student understanding and appreciation for religious diversity and how religion functions in people's lives are beneficial and can challenge misinformation. Democracy is advanced when students confront misconceptions, engage with the religious diversity that exists in Canadian society, and develop what Hanvey (1982) refers to as perspective consciousness: "The recognition or awareness on the part of the individual that he or she has a view of the world that is not universally shared, that this view of the world has been and continues to be shaped by influences that often escape conscious detection, and that others have views of the world that are profoundly different from one's own" (p. 162).

## CULTIVATING STUDENT FLOURISHING: CREATING DIALOGUES AND ENCOUNTERS

Following Parker (2016), we encourage teachers to create opportunities for students to learn about, discuss, and encounter religious diversity. In the following sections, we offer some suggestions for how to create such opportunities.

## Aim for Understanding and Respect Rather than Tolerance

Tolerance alone is insufficient. We might tolerate back pain; that doesn't mean we like it. As Brown (2006) notes, "tolerated individuals will always be those who deviate from the norm, never those who uphold it, but they will also be further articulated as (deviant) individuals through the very discourse of tolerance" (p. 44). In contrast, understanding fosters greater empathy of, and engagement with, people unlike us. A central tenet of religious literacy and engagement with others is that neither understanding nor respect assumes agreement. One can disagree with another's belief about abortion, the afterlife, medical assistance in dying, and so on and still respect the other as a fellow citizen with the right to belief. The intent here is to identify differences, engage from specific belief positions, and then seek common ground across differences.

## Understand That Conflict Isn't Bad

Evidence from civics education research suggests that an open classroom climate where students are encouraged to express their views and examine issues from multiple perspectives is a strong predictor for youth knowledge of and engagement in social and political issues (Torney-Purta & Amadeo, 2012). Hess and McAvoy (2014) argue that the benefits of such pedagogical approaches include increased student engagement and confidence in their ability to discuss complex issues, improved capacity to engage in civil discourse, and the ability to see "disagreements as a normal part of democratic life" (p. 54). Creating the kind of classroom environment where dialogue across difference is safe and productive requires both the teacher and students to agree on certain ground rules, including respect and how to manage disagreements. Collaboratively creating a "Classroom Charter" (UNICEF Canada, n.d.) at the beginning of the year and discussing, articulating, and then practising such expectations can be helpful for ensuring not only that everyone in the classroom is aware of the guidelines for discussion but also that they have ownership over these guidelines because they helped create them. It is crucial to remember that discussion skills do not come naturally to most people; they require practice. Teachers should be explicit about supporting the development of such skills in their classrooms.

## Teach Controversial Public Issues and Critical Thinking

Issues involving religion can be controversial, just like issues involving politics, economics, and culture. Helping students develop sufficient background knowledge on a topic (whether provided by the teacher or acquired through student research), identify individual and multiple perspectives, and learn to identify their own stance on an issue is crucial to their engagement with controversial topics. Using participatory and collaborative strategies such as the Power of 3 Discussion Starter (Kates et al., 2015), inquiry, futures wheel (Mind Tools Content Team, n.d.), interviewing guest speakers, and mapping positions is an effective way to engage students in such work (see also Pace, 2021). Additionally, recounting stories of the people involved can develop empathy as well as critical analysis. Prepare students to recognize emotions as human responses to ideas, events, and feelings rather than something to be feared, but also help students understand how emotions can sometimes hinder our ability to think critically and rationally about a topic. Finally, in a time of immense disinformation and misinformation that hampers understanding and finding common ground, teachers need to teach students how to recognize faulty information. Working from the medical model of prevention, "prebunking" (Garcia & Shane, 2021) teaches students how misinformation and disinformation work beforehand so that when they encounter it, they can recognize it.

## Avoid Inviting Students to Disclose Their Beliefs or Participate in Rituals

Create a safe and inclusive space in which students can research and explore, but never require them to disclose their beliefs. Journalist Linda Wertheimer (2015a, 2015b) documented several controversies that erupted in schools across the United States when teachers invited students to participate in rituals and ceremonies rather than learn about them. In one instance, a teacher invited students to try on religious clothing, and in another case, a teacher had students practise calligraphy by writing words from the Muslim statement of faith. A different group of students visited a mosque, and an attendee invited several male students to participate in prayers. Some students agreed, but when a video of the students praying was made public, a firestorm erupted. While visiting a mosque to learn about Islam has great potential for learning about aspects of that religion, participating in prayers while there (particularly for non-Muslims) is problematic. Rituals and ceremonies are typically reserved for adherents, and participation by nonadherents can be seen as disrespectful.

## Recognize the Multiplicity of Voices That Speak for a Religious/Nonreligious Tradition

Given the shift of focus from institutions to how religion and spirituality are practised at the individual level, it is important to incorporate both practitioners and institutional voices into your classroom. This can include religious and non-religious participants in environmental/creation care movements, those working to end human trafficking, and more. Just as there is no single story about an ethnic group or country, there is similarly no single story about a religious tradition or nonreligious worldview (Adichie, 2009). Importantly, and related to the previous suggestion, ensure that you discuss with your classroom guests *prior* to their visit that their presentations must deliver information rather than proselytization.

## CONCLUSION

In this chapter we supported teachers by providing a self-reflective process to determine their own thinking about religion and nonreligion, provided some background information on the role of religion in both Canadian society and education, and discussed pedagogical considerations that will support student flourishing when discussing world religions, including nonreligious traditions. When teachers are comfortable and confident teaching about religion, students will ask questions and engage in conversation, but they need to trust that the space is safe and that teachers will listen to their voices and correct misinformation or stereotypes. We hope this chapter goes some way toward helping teachers feeling confident and competent to create such spaces. Additionally, teacher assessment of their own understanding of religion and incorporation of the pedagogical suggestions presented in this chapter will further student flourishing as teachers and students reflectively probe more deeply who they are, develop and/or understand their vision for society, and engage with difference (Grant, 2012).

## KEY TERMS

**Controversial public issues:** Social studies scholar Diana Hess (2002) states that "controversial public issues (CPI) are unresolved questions of public policy that spark significant disagreement" (p. 11).

**Flourishing:** This term involves more than just happiness. It is about "people making meaning and sense of important aspects of their life" (Grant, 2012, p. 914) and recognizes that there are a variety of good lives and that not all versions are consumed by the accumulation of wealth. Bokhorst-Heng and Hillier (in the introduction to this volume) locate individual flourishing as occurring within the collective and assert that a whole self and fulfilled life are developed and edified through relationships with diverse others.

**Religious diversity:** At the most basic level, religious diversity refers to the presence of multiple religious traditions and worldviews in a place, community, or society. Such diversity includes nonreligious worldviews. At a higher level, religious diversity is described as religious pluralism, characterized as an "order of equal rights and responsibilities and by a culture of reciprocal commitment to engaging, respecting, and protecting the other—albeit without necessarily conceding equal veracity or moral equivalence to the beliefs and behaviors of others" (Stewart et al., 2020).

## DISCUSSION QUESTIONS AND ACTIVITIES

1. After reflecting on the questions posed in the Teacher Self-Reflection section of this chapter, what misconceptions and/or gaps in your knowledge were you able to identify? What steps will you take to address your misconceptions and gaps?
2. What resources are available to you through your professional organization or local community and/or religious organizations that can assist you in your professional learning about religion?
3. Identify several controversial issues. Then use small-group and whole-class discussions to explore various religious and nonreligious perspectives and how teachers can intentionally create space and use strategies to ensure that all students see themselves and are heard, such as the Classroom Charter discussed above.

## REFERENCES

Adichie, C. N. (2009, July). *The danger of a single story* [video]. Ted Conferences. www.ted.com/talks/chimamanda_ngozi_adichie_the_danger_of_a_single_story/comments

Alameddine, N. (2021). Supporting Muslim students through culturally relevant, responsive, and sustaining pedagogies. *Canadian Social Studies, 52*(2), 22–38. doi.org/10.29173/css20

Asad, T. (1993). *Genealogies of religion: Discipline and reasons of power in Christianity and Islam.* Johns Hopkins University Press.

Banerjee, S., & Coward, H. (2005). Hindus in Canada: Negotiating identity in a "different" homeland. In P. Bramadat & D. Seljak (Eds.), *Religion and ethnicity in Canada* (pp. 30–51). Pearson Education Canada.

Brown, W. (2006). *Regulating aversion: Tolerance in the age of identity and empire.* Princeton University Press.

Cohen, A., Wu, M. S., & Miller, J. (2016). Religion and culture: Individualism and collectivism in the East and West. *Journal of Cross-Cultural Psychology, 47*(9), 1236–1249. doi.org/10.1177/0022022116667895

Cornelissen, L. (2021). *Religiosity in Canada and its evolution from 1985 to 2019*. Statistics Canada. www150.statcan.gc.ca/n1/pub/75-006-x/2021001/article/00010-eng.htm

Garcia, L., & Shane, T. (2021). *A guide to prebunking: A promising way to inoculate against misinformation*. First Draft. https://firstdraftnews.org/articles/a-guide-to-prebunking-a-promising-way-to-inoculate-against-misinformation/

Government of Manitoba. (2019). *Grade 12: World of religions: A Canadian perspective*. Manitoba Education and Training. www.edu.gov.mb.ca/k12/docs/support/world_religions/full_doc.pdf

Grant, C. A. (2012). Cultivating flourishing lives: A robust social justice vision of education. *American Educational Research Journal, 49*(5), 910–934. doi.org/10.3102/0002831212447977

Hanvey, R. G. (1982). An attainable global perspective. *Theory into Practice, 21*(3), 162–167. doi.org/10.1080/00405848209543001

Haque, M. (2019). *Navigating the landscape: Young Muslims' perceptions and experiences of school-based, informal, parental, and Islamic sex-education in Canada* [Master's thesis, University of Regina]. https://ourspace.uregina.ca/handle/10294/9220

Haroun [@hqdada]. (2020, Sept. 10). *With 9/11 tmrw, what was the shittiest thing a teacher said or let other students say in front of you?* … [Tweet]. Twitter. https://twitter.com/hqdada/status/1304192219847561219

Hess, D. (2002). Discussing controversial public issues in secondary social studies classrooms: Learning from skilled teachers. *Theory & Research in Social Education, 30*(1), 10–41. doi.org/10.1080/00933104.2002.10473177

Hess, D., & McAvoy, P. (2014). *The political classroom: Evidence and ethics in democratic education*. Routledge.

Hurd, E. S. (2011). A suspension of (dis)belief: The secular-religious binary and the study of international relations. In C. Calhoun, M. Juergensmeyer, & M. Van Antwerpen (Eds.), *Rethinking secularism* (pp. 166–184). Oxford University Press.

Kates, F. R., Byrd, M., & Haider, M. R. (2015). Every picture tells a story: The power of 3 teaching method. *Journal of Educators Online, 12*(1), 189–211. doi.org/10.9743/JEO.2015.1.1

Keller, T., Camardese, A., & Abbas, R. (2017). "We don't talk about that here": Teachers, religion, public elementary schools and the embodiment of silence, a binational United States and Israel study. *Journal of Childhood and Religion, 7*(February), 1–40. https://mosaic.messiah.edu/edu_ed/27/

Khan, M. (2021). Pedagogy of pain: Pulling passion, potential, and possibility from the pain of silence and truth telling. *Diaspora, Indigenous, and Minority Education, 15*(4), 252–262. doi.org/10.1080/15595692.2021.1944087

Lincoln, B. (2003). *Holy terrors: Thinking about religion after September 11*. University of Chicago Press.

Melnyk, G., & Parker, C. (Eds.). (2021). *Finding refuge in Canada: Narratives of dislocation*. AU Press.

Mind Tools Content Team. (n.d.). *The futures wheel*. Mind Tools. www.mindtools.com/a3w9aym/the-futures-wheel

Moon, R. (2008). Government support for religious practice. In R. Moon (Ed.), *Law and religious pluralism in Canada* (pp. 217–238). UBC Press.

Nicolai-deKoning, J., & Patrick, M. (2021, May 25). Opinion: How to better integrate religion into Alberta's draft curriculum. *Edmonton Journal*. https://edmontonjournal.com/opinion/columnists/opinion-how-to-better-integrate-religion-into-albertas-draft-curriculum

Pace, J. L. (2021). How can educators prepare for teaching controversial issues? Cross-national lessons. *Social Education, 85*(4), 228–233. www.socialstudies.org/system/files/2021-08/se-850421228.pdf

Parker, C. (2016). *Peacebuilding, citizenship, and identity: Empowering conflict and dialogue in multicultural classrooms*. Sense.

Patrick, M. (2023, January 23). Alberta's social studies curriculum pushes religious exceptionalism. *Monitor*. https://monitormag.ca/articles/albertas-social-studies-curriculum-pushes-religious-exceptionalism/

Peck, C. L. (n.d.). *Teaching for diversity*. https://sites.google.com/ualberta.ca/teachingfordiversity/home

Peck, C. L. (2022, January 1). The absurd UCP curriculum. *Alberta Views*. https://albertaviews.ca/the-absurd-ucp-curriculum/

Peck, C. L., & Herriot, L. (2015). Teachers' beliefs about social studies. In Fives, H., & Gill, M. (Eds.), *International handbook of research on teachers' beliefs* (pp. 387–402). Routledge.

Pew Research Center. (2016). *Religion and education around the world*. www.pewresearch.org/religion/2016/12/13/religion-and-education-around-the-world/

Rubertucci, A. (2022, August 10). *Quebec's Bill 21 "disturbing" impact on religious minorities: Study*. CityNews Montreal. https://montreal.citynewsallac22/08/10/quebec-bill-21-religious-secularism

Sears, A., & Herriot, L. (2016). The place of religion in education for citizenship and social justice. In A. Peterson, R. Hattam, M. Zambylas, & J. Arthur (Eds.), *The Palgrave international handbook of education for citizenship and social justice* (pp. 285–304). Palgrave MacMillan.

Somos, C. (2019, October 10). *Sikh teacher moves from Quebec to BC after Bill 21 implemented*. CTV News. www.ctvnews.ca/canada/sikh-teacher-moves-from-quebec-to-b-c-after-bill-21-implemented-1.4633830?cache=%3FclipId%3D64268

Statistics Canada. (2022). The Canadian census: A rich portrait of the country's religious and ethnocultural diversity. *The Daily*. www150.statcan.gc.ca/n1/daily-quotidien/221026/dq221026b-eng.htm

Stewart, W. C., Seiple, C., & Hoover, D. R. (2020). To advance international human rights, first promote covenantal pluralism. *London School of Economics and Political Science, Religion and Global Society* [Blog]. https://blogs.lse.ac.uk/religionglobalsociety/2020/12/to-advance-international-human-rights-first-promote-covenantal-pluralism/

Torney-Purta, J., & Amadeo, J. (2012). The contribution of international large-scale studies in civic education and engagement. In M. von Davier, E. Gonzalez, I. Kirsch, & K. Yamamoto (Eds.), *The role of international large scale assessments: Perspectives from technology, economy, and educational research* (pp. 87–114). Springer.

UNESCO. (2023, January 18). *Let girls and women in Afghanistan learn!* www.unesco.org/en/articles/let-girls-and-women-afghanistan-learn

UNICEF Canada. (n.d.). *Classroom charters.* www.unicef.ca/sites/default/files/legacy/imce_uploads/UTILITY%20NAV/TEACHERS/DOCS/GC/Classroom_Charters_Instructions.pdf

Wertheimer, L. (2015a). *Faith ed: Teaching about religion in an age of intolerance.* Beacon Press.

Wertheimer, L. (2015b, December 18). Teaching about religion in public schools can be risky, but it's worth it. *Washington Post.* www.washingtonpost.com/news/acts-of-faith/wp/2015/12/18/teaching-about-religion-in-public-schools-can-be-risky-but-its-worth-it/

Wilkins-Laflamme, S. (2023). *Religion, spirituality and secularity among Millennials: The generation shaping American and Canadian trends.* Routledge.

# PART VIII

## DISABILITY: NURTURING BELONGING AND FLOURISHING AMONG STUDENTS WITH DISABILITIES

# CHAPTER 16
# Lived Disability Experience in Canadian Schooling: Essential Knowledge for Fostering Disabled Flourishing

*Cynthia Bruce*

Understanding what it means to foster belonging and cultivate flourishing for disabled students in Canadian public schooling is often complicated by ableist beliefs that lead people to accommodate, but rarely welcome or plan for, our presence in schools. It is also made difficult by a pervasive lack of disabled student and educator access to everyday disabled people who have built good, or flourishing, lives on their own terms. Any sense of belonging we may experience is ultimately entangled with messages we receive about the importance of overcoming disability—a covert requirement best facilitated by our diligent utilization, as disabled learners, of the academic accommodations and adaptations we have been granted. This necessity, both real and perceived, is reinforced by the relative societal silence around disability as diversity, valued identity, or legitimate knowledge in multiple educational settings.

Disability is generally a topic of discussion only insofar as it is an individual problem in need of an individual solution (Titchkosky & Michalko, 2012), and disabled students rarely see themselves represented in curriculum, discussions of equity and diversity, or their school staff or leadership. Disability is simply an individual deficit that must be remediated or supported through multiple medical, functional, technical, and/or psychological strategies and interventions, but it is rarely viewed as a good or valued way of living life that can be grounded in rich disability histories and cultures. It can be difficult, therefore, for disabled students and educators alike to imagine a flourishing disabled life.

## CONSIDERING DISABILITY AND FLOURISHING

Disability and flourishing, in my experience as a blind student and teacher educator, are rarely paired in our thinking or teaching about what equitable and inclusive support for disabled learners can be. As Schneider observes in chapter 17 of this volume, course designs in inclusive teacher education programs tend to focus on development of the capacity to identify individual impairment characteristics and formulate remedial strategies that will enable development of normatively conceived and valued academic and/or life skills. Even in jurisdictions where inclusive education is embraced in policy, systemic responses to disability continue to favour the implementation of special education approaches that draw on what Oliver (2009) calls medicalized understandings or definitions of disability as deficit or lack. Accordingly, these jurisdictions rely on what Danforth and Gabel (2006) and Gallagher (2006) have framed as the provision of substantially separate compensatory programs that aim to alleviate the naturally occurring and biologically determined impact of impaired functioning. This deficit-grounded approach is sometimes known colloquially as the *affliction of the week* approach. While it connects teacher education students with the categories used to make decisions about who does and does not receive formal support, it fails to consider disabled people as individuals who can be prepared for global citizenship when supported by educators who have the capacity to engage Nussbaum's (1997) tool of cultivation. Those who engage with Nussbaum's tool are educators who can critically examine self and the exclusionary impacts of traditional or dominant constructions of disability, who can see themselves meaningfully connected to disabled students and recognize their shared humanity, and who can engage with disabled people's stories as an indispensable source of knowledge that can cultivate flourishing through belief in and support for their own life goals and desires.

Grant (2012) compellingly argues, albeit in the context of African American learners in the United States, that teachers who want to cultivate disabled student flourishing must recognize that there are many ways to conceive of living a good life. They must also develop an understanding of culturally specific lived experiences to support minoritized students in conceptualizing and building a good life on their terms. Disabled students in public schools rarely, if ever, have access to rich disabled histories, cultures, and everyday role models that would usefully support this work. The most fervently committed and knowledgeable social justice activists, after all, have tended to know very little about disability and disability issues (Mingus, 2011), so it is hardly surprising when K–12 educators and disability support professionals are unaware of how exposure to disabled role models and disability culture and history can meaningfully support student flourishing. That knowledge, coupled with expanded understandings of critical disability theorizing, can help educators to identify classroom-based, school-based, and systemic opportunities that might disrupt the dominance of medicalized definitions and associated remedial strategies. In fact, theory can play an important role in helping us understand and intervene in the social world—to organize politically and to contest the disableism and **ableism** that pervade the everyday lives of disabled people (Goodley et al., 2019).

Educational access is a broadening priority for Canadian school districts where provincial **accessibility** legislation mandates a regulatory standard in education. Such regulatory standards and legislative frameworks assert accessibility as a human right. However, the extent to which they can support disabled students' belonging and subsequent flourishing is not at all clear. Educational belonging is commonly linked to the desired demonstration of ability, independence, and productivity (Goodley, 2017), aims that reflect "a contemporary society that increasingly seeks to promote the species typical individual citizen: a citizen that is ready and able to work, productively contribute, an atomistic phenomenon bounded and cut off from others, capable, malleable and compliant" (Goodley & Lawthom, 2019, p. 235). Countering such restrictive conditions of belonging requires the capacity to foster accessibility as a process that involves more than the provision of individual accommodation. It is imperative to engage with access as a relational space where one's sense of belonging is inevitably generated during interactions with people and places (Titchkosky, 2011), where the ableist politics of independence, remediation, and overcoming is enacted, and where the politics of interdependence, resistance, and collectivity must be asserted (Hamraie, 2013). Cultivating disabled flourishing, then, means we must leave behind any educational agenda that works to minimize the possibility that disabled people will become a burden on society (see also chapter 17). We must intentionally work to explore, understand, and support disabled students' potential for flourishing within a culturally grounded social justice education framework—one that values disability as legitimate knowledge and a legitimate way of being, knowing, and doing.

## LIVED EXPERIENCE IS KNOWLEDGE

In this chapter, I draw on my own experiences of schooling and my own work as an educator and activist. I also use **critical disability studies** and disability studies in education to argue for the intentional integration of lived disability experience as rich knowledge that can and must be part of contemporary efforts to prepare teachers to foster human flourishing in social justice–grounded education. Grant's (2012) assertion that social justice in education has been too vaguely defined and that there has been inadequate focus on its meaningful realization undergirds the analysis in this chapter. This analysis emanates from the vital assertion that social justice discourses have historically and harmfully excluded disability issues because disability is linked only to the domains of abnormality and individual pathology (Liasidou, 2014). I argue, then, that our stories constitute an important source of knowledge that isn't simply about demonstrating our ability to overcome or triumph in the face of adversity. Our stories can foster capacity-building in teachers by doing the work of cultivating—they can nurture curiosity and make space for the devotion of time and attention to self-improvement that will ultimately benefit others (Grant, 2012). They can prompt essential critical self-reflection to help educators develop an understanding of their connectedness to disabled people. This is done through a sense of shared humanity that necessitates engagement with disability issues in social justice agendas and supports narrative imagination that, more than putting ourselves in the shoes of disabled others, engages disabled people's stories as compelling knowledge that makes occupying the position of the so-called other unnecessary. This latter point is key! Imagining ourselves in disabled people's shoes is often taken literally and mobilized as troubling and contested simulation activities that risk deepening fears about disability and loss of function or about not wanting to be subjected to living such abnormal, impaired lives.

Lived disability experience offers important yet often silenced insight into the inaccessible and unwelcoming nature of the world disabled students are being prepared to enter, but also into the deep creativity of disabled people who carve out life paths while advocating for better access. It offers imaginative alternatives to living, learning, and working environments that privilege competitive individualism over collectivity, and it enables critical engagement with interdependence as a rich way of living that is devalued yet inevitably at the core of what it means to be human (Goodley, 2014).

I begin with my own story of disability and schooling—one that, while decades old, has current relevance in contemporary schooling contexts that continue to centre compensatory strategies supported by special education approaches. I share this story in two different but inevitably connected tellings: one that focuses on a nurturing social world and one that pulls apart the more technical focus of schooling and itinerant support that feels disconnected from notions of flourishing. I then move into an exploration of what it can mean to situate lived disability experience as knowledge, and I finish by explicating strategies I have used to mobilize lived experience as knowledge in teacher education.

## A Story in Two Parts

My story of primary and secondary schooling is complex—a mix of feeling like I belonged and feeling othered by what I now tend to describe as a compensatory support approach that sought to cultivate my ability to emulate normal (Campbell, 2009) for as long as my inevitably dwindling sight would allow. I choose the word *cultivate* with explicit political intent because it centres the deliberate focus on teaching and learning self-improvement strategies that inevitably had a positive impact on others, but it arguably did so by reducing the energy that teachers had to devote to inclusion. It also, however, drew me into the kind of complicity with ableist norms that I would later work to unravel in my doctoral research (Bruce, 2017) and in analyses of how critical disability studies has cultivated increasingly nuanced analyses of my educational encounters with ableism (Bruce, 2016, 2022).

This analysis is inevitably complicated by the fact that I have, in the end, built what I believe to be a flourishing life. The path was not smooth, but I am doing the activist disability work I value in an academic faculty position that has afforded financial stability and career satisfaction. However, flourishing has most substantively been enabled by the deep theoretical analyses I undertook in my doctoral education to unravel the impact of ableism on my educational trajectory. These critical analyses were skilfully supported by Dr. Lynn Aylward, my doctoral supervisor, and were grounded in critical theoretical frameworks that mobilize lived experiences of disability in diverse contexts. I offer two analyses in the following sections: one that traces a path from blind child to blind university instructor and another that drills down into the public school context to consider a support focus that arguably fostered participation and independence without a robust consideration of flourishing as a likely, or even possible, life scenario.

## Growing Up Blind—The Social

I grew up in a relatively small town in Nova Scotia, going to public school in the 1970s and 1980s. My parents had both been raised in the same community and had returned after marrying to settle close to family. Although there were points of distress for me as a young child who learned she would eventually lose her sight, I can say unequivocally that I felt supported and embraced by both family and friends. This support was the primary facilitator of my sense of belonging in both school and community contexts.

Many children who were legally blind in those days completed their schooling in the provincial school for the blind. This was an option tentatively presented to my parents, but it was not one they seriously considered. I still had some functional vision, and I was displaying the cognitive competence that mainstream teachers valued and believed could be fostered—I was "blind but cognitively intact." There was a system of itinerant, or special education, support available, and I began drawing on that service midway through elementary school. So there was no immediate need to consider residential schooling because my parents felt there was sufficient assistance for me to remain in my home setting.

The education of blind and visually impaired students at the time was coordinated by the provincial school for the blind, and itinerant teachers would travel to public schools to provide necessary support. While blind and low-vision students are now supported in their community schools, the itinerant system continues to be used. The itinerant teachers ensured I had access to large-print texts and any existing assistive technology, and they were available to grade-level teachers who had questions pertaining to classroom participation. Orientation and mobility training were made available as I grew and as it became clear that my sight was continuing to diminish. This entailed training around walking with a white cane on predetermined routes consistent with my daily travel patterns. While I have little memory of discussions about learning Braille, I remember being unimpressed with that necessity. I could still read large print, and the itinerants indicated that it was typically the preferred approach to teach students to use their residual vision.

I felt, for the most part, that I fit in or belonged, so I was happy with the plan that involved so-called regular reading rather than Braille. While I did reach the point where the use of my sight became tiring, recorded texts were becoming increasingly available. Therefore, Braille continued to be framed as unnecessary. As an adult, I see the flaw in this normatively-focused strategy. Losing my residual vision was inevitable, and this failing was made real as I entered university and began to experience that loss of sight.

Although not knowing Braille was initially problematic, it became less of an issue as I moved through my university degrees because the availability of assistive technology was growing steadily. The use of laptops, tablets, and smart phones with screen reader technology facilitated my graduate and post-graduate work incredibly, but it has also been indispensable to my work as a university faculty member. It has been vital to my preparation, teaching, and assessment, and it clearly assists disabled students in my undergraduate and graduate classes. Not only does technology enable participation in my courses, but it also facilitates the development of a reciprocal relationship that can attend to the ways our individual impairments intersect.

Certainly, technology is not the answer to all areas where I require support in the university environment. It is an effective tool, but it does not address the deeply held perspectives that raise those ever-present questions about belonging. In some ways, it only serves to entrench those viewpoints more deeply because technology can allow disability to be made invisible and divert institutions from their systemic responsibility to attend to equity—a disappearance of disability that is arguably at the core of how I now understand the lack of explicit attention to flourishing and the focus on problem-solving so I could simply participate. While becoming a blind university faculty member certainly is consistent with a flourishing life, so much of reaching that point has been tied up in responding to instances of marginalization and exclusion, in technical issues of supporting functioning, and in the everyday advocacy that is required to secure access. It often feels like a life marked by lurching from one obstacle to another and one technical or accommodation solution to another. This is not flourishing, and it is not a flourishing life cultivated by educational access to disability histories and cultures or to local, national, and global role models who built good, but ordinary rather than inspirational and extraordinary, flourishing disabled lives.

My story, in this retelling that is excerpted and edited from my dissertation (Bruce, 2017), appears in many ways to articulate a sense of belonging, and there are certainly ways that I experienced that in the friendships I developed and the community my family and I built. Yet, in so many ways, I moved through each educational phase despite a system that was not ready for me and did not expect me, and this will be made evident repeatedly in the more focused retelling in the next section. Being a blind student can be different from being a blind child and friend in a community setting where I occupied a position of privilege and where I was able to develop a close circle of friends, and I am acutely aware that my position of privilege afforded infinitely greater support than others received. Yet even that privilege did not produce the kind of teacher engagement with my intellectual and life potential that made it possible to imagine multiple career pathways that offered me real choices beyond what is arguably stereotypical for blind individuals—musician. This potentially, if inadvertently, links belonging to the pursuit of stereotypical career paths that celebrate disabled success without disrupting the normative order of other professions.

## Being a Blind Learner/Student—The Technical

Reconsidering educational belonging in the context of flourishing generates a different analysis of my learning experiences that is separate from the more social focus articulated above. As a young blind/low-vision student attending small-town Nova Scotian schools in the 1970s and 1980s, I realize now that I was relatively oblivious to the substantive content of discussions that centred on how I would be supported to attend K–12 schools in my home community. What I recall, though, are all the technical hoops associated with school attendance and participation. I remember enduring endless and repeated tests aimed at determining my visual acuity and visual field, experimenting with a wide variety of print magnification tools, and being gradually if reluctantly introduced to orientation and mobility techniques that included sighted guide and white cane use. I explicitly recall using thickly lined white loose-leaf paper so I could produce handwriting that would resemble that of my sighted peers—neat, straight, and well spaced—and reading from a variety of large-print texts that often served as my daily weight-lifting routine as I carried them back and forth from school to home. Perhaps the most vivid recollection I have from my elementary school years, though, is the large and awkward closed-circuit television system that magnified text and that my parents dutifully carted home every weekend—a contraption that was casually, and undoubtedly resentfully on my part, dubbed my machine.

As I moved through middle school and high school, technology improved and I was able to leave behind the machine in favour of photocopy enlargements and tape-recorded texts that, while an improvement, introduced new hurdles connected to delayed receipt of recordings and inevitable memory lapses by those who needed to supply enlarged documents. I wrote tests and exams in different spaces and with extended time as a matter of course, not because of bureaucratically saturated accommodation processes that tend to envision inclusion as an ongoing process of disability management (Titchkosky, 2011). I was also viewed as an academically strong student who had specific musical talent that was fostered, supported, and facilitative of a future, and arguably normalizing, career path (Bruce, 2022). In that context, it is certainly conceivable that music was seen as a path to flourishing, but fostering flourishing was never part of overall discussions that involved me, the blind student who simply wanted to build a life on her own terms.

Music, as mentioned above, is a feasible if stereotypical career path for blind people who possess the requisite talent. It was also an easy way for me to stand out and fit in because it could allow me to accomplish, even if temporarily, the performance of normal that my adolescent self desired and my schooling context valued (Bruce, 2022). Yet I wonder, as I consider the cultivation of flourishing, if it was the easy and logical path to a life that meant that no one engaged, or even thought to engage, with my broader intellectual or life/career potential.

Disability was nowhere in the curriculum except when people like Helen Keller were lauded for their incredible stories of overcoming rather than their radical feminist work. There were no disabled or blind lawyers, teachers, or professors, and I recall being introduced only to older blind people so I could perhaps be convinced that I needed to comply with mobility training, and later Braille learning, to be the best blind person I could be—the one who compensated, overcame, self-advocated, and was minimally disruptive of normative routines of teaching and learning (Bruce, 2020). This notion of the good blind person or the good disabled student (Bruce, 2020) has been an ever-present if under-the-radar current as I have worked to build a flourishing life, and early exposure to the diverse possibilities for living a good disabled life would have painted a very different picture of the kind of flourishing that was possible.

## MOBILIZING LIVED DISABILITY EXPERIENCE

The mobilization of lived disability experience can be as vaguely conceived and ill-defined as the broader project of enacting social justice in schools (Grant, 2012). Because doing so is not about teaching a strategy, approach, or method, it can be difficult to envision how to bring first voice perspectives into the curriculum. It has been my experience, though, that doing so with careful attention to engaging diverse perspectives and experiences of life can be generative and transformative. Critical disability studies scholars have been mobilizing lived experience as knowledge for almost three decades because of its potential to change people's perspectives on the world (Schalk, 2017) and its intentional amplification of the often-silenced perspectives of disabled people themselves. Critical disability studies, as an interdisciplinary field, politicizes the lived experience of impairment in contemporary contexts that value individual ability and achievement over the kinds of alliances and interdependence that define what it means to be human (Goodley, 2014). It engages the lived experience of disability as a potential disruptor of epistemological and methodological assumptions that sustain deficit understandings of and remedial responses to disabled people (Tremain, 2005). So it nurtures imagination and reveals the potential inherent in disability politics, arts, scholarship, and culture to "offer new ways of conceiving and living life, existing with one another and recreating communities that include, augment and emphasize the qualities we all hold as humans" (Goodley et al., 2019, p. 972).

My experience of bringing lived disability knowledge to classrooms has taken place in more than one role. I am a blind activist, educator, and scholar, and it is in this capacity that I have brought lived disability knowledge to many teachers with whom I have engaged. I am, however, also a blind mother of two children, and I always saw this clear connection to schools through their schooling trajectories as a missed opportunity that I didn't know how to address in the absence of a critical disability analysis. I was asked, once, by an educator friend to visit her primary/grade 1 class when they were doing a unit on senses, and I was invited to bring my toddler along to show them that blindness and parenting can and do go together. It was an opportunity for children to engage with me as a blind parent and explore the associated everyday realities, to ask questions, and to simply be in that context, which was, importantly, not a formal presentation about the difficulties of blindness. It showed me how children can so easily engage with the learning that different ways of being and doing can offer, especially when it isn't presented in whole-school presentations that are largely intended to inspire.

My two children, who were born 32 months apart, were in public schools for a combined total of 16 years, and this was the one and only time I was able to bring blindness into the classroom in such an intentional way. Of course, as a past teacher educator and current music therapy educator, I bring blindness into the classroom intentionally and bring broader disability experience into deliberate pedagogical strategies that are variably received by pre-service and professional educators. Graduate students who have witnessed the inequities experienced by disabled students in K–12 classrooms generally appear open to what critical disability studies scholarship and activism can offer. Pre-service teachers, on the other hand, often seem to place greater value on the lived experience of teaching than on the lived experience of disability and learning. The question becomes, then, *How can we mobilize lived disability knowledge early to support a vision of disabled students as people who can and must be supported to flourish, not simply exist?*

## CAREFULLY CURATED READING

I have found a carefully curated course reading list to be very helpful, and my approach to such curation has changed dramatically over the years. It can be tempting, I think, to select readings that are only about disabled student experiences in K–12 classrooms authored by scholars in either a K–12 or a teacher education context. I have found, however, that this approach risks entrenching a narrowly focused disability and social justice agenda that is ultimately and practically disconnected from the real and complex lives that disabled people live. Development of the narrative imagination relies ultimately on being able to imagine disabled people as university students and as citizens who want to participate in all that life has to offer: advanced education, careers, relationships, family, leisure, and the like. Focusing only on schooling contexts makes it almost impossible to imagine disabled lives outside of education contexts, which may inevitably contribute to approaches that aim to prepare people for the workforce as either independent or supported employees who are living but not necessarily flourishing.

I accordingly choose a core text that often facilitates engagement with the full spectrum of lived disability experience as a way of expanding perceptions of what it can mean to live a good disabled life. These are often compilations of activist writings that are produced for the general public and not simply intended for academic audiences. They introduce the reader to a host of complex issues faced daily by disabled people working to build lives in which they can thrive, not simply survive. They also make visible and real the systemic inequities that get in the way, and they can support development of a disposition to social justice work that aims to identify and dismantle them.

As additional core reading, I choose accessible academic readings that orient students to theories of disability that are, in some ways, a remedial intervention aimed at destabilizing the dominance of deficit disability narratives (Linton, 1998). Readers encounter, for example, rich descriptions of the social, cultural, relational, and minority models of disability (see Goodley, 2017). They also engage with theories that centre and account for intersecting experiences of disability and race (see, e.g., Annamma, 2016; Annamma et al., 2018). Finally, and not simply as a supplement, first voice resources are provided in the form of blogs and videos—resources that are equally important to the aim of immersing students in disability experiences, perspectives, and analyses that can transform their beliefs about what is possible for disabled students.

These resources, along with careful mobilization of my own experiences and analyses, are facilitative of critical self-reflection. Students are encouraged, in a focused written assignment, to recall their first life encounters with disability, to consider how those encounters contributed to shaping their understanding of disability and of life possibilities for disabled people, and to reconsider those perspectives with the support of the resources provided in the course. A daily reflexive journal further encourages critical self-reflection by having students engage with what readings and class discussions are making visible about their disability-related beliefs and those advanced by their communities and institutions. This usefully supports, in my experience, a clear analysis of current school and community contexts and ongoing identification of opportunities to contribute to expanded understandings of disability in their schools.

Finally, I encourage critical analysis of disability representation in the public domain. I include, in course resources, academic and activist analyses of disability in journalism, film, television, and the like. An assignment that encourages students to utilize their preferred modes of expression (writing, visual art, drama, poetry, songwriting, etc.) requires engagement with and critical analysis of a particular portrayal of disability in the public domain. This has been a particularly powerful way for them to connect with misrepresentations of lived disability experience and grapple with the ableist tropes that are so often perpetuated in pop culture. It also supports exploration and discussion around the real and everyday lives of diverse disabled people, which cultivates narrative imagination without engaging in contested activities that aim to simulate the experience of specific impairments.

## CONCLUSION

Human flourishing is often excluded from discussions of and planning for disability support in schooling contexts, and lived disability experience is regularly eclipsed by professional and academic special education discourses. We need only examine debates about the use of the word *disability* to understand how unwelcome it is in both health and education settings (Andrews et al., 2019). It is so undesirable, in fact, that it is routinely erased from our vocabulary and replaced with euphemisms like *special needs*, *differently abled*, or even *handi-capable*—erasure that makes the cultivation of flourishing disabled lives unthinkable.

I have argued in this chapter that early intentional integration of lived disability experience is essential for disabled students—students who have as much right to imagine flourishing futures as their nondisabled peers. It is critical knowledge to mobilize in teacher education, especially when working to cultivate democratic K–12 classrooms. Critical disability studies offers an academic and theoretical framework for formulating a first-voice-infused pedagogy, and there is rich activist literature to support this work. There can be no doubt, among those who educate us, that we can flourish. If there is, we will be consigned to existence without meaning, purpose, or growth.

**Important Note about Language**

Our language choices, as disabled people, are often scrutinized by abled others who have been taught that person-first language is the most, and even only, respectful way to speak about disabled people. Many of us, however, explicitly choose to centre disability as a core aspect of our identities—as a valuable part of who we are, how we live and learn, and what we bring to our school communities. Disability, for me, isn't simply an appendage tacked on to my personhood (Titchkosky, 2001). It is a way of being, knowing, and doing that has a history and a culture, brings value, and is ultimately at risk of erasure when we seek to remove it from our vocabulary using euphemisms like *special needs* or *diffAbilities* (Andrews et al., 2019). Language is, for everyone, a decision, and I encourage you to engage thoughtfully and to decide based on careful consideration of diverse disabled perspectives.

# KEY TERMS

**Ableism:** Often defined broadly as discrimination against disabled people or in favour of abled people. However, bringing diverse scholar activists into conversation can help us to understand it as a system of oppression that leads to individual, institutional, and societal assignment of value to people based on their culture, age, language, appearance, religion, birth or living place, health or wellness, and/or their ability to satisfactorily re/produce, excel, and behave (Lewis, 2022). It demands, in neoliberal times, the demonstration of certain preferred abilities equated with normalcy (Campbell, 2009; Wolbring, 2008), that disability be controlled and contained, and that disabled people demonstrate that they are ready and able to work and productively contribute while also being malleable and compliant (Goodley & Lawthom, 2019, p. 235).

**Accessibility:** Most frequently defined as the identification and removal of barriers that prevent full and equal participation in society. Titchkosky (2011) encourages additional considerations of accessibility, or access, as a relational space where one's sense of belonging is generated when disabled people encounter people and physical environments that may or may not expect disability or disabled people. It is where the ableist politics of independence, remediation, and overcoming is enacted and where the politics of interdependence, resistance, and collectivity must be asserted (Hamraie, 2013).

**Critical disability studies:** An activist discipline and methodology that explicitly politicizes the lived experience of impairment and exposes contemporary policy and practice regimes that value individual ability and achievement over the kinds of alliances and interdependence that are at the core of what it means to be human (Goodley, 2014). Critical disability studies facilitates exposure and critique of social norms and conditions that define ways of being as impairment and concentrate them in multiple minoritized communities (Minich, 2016). It is a method, methodology, and perspective that enables critical intersectional pedagogies aimed at changing people's perspectives on the world (Schalk, 2017) and reveals the potential inherent in disability politics, arts, scholarship, and culture to "offer new ways of conceiving and living life, existing with one another and recreating communities that include, augment and emphasize the qualities we all hold as humans" (Goodley et al., 2019, p. 972).

## DISCUSSION QUESTIONS AND ACTIVITIES

1. Identify an early encounter you had with disability, one that occurred in a family, community, or schooling context or setting. Discuss in small groups what the experience taught you about the nature of disability, its place in community and/or school, and how to engage with disability and/or disabled people.
2. In a small group, discuss your perspectives on disability language. Consider first voice perspectives, such as the blog post "Identity-First Language" on the Autistic Self Advocacy Network website (https://autisticadvocacy.org/about-asan/identity-first-language/) or "My Journey with Disability Language and Identity," on the Rooted in Rights website (https://rootedinrights.org/my-journey-with-disability-language-and-identity/). After considering these first voice perspectives, discuss how you might approach a discussion about language in your classrooms.
3. In your group, discuss, from the perspective of critical disability studies and cultivating flourishing, your current encounters with disability. Do they imagine flourishing disabled lives? What kinds of disabled lives do they imagine, encourage, and/or cultivate?
4. Make a plan to bring lived disability experience into your classroom or school community. How would you introduce it and intentionally plan for regular engagement with lived disability knowledge?

## REFERENCES

Andrews, E. E., Forber-Pratt, A. J., Mona, L. R., Lund, E. M., Pilarski, C. R., & Balter, R. (2019). #SaytheWord: A disability culture commentary on the erasure of "disability." *Rehabilitation Psychology, 64*(2), 111–118. doi.org/10.1037/rep0000258

Annamma, S. A. (2016). *DisCrit: Disability studies and critical race theory in education.* Teachers College Press.

Annamma, S. A., Ferri, B., & Connor, D. J. (2018). Disability critical race theory: Exploring the intersectional lineage, emergence, and potential futures of DisCrit. *Review of Research in Education, 42,* 46–71. doi.org/10.3102/0091732X18759041

Bruce, C. (2016). Divergent encounters with normal: Are they really so different after all? *Canadian Journal of Disability Studies, 5*(1), 133–157. doi.org/10.15353/cjds.v5i1.252

Bruce, C. (2017). *Precarious possibilities: Disability, self-advocacy, and university learning* [Doctoral dissertation, Acadia University]. https://scholar.acadiau.ca/islandora/object/theses%3A2158

Bruce, C. (2020). Self-advocacy as precariousness in university education. *Canadian Journal of Disability Studies, 9*(5), 414–440. doi.org/10.15353/cjds.v9i5.703

Bruce, C. (2022). Performing normal: Restless reflections on music's dis/abling potential. *Music Therapy Perspectives, 40*(2), 125–131. doi.org/10.1093/mtp/miab015

Campbell, F. K. (2009). *Contours of ableism: The production of disability and abledness.* Palgrave MacMillan.

Danforth, S., & Gabel, S. L. (2006). Introduction. In S. Danforth & S. L. Gabel (Eds.), *Vital questions facing disability studies in education* (pp. 1–16). Peter Lang.

Gallagher, D. J. (2006). The natural hierarchy undone: Disability studies' contributions to contemporary debates in education. In S. Danforth & S. L. Gabel (Eds.), *Vital questions facing disability studies in education* (pp. 63–76). Peter Lang.

Goodley, D. (2014). *Dis/ability studies: Theorizing disableism and ableism* (iBooks version). Routledge.

Goodley, D. (2017). *Disability studies: An interdisciplinary introduction.* Sage.

Goodley, D., & Lawthom, R. (2019). Critical disability studies, Brexit and Trump: A time of neoliberal-ableism. *Rethinking History, 23*(2), 233–251. doi.org/10.1080/13642529.2019.1607476

Goodley, D., Lawthom, R., Liddiard, K., & Runswick-Cole, K. (2019). Provocations for critical disability studies. *Disability & Society, 34*(6), 972–997. doi.org/10.1080/09687599.2019.1566889

Grant, C. A. (2012). Cultivating flourishing lives: A robust social justice vision of education. *American Educational Research Journal, 49*(5), 910–934. www.jstor.org/stable/23319631

Hamraie, A. (2013). Designing collective access: A feminist disability theory of universal design. *Disability Studies Quarterly, 33*(4). doi.org/10.18061/dsq.v33i4.3871

Lewis, T. L. (2022, January 1). Working definition of ableism—January 2022 update. *Talila A. Lewis* [Blog]. www.talilalewis.com/blog/working-definition-of-ableism-january-2022-update

Liasidou, A. (2014). Critical disability studies and socially just change in higher education. *British Journal of Special Education, 41*(2), 120–135. doi.org/10.1111/1467-8578.12063

Linton, S. (1998). Disability studies/not disability studies. *Disability & Society, 13*(4), 525–539. doi.org/10.1080/09687599826588

Mingus, M. (2011, February 12). *Changing the framework: Disability justice: How our communities can move beyond access to wholeness.* https://leavingevidence.wordpress.com/2011/02/12/changing-the-framework-disability-justice/.

Minich, J. A. (2016). Enabling whom? Critical disability studies now. *Emergent Critical Analytics for Alternative Humanities, 5*(1). https://csalateral.org/issue/5-1/forum-alt-humanities-critical-disability-studies-now-minich/

Nussbaum, M. C. (1997). *Cultivating humanity: A classical defense of reform in liberal education.* Harvard University Press.

Oliver, M. (2009). The social model in context. In T. Titchkosky & R. Michalko (Eds.), *Rethinking normalcy: A disability studies reader* (pp. 19–30). Canadian Scholars.

Schalk, S. (2017). Critical disability studies as methodology. *Lateral, 6*(1). doi.org/10.25158/L6.1.13

Titchkosky, T. (2001). Disability: A rose by any other name? "People-first" language in Canadian society. *Canadian Review of Sociology / Revue canadienne de sociologie, 38*(2), 125–140. doi.org/10.1111/j.1755-618X.2001.tb00967.x

Titchkosky, T. (2011). *The question of access: Disability, space, meaning* (Kindle version). University of Toronto Press.

Titchkosky, T., & Michalko, R. (2012). The body as the problem of individuality: A phenomenological disability studies approach. In D. Goodley, B. Hughes, & L. Davis (Eds.), *Disability and social theory: New developments and directions* (pp. 127–142). Palgrave MacMillan.

Tremain, S. (2005). Foucault, governmentality, and critical disability theory: An introduction. In S. Tremain (Ed.), *Foucault and the government of disability* (pp. 1–26). University of Michigan Press.

Wolbring, G. (2008). The politics of ableism. *Development, 51*(2), 252–258. doi.org/10.1057/dev.2008.17

# CHAPTER 17
# Schools as *Polis*: Fostering Participation and Belonging of Children with Disabilities in Classrooms and Schools

*Cornelia Schneider*

Rethinking disability from a disability studies and disability rights perspective is at the heart of what inclusive education has been trying to accomplish for the past few decades in the field of education. School systems have long been excluding or streaming learners with different learning and social profiles out of the regular classroom into special classrooms, special schools, or institutions. Cultivating diversity and difference in a classroom is a principle that needs to be honoured by any teacher in their own teaching and learning practice. The right of the child with or without disability to be part of the regular classroom and to learn in a heterogeneous group of learners where disability is not considered the only difference among students is a pedagogical challenge. However, where teachers are able to live up to this challenge, all learners benefit and flourish, as the removal of barriers to learning and participation benefits the entire classroom.

This chapter will focus on how the paradigmatic shift from the medical model to the **social or biopsychosocial model of disability** influences how we think about disability in an educational context and in teacher education. If we want to foster human flourishing in the inclusive classroom, we need to think about what will be important to teach pre-service teachers that creates belonging and participation for disabled children in schools. The five core practices of cultivating flourishing lives (Grant, 2012) need to be stretched or complemented so that those practices can be lived in the inclusive classroom. For the purpose of this chapter, we will be focusing mostly on the aspect of "practising democracy" (Grant, 2012, p. 924), where the participation of everyone is not only desired but required. This is where the capabilities approach to rights (Nussbaum, 2003) can join forces with the disability rights movement (Charlton, 1998). Putting students in a position to exercise their rights is what a rights-based approach in the classroom should strive to provide. If we recognize everyone's rights in a classroom, we recognize them as full "citizens" in our classrooms.

Educational theorists in Germany, inspired by John Dewey's work, have recognized schools as an embryonic society (Dewey, 1915; Eikel & Diemer, 2005; von Hentig, 1993, 1996). School can reflect the current society with all its issues but can also model the society we aspire to be in. In this school, students learn to live in a democratic society where students can practise their citizenship in a small setting—**school as polis**. The ancient Greek term *polis* (city state, fortified city) is here not understood in territorial terms. The "topographic *polis* represents the more conventional understanding of political space. It keeps informing most institutional political practices, including policies that seek to promote children's political agency" (Häkli & Kallio, 2014, p. 190). Here, we define *polis* rather as a "relational realm of everyday politics … capturing the many contextual and relational dimensions that pertain to political agency" (Häkli & Kallio, 2014, p. 183). Recognizing children's agency and rights to participate is an essential feature of the school as polis. Flourishing lives can be cultivated only in a context where barriers to participation and belonging are removed, the capability to exercise rights is supported (Nussbaum, 2003), and all children are in a position to participate and contribute. This is where we need to shift our thinking away from what we conceive as the medical model of disability and toward the social model of disability because participation in the polis becomes possible when we strive to remove the barriers to participation in the community of learners. In the following section, I will explain how the social model of disability enables us to think in this way.

## MEDICAL MODEL VERSUS SOCIAL MODEL OF DISABILITY

When it comes to children with disabilities, for a long time, education systems have not found any other responses to learning abilities or behavioural differences than either excluding children from schooling altogether or offering what we know today as *special education*, most often away from regular classrooms or even schools. Disability studies has analyzed these practices in terms of two competing models regarding disabilities (Baglieri et al., 2011; Barnes & Mercer, 2010; Goodley, 2014, 2017). The **medical model of disability** seeks to identify a person's impairment as the issue that needs to be addressed; the issue lies with the individual and their perceived faultiness. In order to join the crowd, proponents of this model argue, the child needs therapy, interventions, and so on to be able to function in the reality of a regular school. While it is uncontested that some of those interventions can be meaningful and helpful for the child in question, they often fail to address an important question related to the context and environment in which disability occurs. They often also isolate the student with a disability. This is where the social model helps us to better understand how disability emerges as a result of a mismatch between the individual's abilities and an environment that presents many barriers to this individual.

In the simplest terms, a wheelchair user cannot access a building unless there is a ramp, which removes the barrier of stairs for this person. In classroom terms, a child with a disability cannot access learning unless barriers are removed (e.g., teacher-centred instruction can constitute a big barrier for many students). Oftentimes, it turns out that those barriers to learning are not specific to a disability but constitute barriers for many students and their learning. For example, relying uniquely on lecture-based teaching or a particular type of activity (e.g. completing worksheets) and rigid deadlines for assignments can impede learning for many learners with or without disabilities, especially if the teaching and learning activity does not connect to the motivations of the students. It can, in worse scenarios, create stigma, marginalization, or exclusion. Good pedagogical practice that removes or compensates for such barriers generally benefits all learners in the classroom and works to remediate the risk of exclusion. If the goal is that all our students flourish in the classroom and in their learning, then we need to make sure that the barriers that could hinder flourishing are removed or at least minimized.

What, then, is the task for teachers who intend to work in an environment that cultivates human flourishing? Previous perspectives or teacher education courses with the underlying lens of the medical model are called *teaching learners with exceptionalities* or *special needs education*. They often tend to be focused on impairments, what their symptoms are, and perhaps how to address them in the classroom (e.g., "What is Down syndrome, and what are typical features of this syndrome? How do we adapt pedagogical practices to these children?"). This "one disability per week" approach is problematic, as it has a tendency to other the child with a disability, and it does not examine underlying assumptions about disability that are often ableist and exclusionary (Parekh, 2022). It puts the onus on the child and the impairment and does not look at practices in the classroom that, in themselves, can constitute barriers to learning. The practices aimed at accommodating the child with a disability then become practices that are targeting only this child while the rest of the classroom continues to learn in traditional ways. Oftentimes, this excludes the child with a disability within the so-called inclusive classroom or puts a spotlight on the difference of the child. This can become increasingly difficult for a growing child who often just wants to be like everybody else and feels that this spotlight stigmatizes them. It also considerably increases the workload for a teacher who is managing several groups in the same classroom and is trying to teach different content to different learners. This is why an approach that has the social model of disability as an underlying model is more productive for any inclusive classroom, as it examines barriers to learning in the classroom whether students with or without disabilities are in attendance (Baglieri & Shapiro, 2017).

The paradigmatic shift to a social model of disability recognizes that disability often results from the mismatch between the learning environment and the abilities that the disabled child brings to the table. It also recognizes that removing barriers to learning benefits all learners in the classroom and not only the child recognized or labelled as disabled. Barriers to learning occur in many instances; they can be physical, psychological, social, or cultural. For students to thrive in the classroom, teachers need to turn their eyes to identifying and removing those barriers and, subsequently, to creating a teaching and learning space that enables the participation and belonging of all learners and allows for flourishing learners to develop in the classroom. In this way, the social model of disability reaches beyond the realm of disabled learners, as it recognizes the removal of barriers as essential for all learners in the classroom. If barriers are cultural or linguistic, removing them remains a crucial task.

In the following sections, I will discuss the aspects that are essential for teachers to consider when creating this barrier-free classroom that will allow all students to flourish as learners in the classroom as well as members of the school polis: rights recognition, teaching and learning in heterogeneous groups, and Universal Design for Learning.

## BUILDING BLOCKS FOR A SCHOOL AS POLIS

### Rights Recognition, Capability Approach

Recognizing education and inclusion as human rights is an essential step in preparing teachers for their task in the school as polis. The presence of children with disabilities in the classroom is not optional but is based on every child's right to an education together with their peers (Schneider, 2016, 2017).

Teachers need to learn about inclusive education models and also the rights-based approaches to disability—such as the Convention on the Rights of Persons with Disabilities (United Nations, 2006) and the Convention on the Rights of the Child (United Nations, 1989)—that are impacting Canadian and provincial accessibility legislation and provincial inclusive education policies (e.g., Nova Scotia Department of Education and Early Childhood Education, 2019). Under this perspective, the first voice of disabled children and their families sharing their lived experiences about their education in the current system is crucial to understanding its shortcomings and to finding ways to transform the system (Peters, 2010). The UN Convention on the Rights of Persons with Disabilities declares the right to an inclusive education and participation essential in Article 24 and mandates that schools in all ratifying countries become ready and accessible for all learners (Schneider, 2017) and respect and recognize (Honneth, 1996; Nussbaum, 2003) the rights of each child to participate in the classroom. The convention is having an enduring impact in Canada at the policy level. For example, in Nova Scotia, the Accessibility Act of 2017 has led to the establishment of accessibility standards for education (Nova Scotia Accessibility Advisory Board, 2020, 2023) applicable to any educational setting in Nova Scotia, and the Inclusive Education Policy (Nova Scotia Department of Education and Early Childhood Education, 2019) is applicable to all Nova Scotia public schools K–12. The implementation of those standards and policies is the next step toward fulfilling the rights of children with disabilities. Any administrator who considers their school a polis recognizes those rights and puts students in the position of participation and contribution in all their activities.

### Teaching and Learning in Heterogeneous Groups

If we want to create a flourishing classroom community, then teachers need to be able to recognize how learning occurs in the brain. Neuroscience allows us to see how the brain functions in the interactions among the brain stem, cortex, limbic system, and prefrontal cortex (Siegel, 2021). It has enabled us to know (or to confirm) under which conditions the brain learns best and what works best to engage the student (Cozolino, 2013; Houdé, 2018). We know now that knowledge creation is only one part of learning (occurring mostly in the cortex of the brain) and that it has to be integrated with the motivation of learning (occurring in the limbic system: Is the student affectively and emotionally in a position to learn? Is there motivation and interest, and if not, how we can we contribute to create this motivation?). And finally, learning needs to be part of the development of the executive functioning of the learner, as the prefrontal cortex matures and learners are able to progressively make better decisions and accurately assess consequences. This foundational neuroscientific knowledge has been used in the creation of Universal Design for Learning (CAST, n.d.) and also applies to other inquiry-based teaching and learning methods that support heterogeneous groups of learners (Houdé, 2018, 2019; Schneider, 2023). It is essential to recognize that barriers to learning often occur due to misunderstandings in the developing brain. Children are more impulsive and have a prefrontal cortex that takes a long time to fully develop. Teachers therefore need to engage learners in ways that connect to their motivations and help to develop their executive functioning over time. This knowledge is essential when we think about methods that support heterogeneous groups of learners.

The formerly innovative term *inclusive education* has, in practice, semantically replaced *special education* or *special education needs* and has not been able to deliver much change. When we hear the term *inclusive eduation* used in schools, it conveys the medical model, with a variety of special supports and special resource centres, often separate from regular classrooms where children with disabilities may frequent the same building as other students but are not learning together in the same classrooms with them. I am deliberately using the phrase *teaching and learning in heterogeneous groups* to distinguish these practices from the ones that we would like to see to create true participation and belonging in the classroom for all. This idea recognizes that heterogeneous groups of any nature are part of any classroom: **heterogeneity** in interests, in upbringing, in learning abilities, possibly in age, in gender expression, in cultural and ethnic background, and so on. The idea is to make this heterogeneity not a weakness but a strength of the classroom. School as a polis (Eikel & Diemer, 2005; von Hentig, 1993) implies that we recognize and include this heterogeneity and not only "accommodate" it in the classroom but make it one of the strongest principles of the classroom, as we are living in an increasingly heterogeneous society that is and should be reflected in the classroom. The school as polis enables all learners to participate and contribute to this microcosm of society and makes learning an activity that helps both the individual and the community to flourish.

Traditionally, the idea of a group of homogeneous learners in one classroom has reigned over how we have organized schooling—by creating what we consider age-appropriate curriculum by grades, by assessing students according to this curriculum, and by centring teaching on the teacher at the front of the classroom. This industrial, one-size-fits-all model of education, and ableist approach to learning and school (Parekh, 2022), has created barriers for many of those who don't fit into this imagined homogeneous classroom in terms of their interests, abilities, racialized and sociocultural backgrounds, and so on. When we do what we call *inclusion*, we are often repeating this form of exclusion, but inside the classroom rather than outside. Teaching in heterogeneous groups needs to address those barriers and analyze how to remove them and create broad accessibility to learning for the content, the curriculum, and the skills.

As trying to shift the thinking from the imagined homogeneous classroom to a heterogeneous group of learners can be overwhelming, guidance on where to begin is needed. A great tool that can help to analyze barriers and create access to learning is the **Index for Inclusion** (Booth, 2011; Booth & Ainscow, 2011). In its threefold approach, which investigates the culture, policies, and practices of a school community, it gives perspectives on some of the elements that need to be examined to create accessibility. It can give pre- and in-service teachers perspective on how to assess accessibility in a school and classroom setting and helps to set goals for transforming one's pedagogical practices and classroom cultures to foster inclusivity and flourishing of all learners. Notably, its indicators also pay attention not only to the students but also to the staff, teachers, and families involved in the school. We often tend to forget about the fact that human flourishing needs to be fostered for those groups, as the exclusive focus on students misses the point of a flourishing school community. If teachers and staff are unhappy, not working in decent conditions, experiencing high levels of stress and burn-out, then students will not benefit from those people. The Index for Inclusion interrogates our cultures, policies, and practices by examining statements such as "Everyone is welcomed" (Indicator A1.1, Booth & Ainscow, 2011, p. 76), "The school has an inclusive approach to leadership" (Indicator B.1.2, Booth & Ainscow, 2011, p. 99), and "Learning activities encourage the participation of all children" (Indicator C.2.2, Booth & Ainscow, 2011, p. 160) with a series of questions that can help identify the gaps of the particular school and make an inclusive improvement plan that supports the development of the school community.

As I mentioned earlier, if we continue to teach in a teacher-centred way in the heterogeneous classroom, several issues will stand in the way of the school as polis. For the child with disabilities, the risk of being excluded or stigmatized within the classroom is high, and this teaching style is not productive to their learning or social experience in the classroom (see, e.g., Schneider, 2011). It also adds stress to the teacher's practice, as they must manage several groups at different learning levels within a single classroom in which all students depend on the teacher as the guide.

In the heterogeneous classroom, reducing or moving away from teacher-centred practices is important, as is supporting the independent learner, who is able to collaborate as much as possible. Working independently is an important skill, and many students can acquire this (in a scaffolded way) early on. If students are enabled to work on, research, and review many things in class by themselves or in collaboration with peers, with minimal support from the teacher, the teacher will become a mentor rather than the adult who is always at the front of the classroom. This will also free up time that the teacher can use to support learners who have more difficulties.

## Universal Design for Learning

The methods that we know foster the independent learner well are the ones that give students increasingly more autonomy in their approach to learning and offer options rather than only one way of acquiring knowledge. **Universal Design for Learning** (UDL; CAST, n.d.; Gargiulo & Metcalfe, 2013) uses a neuroscientific approach to learning and gives learners options in terms of how they will access a field of knowledge (multiple means of engagement), how the knowledge will be represented (multiple means of knowledge), and how they will act out or express this knowledge (multiple means of action and expression) (see also chapters 7 and 13 for more discussion on UDL). Offering these multiple means will, in many cases, remove the barriers to learning that I identified earlier in this chapter, as there are multiple learning paths that students can take. When students become used to the idea that those multiple means are desirable and not an annoying by-product of their learning that disrupts the imagined flow of the class, many will start to create their own learning paths, thus removing the barriers to their learning themselves. Methods such as project-based or inquiry-based learning or the weekly work plan (Schneider, 2023) connect nicely with the UDL approach, as projects create multiple ways of engagement and enable each student to engage at their own learning level. As all of these methods give choice and agency and foster collaboration and engagement, they support the idea of the school as polis and cultivate the flourishing of all learners, who are considered part of the group of heterogeneous learners.

## CONCLUSION

Finally, if the school should function as a polis, connections need to be made with **culturally responsive pedagogy** and similar approaches, as teachers must recognize the intersectionalities among disability, race, gender, and social class. Teaching with equity, diversity, inclusion, and accessibility (EDIA) in mind is a challenge that requires humility and a willingness to grow with the students into a classroom community where everyone can feel involved. The methods and approaches presented in this chapter allow for intersectionality, as the identification of learning barriers in the social model applies for every student, whether they have a disability or not. If we get into the habit of identifying barriers to learning for all of our students, we can open the conversation about barriers that might be cultural or linguistic. Culturally responsive pedagogy can offer responses about how to remove those barriers and how to support students who come from different cultural backgrounds (see also chapter 5). The school as a polis makes room for heterogeneity in all imaginable ways, recognizes everyone as a member of this society, and makes room for their uniqueness, all while creating a dialogue in which all students can partake. Thinking about barriers to participation can constitute an intersectional foundation for conversation about and observation and assessment of classroom practices to move to more productive and inclusive approaches overall. If the goal is to support flourishing classrooms, identifying barriers and how to remove them will support this goal. This is where the teacher remains a lifelong apprentice, as they will need to continue to learn alongside their students, remove the barriers, and open new ways of engagement for their students—for example, by making space for culturally responsive pedagogy to account for the different cultural backgrounds of their students (Waitoller & Thorius, 2016).

The social model of disability in education can be combined with those other approaches that are necessary for the school as polis so students experience visibility and recognition of who they are and what they represent and so they are encouraged to bring their uniqueness—not their conformity—to the classroom. On a final note, just as "Rome was not built in a day," the polis is not something that has to be perfectly constituted within a short period of time. We need to recognize that introducing new practices and approaches takes some time. Tools such as the Index for Inclusion and UDL recognize the need to scaffold and to take small steps toward a more inclusive practice. Changing our ways to organize teaching and learning takes time and allies, but it is essential to take even the smallest steps to benefit the future citizens of this polis.

## KEY TERMS

**Culturally responsive pedagogy:** A student-centred teaching framework that recognizes and cultivates the student's distinctive cultural strengths and stimulates student achievement and cultural flourishing.

**Heterogeneity:** The opposite of homogeneity, this term captures the essence of what our society and classrooms look like today. It recognizes the difference and diversity of all learners as a strength to draw from.

**Index for Inclusion:** A tool that helps school communities create a path toward more inclusivity. It can help to identify barriers to participation and inclusion in the values, policies, and practices of a school and supports the development of a plan that increases participation and belonging for all.

**Medical model of disability:** A model that states that disability is created by an individual's impairment or medical needs and focuses on fixing or remediating those impairments. Contrary to the social model of disability, it does not examine the environment or the context of a person with disabilities in terms of its disabling nature.

**School as polis:** Similarly to how ancient Greek philosophers envisioned the polis to be a place where society would discuss and decide on its affairs, the school as a polis reflects a miniature society where students are considered citizens who participate in and contribute to this *embryonic society*.

**Social or biopsychosocial model of disability:** This model aims at identifying barriers that people with disabilities face in their environment. These barriers can be attitudinal or physical or can relate to barriers in the learning environment. Teachers need to examine their practices and identify and remove barriers in their teaching practices that hinder students' participation in and contribution to the learning process.

**Universal Design for Learning:** An approach that supports teachers in improving and optimizing their teaching and learning practices for all their students. It is based on the knowledge of how the human brain learns best.

## DISCUSSION QUESTIONS AND ACTIVITIES

1. Identify at least three barriers to learning that you might have experienced in a school and create a plan for how you, as a teacher or administrator, could remove those barriers.
2. Discuss the indicator "Everyone is welcomed" from the Index for Inclusion. What do school communities need to do so that everyone who enters a school feels that they are a part of it?
3. What activities or structures could be offered or created in schools to support the school as polis?

4. Carousel activity—thinking about schools as polis (approximately one hour): The goal of this activity is to foster deep thinking about creating a school as a polis and assessing how easy or difficult implementing some of the ideas presented in this chapter would be. Instructions:
    - Split into four groups. Each group starts at a different station, where they will spend 10 minutes making notes and writing down their reflections on chart paper or sticky notes.
    - Switch to the next station. Review, comment on, and add to the notes that the previous group wrote. Repeat until groups have visited all four stations (5–7 minutes at each stations, or more if needed).
    - Groups go back to their original station, review all comments, and underline the most important aspects that they identify (10 minutes).
    - Debrief as a class, present the central aspects of your group discussions, and go into open-ended discussions.

    *Station 1*: Advantages of school as a polis (e.g., What would work well in such a school? What would you appreciate as a teacher? As a student? As a family member?)

    *Station 2*: Disadvantages of school as a polis (e.g., What might create problems? Are there students, teachers, or families who would struggle with this? What are some potential downsides of such an approach?)

    *Station 3*: Opportunities that could open up when starting to work in the vision of school as a polis (What opportunities are related to the removal of barriers in the school?)

    *Station 4*: Aspects of a school that functions as a polis could be difficult to continually deal with (What could hinder the implementation of such a model?)

# REFERENCES

Baglieri, S., Bejoian, L. M., Broderick, A. A., Connor, D. J., & Valle, J. (2011). [Re]claiming "inclusive education" toward cohesion in educational reform: Disability studies unravels the myth of the normal child. *Teachers College Record, 113*(10), 2122–2154. doi.org/10.1177/016146811111301001

Baglieri, S., & Shapiro, A. (2017). *Disability studies and the inclusive classroom: Critical practices for embracing diversity in education*. Routledge.

Barnes, C., & Mercer, G. (2010). *Exploring disability: A sociological introduction* (2nd ed.). Polity Press.

Booth, T. (2011). The name of the rose: Inclusive values into action in teacher education. *Prospects, 41*(3), 303–318. doi.org/10.1007/s11125-011-9200-z

Booth, T., & Ainscow, M. (2011). *Index for inclusion: Developing learning and participation in schools* (3rd ed.). CSIE.

CAST. (n.d.). *Universal Design for Learning guidelines version 2.2.* udlguidelines.cast.org

Charlton, J. I. (1998). *Nothing about us without us: Disability oppression and empowerment.* University of California Press.

Cozolino, L. J. (2013). *The social neuroscience of education: Optimizing attachment and learning in the classroom.* Norton.

Dewey, J., (1915). *The school and society.* University of Chicago Press.

Eikel, A., & Diemer, T. (2005). Schule als polis. *BLK Demokratiebausteine.* doi.org/10.25656/01:250

Gargiulo, R. M., & Metcalfe, D. (2013). *Teaching in today's inclusive classrooms: A universal design for learning approach* (2nd ed.). Wadsworth Cengage Learning.

Goodley, D. (2014). *Dis/ability studies: Theorizing disableism and ableism* (iBooks version). Routledge.

Goodley, D. (2017). *Disability studies: An interdisciplinary introduction* (2nd ed.). Sage.

Grant, C. A. (2012). Cultivating flourishing lives: A robust social justice vision of education. *American Educational Research Journal, 49*(5), 910–934. doi.org/10.3102/0002831212447977

Häkli, J., & Kallio, K. P. (2014). Subject, action and *polis*: Theorizing political agency. *Progress in Human Geography,* 38(2), 181–200. doi.org/10.1177/0309132512473869

Honneth, A. (1996). *The struggle for recognition: The moral grammar of social conflicts.* MIT Press.

Houdé, O. (2018). *L'école du cerveau: De Montessori, Freinet et Piaget aux sciences cognitives.* Éditions Mardaga.

Houdé, O. (2019). La pédagogie Freinet sous l'œil des neurosciences. *Cerveau & Psycho, 116,* 46–51. doi.org/10.3917/cerpsy.116.0046

Nova Scotia Accessibility Advisory Board. (2020). *Recommendations to the minister of justice on an accessibility standard in education: Phase 1.* https://novascotia.ca/accessibility/education-committee/Recommendations-Education-Accessibility-Standards-phase-1.PDF

Nova Scotia Accessibility Advisory Board. (2023). *Recommendations to the minister of justice on an accessibility standard in education: Phase 2.* https://novascotia.ca/accessibility/education-committee/recommendations-education-accessibility-standards-phase-2-en.pdf

Nova Scotia Department of Education and Early Childhood Education. (2019). *Inclusive education policy.* https://www.ednet.ns.ca/sites/default/files/docs/inclusiveeducationpolicyen.pdf

Nussbaum, M. C. (2003). Capabilities as fundamental entitlements: Sen and social justice. *Feminist Economics, 9*(2–3), 33–59. doi.org/10.1080/1354570022000077926

Parekh, G. (2022). *Ableism in education. Rethinking school practices and policies.* Norton.

Peters, S. J. (2010). The heterodoxy of student voice: Challenges to identity in the sociology of disability and education. *British Journal of Sociology of Education, 31*(5), 591–602. doi.org/10.1080/01425692.2010.500092

Schneider, C. (2011). *Une étude comparative de l'éducation inclusive des enfants avec besoins particuliers en France et en Allemagne: Recherches dans onze salles de classe.* Edwin Mellen Press.

Schneider, C. (2016). Recognizing and respecting the rights of children with disabilities in the classroom. *International Journal of Education, 8*(3), 119–133. doi.org/10.5296/ije.v8i3.9444

Schneider, C. (2017). Between children's rights and disability rights: Inclusion and participation of children and youth with disabilities. In X. Chen, R. Raby, & P. Albanese (Eds.), *The sociology of childhood and youth in Canada* (pp. 361–377). Canadian Scholars.

Schneider, C. (2023). (Re)claiming Freinet pedagogy as a tool for inclusive education. *The Inclusive Educator, 6*(1), 21–26. https://www.academia.edu/100181884/_Re_claiming_Freinet_Pedagogy_as_a_tool_for_inclusive_education

Siegel, D. (2021). *Dr. Dan Siegel's hand model of the brain* [Video]. https://drdansiegel.com/hand-model-of-the-brain/

United Nations. (1989). *Convention on the rights of the child.* General Assembly resolution 44/25. www.ohchr.org/en/instruments-mechanisms/instruments/convention-rights-child

United Nations. (2006). *Convention on the rights of persons with disabilities.* General Assembly resolution A/RES/61/106. https://social.desa.un.org/issues/disability/crpd/convention-on-the-rights-of-persons-with-disabilities-crpd

von Hentig, H. (1993). *Die Schule neu denken. Eine Übung in praktischer Vernunft.* Hanser.

von Hentig, H. (1996). *Bildung.* Hanser.

Waitoller, F. R., & Thorius, K. A. K. (2016). Cross-pollinating culturally sustaining pedagogy and Universal Design for Learning: Toward an inclusive pedagogy that accounts for dis/ability. *Harvard Educational Review, 86*(3), 366–389. doi.org/10.17763/1943-5045-86.3.366

# PART IX

## GEOGRAPHY: THE IMPORTANCE OF LOCATION IN SUPPORTING STUDENTS AND TEACHERS

# CHAPTER 18
# The Landscape of Education Inequalities in Northern and Rural Locations in Canada

*Cathlene Hillier and David Zarifa*

This chapter describes how locations shape students' academic outcomes in Canada. We explore the importance of considering *rurality* and *northernness* in discussions of educational inequalities and what that means with respect to students' flourishing. It is well established that sociodemographic categories such as socioeconomic status (SES), gender, culture, disability, and race are key factors that contribute to structural inequalities found in educational achievement and attainment. Rurality has also received attention in the educational inequality literature, as researchers find that many students who reside in rural locations experience unique obstacles that result in lower educational performance compared to their urban peers (e.g., Cartwright & Allen, 2002; Corbett, 2013). Recent work extends beyond rural/urban dichotomies and considers northern/southern differences in students' academic outcomes—including Canada's territorial (Sisco et al., 2012) and provincial North (Hillier et al., 2021; Zarifa et al., 2018; Zarifa et al., 2022). This new research extends previous work on rurality in the educational landscape by adding a consideration of the academic achievement and attainment of students from northern locations in comparison to their southern counterparts.

The concept of human flourishing in a neo-Aristotelian sense outlined by Nussbaum (1997) involves fulfilling one's life potential as a human being in society (see the introduction to this volume for an overview). Access to education, including the tools to truly participate and feel successful in schooling, contributes to the development of students' skills and talents and can pave the way for meaningful future employment. This goal aligns with Nussbaum's (2011) capabilities needed for human flourishing. While there are many important facets of flourishing to consider in children's and youth's education, educational achievement and attainment are two facets that we focus on. We do so to highlight the context of northern/southern and rural/urban inequalities in educational outcomes and the importance of geographical considerations in terms of human flourishing. We conclude by sharing initiatives across Canada that serve to inform educational policy and programming.

## STUDENTS IN NORTHERN AND RURAL COMMUNITIES

There is no doubt that identity is entwined with the geographical location in which one lives (Gollnick & Chinn, 2013). However, to describe what the average student would look like in rural and northern communities would depend highly on each specific area and other family background factors. In learning about any community in which they teach, we recommend that teachers start with the land that they are on and learn about the geographical landscape, the history, and the local social and cultural systems (e.g., chapters 10 and 11 emphasize the importance of land-based education for Indigenous communities). In general, northern regions in Canada have a larger rural populace, higher numbers of Indigenous people, lower levels of parent education, and higher unemployment rates (Allen & Perreault, 2015; Coates & Poelzer, 2014). Northern communities also have younger populations, largely due to Indigenous demographics. Allen and Perrault (2015) report that 36 percent of Indigenous people in the provincial North and 38 percent in the territories are under 18.7 years. Additionally, northern communities tend to have more students living on reserve in comparison to the southern parts of the provinces (Louie & Prince, 2023).

Rural communities also vary by location. Some experience higher rates of poverty in comparison to urban locations. For example, Mitton and Murray-Orr (2021) report that the rural Nova Scotian schools in their study have 30 percent child poverty rates. The rural schools in their study also have larger populations of African Nova Scotian and Mi'kmaq students, which highlights the importance of considering intersectionality among background factors of students' lives, especially socioeconomic status (see chapters 6 and 7). However, it is important to note that the most recent report from the 2021 census indicates poverty rates in rural areas average 5.6 percent in comparison to almost twice the rate in many of Canada's largest urban centres (Statistics Canada, 2022b). Rural areas, once thought of as, and even stereotyped to be, quite homogeneous, can contain as much diversity (e.g., race and ethnicity, culture, religion, sexual orientation, socioeconomic status, abilities) as many urban spaces (Tuters, 2015).

While there has been more focus on teachers' experiences in the rural literature, Corbett's (2007) work in a coastal community in Atlantic Canada examines rural students' sense of place and identity. He notes that students who have travelled to or attended schooling outside of rural communities have developed a "floater" identity position that allows them to easily move in and out of various social groups and that influences more positive interactions with teachers (p. 778). Rural students who have not had many experiences outside of their communities have "localized capital," which can limit their networks to other areas (p. 783). As Corbett (2007) describes, rural youth in his study view their local communities as safe places to live and build community but not necessarily sustainable for future employment. In fact, staying and having the family capital to make a decent living is viewed as a privilege that many participants do not have. At the same time, having the resources to leave home is also a privilege, along with having the cultural capital (cultural know-how) to be successful in urban centres. Academic success is also important to leaving the community for post-secondary education or employment, and being able to interact easily with teachers is seen as a part of being viewed as able and intelligent. One female participant (15 years) noted, "I do good in school because I can talk with my teachers. If I don't understand something I just go up and ask about it. I know they think I'm smart and I get great marks. A lot of kids just hate teachers. They never even try to make that connection. It's like they don't speak the same language. So I think the teachers just end up thinking that they're stupid or something, but they aren't. They just hate school or something" (Corbett, 2007, pp. 782–783). As a result, some youth in Corbett's (2007) study ended up seeing future schooling as either unattainable or not connected to the work they see in their community. These early experiences in school can influence decisions about future education and careers and students' flourishing in terms of their own educational achievement and attainment and feelings of job and life satisfaction.

## RURAL/URBAN CONTEXT OF EDUCATIONAL OUTCOMES IN CANADA

Most of what we know about disparities in educational outcomes related to students' geographical location centres on rural/urban differences. In the broadest sense, researchers have noted that **urban** students tend to perform better academically and experience better educational outcomes in comparison to their **rural** counterparts (Byun et al., 2012; Canadian Council on Learning, 2008; Cartwright & Allen, 2002; Corbett, 2013; Looker, 2010; Looker & Thiessen,

2008). At the same time, these rural/urban differences in educational outcomes generally tend to increase as one follows students from elementary to secondary and post-secondary education.

Taking a closer look at the elementary education level, for instance, Tremblay and colleagues (2001) analyzed results from grade 3 students' math, reading, and writing scores collected by Ontario's Education Quality and Accountability Office (EQAO). Their results indicated that geographical location has a significant impact on EQAO performance, as students who lived in urban areas outperformed their rural counterparts by an average of two percentage points (p. 30). Additional factors that were found to significantly influence test scores were family income (higher income resulted in higher test scores), gender (girls outperformed boys), and language (English-speaking students outperformed French-speaking students).

At the secondary education level, studies have also revealed significant urban/rural disparities in performance on standardized tests. Across all provinces, rural students scored significantly lower on the 2003 Programme for International Student Assessment (PISA) math, science, and reading tests (Canadian Council on Learning, 2008). Similarly, Cartwright and Allen (2002) found that urban students had significantly higher PISA reading averages than rural students in Newfoundland and Labrador, Prince Edward Island, New Brunswick, and Alberta. Rural students scored lower in all provinces (though not all differences were statistically significant) except for Manitoba and Nova Scotia, where rural and urban students had similar scores (Cartwright & Allen, 2002). Rural parents had lower SES overall (except in Ontario, Alberta, and British Columbia), and rural areas had higher unemployment rates, lower levels of post-secondary education (PSE) among adults, and fewer jobs requiring PSE (Cartwright & Allen, 2002). Notably, SES effects are often found to be more influential than location. For example, drawing upon 2006 PISA and Census Canada data, Corbett (2014) reveals that only 3–4 percent of the difference in reading, math, and science scores between students in Nova Scotia and students in Alberta (Canada's top-performing province in PISA scores) were attributable to geography, while income differences accounted for almost 30 percent.

In addition to academic performance at the secondary school level, high school dropout and completion rates are important educational outcomes to consider when examining geographical inequalities (Canadian Council on Learning, 2008; Corbett, 2014; Looker & Naylor, 2009; Uppal, 2017). For instance, in an analysis of nationally representative labour force data from 1990 to 2016, a study by Uppal (2017) found that among individuals 25 to 34 years of age,

14.2 percent of men and 9.9 percent of women outside of census metropolitan areas did not complete high school. These high levels of secondary school non-completion were also shown to contribute to higher unemployment rates (Uppal, 2017). Additionally, Indigenous men were more likely to have less than a high school diploma (20.1 percent) compared to Canadian-born non-Indigenous men (8.5 percent), Indigenous women (15.9 percent), and Canadian-born non-Indigenous women (4.9 percent) (Uppal, 2017). Interestingly, while Corbett's (2014) study reveals differences in standardized test scores, his work also emphasizes the fact that despite these differences in academic performance, Nova Scotia's high school graduation rates were in fact slightly higher than those of Alberta. He highlights the importance of looking beyond rurality, school size, and academic success—what occurs outside of school and in the community has a great influence on success in school. In fact, when controlling for SES and community, rural schools in Nova Scotia outperformed the urban schools (Corbett, 2014).

Looking ahead, it is crucial to also consider rural inequalities in accessing higher education. Finnie and colleagues (2015), for example, found that across provinces, male (59 percent) and female (76 percent) students from rural locations had lower rates of attaining PSE in comparison to male (72 percent) and female (83 percent) students in urban locations. Moreover, about 32 percent of rural and 23 percent of urban students had not accessed any form of PSE at all. Similarly, Newbold and Brown (2015) found that individuals who reside in rural areas had the lowest percentage of university attendance (29 percent) compared to all types of urban areas (small, medium, and large), even when considering other sociodemographics, such as SES. Proximity to the university was another determinant: those who lived more than 40 kilometres away from a university were less likely to attend (29 percent) in comparison to those who lived 40 kilometres from a university or closer (42 percent).

Overall, on average, urban students tend to perform higher on standardized testing, have higher high school completion rates, and be more likely to attend PSE than their rural peers. In seeking answers as to why rural youth are less likely to attend PSE, qualitative research has shed some important light on the mechanisms and barriers behind these differences. Friesen and Purc-Stephenson (2016) indicate that not only does the distance to the closest university have an impact, but concerns around the cost, maintaining a rural identity, social norms (e.g., marrying young and having children), and relationships also influence PSE decisions. Other less-cited factors are fear of the unknown, parental education, traditional gender-role expectations, secondary school preparation, and responsibilities

(Friesen & Purc-Stephenson, 2016). Also, career choices in high school may be influenced by the family's perspective of higher education and whether it is seen as "wasted time" given the local employment opportunities (Corbett, 2009). On the other hand, high-SES families have more mobility in terms of youth aspiring to higher education and moving between rural and urban contexts to achieve educational and occupational goals (Corbett, 2007, 2009, 2013). The discrepancy is exacerbated further when youth view leaving their rural community as a measure of success and the only pathway to social mobility and occupational success (Bourgeois & Kirby, 2012; Corbett, 2007, 2013; Looker, 2021), which can contribute to brain drain from rural to urban locations (Sano et al., 2020).

As outlined above, it is important to note that socioeconomic status does influence many of the disparities in educational achievement and attainment found in rural communities. However, location compounds these differences because of the varied opportunities and resources available across regions. This is especially true when considering the educational outcomes of residents from the northern contexts in Canada.

## NORTHERN/SOUTHERN CONTEXT OF EDUCATIONAL OUTCOMES IN CANADA

Traditionally, studies on Canada's North have typically explored inequalities within the territories (Wilson & Poelzer, 2005). However, as figure 18.1 shows, Canada's more recent definition of the North (see Statistics Canada, 2018) includes not only the three territories but also the northernmost parts of seven provinces constituting **Canada's provincial North**. These areas have similar demographics and share concerns found in the territories (e.g., economies dependent on natural resources, skills shortages, long distance to schooling, network structures) (Alasia & Magnusson, 2005). Thus, a recent body of literature both expands the scope to bring the northernmost parts of Canada's provinces into the conversation on northern inequalities and seeks to understand the compounded disadvantages for youth who grow up in rural areas within the North. Youth from the northern rural contexts within Canada often experience the greatest challenges in their educational performance and attainment. For instance, recent work by Zarifa et al. (2022) using the 2016 census found that 22.2 percent of residents aged 35 to 64 from northern and rural locations reported having less than a high school education. Residents from southern urban locations of the country were half as likely to report the same (11 percent), while about 15 percent of those from northern urban and southern rural locations reported not having completed high school.

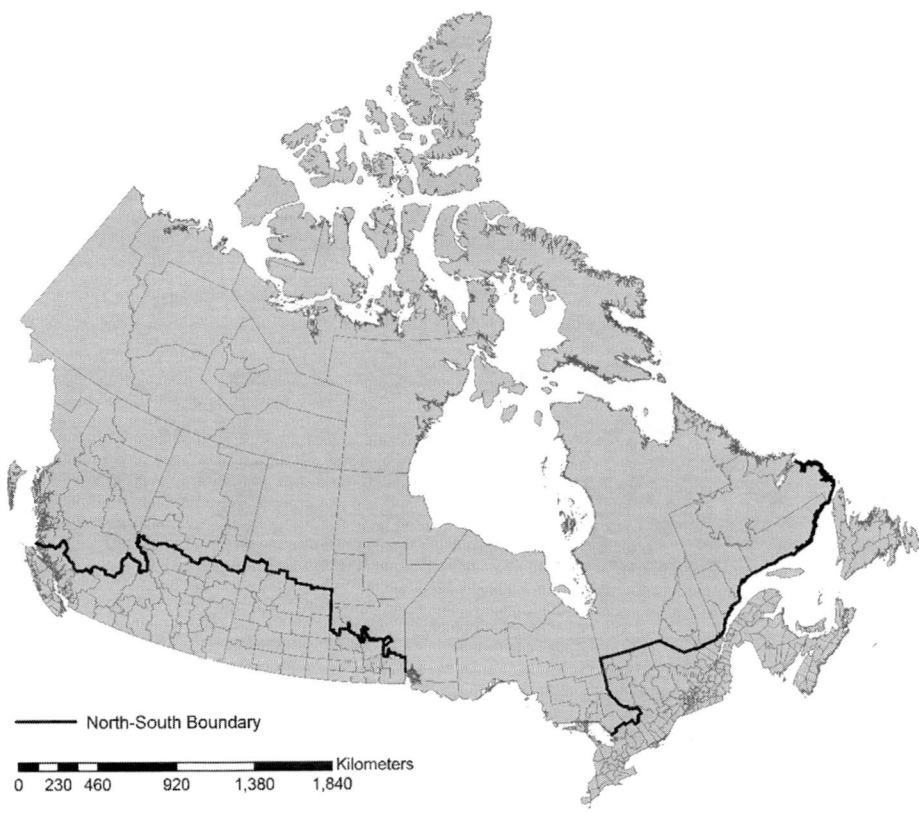

**Figure 18.1: Canada's North–South Boundary**
Source: Map is based on the authors' calculations, derived from Canada's North–South boundary as defined by Statistics Canada (2018).

These unequal outcomes in rural and northern areas of Canada are traced back to differences that occur earlier on in the school system. For example, we observe key geographical differences in academic performance at the elementary school level by taking a closer look at the 2020 numeracy scores for grade 7 students and the reading and writing scores of grade 8 students in Manitoba. The Government of Manitoba (n.d.a) measures grade 7 mathematics and grade 8 reading and writing achievement in its Middle Years Assessment. These tests are scored by teachers at three levels: not meeting, approaching, or meeting level of performance. Average proportions are reported based on a pass/fail basis (*passed* = student met the mid-grade expectations for each test; *failed* = student did not meet the mid-grade expectations for each test).[1] As shown in figure 18.2, students in urban locations have a higher percentage of grade 7 and 8 students meeting provincial expectations in the respective curricular areas in all three

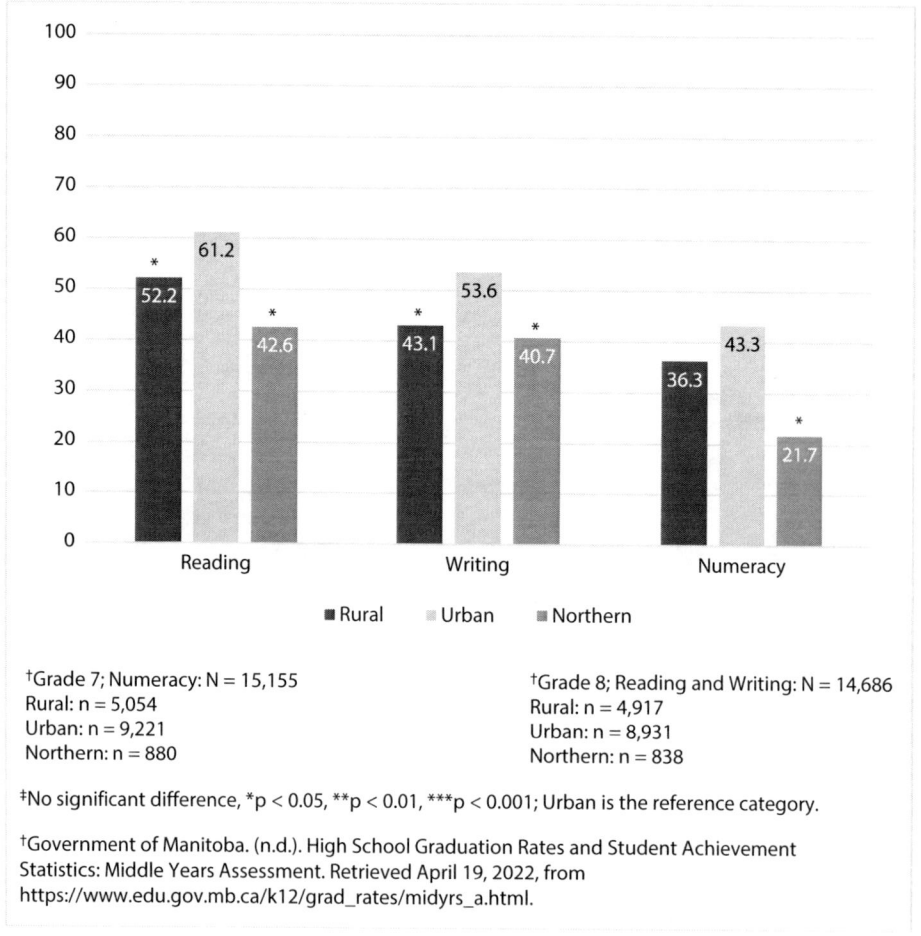

**Figure 18.2: Proportion of Grade 7 and 8 Students Meeting Expectations in Reading, Writing, and Numeracy, Manitoba, 2019–2020**
*Source:* Compiled by the authors based on data from the Government of Manitoba (n.d.a).

assessments. While the percentage of rural students meeting expectations is significantly lower than the percentage of urban students meeting expectations, students in northern Manitoba underperform compared to rural and urban students. Moreover, differences between northern and urban students are sizable, with gaps of 18.6 percent in reading, 12.9 percent in writing, and 21.6 percent in mathematics.

Hillier and colleagues (2021) also found that Canadian youths' math, reading, and science PISA scores at age 15 vary across geographical locations. Even when controlling for a whole host of family background, parent engagement, and student academic measures, students from northern rural locations still show distinct differences across all three PISA outcomes in comparison to their northern urban, southern rural, and southern urban peers. For mathematics performance, southern urban and southern rural students have significantly higher math scores in comparison to northern rural students. Within both reading and science outcomes, southern urban, southern rural, and northern urban students all have significantly higher scores in comparison to their northern rural peers. Notably, all these differences remain even when controlling for sociodemographic, parent engagement, and academic variables. The researchers note other variables that have a negative effect on achievement across the three outcomes, such as being female (negative effect on math and science, positive effect on reading), Indigenous, foreign-born, or low-income; having a parent with high school education or less; having lower parental aspirations for child; and having lower self-aspirations for student. Overall, these findings suggest a multifaceted view of the factors that influence student success in school. They also highlight the importance of understanding more about the achievement gaps of students in Canada's provincial North, and in particular, students in northern rural areas.

In considering high school completion, Gilmore (2012) reports that high school dropout rates in the territories are the highest in the country. Between 2007 and 2010, high school dropout rates in the territories were 15.5 percent in Yukon, 30.1 percent in the Northwest Territories, and 50 percent in Nunavut. Among these, rural, male, and Indigenous youth all have higher dropout rates (Gilmore, 2012). Further, this study found higher rates of unemployment among dropouts compared to high school graduates when they entered the workforce. It is important to note that northern communities in the provinces and territories have higher numbers of Indigenous people within their populations, and academic achievement and attainment has been a concern. Using Canadian census data and the 2001 Aboriginal Peoples Survey, Lamb (2014) found that among Indigenous people, there are higher rates of on-reserve and older individuals who left high school early (specifically, those who attended residential schools). Along with this, being male, living in a rural area, and/or living in the Arctic off-reserve raises the chances that an individual will drop out of high school. More recently, and encouragingly, between 2015 and 2020, the British Columbia Ministry of Education (2021) reported that one of its northern rural districts saw an increase in graduation rates among both Indigenous (64.4 to 72.6 percent) and non-Indigenous (73.2 to 74.3 percent) learners (cited in Louie & Prince, 2023, p. 7).

To further illustrate secondary school differences, in figure 18.3 we compare four-year high school graduation rates across regions, drawing upon several data sources from the Northwest Territories, Nunavut, Ontario, and British Columbia. The graduation measure is based on students successfully achieving provincial or territorial requirements to receive their secondary education diploma.[2] All graduation rates are provided for each province or territory based on geographical location and population. For both British Columbia and Ontario, schools or school boards, respectively, were organized into North/South designations by using Statistics Canada's provincial North and South boundaries for the city where the school or school board is located (Statistics Canada, 2018). Scores in the graph were calculated to show the average score from all northern schools or school boards and all southern schools or school boards.[3] Both Northwest Territories and Nunavut graduation rates were calculated as averages of the available graduation rates in each region in the territory. As seen in figure 18.3, students in northern locations have lower graduation rates. While the differences between Northern (95 percent) and Southern (97.7 percent) British Columbia are minimal, differences between Northern (68.9 percent) and Southern (83.5 percent) Ontario are substantial. Further, by comparison to British Columbia and Ontario, students in Nunavut (47.7 percent) and the Northwest Territories (61.3 percent) have much lower graduation rates.

In the existing literature that examines PSE attainment, studies emphasize the importance of recognizing *remoteness* as a key factor that influences the educational outcomes of those living in Canada's North. For example, Zarifa et al. (2018) discover that geographical location significantly predicts PSE attendance among youth. Youth from southern urban areas are more likely to attend college or university than their peers in northern rural areas, even when controlling for sociodemographic variables, parents' SES, and students' previous academic achievement. Additionally, using the 2016 census data, Leclerc (2022) found that women in very remote areas (just under 40 percent) and remote areas (just under 20 percent) have the highest rates of those with no certificate, diploma, or degree. Further, attainment of a high school diploma or equivalent in very remote (60 percent) and remote (80 percent) areas is below Canada's overall average. In all areas, Indigenous women have lower rates of completion in comparison to non-Indigenous women. Looking at types of degrees obtained, visible minority women and immigrant women have the highest rates of university degrees (and the highest rates of STEM credentials), while Indigenous women have the highest rates of college credentials.

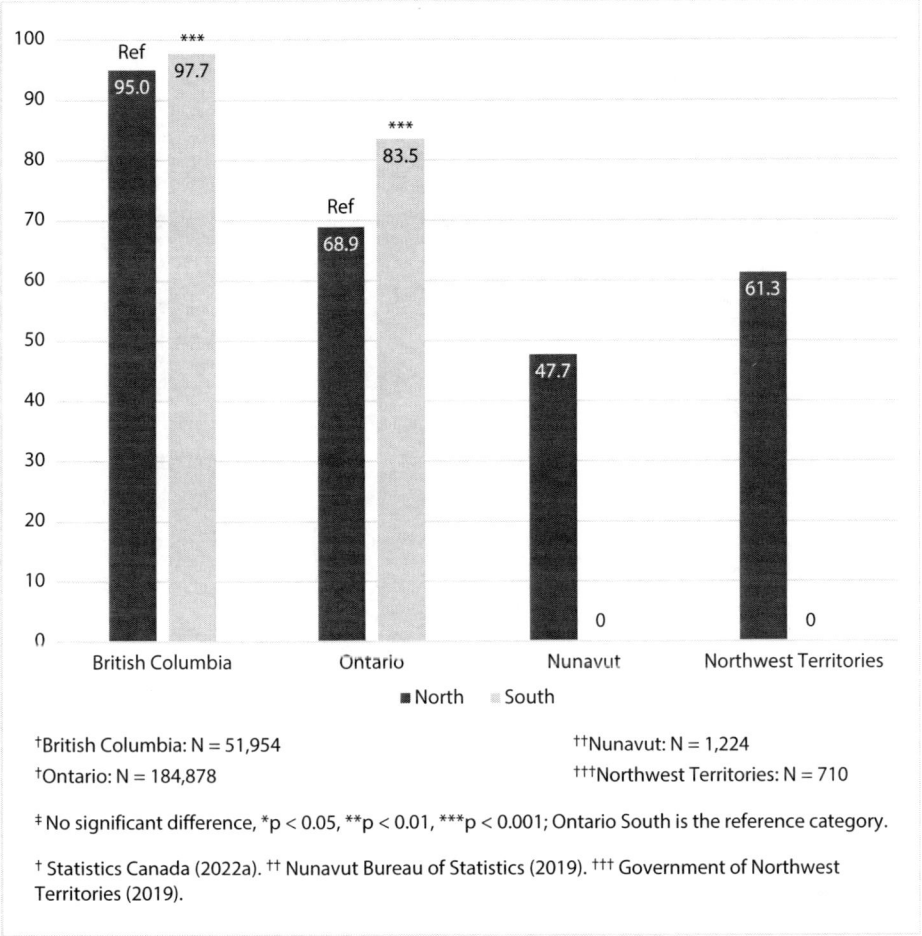

**Figure 18.3: Four-Year Secondary Graduation Rates in Northwest Territories (2017–2018), Nunavut (2016–2017), Ontario (2019–2020), and British Columbia (2018–2019)**
Source: Compiled by the authors based on data from Statistics Canada (2022a), Nunavut Bureau of Statistics (2019), and Government of Northwest Territories (2019).

# RECOMMENDATIONS AND INITIATIVES

In this chapter, we focus on geographical location as an important, and sometimes overlooked, factor in understanding variation in students' performance in school. As noted, rurality has received considerable attention, but adding North/South variants into the mix is crucial to fully understanding how place impacts inequalities in educational outcomes in Canada. In this final section, we employ Nussbaum's (2009, 2011) concept of human flourishing as discussed in this book's introduction and offer some key recommendations and initiatives to address these geographical inequalities.

Rural and northern communities have been responding to these disparities through recommendations informed by research. These initiatives—with the goal of bolstering human capital and resources through school success and future aspirations—can be linked to Martha Nussbaum's (2009, 2011) concept of human flourishing in terms of access to education. In her work, Nussbaum argues that education is essential for the development of human capabilities and is a key factor in enabling individuals to achieve a meaningful and fulfilling life (Nussbaum, 2011). However, in remote rural and northern locations, access to education and other resources can be limited, which can hinder the development of human capabilities. Of Nussbaum's (2011) 10 capabilities that are essential to human flourishing, we see access to education as a key factor in living a life of self-respect, being able to participate in social and political decision-making, developing talents, having access to information, having knowledge of health and nutrition, forming positive relationships with others, and participating in culture and art. We also see K–12 education, and subsequently post-secondary education and training, as being crucial in engaging in meaningful future employment. Therefore, to provide greater access and to address inequalities in educational outcomes, we recommend the following initiatives implemented by northern and/or rural communities in Canada.

First, in Indigenous education, many northern and rural communities have introduced programs that incorporate traditional knowledge and practices into the curriculum (e.g., Government of Canada, n.d.; Government of Nunavut, n.d.; Northwest Territories Education, n.d.; see chapters 10 and 11). This approach aims to help Indigenous students connect with their culture, language, and history and increase their engagement in school. In addition, the importance of *place* in the curriculum has been a focus in Indigenous connections with land (e.g., land-based education). And northern and rural communities benefit from having local communities represented in the curriculum so the focus is not always on urban locations (Burleigh, 2020; Corbett & Gereluk, 2020; Louie & Prince, 2023; Peterson et al., 2018; chapter 19). In STEM fields, the low percentages of Indigenous youth studying and entering STEM occupations is another concern. After interviewing 120 graduates from STEM programs, Cooper (2020a) recommends that K–12 education be aligned with a holistic view of education and Indigenous perspectives and utilize a *culturally responsive curriculum* that brings together Indigenous Knowledge and Western science (see chapters 10 and 11 for a discussion of two-eyed seeing). This approach is respectful of cultural identity and enhances teaching and learning styles that gel with traditional knowledge building (Cooper, 2020a, 2020b; Macpherson, 2020; Sisco et al., 2012). In this initiative, provinces are responding by incorporating Indigenous perspectives into their curriculum. While some provinces are embedding these changes within their science curriculum (e.g., Saskatchewan, British Columbia, Nova Scotia), others are providing external documents and encouraging them as an add-on to pre-existing curriculum (e.g., Alberta, Ontario) (Cooper, 2020b). Additionally, connecting with Indigenous students and families during their elementary education and talking to them about their aspirations for future school and careers can help to build STEM pathways early on (Cooper & Arruda, 2020). As Cooper (2020a, 2020b) notes, there are several points during students' educational experiences when they may decide that STEM fields are not for them; this may happen early on in education, when primary students determine they are "not good" at math and science, or in middle school, when decisions are made about high school courses. Importantly, Louie and Prince's (2023) interviews with Indigenous families from a northern rural community highlight the critical role that teachers play in student engagement and success (see also Burleigh, 2020). Teachers who cultivated relationships with students and who encouraged students' aspirations were noted as being instrumental in students' social and academic success in school.

Second, mentoring and tutoring programs have been implemented in many northern and rural communities to provide extra support to students who are struggling academically (e.g., Northwest Territories Education, n.d.). These programs offer one-on-one or small group support, which can help students overcome academic challenges and improve their confidence and motivation. A multi-tiered approach—at school, family, and community levels—to supporting students in northern and rural communities can assist students in their decisions about PSE. Cooper (2020a, 2020b) recommends that support systems from teachers, guidance counsellors, and student services and information about financial aid and scholarships be in place to help students at these important decision-making junctures (see also Sisco et al., 2012). Additionally, community partnerships can help northern and rural communities address educational gaps by connecting schools with local organizations, businesses, and community leaders (e.g., Government of Manitoba, n.d.b). These partnerships can provide resources, support, and opportunities for students, such as job shadowing, internships, and career guidance.

Third, technology and improved Internet connections have opened new ways for northern and rural communities to access education, especially in remote areas where K–12 and post-secondary schools are quite far away (e.g., Northern

Ontario School of Medicine, 2021). For example, in New Brunswick, where access to learning the French language is a constitutional right, response to the COVID-19 pandemic resulted in the French Language Opportunities for Rural Areas (FLORA) program being shared with families on a broad scope. FLORA is a series of learning modules that incorporate songs, books, and activities (flora.nbed.nb.ca). Since learning French is important for New Brunswick identity (because the province is bilingual) and economic and sociopolitical success, New Brunswick Education provided greater access to FLORA to address the need for quality language programming to continue in remote areas, which were most acutely affected by school closures. This initiative proved to be so effective that it is still available for students to access at home. In addition, Sisco et al. (2012) note that school closures due to weather are another concern, so providing alternatives (e.g., remote learning) on these days could be a solution. To address the concerns of brain drain and students leaving communities for post-secondary education (see Hillier et al., 2020; Sano et al., 2020), training and employment can be offered within these communities to boost employment and economies in these areas (Peterson et al., 2018; Spinu et al., 2021). Significant distance to post-secondary education is a deterrent (Zarifa et al., 2018), so providing local opportunities to complete one's degree is crucial. Increasing local career opportunities would also provide students a reason to aspire to post-secondary education and stay in or return to their communities after PSE (Canadian Council on Learning, 2008).

Fourth, keeping K–12 schools accessible in rural and northern communities is crucial. With school boards closing small schools or amalgamating them into larger schools, it is important to stress that rural and northern communities need their schools to stay open for a variety of reasons. The connection between families and schools is an important one, especially for low-SES (Hillier et al., 2019) and Indigenous (Agbo, 2007) families, and increasing the distance could strain these relationships. Taking the school out of the community also puts it in a precarious position as families might not move to the area if there is no local school (Corbett, 2013), and schools would lose the closeness that families experience with schools in small communities (Peterson et al., 2018). To address this, Corbett (2013) recommends that schools join with other municipal buildings to save on operating costs rather than amalgamating schools. Further, it would be beneficial to decrease the high teacher turnover and increase the number of specialized teachers (e.g., science, mathematics, trades specialists) in rural and northern schools (Kitchenham & Chasteauneuf, 2010; Sisco et al., 2012). Strategies for doing this include offering incentives (e.g., financial) to encourage teachers from rural and northern spaces to come back to their communities to teach and strengthening recruitment strategies to bring teachers into the communities for the long haul (Canadian Council on Learning, 2008; Corbett & Gereluk, 2020; Kitchenham & Chasteauneuf, 2010).

Overall, these initiatives aim to address educational achievement and attainment gaps by providing northern and rural students with the resources, support, and opportunities they need to succeed in school and beyond. Within Nussbaum's (2009, 2011) framework, having access to education and experiencing success in education foster the capabilities necessary for human flourishing.

## KEY TERMS

**Canada's provincial North:** The northernmost areas of seven Canadian provinces (Newfoundland and Labrador, Quebec, Ontario, Manitoba, Saskatchewan, Alberta, and British Columbia) as defined by Statistics Canada, Conference Board of Canada, and Northern Development Ministers Forum (see Statistics Canada, 2018). Considering the northernmost location of the provinces and expanding our understanding of *North* is important because these parts of the provinces share similar resources and sociodemographics with Canada's territories. Notably, New Brunswick, Nova Scotia, and Prince Edward Island are not included, as these provinces lie entirely within Canada's south.

**Rural:** Areas outside of population centres are considered rural. These locations have a population of fewer than 1,000 and/or a population density of fewer than 400 people per square kilometre (Statistics Canada, 2016). In 2021, 17.8 percent of Canada's population lived in rural areas (Statistics Canada, 2022b). Although Canada's territories—Nunavut, Yukon, and Northwest Territories—comprise the largest rural areas in Canada, only 0.3 percent of the population lives there (Statistics Canada, 2022b).

**Urban:** Urban areas—also referred to as population centres—are defined by Statistics Canada as having a population greater than 1,000 and a density greater than 400 people per square kilometre. This definition is divided further into small population centres (1,000–29,999 people), medium population centres (30,000–99,999 people), and large population centres (100,000 or more people) (Statistics Canada, 2016).

## DISCUSSION QUESTIONS AND ACTIVITIES

1. Think about your own time in K–12 schooling. How did geography or location influence your learning or other students' learning? What were some benefits and challenges to learning in that location?
2. How important is educational achievement and attainment to human flourishing? Are there other factors that should be considered in the classroom? What are they?

3. Portfolio activity and/or action research project: Observe teachers in a rural or urban school (whichever you did not attend as a K–12 student). What are some similarities and differences you notice in comparison to your own schooling? What are some benefits and challenges to teaching in that location?
4. In your school, look through some textbooks and children's books in classrooms and the library. How are rural communities and people represented? How are northern communities and people represented? What are your own assumptions about these communities?

## NOTES

1. In figure 18.2, the proportions provided include all available student tabulations, including English, French, and French immersion students. Geographical areas—rural, urban, and northern—are included in the data set, although it is unknown what qualifies an area to be considered one of these categories. Using the proportions available, we calculated the number of students who successfully met the expectations for each geographical area.
2. Ontario requires students to earn at least 30 credits, successfully complete the secondary school literacy requirement, and participate in 40 hours of community involvement (Ontario Ministry of Education, 2022). British Columbia requires students to earn a minimum of 80 credits and successfully complete numeracy and literacy assessments (www2.gov.bc.ca/gov/content/education-training/k-12/administration/legislation-policy/public-schools/graduation-requirements). Both Nunavut and the Northwest Territories require students to earn a minimum of 100 credits (www.ssdec.net/graduation-requirements).
3. The Northwest Territories and Nunavut are considered to be completely in the North, based on Statistics Canada's North and South boundary standards, so there are no southern proportions to include (Statistics Canada, 2018).

## REFERENCES

Agbo, S. A. (2007). Addressing school-community relations in a cross-cultural context: A collaborative action to bridge the gap between First Nations and the school. *Journal of Research in Rural Education, 22*, 1–14. https://eric.ed.gov/?id=EJ768961

Alasia, A., & Magnusson, E. (2005). Occupational skill level: The divide between rural and urban Canada. *Rural and Small Town Canada, 6*(2). http://www.publications.gc.ca/site/eng/9.559291/publication.html

Allen, M., & Perreault, S. (2015). Police-reported crime in Canada's provincial North and territories. *Juristat: Canadian Centre for Justice Statistics, 35*(1), 3–43. https://www.proquest.com/docview/1696027350

Bourgeois, M., & Kirby, D. (2012). Post-secondary education and rural women enrolled in liberal arts undergraduate degrees. *Canadian Journal of Higher Education, 42*(3), 143–169. doi.org/10.47678/cjhe.v42i3.1824

Burleigh, D. (2020). Understanding roles and relationships: Teachers' work in a Northern Ontario remote First Nations community. *Canadian Journal of Education, 43*(3), 689–714. https://journals.sfu.ca/cje/index.php/cje-rce/article/view/4085

Byun, S., Meece, J. L., Irvin, M. J., & Hutchins, B. (2012). The role of social capital in educational aspirations of rural youth. *Rural Sociology, 77*(3), 355–379. doi.org/10.1111/j.1549-0831.2012.00086.x

Canadian Council on Learning. (2008). *Closing Canada's rural/urban literacy gap.* http://hdl.voced.edu.au/10707/99799

Cartwright, F., & Allen, M. K. (2002). *Understanding the rural–urban reading gap.* Statistics Canada. https://publications.gc.ca/collections/Collection/CS81-595-MIE2002001E.pdf

Coates, K., & Poelzer, G. (2014). *The next northern challenge: The reality of the provincial north.* Macdonald-Laurier Institute. www.macdonaldlaurier.ca/files/pdf/MLITheProvincial-North04-14-Final.pdf

Cooper, J. (2020a). *Incorporating indigenous cultures and realities in STEM.* Conference Board of Canada. https://fsc-ccf.ca/wp-content/uploads/2020/07/24559_10697_incorporating-indigenous-culture-and-realitiesprimer.pdf

Cooper, J. (2020b). *Curriculum and reconciliation: Introducing Indigenous perspectives into K–12 science.* Conference Board of Canada. https://csse-scee.ca/blog/news-curriculum-and-reconciliation-introducing-indigenous-perspectives-into-k-12-science/

Cooper, J., & Arruda, N. (2020). *Indigenous STEM access programs: Leading post-secondary inclusion.* Conference Board of Canada. www.conferenceboard.ca/in-fact/abstract-aspx/?did=10872

Corbett, M. (2007). Travels in space and place: Identity and rural schooling. *Canadian Journal of Education, 30*(3), 771–792. https://journals.sfu.ca/cje/index.php/cje-rce/article/view/2974

Corbett, M. (2009). No time to fool around with the wrong education: Socialisation frames, timing and high-stakes educational decision making in changing rural places. *Rural Society, 19*(2), 163–177. doi.org/10.5172/rsj.19.2.163

Corbett, M. (2013). What we know and don't know about small schools: A view from Atlantic Canada. *Country School Journal, 1*, 38–52. https://figshare.utas.edu.au/articles/journal_contribution/What_we_know_and_don_t_know_about_small_schools_A_view_from_Atlantic_Canada/22920677/1

Corbett, M. (2014). Toward a geography of rural education in Canada. *Canadian Journal of Education, 37*(3), 1–22. https://journals.sfu.ca/cje/index.php/cje-rce/article/view/1412

Corbett, M., & Gereluk, D. (2020). Conclusion: Insights and provocations for the future of rural education—reclaiming the conversation for rural education. In M. Corbett & D. Gereluk (Eds.), *Rural teacher education* (pp. 301–318). Springer.

Finnie, R., Wismer, A., & Mueller, R. E. (2015). Access and barriers to postsecondary education: Evidence from the youth in transition survey. *Canadian Journal of Higher Education, 45*(2), 229–262. doi.org/10.47678/cjhe.v45i2.2472

Friesen, L., & Purc-Stephenson, R. J. (2016). Should I stay or should I go? Perceived barriers to pursuing a university education for persons in rural areas. *Canadian Journal of Higher Education, 46*(1), 138–155. doi.org/10.47678/cjhe.v46i1.185944

Gilmore, J. (2012). *Trends in dropout rates and the labour market outcomes of young dropouts.* Statistics Canada. www150.statcan.gc.ca/n1/pub/81-004-x/2010004/article/11339-eng.htm

Gollnick, D. M., & Chinn, P. C. (2013). *Multicultural education in a pluralistic society.* Pearson.

Government of Canada. (n.d.). *First Nations education transformation.* www.sac-isc.gc.ca/eng/1476967841178/1531399315241

Government of Manitoba. (n.d.a). *High school graduation rates and student achievement statistics: Middle years assessment.* www.edu.gov.mb.ca/k12/grad_rates/midyrs_a.html

Government of Manitoba. (n.d.b). *Manitoba's K–12 action plan.* www.edu.gov.mb.ca/k12/action_plan/index.html

Government of Northwest Territories. (2019). *JK–12 education review performance measures technical report.* www.ece.gov.nt.ca/sites/ece/files/resources/jk-12_annual_pm_report_2019-2020_en_-_final.pdf

Government of Nunavut. (n.d.). *Department of education.* www.gov.nu.ca/education

Hillier, C., Milne, E., & Aurini, J. (2019). "It's not just helping your kid with homework anymore": The challenges of aligning education policy with parents and teachers. *Canadian Public Policy, 45*(4), 497–510. doi.org/10.3138/cpp.2019-004

Hillier, C., Sano, Y., Zarifa, D., & Haan, M. (2020). Will they stay or will they go? Examining the brain drain in Canada's provincial North. *Canadian Review of Sociology, 57*(2), 174–196. doi.org/10.1111/cars.12276

Hillier, C., Zarifa, D., & Hango, D. (2021). Mind the gaps: Examining youth's reading, math and science skills across Northern and rural Canada. *Rural Sociology, 87*(1), 264–302. doi.org/10.1111/ruso.12401

Kitchenham, A., & Chasteauneuf, C. (2010). Teacher supply and demand: Issues in Northern Canada. *Canadian Journal of Education, 33*(4), 869–896. https://journals.sfu.ca/cje/index.php/cje-rce/article/view/2190

Lamb, D. (2014). Aboriginal early school leavers on- and off-reserve: An empirical analysis. *Canadian Public Policy, 40*(2), 156–165. doi.org/10.3138/cpp.2012-060

Leclerc, K. (2022). *Portrait of women by relative remoteness of their communities, series 2: Educational attainment.* Statistics Canada. www150.statcan.gc.ca/n1/pub/45-20-0002/452000022022001-eng.htm

Looker, E. D. (2010). Can I get there from here? Canadian rural-urban participation rates in post-secondary education. In R. Finnie (Ed.), *Pursuing higher education in Canada: Economic, social and policy dimensions* (pp. 269–292). McGill-Queen's University Press.

Looker, E. D. (2021). The complex mobilities of rural versus urban youth: Mobility into and out of the parental home and one's community. *International Journal of Child, Youth and Family Studies, 12*(2), 48–64. doi.org/10.18357/ijcyfs122202120233

Looker, E. D., & Naylor, T. D. (2009). "At risk" of being rural? The experience of rural youth in a risk society. *Journal of Rural and Community Development, 4*(2), 39–64. https://journals.brandonu.ca/jrcd/article/view/274

Looker, E. D., & Thiessen, V. (2008). *The second chance system: Results from the three cycles of the youth in transition survey.* Human Resources and Social Development Canada. https://publications.gc.ca/site/eng/9.651080/publication.html

Louie, D. W., & Prince, L. (2023). Achieving equity in graduation rates and other indicators of success for Indigenous learners in Canada. *Canadian Journal of Education, 46*(1), 1–32.

Macpherson, E. (2020). *Learning together: STEM outreach programs for Indigenous students.* Conference Board of Canada. www.conferenceboard.ca/product/learning-together-stem-outreach-programs-for-indigenous-students/

Mitton, J., & Murray-Orr, A. (2021). Identifying the impact of culturally relevant pedagogy: Evidence of academic risk-taking in culturally and economically diverse Nova Scotia classrooms. *Canadian Journal of Education, 44*(4), 1084–1115. doi.org/10.53967/cje-rce.v44i4.4811

Newbold, K. B., & Brown, W. M. (2015). The urban-rural gap in university attendance: Determinants of university participation among Canadian youth. *Journal of Regional Science, 55*(4), 585–608. https://econpapers.repec.org/scripts/redir.pf?u=https%3A%2F%2Fdoi.org%2F10.1111%2Fjors.12197;h=repec:bla:jregsc:v:55:y:2015:i:4:p:585-608

Northern Ontario School of Medicine. (2021). *Revolutionising telemedicine, one consult at a time.* www.nosm.ca/2021/10/26/revolutionising-telemedicine-one-consult-at-a-time/

Northwest Territories Education. (n.d.). *Education, culture, and employment.* www.ece.gov.nt.ca/en/services/student-services

Nunavut Bureau of Statistics. (2019). *Nunavut secondary school graduates, 1998/99 to 2016/17.* Department of Education, Government of Nunavut. http://www.stats.gov.nu.ca/Publications/Historical/Education/Nunavut%20Secondary%20School%20Graduates%201999%20to%202017%20(2%20tables)%20R.xlsx

Nussbaum, M. C. (1997). *Cultivating humanity: A classical defense of reform in liberal education.* Harvard University Press.

Nussbaum, M. C. (2009). Creating capabilities: The human development approach and its implementation. *Hypatia, 24*(3), 211–215. doi:10.1111/j.1527-2001.2009.01053.x

Nussbaum, M. C. (2011). *Creating capabilities: The human development approach.* Belknap Press.

Ontario Ministry of Education. (2022). *School board progress reports: Four-year graduation rate.* www.app.edu.gov.on.ca/eng/bpr/allBoards.asp?chosenIndicator=9&submit.x=16&submit.y=13&submit=GO

Peterson, S. S., McIntyre, L., & Heppner, D. (2018). Northern rural and Indigenous teachers' experiences and perceptions of rural teaching and teacher education. *Journal of Teacher Education and Educators, 7*(3), 189–205. https://dergipark.org.tr/en/pub/jtee/issue/43443/530189

Sano, Y., Hillier, C., Haan, M., & Zarifa, D. (2020). Youth migration in the context of rural brain drain: Longitudinal evidence from Canada. *Journal of Rural and Community Development, 15*(4), 100–119. https://journals.brandonu.ca/jrcd/article/view/1850

Sisco, A., Caron-Vuotari, M., Stonebridge, C., Sutherland, G., & Rheaume, G. (2012). *Lessons learned: Achieving positive educational outcomes in northern communities.* Conference Board of Canada. doi.org/10.13140/RG.2.1.2026.6489

Spinu, O., Van Mulligen, K., & Fiser, A. (2021). *Made in Nunavut: Building Inuit skills for northern offshore fisheries and beyond.* Conference Board of Canada.

Statistics Canada. (2016). *Population centre and rural area classification.* www.statcan.gc.ca/en/subjects/standard/pcrac/2016/introduction

Statistics Canada. (2018). *North and South—variant of SGC 2016.* www23.statcan.gc.ca/imdb/p3VD.pl?Function=getVD&TVD=792561

Statistics Canada. (2022a). *Number of students in regular programs for youth, public elementary and secondary schools, by grade and sex.* www150.statcan.gc.ca/t1/tbl1/en/cv!recreate.action?pid=3710000701&selectedNodeIds=1D7,1D11,2D15&checkedLevels=2D1&refPeriods=20180101,20190101&dimensionLayouts=layout3,layout2,layout2,layout2&vectorDisplay=false

Statistics Canada. (2022b). *Population growth in Canada's rural areas, 2016 to 2021.* www12.statcan.gc.ca/census-recensement/2021/as-sa/98-200-x/2021002/98-200-x2021002-eng.cfm

Tremblay, S., Ross, N., & Berthelot, J.-M. (2001). *Factors affecting grade 3 student performance in Ontario: A multilevel analysis.* Statistics Canada. http://www.geog.mcgill.ca/faculty/grade3ontario.pdf

Tuters, S. (2015). Conceptualising diversity in a rural school. *International Journal of Inclusive Education, 19*(7), 685–696. doi.org/10.1080/13603116.2014.964573u

Uppal, S. (2017). *Young men and women without a high school diploma.* Statistics Canada. www150.statcan.gc.ca/n1/pub/75-006-x/2017001/article/14824-eng.htm

Wilson, G. N., & Poelzer, G. (2005). Still forgotten? The politics and communities of the provincial Norths. *The Northern Review: Exploring Human Experience and the North, 25/26*. https://thenorthernreview.ca/index.php/nr/article/view/148

Zarifa, D., Hango, D., & Pizarro Milian, R. (2018). Proximity, prosperity, and participation: Examining access to postsecondary education among youth in Canada's provincial North. *Rural Sociology, 83*(2), 270–314. doi.org/10.1111/ruso.12183

Zarifa, D., Hillier, C., & Hango, D. (2022). Location matters: Education and employment inequalities in Northern and rural Canada. In M. Hwang, E. Grabb, & J. G. Reitz (Eds.), *Social inequality in Canada* (7th ed.) (pp. 102–116). Oxford University Press.

# CHAPTER 19
# Encountering Rural Narrative/Fiction in Teacher Education: Toward a Conversation

*Michael Corbett*

> As storytelling animals—which human beings are—we are fatally addicted to drama.
>
> —Margaret Atwood

## A STORY ABOUT DEVELOPING PROFESSIONAL SENSIBILITIES

When I was composing the introductory chapter for my doctoral dissertation (Corbett, 2001), a study of the tension between formal education and life in an Eastern Canadian coastal community, I thought that nobody had nailed it better than Alistair MacLeod did in his short story "The Boat."

> On the first day of May the boats raced out as they had always done, laden down almost to the gunwales with their heavy cargoes of traps. They were almost like living things as they plunged through the waters of the spring and maneuvered between the still floating icebergs of crystal white and emerald green on their way to the traditional grounds that they sought out every May. And those of us who sat that day in the high school on the hill, discussing the water imagery in Tennyson, watched them as they passed back and forth beneath us until by afternoon the piles of traps which had been stacked on the wharf were no longer visible but were spread about the bottom of the sea....

And the spring wore on and the summer came and school ended in the third week of June and the lobster season on July first and I wished that the two things I loved so dearly did not exclude each other in a manner that was so blunt and too clear. (MacLeod, 2000, pp. 143–145)

MacLeod's story features conflict within the young protagonist about staying or leaving his community, tension between his parents about the value of books and formal education, the touristic gaze, and something of a gender analysis related to differing parental expectations for the protagonist and his sisters. When I was doing this writing, I was still a public elementary school teacher in a coastal community. I spent my days with students still too young to work in the fishery, though many of them were already more or less putting in time until they could fulfill what they seemed to see as their occupational destiny. This is what I wanted to try to understand.

A few years later, I transitioned into a position in teacher education at Acadia University, where many of southwestern Nova Scotia's coastal community teachers are educated. MacLeod saw the tension between the industrial economies and culture(s) of rural communities and the culture(s) and imagined geographies of schooling (Kramer & Jahnke, 2019), and I could see the same thing in teacher education. Our curriculum paid little explicit attention to rural communities, their structure and social organization, their economies, their histories, their distinctive lifeways, or what kind of education might contribute to human flourishing as opposed to achieving pre-defined outcomes and meeting standards. We seemed to have our eyes on the mechanics of lessons and planning, subject-matter teaching, the individual psychologies of our students, learning theory, and largely abstract problems of educational equity and inclusion. A few of my colleagues were working on things like community asset maps and social change projects, but few paid attention to rurality or **place** in their instruction, even though it was well understood that most of our students would teach in nonmetropolitan schools. I, too, struggled to incorporate thinking about community and place in the unit I taught, which was a half-year crash course in educational history, sociology, philosophy, economics, and geography loosely labelled The Foundations and Contexts of Education.

The longer I worked in teacher education, the more I came to understand that questions concerning the distinctiveness of rural communities, and how teachers might bring sensitivity to this distinctiveness, was a secondary concern in our programs. Most of my students themselves grew up in larger centres and had little experience with rural communities. My own experience was similar. I grew up in a mid-sized Nova Scotian industrial town and found my first teaching position in a Cree-Métis community in Northern Manitoba. I was totally unprepared, not in terms of the mechanics of teaching, but in relation to the culture shock I experienced as a new teacher trying to work in a community that bore little resemblance to the places I'd been (Corbett, 2009). I've written a bit about how my liberal arts degree, and particularly my sociology training, prepared me to see teaching as an inquiry into place more than as a knowledge transmission exercise (Corbett, 2010). It was in this community that I started to see teaching both as a fundamentally relational process and as professional inquiry as well as an opportunity to learn about place, space, and history. The context was the history of settlement, the resilience of hunting, fishing, and trapping in the community despite the imposition of a massively disruptive hydro development, and the residue of residential schooling. To say that schooling was viewed with ambivalence is perhaps a generous assessment, and from a community perspective this ambiguity related directly to how schooling related to flourishing, pleasure, and quality of life.

As a result of my early experience, the question of how to support pre-service and early-career teachers in graduate programs for diverse communities—particularly rural, regional, Indigenous, and isolated communities—has been central to my teacher education pedagogy. While I have encouraged and taught the value of a philosophical, historical, geographical, and sociological sensibility for teachers, it has seemed to me that quality fiction often does a much more authentic and convincing job of conveying the richness and nuance of life and a compelling narrative vision of what might constitute flourishing in rural places.

Fiction takes us places, and my sense of the rural has a lot to do with the experience of/in place. But rurality is also a symbolic construction. MacLeod's "The Boat" is obviously dated, but the complexity and sensitivity of his presentation of rural/coastal Nova Scotian people and place remain compelling and provocative to my pre-service teacher candidates precisely because the story is simultaneously historical, contemporary, and inevitably biased and partial. It is this latter point that is perhaps of most value to teacher readers. Fiction reminds us that there are only partial perspectives (Brooks, 2022), and Donna Haraway (1988) and others have long argued for the importance of standpoint and, in educational contexts, what Kieran Egan (1989) calls teaching as storytelling. Such an approach complicates empirical macronarratives and placeless, scientistic notions of curriculum and pedagogy (Cuervo et al., 2019; Fleet & Britt, 2011). Multiple stories are the heart of what we now call equity, diversity, and inclusion. They represent different visions of human flourishing and confront the ideological pitfalls of the single story. Haraway's point is that more partial perspectives will actually improve and enrich science.

I see novels, short stories, poetry, film, drama, and music to be rich windows on the complexity and ordinariness of the culture (Williams, 1958/1989) that teachers work within day by day. Like Yuval Harari (2020), I am not comfortable with the distinction between fiction and nonfiction. When we try to get our heads around what *rural, regional,* or *remote* means, both as concepts and in terms of their educational impact, it is important, I think, to get beyond a singular demographic focus (which is, of course, important) that situates rurality quantitatively in terms of population density and distance from a metropolis (for this definition, see chapter 18). In addition to providing instructive and often controversial depictions of place, quality **rural fiction** also situates characters within sociocultural, historical, and geographical space that stimulates discussion about the complexity of relationships, decision, compulsion, complexity, psychology, and the multiple variables that influence identity, sociality, behaviour, cognition, and learning, which are the central concerns of professional teachers.

## IMAGES OF THE RURAL

Despite the fluidity of the concept of rurality, the field of **rural education** remains relevant because despite ubiquitous urbanization, there are still more or less unique ways of thinking, acting, and being that characterize life in the myriad places we imagine as rural. The scope of rural education scholarship has both globalized (Gristy et al., 2020; Roberts & Fuqua, 2021; Xue et al., 2023) and expanded to include coastal (Kjørholt et al., 2022) and northern (Bæck & Paulgaard, 2012) social spaces. To use Soja's (1996) characterization of space (which draws on that of Lefebvre [1992]), rurality is real and imagined; it is material, perceived, and conceived. Thus, culture is an important window on different life situations, and various forms of cultural production can be important tools in teacher education that can complicate and problematize mythic stereotypes of rural places. A focus on culture is also an important way to help educators and educational researchers think about how rural people, animals, and things are constructed and conceived by powerful cultural actors like novelists and filmmakers (Reynolds, 2017).

Learning not only happens in place; it is also deeply *embedded* in place (Malpas, 2016). Indeed, a preoccupation with place has been a mainstay of rural education for generations (Corbett, 2021). With its explicit or implied critique of an abstracted, placeless, or metrocentric curriculum, the **place-based education** tradition is alive and well in the field of rural teacher education. Yet work in this pedagogical tradition seldom interrogates how the rural is constructed or the multiple levels of representation and meaning the term signifies. Rurality is demography, economy, symbolic representations, and lived culture all tangled together (Corbett, 2016; Green & Reid, 2021). At the level of lived experience, rurality represents established and emerging ways of seeing and of doing things *around here*, which is the visceral experience of place. Symbolically, rurality takes the form of a set of images, stereotypes, and even mythic origin stories about how particular lands were settled, developed, and transformed into what we generally understand to be modern techno-industrial societies. Some key rural imaginaries include the following:

- *Doctrines of discovery*: The idea of rurality emerges from the notion of terra nullius "discovered" by imperial exploiters, later followed by colonial settlers who "developed" societies, "opened up" the land, and accessed resources. The very idea of rurality is part of the systematic erasure of Indigenous sovereignty that has characterized the establishment of the settler state (John & Ford, 2017). Often associated with this rural imagery is the trope of the resolute and armed libertarian rural pioneer, like Kevin Costner's character in *Yellowstone*.
- *Modernization and the urban teleology*: Within dominant modernization theory, social, economic, and political power evolves from the rural to the urban as societies "develop" more or less quickly. Modernization theory imagines history on a teleological trajectory from the country to the city (Williams, 1974), with so-called developed nations leading the way and providing the template for progress in which the rural is an active, potential, or used-up extraction zone (Edelman, 2021; Fraser, 2022; Sassen, 2014). The human faces of this political economic trajectory are the multiple migration stories of those who leave rural places or who are pushed out of them by forces beyond their control.
- *Dependency of the periphery*: Within the colonial capitalist world system, allegedly underdeveloped hinterlands have been exploited to provide primary resources (principally food, trees, fossil fuels, and formerly fur) for the benefit of the "metropolis" (cf. dependency theory, decolonial theory). A key difference between dependency theory and modernization theory is that in dependency theory, the "left behind" geographies are systematically underdeveloped because of the rapacious growth and exploitation of "advanced" societies.
- *Degradation and ecological damage*: Ravaged resource extraction locations such as Appalachian coal regions, Alberta's Athabasca oil sands, and

Western Australia's Pilbara region are denaturalized and turned into what Edelman (2021) calls "rural sacrifice zones," which have a limited lifespan. Resource extraction zones are not often associated with the term *rural*, but they are often situated demographically in regions designated as rural.

- *Decline and degeneracy*: In contrast to high-amenity tourist areas, declining rural areas with aging and outmigrating youth populations have failed to urbanize, modernize, and develop (cf. culture of poverty, demographic macroanalysis, and modernization theory). Some of these places are abandoned resource extraction zones or places depopulated by agricultural, forestry, or fishery mechanization. Aging populations are said to strain services, inhibiting growth and creating a vicious cycle of decline. Rural areas are often depicted in popular culture as isolated, ignorant, dangerous, and degenerate places in which the trope of decline is often nested in a culture of poverty and/or eugenic framing (e.g., "white trash"; Isenberg, 2017; Reynolds, 2017).
- *Escape and therapy*: Select rural and coastal areas have become *high-amenity* lifestyle migration destinations. These places draw on what is called *natural capital* and are constructed as therapeutic and leisure spaces of escape from urban life for privileged elites. In this imaginary, the rural evokes recreational activity, gourmet tourism, manicured landscapes, ocean views, privacy, and natural beauty. Another face of this phenomenon is the gentrification of high-amenity rural locales, which distorts real estate markets with inflated property prices and property tax structures that make it difficult for elders to remain in their homes and for young people to find affordable housing.
- *Micro agriculture*: In conjunction with high-amenity tourism, rural development also takes the form of niche agriculture as regions develop organic, specialty, and alcohol-related forms of farming that cater to elite consumers.
- *Macro agriculture*: Some rural regions specialize in mechanized and technologized industrial agriculture over vast and increasingly centralized tracts of land. While they represent more or less stable agricultural enterprises, these increasingly large operations ironically create a demand for immigrant and temporary foreign labour due to depopulation and the outmigration of local workforces.
- *The heart of the right shift*: With the rise of populist politics that often use rural imagery to signify divisive anti-science, libertarian, religious,

racialized, or cultural tropes such as *replacement theory*, rural places are often situated as spaces of resentment and reaction. For instance, the provocative and polarized red and blue electoral maps published by the *New York Times* graphically illustrate how support for populist politicians is concentrated in rural areas. Seldom are these data presented with any significant analysis. In the maelstrom of contemporary identity politics, many rural people feel excluded, misunderstood, and somewhat lost, a phenomenon that has been analyzed in rural studies, rural education, and sociological literature (Cervone, 2017; Hochschild, 2016; Wuthnow, 2018).

Each of these imaginaries stimulates multiple implicit analyses of why particular geographies have developed as they have, and these often-competing analyses form the terrain of sociopolitical debates over everything from national economic policy to whether to close rural schools. I will return to these representations toward the end of this chapter.

Much Canadian literary criticism has focused on the ideas of wilderness and what Northrop Frye called the "garrison mentality," which is a political and social consciousness formed behind fortress walls where we cower in fear of what is outside in an enormous, alien land (Frye & Hutcheon, 1995). It probably needs to be said that what Frye and other cultural critics of his generation understood of Canada and its culture is the exclusive and exclusionary experience of European settlers. Frye went on to write that the quintessential Canadian identity question is not "Who am I?" but rather "Where is here?" In this sense, much of Canadian literature is rural literature, as some critics argued for generations that images of rurality have dominated the genre (Atwood, 1972).

Janice Kulyk Keefer (1987) focuses on Maritime Canadian fiction, concluding that this principally conservative, nostalgic communitarian rural genre reflects the marginalization of the region in the sociopolitical development of the Canadian state. There are robust debates in Atlantic and Maritime literature (MacLeod et al., 2019) concerning how Atlantic Canadian fiction looks longingly out from the margins both at lost opportunities and at the relative prosperity of Central and Western Canada and its pre-Confederation trading partner, New England. Most significantly, Kulyk Keefer introduces a powerful regional critique of the Central Canadian (Ontario) garrison, bush garden, and survival metanarratives of Frye and Atwood, arguing that different populations experience place and space in distinct ways.

The idea of rurality often conjures images of farming, farmers, and communities that reflect this industry. At the same time, though, most rural demographic designations offer problematic empirical distinctions that focus on population density and distance from metropolitan centres as well as an analysis of commutability of communities. There are, as I have argued, different ruralities, reflecting different natural bioregions, different settlement histories, different Indigenous Knowledge systems related to these bioregions, and different experiences of industrialization and integration into metrocentric capitalist economies—and different artistic and cultural Canadian literature is a particularly rich resource for depictions of the tensions and problems in rural life and in rural schools.

There is also a long-standing debate within the field of rural studies about the continued usefulness of rurality as a concept and as a field of academic inquiry (Bell, 2007; Copp, 1972). Halfacree (1999) addresses the consequences of what he calls the "effacement" of the rural in the context of neoliberal globalization imaginaries where, as Anthony Giddens (1990) put it, place effectively disappears as a relevant sociological concept. Indeed, from at least the writings of Marx and Engels, the spectre of a vanishing rurality has been a staple of modernist social theory (Corbett, 2006). Regardless, *rural* has not vanished from the roster of state demographic categories that are quantitatively drawn from political discourse mobilized in the pursuit of power or from the confluence of lived experience and consumer "lifestyles" in which rurality is a cultural construction, a performance, and a spectacle (Edensor, 2006; Reynolds, 2017).

The very idea of the rural has also been subjected to critical scrutiny by John and Ford (2017), who argue that "the rural is nowhere" (see also Ford, 2020). This work suggests that the rather singular focus on rural culture as some sort of quintessence of the nation is a deeply problematic gloss over how colonial capitalism produces, shapes, and connects geographies. The authors argue that what is required, rather than an identitarian focus on the mythical uniqueness and exceptionality of settler rurality, is a critique of how urbanization and colonialism have shaped space historically. A recent CBC *Ideas* episode made similar arguments about canonical rural author and essayist Wallace Stegner (Jokinen, 2023).

## SELECT RURAL FICTION

I will conclude by offering a meditation on some fictional and autobiographical pieces I have used in teacher education. This chapter is also an invitation to create and populate a resource bank of fictional resources for rural teacher education and for the larger educational conversation relating to equity, diversity, and inclusion. This is not a complete list; rather, I offer some notes toward a conversation in teacher education and an argument that literature can help our students refine their sensibilities and gain deeper insight into the places where they teach through an engagement with stories in which rural teachers and schools play a central role. Much foundational settler Canadian literature is rurally located; it is a particularly rich resource for depictions of the tensions and problems in rural life and in rural schools. This literature is also a window on the experience of people and it provides multiple visions of how they understand themselves and what, for them, constitutes value and a sense of what it is to flourish. I think that rich and carefully constructed fiction can complicate simple stereotypes, simulated deepfakes, and other forms of destructive textual manipulation that are an increasingly poignant threat to human flourishing today.

Richard Wagamese's opus, particularly *Indian Horse* (2012), and Tomson Highway's (1998) *Kiss of the Fur Queen* have broken a path for many Indigenous fictional perspectives on the travesty of Indian residential schools. Until recently, there were surprisingly few fictional works that took up residential schooling or the wider problem of the linguistic, cultural, and social indoctrination process of schooling. This is no longer the case, and in addition to the large number of recently published books aimed at child and youth audiences, adult novels such as Michelle Good's (2020) *Five Little Indians* and Robert Alexie's (2009) *Porcupines and China Dolls* are notable contributions.

Rural teachers and rural schools are central to a great deal of Canadian fiction. There are several classic Canadian novels in which female rural teachers figure prominently, including Gabrielle Roy's (1950/2010) *Where Nests the Water Hen*, Richard Wright's (2001) *Clara Callan*, and Elizabeth Hay's (2011) *Alone in the Classroom*. Each of these pieces illustrate both the gender dynamics in the history of Canadian education and the sense of isolation rural teaching entails. Each is a period piece, yet these books' content can be used to interrogate what it is to be both a woman and a stranger as a rural teacher. Each of these novels depicts place, power, and the dangerous position of women teaching in rural Canada in the mid-20th century. These stories also describe the social location of teachers prior to unionization and contractual protections.

Given that I teach in Nova Scotia, I have tended toward the use of Nova Scotian fiction. Alistair MacLeod lived much of his life in rural Cape Breton and Ontario. His short stories and his single novel, *No Great Mischief* (2001), are beautifully crafted gems. "The Boat," cited above, is a story of a fishing family in which the two girls grow up and leave the village, but the boy's trajectory is more circuitous and involves difficult negotiations with his parents. MacLeod's short stories collected in *Island* (2000) relate to rural education. I think MacLeod struggled with his own fractured life, academic education, and professorship in Ontario set against the backdrop of his upbringing in rural Cape Breton. Many of his stories straddle the Celtic rural culture of his home province and the industrial and professional labour performed by more or less permanent migrants from that place. There is depth but little romance in MacLeod's depictions of people and place, and the struggle to stay is often juxtaposed with the long-standing economic compulsion to leave rural Nova Scotia. This work continues to resonate with the continuing "long commute" migration of Atlantic Canadian workers to Western and Central Canada (Neis & Lippel, 2019; Walsh, 2012).

Tricia Fish's (1999) *New Waterford Girl* is a movie set in rural Nova Scotia that tells the story of a young woman who wants out of her community. The path out, however, is fraught with difficulty. This film looks at culture as "ordinary" (cf. Williams 1958/1989), which is important for pre- and in-service teachers to think about. The work of Lynn Coady is another example of nicely crafted and gritty depictions of life in rural Atlantic Canada. Her *Strange Heaven* (1998) deals with mental illness, gender, and rural family life. *The Saints of Big Harbour* (2002) is the tale of a working-class Cape Breton boy featuring gender and high school micropolitics in a small community. Her book *Mean Boy* (2006) is the story of a rural youth who makes his way to a small regional university and falls under the sway of a mediocre poet/professor. In the latter two texts particularly, the experience of rural secondary and tertiary education figures prominently in the narrative. In *Mean Boy*, there are many educationally related subtexts, including the difficulty of transitioning from village and small-town life to a university environment. I have also used Christy Ann Conlin's (2002) *Heave*, which opens with a young, rural Nova Scotian bride literally running away from her wedding.

Post-colonial literature is another rich source of insight into rural life and into the power dynamics that operate in schools in national contexts emerging from the nightmare of colonialism and exploitation. A great deal of post-colonial literature situates formal education as an ambivalent and conflicted part of the post-colonial experience. The works of Chinua Achebe (*No Longer at Ease* [1960], among many other titles), Ngugi wa Thiong'o (*Petals of Blood* [1986]), and V. S. Naipaul (*A House for Mr. Biswas* [2003]) are classic examples. In terms of contemporary African fiction, I have taught Tsitsi Dangarembga's (2004) *Nervous Conditions*, a book that explores the intersection of colonial violence and the gendered nature of educational access and achievement in rural South Africa. The disgust of the main character, Tambu, is palpable in the text when her brother is given the opportunity to go to school in the city. When she does get to go to school, though, Tambu doesn't know the codes and expectations of the city school. I think this might fit well with discussions on language and diversity. We learn in Dangarembga's second novel, *This Mournable Body* (2020), that Tambu's journey continued into university and a dismal and complicated post-education life.

Neil Bissoondath is a Canadian novelist who grew up in India. Much of his work speaks to the space between two societies and problems of multiculturalism. In 2006 he published a novel entitled *The Unyielding Clamour of the Night* that is set entirely in rural India. It is the story of a teacher who goes to a small village that has seen political conflict and has had a chequered history of educational provision. As the novel progresses, the reader is given an increasingly rich sense of the challenges and the politics of the place, blended with the teacher's own development. The conclusion is arresting but not entirely unexpected.

*Mr. Pip* is a beautifully written novel by Lloyd Jones (2008). The story is told by a young girl about her teacher. The teacher is an unlikely schoolmaster pressed into service by political conflict in Papua New Guinea in the 1990s. The story is stark, violent, redemptive, and ultimately ambivalent with respect to the way education is imagined in the context of a society simultaneously in transition and in conflict.

Each national context, of course, has its own rural literature, and I hope others will contribute to the conversation by suggesting materials that reflect the tensions in rural places and in rural schools around the world.

Finally, while I have not used them yet in my own teaching, graphic novels have become a mainstay genre of contemporary fiction. Two poignant recent offerings are Akiwenzie-Damm et al.'s (2019) *This Place*, which is a rich historical anthology of Indigenous stories of Turtle Island told across 150 years. The stories are diverse but unified by their focus on place, spiritual power, human dignity, and survival in the face of tremendous challenge. The brilliant illustrations bring to life 10 situated narratives about Indigenous resilience in Canada. Returning to Alistair MacLeod's Cape Breton–based diasporic fiction, Kate Beaton's (2022) *Ducks* begins with a young woman pondering her future and the apparent inevitability of having to leave her rural home despite her university education. The book depicts her journey to the Canadian "oil patch" in Northern Alberta and to the stark isolation, loneliness, and danger of an industrial work camp. This graphic novel offers a biographical tale of the world of work that awaits many young rural Nova Scotians, and indeed, many of my students have found employment in the in-between "long commute" world, working between Atlantic Canada and "out west." *Ducks* offers a poignant gender counterpoint to MacLeod's classic migration stories.

## CONCLUSION

The list of rural fiction that I introduced here in the context of teacher education is a sample of novels I have used productively to stimulate conversations about place with pre-service and graduate teachers. This partial list is an invitation to others to contribute the books they have used. I argue here that pre-service teachers, many of whom will start their teaching careers in rural areas, as well as rurally located graduate teachers pursuing master's degrees will benefit from an engagement with regional fiction.

It is now well established in Canada that teacher education at all levels normally requires an undergraduate degree and at least an additional year of university-based teacher education (although two years is more common). This is a recognition that at least an undergraduate disciplinary formation is basic to the preparation of professional teachers, who are expected to master more than what might be called the instrumental didactic skills taught historically in teachers' colleges. Professionalism is about judgment and refining a practitioner's ability to understand the unpredictability, uniqueness, and complexity of situations and people. I would contend that one part of the academic and practical formation of pre-service teachers in rural regional teacher education programs should include reading and discussing rural-regional fiction to refine sensibilities and connect teachers with compelling and imaginative depictions of people and place as well as how they enact spatially sensitive teaching practice.

But this is all somewhat abstract. How might teacher educators engage in productive readings of these books? I suggest that one answer might be to use my notion of rural imaginaries set against the reader's lived experience and pedagogical and curricular intentions. I think a key challenge for teacher preparation is to connect the stories pre-service teachers bring to the classroom to dialogue with as many other stories as possible. A teacher who reads a lot of fiction should be a teacher better prepared for the messiness of professional practice in unfamiliar contexts. The more stories a teacher knows, the less likely they will be to accept a single story and the more likely they will be to ask critical questions and see complex relationships. A rich knowledge of multiple stories seems to me intimately connected to what constitutes human flourishing, a life well lived, and indeed, an educated person. It is my hope that these reader-teachers will problematize rural stereotypes and subsequently become interested in the beautiful and rich rural-regional places where teacher shortages are chronic.

## KEY TERMS

**Place:** An extremely complex concept that seems entirely ordinary. Place can be understood in terms of physical, social, and cultural geographies. Place is never absolute and is fundamentally relational, and readers are encouraged to remember that all places we can imagine contain other places, while at the same time, all places contain a multitude of other places.

**Place-based education:** This is a movement that draws its roots from several philosophical sources. The fundamental notion is that all education begins with experience and all experience is an engagement with material life. Place-based educators strive to connect educational experiences to the immediate experience of place. There are debates about what counts as place (see the definition above) and how places relate, which has caused some place-based educators to write about place-sensitive, place-conscious (Greenwood, 2013), or place-relational education (Corbett, 2021).

**Rural education:** A field of study that investigates experience and cultures affecting education actors in nonmetropolitan places as well as the structures and systems that impact education delivery in those geographies.

**Rural fiction:** While the lines that separate rural and nonrural as well as fiction and nonfiction are somewhat fuzzy, rural fiction can be understood as works of imaginative storytelling set in a nonmetropolitan space.

## DISCUSSION QUESTIONS AND ACTIVITIES

1. What is your lived experience of rurality, and how does this book challenge and/or affirm that experience?
2. Which of the nine rural imaginaries listed in this chapter do you find operating in the text? How? Are there other imaginaries operating as well?
3. How might you use this fictive reflection to enrich your teaching?
4. Group activity: Work in groups based on the distance between your community of origin and a city (e.g., urban, suburban, rural but within an hour's drive, a one- to three-hour drive, and a drive greater than three hours). Your task is to imagine your community as a character and to write a character sketch describing the community as a teacher.

## REFERENCES

Achebe, C. (1960). *No longer at ease*. Fawcett.

Akiwenzie-Damm, K., Assu, S., Mitchell, B., Qitsualik-Tinsley, R., Qitsualik-Tinsley, S., Robertson, D. A., Sinclair, N. J., Storm, J., Camp, R. V., Vermette, K., Vowel, C., & Elliott, A. (2019). *This place: 150 years retold*. HighWater.

Alexie, R. (2009). *Porcupines and China dolls*. Theytus Books.

Atwood, M. (1972). *Survival: A thematic guide to Canadian literature*. Anansi.

Bæck, U., & Paulgaard, G. (2012). *Rural futures? Finding one's place within changing labour markets*. Orkana Akademisk.

Beaton, K. (2022). *Ducks: Two years in the oil sands*. Drawn & Quarterly.

Bell, M. M. (2007). The two-ness of rural life and the ends of rural scholarship. *Journal of Rural Studies, 23*, 402–415. doi.org/10.1016/j.jrurstud.2007.03.003

Bissoondath, N. (2006). *The unyielding clamour of the night*. Bloomsbury.

Brooks, P. (2022). *Seduced by story: The use and abuse of narrative*. New York Review Books.

Cervone, J. A. (2017). *Corporatizing rural education: Neoliberal globalization and reaction in the United States*. Palgrave Macmillan.

Coady, L. (1998). *Strange heaven*. Goose Lane.

Coady, L. (2002). *The saints of big harbour*. Houghton Mifflin.

Coady, L. (2006). *Mean boy*. Anchor.

Conlin, C. A. (2002). *Heave*. Anchor.

Copp, J. (1972). Rural sociology and rural development. *Rural Sociology, 37*, 515–533. https://eric.ed.gov/?id=EJ069475

Corbett, M. (2001). *Learning to leave: The irony of schooling in a coastal community* [Doctoral dissertation, University of British Columbia].

Corbett, M. (2006). Educating the country out of the child and educating the child out of the country: An excursion in spectrology. *Alberta Journal of Educational Research, 52*(4), 289–301. https://figshare.utas.edu.au/articles/journal_contribution/Educating_the_country_out_of_the_child_and_educating_the_child_out_of_the_country_An_excursion_in_spectrology/22924856/1

Corbett, M. (2009). Rural schooling in mobile modernity: Returning to the places I've been. *Journal of Research in Rural Education, 24*(7), 1–13. https://eric.ed.gov/?id=EJ848520

Corbett, M. (2010). Backing the right horse: Teacher education, sociocultural analysis and literacy in rural education. *Teaching and Teacher Education, 26*(1), 82–86. doi.org/10.1016/j.tate.2009.08.001

Corbett, M. (2016). Reading Lefebvre from the periphery: Thinking globally about the rural. In A. K. Schulte & B. Walker-Gibbs (Eds.), *Self-Studies in Rural Teacher Education* (pp. 141–156). Springer.

Corbett, M. (2021). Re-placing rural education: AERA Special Interest Group on Rural Education Career Achievement Award Lecture. *Journal of Research in Rural Education, 37*(3), 1–14. doi.org/10.26209/jrre3703

Cuervo, H., Corbett, M., & White, S. (2019). Disrupting rural futures and teachers' work. In S. Pinto, S. Hannigan, B. Walker-Gibbs, & E. Charlton (Eds.), *Interdisciplinary unsettlings of place and space: Conversations, investigations and research* (pp. 87–100). Springer.

Dangarembga, T. (2004). *Nervous conditions*. Ayebia Clarke.

Dangarembga, T. (2020). *This mournable body*. Graywolf.

Edelman, M. (2021). Hollowed out heartland, USA: How capital sacrificed communities and paved the way for authoritarian populism. *Journal of Rural Studies, 82*, 505–517. doi.org/10.1016/j.jrurstud.2019.10.045

Edensor, T. (2006). Performing rurality. In P. Cloke, T. Marsden, & P. Mooney (Eds.), *Handbook of rural studies* (pp. 484–495). Sage. doi.org/10.4135/9781848608016.n35

Egan, K. (1989). *Teaching as story telling: An alternative approach to teaching and curriculum in the elementary school*. University of Chicago Press.

Fish, T. (1999). *New Waterford girl*. Genius Products.

Fleet, A., & Britt, C. (2011). Seeing spaces, inhabiting places. In D. Harcourt, B. Perry, & T. Waller (Eds.), *Researching young children's perspectives: Debating the ethics and dilemmas of educational research with children* (pp. 143–162). Routledge.

Ford, D. R. (2020). Educating for social justice. In R. Cordova & W. Reynolds (Eds.), *Afterword: Violent cartographies and the ontology of the rural* (pp. 330–337). Brill.

Fraser, N. (2022). *Cannibal capitalism: How our system is devouring democracy, care, and the planet and what we can do about it*. Verso.

Frye, N., & Hutcheon, L. (1995). *The bush garden: Essays on the Canadian imagination*. Anansi.

Giddens, A. (1990). *The consequences of modernity*. Stanford University Press.

Good, M. (2020). *Five little Indians*. HarperCollins.

Green, B., & Reid, J.-A. (2021). Rural social space: A conceptual-analytical framework for rural (teacher) education and the rural human services. In P. Roberts & M. Fuqua (Eds.), *Ruraling education research* (pp. 29–46). Springer.

Greenwood, D. A. (2013). A critical theory of place-conscious education. In R. B. Stevenson, M. Brody, J. Dillon, & A. E. J. Wals (Eds.), *International handbook of research on environmental education* (pp. 93–100). Routledge.

Gristy, C., Hargreaves, L., & Kučerová, S. R. (Eds.). (2020). *Educational research and schooling in rural Europe: An engagement with changing patterns of education, space and place*. Information Age.

Halfacree, K. (1999). *A new space or spatial effacement? Alternative futures for the post-productivist countryside*. CABI.

Harari, Y. (2020). *21 lessons for the 21st century*. Signal.

Haraway, D. (1988). Situated knowledges: The science question in feminism and the privilege of partial perspective. *Feminist Studies, 14*(3), 575–599. doi.org/10.2307/3178066

Hay, E. (2011). *Alone in the classroom*. McClelland & Stewart.

Highway, T. (1998). *Kiss of the Fur Queen*. Doubleday.

Hochschild, A. R. (2016). *Strangers in their own land: Anger and mourning on the American right*. New Press.

Isenberg, N. (2017). *White trash: The 400-year untold history of class in America*. Penguin.

John, K. D., & Ford, D. (2017). The rural is nowhere: Bringing indigeneity and urbanism into educational research. *Counterpoints, 494*, 3–14. https://www.jstor.org/stable/45177650

Jokinen, T. (2023, February 6). *Why Wallace Stegner believed the American dream was a death sentence for the West*. CBC. www.cbc.ca/radio/ideas/wallace-stegner-protect-wild-west-1.6716689

Jones, L. (2008). *Mister Pip*. Dial Press.

Kjørholt, A. T., Bessell, S., Devine, D., Gaini, F., & Spyrou, S. (Eds.). (2022). *Valuing the past, sustaining the future? Exploring coastal societies, childhood(s) and local knowledge in times of global transition*. Springer.

Kramer, C., & Jahnke, H. (2019). Geographies of schooling: An introduction. In H. Jahnke, C. Kramer, & P. Meusburger (Eds.), *Geographies of schooling* (pp. 1–16). Springer.

Kulyk Keefer, J. K. (1987). *Under Eastern eyes: A critical reading of Maritime fiction*. University of Toronto Press.

Lefebvre, H. (1992). *The production of space*. Wiley-Blackwell.

MacLeod, A., Thompson, P., & Chafe, P. (2019). Passing: Herb Wyile and the future of Atlantic-Canadian literary criticism. *Studies in Canadian Literature, 43*(2), 5–24. https://journals.lib.unb.ca/index.php/SCL/article/view/29288

MacLeod, A. (2000). *Island: The complete stories*. McClelland & Stewart.

MacLeod, A. (2001). *No great mischief: A novel*. Vintage.

Malpas, J. (2016). Placing understanding/understanding place. *Sophia, 56*, 1–13. doi.org/10.1007/s11841-016-0546-9

Naipaul, V. S. (2003). *A house for Mr. Biswas*. Vintage.

Neis, B., & Lippel, K. (2019). Occupational health and safety and the mobile workforce: Insights from a Canadian research program. *New Solutions: A Journal of Environmental and Occupational Health Policy, 29*(3), 297–316. doi.org/10.1177/1048291119876681

Reynolds, W. (2017). Rural place: Media, violent cartographies, and chaotic disruptions. In W. Reynolds (Ed.), *Forgotten places: Critical studies in rural education* (pp. 31–44). Peter Lang.

Roberts, P., & Fuqua, M. (Eds.). (2021). *Ruraling education research: Connections between rurality and the disciplines of educational research*. Springer.

Roy, G. (2010). *Where nests the water hen*. New Canadian Library. (Original work published in 1950).

Sassen, S. (2014). *Expulsions: Brutality and complexity in the global economy*. Belknap Press.

Soja, E. W. (1996). *Thirdspace: Journeys to Los Angeles and other real-and-imagined places*. Blackwell.

Thiong'o, N. (1986). *Petals of blood*. Heinemann International.

Wagamese, R. (2012). *Indian horse*. Douglas & McIntyre.

Walsh, D. E. (2012). Using mobility to gain stability: Rural household strategies and outcomes in long-distance labour mobility. *Journal of Rural and Community Development, 7*(3), Article 3. https://journals.brandonu.ca/jrcd/article/view/613

Williams, R. (1989). Culture is ordinary. In *Resources of hope: Culture, democracy, socialism* (pp. 3–14). Verso. (Original work published in 1958).

Williams, R. (1974). *The country and the city*. Oxford University Press.

Wright, R. (2001). *Clara Callan*. HarperCollins Canada.

Wuthnow, R. (2018). *The left behind: Decline and rage in rural America*. Princeton University Press.

Xue, E., Li, J., & Li, X. (2023). Mapping historical trends of sustainable rural education policy development in China. *Educational Philosophy and Theory, 55*(2), 217–226. doi.org/10.1080/00131857.2021.2008358

# PART X

## INTERSECTIONALITY: TEACHING THE WHOLE CHILD IN CONSIDERATION OF HUMAN FLOURISHING

# CHAPTER 20
# Implicit Inequities in School Practices: Interdisciplinary Perspectives

*Monique Somma, Kim Radersma, Jhonel Morvan, and Leigh Potvin*

As four experienced educators and researchers from various school boards in Canada and the United States, we aim, in this chapter, to challenge the ways that inequities persist in multifaceted ways in the education system. We critically examine injustices that exist in schools through four stories from our own teaching experiences that demonstrate various inequities we witnessed that affected our students daily and were often perpetuated by complicit teachers, even ourselves. We have and continue to wrestle with the agency and power teachers have in allowing inequities to remain unchallenged. Recognizing that our roles as educators are political and that we are either working against inequities or promoting them, we invite educators to consider a critical lens in their practice.

As discussed in the introduction to this volume, Gibson and Grant (2010) describe a commitment to flourishing in the context of education to be one that "encourages all students—regardless of race, ethnicity, socioeconomic status, language, religion, or gender—to imagine and experience flourishing lives and to discover and cultivate individual talents, interest, aptitudes, and commitments" (cited in Grant, 2012, p. 915). Furthermore, Grant (2012) and Nussbaum (1997) argue that human flourishing is not just a goal or an act for oneself; rather, human flourishing is for our communities, both local and global. In the context of education, teachers and administrators "must work intentionally to work against any barriers that would limit the flourishing of students" (Bokhorst-Heng & Hillier, introduction to this volume), particularly those who have been marginalized. The vignettes in this chapter highlight real-life teachers and the challenges they have faced and worked through to ensure that flourishing for marginalized students persists in schools.

## IMPLICIT INEQUITIES IN SCHOOL PRACTICES

"Every student has the opportunity to succeed, regardless of ancestry, culture, ethnicity, gender, gender identity, language, physical and intellectual ability, race, religion, sex, sexual orientation, socioeconomic status or other factors" (Ontario Ministry of Education, 2014, p. 8).

Classrooms are fraught with relations of power among students and teachers that reproduce social norms (Kumashiro, 2004). As Kumashiro (2004) maintains, "it is not a question of whether schools should be addressing issues of oppression. Schools are always and already addressing oppression, often by reinforcing it or at least allowing it to continue playing out unchallenged, and often without realizing that they are doing so" (p. xxxvi). The oppression Kumashiro names here relates directly to the ignorance and complicity that we (the authors) have witnessed daily in our teaching experiences when both teachers and students were confronted with difference. According to Minow (1991), difference is created as long as people have something or someone to compare to. The concept of difference and categorizing items and people based on a trait such as ability is deeply embedded in our schemas. Minow (1991) points out that we teach children to compare difference from an early age, and in order to change the way adults and society view difference as being something less than themselves, these schemas need to be altered. When the *normal* curriculum, *normal* gender roles, *normal* whiteness, and *normal* able bodies that abound in schools across Canada and the United States are uncontested and assumed to be representative of the population, the margins are then assumed *abnormal*. The children who do not see themselves represented in the curriculum or in school personnel, who are held to lower expectations, who do not neatly fit into a clear gender expectation, who are not white, and who are not able-bodied often sit on the sidelines. Teachers who do not understand their participation in these injustices are complicit in perpetuating oppression and impact the child's ability to flourish.

Educators should and can be challenged to disrupt the normalized oppression that surrounds them. We believe that when teachers receive invitations to reconsider teaching practices around them that they have taken for granted, transformative change can occur. Mezirow's transformative learning theory (2018) offers much theoretical hope for this prospect. Holding that adults can transform their thinking using rational and noncoercive dialogue, his theory supports our belief that teachers can challenge their roles when and if they recognize their complicity in oppressive systems. In acknowledging and unlearning privilege as a form of dominance of one group over another (Sensoy & DiAngelo, 2012), activist educators can confront systems of inequity in schools.

Despite good intentions, teachers are commonly drawn to the status quo: the norms, rules, skills, and values that are often taken for granted and unchallenged (Schon, 1983). In our collective experience, teachers often become defensive and self-protective when in a position where norms are being challenged. Schools,

### Box 20.1: Theoretical Frameworks

**Critical Race Theory**

Arising out of the discontent of legal scholars of colour in the United States, critical race theory became a useful theory in education, mainly because it acknowledges that racism is inherent and salient in North America and thrives, mostly unattested and unquestioned (Gillborn, 2005; Ladson-Billings, 1998).

**Queer Theory**

Queer theory emphasizes multiple ways of knowing and being in the world. As a theoretical framework, it resists the gender binary and the set of normalizing assumptions that go along with heterosexism and heteronormativity.

**Critical Whiteness Theory**

Evolving out of critical race theory, critical whiteness studies (CWS) focus on "problematizing the normality of hegemonic whiteness, arguing that in doing so whites deflect, ignore, or dismiss their role, racialization, and privilege in race dynamics" (Matias, 2014, p. 291).

**Critical Disability Theory**

Critical disability theory focuses on a notion that problems lie deeper than the structures that prevent access. When we fail to counteract the unequal position of people with disabilities in society as a whole, including schools, we perpetuate social stigma and all of the attitudes that sustain the exclusion of people with disabilities (Stein, 2007).

The following sections discuss more specifically how each of these four areas of inequity exist in schools and what factors control each individual inequity within the education system.

as social systems, are self-reinforcing, motivated to maintain an equilibrium; as such, they are innately resistant to change and often defensive when challenged with change (Schon, 1983). By examining critical theory (Burghardt, 2011; Horkheimer, 1972; Schon, 1983), this chapter will attempt to challenge the ways in which inequities persist in multifaceted ways in the education system, with particular focus on race, gender, and ability. These identities can be examined from a theoretical standpoint, with critical theory providing an explanation of how these unequal power relations persist in education.

We examine more closely, from a critical theory perspective, the connectedness of the various inequities that exist in the education system, as evident in the race and whiteness, disability, and queer theories that inform this chapter (see Box 20.1; see also chapter 2 and the concluding chapter in this volume).

## CRITICAL WHITENESS (K. RADERSMA)

As a high school English teacher for many years, I did not consider my white skin to be related to the obvious achievement gaps that existed between my **white** students and my racialized students, most commonly measured by student performance on tests and graduation rates. This gap was clearly visible to me but has also been proven by an abundance of research in recent decades. I considered myself neutral and, in my more noble moments, even altruistic. I had chosen to focus my career on helping (as I understood helping) my racialized students succeed and never detected my white identity to be at all problematic in my ability to do this.

Thinking back on those years, I see that my Black and Brown students knew much more about **whiteness**, white identity, and **white privilege** than I did. My students entrusted me with countless stories over the years: from Sikh students who shared intimate and frightening stories about bullying related to their ethnic identity, to Black female students who taught me how challenging it is for them to resist conforming to standards of white beauty, to Latino students who shared their feelings of not being valued in so-called normal society and resigned to being relegated to the sidelines—among many others. My students' experiences of being marginalized, dismissed, and abused were overwhelming and horrific. However, as I listened to them, I did not yet have an understanding of my white identity and what it entailed—how whiteness perpetuated the system that caused them this harm. I did not listen with a sense of responsibility that there was anything I, *personally*, could do to change. I listened to help them, not realizing that I needed to change *myself*. The familiar canary in the coal mine has become an apt metaphor for me as I perceive my own racial identity as a white person in **white supremacy** culture. In my experiences as a high school teacher, I focused on how to help the metaphorical canaries survive the toxic coal mine as I listened to my students and tried to equip them to survive—and somehow thrive—in a toxic environment. Analyzing my own white identity and white supremacy culture has instead shifted my focus to a critique of the toxic mine *itself* by looking for ways to interrupt white dominance, question structural inequities, and challenge the assumptions related to the normative power of whiteness.

I choose to believe that my former students entrusted me with the stories they offered with hope that I could eventually come to understand—and alleviate—their suffering in a way that was not merely paternalistic but revolutionary. I cannot help but share their hope that white teachers can participate in the urgent work of dismantling white supremacy.

There is no uncomplicated definition of the word *white*. It is ironic as much as it is complex. Using *white* as a race signifier runs the risk of reinforcing "uncomplicated, simplistic understandings of race" (Tanner, 2014, p. 183) or identifying an intentional community, like the KKK. White people often prefer to see themselves as individuals and not as members of a culture and, moreover, as individuals whose identities are fluid and constantly shifting. *White* is undoubtedly a problematic identifier, which can "alienate and stigmatize" people from engaging in topics related to racial justice (Bobo, 2001, p. 268).

For clarity, please review the Key Terms section for help in understanding systemic racism. These definitions are intended to be understood as fluid, not fixed. I offer them as a guide to orient this discussion.

Most of the teaching workforce in Ontario is white. In general, racialized teachers are vastly under-represented in the teaching profession in Canada (Abawi, 2021). Disturbing data in Ontario reveal that the hiring of racialized teachers has not kept pace with the increasingly racialized student population (Kodama, 2015). The Ontario Employment Equity Act (1993) was repealed by the Conservative government of Mike Harris, which came to power in 1995. According to the 2006 census, 9.5 percent of the teacher population in Ontario is made up of visible minority teachers, whereas 22.8 percent of the population in Ontario is visible minority (Ryan et al., 2009). This number is expected to reach 48 percent of the population by 2036 (Ontario Ministry of Education, 2017a). Research has proven that having racialized teachers is advantageous to schools for many reasons (Ryan et al., 2009), yet despite policies in place to mandate equitable hiring practices, Ontario has slipped further and further away from a teaching force that matches its population, thus perpetuating "coercive power relations" (Cummins, 2009, p. 261) between white teachers (dominant group) and their students of colour (subordinate group) and reproducing the social norms of a white-dominated country (Cummins, 2009; Matias, 2014). In fact, there has been an increasing dominance of white women in the teaching profession (Feistritzer, 2011). Contributing to this problem is the fact that white teachers act to silence critical discourse about race. Dei (2000) also confirms this: "academic discussions on race are often avoided, negated, or erased in schools" (p. 30).

The following are some considerations to keep in mind as you move forward in your teaching career:

- If you are a white teacher, I invite you to examine the metaphor of the toxic mine and consider how you view racialized students and families. Ask yourself if you consider them people to be saved or humans who are valuable in society (see chapter 2 for more on white saviourism). If you have not already considered your white identity, I invite you to interrogate it and think critically about how whiteness has positioned you as normal and unbiased, as a benevolent benefactor.
- To those of you who are racialized, I am not in a position to offer you advice from my lived experience as a white woman; however, there are many who are. I encourage you to seek mentors in your school board. If a structured system of mentorship with racialized administrators or more experienced teachers does not already exist, seek out racialized mentors who can validate your experiences and help you navigate barriers related to systemic racism. Lastly, know your rights, especially related to your right to be free from discrimination and harassment. Most school boards and districts have clear policies in place related to the human rights legislation in your province or territory.
- Finally, to all, engage in a pedagogy of resistance to the larger systems that subtly and systemically invite us to uphold racial hierarchies. Be attentive to the spaces and cultures in schools, not just in your classrooms, but in the breakrooms and lunchrooms as well. We all have a responsibility to create safe, inclusive, and welcoming spaces that are free from discrimination and harassment, spaces where all teachers have the ability to flourish in their careers. This requires us to be willing to have honest conversations about how race and racism have impacted us all.

## DISABILITY (M. SOMMA)

The foundational understanding that the human rights of people with disabilities are not inherently upheld by society was a concept that I considered throughout my lifetime, but I did not fully understand the social, economic, and political underpinnings of these injustices until more recently in my academic career. As a special education classroom teacher for more than 10 years, I had developed views and beliefs around the unjust treatment of people with disabilities that impacted the way I interacted with the students in my class. My perception of what it meant for my students to be successful was more about providing opportunities for positive school experiences, such as exciting and interactive activities, rather than providing inclusive opportunities. Over the course of the school year, my understandings about what it meant for students with exceptionalities to really be included became more about how the students developed a sense of belonging and community and less about parallel academic programming. A pedagogical shift began in which curriculum became a tool for inclusion rather than a means of othering students who did not have the same academic capabilities.

As I continued to research and examine the discrepancy between achievement and success, I recognized the challenges faced by students with exceptionalities to be more about teacher pedagogy and less about disability. Under critical disability theory, the human rights approach identifies that the problems that exist for individuals with exceptionalities are a result of the structures of systems that society has put in place (Harpur, 2012). When an individual with an exceptionality cannot access a service as a result of a system that is exclusive, this system itself must change in order to allow access for all people regardless of a disability (Harpur, 2012; United Nations, 2007). Systems exist based on the beliefs of those who develop and maintain them. In considering a school being a system, one must consider the individuals (the educators and staff) working in the schools and the belief systems they hold as they relate to disability and teaching practice or pedagogy. A rights-based model of inclusion takes the position that each child, regardless of ability, has a right to participate fully in all aspects of school, including being in a classroom with their peers and taking part in extracurricular activities (United Nations, 2007; Harpur, 2012).

In my own classroom, my conclusion was that although a student was physically in the class most of the day, which had increased their opportunity for interaction with peers, interaction with peers had not been facilitated or supported, and their belongingness in the class was not being fully promoted. I had only initiated a movement toward inclusion in my classroom. This pivotal moment was by no means a complete transformation, yet it marked an initial step toward my ever-developing personal beliefs and understanding of inclusion. I began thinking about inclusion not merely as a student occupying a space, but rather as the alignment of a student's autonomy and sense of belonging. Thinking critically about how environments can be created so that all students can be successful, regardless of their ability (Bennett, 2020), became an essential component of each day in my classroom. In pondering this challenge, there were many questions to be considered, such as *What can I do to make the classroom more inclusive? What does inclusion mean to me?* I came to the understanding that it was not about how much time the student spent in the classroom but rather the quality of interaction that occurred during that time. I continue to reflect on the following:

- Education must adopt a strengths-based approach to students and presume competence. An overarching issue for students with exceptionalities that impacts their flourishing is the ways that education systems focus on individuals as having disabilities rather than on individuals being different or having different needs. The way any student is perceived by members of school organizations is critical to their successful experience in school. The language used to identify, program, and plan for students with exceptionalities and to support in policy is often exclusionary in nature (see also chapters 16 and 17).
- Policy must support inclusion. Despite the notion that special education policies in Ontario are based on Bill 82 and developed to meet the needs of students with exceptionalities, inequity persists. Policies such as Education for All (Ontario Ministry of Education, 2013) and *Special K–12: A Guide for Educators* (Ontario Ministry of Education, 2017c) are in place to ensure that school boards meet the needs of students with exceptionalities by enforcing identification and placement, even though the language within the policies is exclusionary in itself and labelling is essential. From a rights-based perspective, the fault in these policies lies in a focus on identifying exceptionality first and then discussing differentiated programming. We are concerning ourselves with labelling what is *abnormal* in order to establish how to *fix* it in the context of education. Within these types of policies, the "dilemma of difference" reveals an education system situated in "complex and subtle deterministic assumptions about difference, deviance and ability that produced exclusion in the first instance" (Florian, 2007, p.10). Although its discourse is inclusive in

nature, *Special Education K–12: A Guide for Educators* (Ontario Ministry of Education, 2017c) reproduces exclusion by constructing and categorizing students as "different" from their peers and by institutionalizing unequal access to education.

- Schools must be models of inclusion. When systems fail to counteract the unequal position of people with disabilities in society as a whole, including schools, we perpetuate social stigma and all of the attitudes that sustain the exclusion of people with disabilities. Teachers need opportunities to challenge their beliefs about disability and examine their practices to shift practice. When teachers can model inclusive language and behaviour, classrooms and schools can be places where all children can flourish.

## STRAIGHT PRIVILEGE IN SCHOOLS (L. POTVIN)

Despite the role that gay-straight alliances (GSAs) play in creating safe spaces, schools continue to be dominated by unsafe experiences for 2SLGBTQI+ youth (Taylor & Peter, 2011; Taylor et al., 2015). GSAs are important; they provide an opportunity and space for youth to gather in an environment where they can be celebrated. The efforts of teachers and students who start, maintain, and participate in GSAs are often applauded (Kitchen & Bellini, 2013; Short, 2014), and this is justified and warranted. However, the existence of a GSA in a school is not de facto evidence that all gender- and sexuality-based oppression has been solved (Meyer, 2007). GSAs are an important first step but not the final one in the fight for greater gender/sexual equity in schools. Using the work of queer theorists (Britzman, 1995; Foucault, 1978), I argue that schools (and the people in them) need to problematize the role that straight privilege plays in ordering social life in schools (Ingraham & Saunders, 2016). By addressing privilege and not only the oppression faced by 2SLGBTQI+, schools can encourage straight people to recognize the way their lives are ordered differently than those of queer people in schools (Rodriguez & Pinar, 2007). An important reality of GSAs in schools is that straight teachers are most often the leaders for 2SLGBTQI+ youth and their allies (Griffin & Ouellett, 2002). Most often, in Ontario, GSAs are led by straight white women (Kitchen & Bellini, 2013).

I am a former secondary school teacher who now teaches in a post-secondary institution. In the early years of my teaching career, students in my school recruited me to be the teacher lead/staff advisor for the GSA. At the time when the GSA was getting up and running, I had a student in my classes whom I will call Greg.

To say that we had a tense relationship as student-teacher and as individuals is an understatement. Greg liked to challenge authority, and he was good at it. I was teaching him grade 10 civics when the first **International Day of Pink** event was hosted at the school. I was so pleased with the success of the spirited event. Success, for me, was measured in the sheer number of participants (teacher and student) and the general air of excitement. There truly was a wave of pink throughout the school that day, there was a lot of participation in lunchtime activities, and the tone in the school was positive and happy. I taught Greg after lunch. When we all gathered in the class, I was happy to see many of my students wearing pink in support of the event, including Greg. The primary activity in class that day was a group assignment where students were instructed to create an ideal island society, including five guiding laws and/or rules. The activity was used as a way to get students to think about governance and was a creative entry point into teaching about the Canadian Charter of Rights and Freedoms (key parts of the curriculum). Greg, a natural leader, was nominated the presenter for his group to share their ideas. He stood up, in his pink shirt, and read out his group's five rules. The first four rules I can no longer remember, but the last one I will remember forever. Proudly, Greg read out, "No gay people allowed. Will be sent out to sea to hopefully drown." The group, including Greg, giggled as they read their rules. It is possible that they were looking for a reaction from me. I was horrified at the hurtfulness in their words. I tried, as calmly as possible, to address why that particular law was not acceptable. I pointed out the hypocrisy of wearing a pink T-shirt on the International Day of Pink and creating a homophobic rule in a group activity. I asked Greg how he and his group reconciled these two positions. Greg told me that, for his part, he was wearing the shirt because everyone else was—in other words, to fit in. I judged him and the group for their ideas and willingness to share them so openly. I also, however, started to reflect on how I measured the success and effectiveness of the International Day of Pink. Was there substance, critical thinking, and/or careful thought behind the masses of people wearing pink? If Greg was any indication, wearing pink had become the thing to do, and it is quite likely that many students (and maybe even some teachers) were going through the motions. I had to ask myself, *What kind of impact is 2SLGBTQI+ (and other) activism like the International Day of Pink having if people can participate superficially? How do you know whose pink shirt means something and whose does not? What does effective school-based activism look like?* I wish I had a definitive answer to some of these questions. That incident, which occurred more than 10 years ago, was a learning moment for me as an ally, setting the stage for me to think about straight privilege, heterosexism, and heteronormativity—although I did not know that at the time.

The following are some critical observations and suggestions for allyship:

- The proliferation of gay-straight alliances is a response to the existence of homophobia in schools. GSAs and similar organizations have the potential to address not only homophobia, but straight privilege as well. The fact that GSAs exist is positive; 2SLGBTQI+ youth need safe spaces, and schools are often not (Taylor et al., 2015). By simply resisting homophobia, school-based activism is not necessarily shifting away from entrenching the traditional gender binary often reflected in presumed heterosexuality (heterosexism and heteronormativity) (Butler, 2004; Foucault, 1978; Goldstein et al., 2007; see also chapters 8 and 9). In this traditional model, straight people will always be normal and queer people will always be abnormal. A queer model of activism in schools, however, has the potential to recognize and celebrate differences, working outside the lines of the traditional model altogether (Jackson, 2006; Rodriguez & Pinar, 2007). A program that challenges heterosexism and heteronormativity (in addition to homophobia) will not develop unless advocacy and activism in schools focus on the way in which straight privilege operates (Goldstein et al., 2007; Meyer, 2007), allowing straight people subjectivity where queer folks (students with exceptionalities and nonwhite people) are relegated to objectification and/or oppression.
- The role of straight teachers leading GSAs needs to be problematized. Allyship should not be viewed as something that is good in any form, because allies have the potential to reinscribe the oppression of marginalized groups if and when they misstep (Pinar, 2007; Potvin, 2016). This perception of allies as good, right-acting people is too easy for allies to internalize themselves and could limit critical discourse about allyship in schools.
- Queer models of education lend themselves to enhancing experience for all students, not just queer ones (Kumashiro, 2004; MacIntosh, 2007). The gender, racial, and ability narratives we create and perpetuate as educators shape human experiences. Yet if one digs below the surface of the dominant discourses of gender, sexuality, race, and ability, very few people actually feel that these narratives define their lives. So why do we, as educators, uphold these narratives by not problematizing them? I argue here that by shifting toward a model of education rooted in queer theory (valuing diversity and the multiplicity of possibilities in the human experience), schools will become safer for all the people who have

ever felt that these categories were ill-fitting. What this also means is that people with privilege will have to be held accountable to a system that honours and upholds equity of experience, which can look different for everyone.

## INEQUITIES IN SCHOOL MATHEMATICS (J. MORVAN)

In 2007, one of my very few Black students in an International Baccalaureate mathematics class asked me why the students in my academic- and university-level mathematics classes were not proportionally representative of the school student population.

As a Black mathematics educator, Ministry of Education curriculum manager, and now superintendent of education, I have taught and interacted with minority students of many backgrounds. Some strive for the highest level of achievement, and others have struggled in the worst way possible in mathematics. I have witnessed first-hand how important school leadership and teachers can be: setting high expectations, providing good working conditions, and caring for the success of every student, whatever their individual circumstances may be. I continue to be troubled by inequities and inequalities in educational opportunities as well as insinuations regarding some racialized students. The insidious discrimination, by ignorance or by choice, that I have witnessed is something that I find deeply troublesome. Parekh et al. (2018) found that Black students in the Toronto District School Board were more likely to be recommended for and placed in special education classes, and in some areas of the city that had high populations of Black families, advanced academic classes were not offered at secondary schools. Over the last few years, there has been a rise in public debates and political will to address issues of equity in Ontario schools. Various frameworks and policies have been put in place to address the glaring issues of racism in education: an Anti-Racism Directorate, an Education Equity Secretariat, an Equity Knowledge Network, Ontario's Education Equity Action Plan (Ontario Ministry of Education, 2017b), and A Better Way Forward: Ontario's 3-Year Anti-Racism Strategic Plan (Ontario Ministry of Education, 2017a). These initiatives are aimed at addressing issues of racism and racialization in Ontario schools. They are commendable, and the government deserves some credit for its effort. However, the challenge for the education system is to put in place practices coherent to these policies that are presumably based on anti-oppressive research and theories. That may not be an easy task given that "most policy documents position equity and the collective good as their ultimate purpose; [and that] actual implementation in school practices and programs can be very different from the stated policy intent" (Morvan, 2017, p. 36).

One area in school practices where inequities are prevalent is mathematics. Stocker and Wagner (2007) contend, "We are disturbed by the inequities in our world and believe that mathematics educators (consciously or not) contribute to the shaping of this world" (p. 17). For their part, Herbel-Eisenmann et al. (2011) argue that "school mathematics remains a powerful social filter, and understanding and explaining access to and success in school mathematics has been of considerable interest to the research community for some time now" (p. v). Though it is known that more pathways are open to students who do well in mathematics, streaming often precludes some marginalized students from courses leading to mathematics-related fields (engineering, sciences, etc.). Research suggests that "when schools sort students into perceived levels of abilities (tracking), students with the greatest learning needs usually receive the least-qualified teachers, the least rigorous curricula, and teachers with beliefs that may prevent them from investing sufficiently in students" (Theoharis & Brookes, 2012, p. 32). Such practice leads to racial and socioeconomic segregation (Huguley et al., 2007) characterized by some soft bigotry and low expectations (Noddings, 2012).

In the last decade in Ontario, the argument about applied and academic courses as a way of streaming students has been a lively, contentious issue (see also chapter 2). As of September 2021, the Ontario government has implemented destreamed courses in grade 9, including mathematics, in order to address some of these issues. However, many questions remain unanswered. The following list offers critical reflections on three issues discussed in this chapter:

- Public education should allow social mobility. Curtis et al. (2014) argue that "from its origins in the middle of the 19th century, public education in Ontario has worked to ensure that the majority of working-class people will remain in their class of origin, while recruiting a small and select minority of them for social mobility" (p. 2). As Ontario seems to be determined to address the persistent issues of oppression, inequity, and inequality in its school systems, it is legitimate to interrogate how practices in school mathematics perpetuate discriminatory and racist ways that have not been challenged. They may have been in place for so long that they have become the norm.
- Using school mathematics as a social filter limits the pool of talent. Who and what decides which children can access high-quality mathematics courses? Are there forces at play to maintain the patterning of

racial advantage and inequity (Gillborn, 2005) in school mathematics? It is crucial in an increasingly competitive world to offer the best access possible to all students. Preventing some students from accessing high-quality mathematics or other core programming based solely on race or some other demographic factor can only limit the pool of talent from which some sectors could indeed benefit. The Organisation for Economic Co-operation and Development (OECD, 2012) argues that the economic and social costs of students failing and dropping out of school are too high. It is well accepted that "more educated people contribute to more democratic societies and sustainable economies, and are less dependent on public aid and less vulnerable to economic downturns" (OECD, 2012, p. 3).

- Race and racism in school mathematics affect us all. Issues of racism and racialization in school mathematics should not be only for activists, advocates, allies, and those who are systematically and directly affected. Some way or another, most educational stakeholders have to face these issues. Ultimately, the hope is that they will adhere to the principle that "all knowledge is political and that research should be aimed at eliminating social injustice, particularly related to ethnicity, gender, sexual orientation, disability and other marginalized groups" (Savin-Baden & Howell Major, 2013, p. 60).

As illustrated by each educator in the above sections, implicit inequities prevail in schools and school systems. Educators attempting to challenge these structures and beliefs, which continue to marginalize students, must commit to and engage in deconstructing the attitudinal barriers that exist in schools. Considering the recent release of Ontario Ministry of Education documents around the pressing topics addressed in this chapter, we offer several specific and general implications and considerations for moving forward with teaching practice.

## CONCLUSION

As with any new policy or initiative in education, several factors impact the successful implementation of the initiatives discussed here. Many constructed beliefs about inequity are rooted in historical understandings of systematic normalization (Minow, 1991). Changing educators' attitudes and beliefs regarding equity and inclusion can be a challenge, and even more so when the attitudes and beliefs have been embedded in these individuals' belief systems for most of their lives. Teachers are often not aware of the assumptions, theories, or educational beliefs they hold (Somma & Bennett, 2020). As well, the subjective and contextual factors discussed may function to place certain groups at higher rates of disadvantage (Hibel et al., 2010). Hegemonic epistemologies and ideologies of what constitutes the centre (i.e., the normal) and the margin (i.e., the abnormal) influence the referral process. Hegemonic or ideological assumptions of the normative or ideal self include being white, able, straight, and middle class, as opposed to the *other*, which is defined as being nonwhite, disabled, poor, and so on.

For example, the Ontario's 2017 *Education Equity Action Plan* provides a roadmap to further the work of "identifying and eliminating discriminatory practices, systemic barriers and bias from schools and classrooms to support the potential for all students to succeed" (Ontario Ministry of Education, 2017b, p. 4). This plan "opens up new fronts in our efforts to eliminate all forms of discrimination and systemic barriers in our school communities. It is not about a new direction, but rather about refocusing our work and bringing new resources to bear as a means of accelerating our progress towards meeting our goals" (p. 6).

These new fronts include gathering data on suspensions, expulsions, and exclusions, data related to student behaviour, and voluntary identity-based data; collecting and disaggregating data based on race, religion, disability, sexual orientation, gender identity, and parental socioeconomic status; increasing the diversity of faculties of education, teacher candidates, and educators; and increasing focused professional development, among other items. The action plan provides a specific set of action steps that will attempt to further address and "eliminate embedded systemic barriers and discriminatory institutional and instructional practices that negatively impact the achievement and well-being of students and lead to inequitable outcomes" (Ontario Ministry of Education, 2017b, p. 10).

According to Ontario's Bill 13 (an amendment to the Education Act), also known as the Accepting Schools Act (Ontario Legislative Assembly, 2012), teachers in publicly funded schools are mandated to provide safe and positive environments for all children to achieve their highest potential "regardless of race, ancestry, place of origin, colour, ethnic origin, citizenship, creed, sex, sexual orientation, gender identity, gender expression, age, marital status, family status or disability" (p. 1). Despite these initiatives, challenges with implementation ensue. Although ministry documents have been developed to define and support the ideals that teachers and schools are responsible for ensuring that inequalities do not occur, challenges that are deeply embedded in the organizational structures of education systems and society remain.

These implications and recommendations are illustrated in the personal narratives shared and pose several questions for educators to consider: *How do educators attain understandings of critical theory in a way that promotes change within their beliefs and practice? How can current policies be utilized in a way to promote these changes?* We cannot have one without the other. Theory and policy must be included in opportunities for professional development, and time must be a key factor in personal development for teaching more equitably. As Ghosh and Galczynski (2014) eloquently state, "simply changing curricula and policy is insufficient because the problem is embedded in the social consciousness. More destructive and insidious than the formal curriculum is the 'hidden' curriculum. Educational discourse (language and practice) perpetuates racism in subtle ways" (p. 28).

## KEY TERMS

**International Day of Pink:** A day of action when people are called on to wear pink to take a stand against homophobia, transphobia, and transmisogyny. While it often takes place in many workplaces, schools are major participants in the day of action. For more information, visit https://dayofpink.org/.

**White:** This signifies a light skin tone that imparts benefits because of a system that is structured around racial differences (Matias, 2014). Ladson-Billings (2001) claims that being white is about much more than biology, it is about "choosing a system of privilege and power" (p. 81).

**White privilege:** An institutional set of benefits granted to those whose skin tone matches the skin tone of those who hold power positions; it reflects the unearned advantages of being white in a racially stratified society and has been characterized as an expression of institutional power that is largely unacknowledged by most white individuals (Neville et al., 2001).

**White supremacy:** An overarching, persistent system of white Western racial domination that manifests globally and relies on the exploitation of people of colour while locating whites in a structural position of superiority and advantage—offering both material and psychological benefits—and people of colour in a subordinate position of disadvantage (Owen, 2007).

**Whiteness:** A socially constructed, significant, dominant power that creates and upholds the norms of society—giving those with light skin structural advantage, both systemically and personally. This power transforms into "the standard against which all other cultures, groups, and individuals are measured and usually found to be inferior" (Henry et al., 2010, pp. 46–67).

## DISCUSSION QUESTIONS AND ACTIVITIES

1. How do educators attain understandings of critical theory in a way that promotes change within their beliefs and practice?
2. How can current policies be utilized in a way to promote these changes?
3. How does intersectionality impact a student's experience in school, and what can educators do to ensure flourishing?
4. Marshmallow activity (short version): Adapted from https://static1.squarespace.com/static/6052b470dad84918422c787f/t/61423d1316b9067607b0e2c0/1631730964055/Build-Exercises.pdf.

    Materials: Marshmallows, large and small; paper bags; wooden popsicle sticks; toothpicks; timer

    Preparation: For round 1, ensure you have one paper bag for each group of two to three students. Fill one-third of the paper bags with 10 large marshmallows and 10 popsicle sticks. Fill two-thirds of the paper bags with 10 small marshmallows and 10 toothpicks. For round 2, ensure you have one paper bag for each group of two to three students. Fill each bag with 10 large marshmallows and 10 popsicle sticks. (Hide these bags until needed.)

    Activity: Round 1. Create at least five small groups of students. Tell them that they have the exact same number of supplies, and their task is to create the tallest structure. Set a time limit (four to five minutes). Watch carefully and observe how groups react when they notice the obvious disparities. At the end of the time limit, measure and record the height of each structure. Don't let the students touch or tear down their structures after measuring. Debrief by asking questions such as *What did you notice? How did seeing the disparities impact your efforts? Was this fair? Why not?* (This will seem obvious; that's okay.) *How did it make you feel?* Finally, ask, *How could this activity be made more fair?* (Students should suggest that all groups receive the same-size marshmallows and sticks.) Agree with them and distribute the second round of bags.

    Round 2: Tell students they now have a real competition, and let them get excited. Just as they begin, tell them that there's only one rule: they must build the new structure on top of (or using) their existing structure. Let them begin. Allow groups to voice their frustrations. Measure the structures at the end and debrief, asking, *How does this relate to notions of meritocracy? How does this encourage us to think about resources and funding? How does this impact how we think about groups that have experienced injustices? How does this change the ways we think about benevolence and charity?* They will likely have many more insights as well.

## REFERENCES

Abawi, Z. E. (2021). *The effectiveness of educational policy for bias-free teacher hiring: Critical insights to enhance diversity in the Canadian teacher workforce*. Routledge.

Bennett, S. (2020) Rethinking the familiar: It is not about changing our actions, it is about changing our thinking. *Exceptionality Education International, 30*, 19–31. https://ir.lib.uwo.ca/eei/vol30/iss2/4

Bobo, L. D. (2001). Racial attitudes and relations. In N. J. Smelser, J. W. Wilson, & F. Mitchell (Eds.), *America becoming: Racial trends and their consequences* (pp. 264–301). National Academy of Sciences.

Britzman, D. P. (1995). Is there a queer pedagogy? Or, stop reading straight. *Educational Theory, 45*(2), 151–165. doi.org/doi:10.1111/j.1741-5446.1995.00151.x

Burghardt, M. (2011). The human bottom of non-human things: On critical theory and its contributions to critical disability studies. *Critical Disability Discourses / Discours critiques dans le champ du handicap, 3*. https://cdd.journals.yorku.ca/index.php/cdd/article/view/31560/31234

Butler, J. (2004). *Undoing gender*. Routledge. doi.org/10.1080/17457823.2012.717203

Cummins, J. (2009). Pedagogies of choice: Challenging coercive relations of power in classrooms and communities. *International Journal of Bilingual Education and Bilingualism, 12*(3), 261–271. doi.org/10.1080/13670050903003751

Curtis, B., Livingstone, D. W., & Smaller, H. (1992). *Stacking the deck: The streaming of working-class kids in Ontario schools*. Our Schools/Our Selves.

Curtis, B., Livingstone, D. W., & Smaller, H. (2014). *Restacking the deck: Streaming by class, race and gender in Ontario schools*. Canadian Centre for Policy Alternatives.

Dei, G. J. S. (2000). Rethinking the role of Indigenous knowledges in the academy. *International Journal of Inclusive Education, 4*(2), 111–132. doi.org/10.1080/136031100284849

Feistritzer, E. (2011). *Profile of teachers in the U.S. 2011*. National Center for Education Information. https://www.teachertoolkit.co.uk/wp-content/uploads/2016/06/pot2011final-blog.pdf

Florian, L. (2007) Reimagining special education. In L. Florian (Ed.), *The Sage handbook of special education* (pp. 7–20). Sage.

Foucault, M. (1978). *The history of sexuality* (Vol. 1). Random House.

Ghosh, R., & Galczynski, M. (2014). *Redefining multicultural education: Inclusion and the right to be different*. Canadian Scholars.

Gibson, M. L., & Grant, C. A. (2010). Working in small places. In F. S. Hoosain (Ed.), *Democracy and multicultural education* (pp. 43–71). Information Age.

Gillborn, D. (2005). Education policy as an act of white supremacy: Whiteness, critical race theory and education reform. *Journal of Education Policy, 20*(4), 485–505. doi.org/10.1080/02680930500132346

Goldstein, T., Russell, V., & Daley, A. (2007). Safe, positive and queering moments in teaching education and schooling: A conceptual framework. *Teaching Education, 18*(3), 183–199. doi.org/10.1080/10476210701533035

Grant, C. A. (2012). Cultivating flourishing lives: A robust social justice vision of education. *American Educational Research Journal, 49*(5), 910–934. doi.org/10.3102/0002831212447977

Griffin, P., & Ouellett, M. L. (2002). Going beyond gay-straight alliances to make schools safe for lesbian, gay, bisexual, and transgender students. *Angles: The Policy Journal of the Institute for Gay and Lesbian Strategic Studies, 6*(1), 1–7. www.schools-out.org.uk/research/docs/Angles_61.pdf

Harpur, P. (2012). Embracing the new disability rights paradigm: The importance of the Convention on the Rights of Persons with Disabilities. *Disability & Society, 27*(1), 1–14. doi.org/10.1080/09687599.2012.631794

Henry, F., Rees, T., & Tator, C. (2010). *The colour of democracy: Racism in Canadian society.* Nelson Education.

Herbel-Eisenmann, B., Choppin, J., Wagner, D., & Pimm, D. (Eds.). (2011). *Equity in discourse for mathematics education: Theories, practices, and policies.* Springer.

Hibel, J., Farkas, G., & Morgan, P. L. (2010). Who is placed into special education? *Sociology of Education, 83*(4), 312–332. doi.org/10.1177/0038040710383518

Horkheimer, M. (1972). *Critical theory: Selected essays* (Vol. 1). A&C Black.

Huguley, J. P., Kakli, Z., & Rao, R. (2007). The opportunity gap: Achievement and inequality in education. *Harvard Educational Review.* https://eric.ed.gov/?id=ED568853

Ingraham, C., & Saunders, C. (2016). Heterosexual imaginary. In *The Wiley Blackwell encyclopedia of gender and sexuality studies* (pp. 1–4). Wiley-Blackwell. doi.org/10.1002/9781118663219.wbegss762

Jackson, S. (2006). Gender, sexuality and heterosexuality: The complexity (and limits) of heteronormativity. *Feminist Theory, 7*(1), 105–121. doi.org/10.1177/1464700106061462

Kitchen, J., & Bellini, C. (2013). Making schools safe and inclusive: Gay-straight alliances and school climate in Ontario. *Canadian Journal of Educational Administration and Policy, 146*(1), 1–37. www.umanitoba.ca/publications/cjeap/pdf_files/kitchen_bellini.pdf

Kodama, N. (2015). Teacher education and culturally diverse classrooms: A comparative analysis of Japan and Ontario, Canada. In R. DePalma, D. B. Napier, & W. Dze-Ngwa (Eds.), *Revitalizing minority voices* (pp. 91–110). Sense.

Kumashiro, K. K. (2004). *Against common sense: Teaching and learning toward social justice.* Routledge Falmer.

Ladson-Billings, G. (2001). Teaching and cultural competence: What does it take to be a successful teacher in a diverse classroom? *Rethinking Schools Online, 15*(4), 1–5. https://rethinkingschools.org/articles/teaching-and-cultural-competence

MacIntosh, L. B. (2007). Does anyone have a band-aid? Anti-homophobia discourses and pedagogical impossibilities. *Educational Studies, 39*(3), 33–43. doi.org/10.1080/00131940701308874

Matias, C. E. (2014). Tears worth telling: Urban teaching and the possibilities of racial justice. *Multicultural Perspectives, 15*, 187–193. https://eric.ed.gov/?id=EJ1023549

Meyer, E. (2007). "But I'm not gay": What straight teachers need to know about queer theory. In N. M. Rodriguez & W. Pinar (Eds.), *Queering straight teachers: Discourse and identity in education* (pp. 15–29). Peter Lang.

Mezirow, J. (2018). Transformative learning theory. In Illeris, K. (Ed.), *Contemporary theories of learning* (pp. 114–128). Routledge.

Minow, M. (1991). *Making all the difference: Inclusion, exclusion, and American law.* Cornell University Press.

Morvan, J. (2017). Making visible and acting on issues of racism and racialization in school mathematics. *Brock Education Journal, 27*(1), 35–52. doi.org/10.26522/brocked.v27i1.624

Neville, H. A., Worthington, R. L., & Spanierman, L. B. (2001). Race, power, and multicultural counseling psychology: Understanding white privilege and color-blind racial attitudes. In J. G. Ponterotto, J. M. Casas, L. A. Suzuki, & C. M. Alexander (Eds.), *Handbook of Multicultural Counseling* (2nd ed., pp. 257–288). Sage.

Noddings, N. (2012). *Philosophy of education* (3rd ed.). Westview Press.

Nussbaum, M. C. (1997). *Cultivating humanity: A classical defense of reform in liberal education.* Harvard University Press.

Ontario Legislative Assembly. (2012). *Bill 13: Accepting Schools Act.* www.ola.org/en/legislative-business/bills/parliament-40/session-1/bill-13

Ontario Ministry of Education. (2013). *Learning for all.* https://files.ontario.ca/edu-learning-for-all-2013-en-2022-01-28.pdf

Ontario Ministry of Education. (2014). *Achieving excellence.* http://ncee.org/wp-content/uploads/2017/01/Ont-non-AV-10-Ontario-Government-Achieving-Excellence-A-renewed-vision-for-education-in-Ontario.pdf

Ontario Ministry of Education. (2017a). *Anti-black racism strategy.* www.ontario.ca/page/ontarios-anti-black-racism-strategy

Ontario Ministry of Education. (2017b). *Ontario's Education Equity Action Plan.* www.ontario.ca/page/ontarios-education-equity-action-plan

Ontario Ministry of Education. (2017c). *Special education in Ontario K–12: A guide for educators.* https://files.ontario.ca/edu-special-education-policy-resource-guide-en-2022-05-30.pdf

Organisation for Economic Co-operation and Development. (2012). *Equity and quality in education: Supporting disadvantaged students and schools.* doi.org/10.1787/9789264130852-en

Owen, D. S. (2007). Towards a critical theory of whiteness. *Philosophy & Social Criticism, 33*, 203–222. doi.org/10.1177/0191453707074139

Parekh, G., Brown, R. S., & Robson, K. (2018). The social construction of giftedness: The intersectional relationship between whiteness, economic privilege, and the identification of gifted. *Canadian Journal of Disability Studies, 7*(2), 1–32. doi.org/10.15353/cjds.v7i2.421

Pinar, W. F. (2007). Introduction: A queer conversation, toward sustainability. In N. M. Rodriguez & W. Pinar (Eds.), *Queering straight teachers: Discourse and identity in education* (pp. 1–14). Peter Lang.

Potvin, L. (2016). Radical heterosexuality: Straight teacher activism in schools: Does ally-led activism work? *Confero: Essays on Education, Philosophy and Politics, 4*(1), 9–36. doi.org/10.3384/confero.2001-4562.160614

Rodriguez, N. M., & Pinar, W. (2007). *Queering straight teachers: Discourse and identity in education*. Peter Lang.

Ryan, J., Pollock, K., & Antonelli, F. (2009). Teaching diversity in Canada: Leaky pipelines, bottlenecks, and glass ceilings. *Canadian Journal of Education, 32*(3), 591–617. https://journals.sfu.ca/cje/index.php/cje-rce/article/view/3053

Savin-Baden, M., & Howell Major, C. (2013). *Qualitative research: The essential guide to theory and practice*. Routledge.

Schon, D. A. (1983). *The reflective practitioner*. Basic Books.

Sensoy, Ö., & DiAngelo, R. J. (2012). *Is everyone really equal? An introduction to key concepts in social justice education*. Teachers College Press.

Short, D. (2014). Queering schools, gay-straight alliances, and the law. In G. Walton (Ed.), *The gay agenda: Claiming space, identity, and justice* (pp. 327–344). Peter Lang.

Somma, M., & Bennett, S. (2020). Inclusive education and pedagogical change: Experiences from the front lines. *International Journal of Educational Methodology, 6*(2), 285–295. doi.org/10.12973/ijem.6.2.285

Stein, M. (2007). Quick overview of the United Nations convention on the rights of persons with disabilities and its implications for Americans with disabilities. *Mental and Physical Disability Law Reporter, 31*(5), 679–683. https://scholarship.law.wm.edu/facpubs/261

Stocker, D., & Wagner, D. (2007). Talking about teaching mathematics for social justice. *For the Learning of Mathematics, 27*(3), 17–21. https://www.jstor.org/stable/40248579

Tanner, S. J. (2014). *A youth participatory action research (YPAR), theatrical inquiry into whiteness* [Doctoral dissertation, University of Minnesota].

Taylor, C., & Peter, T. (2011). *Every class in every school: Final report on the first national climate survey on homophobia, biphobia, and transphobia in Canadian schools*. Egale Canada. http://egale.ca/wp-content/uploads/2011/05/EgaleFinalReport-web.pdf

Taylor, C., Peter, T., Campbell, C., Meyer, E., Ristock, J., & Short, D. (2015). *The Every Teacher Project on LGBTQ+-inclusive education in Canada's K–12 schools: Final report*. Manitoba

Teachers' Society. http://news-centre.uwinnipeg.ca/wp-content/uploads/2016/01/EveryTeacher_FinalReport_v12.pdf

Theoharis, G., & Brooks, J. S. (Eds.). (2012). *What every principal needs to know to create equitable and excellent schools*. Teachers College Press.

United Nations. (2007). *Convention on the Rights of Persons with Disabilities.* www.un.org/disabilities/documents/convention/convoptprot-e.pdf

# CHAPTER 21
# The Things We Carry: Human Flourishing for Students and Educators Through the Equity Backpack Project

*Vandy Britton, Nerlap Kaur Sidhu, Navtej Nevan Singh Sidhu, and Nathan Ngieng, with Balkaran, Manmeet, Ardra, and Envy*

> We don't need improvement. We need an approach that fundamentally and radically transforms the experiences of children and families at the margins.
> —Shane Safir

How does equity work in K–12 classrooms foster human flourishing? How and why is it important to explore one's identity in relation to school? What follows is a series of personal narratives shared by educators and students who seek to answer these questions in relation to a particular project, the Equity Backpack Project (EBP), undertaken by a group of students and their teacher in a middle school in a city near Vancouver, British Columbia, in 2021. These personal narratives—stories, if you will—are woven together with the words of scholars who have been considering these very same questions for a much longer time than we have. Through these narratives, we hope to inspire you to engage in equity work with your own students.

We begin with Balkaran (age 11):

> In my early school years, I came to school carrying all of my tohfay [gifts], including my Punjabi language, Indian culture, parivar [family] and teachings that my family shared with me. I tossed these tohfay [gifts] aside as I stepped into the classroom in exchange for Western culture and English. You had to act like them

[Western students], and dress like them. I found myself even asking questions like them. My desire to be like them was tiring, and difficult. I woke up each day preparing myself for the information my teacher was going to put on me. The information was not even connected to me, my family, or my culture—not at all. I remember being in grade five, wishing my dark skin away because I wanted to be White. School was erasing my identity and culture. I felt ashamed and I was letting it all happen because I thought that being White was somehow smarter.

According to the Online Etymology Dictionary, the word *withering* comes from the root word *wither* and means to lose vitality, force, and freshness (Online Etymology Dictionary, n.d.a). Through his reflection, Balkaran eloquently shares how he felt that significant aspects of his identity were withering away because of the expectations in place for him at school. His experience is disappointing at best, heartbreaking at worst. The title of Yancy's (2012) article "How Can You Teach Me If You Don't Know Me?" asks educators to consider *the* essential question in relation to human flourishing: How can a student flourish in school if the teacher does not know who the student is and understand what the student is carrying with them? Furthermore, how are the *tohfay* (gifts) that the student is carrying with them into the classroom viewed? Are they considered assets or deficits, or are they completely ignored? Finally, who is responsible, if not schools and educators, for providing a safe and ethical space of engagement (Ermine, 2007) for students to share their lived experiences and explore their identities, thus leading to human flourishing?

Fortunately, Balkaran's story does not end there. He continues:

This school year has been way better. In my classroom, while participating in the Equity Backpack Project, I started to understand the inequities in my life and really empathized with my classmates' life stories. We actually just talked about our lives and celebrated our differences. For the first time in a long time, I felt an overwhelming sense of relief. I felt human. I felt whole. I felt hope. I felt connected to my classmates and the world in a new way—a way that I never thought was possible before. I feel like this year at school I am learning about the importance of understanding and caring for others. I love that I am not losing my roots. I really feel cared for, and I can honestly say that I really care about my schooling. I always wondered why schooling came at the price of losing myself, hiding my language, culture, and all the tohfay [gifts] my family gave me—just to get good grades. The EBP has given me a new confidence, purpose, courage, and hope at school, in the classroom, and in life. I finally feel valued, seen, and heard.

## WHAT IS HUMAN FLOURISHING?

Aristotle's notion of *eudaimonia* (happiness)—now better understood to be human flourishing (Aristotle, 2009; Wolbert et al., 2021)—and the ways in which humans seek to achieve this goal have been the subject of many philosophers. This said, the word *flourish* itself was not documented until the 12th century, when French speakers coined it: *flourish* then meant (and still means) "to blossom" or "to grow," as in the way that a flower blossoms (*floriss, florir*). The metaphoric sense of the word, equating "to flourish" with "to thrive," came into the lexicon for English speakers in the mid-14th century. Interestingly, by the end of the 14th century, another meaning of the word had come into being for English speakers: to "flourish" a weapon, or to hold it in your hand and wave it about (Online Etymology Dictionary, n.d.b). In this context, **agency** was attached to the word. Thus, it is with all three meanings of *flourish* in mind that we consider the "dynamic state" (Wolbert et al., 2015, p. 124) and the role of human flourishing in relation to the EBP.

### To Flourish = To Blossom or to Grow

The EBP, the creation of middle school teacher Nerlap Sidhu, grew out of Nerlap's desire that her students would not struggle with inequities in school in the same ways she had (Sidhu, 2021). The "invisible knapsack" to which McIntosh (1998) refers in her seminal article on white privilege got Sidhu to consider, *What would a* visible *knapsack (backpack) look like, and how could this amplification of students' identities support human flourishing?* Instinctually recognizing that curricula need to act as both "mirrors and windows for all students" (Bishop, 1990, p. xi), and echoing Lorde's passionate plea to use different tools than the master's to make significant change (Lorde, 1979), Sidhu developed the EBP so that her students could see themselves reflected in the curriculum, share their lived experiences as a **living curriculum**, and use that curriculum as a window through which to learn about others. The 10-lesson unit of study, officially entitled *Equity Backpack: Fostering Equity and Inclusion through Lived Experiences* (Sidhu, 2021), supports students in understanding concepts such as equity, inclusion, anti-racism, and intersectionality through the lenses of their own lives. The students engage in arts-based learning experiences, share their personal experiences with each other, interview family and community members, respond to questions that challenge their thinking about identity through both written assignments and classroom discussions, and are inspired to consider the positive impact that they (both individually and collectively) can potentially have upon the world (Sivia et al., 2021). Sidhu created the EBP as a means to disrupt the **hegemonic discourses** that were implicitly prescribed for the school and students in the city where they lived. The EBP effectively broke down the barriers between the school and the larger community through the process of inviting community members to share aspects of their lives with the students. A powerful by-product of the EBP is that it became a way for individual students to re/claim their identity. Educators across Canada have adopted the EBP to undo the damage done by the Eurocentric curriculum and to allow their students and themselves the opportunity to mutually flourish.

Nerlap shares:

> As a student growing up in British Columbia in the 1980s, I was denied the opportunity to explore and share different aspects of my identity as my teachers abided by the Eurocentric curriculum. I lacked agency within the classroom because it was my teachers and the prescribed curriculum that determined whether my knowledge was considered worthwhile. Simply put, I was not allowed to flourish. One of my inspirations for creating the EBP was that as a child I was never given the opportunity to share aspects of myself in the classroom and forge a strong sense of my identity. My name was anglicized to Anita in school as a form of assimilation. Sadly, it was not until high school when I met my first teacher of colour; he reminded me of how far I had drifted from my culture and my roots. It was not until I was in my late thirties that I had the confidence to reclaim my birthname, Nerlap Kaur Sidhu. As an educator, I recognized that my students deserved an opportunity to feel seen, heard, and empowered; my students deserved the opportunity to flourish in school. The EBP created a space within the classroom where my students knew that their story mattered and that they mattered. By controlling whose knowledge is worth sharing, educators prevent their students from celebrating their whole selves and deny them the opportunity to flourish.

The EBP brings students together through the acknowledgement of their differences, the exchange of lived experiences, and the exploration of their identities. Flourishing occurs when students gain a deeper understanding of who they are and how they are connected to each other (Ellyatt, 2022). Through providing students with the opportunity to engage in the reciprocal exchange of their personal stories within the classroom setting, teachers provide students with

**ethical spaces** in which to establish relationships and understandings. Thus, relinquishing control in the classroom is a necessary pedagogical shift for educators to engage in to allow students to explore their identities, feel empowered, and flourish through coming to know themselves and each other (Brown, 2004).

Nerlap continues:

> Through my work on the EBP I have come to understand that human flourishing does not take place in isolation. My students flourished through talking about their lives with each other and understanding their differences. While some educators may believe that acknowledging differences within the classroom creates division amongst students, I have seen firsthand through the EBP how allowing students the opportunity to come to understand their differences brings them closer together. It also has the power to create a strong sense of belonging and agency. It took time, but I eventually found the confidence within myself to begin shifting my pedagogy in order to provide all students, including students of colour, with opportunities to dismantle the hegemonic discourses that surrounded them. Balkaran [the student at the beginning of the chapter] shared with me that he felt "really glad" that we were learning about culture and identity. He had been teased for his long hair and the patka he wears on his head. I recall how he proudly pointed to the patka he was wearing and said, "This is part of my identity, my history, my parents, and my grandparents. Our class is building bridges across cultures and not walls."

Identity-centred work can act as a catalyst for human flourishing by providing students with the place and space to grow and learn together. Aoki (1993) contends that educators must "shift towards a lived curriculum that integrates students' lived experiences, histories, and cultures into the classroom" to rectify some of the ways in which the current education system falls short (p. 259). Culturally relevant and responsive pedagogies seek to address these systemic inequities.

Incorporating culturally relevant pedagogy that involves bringing the individual experiences, histories, and cultures of all students into the classroom can restore that which has been taken away from students who have had to experience education through a purely Eurocentric lens. Education requires this reimagining, as students need opportunities to build cultural bridges that allow for the celebration of differences. Alcoff (2006) reminds us that the erasure of difference leads only to "distrust, miscommunication, and thus disunity" (p. 7). This way of thinking is deeply embedded within the Eurocentric curriculum and is something that can be disrupted by projects such as the EBP.

Nerlap continues:

> Ellie, a grade 6 student, learned about her father's experience as an immigrant from Vietnam. She shared, "He was the only one from his culture in school and he thought there was something wrong with him. It made me feel really heartbroken because there's nothing wrong with the culture and you should celebrate it." Ellie reflected on the challenging experience of her father, and it inspired her to make a conscious decision to share her Vietnamese culture with others. While participating and co-creating the EBP my students shared with me that they felt heard, seen, and that they had the opportunity to change the world in a positive way by bringing people together. By understanding our differences through the EBP, my students and I felt a stronger sense of interconnectedness. We came to recognize that the challenges we face as humans can actually bring us together in unity.

The EBP and other culturally responsive curriculum provides students with the tools to respond in a unified and responsible way to problematic issues like racialization and other societal injustices; they offer real-world opportunities to celebrate differences and to navigate inequities. Conversations around the personal experiences of family members provide entryways for students to reflect and re/connect with their identity.

### To Flourish = To Thrive

Ladson-Billings (2006) encourages educators to foster the growth of cultural competence to support "students to recognize and honor their own cultural beliefs and practices while acquiring access to the wider culture, where they are likely to have a chance in improving their socioeconomic status and making informed decisions about the lives they want to live" (p. 36). Ladson-Billings's (1995) theoretical model of culturally relevant curriculum "not only addresses student achievement, but also helps students to accept and affirm their cultural identity while developing critical perspectives that challenge inequities that schools (and other institutions) perpetuate" (p. 469). This practice asks teachers to draw upon the "funds of knowledge" (Moll & Gonzalez, 1994) that students come to school with; utilize "cultural modeling" (Lee, 1995) as a framework for instruction such that students' own lives inform the curriculum; and actively engage in culturally sustaining pedagogies (Paris, 2012) in order "to perpetuate—and sustain—linguistic, literate, and cultural pluralism as part of the democratic project of schooling" (p. 95).

What we choose to teach, how we interact with students, and how we treat families all play a crucial role in how children come to see the world and how they engage with it. "Youth need opportunities in school to explore multiple facets of selfhood, but also learn about the identities of others who may differ" (Muhammad, 2020, p. 67). According to Egbo (2019), for students to become "accomplished citizens" (p. 128), ultimately teachers need to provide students with the opportunities to come to know and value their own individual cultures as well as to understand and work within the dominant culture. Unfortunately, the cycle of erasure of culture while in the K–12 school system continued for another generation in Nerlap's family with the experiences of her son Navtej:

> I am a Punjabi, middle class, 28-year-old, heterosexual, able-bodied, cisgender man, settler, and educator. Each of these aspects of my identity intersect and contribute to my unique experiences of privilege and oppression on a day-to-day basis. During my time as a student in British Columbia's K–12 education system in the 2000s, the complexities of my identity were not explored. Instead, I was taught to assimilate by learning solely about Eurocentric ways of knowing and being. My language, a central part of my identity, was first silenced, and eventually erased while I was in elementary school. My white teachers would tell me not to speak Punjabi in class as they deemed it inappropriate because they could not understand what I was saying. After each of these experiences I began to grow increasingly anxious whenever I spoke Punjabi, which led to me speaking it less and less, until I lost my ability to speak it entirely. In this case, a significant part of my identity withered away because I was denied the opportunity to speak my home language and was forced to assimilate by only learning how to speak English. When I was older and realized what I was missing, I spent seven years re/learning Punjabi in an after-hours language program offered by a local gurdwara.

As Tatum (2000) states, "dominant groups, by definition, set the parameters within which the subordinates operate" (p. 3), and use of languages other than English within the classroom has certainly been discouraged by many teachers in English Canada (Piccardo & Payre-Ficout, 2022). Sometimes it seems as though "difference within the classroom is being treated as a disruptive force that needs to be erased for the sake of unity" (Alcoff, 2006, p. 6). This "disruptive force" is seen as a threat to the "single story" (Adichie, 2009) narratives that have been such significant parts of the Eurocentric education system, where certain voices are purposely and purposefully excluded. Ortiz Guzman (2017) speaks of the importance of practising "radical inclusion … the intentional act of interrupting inequity where it lives: our separations" (p. 45) within the classroom. "Recognizing the multiplicity of stories, truths, their proximities, their intersections, and the people who own the stories" (p. 45) is integral to the process of equity work. The EBP and other curriculum that includes all students' lives disrupts this "single story" Eurocentric narrative and replaces it with a practice that fosters and nourishes human flourishing. All facets of the human experience must be explored, and all humans, regardless of their differences, must be included in the exploration.

Navtej continues:

> While I was in school, one of the dominant narratives surrounding Punjabi males living in suburban Vancouver was that they are gang-affiliated. Many Punjabi male students, including myself, were thought to be attending "gang schools" and were considered gang-affiliated simply because of the visual markers of our gender and race. My high school was not a "gang school" nor was I part of any "gang"; this was the narrative that the larger community and the media prescribed to me based on me being a Punjabi male and attending a school in a certain part of our city.

The legacy of the notorious Punjabi gangster Bindy Johal and the violent depictions of Punjabi male youth in the media have played a large part in the formation of this hegemonic narrative, and it has cast a long shadow over the identity of Punjabi males (Pabla, 2020). Lorde (1984) speaks to the harmful nature of this "single story" phenomenon: "I find I am constantly being encouraged to pluck out some one aspect of myself and present this as the meaningful whole, eclipsing or denying the other parts of self.… My fullest concentration of energy is available to me only when I integrate all parts of who I am" (p. 121).

Navtej explains further:

> This fragmented way of living, where only my race and gender defined who I was, contributed to the process of withering that I experienced as a student in the K–12 education system. I always wondered why my teachers did not attempt to get to know who I truly was as a person, instead of accepting this hegemonic gang narrative. While the classroom should have been a place to disrupt these harmful narratives and allow me and the other non-white students to flourish, this simply was not the case. It is already difficult for Punjabi male youths to express their vulnerability as the Punjabi gang narrative paints vulnerability

as a weakness; then couple that with no safe space in the classroom where I could express my vulnerability and/or explore identity. Now as an educator in the K–12 system, I see the continued longing for students to be seen, heard, and their differences and identities celebrated. This is precisely why educators need to create safe spaces so students can thrive, express their vulnerability, and explore the intersecting aspects of their identity with their peers.

Projects like the EBP contribute to creating classroom environments that prevent the withering of a person's identity and instead opens doors and windows (Lee, 1995) for students to find strength and agency within themselves.

## To Flourish = Agency

Safir and Dugan (2021) discuss the importance of student agency within the classroom and the particularities of what it looks like: "In the social ecology of the classroom, agency is about connection to self, peers, adults, the community beyond the classroom, and ultimately the world. Agency does not emerge in a vacuum, nor does it flourish in a traditional classroom where the teacher is positioned as a content expert dishing out knowledge. It emerges in a learning space where power is distributed, knowledge is democratized, diverse perspectives are welcomed, and children are intellectually and emotionally nourished" (p. 102).

The following student voices demonstrate the power of an inclusive curriculum that centres students' lives and experiences: a power that inspires agency and change. Manmeet shares:

> When I first came into middle school, I was super nervous. It didn't help that none of my friends were in class at the time. When I walked into class for the first time, I felt like I did not belong. I didn't know anyone there and it was my first day in a completely new school, with a ton of new people. When my teacher first told me about the EBP, I was kind of excited because I had never done any project like it before. At first, I had no idea what equity was. I knew equality, inclusion, and anti-racism but not equity. When we started learning about equity, inclusion, anti-racism, and things of that genre it made me see the world how it truly is. We have always been told that the world is a beautiful place and that it is perfect. But the sad truth is that there are lots of problems in the world and one of them is racism. I felt sad and disappointed that this stuff was still going on. The backpack project helped me feel inspired to make a positive change in the world, especially around the topic of equity. The EBP also helped me to grow as a person. Because of the EBP, I made a ton of new friends and I finally felt like I belonged. We connected, based on our struggles

and challenges in life. We shared our stories with each other, and we bonded like a classroom family. We found ways to celebrate our differences and respect each other's heritage. At first, I didn't think that it was going to be a big thing. I thought that we were just going to do the project for a little while and then move on. But I was wrong. It got on the news twice and the EBP made its way across 70 schools in BC and one in Alberta in less than a year. Now it has made its way across Canada and to think it all started in my grade 6 classroom. Wow! We did this and helped change the world for the better. The backpack project has also impacted my future. Because of the EBP, I got a ton of opportunities to be on the news, in videos, to be in a book, and we were also recognized by the Prime Minister. Since I had all of these opportunities, I can put them on my resume to get a good job or to go to a good university. Not only did I flourish as a person, so has my future. I think the main reason why the EBP became so popular is that it addresses real-world problems, and it educates people about what is going on in the world. Even though we were so young, our teacher still taught us about these serious topics that other educators might have been nervous to talk about. Our teacher felt the need for us to know about this stuff because of what was going on in the world at the time. We used our voices to bring about a positive change to education and the world. Most importantly our teacher let us know that we mattered.

Ardra echoes Manmeet's story:

My name is Ardra and I'm a grade 8 student now. As you can expect, middle school brought many challenges. When I transitioned into my teenage years, I learned a lot about the qualities of life and was exposed to so many new perspectives. Little did I know, understanding these new perspectives and ideas was harder than I expected. Luckily, I was introduced to the EBP. It provided me with a lot of opportunities that I wouldn't have been able to get otherwise. It definitely opened my eyes to a world of new knowledge. I was able to grow and learn in so many different ways—whether it was in building self-confidence and self-esteem, learning about different cultures or making a safe community for those around me. The EBP gave me so many chances to explore, to learn about myself and to ultimately flourish in school. Finding the right environment and bonding with your peers is something that is essential when it comes to middle school. If I were to go back in time to when I was younger, I was a quiet, shy, and closed-minded student. I didn't fit in at school, had a hard time meeting new people, and I was not that open to new challenges. Because of the EBP, I have learned to use my voice to speak up for others and myself. I am an open, compassionate, and adventurous student. Finding your true identity, who you strive to become and the type of people you want to surround yourself with, is easier said than done, but learning more about equity and identity can help you. I hope to keep growing and helping others to grow too. Let's step forward together and make a difference! Let's use our voices to build bridges. We got this.

Envy, also, was deeply impacted by her participation in the EBP project:

The EBP has helped me flourish and grow in a variety of ways. It has impacted my life in such a positive way and has changed me as a student and person. The EBP has most definitely helped me achieve a confidence that I was not aware I had. By sharing my voice, knowledge, and learning with others, and teaching others what I know and learnt, it has made me more comfortable with myself. This project helped me in my journey through middle school. I have become more understanding of others and what they have been through with their experiences. I've learned to take into account my own feelings and moods from our mood meter, and to stick up for myself and others against racism and discrimination in a responsible way. The project didn't just touch on sensitive subjects, it gave me a voice that helped me understand my surroundings and be able to guide myself in a way that didn't make a situation feel awkward. I am proud to be growing up in a generation that has more acceptance of differences. The EBP lets kids like me accept ourselves the way we are and let us be proud of who we are and of others. Without this project I wouldn't have been able to grow into the person I am today and recognize this valuable knowledge I have. All these lessons in the EBP and exchanging our stories with classmates has helped me flourish as a person and will continue to help me grow into a better student and human.

## MOVING FORWARD

Educational equity has been described as the state in which every youth receives what they need to develop to their full academic and social potential (National Equity Project, n.d.). The centrality of voice and agency that has long been suggested in the literature (e.g., Baroutsis et al., 2016) in provoking the awareness of inequitable situations and the role identity plays in this is implicit in the EBP and the foundational equity work occurring in certain school classrooms. Article 12 of the United Nations' (1989) Convention on the Rights of the Child states that "the child who is capable of forming his or her own views [shall be given] the right to express those views freely" (p. 4). In this way, the EBP nurtures "funds of knowledge," constructed through inquiry and reflection, that are reinforced through joint experiences (Watkins et al., 2018). Nathan, an assistant superintendent in the district where Nerlap teaches, shares his story on the importance of equity work:

> I am an assistant superintendent and educator in the large suburban school district in which Nerlap teaches. As an educational leader, I am faced with tackling complex issues related to race, socio-economic status, gender, disability, culture, and sexual orientation on a regular basis. The commitment to equity in our school district, the work happening with the EBP, and my experiences as an inclusive educational leader support my approach of reflection, inclusion, advocacy, and dialogue as key tenets in enacting a socially just leadership approach. The EBP was a catalyst for this stance of empowerment over marginalization and a greater system awareness of positionality and power, attitudes and assumptions of others, and the impact of actions on human flourishing [Celoria, 2016; Theoharis, 2007]. This leadership commitment to care, understanding, and compassion through dialogue and collective hope is what the EBP represents in support of a flourishing education system where "[the spoken] true word [will] transform the world" [Freire, 2018, p. 87].

Nathan highlights the importance of working together, across all levels of education, to address this imperative of system change in the name of human flourishing. A shared purpose of educational equity grounded in a deeper learning theory of change (Watkins et al., 2018) supports system-level change, where dialogical approaches can lead to greater levels of student engagement and the exploration of issues that support the flourishing of students in our classrooms (Stevenson, 2022). Through this systems perspective, inequities move beyond fiscal resource allocation to schools and instead are located in domains related to the social, cultural, and identity realms of students and teachers (Storz, 2008). This supports the collective work of the EBP, where issues of equity, diversity, inclusion, and decolonization are vocalized and situated by those who experience it, in a manner that is invitational and supports the transformation of the Canadian education system into one that is compassionate and responsive to the needs of all of its students.

There is no doubt of the importance of including our students' identities in the curricula of our classrooms, in our schools, and across all levels of education. Their voices and experiences matter; *they* matter. Curriculum must start and end with identity, and we do our students a serious disservice by teaching in any other way. Inclusive curriculum such as the EBP allows educators to carefully unpack the things (heritage, language, privilege, etc.) that students carry with them and creates safe and ethical spaces for student agency and empowerment to flourish. Recognizing our students as agents of change and as the *living curriculum* is what sparks human flourishing and will change our world for the better one classroom at a time. Safir and Dugan (2021) speak of schools "as possibility spaces in which to reimagine society" (p. 11). What a society we could create by working together.

## KEY TERMS

**Agency:** When students feel empowered to make changes in their own lives and in the lives of others. It is fostered through a strong understanding of our interconnectedness within classrooms where students have choice and all of their voices and lived experiences matter.

**Ethical spaces:** The concept of *safe spaces* in classrooms is regularly talked about; however, sometimes safe spaces are mistaken with *comfortable spaces*, meaning that if a student is uncomfortable, then the space is not safe. Sometimes, in conversations, our values or beliefs feel threatened, particularly when cultural beliefs and understandings are part of the conversation. Ermine (2007) introduced the concept of "ethical spaces of engagement" where these differences are surfaced and discussed.

**Hegemonic discourses:** The predominant understanding that is at play within a society and how this way of thinking is perpetuated through people's actions and words. Hegemony is the dominance of one way of thinking or being over all others; *discourse* refers to communication.

**Living curriculum:** Where teachers recognize the *tohfay* (gifts) or assets that students bring with them into the classroom and they incorporate students' cultures, histories, experiences, and stories into the curriculum.

## DISCUSSION QUESTIONS AND ACTIVITIES

1. In what ways did your education support and not support the development of your identity? What could your teachers have done to help you to come to understand yourself and others?

2. Which student story resonated with you? Why? What might help you in knowing who your students truly are so that you can see the things they carry as *tohfay* (gifts) or assets?

3. What do equity work and radical inclusion look like in your context? How could utilizing culturally sustaining pedagogy in the classroom support student agency?
4. Create your own Equity Backpack. Share with others in your class. How could its creation support your continued growth and development as a teacher?

## REFERENCES

Adichie, C. N. (2009, July). *The danger of a single story* [Transcript]. TED Conferences. https://www.classacthr73.org/resources/Documents/Event%20Materials/Chimamanda%20Adichie%20The%20Danger%20of%20a%20Single%20Story.pdf

Alcoff, L. (2006). Introduction: Identity and visibility. In L. Alcoff (Ed.), *Visible identities: Race, gender, and the self* (pp. 5–10). Oxford University Press.

Aoki, T. T. (1993). Legitimating lived curriculum: Towards a curricular landscape of multiplicity. *Journal of Curriculum and Supervision, 8*(3), 255–268. https://eric.ed.gov/?id=EJ461080

Aristotle. (2009). *The Nicomachean ethics* (L. Brown, Ed., D. Ross, Trans.). Oxford University Press.

Baroutsis, A., McGregor, G., & Mills, M. (2016). Pedagogic voice: Student voice in teaching and engagement pedagogies. *Pedagogy, Culture & Society, 24*(1), 123–140. doi.org/10.1080/14681366.2015.1087044

Bishop, R. S. (1990). Mirrors, windows, and sliding glass doors. *Perspectives: Choosing and using books for the classroom, 6*(3), ix–xi. https://digitalscholarship.unlv.edu/taboo/vol22/iss1/6

Brown, K. M. (2004). Leadership for social justice and equity: Weaving a transformative framework and pedagogy. *Educational Administration Quarterly, 40*(1), 77–108. doi.org/10.1177/0013161X03259147

Celoria, D. (2016). The preparation of inclusive social justice education leaders. *Educational Leadership and Administration, 27*, 199–217. https://eric.ed.gov/?id=EJ1094414

Egbo, B. (2019). *Teaching for diversity in Canadian schools* (2nd ed.). Pearson Canada.

Ellyat, W. (2022). Education for human flourishing—a new conceptual framework for promoting ecosystemic wellbeing in schools. *Challenges, 13*(58). doi.org/10.3390/challe13020058

Ermine, W. (2007). The ethical space of engagement. *Indigenous Law Journal, 6*(1), 194–203. https://jps.library.utoronto.ca/index.php/ilj/article/view/27669

Freire, P. (2018). *Pedagogy of the oppressed* (4th ed.). Bloomsbury Academic.

Ladson-Billings, G. (1995). Toward a theory of culturally relevant pedagogy. *American Education Research Journal, 32*(3), 465–491. doi.org/10.3102/00028312032003465

Ladson-Billings, G. (2006). From the achievement gap to the education debt: Understanding achievement in U.S. schools. *Educational Researcher, 35*(7), 3–12. doi.org/10.3102/0013189X035007003

Lee, E. (1995). *Letters to Marcia: A teacher's guide to anti-racist education*. Cross-Cultural Communications.

Lorde, A. (1979). The master's tools will never dismantle the master's house. In R. Lewis & S. Mills (Eds.), *Feminist postcolonial theory* (pp. 25–28). Edinburgh University Press.

Lorde, A. (1984). Age, race, class, and sex: Women redefining difference. In *Sister outsider: Essays and speeches* (pp. 114–123). Crossing Press.

McIntosh, P. (1998). White privilege: Unpacking the invisible knapsack. In M. McGoldrick (Ed.), *Re-visioning family therapy: Race, culture, and gender in clinical practice* (pp. 147–152). Guildford Press.

Moll, L. C., & Gonzalez, N. (1994). Lessons from research with language-minority children. *Journal of Reading Behavior, 26*(4), 439–456. doi.org/10.1080/10862969409547862

Muhammad, G. (2020). *Cultivating genius: An equity framework for culturally and historically responsive literacy*. Scholastic.

National Equity Project. (n.d.). *Educational equity definition*. www.nationalequityproject.org/education-equity-definition

Online Etymology Dictionary. (n.d.a). *Withering*. www.etymonline.com/word/wither

Online Etymology Dictionary. (n.d.b). *Flourish*. www.etymonline.com/word/flourish

Ortiz Guzman, C. M. (2017). *EquityXdesign: Leveraging identity development in the creation of anti-racist equitable design thinking process* [Doctoral dissertation, Harvard Graduate School of Education]. https://dash.harvard.edu/handle/1/33774659

Pabla, M. (2020). The legacies of Bindy Johal: The contemporary folk devil or sympathetic hero. *Sociology and Legal Studies, 11*(5), 228. doi.org/10.3390/rel11050228

Paris, D. (2012). Culturally sustaining pedagogy: A needed change in stance, terminology, and practice. *Educational Researcher, 41*(3), 93–95. doi.org/10.3102/0013189X12441244

Piccardo, E., & Payre-Ficout, C. (2022). Plurilingualism: Integrating languages and cultures in a personally reflective, and socially mediated process. In E. Piccardo, G. Lawrence, A. Germain-Rutherford, & A. Galante (Eds.), *Activating linguistic and cultural diversity in the language classroom* (pp. 15–47). Springer.

Safir, S., & Dugan, J. (2021). *Street data: A next-generation model for equity, pedagogy, and school transformation*. Corwin.

Sidhu, N. K. (2021). *Teacher resource kit for the equity backpack: Fostering equity and inclusion through lived experiences* [Unpublished manuscript]. https://drive.google.com/file/d/1Pi-qirNOCh7yqpWHWZJIBmHwZLAnzwN2/view

Sivia, A., Sidhu, N. K, & Levings, I. (2021). In E. Lyle (Ed.), *Re/humanizing education* (pp. 124–136). Brill. doi.org/10.1163/9789004507593_012

Stevenson, M. (2022). *Education for human flourishing*. Centre for Strategic Education.

Storz, M. G. (2008). Educational inequity from the perspectives of those who live it: Urban middle school students' perspectives on the quality of their education. *The Urban Review, 40*(3), 247–267. doi.org/10.1007/s11256-008-0083-0

Tatum, B. D. (2000). The complexity of identity: "Who am I?" In M. Adams, W. J. Bluemenfeld, H. W. Hackman, X. Zuniga, & M. L. Peters (Eds.), *Readings for diversity and social justice: An anthology on racism, sexism, anti-semitism, heterosexism, classism and ableism* (pp. 9–14). Routledge.

Theoharis, G. (2007). Social justice educational leaders and resistance: Toward a theory of social justice leadership. *Educational Administration Quarterly, 43*(2), 221–258. doi.org/10.1177/0013161X06293717

United Nations. (1989). *Convention on the rights of the child*. www.ohchr.org/Documents/ProfessionalInterest/crc.pdf

Watkins, J., Peterson, A., & Mehta, J. (2018). The deeper learning dozen: Transforming school districts to support deeper learning for all. https://static1.squarespace.com/static/5bae5a3492441bf2930bacd1/t/5c044d39758d469484888c20/1543786237346/Deeper+Learning+Dozen+White+Paper+%28Public+2%29.pdf

Wolbert, L., de Ruyter, D., & Schinkel, A. (2015). Formal criteria for the concept of human flourishing: The first step in defending flourishing as an ideal aim of education. *Ethics and Education, 10*(1), 118–129. doi.org/10.1080/17449642.2014.998032

Wolbert, L., de Ruyter, D., & Schinkel, A. (2021). The flourishing child. *Journal of Philosophy of Education, 55*, 698–709. doi.org/10.1111/1467-9752.12561

Yancy, G. (2012). How can you teach me if you don't know me? Embedded racism and white opacity. In C. Ruitenberg (Ed.), *Philosophy of education* (pp. 44–54). doi.org/10.47925/2012.043

# CONCLUSION

# Pedagogy for Flourishing: Preparing and Equipping the Educator

*Wendy D. Bokhorst-Heng*

In the introduction to this volume, we introduced you to Nussbaum's (2011) three capabilities for human flourishing: critical examination of the self; seeing oneself as a global citizen, bound to the flourishing of humanity; and compassion and empathy through narrative imagination. Implicit in developing these capabilities is the process of personal transformation. I remind you of the quote we shared from Howard (2006): "We cannot fully and fruitfully engage in meaningful dialogue across the differences of race and culture without doing the work of personal transformation.... We must assume that we will be changed in the process of engagement and dialogue" (p. 6). This transformation, in turn, can lead to our flourishing and the flourishing of those around us. The questions that this book seeks to answer are *What do these capabilities and flourishing look like in relation to the various dimensions of diversity in our student populations and our school faculty? And how do we teach for flourishing, especially cultivating the three foundational capabilities?*

The authors of this book addressed these questions in their specific areas, considering both conceptual models and practical pedagogical strategies that will help inform your teaching. To augment their discussions, this chapter explores more deeply strategies for self-reflection and for understanding our own position in relation to others and within the broader conversations regarding inequality and oppression. I will focus on two related constructs: *intersectionality* and *privilege*. As stated in a 2018 report by the Ontario Association of Interval and Transition Houses (OAITH), "Self-reflection ... is even more critical as we advance in our knowledge and understanding of oppression, power and privilege, intersectionality and how we ourselves hold both power and marginality, and we reinforce both oppression and marginalization, in our work, in our personal lives, with our family and anywhere we interact with others" (p. 14).

While the suggested strategies are ones that you can use in your own teaching, they are also meant to guide you in your own journey of reflection and flourishing, without which you cannot effectively guide others.

But first I draw your attention to the Indigenous Medicine Wheel as an Indigenous way of knowing (see chapter 11) to think about the connections between critical self-reflection and flourishing and pedagogy. This discussion is in response to the Truth and Reconciliation Commission's 62nd Call to Action, which calls for educating teachers on how to integrate Indigenous Knowledge and pedagogy into classrooms. I draw from Nicole Bell's (Anishinaabe from the Bear clan from Kitigan Zibi First Nation) (2014) work "Teaching by the Medicine Wheel: An Anishinaabe Framework for Indigenous Education." The Medicine Wheel is an ancient, sacred metaphor used in many Indigenous communities to represent Indigenous knowing. While there are different interpretations and applications of the Medicine Wheel, she notes, they all share the same "underlying web of meaning" regarding the interrelatedness and interconnectivity of all things: the emotional (ways of seeing), the physical (ways of doing), the mental (ways of knowing), and the spiritual (ways of being). The wheel is divided into four equal quadrants, each symbolizing one of the powers/medicines and areas of teaching of the four directions (east, south, west, north) and represented by a different colour, usually red, yellow, black, and white. In addition, the wheel is surrounded by the spirit world, with the Creator above and Mother Earth below. The completed image, Bell (2014) explains, is a model that "resembles a compass for human understanding" (para. 3).

Bell (2014) then considers the wheel in terms of pedagogy, explaining how each of the four directions comprises "gifts" as depicted in the Medicine Wheel designed by Cree Elder Michael Thrasher (see figure 22.1): "In the east, the gift of vision is found, where one is able to 'see.' In the south one spends time in which to relate to the vision. In the west, one uses the gift of reason to figure it out. In the north, one uses the gift of movement to do or actualize the vision" (para. 6).

The interconnectedness of these gifts is essential, Bell (2014) argues, as the fourth direction, involving a healing movement toward change, is possible only when the other components have been acknowledged. Within this model is a form of praxis contingent on continual reflection, "a healing and learning that can only happen through continuous and going reflection of oneself in relation to

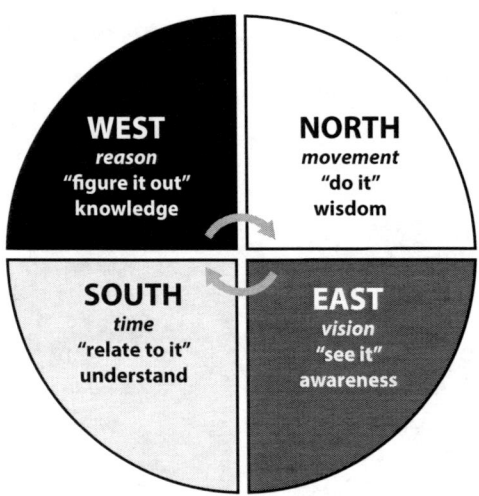

**Figure 22.1: Cree Elder Michael Thrasher's Gifts of the Medicine Wheel**
*Source:* Gifts of the Four Directions, Bell (2014). Used with permission from N. Bell.

others" (para. 7). This continuous process maintains balance and wholeness while embracing change. Included in this model are the core principles of wholeness, interrelationships, interconnections, and balance/respect: human flourishing.

Bell (2014) points out that there are many ways that Elders and traditional teachers have expressed the four directions, each drawing attention to different relationships that can be expressed in sets of four. The Anglophone East School District—in my own location in New Brunswick, in a city located on the unceded traditional territory of the Mi'kmaq people—presents a Medicine Wheel developed by the Indigenous Advisory Group under the guidance of Elder in Residence Donna Augustine of Elsipogtog First Nation. The wheel brings together cultural competence, decolonization, reconciliation, and Indigenization, and the four ways of knowing: mental-cognitive (reflection), spiritual-cultural (awareness), social-emotional (knowledge), and physical (action). The rising sun in the background is a reminder that the school district is located in the traditional territory of the Mi'kmaq people (see figure 22.2).

The Medicine Wheel is juxtaposed with the province's Education Act, its 10-year education plan, and the Truth and Reconciliation Commission's Calls to Action to emphasize the need to move from reflection to action within the province's policy, curriculum, and pedagogy. As my co-editor, Cathlene Hillier, pointed out, these attributes are similar to the head, heart, hands activity (described later in this chapter) that I frequently use in my teaching to encourage

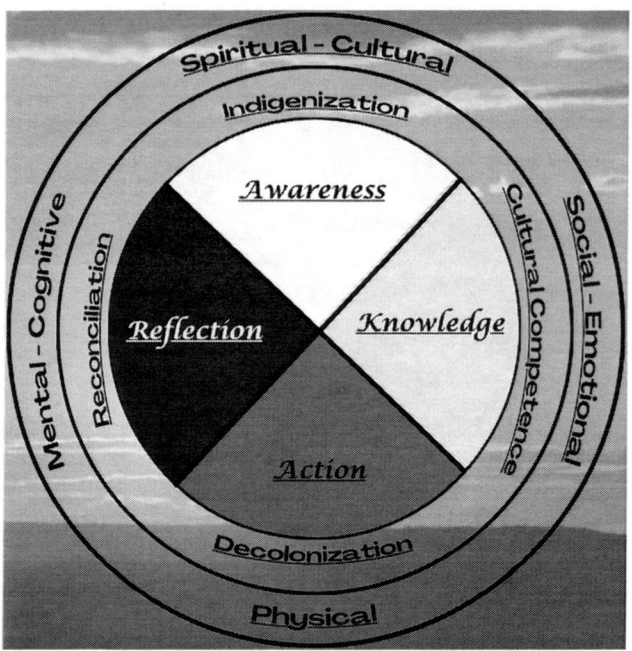

**Figure 22.2: Indigenous Education**
*Source:* Anglophone East School District (2024), Indigenous Education, https://asdeast.nbed.ca/indigenous-education/. Reprinted with permission from Elder Donna Augustine, Thunderbird Turtle Woman, of Elsipogtog First Nation, and Tracy Landry, Indigenous Education Coordinator.

reflection-to-action. However, similar to what LaFever (2020) concludes concerning Bloom's taxonomy in comparison to the Medicine Wheel, absent in the head, heart, hands activity is acknowledgement of the Spirit component of self and hence of learning.

Before you explore the pedagogical strategies described in the rest of this chapter, you may wish to learn a bit more about the Medicine Wheel and its applications to capacity-building for flourishing. Here are some suggested resources:

- Mallory Graham's (Anishinaabe-kwe [Ojibway and Potawotami] from Curve Lake First Nation) video *What Is the Medicine Wheel?* www.youtube.com/watch?v=S7nb4rJ_N14
- Nicole Bell's (2014) article "Teaching by the Medicine Wheel"
- LaFever's (2020) chapter "Using the Medicine Wheel for Curriculum Design in Intercultural Communication"
- Chapters 10 and 11 in this book

Some possible areas of reflection include *How might the Medicine Wheel provide additional insights into the concept of flourishing explored in this book, including chapters 10 and 11? What are some additional levels or outcomes you might add to LaFever's (2020) spiritual domain? What are some additional verbs you might consider? How might consideration of the Medicine Wheel change your approach to teaching and learning?*

The rest of this chapter is organized as follows: I will first introduce you to some key vocabulary that is used throughout the book, using a *quadrant vocabulary chart*. The focus will then turn to a series of pedagogical strategies: critically examining the self by using the tools of *duoethnography* (Brown & Barrett, 2017); identifying intersectionality using the *identity wheel*; exposing privilege (and intersectionality) premised on Mcintosh's (1988) *privilege checklist*; and participating in the *Human Library*, an activity that can be used to expose and break down stereotypes, consider ourselves in relation to others, and build compassion. All of these strategies require critical examination of self and are best employed in dialogue with others.

## BUILDING VOCABULARY: FOUR CORNERS VOCABULARY CHART

Once students are divided into small groups, instruct them to divide their chart paper into four quadrants, with their assigned word in the middle (see figure 22.3).

In the top-left quadrant, groups will write their own definition of the word. To do this, students can explore course readings or Internet resources to help develop the definition, but it is important that the definition is written in their own words. In the bottom-left quadrant, groups will write a sentence that incorporates the word to demonstrate their understanding. In the top-right quadrant, they will draw an illustration of the word, again focusing on its deeper meaning. And finally, in the bottom-right quadrant, the group will provide a personal association with the word based on what they have experienced, seen, or heard about. When groups are finished, instruct them to tape their charts on the wall. When all charts are posted, have the class do a gallery walk, where students will have the opportunity to add their own connections to each word or pose questions using sticky notes. Once everyone has had the opportunity to examine and respond to all of the quadrant charts, the instructor will have a class discussion during which they will review all the words and consider their importance within discussions of diversity and social justice.

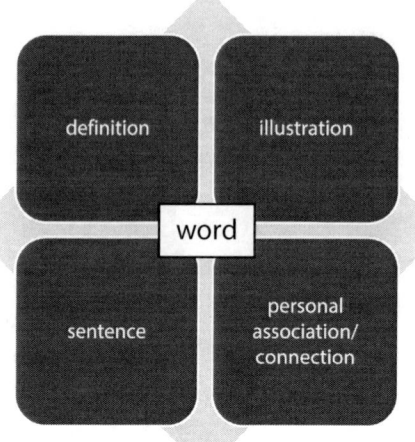

**Figure 22.3: Four Corners Vocabulary Chart**
*Source:* Compiled by the authors.

Note that this four corners vocabulary chart can also be done individually, with each student being assigned a word and developing their own four corners organizer on an index card or piece of paper, for example. After completing their index card, students can join with others who had the same word to compare their responses and then engage in a whole-class discussion to debrief all of the words.

As you engage with the content of this book, either in preparation for reading or perhaps while reading, you can use this four corners vocabulary chart to delve deeper into some of its key vocabulary. You may wish to do this individually or perhaps with your peers and with the guidance of your instructor. You may choose words that are completely new to you or perhaps words that are too familiar to you: words that have a taken-for-granted nuance for you and require your reconsideration. Some suggested vocabulary words are *prejudice, compassion, positionality, discrimination, microaggression, structural oppressions,* and *equity education.*

To get you started, we will work together on two terms that appear throughout this book: *intersectionality* and *privilege.* I chose these words for their significance in critical self-reflection, a foundational capability in flourishing.

## Intersectionality

*Intersectionality* is a term first coined in 1989 by American critical race theorist Kimberlé Williams Crenshaw and used to describe how identity-based systems of oppression overlap and influence one another. As summarized on the University of British Columbia's (UBC's) website (2021), intersectionality "merges many identity markers, including race, class, gender, sexual orientation, age, ethnicity, religion, disability, and more, to create a more truthful and complex identity." It is important to understand intersectionality in terms of its direct relationship to oppression. "Oppression is a force that allows, through the power of norms and systems, the unjust treatment or control of people. Intersectionality shows us that social identities work on multiple levels, resulting in unique experiences, opportunities, and barriers for each person. Therefore, oppression cannot be reduced to only one part of an identity; each oppression is dependent on and shapes the other. Understanding intersectionality is essential to combatting the interwoven prejudices people face in their daily lives" (UBC, 2021). The concept of intersectionality has been taken up by a number of our authors, including in discussions related to refugees (chapter 5), socioeconomic status (chapter 6), queer allyship (chapter 9), religion (chapter 14), and disability (chapter 17), and informs discussions in part X. You may wish to review these chapters in light of intersectionality and think about how this metaphor provides a "more truthful and complex identity." Then, using the four corners template, consider the following questions: In your own words, how do you define intersectionality? How might you use this term in your conversations about inequality and social justice within education? What does intersectionality look like, visually? What experiences might you have with intersectionality, and how does it deepen your understanding of your own identity, experiences with oppression, and privilege? As you discuss your responses with your peers, how do their experiences and connections with intersectionality compare with yours? How do their unique experiences speak to the importance of intersectionality in understanding the multifaceted nature of identity-based oppression?

To gain an even deeper understanding of intersectionality, I encourage you to watch Kimberlé Crenshaw's seminal 2016 TEDx talk, *The Urgency of Intersectionality* (https://www.youtube.com/watch?v=akOe5-UsQ2o). Another important resource is OAITH's intersectionality report, *How Does Intersectionality Work?* (2018), which highlights how intersectionality exists at individual, institutional, and systemic levels.

## Privilege

*Privilege* has to do with how some people are societally granted unearned and often unacknowledged advantages, while others are not. It is not something people choose, and in fact, without critical self-reflection, most are unaware of the privilege they hold. Their advantages may not be discriminatory in and of themselves; however, these advantages are nonetheless linked to systems of oppression[1] that impact people based on identities such as race, gender, sex, social class, and so forth. That is, privilege is made possible by a system and people that maintain it, including policies, laws, institutional practices, attitudes, and so forth. In his essay on privilege, Collins (2018) asks two pertinent questions as a follow-up to McIntosh's exploration of white privilege: Who built that system? Who keeps it going? He gives examples of policies that impact the accumulation of generational wealth that favour white people. Think of a flight of stairs (University of Michigan, 2021a). The ubiquity of stairs in buildings reflects a general assumption that people have the physical ability to walk up the stairs to access higher floors in the building. The design of the build (the system) that privileges some thus contributes to the oppression of others who are not able.

Because privilege is normalized, it can be difficult to even recognize it at first. And because it is normalized and often invisible to those who have privilege, addressing privilege is often met with resistance and defensive reactions or guilt. An instructor's guide to understanding privilege, developed by the University of Michigan (2021a), provides an excellent summary of why discussing and acknowledging privilege is so difficult: it challenges our dominant ideology of individualism and meritocracy, the idea that people have earned their position of privilege; it challenges "the validity of personal achievement and personal struggles"; because it is normalized, it is often "seen as a goalpost instead of how oppressive systems and structures operate to benefit some and inhibit others" (p. 3).

Peggy McIntosh's (1988) paper *White Privilege and Male Privilege: A Personal Account of Coming to See Correspondences through Work in Women's Studies* is often invoked in discussions about privilege. In this paper, McIntosh describes white privilege as follows: "I have come to see white privilege as an invisible package of unearned assets that I can count on cashing in each day, but about which I was 'meant' to remain oblivious." She identifies 46 examples of white privilege (e.g., "21. I am never asked to speak for all the people of my racial group"). Her list could be critiqued for its "softness"—for containing examples of minimal consequence to those who lack these privileges (Collins, 2018). However, the examples and the concept of privilege allow for a way to talk about the ways in which white people and racialized people move through the world in very different ways with very significant consequences.

Our earlier discussion about intersectionality is helpful here because it highlights how we hold both privilege and marginality/oppression. In this case, intersectionality suggests that one person may have privilege in one area (they may be white), while they may lack privilege in another (they may be poor). Some of the categories related to our identity are fixed (e.g., race), and some may change over the course of our lifetime (e.g., class, gender identity, religion), which means our positions of privilege or oppression can also change.

The concept of privilege is discussed by many of the authors in this book, including in relation to race (chapter 3), immigration (chapter 5), sexual orientation (chapter 9), religion (chapter 14), ability (chapter 16), rurality (chapter 18), and intersectionality (chapters 20 and 21). You may wish to examine these chapters in relation to their discussion of privilege, considering how it is taken up in different contexts of identity and how privilege is tied into intersectionality. Then, as before, use the four corners template to explore more deeply the meaning of privilege and to reflect on how this term relates to you. In your own words, how do you define privilege? How might you use this term in your conversations about inequality and social justice within education? What does privilege look like, visually? What personal experiences have you had with privilege or lack of privilege, and how do these experiences deepen your understanding of your own identity? As you discuss your responses with your peers, how do their experiences and connections with privilege compare with yours? How do their unique experiences speak to the importance of privilege in understanding the multifaceted nature of intersectionality and systemic oppression?

There are a number of excellent resources you can use to further your understanding of privilege. The first is "Privilege 101: A Quick and Dirty Guide" by Sian Ferguson (2014) (https://everydayfeminism.com/2014/09/what-is-privilege/). Next are three very different but equally powerful conversations: (1) an interview with Dr. Eddie Moore, founder of the White Privilege Conference (he discusses all forms of privilege as well) (www.pbs.org/video/dr-eddie-moore-1806-0ciopx/); (2) writer and storyteller Phyllis Unterschuetz's very personal account of privilege, *The Promise: A Lesson in White Privilege* (www.youtube.com/watch?v=1Wlf6QflVyc); and (3) activist Tim Wise's lecture *White Like Me: Reflections on Race from a Privileged Son* (he also has a book, and there is a documentary by the same title) (www.youtube.com/watch?v=tplVCp8jqNs). Finally, Chescaleigh's video provides an excellent introduction to the concepts of intersectionality and privilege that could be used in your K–12 classrooms: *Sometimes You're a Caterpillar* (www.youtube.com/watch?v=hRiWgx4sHGg).

While these resources focus primarily on white privilege, remember that the key characteristics and dynamics of white privilege define other forms of privilege as well; they just manifest differently. As you engage in conversations about this topic, consider the overlay of privilege and intersectionality; consider your place and responsibilities in this conversation as both possessor of privilege and as one denied privilege. A simple reflective exercise comes to mind: *head, heart, hands* (think of a gingerbread person cut-out). *Head* (knowledge): As you listen, what new concepts, terms, and arguments do you hear, or what concepts are you reminded of in a new way? *Heart* (emotions): What emotions do you experience as you listen? Do you react with anger? Pain? Guilt? Confusion? *Hands*: Consider an action plan. What is one tangible action you will commit to as a way to counter the damaging effects of privilege? Given the earlier discussion about the Medicine Wheel, consider the spiritual domain as well: How might you expand space for connectedness in your personal life and work and build relationships with others to make space for flourishing?

Having modelled the use of the four corners vocabulary chart, in the next section, I will focus on pedagogical strategies that can be used to develop the capabilities for flourishing noted earlier: exploration of self, seeing oneself in relation to others, and building capacity for compassion and empathy.

## BUILDING YOUR PEDAGOGICAL TOOLKIT

### Duoethnography: Critical Self-Reflection in Conversation with Others

I noted at the beginning of this chapter the importance of beginning with a critical examination of the self. I am grateful to Dr. Hilary Brown, a professor of education at Brock University, for introducing me to duoethnography. While duoethnography is normally understood as a research methodology, she developed it as a pedagogical tool for critical self-reflection and for exploring the vulnerabilities associated with discussions regarding intersectional identities and privilege. She generously shared her assignment materials with me to augment her article (Brown & Barrett, 2017), both of which I have used and adapted in my own teaching.

Norris and Sawyer (2012) define duoethnography as "a collaborative research methodology in which two or more researchers of difference juxtapose their life histories to provide multiple understandings of the world—duoethnography embraces the belief that meanings can be and often are transformed through the research act" (p. 9). This definition prompted Brown and Barrett (2017) to consider duoethnography in their respective fields (diversity and mental health) as a way for students to "[gain] critical awareness of their own narratives of experience through a dialogic process" (Sawyer & Norris, 2013, p. 3). They use the principles of duoethnography to guide teacher candidates to become reflective practitioners at all four levels of reflection: surface, pedagogical, and especially critical and the self. These principles include the following: our life histories are the focus of our research; duoethnographies are polyvocal and dialogic; the goal is to disrupt the metanarrative; participants have the opportunity to question previously held stories or interpretations of the past and to reconceptualize or restory those narratives. A full discussion of duoethnography's principles can be found in Sawyer and Norris (2013) and Brown and Barrett (2017). Ultimately, then, Brown and Barrett (2017) recast duoethnography as a pedagogical tool for students to develop the capabilities of critical reflection of self in relation to others in an "interactive third space": to have "teacher candidates explore, in conversation with another teacher candidate, the autobiographical and cultural events and influences that have shaped their beliefs, personality, and decisions" (p. 88) regarding diversity. "Reflection is at the heart of the duoethnographic process" (p. 88).

With this background to duoethnography as a form of pedagogy, I now provide excerpts from the assignment that Brown developed for her students, also summarized in Brown and Barrett (2017, p. 91–92), and that I adapted in my teaching. This duoethnographic exercise could also be used to prepare you to engage with the content of this book.

In this dialogic third space, then, duoethnography provides opportunities to build Nussbaum's (2011) capabilities that we identified as essential to human flourishing: a critical examination of the self around questions that interrogate one's own life narratives; seeing oneself in relation to others and to the flourishing of humanity when comparing and reflecting on each other's experiences and interpretations; and capacity for compassion and empathy in narrative imagination when interpreting and (re)storying partners' experiences.

## Identity Wheel: Locating Intersectionality and Exposing Privilege

There are many variations of an *identity wheel* available on the Internet. However, I am especially drawn to the one developed by OAITH in its 2018 report (p. 14) for how it juxtaposes intersectionality and privilege. It would be important for you to process this activity for yourself before you present this to your students, allowing yourself time to first reflect and consider how your positions on this wheel might also influence your role as a teacher and your relationships with your students.

*Instructions.* Following OAITH's suggestion (2018, p. 16), use the diagram on page 14 of its report to map your own places of privilege and marginality.

> **Box 22.1:** Duoethnography Exercise

*Instructions.* The assignment has three parts: (1) having the conversation; (2) summarizing the conversation (there are three parts to the written summary); and (3) distilling meaning from the conversation.

1. *Having the conversation*: Find a conversation partner—ideally someone with whom you share some important characteristic but who is also different from you in some significant way. Devote at least one uninterrupted hour to a conversation about diversity. Record your conversation. The following are some possible questions that you could explore in your conversation (but do *not* see this as a question-answer interview nor as a list to work through! These are prompts only):
    - When do you remember first encountering diversity, and what do you remember about that encounter? For example, when did you first become aware of differences in race? In social class? In sexualities?
    - What autobiographical, nonschool experiences (travel, parental influence, religious beliefs, geographical location, influential people or experiences, socioeconomic background, etc.) contributed to your assumptions about and skills related to diversity?
    - What cultural events and community characteristics and values might have been influential in your development as a teacher? For example, your community might have been very homogeneous or very heterogeneous in composition, or the community might have very politically conservative.

    The responses to these prompts and the stories that ensue should be shared in a natural conversational style. You may ask each other probing questions or offer responses that build alternative or shared experiences, or you may be reminded of something that takes the conversation in a different direction. Go deep!

2. *Summarizing the conversation.* The written summary, completed after listening to your recording, comprises three parts:
    i. Write a summary of your own experience as a student as it relates to diversity. This should be written in narrative form, an autobiographical story that incorporates the questions you addressed in the conversation.

ii. Write a similar summary for your conversation partner that captures your interpretation of what you heard in the conversation regarding their experiences.
iii. In a second conversation (in class), share your narratives with each other and discuss how accurate and consistent your interpretations seem to be. Did you hear each other as you heard yourselves or as you intended to be heard by the other person? You will then write a third part of your written response: a few paragraphs on how you responded to each other's summaries. Wherever possible, refer to specific statements or stories from the conversation in supporting or explaining your descriptions.

3. *Distilling meaning from your story.* After you have shared your interpretations, you will search your stories for the impact they are having on your future or current role as a teacher and your effectiveness in the classroom. Some possible questions to prompt you are below. As before, responses should be written with a thematic, narrative flow and not as just a series of answers to the questions below. Refer to specific examples from your conversations with your partner to support your responses.

- Do you see any of the experiences you described as a hindrance to being responsive to new ideas about teaching and learning? If so, how might you address these?
- What biases might you bring to the classroom that could be either beneficial or detrimental to your effectiveness as a teacher?
- How might you need to compensate for or adapt yourself to the biases you hold?
- In terms of diversity, how might your own experiences be used to help you understand or meet the needs of your future students?
- Are there now questions you have about your own education or past experiences that you want to investigate as a result of this activity? If so, what are they?

OAITH suggests placing dots or some other kind of marking to indicate where you hold privilege and where you hold marginality in the various dimensions of the diagram. It is important to understand that your marginal locations do not "cancel out" privilege and power, as noted earlier. Using our earlier example, you may assume that you, as a white person, don't experience white privilege because you are poor. But being poor doesn't cancel out the fact that you, as a white person, are less likely, for example, to be subjected to police brutality, which is a reality for many who are not white (Ferguson, 2014).

Think about the following:

- Which aspects of your identity are most important to you and why? How would you feel if (or how have you felt when) someone ignored one of your identities?
- Reflect on how your identity and privilege intersect. Why it is harder to notice those locations where you hold privilege than those where you do not?
- Consider the three sets of questions OAITH's report poses to interrogate our own privileges (p. 16) (similar to the head, heart, hands activity used earlier), taking your reflection to action. Ask yourself the "feeling" questions: Identify a wedge on the wheel that represents privilege for you. What are you feeling (e.g., guilt? sadness? anger? fear of making mistakes?) and why? How can you move past these feelings? Remember, as well, that while personal experiences are important, the real significance of privilege is that it is linked to systems of oppression. Consider the "thinking" questions: What are the institutional and systemic systems in place (including the beliefs and norms) that perpetuate the system of privilege that you benefit from? What do you actively do, without thinking about it (because that's how privilege works and functions), that reinforces your privilege and your lack of awareness of your privilege? Finally, consider the "action" questions: What can you do to be able to recognize privilege when you experience it? How can you disrupt and interject when those moments happen? If you hold privilege and want to show solidarity with a community that you are not a member of, how can you do this in respectful and helpful ways and with compassion?

If you have the opportunity, share your identity wheel and your reflections with a peer to explore more fully the nuances it represents. Think about how looking closely at ourselves helps us understand others, develop compassion, and think about our responsibilities in building the conditions for human flourishing.

## Privilege Checklist

This activity is an opportunity to explore both privilege and intersectionality. To prepare for this activity, first complete the four corners vocabulary chart regarding *privilege*, discussed earlier. In your classroom, you could have students read Ferguson's (2014) "Privilege 101: A Quick and Dirty Guide." Second, become familiar with Peggy McIntosh's (1988) article on white privilege and her list of everyday situations in which her whiteness affords her privilege.

*Instructions*: Divide the class into groups of two to four. Present them with a list of privileged identities to choose from, including gender, religion, socioeconomic status, ability, and so forth. You can consult OAITH's (2018) identity wheel for additional ideas. Encourage each group to choose an identity that they have not really thought about before, or perhaps the one that makes them feel most uncomfortable; ideally, it should be a privilege that they themselves hold. Using McIntosh's list as a model, students will develop a list of privileges associated with the identity selected. You can find examples of these lists online to help prepare you to guide students if necessary.

When their lists are completed, groups can share them in a gallery walk, digitally, or with a partner group. As students look at each other's lists, have them consider the following (University of Michigan, 2021b):

- What is your reaction to this list?
- Is there anything that surprises you, raises questions for you, or that you find problematic?
- Can you share something on this list that you have experienced in your own life?
- How do you think benefiting from this privilege or not benefiting influences your experience at school?

In their version of this activity, Ghosh and Galczynski (2014) suggest that students also identify what societal norm is assumed in each of their privilege statements and how privilege is granted to the dominant group.

Once students have had a chance to read each other's lists, guide them in a whole-class discussion on systemic structures of power and intersectionality. Here are some questions to include (University of Michigan, 2021b): If you were unaware of privileges or lack of privileges that you hold before this activity, why do you think that is? How do the different privileges or lack of privileges together interact in your everyday life? How do privilege and oppression manifest at school (in the classroom, building, extracurricular activities, facilities)? Why is it important to be aware of privilege and oppression? How might this awareness change how you view others?

In this exercise, students are encouraged to engage in critical reflection of self (where they are positioned in relation to these privileges), consideration of their position in relation to others and the systemic structures of power, and identification of areas for compassion and empathy in narrative imagination as they consider what it might be like for someone who does not live within these privileges.

## Human Library: Building Empathy and Compassion

The Human Library is an educational event that began in Denmark more than 23 years ago and has since spread to six continents and 85 countries. Using the metaphor of libraries and reading, the Human Library "works to create a safe framework for personal conversations that can help to challenge prejudice, help rid discrimination, prevent conflicts, and contribute to greater human cohesion across social, religious, and ethnic divisions"—to "build a more inclusive community" (https://humanlibrary.org). The Human Library thus provides opportunity for students to develop all three capabilities in relation to human flourishing. So what does it look like?

There are different variations, but here I describe what it looked like in my own experience. Each year, Bachelor of Education students in my course on diversity and multicultural education were involved in organizing and hosting a Human Library for the university community. High school students from neighbouring schools were also invited to participate as *readers* in the event. We reserved one room for our *library books*: individuals who defined themselves by a particular topic or identity. Some of the books included topics such as a female mechanic, someone who grew up in the projects, a nun, First Nations, a transgender person, Down syndrome, 2SLGBTQI+, a man with schizophrenia, a former drug addict, an ex-convict, a person who is blind, a refugee, and a Muslim woman. While they waited to be *signed out* by a reader, books would engage in conversation with each other over a light lunch. Just outside of this *library room* was a common area furnished with small round tables, each with two or three chairs. Tables were decorated with tablecloths and flowers, and live or recorded music was playing to help create an atmosphere conducive to conversation. A *circulation desk* provided copies of the collection's catalogue (which included with the book title a brief description of the stereotypes commonly associated with this title) and managed the sign-out processes. Once a *reader* (a member from the university community or the high school) identified a *book* they wanted to read, the book would be signed out, and together the book and reader would sit at a table to engage in conversation. Guidelines were given regarding the terms of engagement, and these aimed to maintain respect and care. Once their conversation was finished, the book would return to the library and the reader could sign out another book.

An essential component for the students in my class was reflection and discussion after the event. First, my students completed a K-W-L (Know, Want to know, Learned) chart during the event. The first two columns were completed prior to reading a book, and the last one was completed afterward: What do I think I know about this book prior to reading? What do I want to know? What have I learned from and about this book, including what turned out to be myth? Students had to the opportunity to share their responses in our post-event discussion. Second, we engaged in broader discussion: Which book will you never forget reading, and why? Which book was the most difficult to read or made you the most uncomfortable, and why? What assumptions about a book did you bring prior to reading, and how did your assumptions change? How will you act differently after reading the books you read today? How might the conversations change your everyday interactions with your peers, colleagues, and future students? How might they change your teaching? It was important not just to explore the empathy developed, but also to consider how that empathy may or may not turn into compassion in the sense of action and social justice. We also talked about systemic oppression and what that looked like in the stories we read. What became clear in students' reflections—which were often very moving—was how, in this "dialogic space" (Wegerif, 2007) created by the Human Library, the seeds of flourishing were sown as students reflected on self, in relation to others, and expressed compassion and desire for action.

## A FINAL WORD: FLOURISHING IN DIALOGIC SPACE

In this chapter, we have explored various pedagogical strategies and platforms that can be used to develop in ourselves and our students the capabilities that are intrinsic to human flourishing. Human flourishing begins with critical self-examination. But this self-examination becomes nothing more than self-indulgent navel-gazing if we do not consider ourselves in the context of the communities and world within which we live and in the context of the systems that uphold our positions within these communities. We also need to engage with others in dialogue to develop capabilities of compassion and empathy and, through narrative imagination, enter someone else's story. It is within that space created by dialogue that flourishing can occur.

This notion of learning and transformation through dialogue is not new. Wegerif (2007) talks about "dialogic space," drawing from the work of Bakhtin (1981). For Wegerif (2007), dialogic space is a space of dialogue "in which creative thought and reflection can occur," thereby enabling "possibility thinking" (p. 79). It requires an other-orientation, a "mutual attunement" (Wegerif, 2007) where we openly explore and engage with other voices and perspectives. As described by Palmgren-Neuvonen et al. (2021), "dialogic space is co-constituted in a linguistic process that engages the participants in the iterative negotiation of shared meanings and maintenance of intersubjectivity, namely, entailing an other-orientation and trust" (p. 411). The goal is not agreement; rather, the goal is understanding and meaning-making in relationship with others. As a framework for pedagogy, dialogic space entails three moves (Wegerif, 2013): *opening* to enable a shared space of possibilities; *broadening* (or expanding, widening) to bring in multiple perspectives; and *deepening* to invite shared reflection of those perspectives, to challenge the participants' assumptions, and to take responsibility for one's perspectives and future actions. With a stance of mutual attunement, the emphasis is on mutual respect and an openness to learn, grow, and transform. The strategies provided in this chapter and throughout this book with respect to diversity in Canadian classrooms contribute to this broader work of creating dialogic space for human flourishing.

## NOTE

1. As defined by the Learning Network (2015), *systems of oppression* "refer to larger forces and structures in society that create inequalities and reinforce exclusion. These systems are built around societal norms, and are constructed by the dominant group(s) in society. They are maintained through language (e.g. 'That's so gay'), social interactions (e.g. 'catcalling' women), institutions (e.g. when school curriculum does not acknowledge residential schools), and laws and policies (e.g. immigration policies that make it difficult for new Canadians to access health services)" (para. 2).

## REFERENCES

Anglophone East School District (2024). *Indigenous education*. https://asdeast.nbed.ca/indigenous-education/

Bakhtin, M. M. (1981). *The dialogic imagination: Four essays* (M. Holquist & C. Emerson, Trans.). University of Texas Press.

Bell, N. (2014). *Teaching by the Medicine Wheel: An Anishinaabe framework for Indigenous education*. EdCan Network. https://www.edcan.ca/articles/teaching-by-the-medicine-wheel/

Brown, H., & Barrett, J. (2017). Duoethnography as a pedagogical tool that encourages deep reflection. In J. Norris & R. D. Sawyer (Eds.), *Theorizing curriculum studies, teacher education, and research through duoethnography pedagogy* (pp. 85–110). Palgrave Macmillan.

Collins, C. (2018). What is white privilege, really? *Learning for Justice, 60*. https://www.learningforjustice.org/magazine/fall-2018/what-is-white-privilege-really

Ferguson, S. (2014). *Privilege 101: A quick and dirty guide*. https://everydayfeminism.com/2014/09/what-is-privilege/

Ghosh, R., & Galczynski, M. (2014). *Redefining multicultural education: Inclusion and the right to be different* (3rd ed.). Canadian Scholars.

Howard, G. R. (2006). *We can't teach what we don't know: White teachers, multiracial schools* (2nd ed.). Teachers College Press.

LaFever, M. (2020). Using the Medicine Wheel for curriculum design in intercultural communication: Rethinking learning outcomes. In Information Resources Management Association (Ed.), *Multicultural instructional design: Concepts, methodologies, tools, and applications* (pp. 686–711). IGI Global. doi.org/10.4018/978-1-5225-9279-2.ch032

The Learning Network. (2015, October). Intersectionality. *The Learning Network, 15*. https://www.learningtoendabuse.ca/resources-events/pdfs/Intersectioanlity_Newsletter_FINAL2.pdf

McIntosh, P. (1988). *White privilege and male privilege: A personal account of coming to see correspondences through work in women's studies* (Working paper 189). Wellesley Centers for Women. https://www.wcwonline.org/Fact-Sheets-Briefs/white-privilege-unpacking-the-invisible-knapsack-2

Norris, J., & Sawyer, R. D. (2012). Toward a dialogic methodology. In J. Norris, D. S. Sawyer, & D. Lund (Eds.), *Duoethnography: Dialogic methods for social, health, and educational research* (pp. 9–39). Left Coast Press.

Nussbaum, M. C. (2011). *Creating capabilities: The human development approach*. Harvard University Press.

Ontario Association of Interval and Transition Houses. (2018). *How does intersectionality work? Understanding intersectionality for women's services*. https://www.oaith.ca/assets/library/FINAL_OAITH_IntersectionalityReport_ENG.pdf

Palmgren-Neuvonen, L., Littleton, K., & Hirvonen, N. (2021). Dialogic spaces in divergent and convergent collaborative learning tasks. *Information and Learning Sciences, 122*(5/6), 409–431. doi.org/10.1108/ILS-02-2020-0043

Sawyer, R. D., & Norris, J. (2013). *Duoethnography: Understanding qualitative research*. Oxford University Press.

Sensoy, Ö., & DiAngelo, R. (2017). *Is everyone really equal? An introduction to key concepts in social justice education* (2nd ed.). Teachers College Press.

Truth and Reconciliation Commission of Canada. (2015). *Calls to action*. http://www.trc.ca/websites/trcinstitution/File/2015/Findings/Calls_to_Action_English2.pdf

University of British Columbia. (2021, March 8). *Intersectionality: What it is and why it matters*. Vice-President Finance and Operations Portfolio. https://vpfo.ubc.ca/2021/03/intersectionality-what-is-it-and-why-it-matters/

University of Michigan. (2021a). *An instructor's guide to understanding privilege*. https://sites.lsa.umich.edu/inclusive-teaching/wp-content/uploads/sites/853/2021/08/An-Instructors-Guide-to-Understanding-Privilege-Draft.pdf

University of Michigan. (2021b). *Examining privilege and oppression*. https://sites.lsa.umich.edu/inclusive-teaching/wp-content/uploads/sites/853/2021/12/Examining-Privilege-and-Oppression.pdf

Wegerif, R. (2007). *Dialogic education and technology: Expanding the space of learning*. Springer.

Wegerif, R. (2013). *Dialogic: Education for the Internet age*. Routledge.

# AUTHOR BIOGRAPHIES

**Zuhra Abawi** (EdD) is an Assistant Professor of Education at Niagara University. Prior to her faculty appointment, she was an elementary teacher and early childhood educator with the Peel District School Board. She is the author of *The Effectiveness of Educational Policy for Bias-Free Hiring* (2021) and co-editor of *Equity as Praxis in Early Childhood Education and Care* (2021) and *Enacting Anti-Racist and Activist Pedagogies in Teacher Education* (2023). Her work focuses on how discourses of race, equity, and identity are negotiated, mediated, and socialized in education. Her research seeks to recentre the voices of racialized and Indigenous children, families, and educators by problematizing whiteness and Eurocentric practices and processes of knowledge production, curricula, and discourses embedded in educational institutions from an anti-racist and critical race framework.

**Sally Abudiab** (MSc, MSW) is a registered social worker practising in Ontario and primarily works with youth at the intersection of child protection, education, and the criminal justice system. She currently attends the Lincoln Alexander School of Law to integrate her rich lived experiences with academic knowledge to drive sustainable, trauma-informed legal transformations. She is committed to inclusive holistic social policies and knowledge co-creation, and her mission revolves around expanding justice for those marginalized in society by pushing the boundaries of what is possible in social work and legal advocacy.

**Katy Arnett** (PhD) is a Professor of Educational Studies at the University of Maryland. Her research, on inclusive teaching practices and methods in second-language classrooms, has been disseminated in both English and French in multiple venues. She has presented at conferences in the United States and Canada and has been invited to speak to various school districts in the United States and provincial ministries of education in Canada. She was a Fulbright Scholar (2012–2013) at the Second Language Research Institute of Canada at the University of New Brunswick. Dr. Arnett has also co-developed, developed, or contributed to multiple textbook programs for teaching French as an additional language to students in Canada.

**Hiba Barek** (PhD) is an Adjunct Assistant Professor at Western University and a certified French teacher. She is a winner of the 2021 CATE Thesis and Dissertation Awards of Recognition. She earned a bachelor's degree and a master's degree in social sciences with particular emphasis on human development and sustainable development. She also earned a doctorate in curriculum studies and studies in applied linguistics from Western University. She is a contributor to the Bloomsbury Education and Childhood Studies encyclopedia. Her research interests focus on anti-racist pedagogies, care ethics in education, refugee education, agency and education, STEM education, and culturally responsive practices.

**Rachel Berman** (PhD) is an immigrant and white settler who grew up in Toronto, which is the traditional territory of many nations, including the Anishinaabe, the Haudenosaunee, and the Wendat Peoples, and is covered by Treaty 13. Rachel is a Professor in the School of Early Childhood Studies at Toronto Metropolitan University. Her research and teaching focus on race in early childhood settings; theoretical frameworks, in particular critical race theory and feminist theories; and critical qualitative methods. Her research has appeared in the *International Critical Childhood Policy Studies Journal*, the *Journal of Childhood Studies*, *Children & Society*, and the *International Journal of Qualitative Methods*, among other journals.

**Marja G. Bertrand** (PhD candidate) is a Senior Research Associate at Western University and a math and science teacher. Ms. Bertrand has received several graduate awards from the Faculty of Education at Western University, specifically the Art Geddis Memorial Award for her use of reflective practice as a critical lens and the Joan Pedersen Memorial Graduate Award for her contribution to early years education research. She has also implemented and designed curriculum documents for STEM, STEAM, and maker education activities with aesthetically rich mathematical experiences. Ms. Bertrand's research interests lie in STEM/STEAM education, makerspaces, culturally responsive pedagogies, and computational thinking tools.

**Wendy D. Bokhorst-Heng** (PhD) is a Research Fellow of Education at Crandall University (retired as Full Professor in 2021) and teaches part time at Wilfrid Laurier University and Western University. She has taught courses related to diversity and multiculturalism to undergraduate, Bachelor of Education, and graduate students, both in the United States and in Canada. She has published extensively on language and education policy in Singapore and its relationship with multicultural policy or national ideologies. Her recent research focuses on intercultural competence within the context of French immersion education in New Brunswick, considering the role of teachers and students, with a focus on human flourishing and ethics of care.

**Renée Bourgoin** (PhD) is an Associate Professor at St. Thomas University. She typically teaches elementary reading and language arts, social studies, language acquisition, and exceptionalities and differentiation courses. Renée's research interests include language/literacy acquisition and pedagogy, biliteracy, multiliteracies, at-risk language learners, cross-curriculum teaching and learning, and inclusion in language learning contexts. Prior to joining the School of Education, Renée worked at the school district level as a subject coordinator and an instructional coach. She is also an Honorary Research Associate at the Second Language Research Institute of Canada.

**Vandy Britton** (PhD) is an Associate Professor of Education at the University of the Fraser Valley. She currently teaches courses in social justice education, Indigenous education, secondary English methods, drama methods, and reflective practice in education to Bachelor of Education students. She also teaches courses in mentorship to Master of Education students. Dr. Britton's research areas include teacher education, language/literacy education, social justice and anti-racist education, arts-based education, and Indigenous education. She is particularly interested in how teacher candidates construct their identities and the ways in which teacher educators can support teacher candidates to decolonize and Indigenize their practice.

**Cynthia Bruce** (PhD) is an Associate Professor of Music Therapy and Chair, Department of Creative Arts Therapies at Concordia University. As a blind activist scholar and educator, she works to bring critical disability studies to music therapy and post-secondary education to amplify disabled voices, make visible and disrupt ableism, and create capacity for progressive systemic change. She teaches courses that bring a critical disability studies focus and analysis to education and music therapy contexts. She also maintains an active research program that mobilizes the lived knowledge of disabled university students and faculty in examinations of post-secondary accessibility and anti-ableist possibilities.

**Alana Butler** (PhD) is an Assistant Professor in the Faculty of Education at Queen's University. She joined Queen's University in 2017 and teaches in the Bachelor of Education and Graduate Studies programs. She has taught graduate courses on critical educational theories and Bachelor of Education courses on social justice education, at-risk learners, and social studies education. Her research interests and publications focus on the academic achievement of low-socioeconomic students, race and schooling, equity and inclusion, and multicultural education.

**W. Y. Alice Chan** (PhD) is the Executive Director and co-founder of the Centre for Civic Religious Literacy (CCRL). As a middle school teacher, she witnessed religious bullying in her Toronto-area classroom. Since then, she has researched religious bullying and religious literacy to help herself, her colleagues, and students of all ages. Her findings have been presented and published internationally, including in her book *Teaching Religious Literacy to Combat Religious Bullying: Insights from North American Secondary Schools* (Routledge). Now at CCRL, she promotes religious literacy across age groups, professions, communities, and sectors to support religious, spiritual, and nonreligious individuals.

**Michael Corbett** (PhD) is a Professor Emeritus in the School of Education at Acadia University. Previously, he worked as a public school teacher, consultant, and principal in Indigenous and rural communities in Manitoba and Nova Scotia. His experience working in small schools in nonmetropolitan places shaped his scholarly focus on the uneven development of modern education systems throughout the world, and particularly in the Canadian context. In addition to publishing more than 200 scholarly contributions, Corbett has worked with rural communities and schools in Australia and Canada as well as doing international comparative work in Norway and Finland. From 2015 to the start of 2018, he was a Professor of Rural and Regional Education at the University of Tasmania.

**Joanie Crandall** (PhD) is an Assistant Professor of Indigenous Education at the University of Northern British Columbia and Adjunct Professor of Education at Yorkville University. She has worked in Gwich'in, Inuvialuit, Inuit, and Cree communities. She has taught emergent literacy, elementary literacy, communications, and social studies to undergraduate education students; literature and composition; and Indigenous perspectives in Canadian education, organizational learning, leadership, proposal writing, self-directed inquiry, and action research to graduate Education students. She has also mentored graduate learners conducting capstone research. Dr. Crandall has published on social justice and allyship in northern educational contexts, decolonizing reading methodologies, and Indigenous videography and music.

**Carmelita Duffy** (BA, BEd) is a classroom teacher in New Brunswick. After completing her undergraduate degree, Carmelita pursued her dream of becoming a teacher. In 2023, she graduated from the Bachelor of Education program at St. Thomas University. When she was growing up, Carmelita tutored children in her neighbourhood. She always had a passion for learning and teaching others new things. She had a particular interest in teaching language. As a French immersion student, many of Carmelita's immersion teachers influenced and motivated her, inspiring her to also become a positive role model for young immersion students. Her goal is to create a positive and inclusive space for her students.

**Ardavan Eizadirad** (PhD) is an Assistant Professor in the Faculty of Education at Wilfrid Laurier University. Dr. Eizadirad is the author of *Decolonizing Educational Assessment: Ontario Elementary Students and the EQAO* (2019) and the co-editor of *Counternarratives of Pain and Suffering as Critical Pedagogy: Disrupting Oppression in Educational Contexts* (2022), *The Power of Oral Culture in Education: Theorizing Proverbs, Idioms, and Folklore Tales* (2023), and *Enacting Anti-Racist and Activist Pedagogies in Teacher Education* (2023). He is also the founder and Director of EDIcation Consulting (www.edication.org), which offers equity, diversity, and inclusion training to organizations and corporations.

**Kate Freeman** (EdD) recently retired from Queen's University, where she served for more than 30 years in various program development, management, research, fundraising, and ally-building capacities in Indigenous education. At Queen's University Faculty of Education, she was closely involved in the development and delivery of Indigenous community-based teacher education programs created and offered in partnership with First Nations stakeholders. She is a graduate of Trent University (Native Studies) and completed her doctoral degree at the University of Toronto with a focus on Indigenous education and program development.

**Cathlene Hillier** (PhD) is an Associate Professor of Education at Crandall University. She teaches social studies education and educational policy courses to Bachelor of Education students. She has also taught undergraduate sociology courses that address diversity and inequality in public policy and schooling. Dr. Hillier is the recipient of the 2024 Stephen and Ella Steeves Award for teaching excellence at Crandall. She has published articles on religious diversity in schools as well as socioeconomic and geographical inequalities in academic outcomes. Dr. Hillier is currently leading a SSHRC-funded project on technology use among children, families, and schools in New Brunswick and Ontario.

**Ben Iheagwara** (PhD) is an independent scholar and public affairs consultant with a strong background in multiculturalism, political philosophy, and international relations. He holds a Master of Arts in International Relations from McMaster University, a doctorate degree in philosophy from the University of Ottawa, and a post-graduate certificate in government relations management from Seneca College, Toronto. He has taught in Nigeria, Trinidad and Tobago, and Canada. He has also worked as a humanitarian aid worker with the Canadian Red Cross and faith-based institutions.

**Jay Kennedy** (PhD) (he/him) is an Adjunct Professor in the Faculty of Education at Lakehead University. He is an experienced primary school teacher and newly minted critical masculinities scholar who has presented his work at IOERC8 and the 2021 AERA Conference, among others. His research interests combine experiential education with issues of social and environmental justice.

**Karen A. Krasny** (PhD) is a Professor of Language and Literacy in the Faculty of Education at York University, where she teaches undergraduate courses in intermediate/senior language arts and English education and graduate seminars in theoretical models of reading and in children's and adolescent literature. As a former K–12 teacher, curriculum coordinator, and provincial language arts specialist (Manitoba), she has a long-standing interest in how Canadian language and multicultural policy shape educational practice. She is the celebrated author of *Collection Imagination*, 18 French-language picture books for children published with Addison-Wesley (Pearson). She is also a former co-editor-in-chief of the *Journal of the Canadian Association for Curriculum Studies*. Dr. Krasny has mentored students and early-career professionals in Canada, the United States, China, Ukraine, the United Kingdom, Saudi Arabia, and Germany.

**Ann E. Lopez** (PhD) is a Jamaican-born Professor of Educational Leadership and Policy at the Ontario Institute for Studies in Education, University of Toronto.

She is the Director of the Centre for Leadership and Diversity and Co-Director of the Centre for Black Studies in Education. She was Provostial Advisor, Access Programs 2017–2023, and Academic Director, Initial Teacher Education 2013–2016. Her research interests include school leadership theorizing and praxis, decoloniality, decolonizing educational leadership, and culturally responsive and socially just leadership. Dr. Lopez is co-editor-in-chief of the *Journal of School Leadership* and co–series editor of Studies in Educational Administration. She is the recipient of the OISE 2020 Award for Distinguished Contributions to Teaching and the 2022 University of Toronto Award of Excellence and Jus Memorial Human Rights Prize—Influential Leader.

**O'nahkwi:yo Kelly Maracle** (PhD candidate) is an Assistant Professor in the Indigenous Studies Program at Queen's University. She is a Mohawk woman and member of the Mohawks of the Bay of Quinte at Tyendinaga Mohawk Territory. Kelly has held numerous roles in the field of Indigenous education over the past 20-plus years in K–12, adult education, post-secondary education, and administration. She is a mother of three children and sits with the Turtle clan. Kelly's areas of focus are developing culturally responsive, land-based educational programming and trauma-informed practice.

**Lindsay Morcom** (PhD) (Ardoch Algonquin First Nation) is the Associate Dean in the Faculty of Education at Queen's University. She is a Canada Research Chair in Language Revitalization and Decolonizing Education. She is an interdisciplinary researcher with experience in education, Aboriginal languages, language revitalization, linguistics, and reconciliation. She is of Anishinaabe, Black Sea German, and French heritage and embraces the distinct responsibility this ancestry brings to her research. She is an active member of the Kingston urban Indigenous community and works collaboratively with the Kingston Indigenous Languages Nest to foster urban Indigenous language revitalization.

**Jhonel Morvan** (PhD) conducts research that focuses on school leadership, inclusion, equity, and mathematics achievement for Black, racialized, and minoritized students. He has authored several book chapters and scholarly articles on issues of equity and inclusion as they relate to mathematics and school leadership. He has more than 25 years of experience in education, in Ontario and internationally, as a teacher, administrator, and system leader. He was a curriculum manager at the Ontario Ministry of Education before his current position as a Superintendent of Education in a Northern Ontario district school board.

**Immaculate K. Namukasa** (PhD) is a Mathematics Education and Curriculum Studies Professor and the Associate Dean at the Faculty of Education, Western University. She was named a Distinguished Teaching Fellow with the Centre for Teaching and Learning at Western University in 2017 and named an "Amazing Human of Thames Valley" by the Thames Valley District School Board in 2022. She is a past journal editor for the *Ontario Mathematics Gazette* and *Math + Code 'Zine*. Her research interests lie in curriculum and pedagogical reforms, mathematics education, and teacher professional development through the integration of technology and computational thinking tools/resources/activities.

**Nathan Ngieng** (EdD) is a Deputy Superintendent with the Abbotsford School District in British Columbia. He has been in public education for more than 25 years, supporting transformational change in the K–12 public education system. Dr. Ngieng has advocated for inclusive education at a provincial policy level, with a focus on collaborative partnerships with community agencies and supports. His recent dissertation focuses on amplifying the voice of "at-promise" middle school students to foster school success and utilizing the promotion of student voice, agency, and empowerment as a catalyst for system change.

**Margaretta Patrick** (PhD) is an Associate Professor of Education at the King's University in Edmonton, Alberta, where she created a course called Religious Diversity in the Classroom that prepares beginning teachers to be confident and competent to teach about religion in all school contexts and within all subjects. Her research foci include how secondary social studies teachers teach about religion, the role of religious literacy in school curriculum, and the role of teacher beliefs with regard to religion.

**Carla L. Peck** (PhD) is a Professor of Social Studies in the Faculty of Education at the University of Alberta and is the Director of the Thinking Historically for Canada's Future SSHRC Partnership Grant. She researches teachers' and students' understandings of democratic concepts and teachers' and students' historical understandings, and is particularly interested in the relationship between students' ethnic identities and their understandings of history. She has held several major research grants and has authored, co-authored, and/or co-edited numerous journal articles, book chapters, and books related to this work.

**Leigh Potvin** (PhD) is the Director of and an Associate Professor in the School of Outdoor Recreation, Parks and Tourism at Lakehead University

(Thunder Bay). Leigh started her career as a K–12 teacher before moving into academia. Her post-secondary teaching focuses on leadership, social justice, equity, diversity, inclusion, and applications of these concepts in outdoor experiential education contexts. Leigh is an equity-focused and community-based researcher. Her current research focuses on fat queer liberation in outdoor recreation and parks contexts. For more on her work, see www.researchstories.ca.

**Kim Radersma** (PhD) is a Human Rights Officer for the Waterloo Region District School Board, where she works with system leaders to address systemic inequities in education both proactively and reactively. Kim has more than 15 years of experience as a high school teacher in the United States and six years as a university instructor in Canada. Her dissertation research focused on interrogating white identity and exploring transformational possibilities for white educators.

**Liv Rondeau** (OCT, MEd) is a Kanyen'kehá:ka (Akwesasne Mohawk Territory) educator and PhD student in cultural studies at Queen's University. She currently holds the title of Vice-Principal of Indigenous Education at the Limestone District School Board. She is a Graduate Teaching Fellow in the Indigenous Teacher Education Program, where she focuses on supporting teacher candidates in developing an understanding of Indigenous educational theory, holistic approaches to education, global Indigenous identities, language revitalization in education, and education for decolonization. As an artist and academic, she focuses her PhD research on the resurgence of Haudenosaunee raised beadwork and the cultural relevance that beadwork holds.

**Sonya Sachar** (PhD) is an Assistant Professor of Language and Literacy in the Faculty of Education at the University of Alberta. Over the past decade, she has taught in both post-secondary and elementary schools in Toronto, Ontario. Her research in applied linguistics is dedicated to promoting social justice in language and literacy education, particularly for racially minoritized students in Canada. Her current research involves exploring the perspectives of pre-service teachers regarding multilingualism in Canadian classrooms. Additionally, she collaborates with members of the South Asian Punjabi-speaking community to underscore the critical importance of preserving heritage languages.

**Cornelia Schneider** (PhD) is an Associate Professor in the Faculty of Education at Mount Saint Vincent University. Dr. Schneider's work focuses on people who are involved in educational processes, especially children and adults who are disabled. She has a comparative education approach that has led her to do work in Germany, France, Canada, and Honduras, among other places. More recently, she has become involved with policy work in Nova Scotia in order to improve equity, diversity, inclusion, and accessibility in public schools and post-secondary education. She is also deeply committed to teacher education, as she considers preparing pre-service teachers for inclusive education a pillar of EDIA work.

**Nerlap Kaur Sidhu** (PhD student) is a public middle school Vice-Principal in British Columbia. Her role as a Vice-Principal, classroom teacher, district curriculum instructional leader, and trustee on a private school board has given her the opportunity to collaborate, innovate, and inspire educators. She teaches social studies, English, social justice, and social-emotional literacy. Her interests include critical social justice, human rights education, and critical Indigenous education. Nerlap designs challenging high-support learning experiences that strengthen student identity formation while addressing inequities in public schooling. She has recently published on re/humanizing education. Nerlap has directly influenced the instructional practices of educators across Canada. She continues to grow and learn from colleagues and students.

**Navtej Nevan Singh Sidhu** (MEd) is a public school classroom teacher in British Columbia. He currently teaches courses in English, social studies, and social justice within elementary, middle school, and secondary school classrooms. He completed the Master of Education program at Simon Fraser University with a focus on Curriculum and Instruction: Equity Studies. The Master of Education provided him with a strong and diverse background in areas such as Eurocentrism in education, anti-racist pedagogy, Indigenous perspectives, and feminist theory. Navtej's interests lie in researching how hegemonic masculinity, Eurocentrism in education, and media representations affect the identity formation of marginalized students.

**Monique Somma** (PhD) is an Assistant Professor in the Department of Educational Studies at Brock University. She teaches courses in child development, cognition, and the inclusion of students with exceptionalities aimed at preparing educators to effectively meet the needs of diverse learners in the classroom. As a former special education and inclusive class teacher, she brings understanding and experience to her teaching and research. Her research focuses on preschool to secondary educator preparedness for inclusive education, from attitudes and beliefs to learning and practice, and strives to support educators to build capacity to include students with special education needs.

**David C. Young** (PhD) is a Professor in the Faculty of Education at St. Francis Xavier University, Director of the Frank McKenna Centre for Leadership, and a Resident Fellow of the Brian Mulroney Institute of Government. Dr. Young is the past chair of the Department of Curriculum and Leadership, and he previously served as chair of the Inter-University Doctoral Program in Educational Studies. Dr. Young's research is focused on the broad topic of educational administration and policy. More particularly, his current writing deals with issues pertaining to law and education. Dr. Young is co-editor of *Teaching Online* (2014), editor of *Education Law in Canada* (2017), co-editor of *Readiness for the Field* (2018), and co-author of *Policy Matters* (2023).

**David Zarifa** (PhD) is a Professor and Tier 2 Canada Research Chair (CRC) in Life Course Transitions in Northern and Rural Communities in the Department of Sociology at Nipissing University and Director of Nipissing's Research Data Centre. Dr. Zarifa has published extensively on issues relating to post-secondary access, educational choices and pathways, school–work transitions, labour market outcomes, skills, and brain drain. His recent research focuses on the unique experiences of northern and rural youth in Canada as they navigate their way through the education system and transition into the workforce.

# INDEX

ableism, 314
    concept of, 305, 315
    in educational spaces, 172, 303, 307, 322, 325
accessibility
    concept of, 315
    legislation, 305, 323
    teacher engagement with, 248, 325, 327
    universal design and, 246–248
Achebe, Chinua (*No Longer at Ease*), 365
achievement gaps
    COVID-19 and, 141
    poverty and, 120, 135
    racialization and, 72, 378
    rural/Northern areas and, 343
    *See also* opportunity gaps
Adichie, Chimamanda, 8, 403
*Adler v. Ontario (Minister of Education)* (1992–1996): 26–27, 32
affiliation, 6–7, 9, 70
    religious, 286, 291
agency
    cultivating learners', 108, 123, 127, 237, 320
    human flourishing and, 70, 375, 399–401, 405, 407, 409
    pedagogical praxis and, 82–85, 326
Akiwenzie-Damm, Kateri, et al. (*This Place*), 366
Alberta, 62
    culturally relevant pedagogy in, 62, 265, 347, 406
    draft social studies curriculum, 283–284, 287
    fictional depictions of, 360, 366
    school funding, 31–32
    socioeconomic status/geography achievement impacts, 117, 338, 349
Alexie, Robert (*Porcupines and China Dolls*), 364
allyship, straight teachers', 286
    challenges with, 173–180
    need for, 160–164, 170–171
    *See also* straight privilege

Amjad, Afshan, 265–266, 269
Anishinaabe perspectives, 176, 190
    on flourishing, 206, 210–212
    Medicine Wheel. *See* Medicine Wheel
    *mino-bimaadiziwin*, 199, 210–211, 219
    Seven Grandfather Teachings, 210–211, 218–219
anti-Black racism/anti-Blackness
    addressing, 48, 77–78, 82–83
    curriculum reinforcement of, 44
    in schools, 46–47, 77
anti-oppressive pedagogy, 40, 66, 171–172, 187, 194, 386
anti-racism
    critical race theory and, 40–41, 47
    educational initiatives, 76, 386, 405
    pedagogy, 66, 85, 102, 187, 194, 399
anti-wokeness, 41, 50, 76
*apoqnmatultl'k jiksktuali'lk*, 187–188, 190, 192, 195–200
Arctic region, 343
    teaching in, 187, 193, 197
Aristotle, 4–7, 21, 71, 228, 335, 399
artificial intelligence (AI), 87, 226, 237–238
aspirations, 30
    concept of, 128
    immigrants', 109, 228
    Indigenous community, 346–347
    parental, 123–28, 233, 343
    socioeconomic status and, 115–116, 122–127
    student, 95, 124, 128, 343
Atlantic Canada, 337, 362, 365–366
attention deficit hyperactivity disorder (ADHD), 138, 143
Atwood, Margaret, 356, 362

backwards design, 248–249
*Bal v. Ontario* (1994): 26–27

barriers
- addressing systemic, 24–25, 127–128, 144–145, 315, 388–389
- concept of, 123, 259, 419
- cultural, 24, 212, 322
- disability and, 248, 251, 321–322, 328
- educators working to dismantle, 133, 249, 254, 258, 319–328, 400
- to flourishing, 15, 30, 50, 159, 319–325, 375
- geographical, 339
- language, 94, 244, 322
- racism and, 46–48, 325, 380
- socioeconomic status, 133–136, 140–141

Battiste, Marie, 61, 70–71
Beaton, Kate (*Ducks*), 366
belonging
- concepts of, 196, 214–215, 219, 328
- disabled students', 303–305, 308–310, 315, 319–320, 381–382
- inclusive education and, 322–324, 328, 382
- liberatory praxis and, 78, 81–83, 88, 145, 401
- multicultural policy and, 230, 232
- racialized/marginalized students', 40, 61, 78, 98, 106, 322–324
- religion and, 267, 276

bilingualism, 23–24, 230–231. *See also* Royal Commission on Bilingualism and Biculturalism
Bissoondath, Neil (*The Unyielding Clamour of the Night*), 366
Black people, 336
- Canada's historical racism against, 40, 44–46, 61
- poverty rates, 117
- systemic racism facing, 8, 10, 68, 79
- teaching history of, 42–46, 63–64, 80, 85
- violence against, 40, 46, 268

Black people, Indigenous Peoples, and people of colour (BIPOC)
- addressing achievement gaps of, 141–142, 145
- discrimination facing, 47–48, 61, 209–210
- elevating perspectives of, 49–51, 67–68, 82–83, 207, 375

Black students, 244
- academic streaming discrimination, 46–48, 63–64, 386–388
- experiences with racism, 2–3, 46, 77, 378
- inequities and oppression facing, 77–78
- literate lives of, 79, 82–83
- support for, 82–83, 86, 304

blind/visually impaired students
- education of, 308
- lived experiences of, 307–312

Bloom, Paul, 8–9
Bourdieu, Pierre, 121, 228–229
boy-crisis, 158–159
British Columbia, 3, 350n2
- curriculum in, 163, 347, 397, 406
- Eurocentrism/racism in schools in, 64, 400, 403
- religion/spirituality in schools, 267–268
- school funding, 31, 267
- socioeconomic status/geography achievement impacts, 117, 338, 343–345, 349

Buddhism, 269, 289–290

capabilities approach (Nussbaum), 3–9, 115–118, 320, 335, 413, 423
Centre for Civic Religious Literacy (CCRL), 271, 274, 276, 278
Charter of Rights and Freedoms, 232, 384
- cases on religion and education, 26–28, 32
- rights/freedoms based on, 25, 33–34

Children of the Earth High School (Winnipeg), 235–236
Chinese people, 270
- Canada's historical racism against, 61, 77, 117
- newcomers, 244, 271

Christianity, 270
- colonialism and, 275, 289–290
- dominance in Canadian society, 154–155, 275
- funding for schools prioritizing, 27, 267
- in schools, 27, 266–267, 287

Coady, Lynn (*Mean Boy*), 365
collaborative learning, 85, 88, 139, 293–294

colonial legacy, 194
    Canada's, 59, 61–62, 72
    residential schools', 29, 40, 234
    United States', 44, 76

colour-blindness, 43, 50–51

Confederation, 23, 230, 267, 362
    concept of, 35

Conlin, Christy Ann (*Heave*), 365

controversial public issues, teaching, 65, 161, 284, 288, 293–295

*Corporation of the Canadian Civil Liberties Association v. Ontario (Minister of Education) and Elgin County Board of Education* (1990): 26–27

cosmopolitan education
    concept of, 66, 71–72
    diagnostic approach of, 66–68
    empowerment approach to, 66, 69–70
    sympathetic imagination, 66–68, 70

counter-narrative/storytelling
    concept of, 43, 51
    as CRT pedagogy, 49–50, 188, 265

covenantal pluralism, 272–274, 276–278

COVID-19 pandemic
    community upheaval amid, 93, 195
    digital divide in, 135, 140–142, 197
    measures for learning amid, 140–144, 197, 348
    poverty amid, 116, 134–135, 140

Crenshaw, Kimberlé, 42–44, 51, 418–419

critical consciousness, 102, 193
    concept of, 83, 88
    fostering in learners, 7, 12, 78, 83, 104–105

critical disability studies, 319, 321
    lived experience and, 306–307, 311–312, 314–316
    theory, 305, 377, 381

critical race theory (CRT), 418
    backlash to, 41, 44, 46–47, 76
    in Canada, 45–51
    concept and history of, 41–42, 47–48, 377
    critiques of, 42, 46–47
    interest convergence, 41–43
    in pedagogy, 48–51, 187–188
    teacher awareness and, 49–51, 194
    tenets of, 42–44
    in United States, 44–45
    *See also* TribalCrit

critical self-examination, 5–6, 429

critical self-reflexivity, 188, 191–192, 286

critical theory (CT), 378, 390
    components of, 97–98

critical thinking
    cultivating, 293–294

cultural capital, 30, 72, 121–122, 126–127, 187, 337

cultural relativism, 6, 272–273, 278

culturally reflective teaching/learning, 143
    concept of, 145
    developing, 142–144, 217, 226

culturally responsive caring, 108
    concept of, 98, 109
    demonstrations of, 106–107
    lack of, 30, 99

culturally responsive curriculum/pedagogy, 99
    concept and benefits of, 81–82, 86–87, 107, 327–328, 401–402
    Indigenous perspectives in, 346, 408

culturally responsive teaching (CRTe), 108, 190, 226
    components of, 97–98, 102
    concept of, 109
    demonstrating, 103–107, 194
    educator struggles with, 2, 95
    principles of, 136–137

curiosity, 5–6
    cultivating, 10–11, 67, 216, 306

Dangarembga, Tsitsi (*Nervous Conditions*; *This Mournable Body*), 365–366

decolonial love. *See* radical decolonial love

decolonization, 52, 65
    concept of, 73
    educator dialogue on, 196, 210, 415
    equity, diversity, inclusion, and (EDID), 190–193, 197–199, 408
    stipulations of, 72, 198, 210, 215

democracy
    participation in societal, 5, 292–293, 388
    school practice of, 4, 271, 278, 314, 320, 402–405

Dewey, John, 320
dialogic space
    duoethnography and, 412–413
    engaging with critical issues, 82, 87, 408
    Human Library and, 429–430
    Indigenous lens and, 189
    religious literacy and, 282, 285
DiAngelo, Robin, 9–10
differentiated instruction, 138, 259, 382
    English language development, 103–106, 258
digital divide/gap, 135, 142–143, 145
disability
    dominant narratives on, 8–9, 245, 303–304, 309–315
    medical model of. *See* medical model of disability
    rights, 319–320, 323, 381
    social model of. *See* social/biopsychosocial model of disability
    studies, 319, 321
disabled people, 408
    exclusion of, 207, 305–307, 322–326, 381–383, 389
    flourishing of, 303–307, 309–311, 313–315
    inclusive education and, 209, 247, 304, 319–327
    language on, 8–9, 303–304, 309–315
    mobilizing lived experiences of, 304, 306, 311–312, 323
    poverty facing, 118, 335
    teacher perceptions of, 8–9, 314, 248, 381–383, 388–389
    technology use by, 308–310
    *See also* blind/visually impaired students; Universal Design for Learning
discrimination
    ableist, 172, 303, 307, 315, 322, 325
    classroom conversations on, 12–13, 285, 418–420, 428
    concept of, 15
    gender/sex, 15, 181
    intersectionality and, 51
    multiculturalism and, 24–25, 29–30
    policies/legislation and, 23–25, 27, 32
    racial, 41–46, 63–64, 77, 271, 380, 386–387
    religious/spiritual, 265, 271, 274–278, 285, 290
    school practices, 41–46, 63–64, 118, 274–278, 386–389
    socioeconomic, 118
    systemic, 2, 47, 63, 69, 418–420
    teacher reflection/work on, 172, 179, 389, 407
diversity, 25
    celebration of, 30, 230, 235, 385–386
    definitions of, 1
    disability as, 303, 319, 327
    duoethnography and, 422–425
    institutionalization of, 25, 29
    intersectionality of, 3–4, 48
    linguistic, 225, 229, 235, 238, 366
    multicultural education/policy and, 23–25, 33, 51, 62–65, 230
    opinions on, 10, 77
    pluralism and, 272–275
    religious. *See* religious diversity
    rural, 336–337
    student, 1–2, 48, 93, 413
    super. *See* superdiversity
    teaching in education, 2–5, 30, 98, 319, 413, 417, 428
diversity, equity, and inclusion (DEI), 41
    and accessibility, 327
    and decolonization, 190–193, 197–199, 408
    increase in, 46, 389
    in rural communities, 336, 357–358, 363–364, 366
    teaching in education, 76, 137–138, 226, 358, 408, 428
dropout rates, 48, 78, 338, 343

Eck, Diana L., 272–274
egalitarianism
    Canadian mythology of, 45–46
    in education, 66–72
    liberal, 66, 69, 71
Egan, Kieran, 358

elementary education, 357
    deaf learner experiences in, 308, 310
    language instruction in, 100, 233, 403
    racism in, 47, 347, 403
    religious discrimination in, 265, 285
    rural, 338, 341
    urban, 122, 131, 265, 338
Ellison, Ralph, 68
embodied capital, 228–229
empathy
    capabilities approach to, 5, 7, 78, 413, 422–423
    concepts of, 7–9
    covenantal pluralism and, 273–274, 278, 293
    cultivating in students, 138, 294
    Human Library and, 428–430
employment,
    disabled student, 309–311, 313
    flourishing and, 72, 127–128, 335–337, 346, 406
    Indigenous, 236, 336, 339, 343, 346
    parental/student aspirations for, 119, 123–128
    policies to increase, 25, 208, 348
    race and, 42–43, 379–380
    rurality/northernness and, 116, 335–340, 343, 347–348, 366
    socioeconomic status and, 115–116, 119–126, 135, 340, 348
    *See also* teaching career experiences
English literacy development (ELD) teachers
    attempting to bridge cultural divides, 100–102
    case study with, 96–98
    challenges with refugee students, 93–96, 108
    culturally responsive caring by, 106–108
    culturally responsive pedagogy by, 102–106
    lack of training for refugee SIFEs, 98–100
equity
    challenges to, 76–77, 197, 379, 383
    concept of, 43, 145

disability and, 303, 309, 327
educational, 62, 357, 407–408
educator self-reflection and, 30, 83, 102, 172–174, 418
liberatory praxis and, 82–85, 87–88
literacy, 30, 35, 82, 85
multiculturalism and, 25, 35, 62
policies, 25, 35, 379, 386–389
teaching for, 2–3, 134–140, 250, 407–408
*See also* diversity, equity, and inclusion (DEI)
Equity Backpack Project (EBP), 397
    flourishing in, 399, 401, 405–407
    as living curriculum, 398–402, 404, 407–409
Erasmus, George, 60
essentialization, 154, 164, 289
ethical spaces, 398, 400–401, 409
*eudaimonia*, 4, 66, 71, 228, 399
Euro-Canadian community
    grand narratives of, 60–62, 64
    multicultural education and, 62–65
    privileging of, 59–60, 63–64, 72
Eurocentrism
    concept of, 61, 73
    dismantling/decentring, 40, 43, 66, 73, 76–80, 400–404
    educator awareness of, 82, 192
    hegemony of, 43, 80, 137, 154, 403
    Indigenous ways of seeing versus, 137, 216
    multiculturalism and, 60–62, 64–66, 72
    racialized students and, 59–60, 69–70, 401

femininity
    stereotypical qualities of, 154–156, 158–159
    whiteness and, 47
feminist critiques, 42, 177, 311
fiction, Canadian, 362
    rural flourishing in, 358–359, 363–368
First Nations people, 28, 36n4, 187, 213, 428
    educational sovereignty, 30–31
    languages, 229, 234
    socioeconomic inequities and, 135
    *See also* Indigenous Peoples

Fish, Tricia (*New Waterfront Girl*), 365
flourishing
    agency in, 70, 375, 399–401, 405, 407, 409
    Anishinaabe perspective on, 206, 210–212
    barriers to, 15, 30, 50, 159, 319–325, 375
    concept of, 15, 295
    conditions for, 71–72
    of disabled people, 303–307, 309–311, 313–315
    employment and, 72, 127–128, 335–337, 346, 406
    gender and, 14, 66–69, 324, 375–376, 389
    global citizenship and, 3–5, 30, 188, 193, 346, 375
    Haudenosaunee perspective on, 206, 210–212, 218–219
    Medicine Wheel and, 210–211, 414–417, 422
    mutuality in, 207, 209–212, 218, 400, 430
    rural, 358–359, 363–368
    socioeconomic status and, 14, 66, 118–123, 134–135, 145–146, 290, 335
    triad of ideas in, 71–72
    well-being and, 115–116, 210, 215, 218
    withering versus, 398, 403–405
Floyd, George, 46, 76, 87
Foucault, Michel, 170
Freire, Paulo, 15, 84, 192, 408
    critical consciousness, 7, 78, 83, 88
French Canadians, 23, 31, 231
French Immersion (FI), 243–244, 350n1
French language learning, 31, 62, 158, 348
French Language Opportunities for Rural Areas (FLORA), 348
funding, 48
    faith-based school, 31–32, 267–268
    multicultural/language initiative, 24, 26, 233, 235
    private school, 27, 32, 267
    Roman Catholic school, 31–32, 267
    socioeconomic status and, 135, 141

gay-straight alliance (GSA) clubs, 162, 171–173, 276, 383–385

geography, 192
    academic achievement and, 336–338, 342–346
    marginalization through, 3, 116, 336–337, 424
    *See also* place; provincial North
gender
    academic test scores and, 338–339, 389
    binary concept of, 153–154, 156–157, 377, 385
    discrimination, 15, 30, 181, 404
    divergent expressions of, 160–161, 164
    fictional depictions of, 357, 364–366
    flourishing and, 14, 66–69, 324, 375–376, 389
    hierarchy, 154, 156, 388
    intersectionality and, 3, 11, 43–44, 51, 274–275, 327, 419–421
    norms, 153–155, 159–161, 339, 376
    school policing of, 157–158, 160–161, 163–164, 383
    school curricula and, 157–158, 162–163, 378
    supports for teachers and students on, 162–164, 403, 408
    teacher biases, 43, 159–160, 179–180
    transmission of knowledge about, 153, 156–157, 159–160
    Western notions of, 153–156
    *See also* 2SLGBTQIA+ community; allyship, straight teachers'
Giddens, Anthony, 363
Giroux, Henry, 84
global citizenship, 304
    cultivating in students, 5–9, 78, 136–137, 188, 199, 413
globalization, 225
    rural education and, 359, 363
    superdiversity and, 226–227, 238
Good, Michelle (*Five Little Indians*), 364
good mind, 211–212, 218
graduation, high school
    rates, 119, 339, 342–345, 388
    skills upon, 208, 346

Grant, Carl, 4, 6, 15, 304, 306, 375
gratitude, sense of, 143, 178, 211–212, 218–219

Harari, Yuval, 359
Haraway, Donna, 358
Hay, Elizabeth (*Alone in the Classroom*), 364
hegemonic discourses, 60–61, 170, 404
    concept of, 409
    disrupting, 236, 236, 377, 389, 400–1
hegemony
    American, 189
    concept of, 73, 409
    Euro-Canadian/white, 48, 61
    of normative narratives/epistemologies, 60–61, 67, 170, 172, 404
    *See also* hegemonic discourses
heritage language
    Indigenous languages, 232, 236
    school programs, 232–236, 238
heterogeneity, 328, 424
    benefits of/strategies for learning space, 128, 319, 322–327
    religion and, 269, 278
heteronormativity
    confronting, 172–175, 179–180, 377, 384–385
    in curriculum, 157, 159, 163, 170
    harm from, 47, 153, 161, 172, 179
heteropatriarchy, 172
heterosexism, 66, 155, 170, 181
    confronting, 172–175, 179–180, 377, 384–385
heterosexuality
    hegemony of, 155, 172–173, 180, 385
    privilege, 2, 181
Highway, Tomson (*Kiss of the Fur Queen*), 364
Hinduism, 268, 270, 275, 289
homophobia, 384–385, 390
    pervasiveness in schools/society, 2, 155, 161, 170, 172–173
    teacher involvement in, 171, 174–175, 178–180
hooks, bell, 207, 209
Howard, Gary, 2, 10–11, 413

human flourishing. *See* flourishing
Human Library, 417, 428–429
Hurd, Elizabeth Shakman, 290

identity-centred education, 83
    Eurocentric versus, 62–63, 137, 193–194, 346–347
    faith-based, 275–277, 285
    importance of inclusive, 48, 210, 398–409
    language development and, 103, 228, 233, 348
    place-based, 336–339, 362
identity wheel, 423, 426–427
immigrants, 344, 361
    Canada's increasing population of, 1, 24, 226–227, 244
    Eurocentrism regarding, 22, 28
    experiences of, 79, 268, 402
    language learning and, 228, 231–233, 243
    multicultural policies and, 1, 22–26, 35
    poverty facing recent, 134
    systemic inequities for, 108, 134, 268, 421
immigration
    laws and policies, 41–42, 230, 243, 266
    status, 274, 291, 440n1
inclusive education, 274–275
    belonging and, 322–324, 328, 382
    concept of, 324
    disability and, 209, 247, 304, 319–327
    identity-centred, 48, 210, 398–409
    language learning and, 243–247, 249–254, 258
    special education versus, 306–307, 314, 321, 324
Index for Inclusion, 325, 327–328
India, 26, 366
    newcomers from, 244, 271, 397
    religious conflict in, 268, 270
Indigenous Peoples
    assimilation of, 22–23, 28–29, 61, 154, 189–190, 231
    (counter-)narratives for teaching, 49–51, 145
    COVID-19 impacts, 195, 197

Indigenous Peoples (*continued*)
  cultural/linguistic genocide of, 29, 40, 61, 64, 229, 275
  culturally responsive education for, 30–31, 190–191, 193–199, 346–348
  curriculum inclusion of, 61–64, 145, 346–348, 358, 364–366
  definitions and terms for, 187–188
  Elders, 187, 195–196, 200, 214, 236, 414–416
  Eurocentric narratives about, 60, 62–64, 192, 198, 207
  flourishing of, 195–196, 198, 206, 210
  gender, understandings of, 154, 172
  intergenerational trauma, 28–29, 40, 50, 61, 64, 72
  land, relationships with, 192, 216–218, 226, 229, 336, 346
  languages, 190, 193–199, 230–232, 234–236
  learning inequities facing, 47, 64, 77–78, 141, 339, 343–344
  liberatory pedagogical practice for, 2, 79–80, 85–88
  liminality of, 188–189, 227
  non-Indigenous educators and, 61–62, 190–192, 196–197, 217–218, 268
  non-Indigenous walking with, 36n4, 171, 187, 197, 200
  ontologies/epistemologies, 193, 200, 210, 414–417
  oral narratives of, 189–190
  as original inhabitants, 22, 45, 62, 64, 230
  population growth of, 1, 236, 336
  poverty facing, 117, 134
  racism facing, 47, 60–61, 189, 274, 360
  reconciliation, 64, 176, 195–197, 235–236, 414–415
  residential schools. *See* residential schools
  resistance, 172, 192, 207, 366
  resources in teaching, 187–188, 197–198, 207
  rights of, 189–190, 192, 234–235
  self-determination/sovereignty, 189–190, 360
  and settler-colonialism, 22, 45–46, 52, 61, 64, 72–73, 189
  traditional knowledge, 189–195, 198–199, 206, 212, 216–217, 363
  Treaties, 61, 192, 235
  TribalCrit and. *See* TribalCrit
  two-eyed seeing. *See* two-eyed seeing (*Etuaptmumk*)
  wellness, perspectives on, 209–210, 212–218
  worldviews/spiritualities, 213, 217–218, 268, 275, 414–417
  *See also* decolonization; Black people, Indigenous Peoples, and people of colour (BIPOC)
inequities
  power, 172, 407–408
  principles to tackle, 35
  racial, 43, 50–52, 197–198
  school practices, 197–198, 376–378, 382, 386–389
  systemic/structural, 76–82, 98, 133–135, 145, 312–313
  teacher attempts to mitigate, 101–102, 108, 137, 143–144, 398–404
Institute for Global Engagement (IGE), 272, 274
interest convergence, 41–43
International Day of Pink, 384, 390
intersectionality, 1, 4, 316
  activities for exploring, 43–44, 417, 420–423, 427
  concept of, 3, 44, 51, 274–275, 418–419
  educators' recognition of, 117, 172, 327, 336, 399, 413–414
Inuit people, 46n4, 187
  languages of, 229, 234
  pedagogical resources for, 188, 197–198
  *See also* Indigenous Peoples
*Islamic Schools Federation of Ontario v. Ottawa Board of Education* (1997): 26–27
Islamophobia, 265–266, 268, 277

Jane and Finch community (Toronto), 133, 140–143
Jewish people, 276
    discrimination facing, 283
    hate crimes against, 268–269
    private school attendance, 27, 32
Jones, Lloyd (*Mr. Pip*), 366

Kaur, Amrit, 283
Keefer, Janice Kulyk, 362
Khan, Momina, 265
Kimmerer, Robin Wall, 210
King, Cecil, 216
King, Thomas, 198
Komagata Maru, 25, 77, 277

Ladson-Billings, Gloria, 44, 81–82, 87–88, 402
land, the
    Euro-Western notions of, 156, 360
    importance of connection to, 138, 214–216, 218, 270
    knowledge about, 210, 336
    *See also* Indigenous Peoples: land, relationships with
language learning
    artificial intelligence (AI) and, 226, 237–238
    bilingual, 23–24, 230–232
    English, 96–98, 102–106
    for all, 243, 245
    French, 31, 62, 158, 243–244, 250n1, 348
    heritage, 232–236, 238, 403
    inclusive, 243–247, 249–254, 258
    Indigenous, 190, 193–199, 230–232, 234–236
    instructional design for, 248–250, 252–254, 257–258
    lesson planning for, 102–106, 252–258
    principles of, 246, 250–252
    Russian, 233–234
    second, 243–246, 248–249, 258
    Ukrainian, 62, 228–229, 231, 233
    *See also* Universal Language Actions (ULAs)
language policies
    bilingual, 23–24, 230–231
    Canada's implementation of, 225
    exclusionary, 234–235, 244–245
    as manipulative mechanisms, 229–230
    plurilingualism and. *See* plurilingualism
    superdiversity and. *See* superdiversity
    *See also* Official Languages Act
learning disabilities, 125, 245
Levine, Glenn S., 4, 8
liberatory praxis, 2, 78
    concept of, 83–85, 88
    engaging, 79–80, 85–88
literacy
    alternative/multiple forms of, 30, 35, 82–83, 85
    Black, 82–83
    critical, 81–82
    digital/media, 82, 87, 271, 278
    English, 96–98, 100–108
    poetic, 82, 87, 314
    religious, 271–272, 278, 282, 293, 284–285
    worldview, 271–272
    *See also* literate lives, valuing
literate lives, valuing
    aspects of, 80–81, 83, 87
    Black students', 79, 82–83
    as liberatory praxis, 78, 85–87
living curriculum, 399, 409
low income
    educational challenges of, 135, 343
    concept/measures of, 128, 134
    rates of, 116–118
    *See also* poverty; low socioeconomic status (SES)
low socioeconomic status (SES)
    aspirations and, 115, 124, 126–127
    educational challenges of, 119–122, 134–135
    hindering flourishing, 115, 127–128
    intersectional identities and, 117, 338
    supporting students with 127–128, 133–134
    *See also* socioeconomic status (SES)
Luke, Allan, 3–4

MacLeod, Alistair (*No Great Mischief; Island*), 356–358, 364–366
Manitoba, 358
    curriculum in, 62, 64, 233, 284, 292
    school funding, 32, 267
    socioeconomic status/geography, achievement impacts, 117, 338, 341–342, 347–349
Marshall, Albert, 187, 200
Marxist theory, 42, 363
masculinity,
    conforming to mainstream, 154, 159
    school subjects and, 157–158
    stereotypical qualities of, 155–156
mathematics
    academic achievement in, 119–120, 208, 338, 341–343, 347
    inequitable student representation in, 155, 386–388
    programming, 140–143, 234, 248
    *See also* STEM (science, technology, engineering, and mathematics) subjects
McIntosh, Peggy, 10, 399, 420, 427
medical model of disability, 320–321, 328
Medicine Wheel
    flourishing and concept of, 210–211, 414–417, 422
    gifts of the (Cree understanding of), 414–415
    Indigenous education depiction (Mi'kmaq), 415–416
    pedagogical resources for, 416
melting pot, 21, 35
mental health, 161, 422
    Indigenous perspectives on, 210–217
    school programming for, 214–215, 217–218
    socioeconomic status and, 115, 119, 121, 135
    Western perspectives on, 95, 208, 212–215
    *See also* well-being
Mental Health Commission of Canada (MHCC) report, 217
mentorship, 139, 175, 191, 326, 347, 380
Métis people, 187, 229, 234, 358. *See also* Indigenous Peoples
métissage, 191
microaggressions, 49, 51, 418
Millennials, beliefs of, 291–292
monoculturalism, 3, 28
monolingualism, 227–228
    translanguaging versus, 236–237, 249
mosaic, 21, 35
*Multani v. Commission Scolaire Marguerite-Bourgeoys* (2006): 33, 267
multicultural education, 97, 99, 195, 287
    concept of, 4, 21, 28–29, 62–63, 74
    cosmopolitan education versus, 60, 66–68, 72
    Eurocentric perspective in, 59–62, 64–65, 69, 72
    evolution of, 62–63
    failures of, 62–65, 72
    four perspectives on, 28–31
    recommendations for, 187, 194, 285
    religious freedom and, 26–28, 32–34
    school funding amid, 31–32
    systemic racism in, 59–60, 63–65, 68–69
multicultural policy, Canadian, 1, 236
    bilingual framework of, 24–25, 61–62, 225, 230–232
    critics of, 6, 26–27, 31, 366
    evolution of, 21–25, 28
    formative stage, 24, 29
    incipient stage, 22–24, 28–29
    institutionalization of, 24–29
    introduction of, 35, 45, 77
multiculturalism, 59, 428
    Canadian policy of. *See* multicultural policy, Canadian
    concept/interpretations of, 15, 21–23, 35
    discourse of, 77
    in education. *See* multicultural education
    Quebec interculturalism versus, 31
Multiculturalism Act, 25, 45, 62, 77, 232–233
multilingualism, 228, 238. *See also* plurilingualism
Muslim people, 26–27, 94, 289–290, 294
    discrimination/hate crimes against, 265–269, 285

wearing the hijab, 177–178, 265
stereotypes about, 265–266, 268, 277, 286
*See also* Islamophobia

Naipaul, V.S. (*A House for Mr. Biswas*), 365
narrative imagination, 313–314
    compassion and empathy requiring, 5, 8–9, 31, 413
    cultivating students', 78, 428–430
    educators', 306, 423
nationalism, 35
    Quebec, 33, 62, 230
nature. *See* land, the
New Brunswick, 35, 267, 349
    curricula in, 173, 415
    socioeconomic status/geography, achievement impacts, 117, 338, 348
Newfoundland and Labrador, 349
    school funding, 233, 267
    socioeconomic status/geography, achievement impacts, 117, 338
Nigeria, 270–271
nonbinary people, 118, 156, 163
nonreligiousness
    secularism and, 270
    students' increasing, 286
Northern areas. *See* provincial North
northernness, 358, 366
Northwest Territories, 349, 350n3
    socioeconomic status/geography, achievement impacts, 117, 338, 343–345, 350n2
Nova Scotia, 35, 347, 349
    experiences with disability in, 307–308, 310, 323
    fiction, 364–366
    growing up in, 307–308, 357–358
    segregation/discrimination in, 40, 46
    school funding, 32, 277
    socioeconomic status/geography, achievement impacts, 117, 336, 338–339
Nunavut, 350n2
    curriculum in, 188
    socioeconomic status/geography, achievement impacts, 116–117, 343–345, 349, 350n3

Nussbaum, Martha, 15, 60, 199
    on affiliation, 6–7, 9, 70
    capabilities approach, 3–9, 115–118, 320, 335, 413, 423
    cosmopolitan education, 66–72
    on critical self-examination, 5–7, 9, 78, 304
    on flourishing/global citizenship, 3–5, 30, 188, 193, 346, 375
    narrative imagination, 8–9, 31
    *See also* cosmopolitan education

Official Languages Act, 23, 230–232
Ontario, 35, 122, 165
    Bill 98 (Better Schools and Student Outcomes Act) passage, 207–208
    curriculum in, 26, 99–100, 104, 108, 163, 347
    equity challenges in, 40, 379, 382–383, 386–390
    fiction set in, 362, 364–365
    language instruction in, 233–234
    religion and education in, 26–27, 32–33, 267–268, 276
    school funding, 26–27, 31–32, 233, 267
    socioeconomic status/geography, achievement impacts, 117, 338, 344–345, 349, 350n2
    systemic racism, 46–51, 63–64, 77–78
    teacher experiences in, 80–82, 96–102, 108, 183–190
    wellness and mental health programming, 214–215
Ontario Association of Interval and Transition Houses (OAITH) reports
    identity wheel, 423–424, 426–427
    on intersectionality and privilege, 413–414, 419
*Ontario Human Rights Commission and Harbhajan Singh Pandori v. Peel Board of Education* (1992): 33
opportunity gaps, 141
    mitigating, 133, 143–145
    socioeconomic status and, 118–120, 134–135
    *See also* achievement gaps

456   INDEX

oppression, 250
    challenging, 76, 78–83, 108, 171–172, 376–377
    colonial, 196, 198, 207, 210, 219
    concept of, 88–89, 430n1
    gender, 383, 385
    intersectional, 44, 171–172, 403, 419–421
    persistence of, 2–3, 11, 387
    racist, 49, 77
    reflection on, 84–88, 413–414, 419–421, 426, 428–429
    structural/systemic, 43–45, 66–67, 290, 315, 418–419, 426
    victims of, 21, 87, 180
    *See also* anti-oppressive pedagogy

Palmer, Parker, 273
parents/caregivers
    aspirations for children, 123–28, 141, 233, 307–310, 343, 357
    curriculum debates, 46–47, 177, 287
    education level of, 122–125, 128, 141, 343
    engagement in children's education, 120–122, 125–126, 137, 342–343
    immigrant, 1, 411
    lack of support for, 120, 136
    language education, 231, 233–234
    private/religious education debates, 27, 32, 34, 46, 265–268
    resources for, 140, 142–144, 197
    responses to gender/sexual health education, 160, 162–164, 286
    rural, 338, 365
    socioeconomic status, influence of, 141, 336, 339–340, 344, 389
    *See also* single-parent households
Peel District School Board, 33, 46, 268, 276
Pentecostalism, 270
Philippines, the, 233, 244, 271
physical education curriculum, 158, 163, 233
place, 60, 328, 345
    concept of, 368
    decolonial/Indigenous notions of, 191, 212, 216–217, 346
    learning as embedded in, 28, 133, 357–360, 404
    of origin, 66, 315, 389
    religion and, 270, 278, 296
    rural sense of, 337, 357–359, 362–367
    wellness and, 212, 216–217, 401
place-based education, 359–360, 368
pluralism
    covenantal. *See* covenantal pluralism
    multiculturalism and, 29–31
    religious diversity and, 272–275, 296
    schools and, 29, 402–403
    societal, 29–30, 402
    tolerance versus, 272–273, 278, 293
plurilingualism, 236–237
    concept of, 227, 238
    promise of, 225, 228
    *See also* multilingualism
police
    hate crime reporting, 268–269
    violence toward racialized people, 46, 426
policing of gender, 157–158, 164
policy
    definitions/functions of, 229–230
    immigration, 230
    inclusion, supporting, 382
    language. *See* language policies
    multicultural. *See* multicultural policy, Canadian
positionality, 79–80, 190–191
    educator examination of, 11, 49, 84–86, 234, 418
    oppression/experiences based on, 51, 195
    understanding students', 2, 84, 138, 199, 408
post-secondary education, 159, 277
    aspirations for, 122–126, 128
    employment prospects and, 346
    Indigenous, 190, 196
    parents with, 122–125
    rurality and, 337–338, 343–344, 348
    socioeconomic status and, 47, 63, 115, 119, 122–124
    teaching in, 48, 383
    technology access/use and, 238, 347–348

poverty
    community, 136, 141, 144–145
    education gaps and, 115–116, 118–120, 133–135
    intersectional identities and, 53, 117–118, 127–128, 134, 144
    measures of, 116, 128, 134
    rates of, 116–118, 134, 336
    rural, 336, 361
    supportive teaching strategies for, 136–140, 144–145
power relations, 8, 97, 189
    agency and, 375, 405, 408
    awareness of, 83–84, 230, 285–286, 414, 419
    challenging inequitable, 72, 172, 250, 427–428
    colonial, 207, 228–229, 274, 365
    cultural analysis of, 360, 363–364
    flourishing and, 78–79
    political/institutional, 72, 88, 156, 227, 360, 379
    racial, 49–51, 73, 99, 379, 390
    school, 50, 170, 236
    student-teacher, 83–84, 97–99, 107, 376–380
praxis, 272
    concept of, 83, 89
    critical, 192, 200
    liberatory. *See* liberatory praxis
    self-reflective, 49, 88, 192, 414
pre-service teachers
    marginalized students and, 2, 177–178, 194
    pedagogical training of, 246–247, 252, 312, 319
    in rural/Indigenous communities, 191, 194, 358, 367
    sharing personal stories, 160, 194, 367
Prince Edward Island, 349
    school funding in, 233, 267
    socioeconomic status/geography, achievement impacts, 117, 338
privilege, 337, 361
    checklist, 427–428
    concept of, 10, 15, 419–420
    defensiveness when confronting, 11, 377–378, 420
    dismantling, 377, 409, 417, 419–423, 426
    heterosexual, 2, 181, 188–191, 383–385
    intersectionality and, 413–414, 419–421
    passivity enabling, 6, 272, 419–420
    power and, 8, 97, 419
    racial, 41–43
    teacher self-reflection on, 3, 171–173, 309, 403, 419–423, 426
    unacknowledged, 2, 174–178, 377, 419–420
    white. *See* white privilege
Program for International Student Assessment (PISA) achievement gaps
    geographical location, 338, 342–343
    socioeconomic status and, 120
programmatic curriculum, 98, 142
    concept of, 109
    lack of relevance/representation in, 99–100, 103–104
Protestantism, 267, 270, 289
provincial North, 335–336, 349, 358
    educational challenges/differences in, 340–344
publicly funded schools,
    efforts to increase safety in, 46, 226, 389
    racism in, 46, 48, 268, 285, 387
    religious education in, 32, 34, 287
Punjabi students, 233, 397, 403
    male youth depictions, 404–405

Quebec, 35
    Bill 21, passage of, 34, 268, 283
    interculturalism and, 31
    Islamophobia in, 267, 277, 283
    nationalism, 23, 62, 230
    school funding in, 32, 233, 267
    secularism debates in, 34, 267, 283
    socioeconomic status/geography, achievement impacts, 117, 349
    *See also* French Canadians

queer people, 171–178, 180, 385
queer theory, 276, 377, 383, 385–386

*R. v. Big M Drug Mart* (1985): 33
racial justice, 97, 379
    conditions for, 41–42, 60, 65
racialization, 377
    addressing in schools, 386, 388, 402
    concept of, 52
    of religion, 271, 278
racism
    anti-Black, 44, 46–48, 77–78, 82–83
    anti-Indigenous, 47, 60–61, 189, 274, 360
    barriers due to, 46–48, 325, 380
    Canada's historical, 40, 44–46, 61
    in mathematics, 386–388
    multicultural education, 59–60, 63–65, 68–69
    school-based, 46–48, 64, 268, 347, 400, 403
    stereotypes and, 43–44, 50, 86, 276–277
    student experiences with, 2–3, 285, 378, 387
    systemic, 8, 10, 46–51, 63–64, 68, 77–79
    *See also* anti-racism
radical decolonial love, 206, 219
    educational approach of, 209–210, 216
    tenets of, 207, 211–212, 214–215
reading and writing
    academic performance in, 338, 341–342
    Indigenous language programs and, 236
refugee students with interrupted formal education (SIFEs), 97
    challenges responding to, 93–95, 98–100, 108
    cultural divides for, 100–102
    culturally responsive caring for, 106–108
    culturally responsive pedagogy for, 102–106, 108
    curricular irrelevance for refugee SIFEs, 98–100
refugees, 23, 419, 428
    poverty/inequities facing, 77, 118
    Syrian, 93–94, 275, 291

relational knowing, 193–194, 315
relational responsibility, 85, 211–212, 218, 278
relationality, 191–192
    disability and, 305, 313, 315
    in places/schools, 320, 358, 368
religion
    belonging and, 267, 269, 276, 278, 285–286, 291
    Charter cases on education and, 26–28, 32
    concepts of, 266, 278, 289, 293
    contentiousness of, 268–269, 283–284
    creating opportunities to encounter, 292–295
    discrimination due to, 265, 271, 274–278, 285, 290
    hate crimes based on, 268–269
    history in Canada, 267–269
    literacy. *See* religious literacy
    parental debates on, 27, 32, 34, 46, 265–268
    pluralism and, 272–275, 296
    racialization of, 271, 278
    role in schools/society, 266–267, 289–290
    in schools, 26–27, 32–34, 283–284, 267–268, 276, 287
    secularism and, 275, 269–271
    teacher self-reflection on, 288, 295
    2SLGBTQI+ and, 276
    *See also* nonreligiousness
religious diversity, 266, 269
    concept of, 296
    pluralism and, 272–275
    student engagement with, 276, 284–285, 287, 292
    teaching resources for, 271, 277–278, 292
religious freedom, 268
    Charter right to, 26–28, 32–34
religious literacy
    concepts of, 271–272, 278, 293, 284–285
    cross-cultural, 266, 272–274, 276–278
    inclusive notions of, 274–275
    need for, 268, 277–278
remote learning, 142–143, 226, 348

residential schools, 190
    forced attendance, 28, 343
    genocidal legacy of, 29, 40, 77, 234, 358
    settler narratives about, 64, 430n1
    trauma from, 28, 64, 72
    violence at, 28–29, 269
    white/Christian assimilationism at, 46, 154, 231, 290, 364
resource extraction, 360–361, 366
reverence, sense of, 211, 218
Roman Catholic schools, 31–32, 268
Roy, Gabrielle (*Where Nests the Water Hen*), 364
Royal Commission on Bilingualism and Biculturalism, 23, 225, 230–231
rural areas, 3
    agriculture in, 361
    concept of, 349
    depictions of flourishing in, 358–359, 363–368
    diversity, equity, and inclusion in, 336, 357–358, 363–364, 366
    elementary education, 338, 341
    employment, 116, 335–340, 343, 347–348, 366
    French language learning in, 348
    post-secondary education and, 337–338, 343–344, 348
    poverty, 134, 336, 361
    pre-service teachers in, 191, 194, 358, 367
    sense of place, 337, 357–359, 362–367
    socioeconomic status and academic performance, 338–345, 349
    stereotypes of, 336, 359–360, 367
    student support programs in, 347–348
rural education, 359, 362, 365, 368
rural fiction, 358–359, 363–368
rurality
    academic outcomes and, 335, 337–338
    attention to, 345, 357, 359
    concept of, 359–360, 363
    imaginaries of, 358, 360–363
    modernization versus, 360–361

*S. L. v. Commission Scolaire des Chenes* (2012): 34
Saskatchewan, 163
    curricula in, 62, 347
    school funding in, 31–32
    socioeconomic status/geography, achievement impacts, 117, 349
scaffolding, 238, 247–251, 256, 326–327
Scheer, Andrew, 32
school as polis, 320, 323–328
secondary schools, 80, 235–236, 365, 375, 428–429
    completion of, 119, 122–125, 338–339
    gay-straight alliances in, 171, 276, 383–384
    racism in, 47–48, 378–379, 400, 404
    refugee student experiences in, 95–96, 99–100, 108
    rural/urban achievement differences in, 338–346, 350n2
    streaming/gaps for courses in, 47, 127–128, 157, 386
secularism, 155
    concept of, 280, 290
    multicultural education and, 27–28, 285
    narratives of, 166–167
    Quebec and. *See* Quebec: secularism debates in
    religion and, 275, 269–271, 290–291
segregation in schooling, 40, 45–46, 387
Sensoy, Öslem, 9–10
*Servatius v. Alberni School District No. 70* (2022): 268
settler-colonialism
    Canada's history of, 46, 77
    concept of, 52
    dehumanization in, 207–208, 210
    lack of engagement with, 50–51, 64
    ongoing, 46, 234
Seven Grandfather Teachings, 210–211, 218–219
sex
    concepts of, 156–157
    curriculum teaching about, 162–163, 286–287
    viewed as essentialized, binary concept, 154–156
    *See also* gender

sexism, 66, 185
    confronting, 172–174
    *See also* heterosexism
sexuality, 383
    diverse expressions of, 1, 155, 274, 336, 385
    intersectionality and, 3, 44, 170, 408, 419–420
    norms, 153, 157, 161–164, 172–173
    teacher reflection/training on, 11, 159, 162–164
    transmission of knowledge about, 153, 159–161
    viewed as binary concept, 154
    *See also* heterosexism
Sikhism, 267–269, 275, 283, 278
single-parent households
    experiences of, 123
    poverty facing, 116–118, 134, 138–141
social/biopsychosocial model of disability, 327–328
    medical model versus, 319–322
social capital, 30, 72, 121–122, 140, 158, 238
social-emotional learning (SEL) and knowledge, 72, 138–139, 276
    Indigenous communities honouring, 217, 415
social justice, 25, 79
    allyship and, 174, 176
    classroom integration of, 102, 105, 137, 154, 417–421
    conservative perceptions of, 41
    critical consciousness and, 7, 51, 429
    disability and, 305–306, 311–313
    in education/curricula, 6, 9–10, 145, 311–313
    Indigenous perspectives and, 189, 191, 198
    religious literacy and, 271, 291
sociocultural structures, 98, 102, 108, 144, 325
sociocultural theory (SCT), 247–248
socioeconomic status (SES), 116, 207, 277, 389, 424
    aspirations and, 115–116, 122–127
    concept of, 128
    goal of flourishing despite, 14, 66, 145–146, 375–376, 402

high, 115, 119–122, 126, 340
low. *See* low socioeconomic status (SES)
marginalization due to, 115, 387, 419, 427–128
as predictor of flourishing, 118–123, 134–135, 290, 335
rural areas and, 338–340, 344
*See also* poverty
Socrates, 5–6, 66
solidarity, 426
    Indigenous, 194–195, 197–200
South Asian people, 25, 86, 117, 268, 275
special education, 381
    exclusionary policies and resources, 304, 382–383
    inclusive education versus, 306–307, 314, 321, 324, 383
    placement in, 119, 308, 386
Spirit of Math, Community School Initiative (CSI), 141–143
spiritualities, 272, 276–277, 422
    Indigenous, 210–217, 268, 275, 366, 414–417
    student, 286, 291, 294
standardized testing, 76, 158
    emphasis on, 32, 207
    liberatory praxis versus, 78, 88
    socioeconomic/geographical differences in, 120, 338–339
    student well-being versus, 215
Stegner, Wallace, 363
STEM (science, technology, engineering, and mathematics) subjects, 345
    Indigenous students in, 346–347
    women studying, 157, 354
stereotypes, 73
    concept of, 15
    of disabled people, 309–311
    gender, 153–161
    Human Library breaking down, 417, 428–429
    Islamophobic, 265–266, 268, 277
    perpetuation/persistence of, 8, 156–160, 179

racial, 43–44, 50, 86, 276–277
recognition of holding, 10, 277–278, 295
of rural places, 336, 359–360, 367
student/teacher grappling with, 82, 107, 160–161, 287, 364
stigmatization, 135, 379
disability and, 321–322, 325–326, 377, 383
campaigns against, 217
Stoic philosophy, 8, 66, 71
storytelling
counter-. *See* counter-narrative/storytelling
culturally responsive teaching and, 103, 105, 398–491, 406–409
literate lives and, 79–82
teaching as, 138, 198, 358–360, 364–367, 424–425
straight privilege, 2, 188–191, 383–385
suicide, 176
superdiversity, 225–227, 238–239

teaching career experiences, 307, 309–311, 378
considerations for, 380–381, 383–384
early, 3, 179, 358, 367
Teaching for Diversity, 292
teaching profession, 11
dominance of whiteness and women in, 46–47, 379–380
terra nullius, 60, 360
Thiong'o, Ngugi wa (*Petals of Blood*), 365
tolerance, 33, 162
religious pluralism versus, 272–273, 278, 293
Toronto
discrimination facing racialized students in, 47–48, 119, 141, 386
District School Board, 47–48, 63, 119, 141, 386
support for student flourishing in, 140–144
Tory, John, 32, 267–268
transgender people
increasing visibility of, 156, 161, 428
poverty facing, 118

teacher interactions with, 161, 163, 174, 177
*See also* 2SLGBTQIA+ community
translanguaging theory, 236–239
transphobia, 170, 179, 390
TribalCrit, 190
building human flourishing through, 195–198
framework/lens of, 187–188, 193, 196–200
tenets for engaging, 189, 191–192, 194–195
Trudeau, Justin, 35
Trudeau, Pierre Elliott, 24, 45, 225, 232
Truth and Reconciliation Commission, 29, 195
Calls to Action, 196, 199, 226, 229, 414–415
Indigenous languages, 234–236
tutoring, 119, 127, 139, 347
2SLGBTQIA+ community, 41, 153, 428
educator allyship with, 160–164, 170–171, 173–175, 178, 286
gay-straight alliance (GSA) clubs, 162, 171–173, 276, 383–385
violence/harm toward, 162–163, 172–173, 180–181, 383–385
two-eyed seeing (*Etuaptmumk*), 187, 206, 216–217, 219, 346

Ukrainian language, 62, 228–229, 231, 233
Understanding by Design (UBD). *See* backwards design
under-resourced communities
racialized students in, 78
support for, 141–145
United Nations, 118
Convention on the Rights of the Child, 323, 407
Convention on the Rights of Persons with Disabilities, 323
Educational, Scientific and Cultural Organization (UNESCO), 173, 234–235
Human Rights Committee, 32
United States, 173, 238, 285, 314, 377
Indigenous Peoples in, 188–190, 294

Universal Design for Learning (UDL), 244, 324, 326, 328
    principles/guidelines, 138, 246–247, 249
Universal Language Actions (ULAs), 249–250, 253, 259
urban areas, 349

Vygotsky, Lev, 244, 247, 249
Wagamese, Richard (*Indian Horse*), 364
wâhkôhtowin, 187–188, 190, 192, 195–200
*Waldman v. Canada* (1999): 32
well-being, 315
    capabilities approach, 65–66, 69–72, 88
    flourishing and, 115–116, 210, 215, 218
    Indigenous perspectives on, 210–218
    of the land and more-than-human, 210, 214–216, 218
    racialized people and, 42, 51, 65–66
    radical decolonial love and, 209–210
    refugee students' 98, 106–109
    religion and, 269, 276
    socioeconomic status and, 135, 389
    Western notions of, 9, 206–208, 212–217
    *See also* mental health
Western Canada, 229, 231, 362
Western worldviews, 346, 390
    on education, 207, 209, 216
    on educator distance, 209, 212–213
    on multiculturalism, 59–62, 64–65, 69, 72, 397–398
    on secularism/religion, 270–271
    sex/gender norms, 153–156
    on student individual choices, 208–209, 214
    of well-being, 9, 206–208, 212–217
    *See also* Eurocentrism
white, 154
    concept of, 10, 379–380, 390
    racial frameworks, 46, 50, 77–78, 389, 398
    saviourism, 49, 52, 380
    settler colonialism, 51, 189, 234
    societal paradigms, 40, 42, 68, 228, 292, 361
    students, 2–3, 40, 47–48, 51, 177, 378
    teachers, 2, 47, 153, 177–179, 194, 379–380
    women, 46–47, 177, 378, 380, 383
white privilege, 170–171
    centrality of, 64, 399, 403
    classroom discussion/activities, 2–3, 378, 420–421, 426–427
    concept of, 390, 399, 420
white supremacy, 65, 379
    concept of, 73, 390
    CRT on, 42, 50
    in education system, 46, 50–51, 78
    harms of, 76
    persistence of, 61, 88
    white discomfort with, 46, 50
whiteness
    concept of, 390
    critical, 377–380
    hegemony of, 47, 49–50, 376, 427
    self-awareness of, 46, 49
    of teaching profession, 46
Wilkins-Laflamme, Sarah, 291
Wolterstorff, Nicholas, 7, 9
worldviews, 66
    diversity and distinctness of, 265, 271–276, 289–291, 296
    hegemonic, 83
    Indigenous, 213–218, 268
    as informing and informed, 275
    nonreligious. *See* nonreligiousness
    personal meaning of, 276
    teacher self-awareness of, 86, 286
    Western. *See* Western worldviews
    white, 50
Wright, Richard (*Clara Callan*), 364

Youth Association for Academics, Athletics, and Character Education (YAAACE), Community School Initiative (CSI), 141–143
Yukon, 117, 343, 349

*Zylberberg et al. v. Sudbury Board of Education* (1988): 26–27